International Bank Accounting

Prepared by Ernst & Whinney

Published by Euromoney Publications

Published by
Euromoney Publications Limited
Nestor House, Playhouse Yard,
London EC4V 5EX

Data Processed by Avonset, Midsomer Norton, Bath
Printed in Great Britain at The Bath Press, Bath

CONTENTS

ACKNOWLEDGEMENTS

We are grateful to Ernst & Whinney's banking experts around the world for their willing co-operation in compiling this book.

We are particularly indebted to Edward Woolfenden, our consultant editor in London, for his perseverance over the past six months and his willing assistance in the myriad problems of editing and reading. Overall editing of the book in London has been under the direction of Howard Brown and Bob Sharpe, and has been co-ordinated through the Ernst & Whinney International Banking Committee.

While every effort has been made to ensure the accuracy of the material in this book, reference should be made to professional advisers in the relevant country before acting upon it, in order to ascertain the current position.

Ernst & Whinney
December 1984

v

PROFILE

ABOUT THE AUTHORS

Ernst & Whinney is one of the world's foremost firms of public accountants. Its success stems both from its strength in auditing, particularly in key sectors such as financial services, oil and aerospace, and from its management consultancy and other non-audit based advisory services.

Ernst & Whinney has extensive worldwide expertise in banking and finance and the strength of its banking practice is reflected in the spread of these clients throughout the world. For instance, its clients include four of the eleven clearing banks in the United Kingdom, 49 of the 200 top ranking banks in the United States and 40 banks in the Middle East, including a number of government monetary agencies.

The ability of Ernst & Whinney to draw on its international expertise is clearly demonstrated by this book which has been described as a definitive work on international bank accounting. It will be of use not only to bankers but also to all those working in the international monetary system, whatever their role.

INTRODUCTION

GENERAL

International banking has been one of the major growth industries of the 1970s and 80s. New financial centres have sprung up during this period and any bank which has any pretentions or ambitions for growth can no longer afford to operate just within its home country. We, as a firm with many banking clients throughout the world, felt there was a need for an internal manual so as to keep ourselves up to date with accounting requirements for banks throughout the world. When the publishers of *Euromoney* approached us to write such a book for them, we readily agreed to undertake this task because we could appreciate the problems that bankers and investors have in making a proper appraisal of the accounts of banks which are prepared under the many differing laws and practices existing around the world.

We set about this task by asking each of our offices in the major financial centres of the world to write a chapter, setting out the laws, regulations and best accounting practice concerning the preparation of financial statements of banks in their own country. Each country has found it necessary, because of the importance of banking to its economy, to set up a supervisory regime to ensure that banks conduct their business in a prudent manner, and therefore keep the confidence of their depositors, and that the banks observe the monetary requirements of the government's economic policy. The supervisory authorities' reporting requirements impact on a bank's accounts and therefore we considered it essential to broaden the scope of the book so as to give details of the supervisory authorities and the obligations they impose on banks to provide information to them. Details are also given of the ability of a foreign bank to operate in another country and the necessary approvals it must obtain before it commences business.

Each country chapter has therefore been written to a standard format and details of this are shown in the layout of country chapters on page xv. The format has been divided into 10 main sections:

General Information − including details of the supervisory authorities, laws and regulations affecting banking and the ability of foreign banks to operate in a country

Accounting − including the laws and regulations affecting accounts, the obligation to furnish accounts, mandatory accounting dates, audit requirements and availability of accounts for public inspection

Format, Style and Contents of Accounts

Accounting Policies

Window Dressing

Amounts to be Maintained by Law − including minimum capital requirement

Key Ratios − as prescribed by supervisory authorities

Accounting Returns other than Accounts

Taxation

Interpretation of Accounts

It has not been easy to decide on a logical order for the country chapters but the UK and US head the list because of the leading financial centres in London and New York and, in certain respects, they tend to set patterns which other countries follow. These are followed by the European Economic Community chapter and then the European countries in alphabetical order, both within the EEC and outside.

The other countries then follow in alphabetical order with certain Middle Eastern countries being included in one chapter.

Accounting terminology

By and large, accounting terminology is standard throughout the countries surveyed in this book, although there are certain differences, especially in the area of provisions for bad and doubtful debts. Each author has used the nomenclature standard in his country and it will be necessary to take this into account when reading each chapter.

OVERVIEW OF COUNTRY CHAPTERS

The remainder of this introduction is devoted to an overview of the separate sections of the country chapters.

Supervisory authorities

As already mentioned, all countries exercise supervisory control over banking operations in their country but the degree of control varies from one country to another. On the one hand, countries such as Japan exercise very strict control over banks with almost every aspect of banking being controlled by law, regulation or edict from the supervisory authority, while on the other hand countries such as the UK look at each bank on its own merits rather than having a prescriptive set of rules applying to all banks. Many countries of course lie between these extremes.

It is appropriate to mention here that there is increasing co-operation between the supervisory authorities of individual countries to ensure that all aspects of international banking are properly supervised. The initiative for this was taken by a committee of the Bank for International Settlements known as the Committee of Supervisors which is based at Basle. The original paper was drawn up in 1975 and a revised version published in 1983 and there is now effective agreement to allocate responsibilities between the supervisory authority of the country of the parent bank and that of the host country in which a branch or subsidiary is operating. The emphasis is on supervision to be carried out on a group basis, although the host authority has defined responsibilities in respect of the operations carried out in its country. This concordat (the 'Basle Concordat') was originally between the supervisory authorities of the Group of Ten countries, together with Switzerland and Luxembourg, but it has since been endorsed by many other countries. The EEC also endorsed this policy when it issued a Directive in June 1983 requiring its member countries to arrange for supervision to be carried out on a group basis (see Chapter 3).

Ability of foreign banks to operate through branches and subsidiaries

Many countries will allow a foreign bank to operate in their country, provided an economic need is proven and there are reciprocal arrangements in the other country. However, it should be noted that certain countries prevent or make it very difficult for foreign banks to have a presence in their country, other than by way of representative office; examples are Australia, South Africa, Saudi Arabia and Kuwait, although Australia is currently reviewing its position in this matter.

Bank accounts subject to special laws

In most countries a bank is generally organised as a company or corporation with limited liability and as such it is subject to the general requirements of company law in that country. However, there are many countries which have special laws or regulations affecting the format and content of bank accounts. These are generally part of a banking law which regulates the way in which a bank can conduct its business and imposes comprehensive reporting requirements, not only to the supervisory authorities but, quite often, to the shareholders and the general public.

Where the format and content of accounts are prescribed by law or regulation, the accounts generally consist of a balance sheet and profit and loss account, often in some detail but rarely supported by comprehensive footnotes. This is fairly common on the Continent of Europe where countries tend to have a chart of accounts, with the annual financial statements being a summarised form of this chart of accounts. In this connection the EEC will perhaps raise as well as unify reporting standards, for when the draft Directive on Bank Accounts is finally agreed it will not only require a uniform format but also the disclosure of accounting policies and supplementary information by way of notes to be included with the accounts.

In most countries a limited liability company is obliged to prepare annual accounts and to file them at an official registry where they are available for public inspection. Therefore the appropriate legislation is concerned with the content and format of these annual accounts.

Legislation concerning the inclusion of financial information in a prospectus inviting the public subscription of shares and other securities will therefore be based on the information required to be disclosed in the annual accounts.

In the US, however, there is no corporate law requirement *per se* to prepare and file annual accounts and it is only when a corporation makes a public offering of securities that the law prescribes the information to be disclosed in a prospectus which has to be filed with the appropriate authority, namely the Securities and Exchange Commission (SEC). Annual and other periodic reports filed with the SEC are the means by which information about corporations is updated.

Mandatory accounting date

Several countries require accounts to be made up to a specified date in the year, 31 December and 31 March being the most common dates although in Canada it is 31 October. In those countries where a choice is allowed 31 December is the most popular date.

Audit requirements

All countries with the exception of Spain require the accounts of banks to be audited. The auditors' obligation is to report to the shareholders, although in some countries, e.g. Canada, Germany and Switzerland, they also have a duty to report to the supervisory authority on certain matters.

Audits tend to be of two types, those where the auditors concentrate on whether the accounts are properly prepared in accordance with the law or regulations, and those of the Anglo-Saxon type where a more fundamental review of the organisation and of the individual transactions take place, to ensure not only that the accounts are properly drawn up in accordance with the law, etc., but also that they reflect a 'true and fair view' of the bank's state of affairs at its accounting date and of the operations for the accounting period.

In addition, the supervisory authorities may use inspectors to conduct their own enquiries, either on a routine basis or where they consider there are particular circumstances which make such an inspection necessary.

Submission of accounts to other authorities

Where a bank is listed on a stock exchange, it normally has to enter into an agreement (the listing agreement) with that stock exchange setting out its responsibilities. The bank would be required to file copies of all notices and other documents sent to shareholders, including the annual accounts. There are often disclosure requirements which are in excess of the statutory requirements, e.g. in France a listed bank would have to prepare consolidated accounts, make comprehensive footnote disclosures and include a management report on the results for the year. None of these are required for the statutory accounts.

Extent to which format and content are prescribed

In every country the accounts sent to the supervisory authority have their format and content prescribed by law, regulation or edict from the supervisory authority. In some cases these accounts also form the statutory accounts, e.g. in Canada, but in other cases they are used solely by the supervisory authority for their own purposes in conjunction with additional statistical returns which the banks are required to make, e.g. the balance sheet (Form BS) in the UK.

Even if the statutory accounts are separate from those required by the supervisory authorities, in most countries they will have to conform with the law, regulations and/or generally accepted accounting principles (as recognised in each country).

Generally accepted accounting principles are constantly changing in order to meet the current needs of a country. They are normally codified by the issue of accounting standards by an appropriate body, which can be either an official organisation backed by law or a representative organisation set up by the accounting profession of a country together with users and preparers of accounts. It is interesting to note in these days of international banking that the laws and requirements of one country often affect the way information is disclosed in another resulting in banks disclosing more information than they are required to do by the law of their own country. For example, when a bank wishes to raise public capital on the US market, it must produce a prospectus complying with the detailed requirements of the SEC. As the prospectus is a public document, many such banks take the view that their own local accounts should disclose similar information, either in the accounts themselves or as supplementary information.

Disclosure and exemption from disclosure of specific items

One of the biggest controversies in preparing accounts of banks is how much information should be disclosed. To be successful in business a bank must retain the confidence of its depositors. It must therefore be seen to adopt prudent policies and have the ability to withstand a crisis.

Traditionally, banks have tended to be secretive by nature and conservative in the accounting policies they adopt. The practice therefore was to disclose as little information as possible in the belief that this was the best way to preserve confidence.

This policy received official support and most countries built into their laws provisions to allow a bank to retrain from disclosing sensitive information, the disclosure of which was regarded as likely to affect its ability to continue to attract deposits.

During the last two decades, however, attitudes have begun to change. The US took the lead in this matter so that the US banks provide detailed information about most aspects of their operations, including sensitive

items such as interest margins, movements on bad debt provisions (in US parlance, allowance for loan losses), non-performing loans and country exposure. However, there are still countries which believe it is necessary to preserve secrecy and, in this respect, Germany and Switzerland are two countries where it is permissible to withhold from the public at large, including shareholders and depositors, certain information such as doubtful debt provisions and market value of investments.

In the UK opinion is divided as the Clearing Banks make full disclosure but the Accepting Houses (Merchant Banks) still take advantage of the exemption provisions of the Companies Acts.

The other Continental European countries tend towards the German attitude, while Canada and Australia have moved towards greater disclosure.

Hidden reserves

The question of whether a bank should be allowed to maintain hidden reserves is very much bound up with the previous topic of disclosure.

Traditionally, it was accepted that in order to maintain depositors' confidence in a bank it was perfectly right and proper for a bank to maintain secret or hidden reserves, so that it could smooth out its reported profits by making transfers to or from its hidden reserves. One of the principal proponents of this policy is Germany, which still has memories of the problems caused by hyperinflation in the 1930s, and of the consequential financial crisis.

In the UK those banks which are exempt from full disclosure are also permitted to maintain inner reserves but this fact has to be indicated on the balance sheet. Other countries where this is permitted include Switzerland, Hong Kong, South Africa, Singapore and certain countries in the Middle East.

Hidden reserves are maintained in two ways. One way is to have certain inner reserves or contingency accounts which are included in deposits and other accounts on the balance sheet. The other way is deliberately to under-value certain assets such as investments, advances or fixed assets by making excessive provisions. Exempt banks in the UK predominantly adopt the first method and the other method finds favour in Germany. It is interesting to note that the EEC draft Directive on Bank Accounts allows certain assets to be undervalued by up to 5% of their value, but still requires the accounts to show a 'true and fair' view. At first sight the two policies appear incompatible and may cause problems for auditors of banks in EEC countries.

Consolidation

Nearly half the countries surveyed require bank groups to prepare consolidated accounts and in this respect they are treated no differently from any other group of companies.

In some of the other countries where there is no legal requirement to produce consolidated accounts it should be noted that if the bank is listed on a stock exchange it will often be required under the terms of the listing agreement to produce consolidated accounts for circulation to the shareholders. Furthermore, many supervisory authorities are stipulating that consolidated accounts should be submitted to them even if there is no requirement to publish such accounts and this trend will be given impetus by the Basle Concordat where it was agreed that the supervisory authority of the parent bank would exercise control on a group basis.

Accounting policies

In many countries accounting policies for banks are prescribed by law, regulation or edict from the supervisory authorities and all banks in those countries are obliged to comply with these requirements. However, there are a number of countries notably the UK, Australia, South Africa, Singapore and Hong Kong where the overriding consideration is for accounts to show a true and fair view and it is left to the directors of each bank to decide which policies are appropriate for that bank. In this connection the development of generally accepted accounting principles (GAAP) should be noted. They are normally codified by the accounting bodies in each country issuing an accounting standard on a particular subject after consultation with all interested parties. A bank would be expected to follow GAAP unless there are sound reasons why an alternative policy should be adopted. Normally the effect of the deviation from GAAP would have to be quantified and the auditors would have to qualify their report if they considered the deviation not justified under the circumstances.

Notes to the accounts including accounting policies adopted

In those countries where there is a legal format for the accounts of banks it is quite often considered unnecessary to provide additional information by way of notes to the accounts or to describe the accounting policies adopted as these will also be prescribed by law or regulation.

However, banks in the UK, US, The Netherlands, Canada, Japan, Hong Kong, Singapore and South Africa generally provide adequate details of accounting policies and additional accounting information to support the balance sheet and profit and loss account. This information is generally disclosed to conform with the law and GAAP or, quite simply, to enable the accounts to show a true and fair view.

It is interesting to note that the EEC draft Directive on Bank Accounts requires adequate footnote disclosure and this will represent a major change for some Continental European countries. However, the major banks in countries where there is no legal obligation to provide full disclosure will often voluntarily prepare accounts for circulation to their shareholders and their international banking connections, which provide adequate information and bear comparison with the best in the world.

Foreign exchange

Almost all countries use the closing rate of exchange at the balance sheet date to translate foreign currency assets and liabilities into the local currency. With regard to foreign exchange dealing, forward contracts are valued at the closing rate or the closing forward rate. However, practices vary as to whether any forward profits are taken up. Some countries take in both forward profits and losses while other countries will not take up forward profits until they are realised but will require losses to be provided for. Another variant is to use unrealised forward profits to offset unrealised forward losses and only provide for any net unrealised loss.

Deferred tax

In some countries the treatment for taxation purposes in respect of a particular item can differ from its accounting treatment and this normally results in a timing difference. For example, interest for tax purposes may be treated on a paid or received basis while for accounting purposes it may be treated on a payable or receivable basis so that the incidence of taxation on net interest will be out of phase with the net interest figure reflected in the accounts. Again, the tax allowances on the acquisition of fixed assets are often front-ended whereas the depreciation charge is generally written off against profits over the economic life of the asset. Therefore, to prevent the after tax profit figure from fluctuating widely when compared with the pre-tax profit, the charge for taxation included in the profit and loss account is computed on the accounting basis and any difference attributable to timing differences is taken to a deferred tax account to be released in later years as appropriate.

The two principal countries which adopt a deferred tax policy are the US and the UK and the main difference between the two is that in the US deferred tax is taken up on all timing differences, whereas in the UK it is necessary to provide for deferred taxation only if the directors consider that the taxation liability will crystallise in the future.

Provision for bad and doubtful debts

The provision for bad and doubtful debts is generally regarded as being in two parts — the specific provision which covers all identified losses and the general provision which is intended to cover risks which are known to exist but which have not been identified at the balance sheet date.

The amount of the specific provision is generally ascertained by reviewing the loan portfolio and identifying the problem loans. In the case of the general provision there are a number of methods adopted to determine its size.

In Japan, Germany and Spain the amounts to be set aside are fixed by law or regulation. In other countries, such as Italy, a general provision up to a given percentage of loans, etc., is treated as tax deductible and this will generally be the minimum figure provided, although banks often set aside additional amounts beyond that allowable for taxation purposes.

In the UK the general provision is not deductible for taxation purposes and its size is determined by management in the light of the particular circumstances of each bank. In the US identified bad debts are charged off and in addition to this an allowance for loan losses is maintained. Part of this is tax deductible and banks are required to divide the reserve into allocated and unallocated parts. The allocated part is regarded as covering those loans which are regarded as doubtful, and the unallocated part equated to a general provision.

There is no consistent treatment of provisions for bad and doubtful debts in the balance sheet among the countries surveyed. Some countries opt to offset both the specific and general provisions against the appropriate assets, and others treat the specific provision as a deduction from the asset but require the general provision to be included on the liabilities side. A third method is for both the specific and general provisions to be included on the liabilities side leaving the assets to be shown at their gross value.

Amortisation of premiums and discounts on investments

The majority of countries regard it as acceptable accounting practice to amortise both premiums and discounts on the purchase of investments with a fixed redemption date. However, it should be noted that the draft EEC Directive on Bank Accounts does not permit investments to be written up above acquisition cost although it would appear to permit the amortisation of premiums.

Offsets (i.e. to what extent can assets and liabilities be set off against each other)

Many of the Continental European countries do not permit the offsetting of assets against liabilities even if the debits and credits relate to the same customer. However, other countries allow setoffs if there is a legal right of set off and amounts are for the same term and in the same currency.

Goodwill

Almost without exception banks are required either to write off goodwill in the year of acquisition or to amortise it over a period of years. Some countries specify a fixed period of time varying from five to 40 years but others require it to be written off over its economic life.

Revaluation of assets

Many countries will permit the revaluation of assets provided any surplus is taken to a revaluation reserve and is not regarded as distributable by way of dividend. However, some countries will only permit a revaluation under a particular law which specifies the date when the revaluation may be undertaken, and at least one country would regard any revaluation surplus put through the books of account as taxable income.

Instalment finance and leasing

It is generally accepted that leased assets should be a separate item in the balance sheet but some countries show this item as a separate sub-division of lending to customers. Instalment finance is almost always shown as a sub-division of lending although not every country requires separate disclosure of this item.

Practices vary concerning the recognition of income but banks in those countries where a substantial amount of leasing is undertaken generally recognise income in proportion to the balance of the net investment in the leased asset. In the case of instalment finance the 'rule of 78' is often adopted. However, there are some countries where income is released on the straight line basis.

Dealing assets

Most countries recognise that it is part of a bank's business to hold assets with a view to making a profit on their resale. In most countries these assets are valued at the lower of cost and market value. Some countries, e.g. Germany, will permit a lower valuation but others allow dealing assets to be carried at market value.

Pension disclosure

Generally speaking there is little disclosure concerning the cost of providing pension benefits. In a number of countries pensions are secured by a policy with an insurance company to whom the bank pays a premium but it is not common practice to disclose the annual premium or even describe the method used to provide for the future cost of employees' pensions.

In the UK and the US banks generally maintain a pension fund as a separate fund outside the bank and under the control of trustees. In the US GAAP requires that disclosure be made of the fund's existence, the bank's accounting and funding policies and the pension cost for the period. For certain pension plans further actuarially derived disclosure is also required. In the UK best practice is to include a note stating whether the pension scheme is adequately funded on an actuarial basis and describing the basis upon which this has been determined.

Depreciation

Generally speaking it is accepted practice for banks to depreciate property and equipment over their expected economic lives, although in assessing the latter, banks in many countries will adopt the depreciation rates approved for taxation purposes. Spain, perhaps, is alone in having depreciation rates prescribed by law.

Window dressing

Window dressing may be defined as the entering into of transactions before the accounting date which mature immediately after it, the substance of which was primarily to alter the appearance of the balance sheet.

Although window dressing is still practised in some countries it is increasingly finding disfavour with the supervisory authorities. It is practised mainly to improve the apparent liquidity of a balance sheet or to increase its footings.

Minimum capital requirement

All countries now have minimum capital requirements which a bank must meet before it will be granted approval to commence business. In many countries where a minimum sum is specified by the law the supervisory authority is empowered to require a larger figure which it deems to be appropriate having regard to all the circumstances. Another practice adopted by many countries is to require a statutory reserve to be built up by setting aside a defined proportion of the profits available for distribution until the reserve has reached a certain size which is generally defined in relation to the size of the issued share capital.

Key ratios

Each supervisory authority has a number of ratios which it expects the banks under its control to observe. At the present time there is little standardisation in the definitions used although attempts are being made by the EEC to reach common definition of ratios to be used within the Common Market. The most commonly used ratios are

> own funds to public liabilities
> own funds to total assets
> own funds to risk assets
> own funds to fixed assets

The definition of own funds will include equity capital and reserves and may also include a proportion of loan capital issued, e.g. subordinated loan capital with a minimum life outstanding, any hidden reserves and sometimes the general provision for doubtful debts. In some countries the infrastructure, i.e. premises, equipment, investment in subsidiaries and trade investments, is deducted from the total of own funds to give a figure of free resources which is compared against public liabilities or risk assets. The latter is determined by taking the various classes of assets, both on and off the balance sheet, and weighting each with an appropriate risk factor.

Liquidity ratios are also employed and these take various forms such as minimum cash or liquid assets ratios, or a bank may be required to maintain liquid assets as a defined proportion of various maturity bands of deposit liabilities.

Restraints are often placed on the granting of large loans. The basis of comparison is generally own funds and the restrictions can take the form of a limit on an individual loan to a single connected party and also the total of such loans.

Accounting returns other than accounts

The supervisory authorities of all countries require information to be submitted to them in addition to the annual accounts. This information is used in connection with their supervisory duties, to enable them to calculate the various key ratios mentioned above and also to prepare statistics concerning the banking industry and the economy of the country concerned.

There is no standard pattern for the additional information to be provided and it is necessary to examine carefully the requirements of each country. The frequency of submission varies with each country, with the information to be provided and, sometimes, with the rating or standing of a particular bank, and it can be daily, weekly, monthly, quarterly, half yearly or on an annual basis.

Taxation

Banks in all countries, with the exception of those in the Middle East where there is little or no taxation, are subject to taxation and generally they are taxed in the same way as any other business. In France, however, banks are also subject to a special tax on deposits.

In most countries the statutory accounts are accepted as the basis for computing the taxable profits but, almost invariably, adjustments are made because items included in the accounts are not taxable or allowable as a deduction for tax purposes and also certain deductions may be allowed for tax purposes which are not included in the statutory accounts. However, there are certain countries such as Germany, France, Italy and Luxembourg where it is often necessary for an item to be charged in the statutory accounts before it can be allowed as a deduction for tax purposes. It is obvious that in these instances tax considerations will influence the presentation of the accounts.

Interpretation of accounts

From the foregoing it will be apparent that there are differing reporting requirements in the countries surveyed in this book. It is therefore very difficult to compare the accounts of banks from one country against those in another country because of the different legal requirements and accounting practices of the individual countries. Even when examining the accounts of banks from the same country it is often difficult to make a proper comparison because of the absence of detailed information supporting the published accounts. This is very noticeable in those countries which permit hidden reserves to be maintained and allow profit smoothing to take place. However, the accounts of banks in the US and the Clearing Banks in the UK make adequate disclosure for a proper analysis to be made.

The fact that banks are supervised and that their accounts are audited does ensure generally that the information published is reliable but as there are no uniform standards of reporting throughout the world it does mean that the information published varies as to adequacy of disclosure.

In this connection the EEC Directive on Bank Accounts, once it has been agreed, will standardise bank reporting within the EEC but, as currently drafted, it does suffer from the defect of allowing hidden reserves to be maintained. However, it will be some time before the final text is agreed and brought into local legislation.

CONCLUSION

It is apparent that there is little comparability between the accounts of banks in different countries, or even within the same country. Careful study of each chapter is therefore recommended before making comparative judgements. The comparative table of accounting and other requirements has been prepared to facilitate comparisons.

LAYOUT OF COUNTRY CHAPTERS

Comparative table of accounting and other requirements

		UK	US	EEC	Belgium	France	Germany	Italy	Luxembourg	The Netherlands	Spain	Switzerland
1	Supervisory authority separate from central bank	No	No*	N/A	Yes*	Yes	Yes	Yes	Yes	No*	No*	Yes
2	Ability of foreign bank to operate as a											
	— branch	Yes	Yes	Yes	Yes	Yes	Yes	Yes	Yes	Yes	Yes	Yes
	— subsidiary	Yes	Yes	Yes	Yes	Yes	Yes	Yes	Yes	Yes	Yes	Yes
3	Bank accounts subject to own law	No	Yes*	Yes*	Yes*	Yes	Yes	No*	Yes*	Yes*	No*	Yes
4	Format and content fixed by law	Partly*	Yes	Yes	Yes	Yes	Yes	Yes*	Yes	Yes*	Yes	Yes
5	Mandatory year end date	No	No*	No	No*	Yes	No*	Yes*	No*	Yes	Yes	No*
6	Auditors responsible to supervisory authority as well as shareholders	No	No	N/A	No*	Yes	Yes	No	No	Yes	No	Yes
7	Hidden reserves permitted	Yes*	No	Yes*	Yes	No*	Yes	Yes*	Yes	No	No	Yes
8	Requirement to produce consolidated accounts	Yes	Yes	Yes*	Yes*	No*	Yes*	No*	No*	Yes	No	Yes*
9	Accounting policies fixed by law	No	Yes*	Yes*	No*	No*	Yes	No*	No*	Yes*	Yes	Yes
10	Accounting policies published	Yes	Yes	Yes	No	No	No	No	No	Yes	No	No
11	Footnotes included as part of accounts	Yes	Yes	Yes	No	No	No	No	No	Yes	No	No
12	Foreign exchange translation											
	— at closing rate	Yes	Yes*	Yes	Yes*	Yes	Yes*	Yes	Yes	Yes	Yes	Yes
	forward deals — bring in profits	Yes*	Yes	Yes*	Yes*	Yes*	No*	No*	No	No	Yes	No
	— bring in losses	Yes*	Yes	Yes	Yes*	Yes*	Yes*	No*	Yes	Yes	Yes	Yes
13	Deferred tax accounting	Yes	Yes	N/A	No	No	No	No	No	Yes	No	No
14	Bad debt provisions											
	— Specific provision	Yes	Yes*	Yes	Yes	Yes	Yes	Yes*	Yes	Yes	Yes	Yes
	— General provision permitted	Yes	Yes*	Yes	Yes	Yes	Yes	Yes	Yes	Yes	Yes	Yes
	size fixed by law	No	No	No	No	No	Yes*	No*	No	No	Yes	No
	— Details disclosed	Yes*	Yes	No	No	No	No	Yes	No	No	No	No
	— Treatment in accounts											
	— both netted against assets	Yes	Yes	Yes	Yes							
	— specific netted but general shown gross					Yes	Yes			Yes		
	— both shown gross							Yes	Yes		Yes	Yes*
15	Premiums and discounts on purchase of investments amortised	Yes	Yes	No	Yes	No*	No	Yes	No	Yes	No*	Yes*
16	Offsets allowed if legal right exists	Yes	Yes	No	No	No	Yes*	No	No	Yes*	No	Yes*
17	Treatment of goodwill											
	— amortise	Yes*	Yes*	Yes	Yes	Yes	Yes	Yes	No	Yes	No	Yes*
	— write off	Yes*	No	Yes	Yes	Yes	No	No	No	Yes	No	Yes*
	— other	Yes*	No	No	Yes	Yes*	No	No	Yes*	No	Yes*	No

* See text in country chapter for precise details

Australia	Canada	Hong Kong	Japan	Middle East	Bahrain	Kuwait	Saudi Arabia	UAE	Singapore	South Africa		
No*	Yes	Yes	Yes		No	No	No	No	No*	Yes	Supervisory authority separate from central bank	1
											Ability of foreign bank to operate as a	2
No*	No	Yes	Yes		Yes	No	No*	Yes*	Yes*	No*	− branch	
No*	Yes	Yes	Yes*		Yes	No*	No*	No*	No	No*	− subsidiary	
Yes*	Yes	No	Yes		Yes	No	No	No	Yes*	Yes*	Bank accounts subject to own law	3
Yes*	Yes	No	Yes		No*	No	No	No	Yes*	No*	Format and content fixed by law	4
No	Yes	No	Yes		Yes	Yes	No*	Yes	No	No	Mandatory year end date	5
No*	Yes	No*	No		No*	No	No*	No	Yes	No*	Auditors responsible to supervisory authority as well as shareholders	6
No	Yes*	Yes	No*		No	Yes	No*	Yes	Yes	Yes	Hidden reserves permitted	7
No*	Yes	Yes	No*		No*	No	No	No	Yes*	Yes	Requirement to produce consolidated accounts	8
No*	Yes*	No*	Yes		No	No	No	No	No	No	Accounting policies fixed by law	9
Yes*	Yes*	Yes	No*	Yes*					Yes	Yes	Accounting policies published	10
Yes*	Yes*	Yes	No*	Yes*					Yes	Yes	Footnotes included as part of accounts	11
											Foreign exchange translation	12
Yes	Yes	Yes	Yes	Yes					Yes	Yes	− at closing rate	
Yes*	Yes	Yes*	Yes*	Yes*					Yes	Yes*	forward deals − bring in profits	
Yes*	Yes	Yes*	Yes*	Yes*					Yes	Yes*	− bring in losses	
Yes	Yes	No	No	No					Yes	Yes*	Deferred tax accounting	13
											Bad debt provisions	14
Yes	Yes	Yes	Yes*	Yes					Yes	Yes	− Specific provision	
Yes	Yes*	Yes	Yes	Yes					Yes	Yes	− General provision permitted	
No	No	No	Yes*	No					No	No	size fixed by law	
Yes	No	No	Yes*	No*					No	No	− Details disclosed	
											− Treatment in accounts	
Yes		Yes		Yes					Yes	Yes	− both netted against assets	
	Yes										− specific netted but general shown gross	
		Yes*									− both shown gross	
Yes	Yes	Yes	Yes*	Yes*					Yes*	Yes	Premiums and discounts on purchase of investments amortised	15
Yes	Yes*	Yes*	Yes	No*					Yes*	Yes*	Offsets allowed if legal right exists	16
											Treatment of goodwill	17
N/A	Yes	Yes*	Yes	No					Yes	No	− amortise	
N/A	No	Yes*	No	Yes*					Yes	Yes	− write off	
N/A	No	Yes*	No	Yes*					No	No	− other	

* See text in country chapter for precise details

Comparative table of accounting and other requirements

		UK	US	EEC	Belgium	France	Germany	Italy	Luxembourg	The Netherlands	Spain	Switzerland
18	Revaluation of assets permitted	Yes	No*	Yes	Yes	Yes*	No	No*	Yes*	Yes	Yes*	No*
19	Leasing and release of income											
	— straight line	No	No		Yes*	Yes*	Yes	No	N/A	No	Yes*	Yes*
	— investment in lease	Yes	Yes		Yes*	No*	No	Yes	N/A	Yes	No	Yes*
	— 'rule of 78'	Yes	No		Yes*	No*	No	No	N/A	No	No	Yes*
20	Valuation of dealing assets											
	— lower of cost and market value	Yes*	No	Yes	Yes	Yes*	Yes*	Yes*	Yes	No	Yes	Yes*
	— market value	Yes*	Yes	No	No	No	No	No	No	Yes	No	Yes*
21	Pensions											
	—disclosure of basis of accounting	Yes	Yes		No	No	No	No	No	No	No*	No
	— charge to profits	No	No	No	No	No	Yes*	No	No	No	No	Yes
22	Depreciation rates											
	— fixed by law	No	No	No	No	No	No	No	No	No	Yes	No
	— governed by tax requirements	No	No		Yes	Yes	Yes	Yes	Yes	No	No	No
23	Minimum capital requirements	Yes*	Yes	Yes	Yes	Yes	Yes	Yes	Yes	Yes	Yes	Yes
24	Key ratios prescribed by supervisory authorities											
	— capital adequacy, e.g. own funds to public liabilities or total assets	Yes	Yes		Yes	Yes	Yes	Yes	Yes	Yes	Yes	Yes
	— minimum liquid assets	Yes	Yes		No	Yes	Yes	No	Yes	No	Yes	Yes
	— other liquidity ratios	Yes	Yes		Yes	Yes	Yes	Yes	Yes	Yes	No	Yes
	— other ratios	Yes	Yes*		Yes*	Yes	Yes	Yes	Yes	Yes	Yes	Yes
25	Special tax on banks	No	No		No	Yes	No	No	No	No	No	No
26	Items to be included in accounts as a condition of being allowed as a deduction for taxation purposes	No	No		Yes	No	Yes	Yes	Yes	No	No	No

* See text in country chapter for precise details

Australia	Canada	Hong Kong	Japan	Middle East	Bahrain	Kuwait	Saudi Arabia	UAE	Singapore	South Africa		
Yes	No*	Yes	No	Yes*					No*	No*	Revaluation of assets permitted	18
											Leasing and release of income	19
No	No	Yes*	No	No					Yes	No	— straight line	
Yes	Yes	Yes*	Yes	No					No	Yes	— investment in lease	
No	Yes*	Yes*	No	Yes*					Yes	No	— 'rule of 78'	
											Valuation of dealing assets	20
Yes	No	Yes	Yes	Yes*					Yes	No	— lower of cost and market value	
No	Yes	No	No	Yes*					No	Yes	— market value	
											Pensions	21
No	Yes*	No	No	No					Yes*	No*	—disclosure of basis of accounting	
No	No*	No	No	No					Yes*	No*	— charge to profits	
											Depreciation rates	22
No	No	No	Yes	No					No	No	— fixed by law	
No	No	No	Yes	No					No	No	— governed by tax requirements	
No*	Yes	Yes*	Yes		Yes	Yes	Yes	No	Yes	Yes	Minimum capital requirements	23
											Key ratios prescribed by supervisory authorities	24
Yes*	No*	No	**		Yes	No	Yes	Yes	No*	Yes	— capital adequacy, e.g. own funds to public liabilities or total assets	
Yes	Yes*	Yes*	**		Yes	No	Yes	No	Yes*	Yes	— minimum liquid assets	
Yes	Yes*	Yes*	**		Yes	No	Yes	No	Yes*	No	— other liquidity ratios	
Yes	Yes	Yes*	**		Yes	No	No	No	Yes*	Yes	— other ratios	
No	No	No	No		No	No	No	Yes*	No	No	Special tax on banks	25
											Items to be included in accounts as a condition of being allowed as a deduction for taxation purposes	26
No	No	No	No*	N/A	N/A	No	N/A	No*	No			

* See text in country chapter for precise details

** See Japan, Appendix VII

meeting in each year, other than the year of incorporation, and it must take place not more than 15 months after the previous annual general meeting.[28] The first annual general meeting must take place within 18 months of incorporation. The accounts which have been submitted to the members prior to the annual general meeting must be filed with the Registrar of Companies not less than 42 days after the annual general meeting and not less than 10 months (seven months in the case of a public company) after the end of the financial period to which they refer.[29]

2.5.2 *Form of accounts to be furnished*

The directors of a company are required to prepare for each accounting period accounts[30] comprising a balance sheet and a profit and loss account.[31] The form and content of the balance sheet and profit and loss account are contained in schedules 8 and 8A to the Companies Act 1948. The balance sheet is required to give a true and fair view of the state of affairs of the company as at the end of its financial year and the profit and loss account is required to give a true and fair view of the profit or loss of the company for the financial year.[32] There must be annexed to these accounts a report of the auditors[33] and a report of the directors.[34]

This latter report must include reviews of the business of the company and its subsidiaries, recommended dividends, the names of all directors during the financial year, significant differences between the book and market values of land and buildings of the company or its subsidiaries, information regarding directors' interests in capital, details of United Kingdom political and charitable contributions and information regarding employees.

2.5.3 *Mandatory accounting dates*

Companies may give notice to the Registrar of Companies specifying a date (the accounting reference date) in the calendar year as being the date on which in each successive year accounts will be made up to.[35] In the case of banks the usual date used is 31 December. If the company does not give such notice, then the company's accounting reference date will be 31 March.[36] The accounting reference date may not be altered unless specific procedures are complied with.[37]

2.6 Requirements as to accounts (a) prior to incorporation (b) prior to commencement of trading and (c) in order to continue trading

Accounts are not required to be furnished to the Registrar of Companies either prior to incorporation or prior to commencement of trading. Thereafter, if annual returns are not made to the Registrar of Companies within the prescribed periods which start from the date of incorporation, he has the power to strike companies from the register and this would affect its ability to continue trading. The Banking Act makes no stipulation as to when accounts must be furnished. However, the Bank of England clearly may require accounts at any time in order to satisfy itself that it may grant a licence[38] and also that the recognition and licensing should continue.[39]

2.7 Audit requirements

All companies are required to appoint auditors and the first auditors should be appointed by the directors. Thereafter, these auditors should be appointed by members at the annual general meeting and there are rules governing both their appointment, removal and resignation.[40] Auditors have a right of access at all times to the books, accounts and vouchers of the company and are entitled to require from the officers of the company such information and explanations as the auditor thinks necessary for the performance of his duties. In preparing their report on the accounts, auditors are required to carry out such investigations as will enable them to form an opinion whether or not proper books of account have been kept by the company and whether or not the accounts are in agreement with the books of account. In their report, the auditors are required to state whether in their opinion the accounts comply with the requirements of the CA 1948, etc. and show a true and fair view of both the financial position at the year end and of the profit or loss for the year. The auditors must also report if, in their opinion, proper books of account have not been kept and if they have not received adequate information and explanations.[41] There is no obligation to report on these two matters if the auditors are satisfied.

The auditors are also required to consider whether the information given in the directors' report relating to a financial year is consistent with the financial accounts for that year.[42]

Auditors must be members of defined professional bodies[43] which have laid down auditing standards with which members of those bodies must comply. The standards require *inter alia* that auditors should disclose in their report whether or not the audit has been carried out in accordance with those standards.

Directors, officers and employees of a company are not permitted to hold office as auditors of that company.[44]

2.8 Acceptability to fiscal authorities of accounts submitted to supervisory authority

The accounts submitted to the Registrar of Companies will be accepted by the fiscal authorities in the case of companies incorporated in the United Kingdom. However, greater detail will be required and in order to compute the liability to taxation they will be subject to amendment as required by the relevant tax legislation. In the case of overseas companies trading in the United Kingdom, accounts for the trading operation will be required for submission to the fiscal authorities.

---

[28] CA 1948 ss.131, 158
[29] CA 1948 s.126, CA 1976 s.6
[30] CA 1976 s.1
[31] CA 1948 ss. 149, 149A
[32] CA 1948 ss.149(2), 149A(1)
[33] CA 1948 s.156(1)
[34] CA 1948 s.157
[35] CA 1976 s.2(1)
[36] CA 1976 s.2(2)
[37] CA 1976 s.3
[38] BA 1979 s.3, sch 2
[39] BA 1979 s.16
[40] CA 1976 ss.14 to 17
[41] CA 1967 s.14
[42] CA 1981 s.15
[43] CA 1948 s.161 as amended
[44] CA 1948 s.161

2.9 Submission of accounts to any authority other than by requirement of law

Listed companies are required to file with the stock exchange copies of all documents, including the accounts, issued to members. They are also required to prepare, and send to members, an interim financial statement showing the profit earned in the first half of the financial year. The interim statement, which is not required by law, is not subject to audit.

2.10 Application of laws and regulations to foreign banks operating through branches and subsidiaries

Where a foreign bank operates through a subsidiary incorporated in the United Kingdom, the subsidiary will have to comply with all the legal requirements and the foreign bank will be unaffected by those requirements.

In the case of a foreign bank operating through a branch, the bank itself has to comply with all the requirements,[45] except that it does not have to comply with certain of the requirements including *inter alia* to submit a directors' report[46] and auditors' report.

2.11 Availability of accounts for public inspection

All documents including accounts which are filed with the Registrar of Companies are available for public inspection.[47] Information is also publicly available as companies are required to maintain the following registers which are open to inspection by members:
- Members.[48]
- Directors and secretary.[49]
- Charges.[50]
- Shareholdings of directors, spouses and their children.[51]

The accounts of partnerships are not required under partnership law to be available for public inspection. However, a licensed institution must make available at each place of business within the United Kingdom a copy of its most recent audited accounts.[52]

3 FORMAT, STYLE AND CONTENTS OF ACCOUNTS

In Great Britain, that is to say England, Wales and Scotland, the general provisions as to the content and form of companies' accounts including format are contained in section 149 of and schedule 8 to the CA 1948 (as inserted by section 1 of the CA 1981).

The format laid down is not suitable for banks, other financial institutions and insurance companies, for whom the EEC Commission is preparing separate Directives on the form and content of their annual accounts. Therefore, for the time being, these classes of companies may[53] prepare their accounts in accordance with section 149A of and schedule 8A to the CA 1948. These are the original section 149 and schedule 8 before they were renumbered by the CA 1981.

Companies taking advantage of this provision must state in their accounts the fact that they are prepared in compliance with section 149A of and schedule 8A to the CA 1948.

Similar legislation applies to Northern Ireland.

3.1 Extent to which format is laid down by statute, supervisory authority, generally accepted accounting practice or otherwise

In contrast to schedule 8 to CA 1948 (which prescribes a strict format for annual accounts) schedule 8A does not lay down a format for the accounts of banks. However, while neither the supervisory authority nor generally accepted accounting practice have stipulated a format, there is a consensus in the industry which suggests that the balance sheet should show all the assets and liabilities in descending order of liquidity.

3.2 Description of format

As stated in the preceding paragraph there are no laid down formats for the accounts of banks. However, the directors of a company are required to prepare a profit and loss account in respect of each accounting period and a balance sheet as at the date to which the profit and loss account is made up.[54] To these a directors' report[55] and the report of the auditors must be annexed.[56] In addition, generally accepted accounting practice prescribes that there should be a statement of source and application of funds[57] and current cost accounts.[58] The accounts and accompanying documents will, therefore, normally comprise:
- Directors' report.
- Auditors' report.
- Profit and loss account (if the bank has subsidiaries, only a consolidated profit and loss account need be presented).
- Consolidated balance sheet (if the bank has subsidiaries).
- Balance sheet.
- Statement of source and application of funds.
- Notes to the accounts.
- Current cost accounts.

A typical set of accounts is set out in Appendix II.

3.3 Extent to which contents are prescribed by statute, supervisory authority, generally accepted accounting practice or otherwise

In the case of a bank, the contents of its accounts are not rigidly prescribed by statute but there are minimum disclosure rules[59] and these are summarised as follows:
(a) The authorised share capital, issued share capital, liabilities and assets shall be summarised with such particulars as are necessary to disclose the general nature of the assets and liabilities.

[45] CA 1976 ss.9, 10
[46] SI 1982 No. 676
[47] CA 1948 s.426 as amended
[48] CA 1948 s.110
[49] CA 1948 s.200
[50] CA 1948 s.104
[51] CA 1967 ss.27 to 31
[52] BA 1979 s.15
[53] CA 1981 sch 2 para 1
[54] CA 1976 s.1
[55] CA 1948 s.157(1)
[56] CA 1948 s.156(1)
[57] SSAP 10
[58] SSAP 16
[59] CA 1948 s.149A, sch 8A

(b) The balance sheet shall give a true and fair view of the state of affairs at the end of the financial period and the profit and loss account shall give a true and fair view of the profit or loss for the financial period.

(c) The reserves, provisions, liabilities and assets shall be classified under headings appropriate to the company's business.

(d) Fixed assets, current assets and assets that are neither fixed nor current shall be separately identified.

(e) The method or methods used to arrive at the amount of fixed assets under each heading shall be stated.

(f) Provision must be made for any diminution in the value of current assets.

(g) Any notes to the accounts, or documents annexed thereto, shall be deemed to be part of the accounts.

In the case of both the balance sheet and profit and loss account there are specific disclosure requirements and in respect of each item disclosed there must be shown the corresponding figure for the immediately preceding financial period. There must also be disclosed the name and country of incorporation of the ultimate holding company, if any, the basis on which foreign currencies have been converted, and details regarding companies, whether subsidiaries or not, in which more than 10% of any class of equity share capital is held. These requirements are dealt with in more detail in Appendix II.

The disclosure requirements for banks and their holding companies are different from those of other companies in relation to transactions involving directors. The general disclosure requirement is that a company must disclose in its accounts particulars of transactions entered into or subsisting at any time during the accounting period by the company, or its subsidiary, to a director of the company or its holding company, or to a person connected with such a director.[60] However, in the case of banks and their holding companies a register must be maintained containing a copy of every agreement or arrangement, the details of which would have been required to be disclosed in the accounts of the current year and those of each of the preceding 10 years. Furthermore, such companies must prepare a statement, based on the register, of particulars of all the transactions subsisting during the preceding financial year and make the statement available for inspection by members at the annual general meeting and for the preceding 15 days at the company's registered office. The statement must be examined by the auditors who must state in a report attached to the statement whether, in their opinion, it has been properly prepared in accordance with the Act.[61]

The supervisory authority does not prescribe the contents of the accounts but occasionally offers guidelines concerning the treatment of contentious items, e.g. deferred tax.

In the United Kingdom generally accepted accounting practice is codified in Statements of Standard Accounting Practice (SSAPs) issued jointly by the accountancy bodies and which are expected to apply to all accounts intending to give a true and fair view. While these statements do not have the force of law they are mandatory for all listed companies, since the stock exchange will not grant a listing unless a company agrees to apply the statements in the preparation of its accounts. They are also binding on all members of the accountancy bodies concerned and therefore on the auditors. The standards cover a wide range of accounting matters, are added to from time to time, are constantly under review and identify a number of matters which are necessary to the understanding of all accounts produced in the United Kingdom.

Significant departures from standards are required to be disclosed and explained in the accounts and the effect, if material, should also be disclosed. Auditors are required to ensure that significant departures are disclosed and they must accept that the departure is necessary for the accounts to show a true and fair view. If they cannot agree to this they will have to qualify their report.

In particular there are four fundamental accounting concepts which, unless there is a clear statement to the contrary, it must be assumed have been adopted in the preparation of accounts.[62] These are:

(i) The going concern concept:
the business will continue in operational existence for the foreseeable future.

(ii) The accruals concept:
revenue and costs are recognised as they are earned or incurred and are matched in so far as is practicable in the profit and loss account of the period to which they relate.

(iii) The consistency concept:
accountancy treatment is consistent within each accounting period and between one period and the next.

(iv) The prudence concept:
revenue and profits are not anticipated but are dealt with in the accounts of the financial period in which they are realised; provision is made for all known expenses and losses.

Material accounting policies which management has adopted as being best suited to its particular circumstances must be disclosed in the notes to the accounts.

It is interesting to note that the Fourth Council Directive on Company Law[63] adopted these four accounting concepts, together with a fifth, namely that the components of assets and liabilities must be valued separately. These five accounting principles have been incorporated into schedule 8 to the CA 1981 and therefore must be followed in the preparation of accounts generally[64] but are not mandatory for banks at present.

3.4 Disclosure of specific items required other than those required by general law

Banks are not required to disclose information in their accounts other than that which is required for companies as a whole. However, in the case of companies which are listed it must be remembered that there are additional disclosure requirements in force. Certain banks (notably the clearers) now disclose more information and in greater detail than that required by the Companies Acts and, in

---

[60] CA 1980 s.54
[61] CA 1980 s.57
[62] SSAP 2
[63] 78/660/EEC
[64] CA 1948 sch 8 paras 10-14

respect of some items more than is required under the EEC's proposed bank accounts directive.

One of the reasons for this is that certain banks have raised additional long-term funds on overseas markets, particularly in the US where they have had to file prospectuses with the Securities and Exchange Commission and therefore they have had to include in these prospectuses detailed information similar to that provided by US banks. As these documents are available for public inspection the UK banks considered that they should provide their own shareholders with equivalent information.

3.5 Exemptions from disclosure allowed in respect of banking items

Although a banking company may be granted certain exemptions from disclosure by the Department of Trade[65] these are primarily of a general nature rather than being related to specific banking items. Banks granted exemptions are permitted not to disclose:

– The aggregate amount and an analysis of their reserves.

– Movements in their reserves.

– The market value of their listed investments.

– The directors' valuation of their unlisted investments.

– Their operating profit and tax charge.

– Material factors affecting the profit or loss for the year.

It must be emphasised that these exemptions from disclosure are permissive and not mandatory. In practice it is unlikely that any further banks will be granted exemption from disclosure by the Department of Trade.

The exemption granted is from disclosure and not from the use of proper accounting principles in the preparation of the accounts. In particular, the accounts should conform with SSAPs.

A typical set of accounts for a company which has been granted exemption is set out in Appendix III.

3.6 Hidden reserves

Banks who have been granted exemption from disclosure by the Department of Trade are able to maintain hidden, or inner, reserves which are not required to be disclosed, nor are transfers to and from those inner reserves.

Prior to 1969 practically all banks in the United Kingdom were exempt, but the clearing banks disclosed their full reserves for the first time in their 1969 accounts and over the years since then many other banks have elected for full disclosure, until today when it is principally the merchant banks and discount houses which continue to claim exemption status. They consider that they are in competition with similar banks on the continent and they feel that they would give their competitors an unfair advantage if they had to disclose their inner reserves while their continental rivals did not.

Besides maintaining inner reserves, exempt banks tend to follow conservative accounting policies like writing down their premises and other fixed assets, not revaluing their property at current prices and maintaining investments at the lower of cost and market value.

3.7 Requirements as to consolidated accounts

Where at the end of its financial period a company has a subsidiary, and is not itself a wholly-owned subsidiary of another body corporate incorporated in Great Britain, it is required to prepare group accounts dealing with the state of affairs and profit or loss of the company and its subsidiaries.[66]

The accounts prepared must comply, in so far as is practicable, with the requirements of the Companies Acts as if they were the accounts of any actual company[67] and are therefore subject to the same disclosure requirements, except that they are not required to contain certain information relating to directors' and employees' emoluments, investments[68] and transactions involving directors.[69] In combining the accounts of the companies in the group the directors may make such adjustments as they think necessary.[70] SSAP 14 sets out the standard accounting practice in respect of group accounts.

These group accounts have to be included among the documents comprising the accounts of the company. They will, therefore, be sent to every member of the company and to every holder of debentures of the company, and must also be filed with the Registrar of Companies and are subject to audit.

Group accounts need not deal with a subsidiary if the directors of the company are of the opinion that:
(a) It is impracticable, or would be of no real value to the members of the company in view of the insignificant amounts involved, or would involve expense or delay out of proportion to the value to members of the company; or
(b) The result would be misleading, or harmful to the business of the company or any of its subsidiaries; or
(c) The business of the company and the subsidiary are so different that they cannot reasonably be treated as a single undertaking.

The approval of the Department of Trade is necessary if the grounds for exclusion are that it would be harmful or that the businesses are different.[71]

The group accounts required are, subject to certain exceptions, to comprise a consolidated balance sheet and a consolidated profit and loss account dealing with the profit or loss of the company and all the subsidiaries to be dealt with in the group accounts.[72] The exceptions to this are where the directors are of the opinion that the group accounts would be more readily appreciated by the members if they were presented in a different form.[73] If this is the case the same or equivalent information must be disclosed. Under standard accounting practice the onus is on the directors to justify and state the reasons for not presenting group accounts in the form of consolidated statements.[74]

Standard Accounting Practice is that the group accounts should be prepared in the form of a single set of consolidated financial statements covering the holding company and its subsidiary companies in the United Kingdom and overseas.[75] Grounds for exclusion of a

---

[65] CA 1948 sch 8A para 23
[66] CA 1948 s.150(1)
[67] CA 1948 sch 8A para 18
[68] CA 1948 sch 8A para 19
[69] CA 1980 ss. 54, 56
[70] CA 1948 sch 8A para 17
[71] CA 1948 s.150(2)
[72] CA 1948 s.151(1)
[73] CA 1948 s.151(2)
[74] SSAP 14 para 22
[75] SSAP 14 para 15

subsidiary from the consolidation are dissimilarity in business, lack of control either by way of voting rights or by the ability to appoint directors, and the existence of restrictions which impair the holding company's control and temporary control.[76] If these grounds are used for excluding a subsidiary the onus is on the directors to justify and to state the reasons for reaching the conclusion that the resulting group accounts give a fairer view of the financial position of the group as a whole.[77]

4 ACCOUNTING POLICIES

4.1 Responsibility for laying down accounting policies

Both company law[78] and general accounting principles[79] provide that:

(a) Specific accounting concepts must be followed in the preparation of company accounts.

(b) Accounting policies must be applied consistently from year to year and those adopted in the preparation of the accounts must be disclosed by way of note to the accounts.

Further general accounting principles lay down the basis on which specific items should be accounted for. The specific accounting policies used in the preparation of the accounts are the responsibility of the directors since they are required to prepare accounts for each accounting period.[80] At present, schedule 8 to the CA 1948 does not apply to banks.

4.2 Particular accounting policies

4.2.1 Foreign exchange

Assets and liabilities maintained in foreign currencies including commitments for future purchases and sales are normally translated at exchange rates current at the balance sheet date and any differences taken to profit and loss account.

In the case of consolidated accounts the assets and liabilities of foreign subsidiaries are translated at the rates of exchange current at their balance sheet date. Profits and losses are translated at either the average rate for the year or the closing rate. Any difference arising from the translation of the net opening assets at the closing rates is taken to reserves.

4.2.2 Deferred tax

Accounting for deferred taxation is dealt with in Standard Accounting Practice.[81] This standard provides that the liability should be provided where the timing difference which gave rise to the deferral is likely to be reversed in the foreseeable future. The resultant amount should be disclosed in the accounts. In the case of other timing differences the extent of the liability should be determined and the amount disclosed by way of note to the accounts. The requirements of this standard are followed by banks, although in the case of those granted exemption from disclosure the amounts referred to above will not be shown. The policy followed will, however, be described.

4.2.3 Specific and general provisions for bad and doubtful debts

As a matter of prudent financial policy, banks will make provisions against bad and doubtful debts. This is normally assessed on a case-by-case basis and a provision is raised against each loan or advance where it is anticipated there will be a loss, after taking into account the value of any security held.

In the case of consumer credit, due to the large number of loans made it may not be practical to review each loan separately. The provision required will be calculated using a statistical formula based on actual bad debt experience.

Where interest on a loan is not likely to be received, either a provision will be raised against the likely loss or the interest will not be credited to income.

The assessment of the potential loss is always a matter of management judgement and to ensure that a bank is covered against loss it is usual for a bank to raise a general provision for bad and doubtful debts, in addition to the specific provisions raised. The size of this general provision is again a matter of management judgement, taking into account the economic outlook, and in some cases it is assessed at a percentage of the outstanding advances.

Provisions are generally applied against the advance when the extent of the loss has been determined.

4.2.4 Treatment of provisions in accounts

In the United Kingdom a provision is an amount set aside as reasonably necessary for the purpose of providing for any liability or loss which is either likely to be incurred, or certain to be incurred, but uncertain as to amount or as to the date on which it will arise. In the case of those provisions which arise out of the diminution in value of an asset they will normally be netted off against that asset in preparing the balance sheet. Other provisions will normally be dealt with under liabilities and in certain instances may be separately disclosed.

4.2.5 Premiums and discounts on investments (amortise, write off, etc.)

In the case of fixed interest investments with a fixed redemption date, other than those held as current assets for resale, the premiums or discounts are normally amortised on a straight line basis over the period from the date of purchase to the date of maturity.

4.2.6 Offsets, i.e. to what extent can assets and liabilities be set off against each other (legally or in practice)

The netting-off of assets and liabilities does not normally take place except where one can be legally set off against the other for settlement. In the case of individual customers where particular assets and liabilities exist, the

---

[76] SSAP 14 para 21
[77] SSAP 14 para 22
[78] CA 1948 sch 8 paras 9-16 and 36
[79] SSAP 2
[80] CA 1976 s.1
[81] SSAP 15

extent to which their maturity dates and currency are compatible will determine the amount of the set-off. This treatment accords with both the need to disclose the true and fair view of the state of affairs at the balance sheet date and the supervisory approach of the Bank of England dividing all assets into maturity bands (see Section 7).

4.2.7 Goodwill

The amount and the basis on which goodwill is stated in the balance sheet must be disclosed.[82] In the case of a bank there is no statutory requirement for it to be depreciated over its estimated useful life as is the case with other companies[83] and will be the case if the proposed EEC Bank Accounts Directive is adopted.

Goodwill arising on consolidation, that is to say the excess of the cost of acquiring a subsidiary company over the value of the net tangible assets acquired, is treated in a similar manner. In the accounts it is commonly described as 'Premium on acquisition of shares in subsidiaries'. There is neither a statutory requirement nor a requirement under accounting practice to write off such goodwill over its estimated useful life.

However, in practice it is usual either to write off goodwill to reserves in the year of acquisition or to amortise it over its estimated useful life and this is true whether it is purchased goodwill or arising on consolidation.

Goodwill arising on consolidation is defined in SSAP 14 which states that the purchase consideration when a subsidiary is purchased should be allocated between the underlying net tangible and intangible assets, other than goodwill, on the basis of the fair value to the acquiring company. The difference between the purchase consideration and the value ascribed will represent the premium or discount on acquisition. The standard also states that if the values are not adjusted in the books of the acquired company the adjustment must be dealt with on consolidation.

4.2.8 Consolidation

The requirements for consolidated accounts are set out in Section 3.7. The following matters must be taken into account in preparing the consolidated accounts which should be in the form of a single set of accounts and should cover the holding company and all its subsidiary companies at home and overseas:

(a) Uniform accounting policies should be followed by the group and where such policies have not been followed in the accounts of a subsidiary appropriate adjustments should be made if they are material. If this is impracticable, appropriate disclosure will need to be made.

(b) Common accounting dates should be used. If this is not practicable in defined circumstances, appropriate adjustments should be made for any abnormal transactions in the intervening period and details should be given naming the subsidiary, its accounting date and the reason for using a different accounting date.

(c) Changes in the composition of the group. The effective dates of acquisition or disposal must be decided so that the correct profits or losses may be dealt with properly in the consolidated accounts.

(d) Outside or minority interests in the share capital and reserves of subsidiary companies must be disclosed, as must their share of profits. Debit balances should be recognised only if there is a binding obligation on minority shareholders to make them good.

(e) If there are significant restrictions on distributions by subsidiary companies the extent of these restrictions should be indicated.

(f) All inter-group transactions should be eliminated from the consolidated accounts. Particular care should be taken to eliminate all inter-group profits which have not been realised outside the group.

4.2.9 Revaluations of assets

Where appropriate the revaluation, both upwards and downwards, of assets is permitted. If such revaluations are carried out, the fact and the basis thereof should normally be disclosed in the accounts.

Where assets have suffered permanent diminution in value, provision should be considered against such assets, firstly in order that the true and fair view of the state of affairs of the company may be disclosed, and secondly because the directors are required to state if in their opinion any of the current assets have not a value on realisation, in the ordinary course of business, at least equal to the amount at which they are stated in the accounts. Any provision made should be dealt with through profit and loss account.

In the case of fixed assets the Companies Acts require disclosure as to whether assets are carried at cost or valuation. If assets are carried at valuation there are requirements for the bases to be disclosed. In particular it is normal for premises to be revalued on a regular basis since the directors' report is required to disclose significant differences between the book and market values.

Revaluation surpluses, being unrealised, are not available for distribution to shareholders as dividends, although they may be used to pay up shares issued to members as a bonus issue.

In the case of those banks granted exemption from disclosure neither the revaluation surpluses or deficits, nor the fact that assets have been revalued, will be disclosed.

4.2.10 Instalment finance and leasing including basis of recognition of income

In most cases income is recognised over the primary period of the contracts and is credited to profit and loss account in proportion to the net funds invested. The asset is stated in the balance sheet after deducting a provision for unearned income.

4.2.11 Dealing assets

Some banks show as a separate category in their balance sheet assets held with a view to reselling them at a profit in the short-term. These assets are normally valued at the lower of cost and market value but occasionally at market value.

---

[82] CA 1948 sch 8A para 5   [83] CA 1948 sch 8 para 20

4.2.12 Pensions

In the United Kingdom retirement benefits are normally provided through trustees, separate from the employers, who administer what is known as a pension fund. The trustees receive contributions from the employer and invest these so that funds are available to pay pensions as and when they become due. The contributions are normally calculated by actuaries, who take into account both present and future levels of salaries and past short-falls in contributions when they assess current contributions.

4.2.13 Depreciation

Accounting for depreciation is dealt with in SSAP 12 which defines depreciation as 'the measure of the wearing out, consumption or other loss of value of a fixed asset whether arising from use, effluxion of time or obsolescence through technology and market changes'. It lays down that fixed assets having a finite useful life should be depreciated by allocating the cost (or revalued amount) less the estimated residual value over the periods expected to benefit from its use. In respect of each major class of depreciable asset the accounts should disclose the depreciation methods used, the useful lives or depreciation rates, depreciation for the period and the gross amount of depreciable assets and the related accumulated depreciation. The requirements of the standard are an amplification of the information required under the Companies Acts.[84]

Depreciation provided against fixed assets will be deducted from cost or valuation to arrive at the balance sheet value of the assets concerned. However, in the case of those banks granted exemption from disclosure, although they are required to comply with the standard, the information referred to above will not be disclosed.

A review of accounts indicates that the following rates of depreciation are used mainly on a straight line basis:

Freehold property	not less than 50 years
Leasehold property long leases	50 years
short leases	the period of the lease
Motor vehicles	3–5 years
Computers	5–8 years
Other items	1–15 years

5 WINDOW DRESSING

To 'window dress' a balance sheet is generally taken to mean the improvement of its liquidity or possibly the increase of balance sheet totals and it is normally effected by the making of a number of transactions just before the year end which are subsequently reversed after that date. This is a practice which is not approved of in the UK and indeed under SSAP 17 'Accounting for post balance sheet events' an auditor would have to qualify his report if he found any evidence of such a practice.

However, it must be appreciated that a bank, as part of its management of liquidity, will always have a portfolio of short-term assets, the total of which varies from day to day in accordance with the fluctuation of deposits and advances.

6 AMOUNTS REQUIRED TO BE MAINTAINED BY LAW OR OTHERWISE

A recognised bank is required at the time it is granted recognition to have, if it is an institution which provides, or will provide, a wide range of banking services, net assets which amount to not less that £5 million. An institution which provides, or will provide, a highly specialised banking service is required at the time it is granted recognition to have net assets of not less than £250,000.[85] Thereafter must be maintained at all times 'net assets, which, together with other financial resources available to the institution of such a nature and amount as considered appropriate by the Bank, are of an amount which is commensurate with the scale of the institution's operations'.[86]

A licensed institution must at the time it is granted a licence have net assets of not less than £250,000[87] and it must maintain net assets, together with other financial resources available to it, sufficient to safeguard the interests of its depositors. In calculating these net assets regard must be had to the scale and nature of the liabilities of the institution, the source and amounts of deposits accepted by it and the nature of its assets and the degree of risk attached to them. There must also be maintained adequate liquidity, having regard to the relationship between liquid assets and liabilities and the times at which liabilities fall due and assets mature, and provisions for bad and doubtful debts and obligations of a contingent nature.[88]

These amounts may be changed by means of a SI issued by the Treasury after consultation with the Bank of England.

Net assets are defined as paid-up capital and reserves.

The Bank of England requires the larger recognised banks and licensed deposit-takers to maintain a non-interest bearing deposit account with the Bank. The levels of these accounts are fixed twice a year at ½% of the institution's average eligible liabilities over the previous six months. All institutions with eligible liabilities of £10 million or more have to comply with this requirement. Furthermore, the clearers have to maintain an additional booking balance with the Bank of England to cover settlement of their daily clearings.

Eligible liabilities are basically the sterling deposits of the banking system as a whole.

In addition, eligible banks, that is to say those recognised banks whose acceptance of a bill makes it eligible for rediscount at the Bank of England, are required to keep deposits with members of the London Discount Market Association (LDMA) totalling an average of 6% of their eligible liabilities with a minimum on any one day of 4%.

7 KEY RATIOS

BA 1979 lays down minimum net assets which must exist before recognition or a licence are granted and provides

---

84 CA 1948 sch 8A
85 BA 1979 sch 2 para 5
86 BA 1979 sch 2 para 6
87 BA 1979 sch 2 para 9
88 BA 1979 sch 2 para 10

that in the case of recognised banks the institution shall at all times maintain net assets commensurate with the scale of the institution's operations and that in the case of licensed institutions adequate liquidity shall be maintained.[89] The appropriate measurements and ratios have been developed by the Bank of England in consultation with the banks and reference should be made to papers issued from time to time by the Bank. Important among these are:

(a) The measurement of capital (September 1980).
(b) The liquidity of banks (March 1981).
(c) Foreign currency exposure (April 1981).
(d) The measurement of liquidity (July 1982).

7.1 Capital adequacy

The Bank's approach to the assessment of capital adequacy is a flexible one which takes account of the character of each institution, is concerned with the capital required for a continuing business and has regard 'not only to the interests of depositors with particular institutions but also to the maintenance of confidence in the system as a whole'. In consequence it is considered inappropriate to have precise numerical guidelines for the needs of individual businesses. Since the ultimate assessments will depend upon qualitative judgements, based on such matters as profitability and the nature of the business, there is a range of capital ratios which may be regarded as adequate.

When the Bank assesses the capital adequacy of United Kingdom incorporated deposit-taking businesses it takes into account both their consolidated operations on a worldwide basis and whether or not deposit-taking subsidiaries in the United Kingdom are adequately capitalised in their own right.

The Bank has identified the two most important objectives of capital ratios as being:

(a) To ensure that the capital position of an institution is regarded as acceptable by its depositors and other creditors.
(b) To test the adequacy of capital in relation to the risk of losses which may be sustained.

It therefore considers it desirable that one of the measures of capital to be used by the Bank should be made up of items which are as far as possible available to the public, because the public's judgement based upon such information will have an important bearing on the stability of particular institutions. The second objective requires information which may only be available to the institution itself and the supervisory authority, and the measure devised will, therefore, not be based on information normally available to the public.

The Bank has concluded that the objectives will best be met by the following ratios:

(a) Free capital ratio: the measurement of the adjusted capital base against all other non-capital liabilities apart from contingent liabilities which are incorporated within the balance sheet.
(b) Risk asset ratio: the measurement of the adjusted capital base against the adjusted total of risk assets.

In the succeeding paragraphs the way in which these items are calculated is set out and consideration is given to the reasons for specific adjustments.

The capital base is made up as follows:

(a) Share capital. The amount paid-up on issued ordinary and non-redeemable preference shares and share premium account. Neither authorised but unissued shares nor amounts not paid-up on issued shares are included. Redeemable preference shares are dealt with as subordinated loan capital.

(b) Loan capital. Items which are fully subordinated to other creditors, including depositors, which have an initial term of not less than five years to maturity and which have no restrictive covenants. The maximum amount which may be included is limited to one third of the capital base net of outstanding goodwill and amounts are subject to straight line amortisation in the last five years of life.

(c) Minority interests arising on consolidation. These are included in the capital base for the assessment of group capital adequacy although they may be excluded in whole or part if the Bank considers their availability to be restricted.

(d) Reserves. Balance on profit and loss account and general reserves, however described.

(e) Provisions. General bad debt provisions less any associated deferred tax asset. Provisions for specific bad debts, for interest suspended and for current and deferred taxation are excluded.

In order to arrive at the adjusted capital base for gearing ratio purposes the following additional deductions have to be made:

(a) Investments in subsidiaries and associated companies and trade investments. The deduction should also include lending to such companies which have the character of capital.
(b) Goodwill.
(c) Premises from which the bank operates.
(d) Equipment and other fixed assets used in those premises.

In calculating all other non-capital liabilities the following will not be included:

(a) Subordinated loan stocks disallowed by the qualifying criteria for the capital base.
(b) The liability of Scottish and Northern Irish banks for their own note issue to the extent that it is covered by Bank of England notes and by coin. Banks in England and Wales are not entitled to issue their own bank notes.

Different criteria are considered appropriate in arriving at the capital base used for calculating the risk asset ratio as compared with that used for calculating the gearing ratio. Accordingly, no deduction is made for premises from which the bank operates, since it is considered that they are no more vulnerable than other property assets, and regard will be had to any genuine hidden values in the balance sheet and to any overstatement of assets in relation to their market value. Deductions will continue to be made for investments in subsidiary and associated companies, trade investments, goodwill and equipment and other fixed assets.

Three types of risk — credit, investment and forced sale — inherent in the assets themselves are taken into account in the standard risk asset calculation by applying

---

[89] BA 1979 sch 2

12

weightings to different assets reflecting the extent to which they are susceptible to these risks. The relevant weightings are set out by multiplying each balance sheet asset by its weighting and adding them together.

In considering the risk asset ratio it must be emphasised that the calculation is only the first step in the assessment of capital adequacy by this method. There remains the qualitative judgement to be made, which will take into account the particular circumstances of each bank or licensed institution.

7.2 Liquidity

As in the case of capital adequacy the Bank of England does not seek to impose a standard ratio but instead takes into account the particular circumstances of each institution and its place within the banking system. Its objective 'is to ensure that banks' management policies apply a prudent mix of liquidity . . . appropriate to the circumstances of that bank and that these policies are sustained at all times'. In order to achieve this the Bank of England will hold regular meetings with senior management and will wish to consider liquidity in the light of a bank's own internal management policies.

The basis of measurement adopted by the Bank is based on a cash flow approach and may deal with all currencies together, although it may be used for a particular currency or for groups of currency. In principle the measurement takes into account all assets and liabilities and is not confined to banking assets and liabilities. This means that significant items such as tax liabilities are taken into account.

All assets and liabilities are divided into maturity bands with the net positions in each band being accumulated specifically. Marketable assets, subject to agreed discounts, will be included in the earliest bands and commitments will be recognised as liabilities and dealt with in the appropriate band. However, various items, such as undrawn overdraft facilities and lending repayable only nominally on demand, will have to be discussed with the Bank before their treatment is determined.

The system of measurement is illustrated in the following table:

	Sight-8 days	8 days-1 month	1-3 months	3-6 months	6-12 months
Liabilities					
Deposits					
Commitments					
Less:					
Assets					
Marketable					
Non-marketable					
Standby facilities available					
= Net position					
+/−Carried forward					
= Net cumulative position					

Contractual standby facilities made available by other banks are to be taken into account as sight assets, although regard must be paid to their remaining term and the possibility that they may not be renewed. Facilities made available to other banks are treated in the same way as commitments to lend at some uncertain future date.

The liquidity calculations form the basis for discussions with the senior management of particular banks about their liquidity policies and its management, and for the establishment of guidelines of liquidity adequacy. These guidelines will vary according to the circumstances of individual banks.

8 ACCOUNTING RETURNS OTHER THAN ACCOUNTS
8.1 By whom required
8.2 Nature of requirements

The Bank of England requires returns on a regular basis setting out accounting information for both supervisory and statistical purposes. The returns are not subject to audit and they may be broadly categorised under the following headings:
− Accounts on a more detailed basis than those required under the Companies Acts.
− Maturity analyses of assets and liabilities in both sterling and other currencies.
− Foreign currency exposure.
− Annual valuations.

Depending upon the particular returns, these are required to be submitted on weekly, monthly, quarterly or annual bases within fixed periods from the reporting date. There is available a 'Banking statistics definition folder' which gives details of the items referred to in the various forms.

The principal accounting form is a balance sheet return which is required to be completed monthly as at third Wednesday (second Wednesday in December) and quarterly as at end of March, June, September and December to be returned within seven calendar days of the reporting date. The information in the form is set out in two columns, namely sterling and other currencies.

Liabilities are set out under the following main headings, each of which is further subdivided.
(a) Notes in circulation.
(b) Deposit liabilities.
(c) Items in suspense.
(d) Credit terms in course of transmission.
(e) Capital and other funds.

Assets are set out under the following main headings, each of which is further subdivided:
(a) Cash.
(b) Debit items in course of collection.
(c) Market loans.
(d) Special deposits and cash ratio deposits with Bank of England.
(e) Bills (excluding lending under special schemes).
(f) Lending under special schemes for exports and ship building.
(g) Other loans and advances.
(h) Assets leased to customers.
(i) Investments.

(j) Items in suspense.

(k) Other assets.

Details of acceptances, refinanced lending at fixed rates and the total amount of overdraft, loan and acceptance facilities must also be given.

The information given in the returns is used by the Bank in calculating the ratios referred to in Section 7.

The returns are not available for public inspection although in some instances they form the basis for published industry and economic statistics in aggregate.

9 TAXATION

9.1 General method of taxation

The United Kingdom's fiscal year ends on 5 April in each year and the Treasury budgets are presented, usually annually, to parliament in March or April. The proposals as amended become law in the Finance Act for that year which is usually passed in July or August. The budgets cover *inter alia* company taxation (corporation tax and capital gains tax), personal taxation (income tax and capital gains tax), taxes on goods and services (value added tax and customs and excise duties) and social security payments. In addition to taxation raised by central government, local authorities raise money by means of property taxes (rates). The law relating to taxation is contained in the Income and Corporation Taxes Act 1970 and subsequent Finance Acts. The Acts need to be read in conjunction with relevant decisions of the courts.

(a) Company taxation

This is administered on behalf of the government by the Board of Inland Revenue, which operates through local Inspectors of Taxes, and a company or branch deals with the Inspector for the district in which its registered office is situated. Assessments to taxation will be made by the Inspector before the due date. If agreement has been reached between the Inspector and the taxpayer the agreed figure will be assessed. Otherwise, an estimate figure will be assessed. Appeals against estimated assessments must be made in order to keep the position open until the correct liability can be determined and in disputed cases this may involve reference to the courts. Taxation is payable to the Collector of Taxes.

Corporation tax payable by a company is divided into that payable on trading income and that payable on disposal of capital assets.

The rate of corporation tax on trading income is fixed, normally retrospectively, in the Annual Budget and this rate applies to accounting periods or parts thereof falling within the financial year ended 31 March, i.e. the tax year. Although the rate has remained unchanged for several years at 52%, the 1984 Finance Act gradually reduces the rate in annual steps to 35% in the financial year commencing 1 April 1986. There are provisions for lower rates for companies with small taxable profits (£100,000 or less) and there is marginal relief where the profits are between £100,000 and £500,000. However, if the small company is a part of a group the concession is affected by the number of companies, wherever located, in that group.

The effective rate of taxation for capital gains is 30% and has remained unchanged for some time.

Taxes are payable nine months after the end of the accounting period to which they relate. However, in respect of businesses established prior to April 1964 tax is payable on 1 January in the financial year after that in which the accounting period ends. In no case will the delay in payment be less than nine months although it may be as long as 23 months. There are provisions for payment of interest on overdue payments and such interest is not allowable as an expense in computing income for taxation purposes.

It should be noted, however, that where a company pays a dividend it is also required to make an advance payment of corporation tax on trading income. This is explained in some detail later on in this section.

In the case of both subsidiaries and branches the trading profit for taxation purposes will be based on the results shown in the accounts, but adjustments will be made to convert results ascertained from accounts prepared in accordance with normal accounting principles into profits for taxation purposes. In the case of representative offices there are no taxable profits or losses since the bank concerned is not trading in the United Kingdom.

Trading losses may be set against chargeable gains or other profits arising in the same company or branch in the same accounting period. They may also be surrendered, where the appropriate relationship exists, for offset against the profits of another group company in the same accounting period. The necessary relationship exists if both are resident in the United Kingdom and one owns 75% or more of the equity capital of the other or another resident United Kingdom company owns 75% or more of each of them. The relationship does not exist if their immediate holding company is not a resident company.

If trading losses cannot be used in this way they may be used to offset any profits arising in the preceding accounting period, provided the company was, in that period, carrying on the same trade, or may be carried forward indefinitely for offset only against profits arising from the same trade in succeeding accounting periods. It must, however, be stressed in relation to losses carried forward or back, that surrenders against the profits of other group companies are not permitted.

A branch of a foreign bank may remit profits after taxation has been charged to its head office without a further deduction of withholding tax or any other United Kingdom taxation consequences. Such a remittance is not regarded as a dividend.

A United Kingdom company can only distribute its profits by way of dividend and when doing so it must account to the Revenue Authorities for Advance Corporation Tax (ACT) which is calculated on the amount of the dividend. Any payment due must be made immediately following the end of the quarter in which the dividend was paid. So far as the company is concerned this is an advance payment of corporation tax in respect of the period in which the dividend is paid. When the corporation tax liability is agreed this payment may, subject to certain limitations, be set off against it.

Any amounts of ACT unrelieved (that is to say not off-set against the corporation tax liability for the year) may be carried forward indefinitely for offset against future corporation tax liabilities. Alternatively they may be offset against corporation tax liabilities of the six preceding years or against the liability of another United Kingdom company in which more than 50% of the equity capital is held. The treatment of ACT in the accounts is dealt with in SSAP 8. This provides that amounts unrelieved may be carried forward as deferred taxation unless they cannot be offset in the foreseeable future, in which case they must be written off in the profit and loss account.

The rate of ACT varies with the personal rate of income tax. The rate has for some time been three sevenths of the dividend, equivalent to 30% of the aggregate of the dividend and the ACT.

A United Kingdom resident company may make a claim to offset foreign tax already suffered on overseas income against its corporation tax liability. The foreign tax, if claimed for such offset, must be offset before ACT has been offset and if the rate at which foreign tax was suffered exceeds the current rate of corporation tax then relief is restricted to that rate. There is a further restriction in the case of foreign withholding taxes: only 15% can qualify for credit relief (tax against tax) as above. If the withholding tax is at a rate greater than 15% the excess is treated as an expense. Any other tax not claimed for credit relief will be treated as an expense in arriving at taxable profits.

Capital gains fall within the scope of corporation tax as chargeable gain, with only a proportion of the gain being treated as taxable, hence the lower effective rate. Trading losses may be offset against chargeable gains of the same or the immediately preceding period but trading losses brought forward may not be offset against the chargeable gains of a succeeding period. Where the proceeds of the sale of an asset are subsequently reinvested in another asset used in the business there are provisions for 'rollover relief', that is to say postponing the tax liability until the new asset is sold.

Capital losses cannot be offset against trading profits or chargeable gains in other group companies. They may only be carried forward (not backward) against subsequent capital gains arising in the same company.

(b) Property taxes (rates)

All properties in the United Kingdom have a rateable value and local authorities levy rates expressed as an amount per £ of rateable value. The rate is fixed in February or March of each year, for the following year to 31 March. The timing of payments varies from local authority to local authority but is likely to be on a quarterly or half-yearly basis.

Rates are treated as an expense for corporation tax purposes.

9.2 Accounts as basis for taxation

United Kingdom taxation will be assessed on the basis of computations sent to the local Inspector of Taxes for the area in which the company or branch is situated. The tax period for which computations are submitted will be the same as the relevant financial accounting period. The computations should be supported by the accounts, and by other relevant data.

In the case of a company, the accounts submitted to the Inspector of Taxes will be those approved by the shareholders supplemented by additional data including a detailed trading and profit and loss account. In the case of a branch, the accounts should comprise balance sheet and detailed trading and profit and loss account and should include all income and expenses arising from the operations of the branch in the United Kingdom.

The Inland Revenue are entitled to carry out their own investigations of the underlying records but it is unusual for them to do so. This is probably because all company accounts are audited by recognised auditors and the use of professional advisers to present the computations is widespread.

9.3 Adjustments permitted or required

Adjustments are required to convert the results ascertained from accounts prepared in accordance with normal accounting principles into profits for taxation purposes. These are contained in the computations submitted to the Inspector of Taxes and fall broadly into the following categories:

(a) Expenses specifically disallowed by statute, e.g. entertainment expenses.

(b) Expenditure to be disallowed as not incurred wholly and exclusively for the purpose of the trade (this relates mainly to personal expenditure in proprietary companies but could arise in the case of non-proprietary companies, e.g. expenditure for the benefit of another company in the same group or contributions to a political party).

(c) The elimination of capital expenditure, depreciation or capital gain from the accounts and the substitution for it of any available tax allowance or gain calculated under capital gains rule.

(d) Amounts, including provisions, set aside in the accounts for the period but allowed as a charge against taxable profit when a loss is sustained or cash is paid out.

Specific adjustments for tax purposes in the case of banks
Capital allowances

Depreciation charges are not allowed in tax computations but capital allowances may be set against trading income. Capital allowances are calculated by reference to the cost of capital assets acquired for the purposes of trade. Different classes of asset attract different types of allowance and the basic rules for the principal categories are set out below:

(a) Buildings rank for allowances only where they are classified as industrial; banking premises do not fall within this category.

(b) Premiums payable on the acquisition of leasehold premises will not normally attract allowance, unless they can properly be allocated to furniture and equipment included, in which case they may be treated as plant and machinery. If, however, a new lease is granted by the freeholder (as opposed to the bank being assigned an existing lease), with less than 50 years to run, a proportion of any premium paid may be deemed to be rent and allowed as a deduction over the period of the lease. In such cases, the shorter the term of the lease, the higher the proportion of the premium which may be treated as rent.

(c) Leasehold improvements and refurbishments do not normally rank for capital allowances and this restriction will usually apply where the work relates to the structure or fabric of the building. Some improvements, for instance the installation of an air conditioning system, may rank as plant and machinery and attract the corresponding allowances. Furthermore, expenditure correctly classified as repairs, rather than improvements, may properly be charged as a normal trading expense.

(d) Motor vehicles for use by bank employees in the course of their employment attract capital allowances at 25% p.a. on the written down balance at the start of each accounting period. The annual allowance is not to exceed a specified amount for any one vehicle.

(e) Plant and machinery is the major source of capital allowances. As noted above, the precise definition of plant and machinery is complex but items which would certainly fall within this category include telephone and telex, heating and ventilation equipment, accounting machines and computers, carpets and curtains, office furniture and commercial vehicles. Office partitioning may also be allowed in certain circumstances. On all such items, a 'first year allowance' (at present 75%) may be claimed, based on 100% of the acquisition cost. This allowance can be claimed whether the goods are new or secondhand, although it will not apply if the goods are acquired from a connected party. The purchaser is permitted to disclaim all or part of the first year allowance (in which case any unclaimed balance of cost of the assets is carried forward and claimed at 25% p.a. on the reducing balance in succeeding periods). The 1984 Finance Act has brought in legislation to phase out first year allowances by 31 March 1986, after which capital allowances will be available at 25% per annum on the reducing balance.

(f) The availability of capital allowances on leased plant or machinery will depend on the terms of the lease, but it is common for capital allowances to be available to the lessor provided that the lessee would have been able to claim such allowances in the case of outright purchase.

Provisions against loans

General provisions against the loan portfolio as a whole are not allowable for tax purposes. Specific provisions against particular loans are deductible, but it may be necessary to substantiate the requirement for a provision and the Inland Revenue could and does question the need for the provision. An event of default, even if it has not yet resulted in the loans being called in, would provide persuasive, though not conclusive evidence in such circumstances.

Provisions against securities

Provisions against securities (reducing cost prices to market values, where this is appropriate) will in general only be treated as deductible for tax if the securities are held as current assets purchased with the intention of resale. It may be necessary to demonstrate that there is a trade of dealing in securities, that the securities concerned are managed and accounted for separately from other securities held for the longer term and that the volume of purchase and sales is large enough to indicate an active trade. In the case of other securities, any profit or loss arising will be dealt with for taxation purposes on maturity or disposal, and amortisation of the original premium or discount in the original cost debited or credited to the profit and loss account while the securities are held, will be ignored for tax purposes.

Discounted bills

Discounts arising on bills of exchange will also usually be taken evenly to profit in the accounts over the period to maturity. For taxation purposes, however, there is an alternative basis under which no income is recognised until the bill matures.

Foreign exchange

Trading in foreign exchange is part of a bank's normal activity and taxation treatment will follow normal accounting treatment for profits or losses arising on the translation at different rates of current assets and liabilities expressed in foreign currency and of outstanding forward contracts. Different considerations apply when exchange differences arise on assets and liabilities which are longer term in nature. Exchange differences arising on capital investments will be treated in the same way as any other changes in the value of such investments; profits and losses will be recognised for tax only on disposal of the investment, and be incorporated in the calculation of the capital gain or loss.

Interest

(a) If recognition is obtained from the Inland Revenue that a bona fide banking business is being carried on then subject to (c) below virtually all interest will be received and paid without the withholding of any UK income tax, although foreign withholding taxes will obviously have been deducted where applicable. The only case where UK income tax might need to be deducted would be in the payment of interest on long-term borrowings which are regarded as part of the bank's capital structure rather than deposits taken in the ordinary course of banking business.

(b) Before granting recognition, the Inland Revenue is likely to need to be satisfied that the bank is offering a full range of banking services, including current accounts and cheque books. If recognition is not obtained, the institution will be required to receive and pay certain interest net of UK income tax (presently 30%) including all interest paid to foreign residents (subject to the provisions of relevant double tax agreements) and all interest paid to UK depositors or received from UK borrowers unless they are themselves recognised as banks by the Inland Revenue.

(c) It should be noted however, that from 6 April 1985 interest paid by banks and certain other financial institutions on deposits placed with them by individuals resident in the UK will in effect be paid at a 'net' level. This results from the banks being required to pay over to the Inland Revenue tax on such interest at a composite rate. This rate will be less than the standard rate of income tax and it will be fixed by the Inland Revenue each year before 31 December for the next tax year commencing on the 6 April.

16

This will bring bank interest paid to individuals onto the same footing as building society interest and banks will have to account for this tax when paying the relevant interest. However, the interest will only be paid over to the Inland Revenue on a quarterly basis and any income tax suffered on income received by the bank may be deducted from the amount due. Interest on certain deposits, e.g. certificates of deposit and time deposits of over £50,000 and for more than 28 days, is outside this arrangement.

(d) So far as concerns UK tax suffered on interest receivable (which is unusual, as indicated above) the tax suffered can be subsequently recovered by deduction from corporation tax liabilities or in cash.

(e) Interest payable under deduction of tax per the final sentence of (a) above is in general treated as a charge on income rather than as a trading expense. It will be allowable as and when paid rather than when accrued, and this will give rise to adverse timing differences in the corporation tax computations. Furthermore, if charges exceed trading profit in any accounting period, they may not be carried back and offset against the trading profit of the previous period (as a trading loss could), although they may be carried forward for offset against future profits.

(f) The doubtful areas, in relation to deductibility of interest paid by a bank on its long-term funding, are:

(i) Payment of interest by a branch on long-term funding raised from non-residents.

(ii) Payment of interest whether by a branch or a subsidiary on such long-term funding, where the interest is payable to a separate but affiliated company which is not resident in the UK.

In both cases, the difficulty may be removed by a double tax treaty between the UK and the country of the recipient. The rules are complex, however, and advice should be sought from accountants.

Management charges between group companies

For either a subsidiary or a branch, it is reasonable that a management charge should be made by head office, or other relevant group company, for the various supervision, administrative and support services offered. This should cover all direct expenses incurred (including secondment of staff, travelling, telephone and telex, time allocated by head office supervisory, operational and audit personnel) and is likely to include a proportion of general overhead expenditure not directly identifiable to the UK operation. The Inland Revenue are likely to wish to scrutinise such charges closely to ensure that they are reasonable, reflect fairly the relationship between the parties and are applied consistently from year to year (and applied consistently between the UK operation and others elsewhere in the world). This applies equally whether the charge is a notional deduction for tax purposes in a branch's books or a formally invoiced charge to a subsidiary company. In the former instance, the Inland Revenue may renegotiate the figure, in the latter case it could disallow a proportion of the charge as not incurred wholly and necessarily for the purpose of the United Kingdom trade.

Interest charges between group companies

(a) Banking operations may lend significant sums to their head office or parent company, and it is important that such loans carry an appropriate rate of interest. It is now generally accepted that the margin made by the UK branch or subsidiary should be equivalent to that which it would expect to earn on lending to another bank of similar size and standing. If the Inland Revenue are dissatisfied with interest income calculations made on this basis, they are entitled to argue for the substitution of higher rates.

(b) Similar criteria apply to the charging of interest on loans which have been negotiated in the United Kingdom and booked abroad or vice versa. The primary consideration in allocating profits will be the country where the credit risk is taken, but adequate compensation would also be expected for negotiation or managing the loan at another location. Borrowings from connected companies abroad also require to be dealt with on a similar basis and the Inland Revenue would seek to disallow excessive interest charges on deposits.

Free capital

In the case of a United Kingdom branch of an overseas company branch, a further adjustment requires to be made to allow for 'free capital'. This adjustment is designed to compensate for the fact that a United Kingdom subsidiary company operates with a base of share capital and reserves from which its shareholders do not receive a return in a form which gives the company a tax deduction, whereas a London branch may often be funded from its head office and the amount of its 'free capital' cannot be assessed as objectively. The Inland Revenue will seek to disallow interest on those borrowings which are considered to constitute 'free capital', and the calculation of this capital for a specific branch will be the subject of detailed discussion with the Inland Revenue.

9.4 Effect of tax considerations on presentation of accounts

Since the profits shown by the statutory accounts are required to be adjusted as explained in Section 9.3, in order that profits for tax purposes may be calculated, tax considerations will not normally affect the presentation of the accounts.

10 INTERPRETATION OF ACCOUNTS

10.1 Adequacy of information as to contents and disclosure

In the case of those companies which take advantage of the exemptions provided for banks under the Acts[90] information relative to profits (both before and after taxation), bad debt reserves, taxation, movements in reserves and provisions, the classification of liabilities, fixed assets and the valuation of investments will not be available. A reader of the accounts will therefore have

---

[90] CA 1948 Sch 8A para 23

inadequate information on which to make a full assessment of the bank's position. In the case of other companies adequate information should be disclosed.

10.2 Audit and reliability of information

As mentioned in Section 2.7 in the United Kingdom all companies are required to appoint auditors whose duties in connection with the examination of the accounts are laid down by statute.

In addition Standard Accounting Practice requires that the auditors must ensure that significant departures from that practice are disclosed and the effect of the departure is quantified.

These provisions ensure that the information contained in the accounts of companies should be reliable.

In the case of partnerships there are no comparable statutory provisions regarding the preparation of accounts, their contents or their audit, although the BA 1979 stipulates that in the case of licensed institutions a copy of its most recent audited accounts must be available for inspection at each place of business within the United Kingdom. On the presumption that the Bank of England would not allow such accounts to be markedly different from the accounts displayed by other licensed institutions, it may be assumed that similar standards of reliability will apply.

10.3 Comparability between different banks on the basis of published accounts or publicly available returns

In the case of a bank which has been granted exemption from the disclosure of certain items there will be insufficient information available for a satisfactory comparison to be made with other banks. In particular there will be no information available as to the full extent of reserves, and the disclosed net profit will be shown after taxation and transfers to or from inner reserves.

In the case of a bank which has not taken advantage of the exemptions from disclosure there will be more information available for comparison purposes. However, in making such comparisons full regard must be had to the accounting policies adopted by individual banks. These may not necessarily be the same since the requirement is that each company must adopt policies on a consistent basis, that such policies must be appropriate to the business and that the policies must be disclosed. In general, accounting practice does not require that the policies adopted should be identical for all companies. Comparability will be particularly affected by the policies adopted in connection with provisions for bad and doubtful debts, leasing finance and foreign currency translation.

APPENDIX I

Laws and regulations governing banks

Bank Charter Act 1844

Bank Notes (Scotland) Act 1845

Stamp Act 1853

Bankers Books Evidence Act 1879

The Bills of Exchange Act 1882

Bank of England Act 1946

Cheques Act 1957

Prevention of Fraud Investments Act 1958

Building Societies Act 1962

Consumer Credit Act 1974

Banking Act 1979

A typical set of accounts

A Bank plc

Directors' Report

The directors' reports must deal with the following matters:

(1) A fair view of the development of the business of the company and its subsidiaries during the financial year and of the position at the end of it. In particular it must refer to:

(a) Particulars of important events affecting the company or its subsidiaries occurring after the year end.

(b) Likely future developments in the business of the company.

(c) The activities, if any, of the company in the field of research and development.

(2) Recommended dividend.

(3) Names of all directors during financial year.

(4) Principal activities of company and its subsidiaries, including significant changes during year.

(5) Indication of any significant difference between book and market value of land and buildings of company, or any of its subsidiaries.

(6) Loans to directors if over £100,000 at any time during year.

(7) Particulars of arrangements to enable directors to benefit from acquisition of shares or debentures.

(8) Directors' interests, as recorded in register, in shares or debentures of group companies, give details at beginning (or at later date of appointment) and end of year. This may be given by way of note to the company's accounts instead of in the directors' report (CA81 s13(4)).

(9) Totals of UK political and charitable contributions respectively of the company or group, if together more than £200; for each political contribution of £200 name person or party. (Wholly owned subsidiaries of UK companies are exempt.)

(10) If the company has more than 250 employees under contracts of service working wholly or mainly in the UK, a statement describing the policy applied during the year:

(a) For giving full and fair consideration to applications for employment made by disabled persons, having regard to their particular aptitudes and abilities.

(b) For continuing the employment of, and for arranging appropriate training for, employees of the company who have become disabled persons during the period when they were employed by the company.

(c) For the training, career development and promotion of disabled persons employed by the company.

A Bank plc

Analysis of operating profit for the year ended...

	This year (£000)		Preceding year (£000)	
Interest income	xxx		xxx	
Investment income	xxx		xxx	
Commissions receivable	xxx		xxx	
Other income	xxx	xxx	xxx	xxx
Interest payable	xxx		xxx	
Bad and doubtful debts	xxx	xxx	xxx	xxx
		xxx		xxx
Operating expenses	xxx		xxx	
Personnel	xxx		xxx	
Premises and equipment	xxx		xxx	
Other	xxx	xxx	xxx	xxx
Operating profit		xxx		xxx

The notes on pages x to x form part of these accounts.

A Bank plc

Consolidated profit and loss account for the year ended...

	This year (£000)	Preceding year (£000)
Operating profit	xxx	xxx
Share of profits of associated companies	xxx	xxx
Interest on loan capital	xxx	xxx
Profit before taxation	xxx	xxx
Taxation	xxx	xxx
	xxx	xxx
Minority interests in subsidiary companies	xxx	xxx
	xxx	xxx
Extraordinary items	xxx	xxx
Profit attributable to ordinary shareholders	xxx	xxx
Dividends	xxx	xxx
Retained profit	xxx	xxx
Earnings per share	x	x

The notes on pages x to x form part of these accounts.

A Bank plc

Consolidated balance sheet

Liabilities	This year (£000)		Preceding year (£000)		Assets	This year (£000)		Preceding year (£000)	
Current, deposit and other accounts	xxx		xxx		Cash in hand and with central banks	xxx		xxx	
Current taxation	xxx		xxx		Money at call and short notice	xxx		xxx	
Dividend	xxx	xxx	xxx	xxx	Bills discounted	xxx	xxx	xxx	xxx
Deferred taxation		xxx		xxx	Cheques in course of collection		xxx		xxx
Loan capital		xxx		xxx	Investments other than trade investments		xxx		xxx
Minority interests in subsidiaries		xxx		xxx	Advances and other accounts		xxx		xxx
Share capital and reserves					Trade investments		xxx		xxx
Issued share capital	xxx		xxx		Investments in associated companies		xxx		xxx
Reserves	xxx	xxx	xxx	xxx	Premises and equipment		xxx		xxx
		xxx		xxx			xxx		xxx

Signatures of at least two directors

Date of signing

The notes on pages x to x form part of these accounts.

A Bank plc

Balance sheet

Liabilities	This year (£000)		Preceding year (£000)		Assets	This year (£000)		Preceding year (£000)	
Current, deposit and other accounts	xxx		xxx		Cash in hand and with central banks	xxx		xxx	
Current taxation	xxx		xxx		Money at call and short notice	xxx		xxx	
Dividends	xxx	xxx	xxx	xxx	Bills discounted	xxx	xxx	xxx	xxx
Amounts due to subsidiaries		xxx	xxx	xxx	Cheques in course of collection		xxx		xxx
Deferred taxation		xxx	xxx	xxx	Investments other than trade investments		xxx		xxx
Loan capital		xxx	xxx	xxx	Advances and other accounts		xxx		xxx
Share capital and reserves					Balances due from subsidiaries		xxx		xxx
Issued share capital	xxx		xxx		Trade investments		xxx		xxx
Reserves	xxx	xxx	xxx	xxx	Investments in associated companies		xxx		xxx
					Investments in subsidiaries		xxx		xxx
					Premises and equipment		xxx		xxx
		xxx		xxx			xxx		xxx

Signatures of at least two directors

Date of signing

The notes on pages x to x form part of these accounts.

21

A Bank plc

Statement of source and application of funds

	This year (£000)	Preceding year (£000)
Source of funds		
Profit before taxation	xxx	xxx
Items not involving the movement of funds	xxx	xxx
Depreciation	xxx	xxx
Amounts retained by associated companies	xxx	xxx
Minority interests	xxx	xxx
Exchange adjustments	xxx	xxx
Funds generated by operations	xxx	xxx
Funds from other sources		
Disposal of trade investments	xxx	xxx
Disposal of fixed assets	xxx	xxx
Issue of shares	xxx	xxx
Issue of loan capital	xxx	xxx
	xxx	xxx
	xxx	xxx
Application of funds		
Additions to trade investments, associated companies and fixed assets	xxx	xxx
Taxation paid	xxx	xxx
Dividends paid	xxx	xxx
Increase in working capital	xxx	xxx
	xxx	xxx
Increase in working capital is represented by		
Increase in advances and other accounts	xxx	xxx
Increase/(decrease) in other monetary assets	xxx	xxx
	xxx	xxx
Increase in current and deposit accounts and other liabilities	xxx	xxx
	xxx	xxx

The notes on pages x to x form part of these accounts.

A Bank plc

Notes to the accounts

(1) The accounts are prepared in accordance with the provisions of Companies Act 1948 S 149A and schedule 8A.

(2) Basis of consolidation, i.e. a description of how the assets, liabilities, profits and losses of subsidiaries and associated companies have been dealt with in the group accounts.

(3) Accounting policies, including those relating to bad and doubtful debts, investments, depreciation of fixed assets, instalment finance, leased assets, pension contributions, deferred taxation and foreign currencies and the basis of conversion.

(4) Disclosure of various items taken into account in arriving at operating profit including auditors' remuneration, interest receivable and payable, investment income, hire of equipment and depreciation of fixed assets.

(5) Analysis of directors' and employees' emoluments (not only does the aggregate directors remuneration have to be disclosed but the emoluments of directors (and employees earning more than £30,000 per annum) have to be analysed into bands of £5,000 and the total number each of directors and employees in each band has to be disclosed).

(6) Taxation. The charge split between United Kingdom and overseas taxation and the basis thereof and information regarding deferred taxation.

(7) Extraordinary items. Details thereof.

(8) The amount of profit dealt with in the accounts of the holding company.

(9) Dividends. Amounts paid, payable and proposed.

(10) Earnings per share. Basis of calculation.

(11) Share capital. Authorised and issued share capital and details of various classes.

(12) Reserves. Details of opening and closing reserves and movements thereon. Also share premium account and preliminary expenses.

(13) Details of loan capital.

(14) Deferred taxation. Details of potential liability and amount provided for in accounts.

(15) Bills discounted. Split between government and other bills.

(16) Investments – other than trade investments. Basis of valuation. Analysis between listed, whether in Great Britain or elsewhere, and unlisted investments and comparison between book amount and valuation.

(17) Advances and other accounts. Broad analysis of heading and details of provision for bad and doubtful debts including total provision at beginning and end of period and charge against profits.

(18) Trade investments and investments in associated companies. Basis of valuation. Analysis between listed, whether in Great Britain or elsewhere, and unlisted investments and comparison between book amount and valuation. Information is also given regarding the issued share capital, country of incorporation and interest held.

(19) List of principal subsidiaries, their country of incorporation and operation and interest held.

(20) Premises and equipment. Analysis by type of asset of opening cost, additions and disposals during the period, closing cost, accumulated depreciation and opening and closing net book amount. Method of valuation.

(21) Contracts with directors and connected persons.

(22) Contingent liabilities and commitments.

(23) Commitments for capital expenditure not provided for in the accounts.

(24) Identity of the holding company if the company is a subsidiary company.

Current cost accounts.

Auditors' report.

APPENDIX III

A typical set of accounts for an exempt bank

An Exempt Bank plc

Consolidated profit and loss account for the year ended...

	This year (£000)	Preceding year (£000)
Profit for the year, after taxation, of the company, its subsidiaries and its share of profits of associated companies after deducting minority interests and transfers to inner reserves out of which provision has been made for diminution in value of assets	xxx	xxx
Dividends	xxx	xxx
Profit retained	xxx	xxx
	xxx	xxx

The notes on pages x to x form part of these accounts.

An Exempt Bank plc

Consolidated balance sheet

Liabilities	This year (£000)		Preceding year (£000)		Assets	This year (£000)		Preceding year (£000)	
Current, deposit and other accounts including inner reserves	xxx		xxx		Cash in hand and with central banks	xxx		xxx	
Dividends	xxx	xxx	xxx	xxx	Money at call and short notice	xxx		xxx	
Loan capital		xxx		xxx	Bills discounted	xxx	xxx	xxx	xxx
Minority interests in subsidiaries		xxx		xxx	Cheques in course of collection		xxx		xxx
Share capital and reserves					Investments other than trade investments		xxx		xxx
Issued share capital	xxx		xxx		Advances and other accounts		xxx		xxx
Reserves	xxx	xxx	xxx	xxx	Trade investments		xxx		xxx
					Investments in associated companies		xxx		xxx
					Premises and equipment		xxx		xxx
		xxx		xxx			xxx		xxx

Signatures of at least two directors

Date of signing

The notes on pages x to x form part of these accounts.

An Exempt Bank plc

Balance sheet

Liabilities	This year (£000)		Preceding year (£000)		Assets	This year (£000)		Preceding year (£000)	
Current, deposit and other accounts including inner reserves	xxx		xxx		Cash in hand and with central banks	xxx		xxx	
Dividends	xxx		xxx		Money at call and short notice	xxx		xxx	
Amounts due to subsidiaries	xxx	xxx	xxx	xxx	Bills discounted	xxx	xxx	xxx	xxx
					Cheques in course of collection		xxx		xxx
Loan capital		xxx		xxx	Investments other than trade investments		xxx		xxx
Share capital and reserves					Advances and other accounts		xxx		xxx
Issued share capital	xxx		xxx		Balances due from subsidiaries		xxx		xxx
Reserves	xxx	xxx	xxx	xxx	Trade investments		xxx		xxx
					Investments in associated companies		xxx		xxx
					Investments in subsidiaries		xxx		xxx
					Premises and equipment		xxx		xxx
		xxx		xxx			xxx		xxx

Signatures of at least two directors

Date of signing

The notes on pages x to x form part of these accounts.

An Exempt Bank plc

Notes to the accounts

(1) The accounts are prepared in accordance with the provisions of Companies Act 1948 S 149A and schedule 8A.

(2) Basis of consolidation, i.e. a description of how the assets, liabilities, profits and losses of subsidiaries and associated companies have been dealt with in the group accounts.

(3) Accounting policies, including those relating to bad and doubtful debts, investments, depreciation of fixed assets, instalment finance, leased assets, pension contributions, deferred taxation and foreign currencies and the basis of conversion.

(4) Auditors' remuneration.

(5) Analysis of directors' and employees' emoluments (not only does the aggregate directors remuneration have to be disclosed but the emoluments of directors (and employees earning more than £30,000 per annum) have to be analysed into bands of £5,000 and the total number each of directors and employees in each band has to be disclosed).

(6) Extraordinary items. Details thereof.

(7) The amount of profit dealt with in the accounts of the holding company.

(8) Dividends. Amounts paid, payable and proposed.

(9) Share capital. Details of authorised and issued share capital.

(10) Reserves. Details of opening and closing reserves and movements thereon.

(11) Details of loan capital.

(12) Bills discounted. Split between government and other bills.

(13) Investments – other than trade investments. Analysis between listed, whether in Great Britain or elsewhere, and unlisted investments and comparison between book amount and valuation.

(14) Trade investments and investments in associated companies.

Analysis between listed, whether in Great Britain or elsewhere, and unlisted investments and comparison between book amount and valuation. Information is also given regarding the issued share capital, country of incorporation and interest held.

(15) List of principal subsidiaries, their country of incorporation and operation and interest held.

(16) Contingent liabilities and commitments.

(17) Commitments for capital expenditure not provided for in the accounts.

(18) Material post balance sheet events.

(19) Identity of the holding company if the company is a subsidiary company.

Auditors' report.

APPENDIX IV

Classification of assets and risk weights held by UK offices of reporting banks

(i) Nil weight — Bank of England notes and UK coin
Other sterling notes
Balances with Bank of England
Special deposits with Bank of England
Debits in course of collection on banks in the United Kingdom
Balances with overseas offices of the reporting bank
Lending under special schemes for exports and shipbuilding
Certificates of tax deposit
Items in suspense
Refinanced lending at fixed rates
Gold physically held in own vaults
Gold held elsewhere on an allocated basis

(ii) 0.1 weight — Foreign currency notes and coin
UK and Northern Ireland treasury bills

(iii) 0.2 weight — Debit items in course of collection on overseas banks
Market loans with listed banks, discount market, etc.
Market loans to UK local authorities and public corporations
Balances with banks overseas with a maximum term of up to one year (including claims in gold)
Bills other than UK and Northern Ireland treasury bills
Other loans and advances to Northern Ireland government, UK local authorities, public corporations and other public sector
British government stocks with up to 18 months to final maturity
Acceptances drawn by UK and overseas banks and UK public sector
Claims in gold on UK banks and members of the London Gold Market

(iv) 0.5 weight — British government stocks with over 18 months to final maturity
Northern Ireland government stocks
UK local authority and other public sector stocks and bonds
Guarantees and other contingent liabilities

(v) 1.0 weight — Acceptances drawn by other UK and overseas residents
Market loans placed with other UK residents
Other loans and advances, net of specific provisions for bad debts, but excluding connected lending
Assets leased to customers
Working capital provided for overseas offices of the reporting bank, both in the form of deposits and in other forms
Balances with banks overseas with a term of one year or over (including claims in gold)
Claims in gold on non-banks
Aggregate foreign currency position (defined in the Bank's paper on 'Foreign Currency Exposure')
Other assets 'other', e.g. silver, commodities and other goods beneficially owned by the reporting bank
Other quoted investments, not connected

(vi) 1.5 weight — Connected lending (to be looked at case-by-case and to exclude market-type lending where this can be separately identified)
Unquoted investments (subject to case-by-case treatment)

(vii) 2.0 weight — Property (includes all land and premises beneficially owned by the reporting bank)

Items to be deducted from capital — Plant and equipment
Intangible assets
Investments in subsidiary and associated companies and trade investments

25

CHAPTER 2

UNITED STATES

GERALD LINDSTROM and GALE PFUND

1 GENERAL INFORMATION

The United States of America is a federal republic of 50 states. The federal government is comprised of three branches: executive, legislative and judicial. These functions were intentionally separated to achieve a 'balance of power' in the government. The executive branch consists of the President, a number of departments each headed by a Secretary and a number of independent agencies. The Secretaries comprise the President's Cabinet and the agencies include certain regulatory agencies of interest to banks such as the Federal Reserve System and the Securities and Exchange Commission.

The legislative branch consists of the Senate and the House of Representatives and a law has to be passed through both chambers and be signed by the President before it becomes effective.

The judicial branch consists of the court system with the Supreme Court serving as the ultimate appellate body. There are no special courts to address banking matters.

The separate governments of each of the 50 states are structured along similar lines to that of the federal government.

Commercial banking in the United States marked its institutional beginning in 1782 with the formation of the Bank of North America. Since that time it has been in a constant state of change. The essential functions of commercial banking have continued although they are being shared to a greater and greater degree by non-commercial banks (thrifts) and other financial institutions. In addition, the commercial banking system has grown more complex over the years and the rate of change has begun to accelerate.

Three events following 1782 mark distinct phases in the evolution of banking in the United States. In 1838 the State of New York passed the Free Banking Act which simplified the process of obtaining a bank charter while at the same time it imposed requirements for pledging securities to back up circulating bank notes.

In 1863 the Congress of the United States passed the National Banking Act which re-established the federal government's role in chartering and regulating banks. Finally, in 1913 Congress established the Federal Reserve System which provided for a central banking function to control bank reserves.

Today the US banking industry is predominant in the world. Major financial centres have grown up in New York, San Francisco, Los Angeles, Houston and Chicago coordinating business on a worldwide basis. There are over 14,000 commercial banks in the US but the top 25 banks account for approximately 40% of the assets held.

The changes occurring in the commercial banking system of the US are fundamental, affecting the structure, regulatory process, accounting policies and basic functions of the system. No abatement of this process of change is expected. The reader is cautioned, therefore, not to rely on the information in this chapter without considering the effect of any developments since its publication.

1.1 Organisations covered by banking regulations

1.2 Summary of major types of banks

The depository institutions which are covered by banking regulations can be divided into two categories, namely commercial banks and thrifts.

One trend in deregulation is to reduce the differences between financial institutions. Historically the thrift institutions were similar in many respect to commercial banks but with strict limitations that, among other things, prohibited their offering checking accounts, trust services, credit cards and commercial loans. They were formed primarily to serve the savings needs of the individual consumer and provide financing primarily for real estate purchases. For a long time they were permitted by law to pay an interest rate differential of ¼% over bank rates to compete for savings deposits. Legislation passed in 1982 greatly expanded the powers of thrifts while at the same time reduced the advantage of the interest rate differential.

Commercial banks in the US can be classified in a number of different ways, depending on whether the reference is to charter source, country of organisation, legal or organisational structure, or market influence and size. Consequently the categories frequently overlap and any given bank will fit a number of them. The following is a description of the most commonly used classifications:

(a) Charter

Under the dual banking system, banks can be chartered by either the federal government or any one of the 50 state governments, as the bank desires. Federally chartered banks receive their charter from the

Comptroller of the Currency, and are referred to as national banks. State chartered banks receive their charter from the superintendent of banks or banking department of the related state government, and are referred to as state banks.

(b) Country of organisation

From the perspective of the United States, any organisation that is organised under the laws of a foreign country and engages in the business of banking is considered a 'foreign bank'. All others are therefore local, domestic or United States banks.

(c) Legal structure

Holding company

A bank holding company is defined in law as any organisation having direct or indirect control over a bank. Virtually all major United States banks are organised as subsidiaries of bank holding companies. A foreign bank that purchases or organises a bank subsidiary in the United States would become a bank holding company. In addition to owning one or more banks in a given state, bank holding companies may also own subsidiaries engaged in permissible non-banking activities.

Bank

A bank is defined in law as an institution that accepts demand deposits and makes commercial loans. There are approximately 560 separately incorporated and publicly held banks with over 500 shareholders in the United States that are not part of a bank holding company group.

(d) Organisational structure

Unit banks

Banks that operate out of only one location in a given state are referred to as unit or single location banks. Such banks are limited to one location normally because either they are too small to permit expansion or because state laws restrict expansion within the state through branching or owning subsidiaries.

Multiple location banking systems

Banks can operate in more than one location, when permitted by state law, by use of branches, or group banks which are separate affiliates or subsidiaries of bank holding companies. Chain banks are those that operate in several locations under the ownership and control of an individual or group of individuals.

(e) Market influence and size

US banks are frequently referred to by their size or position they hold in the market place. Most of those among the largest 20 or 25 banks in the country are located in major cities and are considered to be money centre banks which also generally have multinational operations throughout the world. They lend extensively to companies across the United States and also abroad. They perform the major correspondent banking services for other banks and generally serve the wholesale market more than the consumer or retail markets.

The next group of banks are referred to as regional banks which primarily serve the business needs of their geographic region. They range in size from $1 to $10 billion in assets.

Banks below that size are generally referred to as community or independent banks. They are normally locally or privately owned and are organised primarily to serve the needs of the local community. Many are fiercely independent and are represented by a separate trade association known as the Independent Bankers Association of America.

In addition to the types or classifications of banks discussed above, there are several specialised types of banks that have been created by law to meet specific needs. The most significant of these are the following:

(f) Edge Act Bank or Agreement Corporation

Edge Act Banks were permitted by legislation, sponsored by Senator Edge in 1919, to promote international commerce. Edge Act Banks are federally chartered. They can be owned by foreign or domestic banks and can operate in any state as a separate corporation or a branch of an Edge Act Bank. They are restricted to deposit taking, lending, and investing and other banking functions that are directly related to international finance. Edge Act Banks must maintain reserves against deposits, and are required to have equity capital of 7% of risk assets with a $2 million minimum.

Loans to a single borrower are limited by regulation to 10% of capital and surplus. Regulation K of the Federal Reserve governs the activities of Edge Act Banks.

Agreement Corporations are state chartered banks that have entered into an agreement with the Federal Reserve. They have virtually all the same powers and restrictions as Edge Act Banks.

(g) International Banking Facility (IBF)

In December 1981 the Federal Reserve amended its Regulations D (reserve requirements) and Q (interest on deposits) to permit the operation of International Banking Facilities (IBFs) by US depository institutions, Edge Act Banks and Agreement Corporations, and US branches or agencies of foreign banks. The purpose of the IBF is to enable banks operating in the US to compete more effectively with foreign banks without using an offshore operation. IBFs are free of interest rate restrictions and reserve requirements on deposits that are from non-US residents, foreign affiliates of US corporations or other IBFs and their sponsors. Loans are also restricted to foreign customers, other IBFs, their sponsors, and other organisations that will use such funds outside the US. Deposit accounts have a minimum transaction size of $100,000 and are subject to a two-day withdrawal notice requirement. IBFs can be established merely by segregating ledger accounts without a separate legal structure and without prior regulatory approval. Notification to the district Federal Reserve Bank and agreement to abide by certain operating rules is all that is required. Income is subject to US tax but is generally exempt from the franchise taxes of many states.

(h) Bankers' banks

These banks are so named because they are owned by other banks or depository institutions and are engaged exclusively in providing services for other depository institutions and do not do business with the general public. As a result they are exempt from reserve requirements. They normally provide correspondent banking and other services and are authorised to act as pass-through correspondents for non-member banks that are required to maintain reserves. Bankers' banks may be state or federally chartered and may be owned by a holding company. National banks are limited in their investments in bankers' banks to 10% of their capital and surplus. In addition they are prohibited from owning more than 5% of a bankers' bank.

The following are the major types of thrift institutions in the United States:

(i) Savings banks

State chartered savings banks trace their history to 1816 when they were first organised in mutual form, being owned by their depositors. Today savings banks can obtain either state charters or federal charters from the Federal Home Loan Bank Board, can be either mutual or stock companies, and have their deposits insured by the Federal Deposit Insurance Corporation. Recently the powers of savings banks to engage in commercial lending activities has been expanded.

(j) Savings and loan associations

The Federal Savings and Loan System was created by the Home Owners' Loan Act of 1939 and is administered and supervised by the Federal Home Loan Bank Board. It also provides credit reserves to member associations and supervises the Federal Savings and Loan Insurance Corporation which provides deposit insurance on accounts with savings and loan associations. Savings and loan associations may be stock or mutual companies, may be chartered by the states or the Federal Home Loan Bank Board, and have started to exercise recently expanded powers beyond their traditional savings deposit and real estate lending role.

(k) Credit unions

Credit unions were defined by the Federal Credit Union Act of 1934 as co-operative associations designed to promote thrift among members who are united by some common bond. Today most credit unions are associated with governmental or private sector employers and draw their memberships from the related employee groups. Credit unions can be state or federally chartered. Accounts are insured by the National Credit Union Administration and liquidity reserves are provided by the National Credit Union Central Liquidity Facility. Credit unions are becoming full service financial institutions for their members and providing additional competition for the banking industry.

(l) Government owned or sponsored banks

In addition to the private sector banks and institutions described above, there are a number of government-owned or sponsored banks that play an essential role in the financial system of the United States and these have been formed to achieve specific social or economic purposes such as channelling funds into agriculture, education or housing. These government banks do not take deposits but obtain their financing through the sale of bonds or other debt instruments. Included among these institutions are the banks for co-operatives, federal home loan banks, federal intermediate credit banks and federal land banks, together with the Federal Home Loan Mortgage Corporation, the Federal National Mortgage Association and the Student Loan Marketing Association.

(m) Federal Reserve System

The Federal Reserve Bank, created by the Federal Reserve Act of 1913, was established as a central bank to co-ordinate and serve as a bankers' bank for the many individual banks throughout the country and acts as the lynch-pin of the Federal Reserve System the primary functions of which are to:
  - Regulate the money supply.
  - Hold legal reserves.
  - Supply needed currency.
  - Provide funds transfer.
  - Facilitate clearance of checks.
  - Act as government fiscal agent and depository.
  - Provide economic analysis.
  - Examine and supervise state chartered member banks, bank holding companies. and non-banking affiliates and Edge Act Banks.

The Federal Reserve System is organised as follows:

The Board of Governors of the Federal Reserve System consists of seven members appointed by the President of the United States. Their function is to determine monetary policy and exercise supervision over the system.

The Federal Open Market Committee sets policy regarding the purchase and sale of securities in the open market as a tool of monetary policy.

The Federal Advisory Council consists of one member from each of the 12 Federal Reserve districts to provide advisory services.

The country is divided into 12 districts each with its own Federal Reserve Bank which provides the operational services of the system for the benefit of member banks.

Membership of the Federal Reserve System is mandatory for all national banks and is voluntary for state banks. Members are required to subscribe to stock in the related district Federal Reserve Bank in an amount equal to 6% of their capital and maintain deposits at the district Federal Reserve Bank as required reserves.

Most other depository institutions are now required to maintain reserves whether or not they are members of the Federal Reserve System.

Balances on deposit with the district Federal Reserve Bank are used in the payments mechanism to provide immediately available funds for transfer between banks. These deposits are called federal funds and banks have created an active market in buying and selling federal funds so that these balances can be made available as needed to meet reserve requirements and effect transfers. The rates charged for these funds can be quite volatile as they directly reflect the amount of liquidity in the banking system.

Control of the money supply of the country is one of the most important functions of the Federal Reserve because of its effect on inflation and the rate of economic growth. This control is accomplished by either adjusting the legal reserve requirements, buying and selling securities in the open market to replenish or draw reserves from the system, adjusting the discount rate charged to banks that borrow from the Federal Reserve, or some combination thereof.

Finally, another important function of the Federal Reserve is to act as lender of last resort to depository institutions that require funds in unusual or emergency situations.

1.3 Supervisory authorities

1.4 Status of supervisory authorities

The United States has a dual (federal and state) system for chartering and supervising depository institutions including banks and thrift institutions. The system has developed over the last 120 years as the result of state and federal legislation that created the various banking systems and their related regulatory agencies. As a consequence there has developed a complex structure for the regulatory control of depository institutions.

The primary federal regulators of the banking system are the Office of the Comptroller of the Currency, the Board of Governors of the Federal Reserve System and the Federal Deposit Insurance Corporation (FDIC). The Comptroller of the Currency is the head of the Office of the Comptroller of the Currency (OCC) within the Treasury Department. This office was created by the National Banking Act of 1863 and is now solely responsible for chartering and supervising all national or federally chartered banks. All national banks are required to be members of the Federal Reserve System (FRS) and are required to have their deposits insured by the FDIC.

Banks chartered by the various states are supervised by their local state banking departments. Approximately 10% of these state banks have chosen to join the FRS, and are referred to as state member banks. By joining the FRS they are required to have their deposits insured by the FDIC and to come under the regulatory jurisdiction of the FRS which then shares supervisory responsibility with the local state banking department.

While most state banks have chosen not to become members of the FRS, they have elected to avail themselves of deposit insurance from the FDIC. These banks are referred to as state insured non-member banks. They are under the jurisdiction of the FDIC as the primary federal regulator which shares supervisory responsibility with the local state banking department. A small number

of state chartered banks are uninsured and are regulated only by their local state banking department.

In addition, the OCC is responsible for approving the establishment and supervising federal branches or agencies of foreign banks. Deposit insurance from the FDIC is available for these branches and agencies and is mandatory if they accept retail deposits which are defined as domestic non-corporate deposits under $100,000.

The FRS has further responsibility for approving and supervising bank holding companies, non-banking subsidiaries of bank holding companies, and Edge Act Banks and foreign branches of US banks. They share responsibility for Agreement Corporations with the local state banking department.

In addition to administering the system of nationwide deposit insurance, the FDIC by law becomes the receiver for all failed or insolvent national banks and, when appointed by state authorities, all state banks that are placed in receivership.

The thrift institutions have a slightly different but parallel regulatory structure. They have a similar dual system of state and federal charters. The Federal Home Loan Bank Board (FHLBB) is the federal regulator for savings and loan associations, and the National Credit Union Administration (NCUA) is the federal regulator for credit unions. In contrast to the bank regulatory structure, both the FHLBB and the NCUA provide their respective members with liquidity reserves, deposit insurance, and supervisory control from one regulatory body.

Each of these regulatory authorities of the depository institutions exercises supervisory control by conducting on-site examinations of the institutions, monitoring periodic (quarterly) financial reports, and approving or denying charters, memberships and insurance. Over the years each of these agencies has developed its own procedures, rules and requirements for carrying out its regulatory responsibility. For the last 20 years concern has been expressed within the government about the lack of coordination between the various regulatory agencies and the development of conflicting, overlapping, non-standard and inefficient procedures. The Federal Financial Institutions Examination Council was established in 1979 by the Federal Financial Institutions Regulatory and Interest Rate Control Act of 1978 to address these concerns. The primary purpose of the Council was to establish uniform examination standards and uniform reporting systems for monitoring the financial condition of the supervised institutions and to establish schools for examiners. The overall objective was to promote uniformity among the agencies and improve the quality of supervision.

The Council consists of representatives from all five federal agencies (OCC, FRS, FDIC, FHLBB, NCUA) as well as an advisory group of state agencies. To date the Council has developed uniform call report formats and instructions for reporting quarterly financial information to the respective regulatory bodies. In addition it has made some progress in establishing schools for examiners and developing uniform examination standards.

In the view of many, a great deal more needs to be done to improve the regulatory structure and process. The most significant development in this regard is from Vice

President Bush's Task Group on Regulation of Financial Services which has recently proposed a complete re-organisation and consolidation of these regulatory agencies.

In addition to the governmental regulatory authorities, there are several private industry associations that play a vital role in many aspects of the banking system. They are instrumental in developing concepts that ultimately influence banking legislation and in actively representing their members in forums that discuss these issues. They provide many training and educational programmes, extensive publications, maintain libraries and conduct a variety of research studies. Among the larger of these organisations are the Association of Bank Holding Companies, the American Bankers Association, the Bank Administration Institute and the Robert Morris Associates. In addition, the bankers in each state have formed separate state banking associations.

The table below gives an overview of the various depository institutions of the US in terms of their number, assets and related federal supervisory authority as a summary of the information covered thus far. The data is as of 31 December 1982.

Type of institution	Federal regulator	Number of institutions	Total assets of institutions supervised ($ billions)
National banks	OCC	4,579	1,297
State member banks	FRS	1,054	423
State insured non-member banks	FDIC	8,831	475
Mutual savings banks	FDIC	315	155
Federal savings and loan associations	FHLBB	1,727	479
State savings and loan associations	FHLBB	1,616	207
Federal credit unions	NCUA	11,430	46
State credit unions	NCUA	5,034	24
Total		34,586	3,106

OCC, Office of the Comptroller of the Currency; FRS, Federal Reserve System; FDIC, Federal Deposit Insurance Corporation; FHLBB, Federal Home Loan Bank Board; NCUA, National Credit Union Administration

In addition there were 526 banks and 103 thrifts operating as uninsured state chartered depository institutions which are not regulated by a federal agency.

The rest of this chapter will be confined to commercial banks.

1.5 Laws and regulations governing banks

Banking is governed by many laws and regulations at both the state and federal level. Federal law in the form originally enacted by Congress is published in the Statutes at Large. The federal banking laws are codified in Title 12 of the United States Code. Referenced compilations of these laws, and regulations issued by supervisory agencies pursuant to these laws, are available from the bank law reporting services.

The following are the more significant banking laws that have been enacted at the federal level:

(a) National Bank Act

Originally passed in 1863 and amended significantly in 1864 and 1874, this law established the national banking system and continues as the basic banking law for national banks. It created the Office of the Comptroller of the Currency with provisions to regulate the chartering, organisation, operation and liquidation of national banks. The law also provided for a uniform national currency of national bank notes backed by US government bonds. This system was finally replaced in 1935 and all currency is now issued by the US Treasury.

(b) Federal Reserve Act of 1913

This law and the many subsequent amendments thereto created the Federal Reserve System to serve as the central bank of the United States. It was designed to cure defects in the prior system by providing elasticity of the money supply, control over the money markets, centralisation of bank reserves, provision of rediscount facilities and a system of collecting out-of-state checks. Regulations issued by the Federal Reserve pursuant to this Act are designated alphabetically A to Z and AA and BB.

Of interest in this text are the following:
Regulation D — reserve requirements
Regulation F — securities of member banks
Regulation K — international banking operations
Regulation Q — interest on deposits
Regulation Y — bank holding companies and change in bank control.

(c) Edge Act of 1919

Section 25 of the Federal Reserve Act authorised national banks to establish branches in foreign countries. The Edge Act amended the Federal Reserve Act as section 25a entitled 'Banking Corporations Authorised to do Foreign Banking Business' which provided for national banks to invest in US banks engaged in foreign banking. This law was passed to enable US businesses to obtain a larger share of the growing foreign trade market. Subsequent amendments have greatly expanded the powers of Edge Act Banks.

(d) McFadden Act of 1927

This law was designed to equalise the branching powers of national and state banks by permitting branch banking for national banks where it was permitted for state banks. This was done to stop the trend for national banks to convert to state banks because of the more liberal state laws. The result was that national banks were not permitted to branch across state lines because that was the limit imposed on state banks. National banks were also prohibited from branching outside the cities where they were located, until passage of the Banking Act of 1933.

(e) Banking Act of 1933 (Glass-Steagall Act)

This was the first of two major banking laws of the depression era. It was a comprehensive Act covering a number of matters including Federal Reserve open market operations, limitation of borrowing by executive officers from member banks, regulation of interbank control by directors and investment and branching matters. It is most famous, however, for creating the Federal Deposit Insurance Corporation and separating the business of banking from the business of securities.

(f) Banking Act of 1935

This law was primarily an amendment of the Banking Act of 1933, the Federal Reserve Act and other banking statutes.

(g) Federal Deposit Insurance Act of 1950

This Act revised the deposit insurance section of the Federal Reserve Act and established it as a separate independent law. In addition, the Act increased the deposit insurance coverage, provided for the assessment rebate system, and clarified the powers of the FDIC to facilitate mergers or consolidations of insured banks and to take other measures to prevent the closing of insured banks.

(h) Bank Holding Company Act of 1956

This law resulted in the first comprehensive regulation of bank holding companies. Combined with amendments in 1966 and 1970 it defined a bank holding company as one that controls 25% or more of the stock of a bank. It transferred regulatory control of bank holding companies to the Federal Reserve. Section 3d of the Act, referred to as the Douglas Amendment, prohibits acquisition of an additional bank outside the state where the company maintains its principal office unless such acquisition is specifically authorised by the state in which the bank to be acquired is located. This section, along with the McFadden Act, has restricted the development of inter-state banking to those instances permitted by state law.

(i) International Banking Act of 1978

This law was the first general banking legislation for foreign banks and was designed to put foreign banks on an equal competitive basis with US banks. The major provisions of the Act are as follows:
(1) Permitted foreign directors of national banks.
(2) Permitted foreign ownership and directors of Edge Act Banks.
(3) Revised regulations of Edge Act Banks including changing reserve requirements to be the same as member banks and removing statutory limits on issuance of debentures, bonds and notes.
(4) Permitted federal licensing of branches and agencies of foreign banks by the Comptroller of the Currency.
(5) Limited deposits of foreign bank branches outside 'home state' to those permissible for Edge Act Banks.
(6) Required deposit insurance on most branches of foreign banks.

(7) Imposed reserve requirements and interest rate limitations on foreign branches and agencies of large foreign banks.
(8) Subjected most foreign banks to the Bank Holding Company Act.

(j) Federal Institutions Regulatory and Interest Rate Control Act of 1978

This law is the first in a current series of major reform and deregulation legislation. The major provisions are as follows:
(1) Increased supervisory authority by authorising harsh civil penalties for violating laws and cease and desist orders, provided tougher rules regarding insider loans and increased regulatory authority to remove officers and directors.
(2) Prohibited certain interlocking directorates at competing institutions.
(3) Increased FDIC authority to regulate foreign operations of state non-member banks.
(4) Provided for prior written notification of proposed acquisition (change in control) of insured banks or savings and loan associations and granted regulatory agencies power to disapprove the acquisition.
(5) Prohibited preferential treatment of loans by correspondent banks.
(6) Required annual reporting available for public inspection of loans to officers and directors at banks.
(7) Established the Federal Financial Institution Examination Council.
(8) Provided privacy protection to bank customers with respect to their bank records.
(9) Provided for federal chartering of mutual savings banks under the FHLBB.
(10) Extended Regulation Q and eliminated the thrift interest differential on certain accounts.
(11) Created a central liquidity facility for credit unions.

(k) Depository Institutions Deregulation and Monetary Control Act of 1980

This law was designed to promote competitive balance among depository institutions and provide the Federal Reserve with better tools for implementing monetary policy. The major provisions of this law are as follows:
(1) Implemented uniform reserve requirements for all depository institutions.
(2) Provided for a phase-out of interest rate controls under Regulation Q and established the Depository Institutions Deregulation Committee to implement the phase-out.
(3) Authorised nationwide use of NOW (Negotiable Order of Withdrawal) accounts and permanent authority for automatic transfer services for banks and share draft services for savings and loans.
(4) Federal deposit insurance was increased from $40,000 to $100,000.

(l) Garn-St. Germain Depository Institutions Act of 1982

This law was passed during a period when high interest rates were threatening the survival of mortgage lending institutions, principally thrifts, and consequently having an adverse impact on the housing industry. The objective of the Act was to strengthen these institutions. The major provisions of the Act were as follows:

(1) Provided for deposit insurance flexibility by expanding the alternatives available in offering assistance to troubled institutions.

(2) Provided for 'Net worth certificates' to be issued by troubled institutions to insuring agencies in exchange for promissory notes under a capital assistance programme.

(3) Provided for increased investment and commercial lending powers to federal thrift institutions.

(4) Provided for money market accounts.

(m) International Lending Supervision Act of 1983

This law set guidelines for fee recognition associated with restructured international lending arrangements and non-refundable fees associated with other international loans. It directed bank regulatory agencies to issue regulations on accounting for these fees, but prohibited banks from charging certain fees unless they are recognised as a yield adjustment over the effective life of the loan. This law was intended to discourage excessive international lending motivated by early recognition of high front end fees.

(n) Garn-St. Germain Financial Institutions Competitive Equity Act of 1984

This law was under consideration by the joint banking committee at the time of writing. The final version of the law, if passed, cannot be predicted with certainty. Currently, however, this legislation is expected to cover the following matters.

(1) Redefining a bank to be any institution that is covered by deposit insurance or makes commercial loans and accepts demand deposits.

(2) Expanding underwriting powers of banks in private mortgage-backed securities and municipal revenue bonds, authorising bank holding companies to underwrite and deal in commercial paper, affirming discount brokerage for banks.

(3) Restricting insurance activities of banks.

(4) Authorising regional interstate banking arrangements by states.

(5) Requiring the Federal Reserve to pay interest on legal reserves.

(6) Preventing institutions not meeting minimum net worth requirements from accepting brokered deposits.

1.6 Application of general company law to banks

A bank organised as a corporation will have to comply with the requirements of the corporation law of the state in which it was incorporated as there is no federal corporation law. State corporation law is not very onerous and the charter and bylaws will regulate matters such as the basic business purpose of the corporation, the ability to appoint directors, their powers and duties, and the right to call meetings both of directors and shareholders. There is an obligation to call a shareholders'

annual general meeting but directors normally have the right to declare dividends.

An annual return has to be filed wth the state authorities giving details of such items as the number and amount of shares authorised and in issue, and details of the directors and offices, etc. There is no requirement to file a copy of the annual accounts.

1.7 Sources of laws and regulations

As mentioned earlier the legislative branch of government consists of the Senate and the House of Representatives. Each chamber has a separate Banking Committee and staff which researches and sponsors banking legislation. Any differences in the separate versions of any banking bills proposed are reconciled and adopted in final form by a joint committee before being given back to the separate chambers for final vote.

Regulations can only be made by the supervisory authorities under specific powers given to them by a particular law.

1.8 Ability of foreign banks to operate through branches and subsidiaries

1.9 Level of supervisory control for branches and subsidiaries of foreign banks

Since the passage of the International Banking Act of 1978, foreign banks have powers virtually equivalent to those of US banks. They can apply for state or federally chartered branches or agencies, separately incorporated state or national banks as bank holding companies, Edge Act Banks, IBFs or representative offices. They can also apply to carry on trust activities. The level of supervisory controls is the same for foreign and domestic banks.

The various ways in which a foreign bank can organise its banking operation in the US are as follows:

(a) Subsidiary

A foreign bank can own and operate either a state or national bank as a separate subsidiary with full banking powers.

(b) Branch

A foreign bank can establish either a state or federally chartered unincorporated branch where permitted by state law. A federally chartered branch may be a full branch with authority to accept retail deposits or a limited branch with limited deposit taking authority. State chartered branches generally have similar ranges of deposit taking authority available. A foreign bank can operate a full deposit taking facility in only one state designated by the bank as its 'home' state.

(c) Agency

A foreign bank can establish either a state or federally chartered unincorporated agency where permitted by state law. The rules governing agencies are similar to those for branches except that agencies are normally prohibited from accepting demand or time deposits and performing trust services.

(d) Representative office

A foreign bank can establish a representative office by applying to the appropriate state banking department and registering with the Secretary of the Treasury of the United States. Representative offices cannot perform banking functions such as taking deposits or making loans, but can represent their head office in business development, loan production, customer relations and communication with correspondent banks.

Foreign banks, like US banks, can exercise full deposit taking powers in only one state which they must designate as their home state. Deposit taking powers of their banking operations in other states are limited to those available to Edge Act Banks.

Deposit insurance is required when the organisation accepts retail deposits or non-corporate deposits under $100,000, or when required by state law. Banks can apply for deposit insurance if it is not otherwise required, except that it is not available for Edge Act Banks, IBFs and credit balances of agencies. Insured foreign branches have to pledge certain assets and maintain other assets equal to certain liabilities.

Deposit reserves are required under Regulation D of all branches or agencies of foreign banks with worldwide consolidated assets over $1 billion or when the branch is eligible to apply for deposit insurance.

Foreign banks establishing almost any kind of banking operation in the United States must abide by the requirements of the Bank Holding Company Act and the restrictions on non-banking activities in the United States. Permissible non-banking activities are detailed in Regulation Y and consist of those functions so closely related to banking as to be a proper incident thereto.

If a foreign bank wishes to acquire a bank in the United States, it would have to (1) comply with the applicable provisions of state and federal law depending upon the type of bank charter and (2) obtain the approval of the Federal Reserve to become a foreign bank holding company. Application to the Federal Reserve is made on Form FR Y-1F which requires disclosure of substantial information about the applicant including (1) details of non-US companies in which the foreign bank has a direct or indirect interest of 25% or more and also a list of all companies engaged in business in the US in which the foreign bank (or one of the companies controlled by it under the 25% rule) has an interest of 5% or more, (2) detailed financial information about the applicant and (3) financial information regarding shareholders owning more than 10% of the equity of the foreign bank.

Other matters include the effect the proposed acquisition would have on competition and the benefits to be derived from it. The restrictions of the Bank Holding Act concerning interests in other banks and businesses not compatible with the business of banking apply to directly and indirectly owned companies in the United States and directly and indirectly owned foreign companies engaged in business in the US.

While the FR Y-1F will be of public record once it is filed, it is possible to request that certain information be accorded confidential treatment. This may relate to certain financial information, and details of shareholdings which the foreign bank may wish to keep confidential. Such request may not necessarily be granted.

In addition to compliance with applicable federal and state banking laws, it is necessary to comply with federal and state securities laws if the bank being purchased or its holding company is a publicly traded company.

The process of obtaining the necessary approvals can be lengthy and can easily take over one year after the initial negotiations to purchase the US bank have commenced.

To establish a federal branch or agency, a foreign bank must submit a Form CC7030-01 'Application to Establish a Federal Branch or Agency' with the Comptroller of the Currency. Once an application has been accepted for processing the approval process can be completed in 90 to 180 days. Information required in the application includes three-year pro forma financial statements of the proposed facility, legal and organisational information and a description of how the convenience and needs of the community will be served. The applicant may request confidential treatment for certain information which it may not wish to have available to the public, such as extent of ownership and financial disclosures related to other business affiliations. Similar types of applications are required by the various states to establish a state branch or agency. Representative offices are established by filing an application with the appropriate state banking authority and registering with the Treasury Department. Applications to establish an Edge Act Bank are filed with the Board of Governors of the Federal Reserve System through the district Federal Reserve Bank.

1.10 Methods of incorporation

Applications to establish a national bank are filed with the Comptroller of the Currency and the Federal Reserve. Applications to establish a state chartered bank are filed with the appropriate state banking authority. A corporation is created only at state level as there is no federal corporation law and each of the 50 states and the District of Columbia has its own corporation law. While state laws are similar to some extent, there are wide variations in the requirements for incorporation and operation of a corporation. Delaware corporation law is considered the most liberal, and the majority of US corporations are incorporated in Delaware. It is common practice to be incorporated in a state, such as Delaware, with a liberal corporation law and to qualify the corporation in the state in which it does business. Qualifying to do business in a state is usually a formality. State law generally does not require a minimum capitalisation for corporations, but most states do require that subscribed capital be fully paid-in before the issuance of authorised stock. Capital stock may be issued on a par or no-par basis, and certain issues may be granted preferential rights concerning dividends and receipt of distributions on liquidation, but such treatment must be indicated in the certificate of incorporation.

A corporation can be formed for any legal purpose not prohibited by state statute and it comes into existence as soon as its certificate of incorporation is issued by the state.

Unless required by the certificate of incorporation or the company's bylaws, a director need be neither a state or US resident nor a shareholder in the corporation. Though management of the corporation is technically in the hands of the board of directors, actual operation is by the corporation officers, who are appointed by the board. The officers generally include a president, secretary and treasurer; the bylaws may provide for one or more vice presidents. Generally an officer can hold two or more offices except that the offices of president and secretary cannot be held by the same person. The authority of the officers is spelled out by the bylaws or by a resolution of the board of directors.

1.11 Areas in the country subject to special laws

There are presently no areas of the country subject to special laws of any significance.

2 ACCOUNTING

2.1 Laws and regulations governing accounts

2.2 Application of general company law

2.3 Roles of legislature and supervisory authority

2.4 Extent to which requirements as to returns and accounts are prescribed by laws and regulations

General corporation law does not apply to accounts and the primary laws governing these are the Securities Act of 1933 and the Securities Exchange Act of 1934 which only apply to corporations which offer for sale to the public corporate debt and equity securities. These laws were passed during the great depression following the stock market crash of 1929 to regulate and reform the offering and sale of securities to the general public. The Securities and Exchange Commission (SEC) was created as the primary federal regulator to enforce the securities laws which cover the sale of securities by issuers as well as the underwriting and distribution of those securities by securities firms.

The reporting requirements for issuers of securities cover the following range of activities or events:
- Initial registration.
- Annual reports to shareholders.
- Reports of specific events.
- Quarterly reports.
- Shareholder proxy solicitations.

All of these require financial statements and/or financial disclosures.

Responsibility for enforcement of the securities laws is vested in the bank regulatory authorities for banks and in the SEC for other issuers including bank holding companies. However, the SEC plays the leading role in setting financial reporting and disclosure requirements and bank regulatory authorities are generally required by Public Law 93-495, passed in 1974, to issue regulations substantially identical to those issued by the SEC.

The Securities Act of 1933 governs the registration and financial disclosures applicable to the public distribution of securities. Under Title I, section 3(a)(2), banks were exempted from the provision of the Act and registration with the SEC.

The Securities Exchange Act of 1934 governs the registration and periodic reporting of companies with securities traded over the counter or listed on an exchange. Companies with securities traded over the counter (or by use of the mails) are exempt if they have less than $3 million in assets or under 500 shareholders. These companies are still required to comply with state law regarding the issuance of securities. Title I, section 12(i) of this Act vests the responsibility of the SEC for the regulation of securities, shareholder proxies and current financial reporting for banks in the federal bank regulatory authorities.

The jurisdiction of the federal regulatory agencies in these matters parallels their other supervisory responsibilities as follows:

Type of bank	Regulatory authority	Reference (code of federal regulations)
National bank	Comptroller	12 CFR, part 11
Member state bank	Federal Reserve	12 CFR, part 206 Regulation F
Insured non-member state bank	FDIC	12 CFR, part 335

Regulation F issued by the Federal Reserve is a comprehensive regulation covering the securities activities of banks. Section 206.7 of Regulation F sets forth requirements concerning the form and content of financial statements. Form F-9 gives detailed filing instructions. Similar regulations have been adopted by the Comptroller of the Currency, although minor differences exist among the agencies.

The Comptroller of the Currency has adopted comprehensive rules regarding disclosures in offering circulars used to describe new issues for potential investors. The FDIC has adopted a policy statement containing guidelines on 12 items for the minimum information required, with reference to the Comptroller's regulations for further guidance. The Federal Reserve has no formal requirements for offering circulars but generally follows the guidelines of the OCC and the SEC.

The SEC has extensive instructions and regulations and forms dealing with financial reporting. These are summarised as follows:

(1) Regulation S-X prescribes the form and content of financial statements required to be filed with the SEC. Article 9 of Regulation S-X covers bank holding companies and banks.

(2) Staff Accounting Bulletins issued by the staff of the SEC offer additional guidance in accounting matters and should be considered together with Regulation S-X.

(3) Regulation S-K is the integrated disclosure regulation which states the requirements applicable to the non-financial statements portion of registration statements and annual reports. Included in Regulation S-K are the industry guides. Guide 3 deals with statistical disclosures by bank holding companies.

(4) Regulation 14A covers the rules governing solicitation of proxies and schedule 14A covers the information required in proxy statements.

(5) Forms of annual and quarterly reports and registration statements detail the information required therein.

The following table provides a comparison of the forms required by the bank regulators and the SEC for each of the aspects of the securities laws requiring financial reporting and disclosure by issuers:

	Bank regulators	SEC
Registration	Form F-1	Form 10
Annual reports	Form F-2	Form 10-K
Current reports of certain events	Form F-3	Form 8-K
Quarterly reports	Form F-4	Form 10-Q
Proxies	Form F-5	Schedule 14A

In addition the SEC has specific forms for registration statements for registering securities under the securities acts. These are summarised as follows:

Form S-3

This form is for registrants that have a large following for their securities in the market, have filed required reports with the SEC for the last three years and meet certain other criteria. This form utilises information in previous filings which are incorporated by reference.

Form S-2

This form is generally for registrants that meet the registrant requirements for use of Form S-3 but do not meet the transaction or market following thresholds.

Form S-1

This form is for any registrant not qualified to use Forms S-3 and S-2 such as companies with initial public offerings. Required information is provided in the form rather than being incorporated by reference to other filings.

Forms S-14 and S-15

These forms are used in mergers and acquisitions. They are presently under review by the SEC which has proposed a new Form S-4 to replace them.

Foreign issues of securities that are subject to the US securities laws are required to file similar forms and these are discussed in Appendix I.

The rules and regulations described above are prescribed by law and are directed primarily at the public reporting requirements for the registration and sale of securities and the subsequent reporting of quarterly and annual results.

In addition, every national bank, state member bank and insured non-member bank is required to file quarterly consolidated Reports of Condition (balance sheets) and Income. These reports are referred to as call reports. The federal bank regulatory agencies have agreed on a common format and instructions as promulgated by the Federal Financial Institutions Examination Council (FFIEC).

Call reports are designed primarily to provide detailed information for use by regulators in monitoring bank performance and detecting adverse trends. However, the instructions to the call reports are incorporated by reference in Form F-9 and the Comptroller of the Currency has authorised banks with less than 500 shareholders to provide the call report in lieu of an annual report to requesting shareholders.

Four versions of the call reports are used, depending on the size of the bank and whether or not it has foreign offices, as indicated in the titles below:

Form FFIEC 031

Consolidated Reports of Condition and Income for a bank with domestic and foreign offices

Form FFIEC 032

Consolidated Reports of Condition and Income for a bank with domestic offices only and total assets of $300 million or more.

Form FFIEC 033

Consolidated Reports of Condition and Income for a bank with domestic offices only and total assets of $100 million or more but less than $300 million.

Form FFIEC 034

Consolidated Reports of Condition and Income for a bank with domestic offices only and total assets of less than $100 million.

These reports are on the consolidated bank only and do not include accounts of bank holding companies or other bank subsidiaries of bank holding companies.

For purposes of using these forms, a foreign office includes an IBF, a branch or consolidated subsidiary in a foreign country, Puerto Rico, or a US territory or possession and majority-owned Edge Act or Agreement subsidiaries.

The forms and related schedules vary in the amount of detailed information requested. For example, FFIEC 031 requires more detailed information than FFIEC 034. Appendix II lists the schedules which have to be provided in FFIEC 031 and shows the detailed format of the balance sheet (schedule RC) and statement of income (schedule RI).

2.5 Obligations to furnish accounts

2.5.1 Accounting periods and times of furnishing

2.5.2 Form of accounts to be furnished

2.5.3 Mandatory accounting dates

General corporation law does not require a corporation, including a bank, to furnish its shareholders with copies of its accounts. However, a corporation subject to the requirements of the SEC has to despatch to its shareholders copies of quarterly and annual accounts filed with the SEC. The annual report on Form 10-K must be filed within 90 days of the end of the year and the quarterly report on Form 10-Q must be filed within 45 days of the end of the quarter.

The call reports by national banks and state non-member banks are submitted to the FDIC. The reports by state member banks are submitted to the appropriate district Federal Reserve Bank. In addition, national banks must provide one copy to the appropriate district Federal Reserve Bank and district Deputy Comptroller. As stated above they must make available to shareholders a copy of the call report upon request.

There is currently no mandatory accounting date or fiscal year for banks or bank holding companies. Because of the need to meet the regulatory quarterly call report requirements, however, banks and bank holding companies have universally adopted the calendar year as their accounting year.

2.6 Requirements as to accounts (a) prior to incorporation (b) prior to commencement of trading and (c) in order to continue trading

No accounts as such have to be prepared prior to incorporation or commencement of trading but certain financial data have to be included in the application for approval to commence operations in the US submitted to the regulatory authorities.

Once a bank has commenced trading non-submission of accounts could ultimately result in the revocation of its licence to trade. In the case of a bank holding company reporting to the SEC the ultimate sanction would be the cancellation of its stock quotation.

2.7 Audit requirements

Financial statements filed with the SEC by US domestic registrants must be audited by independent certified public accountants. The SEC has very stringent rules covering the form of the accountants' report, independence of the accountant and other related matters. These are detailed in Regulation S-X.

Federal banking regulators do not have a formal audit requirement for financial statements filed with them. They do require that the quarterly call reports be signed by certain officers and attested to by certain directors indicating that the forms have been prepared in accordance with appropriate instructions and are true and correct to the best of their knowledge.

Although there is no requirement by banking regulators for independent audits, charters for most national banks and many state banks are not issued unless the by-laws of the bank provide for periodic directors' examinations. The overall objective of a directors' examination is to assist the directors in meeting their responsibility to determine the adequacy of management and the soundness of the bank's financial condition. The OCC has published suggested procedures to be followed in such an examination in a pamphlet 'Duties and Liabilities of Directors of National Banks'. The requirements for state banks vary from state to state.

The examination of a national bank may be performed by the directors themselves, internal auditors, independent accountants, or any combination of these. However, directors are not relieved of their responsibility by the delegation of their examination function. They are responsible for significant limitations or omissions in the scope of the examination. Accordingly, the board of directors or its examining committee must take an active role in determining the scope of a directors' examination.

The OCC suggests that the directors participate in the examinations at least to the extent of appraising the bank's policies with respect to loans, investments, earnings and dividends, verifying the existence of fixed assets and the propriety of depreciation, and appraising the adequacy of insurance and surety coverage. In addition, the directors should review and understand the significant details of the directors' examination report.

The assurance obtainable from the directors' examination procedures carried out by internal auditors is limited by the degree of independence and authority that they are permitted to exercise. Situations in which independence and authority are limited are particularly prevalent in small banks where the internal auditor may be only in a part-time position or where internal auditors also have operational duties.

The difference between the audit requirements of the SEC and the federal bank regulatory agencies reflects in part the difference in their objectives. The SEC is concerned primarily with the protection of investors, and concentrates on matters related to full disclosure of financial information in the accounts and enforces compliance by requiring independent audits. Bank regulatory authorities, on the other hand, are concerned primarily with the safety of customer deposits and the survival of the banking institution. Their regulatory procedures are directed primarily toward those goals. While these agencies have various tools to regulate the financial institutions under their jurisdiction, the most important of them is their ability to conduct their own extensive on-site examinations. For example, the Comptroller of the Currency has a staff of over 2,000 bank examiners who comprise most of the employees of that agency. The examinations of each institution are conducted at least once every year. They focus on five areas: safety and soundness, trust, international banking, electronic data processing, and consumer compliance. Most of the time is spent in the area of safety and soundness and much of that time is devoted to a review of the loan portfolio as it often represents the greatest risk to the bank. The examiner's conclusions regarding the soundness of the loan portfolio are expressed by classifying loans of questionable quality into four categories as follows:

Loss: loans determined to be worthless
Doubtful: loans where collection in full is questionable
Substandard: loans with a defined weakness
Other mentioned: loans where adverse trends are developing.

Regulators insist that loans classified loss be charged off promptly. The volume of loans in the other categories are used by management, regulators and independent accountants in evaluating the adequacy of the reserve.

The results of these examinations are confidential and are not used in offering circulars or other public documents.

2.8 Acceptability to fiscal authorities of accounts submitted to supervisory authorities

The rules governing the determination of taxable income for federal purposes are set forth in the US Internal Revenue Code and related regulations. The federal tax system is administered by the Internal Revenue Service (IRS). While the tax laws tend to follow general commercial accounting practices, there are often great differences between them and the rules for calculating net income under either regulatory or generally accepted accounting principles.

These differences can be categorised as either permanent differences or timing differences. Permanent differences exist when certain income items are tax free or when certain expense items are not deductible. Examples of permanent differences are interest on municipal securities which is free of federal tax and amortisation of goodwill which is not deductible for federal purposes.

Timing differences occur when items of income or expense are included in taxable income in different periods than they are included in book accounting income. Timing differences normally arise from use of different accounting methods for books than are used for tax purposes, such as accrual versus cash basis accounting for interest or accelerated versus straight line depreciation of assets. Deferred taxes are provided on timing differences in the accounts.

Of even greater significance, however, is the fact that the tax laws are very complex and the correct treatment of an item of income or expense for tax purposes is not always clear. Consequently the tax returns submitted by the bank to the IRS are subject to audit and examination by revenue agents. Administrative proceedings and an appeals process through the court system are available to resolve differences between the taxpayer and the IRS.

To further complicate matters, most states and some municipalities impose a separate tax on corporate income and there are frequently differences between state and federal rules for calculating taxable income. For example, some states do not allow corporations to carry back net operating losses to claim a refund of taxes paid in prior periods or carry forward net operating losses to reduce taxable income in future periods.

The accounts submitted to supervising authorities are therefore not necessarily unacceptable to the fiscal authorities. Rather, they form the basis or point of departure in subsequent determinations of the propriety of calculations of taxable income.

2.9 Submission of accounts to any authority other than by requirement of law

The stock exchanges normally require a copy of the annual reports of companies that are traded on the exchanges. Other requirements for accounts of banks originate primarily from customers, particularly those using services unrelated to deposit taking and lending. Because they have the resources and abilities, many banks provide servicing of investor loan portfolios, data processing services or other business services such as payroll processing, among many others. Users of these services often require annual reports of the bank as well as special reports on review of internal control or compliance with servicing agreements conducted by the bank's independent accountants.

2.10 Application of laws and regulations to foreign banks operating through branches and subsidiaries

US bank subsidiaries and branches of foreign banks are subject to the same laws and regulations as domestic banks but in addition they have the following obligations:

Form FFIEC 002 'Report of Assets and Liabilities of US Branches and Agencies of Foreign Banks' must be filed quarterly with the appropriate district Federal Reserve Bank where the foreign bank branch or agency is located. It is required of all federally or state chartered branches and agencies. It is similar to the call reports for domestic branches but does not contain an income statement. However, the FFEIC has proposed to change the requirements for foreign banks effective with the 31 March 1985 filing date. If approved, these changes would require that foreign branches and agencies submit an income statement and balance sheet and provide more detail in a form similar to that presently required of US banks using FFEIC Forms 031, 032, 033 or 034.

Foreign branches or agencies that are required to file the FFIEC 002 must also file a FR 2073 'Quarterly Report of International Banking Facility Accounts for US Branches and Agencies of Foreign Banks' if they have established an IBF.

Reporting requirements of the state banking authorities vary. Some have adopted the FFIEC 002 form to meet their requirements.

The Federal Reserve also requires foreign banks operating branches or agencies in the United States or foreign bank holding companies operating a subsidiary in the US to file Form FR Y-7 'Annual Report of Foreign Banking Organisations'. This report covers worldwide financial and managerial information on the bank and information on non-banking activities conducted in the US. A separate Form FR 2068 'Foreign Banking Organisation Confidential Report of Operations' is used for confidential financial information of the bank in addition to that disclosed in the FR Y-7. Another report, Form FR Y-8f 'Report of Intercompany Transactions of Foreign Bank Holding Companies and their US Bank Subsidiaries', is requested quarterly to monitor those transactions.

2.11 Availability of accounts for public inspection

As a general rule, most accounts submitted by banks to governmental authorities are available for public inspection. Accounts filed with the SEC and bank regulators as a result of requirements for the issuance of securities must be delivered to stockholders in accordance with a timetable and in a manner prescribed by the proxy rules. All schedules of the Reports of Condition and Income submitted by each reporting bank will be made available to the public upon request. The only exception to this is the loan information in column A of schedule RC-N 'Past due 30 through 89 days and still accruing'. The information provided by branches and agencies of foreign banks on Form FFIEC 002 is put on a computer file by the FDIC and is available on request.

The statements of condition or balance sheets of national banks and state member banks are required to be published in a newspaper of general circulation within a short period of time after they are submitted to the regulatory authorities.

3 FORMAT, STYLE AND CONTENTS OF ACCOUNTS

3.1 Extent to which format is laid down by statute, supervisory authority, generally accepted accounting practice or otherwise

3.2 Description of format

3.3 Extent to which contents are prescribed by statute, supervisory authority, generally accepted accounting practice or otherwise

The form and contents of all reports filed with the bank regulatory authorities is very rigidly defined by the forms and the instructions to the forms. These reports do not purport to represent financial position or results of operations prepared in accordance with generally accepted accounting principles. Rather they are designed to obtain information required by the regulators to monitor these institutions and to reflect their position somewhat conservatively.

The form and content of financial statements filed with the SEC is governed by Regulation S-X and the related SEC Staff Accounting Bulletins.

Article 9 of Regulation S-X covers financial statements of bank holding companies and banks.

As part of the SEC's process of developing integrated reporting rules, the SEC changed the proxy rules so that financial statements in annual reports to shareholders of companies registered with the SEC must now also be prepared in accordance with Regulation S-X. The form and content of financial statements filed with bank regulatory authorities in annual, quarterly, and current reports and proxy statements is governed by Form F-9 in Regulation F which is required by law to be substantially in compliance with the Regulations of the SEC.

The requirements set forth in Regulation S-X and Form F-9 reflect in large measure what are considered to be generally accepted accounting principles. Generally accepted accounting principles, however, are developed for the most part in the private sector, principally by the Financial Accounting Standards Board (FASB) which is recognised by the SEC as the authoritative body for determining accounting principles. The American Institute of Certified Public Accountants (AICPA) is also very active in this area. In November 1982 the Committee on Bank Accounting and Auditing of the AICPA issued its revised Industry Audit Guide 'Audit of Banks'. It codifies many generally accepted accounting principles for banks and is effective for years beginning after 31 December 1983. The Audit Guide is helpful as a reference when regulatory reporting requirements and generally accepted accounting principles differ.

Financial statements, whether or not filed with the SEC, must be prepared in accordance with generally accepted accounting principles (GAAP) if independent auditors are to render an unqualified opinion thereon. When there are differences between regulatory accounting principles and generally accepted accounting principles, these differences can result in different amounts being reported to the regulators than are reported to the SEC or provided by the bank in audited financial statements.

The accounting profession, the bank regulators and the SEC have been working together to eliminate the differences between RAP and GAAP. Because of rapid changes in the banking industry, however, new transactions have developed that were not adequately covered by previously existing pronouncements. The practices followed by banks in those areas resulted in *de facto* generally accepted accounting principles that may be subsequently either sanctioned or modified by the regulatory authorities.

Currently the major differences in established accounting principles between the regulators and the accounting profession are in the following areas:

(1) Trading account securities are required by the Bank Audit Guide to be valued at market value. Bank regulators permit the use of either cost, lower of cost and market value, or market value.

(2) Intangibles consist of identified intangibles and unidentified intangibles. Identified intangibles in financial institutions include mortgage servicing rights discussed in FASB No. 65 and core deposit intangibles discussed in FASB No. 72. Core deposits are a bank's stable deposit base of demand and savings accounts. They have value because they represent a favourable source of funds for the generation of future revenue and are assigned a value in a bank or thrift acquisition. Goodwill is the unidentified intangible representing the excess of cost over identified net assets acquired in a business combination accounted for as a purchase transaction.

Bank regulatory authorities normally will not permit banks to capitalise goodwill as it does not represent an asset that can be liquidated to pay depositors. The FRS however permits recording of goodwill by bank holding companies. Goodwill written off by a bank can be restored in audited financial statements prepared in accordance with generally accepted accounting principles when appropriate.

Core deposit intangibles can be recorded by national banks, but only 25% of all intangibles are included in the calculation of primary capital.

(3) Equity notes issued by banks are long-term interest bearing instruments that can be redeemed only by the issuance of capital. Such notes are considered as capital for regulatory purposes; however, under GAAP they are considered debt until redeemed.

(4) Redeemable preferred stock is treated as capital for regulatory purposes. The SEC requires that it be reported as a separate caption and not included in equity.

Many foreign banks with only branches, agencies, Edge Act Banks or IBFs are not required to register with

39

the SEC. However, they may be involved with three sets of financial statements, each with different rules governing their form and content. Call reports filed with the bank regulatory authorities must be prepared in accordance with the instructions for those forms. Normally the bank will also have to prepare internal reports to the bank's head office following the bank's internally developed guidelines. Finally, the bank may engage independent accountants to audit the financial statements of its branch, agency or Edge Act Bank. These statements will be prepared in accordance with generally accepted accounting principles using the Bank Audit Guide as the primary reference source.

The formats prescribed for bank balance sheets and income statements by the SEC, Form F-9 and the Bank Audit Guide are generally very similar. The example format shown in Appendix III is generalised and reflects most of the requirements in article 9, Form F-9 and the Bank Audit Guide.

3.4 Disclosure of specific items required other than those required by general law

Disclosures in bank financial statements are subject to the same criteria that apply to all financial statements prepared in accordance with generally accepted accounting principles. Banks must provide the normal disclosures mandated by the SEC and generally accepted accounting principles that are required of all companies when appropriate.

To meet the standards of adequate and informative disclosure, the following items peculiar to the banking industry are normally included in the first footnote to the financial statements which provides a summary of significant accounting policies:
- Securities valuation.
- Futures and forward contracts.
- Trading account valuation basis and income recognition practices.
- Revenue recognition on loans.
- Policies for placing loans on non-accrual status.
- Methods of determining the allowance for loan losses.
- Basis and market value of other real estate owned.
- Trust department income recognition.

In addition, footnote disclosure would be made of the cost and market value, by type, of the investment securities portfolio and the detail of movements in the allowance for loan losses. Loans would be detailed by type either on the face of the balance sheet or in footnotes to the financial statements.

Bank holding companies filing with the SEC are required by Regulation 5-K to provide the additional information called for in Guide 3 'Statistical Disclosures by Bank Holding Companies' in the description of business section of those registration statements for which financial statements are required and annual report filings. The information is generally required for three years for all items except loans and allowance for loan losses where the information is required for five years. The disclosures required by Guide 3 are in the following categories:

(i)   Distribution of assets, liabilities and stockholders' equity; interest rate and interest differential
(ii) Investment portfolio
(iii) Loan portfolio
(iv) Summary of loan loss experience
(v)   Deposits
(vi) Return on equity and assets
(vii) Short-term borrowings

These disclosures require data and average balance information that may not be maintained or readily available by foreign banks in the form required. For new registrants with the SEC the Guide 3 disclosure requirements may require extensive recasting of financial information to comply. For example, the Guide requires that foreign loans be reported by domicile of the borrower rather than booking office of the bank which is the way records would typically be kept.

3.5 Exemptions from disclosure allowed in respect of banking items

There are no particular exemptions from disclosure requirements for banks or bank holding companies. In several instances certain disclosure requirements affect banks and bank holding companies less severely than many other types of business. For example, extensive business segment information reporting by public companies is required by FASB No. 14 and subsequent pronouncements. Although banks and bank holding companies operate in a variety of areas, they are all considered to be banking which is one segment for purposes of complying with this requirement. Banks with significant foreign operations, normally over 10% of the total, will have to provide geographic segment information.

3.6 Hidden reserves

Hidden reserves are not permitted in financial statements of banks or bank holding companies prepared in accordance with generally accepted accounting principles or regulatory accounting principles.

3.7 Requirements as to consolidated accounts

Generally, consolidated accounts are required by both bank regulatory authorities and the SEC. The General Instructions to the call reports detail the consolidation requirements of commercial banks for Reports of Condition and Income filed with the bank regulators. They require the inclusion in consolidated statements of all majority-owned 'significant' subsidiaries and any non-significant subsidiaries the bank has elected to consolidate. Significant subsidiaries are basically those where the bank's investment exceeds 5% of its capital, or the bank's share of the subsidiary's revenue exceeds 5% of consolidated revenue or where the subsidiary's income before tax exceeds 5% of the parent's income. The instructions preclude consolidation with 'domestic subsidiaries that are commercial banks, savings banks, or savings and loan associations that must file separate Reports of Condition and Income'. Investments in unconsolidated subsidiaries or other associated companies where the bank exercises significant influence should be accounted for by the equity method. Form F-9, which details requirements for financial statements of banks filed under the securities laws, refers to the call report instructions for preparation of consolidated balance sheets and statements of income.

The SEC has very similar requirements for filing consolidated financial statements of bank holding companies. Two major differences should be noted. First, they define 'significant' subsidiary in terms of either investments in the subsidiary as a percentage of consolidated assets, or share of subsidiary assets as a percentage of total assets, or share in income before tax as a percentage of consolidated income. Under rule 3.09 of Regulation S-X, separate financial statements of unconsolidated subsidiaries and 50% or less owned companies may be required if they meet any of the investment, asset or income tests described above using a threshold of 20%. In addition, under rule 9.06 of Regulation S-X, condensed financial statements of the registrant or unconsolidated holding company may be required to be disclosed in a note to the financial statements if restricted net assets of the subsidiaries exceed 25% of consolidated net assets. Restricted net assets are those that cannot be transferred to the holding company without consent of a third party such as a bank regulatory agency. For example, national banks must have approval from the OCC to pay dividends in excess of the earnings of the current year plus the earnings retained from the prior two years.

4 ACCOUNTING POLICIES

4.1 Responsibility for laying down accounting policies

The Council of the American Institute of Certified Public Accountants (AICPA) has designated the Financial Accounting Standards Board (FASB), which was established in 1973, as the body responsible for establishing accounting principles. The Securities and Exchange Commission (SEC) in its Accounting Series Release (ASR) No. 150 issued 20 December 1973 recognised the FASB and stated its position that pronouncements of the FASB will be looked to as substantial authoritative support for the accounting practices they address. ASR No. 150 represents continued expression of the SEC's long-standing policy to look primarily to the standard-setting process of the accounting profession. However, in so doing, the SEC also reaffirmed its recognition of its overriding authority under the securities laws to prescribe accounting policy when necessary to meet investor needs.

Rule 203 of the Rules of Conduct of the AICPA restricts members in expressing opinions on financial statements that contain any departure from the accounting principles of the body designated by Council to establish such principles. The principles currently covered by this rule are the AICPA Accounting Research Bulletins, Opinions of the Accounting Principles Board (a predecessor to the FASB), FASB Statements of Financial Accounting Standards and FASB Interpretations.

These documents are published in an integrated fashion by the FASB in a two-volume 'Current Text' which also incorporates supplemental guidance in FASB Technical Bulletins and AICPA Accounting Interpretations.

Other pronouncements of interest not included in the 'Current Text' are FASB Statements of Financial Accounting Concepts, APB Statements and AICPA Terminology Bulletins. These, along with those in the 'Current Text', are available in chronological sequence in a two-volume companion publication entitled 'Original Pronouncements'.

In addition the AICPA has issued a series of 'Statements of Position' on various accounting matters and a series of 'Industry Accounting or Audit Guides', one of which covers the banking industry. The Audit Guides do not have the same authority as the pronouncements covered by rule 203. However, they do represent a compilation of recognised accounting principles that a member of the AICPA should consider in rendering an opinion on financial statements.

The information that follows on specific or particular accounting policies was obtained primarily from the 'Current Text' and the Audit Guide 'Audit of Banks'. Reference is also made to specific FASB Statements or APB Opinions when they constitute in themselves the preponderance of authoritative literature on the subject.

4.2 Particular accounting policies

4.2.1 Foreign exchange

The key to US accounting policy for foreign exchange is determining the entity's functional currency, or the currency of the environment in which the entity primarily generates and expends cash. For most US banks their functional currency is the US dollar. Transactions denominated in currencies other than the US dollar will result in gains or losses during periods when the exchange rate changes. These gains or losses are recognised in net income during the period the rate changes unless the transaction hedges a foreign currency commitment or a net investment in a foreign entity.

If the bank owns a foreign subsidiary or other entity whose functional currency is also the US dollar but maintains its books in another currency, the accounts must be remeasured into the functional currency. The remeasurement should produce the same results as if the records had been maintained in the functional currency. Remeasurement is accomplished by using current exchange rates for monetary items and historical rates for items carried at cost such as securities, property and equipment and deferred charges and credits. Exchange gains and losses from remeasurement are included in net income. Since the functional currency is also the reporting currency, there is no need for translation.

If the bank owns a foreign subsidiary or other foreign entity whose functional currency is other than the US dollar, the transactions of the entity should be measured in its functional currency. Those statements are then translated to the reporting currency, US dollars, using current rates of exchange for the balance sheet and average rates of exchange for the income statement. Translation adjustments are not included in determining net income but are reported and accumulated as a separate component of stockholders' equity until such time as the foreign entity is sold or liquidated.

Gains or losses on forward exchange contracts that are still open at the balance sheet date and that are not hedges of net investments in a foreign entity or a foreign currency commitment are included in determining net income. Gains or losses on speculative contracts are computed using the difference between the contracted forward rate and the market rate available for the remainder of the contract. Gains and losses on other contracts, whether or not deferred, are computed by the difference in spot rates with separate recognition given to the discount or premium.

The current authoritative source for foreign exchange accounting policies is FASB No. 52.

4.2.2 Deferred tax

Accounting for income taxes is based on comprehensive interperiod tax allocation whereby the tax effects of current timing differences are deferred and allocated to tax expense in future periods when the timing differences reverse. Timing differences are differences between the periods when items of income or expense are included in taxable income and when they are included in pretax accounting income. The method used is called the deferred method which calculates the amount of the tax effect currently by the difference between taxable income and pretax accounting income with and without the timing difference. The tax effect is allocated to future periods when the timing difference reverses without regard to new taxes or changes in future tax rates.

When multiple timing differences exist with items originating and reversing in a given period the change in deferred taxes can be determined by either the gross change method or the net change method. Common transactions that frequently give rise to deferred taxes because of different accounting methods used for book and tax purposes are loan loss provisions, depreciation, discount accretion in securities and lease financing. The basic authoritative source for policies on accounting for deferred taxes is APBO No. 11.

4.2.3 Specific and general provisions for bad and doubtful debts

4.2.4 Treatment of provisions in accounts

The allowance for loan losses is a valuation reserve separately disclosed on the balance sheet as a reduction of the total loan portfolio. The allowance is to be maintained at an amount determined by management to be adequate in their judgement to cover all reasonably estimable losses inherent in the existing loan portfolio. This would also normally cover projected losses of any related interest receivable. Known and identified losses are to be promptly charged off against the allowance along with interest accrued in prior periods. Current period interest accruals are reversed against current period income. The allowance is established by periodic provisions that are charged against income, and subsequent recoveries of previously charged off loans are credited to the allowance. The provision is reported on the income statement as a reduction of net interest income. FASB No. 5 on contingencies provides the basis for accruing for losses when it is probable that an asset has been impaired and the amount of the loss can be reasonably estimated.

To implement the requirements of the International Lending Supervision Act of 1983, bank regulatory authorities established new classification categories for foreign loans with mandatory reserve percentages for countries whose loans are deemed to be in the category of 'value impaired'. These reserves are called Allocated Transfer Risk Reserves. They are not considered with the other loan reserves as part of the regulator's definition of bank capital.

With the exception of Allocated Transfer Risk Reserves, minimum reserves are no longer mandated by supervisory authorities unless they have determined that management has not estimated reserves based on a realistic assessment of the risks in the loan portfolio. Such an assessment would typically include consideration of delinquencies, the level of 'non-performing loans', loans classified or criticised by the bank examiners, the results of the bank's own credit review procedures and general economic factors as well as other procedures including a review of historical trends.

Additional disclosures of the risk elements of the loan portfolio are required by the SEC in Guide 3 'Statistical Disclosures by Bank Holding Companies'. These disclosures include the following:
(1) Non-accrual, past due and restructured loans for the past five years.
(2) Potential problem loans as of the end of the current year.
(3) Outstandings to foreign countries individually over 1% of bank assets and aggregate outstandings to foreign countries between 0.75% and 1% of bank assets.
(4) Loan concentrations over 10% of the current loan portfolio.

In addition SEC Staff Accounting Bulletin No. 49A requires that foreign loan disclosures include 'material subsequent developments' such as the various problems currently being encountered regarding restructuring and collecting foreign loans.

4.2.5 Premiums and discounts on investments (amortise, write off, etc.)

Premiums and discounts resulting from the acquisition of fixed income securities held in the investment portfolio are amortised to income to reflect in earnings the market yield at the purchase date. Securities in the investment portfolio are normally intended to be held to maturity, and are carried at cost adjusted for premium or discount amortisation. The period of amortisation or accretion is normally from the date of acquisition to the date of maturity. Premiums on securities carrying an earlier call date at a price above par can be amortised to either the maturity date or the call date. The prevalent methods used for amortisation and accretion are the straight line method, which is easy to use, or the interest method, which results in a constant yield over the life of the security. Gains or losses from early sale or disposition of investment securities are recognised in income when they occur.

4.2.6 Offsets, i.e. to what extent can assets and liabilities be set off against each other (legally or in practice)

In most cases, generally accepted accounting principles require that assets and liabilities be reported gross on the balance sheet so that the full measure of the liabilities of the reporting entity are properly disclosed. The following are the most common examples within the banking industry where offsets are specifically permitted.

(1) Reciprocal due from and due to balances with the same correspondent are offset.

(2) Investments in leveraged leases are recorded net of related nonrecourse debt.

(3) Insubstance defeasance of debt, whereby securities are placed in an irrevocable trust to pay debt at maturity, is reported by offsetting the securities against the outstanding debt, although bank regulatory authorities are generally opposed to this treatment.

(4) For newly organised banks, regulators often require that accumulated losses be netted against paid-in capital so that no deficits are shown on the financial statements. These presentations are typically reversed in the preparation of audited financial statements prepared in accordance with GAAP.

(5) Some banks have 'sold a participation interest' in the acceptances they have issued. The Federal Reserve has indicated its opposition to reducing acceptance liabilities by the amount participated to other banks, but is continuing to investigate this subject and has not issued a formal rule. The Federal Reserve believes that removal of the participated amounts understates the bank's legal liability and since the participating banks report only their portion as a contingency, the effect of the statutory limitation on amounts of acceptances outstanding may be nullified. If participated acceptances are netted, prominent disclosure should probably be made (preferably on the face of the balance sheet) of the gross amounts of acceptances outstanding.

Other uses where offsets may occur in practice are when 'daylight overdrafts' are netted against 'due to' accounts when not covered, or when short sales of securities in the trading account are netted against cash positions in the investment account.

Contra accounts that are typically reported on a net basis are the allowance for loan losses, unearned discount or interest, undisbursed proceeds and participations sold which are all deducted from loans, discount on long-term debt which is deducted from debt outstanding, and accumulated depreciation and amortisation which are deducted from the related assets.

Letters of credit (except those sold for cash) and unused lines are not recorded on the balance sheet but are maintained in memorandum accounts in the books of the bank. Amounts of standby letters of credit outstanding are disclosed in a footnote to the financial statements.

4.2.7 Goodwill

Goodwill is defined as the excess of the cost of an acquired enterprise over the sum of the identifiable net assets. Goodwill is an unidentified intangible asset that is recorded at cost and amortised by systematic charges to income over the estimated benefit period which is not, however, to exceed 40 years. In many cases the SEC recommends 15 to 25 years, depending on the circumstances in the individual case. Normally the straight line method of amortisation is used. Estimates of value and remaining useful life are to be continually evaluated and reductions made if appropriate. Goodwill is disposed of by disposing of the acquired enterprise as a whole.

In the acquisition of a bank or thrift institution, the value of the deposit base, if any, is considered an identified intangible asset to be amortised over the estimated life of the deposit relationship. Also, if in the acquisition of a thrift institution liabilities assumed exceed the fair value of assets acquired, the excess is an intangible which must be amortised over a period not to exceed the remaining life of the long-term interest bearing assets or deposit base.

Traditionally, bank regulatory agencies would not permit banks to record goodwill or other intangibles. The Federal Reserve does permit bank holding companies to record goodwill. Recently the Comptroller of the Currency issued a policy statement related to the recording of deposit base intangibles wherein he stated national banks may now record intangibles, but only 25% of their value will be allowed in calculating bank capital. Also, recording of goodwill has been permitted to facilitate acquisitions of troubled institutions.

4.2.8 Consolidation

Consolidated financial statements are considered more meaningful than separate statements of members of a group when one member directly or indirectly controls the others. Consolidated statements present the position of the group as a single economic entity and are required by the SEC and bank regulatory authorities. Control generally means ownership of over 50% of the outstanding voting shares. Majority-owned subsidiaries would be included in consolidated financial statements unless control is temporary or when control does not rest with the majority owners. Intercompany profits, transactions and balances are eliminated in consolidated statements. The equity method is used for affiliates owned 20-50%, unconsolidated subsidiaries and corporate joint ventures, and this involves bringing into the consolidated financial statement the attributable share of their profits, losses, assets and liabilities. Historically, adjustments resulting from the acquisition of subsidiaries in purchase transactions were recorded only in the investment accounts of the parent corporation and the consolidated statements.

4.2.9 Revaluations of assets

Generally accepted accounting principles in the United States are based on the historical cost accounting theory and revaluations of assets are normally prohibited. Accounting policies in selected areas, however, require the use of market values and subsequent changes in market values for recording assets. The following are among the most common examples:

(1) Trading account securities are carried at market value under generally accepted accounting principles and at market value, lower of cost and market value or cost under bank regulatory requirements.

(2) Marketable equity securities included in investment securities portfolios are required to be written down to market value for both temporary and permanent declines per FASB No. 15.

(3) Other real estate owned is required to be carried at the lower of cost and market value.

(4) Buildings under capital leases are valued at the lesser of fair market value and the present value of the lease payments.

(5) Interest rate futures contracts and option contracts are carried at market value.

(6) Foreign exchange futures contracts are carried at market value.

(7) Goodwill is initially calculated by revaluing the assets acquired in a purchase transaction.

Supplementary disclosure of the effects of changing prices (inflation) is required of certain large publicly held companies by FASB No. 33 and subsequent pronouncements.

4.2.10 Instalment finance and leasing including basis of recognition of income

Instalment finance loans typically originate to finance consumer purchases. They may be direct loans to the individual consumer or indirect loans resulting from the purchase by the bank of instalment sales contracts written by dealers in the merchandise financed. The loans are written on either a simple interest basis or on a discount basis whereby the total finance charge is added to the principal amount and repaid by the borrower in equal monthly instalments over a period of time, generally from 12 to 48 months. In both cases it is preferable to recognise income on a simple interest basis so the income produces a constant yield on the unpaid principal. Historically it was prevalent for banks to recognise unearned discount using the sum of the digits method commonly known as the 'rule of 78'. While this method is no longer formally permitted it is probably used by smaller banks for loans of short maturity.

National banks were first permitted to engage in direct lease financing by the OCC in 1963. Non-bank subsidiaries of bank holding companies have been engaged in providing operating leases but have been required to obtain insurance or some other guarantee to insure full recovery of the principal balance.

Banks are limited to full-payout leases that provide for recovery of the principal and financing cost. These are classified as direct finance or leveraged leases in FASB No. 13 and subsequent pronouncements which prescribe the lease accounting rules. Banks carry direct financing leases at the sum of the minimum lease payments plus the unguaranteed residual value less unearned income as its net investment. Unearned income is recognised over the lease term to realise a constant rate of return on the net investment. Leveraged leases are recorded net of non-recourse debt and income is recognised only when the net investment is positive.

Lessors are permitted to charge initial direct costs directly associated with negotiating and completing lease transactions against income when incurred and to recognise an equal portion of unearned income in the same period. Finance companies are permitted similar treatment of acquisition costs associated with instalment lending transactions, but banks are not permitted to do so under present accounting rules.

4.2.11 Dealing assets

The primary dealing assets of US banks are certain securities that banks are permitted to underwrite and trade. These are normally US government securities and federal agency securities where banks are major dealers, and certain municipal securities where banks are the primary underwriters and dealers. In some securities the only markets available are those made by banks.

Positions in trading securities are recorded as of the trade date rather than the settlement date, and are reported on the balance sheet at market value as the best way to measure the bank's trading decisions.

Securities held in the investment account are carried at cost because they are normally held to maturity. In rare cases when a bank transfers securities from the trading account to the investment account, the transfer should be made at current market value which becomes the new cost basis for the security. Transfers from the investment account to the trading account may occur when current market values are either above or below cost. When market values are below cost a loss should be recognised in the investment account upon transfer. When market values are above cost, no gain is recognised until the security is finally sold because it was identified as a trading account security when acquired.

Short sales in the trading account create a liability which is carried at market value. If the security is also held in the investment portfolio it is still considered a short sale if that is the bank's intention and portfolio securities are not borrowed to cover.

4.2.12 Pensions

The cost of future pension benefits is to be accounted for on the accrual basis so that each period bears its share through an annual provision charged to expense. This rule applies to any of a variety of schemes whereby a company provides benefits to retired employees that can be determined in advance from a written plan or practice. These include both defined benefit and certain defined contribution plans.

Determining the annual provision requires an actuary's study using acceptable actuarial cost methods which may not be the same as those used for funding the plan. Generally accepted accounting principles, outlined in APBO No. 8 and subsequent pronouncements, require that the annual provision fall between a defined minimum and maximum amount to be acceptable. The annual provision always includes normal cost. The primary difference between the minimum and maximum amounts depends on the amount of and the basis used for providing for any additional costs in respect of past service.

This must be amortised over a period of not less than 10 and not exceeding 40 years.

Neither pension plan assets nor retirement payment liabilities are carried on the books of the bank. The bank must disclose in a financial statement footnote the net assets available for plan benefits and the actuarial present value of both vested and non-vested plan benefits as of the most recent benefit information date.

Significant proposed changes to these accounting policies are currently under consideration by the FASB. These changes include moving plan assets and liabilities to the balance sheet of the employer. The treatment of unfunded liabilities under this proposal is not yet clear and has created a great deal of controversy.

4.2.13 Depreciation

Tangible capital assets acquired for use in a business are recorded at cost and are not to be written up above cost. Cost is allocated by depreciation accounting over the expected useful lives of the assets in a manner that is both systematic and rational. Both the straight line method and accelerated methods such as declining balance and sum of the years digits meet the test of systematic and rational.

Companies are required to disclose depreciation expense for the period, balances of major classes of depreciable assets, accumulated depreciation and a general description of the methods used. Often companies use different methods for financial accounting purposes than are used for tax purposes, creating the need to provide for deferred taxes on the timing differences.

5 WINDOW DRESSING

Window dressing, or artificial manipulation or distortion of balance sheets in quarterly or annual reports, is now expressly prohibited by bank regulatory authorities.

While window dressing does not usually have a significant effect on earnings, the practice results in reporting larger deposits and assets on reporting dates, which improves the standing of banks in national rankings. Although unsophisticated investors might be misled, most investment analysts and investors look at average balances and rates and yields as required to be disclosed by SEC reporting banks. In addition, separate financial statement disclosure is required in the notes to the financial statements of rates paid and high and average balances of borrowed funds throughout the year. Any period end balances significantly out of line with reported averages should be detectable by sophisticated readers.

Window dressing can be accomplished in a variety of ways. These include increasing money market activities such as trading in repurchase agreements and federal funds, selling certificates of deposit, building a matched book arbitrage with foreign placements in Eurodollar trading, and holding clearing items (cash letters) to build up demand deposit and correspondent account balances. In addition branches and subsidiaries can affect the appearance of their separate statements by borrowing from their head office or parent company.

6 AMOUNTS REQUIRED TO BE MAINTAINED BY LAW OR OTHERWISE

Minimum capital requirements vary from state to state and, for federally chartered institutions, by type of bank. For newly organised national banks, depending on the location, the Comptroller generally requires initial capital in excess of $1 million after deducting any organisation expenses. Most states would also generally require at least $1 million in capital. Edge Act Banks must have a minimum of $2 million in capital which is to be maintained at 7% of risk assets. Federally chartered branches and agencies have no minimum capitalisation requirements but do have capital equivalency requirements in the form of qualifying deposits of certain assets that must be maintained with an approved depository bank. The amount of these deposits must be the greater of the capital that would ordinarily be required of a national bank or 5% of selected liabilities of the branch or agency. These minimum amounts may be increased by the Comptroller when deemed necessary. In order to obtain deposit insurance, the FDIC also requires that US branches of foreign banks pledge assets on deposit with an acceptable institution equal to 10% of the third party average liabilities outstanding for the last month of each quarter. Deposits otherwise required by state regulators or the OCC can also be used for FDIC purposes up to certain limits.

In addition to capital requirements, national banks are restricted in the amount of cash dividends paid in any one year. Until the amount of capital surplus is equal to common capital, 10% of net profits earned during the year must be transferred to capital surplus before any cash dividends can be paid. Approval of the Comptroller is required if cash dividends paid for any year exceeds the total of the net profits for the year plus retained net profits of the prior two years. Furthermore, the Comptroller specifically prohibits cash dividends that would impair the overall capital of the bank.

In 1983 the Board of Governors of the Federal Reserve System and the Office of the Comptroller of the Currency issued minimum capital guidelines to be used in the supervisory and examination process. The guidelines used are the ratio of primary capital to total assets and the ratio of total capital to total assets. Primary capital is defined as the sum of common stock, perpetual preferred stock, capital surplus, undivided profits, reserves for contingencies and other capital reserves, mandatory convertible instruments, the allowance for possible loan and lease losses and any minority interest in the equity accounts of consolidated subsidiaries. Total capital is defined as the sum of primary capital and limited life preferred stock and qualifying notes payable and subordinated debentures.

The ratios used depend on the size of the bank or bank holding company. The regulators have identified 17 of the largest bank holding companies as multinational, and other institutions with assets over $1 billion as regional. Banks below that size are referred to as community banks. The minimum level of primary capital for multinational and regional banks is set at 5% and for community banks at 6%. Ratios for total capital are set in guideline zones as follows:

Zones	Multinational and regional	Community
1	Above 6.5%	Above 7.0%
2	5.5%–6.5%	6.0%–7.0%
3	Below 5.5%	Below 6.0%

Banks operating in Zone 1 are presumed to have adequate capital if the primary capital ratio is above the minimum. Banks in Zone 2 are presumed to be under-capitalised particularly if the primary capital ratio is at a minimal level. Banks in Zone 3 are strongly presumed to be undercapitalised and must submit a capital augmentation plan. Other supervisory actions are also prescribed depending on the apparent severity of the capital adequacy problem.

Historically, only members of the FRS were required to maintain reserves against deposits. With enactment of the Monetary Control Act of 1980 and revisions to Regulation D, reserve requirements were also extended to almost all foreign branches and agencies and most other depository institutions.

The required deposit reserves can consist of vault cash, balances maintained on deposit at the district Federal Reserve Bank and 'pass through' account balances with member banks. Reserves are currently required on certain types of accounts as follows:

Account	Required reserve
Net transaction accounts	
Up to $28.9 million	3% of balance
Over $28.9 million	$789,000 plus 12% of amount over $28.9 million
Non-personal time deposits under 2½ years	3%
Eurocurrency liabilities	3%

No reserves are currently required until the aggregate of these accounts exceed $2.2 million. Reserves on transaction accounts must be maintained contemporaneously during the time the deposit account balances used to compute the reserves are carried, except for a two-day lag. Reserves for the other deposit accounts must be maintained beginning 17 days after the computation period. In both cases the computation period and the maintenance period run for two weeks. The reserves are calculated based on weekly reports filed with the district Federal Reserve Bank. Certain carry-overs of reserve excesses and deficiencies are permitted and penalties are assessed for certain deficiencies. The details of these requirements are spelled out in Regulation D of the Federal Reserve.

7 KEY RATIOS

Bank regulatory authorities use a number of ratios that measure bank performance in carrying out their supervisory responsibilities. These ratios are computed by the FFIEC from information provided in the call reports and are presented in the Uniform Bank Performance Report (UBPR) which is available to anyone upon request. The UBPR contains five periods, including quarterly, semi-annual, and annual information, of income statement and balance sheet data for the bank as well as the average of the peer group banks. The primary summary ratios produced in the UBPR include the following:

Earnings and profitability

(1) Taxable equivalent pretax net operating income as a percent of average assets.
(2) Taxable equivalent interest income, interest expense and net interest income as a percent of average earning assets.

Loan loss history

(1) Net loan losses to average total loans.
(2) Earnings cover of net loan losses.

Loan loss reserve

(1) Loss reserve to net loan losses.
(2) Loss reserve to total loans.

Liquidity and rate sensitivity

(1) Volatile liability dependence.
(2) Net loans to total assets.
(3) Net market rate position to assets.

Capitalisation

(1) Primary capital to total assets and reserves.
(2) Cash dividends to net income.
(3) Retained earnings to average equity.

Growth rates

(1) Assets.
(2) Primary capital.
(3) Total loans.
(4) Volatile liabilities.

Included in the UBPR is extensive further analysis of these ratios as well as other analyses of the financial statements of the bank to its peers. There are no published minimum or maximum levels for any of the ratios in the UBPR, and the FFEIC cautions that the information therein is not to be used as a rating system.

In addition to the UBPR, bank regulators have adopted a uniform system for rating the condition of banks. The system is called the Uniform Interagency Bank Rating System and is designated by the acronym CAMEL which describes the attributes covered as follows:

C Capital adequacy
A Asset quality
M Management
E Earnings
L Liquidity

For a given bank, each of these attributes is rated on a scale of 1 to 5, and then the bank is given a composite rating of 1 to 5 based on an overall evaluation of each area. The composite ratings are defined approximately as follows:

(1) Banks in this group are considered sound.

(2) Banks in this group are also sound but reflect slight correctible weaknesses.

(3) Banks in this group show greater weaknesses that could deteriorate if corrective action is not taken.

(4) Banks in this group have severe weaknesses that require prompt action.

(5) Banks in this group have a high probability of failure.

The CAMEL ratings on individual banks are considered confidential and are not made available to the public.

Lending limits are imposed on most banks in terms of the ratio of loans to a single individual or entity to capital. For national banks that ratio is 15% of capital. Edge Act Banks and Agreement Corporations are limited to 10% of capital. Federal branches and agencies are limited to 15% of the capital of the parent bank. Ratios for state banks vary but most would normally be in the range of ratios required for federally chartered institutions.

8 ACCOUNTING RETURNS OTHER THAN ACCOUNTS

Most of the banking statistical information collected and disseminated by the Federal Reserve (FR) is obtained from the call reports submitted on FFEIC forms to the bank regulatory authorities. This information is not required to be audited.

In addition to the call reports there are other reports or returns submitted to the regulatory authorities that contain accounting or financial information. The most significant of these are listed below:

(1) Report of Transaction Accounts, Other Deposits, and Vault Cash (Form FR 2900) (weekly to district FR bank for deposit reserve calculations).

(2) Report of Certain Eurocurrency Transactions (Form FR 2951) (weekly to district FR bank for deposit reserve calculations).

(3) Country Exposure Information Report (required quarterly from banks with extensive foreign loans).

(4) Annual Report of Foreign Banking Organisations (Form FR Y-7) (annualy to district FR bank).

(5) Foreign Banking Organisation Confidential Report on Operations (Form FR 2068) (confidential portion of FR Y-7).

(6) Report of Intercompany Transactions of Foreign Bank Holding Companies and their US Bank Subsidiaries (Form FR Y-8f) (quarterly report to district FR bank to monitor these transactions).

9 TAXATION

9.1 General

In the United States, taxes are levied by the federal, state, and local governments in a variety of forms, including income, payroll, sales and property taxes. This section is devoted to income taxes and includes a brief explanation of withholding taxes on fixed and periodic income, such as interest and dividends, and the allowable credit for foreign taxes.

9.2 Federal income taxation of US corporations

Companies incorporated in the United States are liable for federal tax on their worldwide income. A tax credit is allowed for foreign income taxes paid, but the credit is limited to the US tax otherwise payable on the foreign income of the corporation.

Corporate federal income taxes currently are imposed on ordinary taxable income at a maximum rate of 46%, which takes effect for taxable net income in excess of $100,000 (lower rates are in place for taxable income under $100,000). The current rate on long-term capital gains is the lesser of a flat 28% or the regular rate based upon total taxable income. An additional federal tax, known as the minimum tax, is assessed on certain so-called tax preference items. Tax preferences of banks consist primarily of excess loan loss deductions, excess depreciation on real property and a portion of capital gain income. The federal minimum tax is currently 15% of total tax preference amounts minus the regular federal income tax computed on taxable income after deduction of tax preference items.

US banks are required to file annual federal income tax returns reporting the amount of their taxable income and corresponding tax liability. The reporting period, or tax year, usually coincides with the period used for regulatory and financial reporting purposes, typically the calendar year. Estimated tax payments generally are required during the year and the balance of tax must be paid with the filing of the federal return – two and a half months after year end. A six-month extension of the tax return filing, but not of the payment of tax, is automatically available upon request.

Banks generally compute their taxable income under the same rules applicable to other corporate taxpayers with a few notable exceptions. Special rules apply to allow banks and savings associations a larger bad debt deduction under a unique reserve formula. Banks are able to provide to a loan loss reserve on the basis of their actual loss experience or, alternatively, on the basis of a percentage of loans outstanding (the current allowable percentage is 0.6%). Banks generally report the gain or loss on sale of securities and other debt obligations as ordinary rather than as capital transactions. Furthermore, banks are entitled to carry tax losses back 10 years to recover taxes previously paid whereas non-banking corporations may only carry losses back three years against prior taxable income. However, banks are entitled to only a five-year carry-forward of unused tax losses whereas non-banking corporations may carry tax losses forward 15 years.

The federal income tax law generally requires income to be determined under the method of accounting which the corporate taxpayer regularly employs in keeping its books. However, the IRS has ruled that a bank may continue to file its federal income tax return on the cash method while using the accrual method for its books pursuant to bank regulatory authority. Moreover, many tax accounting methods specifically authorised by the tax law and regulations may be used without regard to the book method of accounting for a particular item of revenue or expense. For example, fixed assets may be depreciated under different lives and methods for tax and book purposes.

Certain group taxation reliefs apply. When a US corporation receives dividends from another US corporation, generally only 15% of the dividend is taxable. When two or more US corporations are connected in a chain consisting of at least 80% stock ownership, they may be able to file a consolidated federal return in which intercompany dividends are eliminated and losses of one corporation may be offset against income of another corporation.

US income taxes are withheld on dividends, interest, rents and royalties when paid to a nonresident corporation, partnership or individual (i.e. a foreign 'person'), and then only if the income is not effectively connected with the foreign recipient's US trade or business. The normal withholding rate is 30%; however, this usually is reduced if the United States has a tax treaty with the recipient's country of residence. Beginning in July 1984, the 30% withholding tax was eliminated for interest paid to foreign persons on certain investment securities. The withholding tax still applies, however, to interest on loans by foreign banks to US persons and to interest on debt held by foreign persons that hold 10% or more of the stock of the paying US corporation.

9.3 Taxation of foreign banks operating in the United States

As noted earlier, foreign banks may operate in the United States in a variety of forms, including branches, agencies, or subsidiaries. For taxation purposes, branches and agencies are treated alike when organised under federal or state law. Taxation of subsidiaries and branches (or agencies) differs with respect to the taxes levied on profits remitted to the parent or home office and in the deduction for interest paid. US subsidiaries of foreign corporations may remit profits in dividend form only, and unless the parent also is doing business in the US and dividends remitted are effectively connected with this business, such dividends are subject to a 30% withholding tax (unless lower tax rates are established through a tax treaty). A branch of a foreign bank may remit profits tax-free. However, the foreign bank will be taxed on branch profits as follows:

(1) Foreign bank branches generally will be taxed on their net income at regular US corporate rates if such income is effectively connected with the conduct of a business in the US.

(2) Gross interest and other investment income from US customers that is not effectively connected with the conduct of the US business of the branch is taxed at a flat 30% withholding rate or a lower treaty rate.

Two criteria are used for determining whether income of a US branch is 'effectively connected'. The first is whether the income is derived from assets used in, or held for use in, the conduct of a US business. The second factor is whether the activity of the US business was a material factor in the realisation of the income. In other words, if the foreign corporation has a business presence in the US, it will generally be subject to the corporate federal and local tax on the US business's net income rather than a federal withholding tax on gross investment income of the US business.

It is necessary for a US branch of a foreign corporation to allocate and apportion expenses to its effectively connected income. The interest expense apportionment rules require foreign banks to choose between one of two methods to compute its US interest deduction: the branch/book dollar pool method or the separate currency pools method. Both methods depart from earlier interest deduction rules that embodied a fungibility concept; i.e. that the total interest cost of the foreign bank was fungible and could be allocated to the US branch operation on the basis of gross income or gross assets. The new methods are complex and will impose additional recordkeeping burdens on foreign banks doing business in the United States.

9.4 State and local taxes

Banks generally are subject to franchise taxes of states and certain cities within whose borders they operate. Franchise taxes typically are based on income but in some states are imposed on bank capital. Rates vary by state and the rules for computing taxable income or capital differ. States and municipalities that impose their tax on income generally use federal taxable income as the starting point. However, modifications to federal taxable income are usually contained in the local law. Income tax rates range from about 3% to 13%. In New York, the combined state and city rate is presently 25.8%. However, state and local franchise taxes are allowed as a deduction in determining the bank's federal income tax.

The concept of unitary taxation has received considerable attention lately, particularly as it relates to multinational corporations. Unitary taxation has become a shorthand term for referring to the various formulary apportionment methods used by the states to apportion a corporation's income among the different jurisdictions where it does business. For a state to apply its formulary apportionment method, the underlying business activities of the corporation (or its affiliates) must be unitary.

A unitary business is one in which there is a high degree of interrelationship and interdependence among the activities of the company or related companies. Although the exact degree of interdependence that is required has not been clearly established, the importance of determining whether a company or an affiliated group is involved in a unitary business cannot be overemphasised.

Presently, the following states use worldwide combined reporting: Alaska, California, Colorado, Florida, Idaho, Indiana, Massachusetts, Montana, New Hampshire, North Dakota, Oregon and Utah. (Several of these states are now considering repeal of their worldwide unitary tax.) The extent to which these states employ this method varies. For example, California and Oregon have aggresively pursued the use of this method whereas states such as Indiana and New Hampshire have not.

10 INTERPRETATION OF ACCOUNTS

10.1 Adequacy of information as to contents and disclosure

Bank holding companies that are registered with the SEC generally have the fullest disclosure as they must file an annual report on Form 10-K and distribute annual reports to shareholders pursuant to the SEC's proxy rules. Both Form 10-K and the annual shareholders report include financial statements and other financial and supplementary data as required by Guide 3 'Statistical Disclosures of Bank Holding Companies'. SEC reporting requirements are complex and subject to constant changes as a result of current practices, events, and pronouncements. Audited banks that do not file with the SEC have the full measure of disclosure required by generally accepted auditing standards and generally accepted accounting principles in order for a Certified Public Accountant to render an opinion on the financial statements. Unaudited banks would provide information to shareholders pursuant to requirements of the bank regulatory authorities, which also includes significant financial disclosures.

10.2 Audit and reliability of information

Audited financial statements covered by opinions of Certified Public Accountants are generally considered to be reliable by users of those statements. Although exact statistics are not available, most of the major commercial banks in the US are likely to engage independent accountants even when not specifically required by law to do so. Unaudited financial statements prepared by banks and submitted to regulatory agencies would normally be considered to be reliable by the business community because of the extent of regulatory involvement in the banking process. However, unaudited financial statements, attested to by senior officers and/or directors of banks, lack independent verification by external auditors as to their reliability.

10.3 Comparability between different banks on the basis of published accounts or publicly available returns

Over the past 10 years the standards for public reporting by banks have improved dramatically under the leadership of the SEC, the bank regulatory agencies and the accounting profession. Most bank reporting now follows the standards prescribed by the accounting profession, SEC pronouncements and the bank regulatory agencies, whose rules must now conform to those of the SEC. The disclosures are generally quite extensive and result in virtually as much comparability as is possible without divulging proprietary information or data on individual customers.

11 OTHER RELEVANT INFORMATION

11.1 The changing scene in banking

The changes currently affecting the commercial banking system are part of a process of deregulation driven by competitive pressures and technology that affects most financial institutions in the United States today. In summary, these institutions consist of the following major types:

(a) Thrifts or non-commercial banks

These institutions were originally formed to promote individual savings and to channel loans into the housing and consumer sectors of the economy. They are considered along with commercial banks to be the primary depository institutions of the country. They consist principally of savings and loans associations, savings banks, and credit unions each with its own governmental regulatory structure.

(b) Insurance

This industry includes the traditional property and casualty, life and liability lines as well as credit life and disability used frequently in consumer lending. Insurance is currently an industry aggressively pursued by commercial banks in spite of existing regulatory barriers that limit the banks' ability to participate.

(c) Securities firms

The securities business includes underwriting, dealing, brokerage and advisory services involving principally government debt and corporate debt and equity issues. Banks play an active role in the government markets and are again aggressively seeking to establish a role in the corporate securities arena, which is currently limited by law.

(d) Leasing, commercial and consumer finance companies

A significant volume of asset based financing of accounts receivable and inventories as well as equipment is provided by leasing and commercial finance companies. Consumer finance companies provide financing of automobiles and other consumer goods. These industries are relatively unregulated because they do not take deposits to finance their activities. Many are owned by bank holding companies, the manufacturers of the products financed or other independent companies.

(e) Mortgage bankers

The mortgage banking industry provides a service of underwriting, packaging, selling and servicing mortgage loans for governmental or private institutions who wish to purchase and hold real estate loans to maturity. They are regulated in many respects by the government agencies such as the Federal National Mortgage Association that were formed to assure a viable secondary mortgage market. Banks have long played a major role in the mortgage banking industry.

(f) Registered investment companies

Registered investment companies or mutual funds were brought under the jurisdiction of the Securities and

Exchange Commission by the Investment Company Act of 1940. They enable investors to have an interest in a wider range of investments than they could as individuals. Banks are restricted from owning mutual funds that are sold to the public, although subsidiaries of bank holding companies can provide advisory services to mutual funds. Bank trust departments are permitted to provide conceptually similar pooled investments to their trust accounts with the use of common trust funds. Recently, before interest rate deregulation, money market mutual funds were competing fiercely with banks for time and savings type account balances.

(g) Real estate investment trusts

REITS were created as a device of the tax law to permit investors to have an interest in a wider range of real estate investments than they could acting individually. Like registered investment companies, no tax is imposed on the trust, only on the investors, provided a sufficient portion of otherwise taxable income is distributed to investors annually. Many REITS were formed and subsequently managed by bank holding companies.

Of all the financial institutions discussed so far, banks were and still are the most strictly regulated by governmental authorities at the state and federal levels. These regulations cover virtually every aspect of the business of banking, such as:

- Prices paid for deposits.
- Products or permissible services offered.
- Customers that could use various services.
- Geographic market areas allowed.
- Ease of entry or ability to obtain a charter.
- Availability of bank records to examination and reporting by regulators.
- Management and control of the banking organisation.
- Ability to provide trust and other fucidary services.

Historically, this extensive regulation was considered necessary because of concern over the safety of deposits held by banks for the general public. At one time this role was unique to banks. Recently other financial institutions have come to assume roles very closely resembling those traditionally regarded as the preserve of banking. The result is growing and fierce competition between commercial banks and other institutions such as insurance companies, securities firms and even retailers who are providing deposit services through thrifts and money market mutual funds along with a variety of other services to offer consumers one-stop financial supermarkets. The banks feel threatened and are fighting for a more equitable regulatory framework in which to operate.

Under the Reagan presidential administration, which promotes deregulation generally, these competitive pressures have resulted in growing deregulation of the commercial banking system. The high points of this process to date have been:

- A phase-out of interest rate ceilings under Regulation Q.
- A phase-in of reserve requirements for all deposit taking institutions as a tool of monetary policy to improve control of the money supply.
- Continuing expansion of permissible activities for bank holding companies.
- Some expansion of multi-bank holding companies in various states.
- Growing interstate banking with regional reciprocity and use of consumer banks.
- A gradual erosion of the historical barriers between banking and commerce (with the advent of export trading companies) and banking and securities (with the advent of discount brokerage) that were designed to keep banks from pursuing practices considered to be unsafe.

Recent problems at troubled banks have resulted in some deregulation backlash in Congress. There is a growing mood to limit permissible activities of bank holding companies and a specific proposal to increase minimum capital ratios.

Within this environment, banks and other institutions are testing the limits and loopholes of existing regulations and experimenting with innovative approaches to achieving the benefits of deregulation in advance of formal legal sanction.

A recent and controversial development in this regard is the creation of consumer or 'non-bank' banks. Many of the existing regulatory restraints arise from the Bank Holding Company Act which defines a bank as an institution accepting demand deposits and making commercial loans. Many companies including bank holding companies have purchased a bank, divested the commercial loan portfolio and declared the institution outside of the regulatory restraints because it was no longer a bank as defined in the law. While this technique has met with some initial success, it has caused Congress to re-examine the definition in the Act and may be the object of further 'backlash'. A bank holding company is defined under the Bank Holding Company Act as any company that has direct or indirect control of a bank or a company that controls another bank or bank holding company. For this purpose, control is defined as ownership of 25% or more of the voting shares or the ability to control the management or policies of a bank.

The Bank Holding Company Act imposes restrictions on bank holding companies from acquiring banks in more than one state. The Act prohibits a bank holding company from acquiring 5% or more of the shares of a bank or bank holding company located in another state. Various legislative proposals have been introduced on the federal level to authorise interstate banking but they have been unsuccessful to date. In anticipation of further changes in the Act and perceiving a need to accumulate 'bargaining chips' should it occur, many bank holding companies are acquiring an ownership interest of less than 5% of banks or bank holding companies. In the meantime, banks and bank holding companies are also pursuing other devices to achieve the benefits of interstate banking which is presently restricted. These include selling franchises for use of the name of a bank holding company by another bank without purchasing any interest in the bank. In addition, certain banks and bank holding companies are forming networks to provide on a co-operative basis electronic and other services.

11.2 Secrecy

Banks are generally not required to disclose the details of any deposit or loan relationships except in certain instances, such as certain types of cash transactions, material related party transactions and pursuant to government or judicial inquiry.

APPENDIX I

Filing requirements for foreign issuers of securities registered with the Securities and Exchange Commission

Foreign issuers of securities that are subject to the US securities laws are required to file with the SEC forms similar to those used by domestic registrants but which are designed to accommodate their unique circumstances. Foreign issuers of securities could be a foreign government, a corporation or other entity organised under the laws of a foreign country, or a foreign national. The required forms are summarised as follows:

Form F-1

This is the basic registration statement used for initial public offerings of securities under the Securities Act of 1933 by foreign private issuers that do not qualify to use Forms F-2 or F-3. Most foreign companies coming to the US market for the first time and those registering exchange offers must use Form F-1. All required information must be provided in the form and cannot be incorporated by reference.

Form F-2

This is an abbreviated form used generally by foreign private issuers whose securities are less widely held but who have met the registration and reporting requirements for the past three years or if they have filed at least one annual report with the SEC (Form 20-F). Financial statements and other information can be incorporated by reference from Form 20-F annual report (and other periodic reports, as applicable) so long as the incorporated reports are delivered to potential investors with the prospectus.

Form F-3

This is the most abbreviated form used by foreign private investors who have been subject to the Exchange Act and have filed all required reports for the last three years and have a wide following for their securities in the market place. Financial statements and other information can be incorporated by reference from the issuer's latest Form 20-F annual report (and other periodic reports as applicable) but does not require delivery of the latest Form 20-F to potential investors.

Form 20-F

Form 20-F is used for an initial registration and annual reporting to the SEC by foreign private issuers under the Exchange Act of 1934. This form is used like the Form 10 and Form 10-K for domestic registrants.

Financial statements of foreign issuers required to be included in these forms may be prepared in accordance with the appropriate accounting policies of the foreign issuer's country. However, a discussion of the nature and amounts of the natural variations in the principles, practice and methods used is required. For each income statement and balance sheet presented a reconciliation of net income, earnings per share and shareholders' equity to US is also required.

Annual Reporting

As indicated above Form 20-F is used to report the annual results and it must be filed with the SEC within six months of the end of the year. Unless required by a US stock exchange quarterly reports are not required but Form 6-K is used by foreign registrants to furnish promptly to the SEC information regarded as significant including any published interim results.

APPENDIX II

Form FFIEC 031

Consolidated reports of condition and income for a bank with domestic and foreign offices

Table of Contents

Schedule RC — Balance sheet

Assets	($000)	($000)
1 Cash and balances due from depository institutions (from Schedule RC-A):		
a. Noninterest-bearing balances and currency and coin		xxx
b. Interest bearing balances		xxx
2 Securities (from Schedule RC-B)		xxx
3 Federal funds sold and securities purchased under agreements to resell in domestic offices of the bank and of its Edge and Agreement subsidiaries, and in IBFs		xxx
4 Loans and lease financing receivables:		
a. Loans and leases, net of unearned income (from Schedule RC-C)	xxx	
b. LESS: Allowance for loan and lease losses	xxx	
c. Loans and leases, net of unearned income and allowance for losses		xxx
5 Assets held in trading accounts		xxx
6 Premises and fixed assets (including capitalized leases)		xxx
7 Other real estate owned		xxx
8 Investments in unconsolidated subsidiaries and associated companies		xxx
9 Customers' liability to this bank on acceptances outstanding		xxx
10 Intangible assets		xxx
11 Other assets (from Schedule RC-F)		xxx
12 Total assets (sum of items 1 through 11)		xxx

Liabilities	($000)	($000)
13 Deposits:		
a. In domestic offices (sum of totals of columns A and C, Schedule RC-E, part I)		xxx
(1) Noninterest bearing	xxx	
(2) Interest bearing	xxx	
b. In foreign offices, Edge and Agreement subsidiaries, and IBFs (from Schedule RC-E, part II)		xxx
(1) Noninterest bearing	xxx	
(2) Interest bearing	xxx	
14 Federal funds purchased and securities sold under agreements to repurchase in domestic offices of the bank and of its Edge and Agreement subsidiaries, and in IBFs		xxx
15 Demand notes issued to the US Treasury		xxx
16 Other borrowed money		xxx
17 Mortgage indebtedness and obligations under capitalized leases		xxx
18 Bank's liability on acceptances executed and outstanding		xxx
19 Notes and debentures subordinated to deposits		xxx
20 Other liabilities (from Schedule RC-G)	xxx	
21 Total liabilities (sum of items 13 through 20)		xxx
22 Limited-life preferred stock		xxx

Equity capital	($000)	($000)
23 Perpetual preferred stock	xxx	
24 Common stock	xxx	
25 Surplus	xxx	
26 Undivided profits and capital reserves	xxx	
27 Cumulative foreign currency translation adjustments	xxx	
28 Total equity capital (sum of items 23 through 27)		xxx
29 Total liabilities, limited-life preferred stock, and equity capital (sum of items 21, 22, and 28)		xxx

Schedule RI — Income statement

1 Interest income:	($000)	($000)
a. Interest and fee income on loans:		
(1) In domestic offices:		
(a) Loans secured by real estate	xxx	
(b) Loans to depository institutions	xxx	
(c) Loans to finance agricultural production and other loans to farmers	xxx	
(d) Commercial and industrial loans	xxx	
(e) Acceptances of other banks	xxx	

2 Interest expense:	($000)	($000)
a. Interest on deposits:		
(1) Interest on deposits in domestic offices:		
(a) Interest on time certificates of deposit of $100,000 or more	xxx	
(b) Interest on other deposits	xxx	
(2) Interest on deposits in foreign offices, Edge and Agreement subsidiaries, and IBFs	xxx	

54

	($000)	($000)

Interest income (*contd*)

- (f) Loans to individuals for house-hold, family, and other personal expenditures:
  - (1) Credit cards and related plans — xxx
  - (2) Other — xxx
- (g) Loans to foreign governments and official institutions — xxx
- (h) Obligations (other than securities) of states and political subdivisions in the US — xxx
- (i) All other loans in domestic offices — xxx
- (2) In foreign offices, Edge and Agreement subsidiaries, and IBFs — xxx
- b. Income from lease financing receivables — xxx
- c. Interest income on balances due from depository institutions:
  - (1) In domestic offices — xxx
  - (2) In foreign offices, Edge and Agreement subsidiaries, and IBFs — xxx
- d. Interest and dividend income on securities:
  - (1) US Treasury securities and US government agency and corporation obligations — xxx
  - (2) Securities issued by states and political subdivisions in the US — xxx
  - (3) Other domestic securities (debt and equity) — xxx
  - (4) Foreign securities (debt and equity) — xxx
- e. Interest income from assets held in trading accounts — xxx
- f. Interest income on federal funds sold and securities purchased under agreements to resell in domestic offices of the bank and of its Edge and Agreement subsidiaries, and in IBFs — xxx
- g. Total interest income (sum of items 1a through 1f) — — xxx

Interest expense (*contd*)

- b. Expense of federal funds purchased and securities sold under agreements to repurchase in domestic offices of the bank and of its Edge and Agreement subsidiaries, and in IBFs — xxx
- c. Interest on demand notes issued to the US Treasury and on other borrowed money — xxx
- d. Interest on mortgage indebtedness and obligations under capitalized leases — xxx
- e. Interest on notes and debentures subordinated to deposits — xxx
- f. Total interest expense (sum of items 2a through 2e) — — xxx
3. Net interest income (item 1g minus 2f) — — xxx
4. Provision for loan and lease losses — — xxx
5. Noninterest income:
  - a. Income from fiduciary activities — xxx
  - b. Service charges on deposit accounts in domestic offices — xxx
  - c. Trading gains (losses) and fees from foreign exchange transactions — xxx
  - d. Other foreign transaction gains (losses) — xxx
  - e. Gains (losses) and fees from assets held in trading accounts — xxx
  - f. Other noninterest income — xxx
  - g. Total noninterest income (sum of items 5a through 5f) — — xxx
6. Gains (losses) on securities not held in trading accounts — — xxx
7. Noninterest expense:
  - a. Salaries and employee benefits — xxx
  - b. Expenses of premises and fixed assets (net of rental income) (excluding salaries and employee benefits and mortgage interest) — xxx
  - c. Other noninterest expense — xxx
  - d. Total noninterest expense (sum of items 7a through 7c) — — xxx
8. Income (loss) before income taxes and extraordinary items and other adjustments (sum of items 3, 4, 5g, 6, and 7d) — — xxx
9. Applicable income taxes (on item 8) — — xxx
10. Income (loss) before extraordinary items and other adjustments (item 8 minus 9) — — xxx
11. Extraordinary items and other adjustments:
  - a. Extraordinary items and other adjustments, gross of income taxes — xxx
  - b. Applicable income taxes (on item 11a) — xxx
  - c. Extraordinary items and other adjustments, net of income taxes (item 11a minus 11b) — xxx
12. Net income (loss) (sum of items 10 and 11c) — — xxx
— — xxx

Memoranda

1. Interest on deposits that are subject to *fixed* federal interest rate ceilings in domestic offices — xxx
2. Estimated tax-exempt lease income — xxx
3. Estimated investment tax credit — xxx
4. Estimated foreign tax credit included in applicable income taxes, items 9 and 11b — xxx

5. Income taxes applicable to gains (losses) on securities not held in trading accounts (included in item 9 above) — xxx
6. Number of full-time equivalent employees on payroll at end of current period xxx

APPENDIX III

Example bank corporation and subsidiaries

Consolidated balance sheet

Assets	December 31 19x5 ($000)	December 31 19x4 ($000)	Liabilities and shareholders' equity	December 31 19x5 ($000)	December 31 19x4 ($000)
Cash and due from banks	xxx	xxx	Domestic deposits:		
Interest bearing deposits with other banks	xxx	xxx	Non-interest bearing	xxx	xxx
			Interest bearing	xxx	xxx
Federal funds sold and securities purchased			Foreign deposits:		
under agreements to resell	xxx	xxx	Non-interest bearing	xxx	xxx
Trading account securities	xxx	xxx	Interest bearing	xxx	xxx
Investment securities (market value			Total deposits	xxx	xxx
$xxx at December 31, 19x5;			Short-term borrowings:		
$xxx at December 31, 19x4)	xxx	xxx	Federal funds purchased and securities		
Loans			sold under agreements to repurchase	xxx	xxx
Commercial, financial, and agriculture	xxx	xxx	Commercial paper borrowings	xxx	xxx
Real estate − construction	xxx	xxx	Other	xxx	xxx
Real estate − mortgage	xxx	xxx			
Instalment	xxx	xxx		xxx	xxx
Lease financing	xxx	xxx			
Foreign	xxx	xxx	Bankers acceptances outstanding	xxx	xxx
			Other liabilities	xxx	xxx
Total loans	xxx	xxx	Capital lease obligations	xxx	xxx
Less: Unearned income	(xxx)	(xxx)	x% convertible capital notes due 19x6	xxx	xxx
Allowance for loan losses	(xxx)	(xxx)			
			Total liabilities	xxx	xxx
Net loans	xxx	xxx	**Shareholders' equity**		
Premises and equipment	xxx	xxx			
Customers' acceptance liability	xxx	xxx	Common stock, par value $x a share:		
Other assets	xxx	xxx	Authorized − xxx shares		
			Issued − xxx shares in 19x5 and xxx in		
			19x4, including shares in treasury of		
			xxx in 19x5 and xxx in 19x4	xxx	xxx
			Capital surplus	xxx	xxx
			Retained earnings	xxx	xxx
			Cost of common stock in treasury	(xxx)	(xxx)
				xxx	xxx
	xxx	xxx		xxx	xxx

See notes to consolidated financial statements.

Example bank corporation and subsidiaries

Consolidated statement of income

	Year ended December 31		
	19x5	19x4	19x3
	($000, except per share data)		
Interest income:			
Loans, including fees	xxx	xxx	xxx
Investment securities			
Taxable	xxx	xxx	xxx
Tax-exempt	xxx	xxx	xxx
	xxx	xxx	xxx
Trading account	xxx	xxx	xxx
Other	xxx	xxx	xxx
Total interest income	xxx	xxx	xxx
Interest expense:			
Deposits	xxx	xxx	xxx
Short-term borrowings	xxx	xxx	xxx
Capital lease obligations	xxx	xxx	xxx
x% covertible capital notes	xxx	xxx	xxx
Total interest expense	xxx	xxx	xxx
Net interest income	xxx	xxx	xxx
Provision for loan losses	xxx	xxx	xxx
Net interest income after provision for loan losses	xxx	xxx	xxx
Other income:			
Trust department income	xxx	xxx	xxx
Service charges on deposit accounts	xxx	xxx	xxx
Other service charges and fees	xxx	xxx	xxx
Trading account income	xxx	xxx	xxx
Investment securities gains (losses)	xxx	xxx	xxx
Other	xxx	xxx	xxx
	xxx	xxx	xxx
Other expenses:			
Salaries and employee benefits	xxx	xxx	xxx
Net occupancy expense	xxx	xxx	xxx
Equipment expense	xxx	xxx	xxx
Operation of other real estate	xxx	xxx	xxx
Other	xxx	xxx	xxx
	xxx	xxx	xxx
Income before income taxes	xxx	xxx	xxx
Applicable income taxes	xxx	xxx	xxx
Net income	xxx	xxx	xxx
Net income per common share:			
Primary	xxx	xxx	xxx
Fully diluted	xxx	xxx	xxx
Average shares outstanding (in thousands):	xxx	xxx	xxx

See notes to consolidated financial statements.

Notes to consolidated financial statements

In addition to the balance sheets and statements of income there would be statements of shareholders' equity and statements of changes in financial position. Both of these would cover the same period of time covered by the income statements.

Footnotes to these financial statements would generally follow and cover the following topics:

Note A: Accounting policies
Note B: Restrictions on cash and due from bank accounts
Note C: Investment securities
Note D: Other real estate and troubled debt restructurings
Note E: Loans to related parties
Note F: Allowance for loan losses
Note G: Premises and equipment
Note H: Convertible capital notes
Note I: Restrictions on subsidiary dividends, loans or advances
Note J: Common stock
Note K: Income taxes
Note L: Pension plans
Note M: Leases
Note N: Foreign activities
Note O: Commitments and contingent liabilities
Note P: Condensed financial information on the parent company

57

CHAPTER 3

EEC

PETER THRING

1 GENERAL INFORMATION

1.1 The EEC legal framework

Since its formation the European Economic Community has been working towards a removal of the economic and political barriers between its member states. To achieve this objective the Community has been following a programme for the progressive harmonisation of those laws of member states that affect economic conditions. The harmonisation process is carried out by the creation of a body of EEC law, which member states are obliged to incorporate into their own national legal systems.

EEC law relies for its authority upon the Treaty of Rome, which established the EEC and to which all member states are parties. While certain articles of the treaty have been held by the European Court of Justice to have the force of law in member states without the need for national legislation, most EEC law, in the form of adopted Directives and secondary legislation, is not effective until member states have incorporated it into their own legal framework by means of national legislation, which they are required to do within specified time limits. The body of law that has been built up in the EEC in this way, although continually increasing, falls far short of the developed systems to be found in each member state and many areas of economic activity are still little affected by EEC regulation.

1.2 The place of banks within EEC legislation

EEC legislation does not define banks as such; they fall within the class of organisation described as a 'credit institution', defined as an undertaking whose business it is to receive deposits or other repayable funds from the public and to grant credits for its own account.[1] While any business normally regarded as a bank may be expected to fall within this definition, it also covers other financial institutions such as building societies, credit unions and finance companies.

Many, but not all, credit institutions are constituted as companies falling within the ambit of EEC Company Law Directives and are therefore governed by those Directives so far as they have been incorporated in relevant national legislation and subject to any express exceptions for credit institutions or banks.

1.3 EEC legislation relating to bank accounting and supervision

Four Directives relevant to bank accounting and supervision have been adopted by the EEC, commonly referred to as the First Directive on Banking Law,[2] the Fourth Directive on Company Law,[3] the Seventh Directive on Company Law[4] and the Directive on the supervision of credit institutions on a consolidated basis.[5] On 9 March 1981 a further proposed Directive[6] was published by the EEC Commission, which may in due course form the basis of a further Directive on Banking Law.

The First Directive on Banking Law, adopted by the Council of the European Committee (the Council) on 12 December 1977, aims to reduce the differences between the laws of member states relating to the authorisation and supervision of banks and similar enterprises. The Directive on the supervision of credit institutions on a consolidated basis, adopted on 13 June 1983, takes a further step towards the elimination of differences in supervisory controls and practices in member states by laying down the general principle that supervision should primarily be exercised on a consolidated basis by the member state in which the credit institution has its head office.

The Fourth Directive on Company Law, adopted on 25 July 1978, has the objective of harmonising laws relating to the preparation, audit and publication of the annual accounts of companies and the Seventh Directive on Company Law, which the Council adopted on 13 June 1983, has the same objective with regard to consolidated accounts of holding companies. Banks and other financial institutions are given a temporary exemption from the provisions of both the Fourth and the Seventh Directives 'pending subsequent co-ordination'.[7] The objective of the proposed Directive published on 9 March 1981 and commonly known as the proposed Bank Accounts Directive is to provide this co-ordination by modifying the provisions of the Fourth Directive, and consequently those provisions of the Seventh Directive which are related to those in the Fourth Directive, and applying these modified provisions to credit institutions including banks.

---

[1] Directive 77/780/EEC, article 1
[2] Directive 77/780/EEC
[3] Directive 78/660/EEC
[4] Directive 83/349/EEC
[5] Directive 83/350/EEC
[6] OJ No. C130, 1.6.81
[7] Directive 78/660/EEC, article 1.2

1.4 Bank supervision

No supra-national EEC supervisory authority for banks is set up or envisaged by EEC legislation. The intentions are that each member state should exercise its powers of authorising and supervising banks in a uniform manner, that responsibility for supervision should rest with the member state in which the bank has its head office, so that a bank setting up branches in another member state should be exempt from national authorisation relating to those branches, and that equal conditions of competition between credit institutions should be created as far as practicable. The First Directive on Banking Law and the Directive on the supervision of credit institutions on a consolidated basis represent stages towards the fulfilment of these intentions.

1.5 The First Directive on Banking Law[8]

The Directive was adopted by the Council on 12 December 1977 and member states were required to have brought its provisions into force by 12 December 1979. It applies to credit institutions (as defined in Section 1.2) other than the following:[9]

− Central banks of member states.

− Post Office giro institutions.

− In Belgium, the communal savings banks, the Institut de Réescompte et de Garantie − Herdisconterings- en Waarborginstituut, the Société Nationale d'Investissement − National Investeringsmaatschappij, the regional development companies, the Société Nationale du Logement − National Maatschappij voor de Huisvesting and its authorised companies and the Société Nationale Terrienne − Nationale Landmaatschappij and its authorised companies.

− In Denmark, the Dansk Eksportfinansieringsfond and Danmarks Skibskreditfond.

− In France, the Caisse des Dépôts et Consignations, the Crédit Foncier and the Crédit National.

− In Germany, the Kreditanstalt für Wiederaufbau, undertakings which are recognised under the Wohnungsgemeinnützigkeitsgesetz as bodies of state housing policy and are not mainly engaged in banking transactions and undertakings recognised under that law as non-profit housing undertakings.

− In Ireland, credit unions.

− In Italy, the Cassa Depositi e Prestiti.

− In The Netherlands, the NV Export-Financieringsmaatschappij, the Nederlandse Financieringsmaatschappij voor Ontwikkelingslanden NV, the Nederlandse Investeringsbank voor Ontwikkelingslanden NV, the Nationale Investeringsbank NV, the NV Bank van Nederlandse Gemeenten, the Nederlandse Waterschapsbank NV, the Financieringsmaatschappij Industrieel Guarantiefonds Amsterdam NV, the Financieringsmaatschappij Industrieel Guarantiefonds 'sGravenhage NV, the NV Noordelijke Ontwikkelings Maatschappij, the NV Industriebank Limburgs Instituut voor ontwikkeling en financiering and the Overijsselse Ontwikkelingsmaatschappij NV.

− In the United Kingdom, the National Savings Bank, the Commonwealth Development Finance Company Limited, the Agricultural Mortgage Corporation Limited, the Scottish Agricultural Securities Corporation Limited, the Crown Agents for overseas governments and administrations, credit unions and municipal banks.

The Directive also empowers member states to defer for a limited period the application of its provisions to certain groups of institutions if they are already subject to a supervisory system differing from that applying to banks.[10]

The Directive requires credit institutions to be authorised by competent national authorities before commencing business[11] and provides the following minimum conditions for authorisation:

− The credit institution must possess separate own funds.

− The credit institution must possess adequate minimum own funds.

− There shall be at least two persons who effectively direct the business of the credit institution. Authorisation must not be granted if these persons are not of sufficiently good repute or lack sufficient experience to perform their duties.

To a limited extent member states are permitted to exempt certain credit institutions already in existence at the date of adoption of the Directive from these minimum conditions;[12] for example, 'one-man banks' in existence at 12 December 1977, if any, may continue in business indefinitely, even though they cannot comply with the condition that the institution possesses separate own funds.

A credit institution is not restricted by the Directive in the opening of branches within the member state in which it has its head office. Where branches are to be opened in another member state, the Directive allows that member state to apply the same authorisation procedures as apply to its own national credit institutions,[13] but authorisation cannot be refused solely on the ground that the credit institution has been established with a legal form that would not be permitted by the host country (except in the case of credit institutions not possessing their own funds, e.g. 'one-man' banks). Member states are also prohibited from according more favourable treatment to non-EEC bank branches than to branches of EEC banks.[14]

An Advisory Committee is established by the Directive, with the task of assisting the EEC Commission in the implementation of the Directive.[15] Among its tasks the Advisory Committee is required to decide upon observation ratios for the purpose of monitoring solvency and liquidity by the national supervisory authorities.[16] No observation ratios have been finally established but the latest proposals from the Committee are that two solvency ratios should be adopted, namely:

    risk assets ratio − own funds to risk asset

    gearing ratio   − own funds to other liabilities.

---

[8] Directive 77/780/EEC
[9] Directive 77/780/EEC, article 2.2
[10] Directive 77/780/EEC, articles 2.5 and 2.6
[11] Directive 77/780/EEC, article 3
[12] Directive 77/780/EEC, articles 2.4 and 10.1
[13] Directive 77/780/EEC, article 4
[14] Directive 77/780/EEC, article 9
[15] Directive 77/780/EEC, article 11
[16] Directive 77/780/EEC, article 6.1

Own funds is defined as capital and reserves (including asset revaluation reserves and provisions having the character of reserves) plus fully subordinated loans but after deducting intangible assets and participations in other credit institutions. For the risk assets ratio the denominator is obtained by weighting assets according to the degree of risk; for the gearing ratio it is total non-capital liabilities including acceptances and other contingent liabilities.

Two further solvency ratios had been proposed but one has been dropped and the large exposure ratio has been deferred because of definition problems.

In addition to the solvency ratios, other ratios proposed are a liquidity ratio, i.e. liquid assets to short-term liabilities, and two profitability ratios, i.e. gross profit to total assets and net profit to total assets. These ratios are being calculated on a trial basis for the larger institutions at six-monthly intervals and are being used for comparative purposes only. They are not replacing, at least for the time being, the ratios used by the supervisory authorities to monitor the banks in their own countries.

2 ACCOUNTING

2.1 Laws and regulations affecting accounts

The Fourth Directive on Company Law,[17] adopted by the Council on 25 July 1978, harmonised the laws relating to the content and format of the annual accounts of companies and to their audit and publication. However, pending subsequent co-ordination, member states were not required to apply the provisions of this Directive to banks and other financial institutions or to insurance companies. It was recognised that the nature of these exempted businesses and their economic importance required special consideration. It was not until 9 March 1981 that the Commission of the EEC published the proposed Bank Accounts Directive[18] amending the Fourth Directive for application to credit institutions. This proposed Directive is now subject to the lengthy consultation processes of the EEC, which can continue for several years. Only when this consultation process has been completed will a Directive be adopted and a further period, probably of four or more years, will elapse before the member states have incorporated its provisions into their national legal systems and brought the laws into effect. The remainder of this chapter is based upon the provisions of the proposed Directive, although any Directive which is eventually adopted may differ from it and effective national legislation may not exist for several years.

2.2 Application of the proposed Bank Accounts Directive

The proposed Bank Accounts Directive would apply to all credit institutions, as defined in the First Directive on Banking Law (see Section 1.5 above), which are companies or firms within the meaning of article 58 of the Treaty of Rome, i.e. companies or firms constituted under civil or commercial law, including co-operative societies, and other legal persons governed by public or private law, save for those which are non-profit-making.[19] It would also apply to all other companies or firms whose principal activity is to receive deposits or other repayable funds, for their own account, or to grant credits (including guarantees), to acquire participating interests or to make investments, in so far as such companies or firms have not been made subject to the Fourth Directive.[20] Thus the proposed Directive will apply not only to credit institutions which are defined as undertakings which take deposits *and* grant credit (see Section 1.5 above), but also to undertakings which take deposits *or* grant credit, so that nondeposit-takers which grant credit will be included, unless they are limited companies already covered by the Fourth Directive.

The Fourth Directive permits some relaxation in its provisions for small and medium-sized companies; no similar relaxations are contained in the proposed Bank Accounts Directive and all credit institutions of any size would be subject to the same rules. Partnerships engaged in banking would fall within the scope of the proposed Directive, although bank branches would not. The EEC Commission has considered the preparation of a separate Directive dealing with the accounts of branches of credit institutions with head offices situated outside the EEC but no firm proposals have yet been considered by member states and it seems unlikely that any such Directive will be prepared (see Section 7.1).

Exempted from the proposed Directive would be those credit institutions outside the scope of the First Directive on Banking Law (see Section 1.5 above) and also:

− In The Netherlands, credit institutions which by virtue of article 8 of the Wet Toezicht Kredietwezen are not subject to article 11 of the aforesaid law.
− In the United Kingdom, Friendly Societies and Industrial and Provident Societies.

(Author's note: references to an article without reference to a Directive are references to articles in the proposed Bank Accounts Directive.)

Member states would also be permitted to defer application of the Directive to certain groups of institutions already subject to supervisory systems differing from that applying to banks, so long as the application to those institutions of the First Directive on Banking Law was also deferred (see Section 1.5 above), and to other specialised credit institutions where, because of the nature of their business, immediate application would create serious problems.[21]

2.3 Relationship of the Fourth Directive to the proposed Bank Accounts Directive

While the proposed Directive prescribes the format and content of the accounts and certain of the notes and valuation rules, it should be noted that the whole of the Fourth Directive, except for those articles which are specifically amended or deleted by the proposed Directive, will also apply[22] to those credit and other institutions covered by the proposed Directive.

[17] Directive 78/660/EEC
[18] OJ No. C130, 1.6.81
[19] Article 2.1
[20] Article 2.2
[21] Article 2.4
[22] Article 1.1

2.4 Obligations to furnish accounts

While the proposed Bank Accounts Directive would specify the format and content of the bank's annual accounts, comprising a balance sheet, a profit and loss account and notes on the accounts, and would require their publication together with an annual report and an auditor's report, the method and timing of publication and provisions relating to accounting periods and accounting dates are left to member states to determine by way of national legislation.[23]

2.5 Audit requirements

All annual accounts of banks would be required to be audited by one or more persons authorised by national law to audit accounts, who must also verify that the annual report is consistent with the annual accounts.[24] The proposed EEC legislation does not specify the auditor's duties nor the matters upon which he should report and these would be the subject of national legal requirements or future EEC legislation.

2.6 Application to branches and subsidiaries

Bank branches would not be required to prepare separate accounts. A member state of the EEC need not apply the proposed Bank Accounts Directive to the accounts of a subsidiary, provided that the accounts of the subsidiary are consolidated in the group accounts, all shareholders of the subsidiary declare each year their agreement to the exemption, the holding company declares that it has guaranteed the subsidiary's commitments, the declarations by the shareholders and holding company are published by the subsidiary, and the exemption from the obligation to prepare, audit and publish the subsidiary's accounts is disclosed in the notes on the group accounts.[25]

3 FORMAT, STYLE AND CONTENTS OF ACCOUNTS

3.1 Extent to which format is laid down

The proposed Bank Accounts Directive prescribes a compulsory layout of the balance sheet[26] and two alternative layouts for the profit and loss account.[27] Member states may prescribe one of the alternative profit and loss account layouts or allow banks a choice between the two.

3.2 Description of format

The balance sheet layout takes the form of a horizontal balance sheet with assets listed on the left, broadly in descending order of liquidity, and liabilities, capital and reserves on the right, with liabilities listed generally in order of increasing maturity period. The profit and loss account layouts contain identical items, in the one case presented in a vertical form and in the other in a horizontal layout.

The layouts are illustrated in the Appendices.

3.3 Extent to which contents are prescribed in law

As a general rule banks would be required by the proposed Bank Accounts Directive to present their annual accounts precisely in accordance with the prescribed layouts. However, a more detailed subdivision of the items in the layouts would be allowed and new items could be added, provided that their contents were not covered by any of the prescribed items.[28] In addition, items preceded in the layouts by lower-case letters could be combined if they were immaterial in amount and if the combination made for greater clarity, provided that the combined items were shown separately in the notes.[29]

In exceptional cases, where the prescribed layouts would not be sufficient to give a true and fair view of the bank's assets, liabilities, financial position and profit or loss, additional information must be given. It is an overriding requirement of the proposed Directive that the accounts should give this true and fair view and, if the application of any provision of the proposed Directive prevented this, that provision must be departed from and the departure disclosed in the notes with an explanation and a statement of its effect.[30]

The proposed Directive also contains extensive provisions further describing the nature of the assets, liabilities, revenues and charges to which the balance sheet and profit and loss account headings relate and specifying the valuation bases to be applied in determining certain of these items. These provisions are described in Section 4.2 below.

3.4 Disclosure of specific items

Notes on the accounts would be required by the proposed Directive to contain the following minimum information:
(a) Valuation methods applied to the various items in the accounts, including the basis used to translate foreign currency items into local currency, and the methods used to calculate value adjustments.[31]
(b) The name and registered office of each of the undertakings in which the bank holds directly or through a nominee a percentage (to be fixed by member states) of the capital; the percentage cannot be fixed by member states at more than 20%. The note must also disclose the proportion of capital held, the amount of capital and reserves and the profit or loss for the latest financial year of the undertaking for which accounts have been adopted, unless this information is only of negligible importance to the true and fair view to be given by the bank's accounts. The information concerning capital and reserves and the profit or loss may also be omitted if the undertaking concerned does not publish its balance sheet and less than 50% of its capital is held by the bank.[31]

---

[23] Article 42
[24] Directive 78/660/EEC, article 51.1
[25] Directive 78/660/EEC, article 57
[26] Article 4
[27] Articles 29 and 30
[28] Directive 78/660/EEC, article 4.1
[29] Article 3.1
[30] Directive 78/660/EEC, article 2
[31] Directive 78/660/EEC, article 43.1

(c) The number and nominal value (or accounting par value) of shares subscribed during the financial period.[31]

(d) The number and nominal value (or accounting par value) for each class if there is more than one class of shares.[31]

(e) The existence of any participation certificates, convertible debentures or similar securities or rights, with an indication of their number and the rights conferred by them.[31]

(f) An analysis by original maturity date of the balance sheet items:

Assets 3(b)(bb)	– Loans and advances to credit institutions with agreed maturity dates or periods of notice of three months or more
Assets 7	– Loans and advances to customers with agreed maturity dates or periods of notice
Liabilities 1(b)(bb)	– Amounts owed to credit institutions with dates or periods of notice of three months or more
Liabilities 2(b) and 2(c)	– Amounts owed to customers other than credit institutions with agreed maturity dates or periods of notice or in the form of savings deposits and savings bonds
Liabilities 3(b)	– Commitments represented by certificates (other than debt securities issued)
Liabilities 8	– Subordinated liabilities

The analysis must disclose items (i) up to and including one year; (ii) more than one year but less than five years; (iii) five years and over.

Furthermore, banks must disclose the proportions of assets or liabilities within the 'five years and over' categories which will become due within one year of the balance sheet date, and this further information is also required for:

Assets 6	– Debt securities held in portfolio, and
Liabilities 3(a)	– Commitments represented by debt securities issued

Member states are permitted to require this information analysing maturity dates to be given in the balance sheet instead of in the notes on the accounts.[32]

(g) Information on assets pledged as security for a bank's liabilities and contingent liabilities, sufficient to indicate for each liability category the total amount of assets pledged as security.[32]

(h) The total amount of financial commitments not included in the balance sheet or in items below the line on the balance sheet, disclosing separately commitments concerning pensions and affiliated undertakings.[33, 34]

(i) The proportion of operating income (i.e. interest receivable, income from shares, other variable-yield securities and participating interests, commissions receivable and other operating income) arising from domestic and foreign markets respectively.[35]

(j) Average number of persons employed during the financial year, analysed by category.[33]

(k) The extent to which the profit or loss for the financial year has been affected by valuations differing from those prescribed and made in the year or in earlier years with a view to obtaining tax relief. If the influence of such valuation on future tax charges is material, details must be disclosed.[33]

(l) The difference between the tax charged for the financial year and for earlier financial years and the amount of tax payable in respect of those years, if material for the purposes of future taxation. The amount may also be disclosed in the balance sheet under a separate item as a cumulative total (e.g. deferred taxation).[33]

(m) The emoluments in respect of the financial year of members of the administrative, managerial and supervisory bodies by reason of their responsibilities and any commitments for retirement pensions for former members of those bodies, with an indication of the total for each category.[33]

(n) The amounts of advances and credits granted to members of the administrative, managerial and supervisory bodies and the commitments entered into on their behalf by way of guarantees of any kind.[36]

(o) If not shown in the balance sheet, movements in the various fixed asset items, i.e. purchase price or production cost for each item, additions, disposals and transfers and cumulative depreciation or value adjustments at the balance sheet date and rectifications made during the financial year to the depreciation or value adjustments of previous years.[37] Assets to be treated as fixed assets are defined (see Section 4.2.13 below).

(p) A breakdown of the securities included in:
Assets 6 – Debt securities held in portfolio
Assets 7 – Subordinated claims and debt securities, and
Assets 8 – Shares and other variable-yield securities
into listed and unlisted securities and into securities which were or were not valued as fixed assets (see Section 4.2.13 below).[38]

(q) Information on the value of leasing transactions apportioned between the relevant balance sheet items.[38]

(r) The book values, separately, of land and buildings occupied by the bank and land and buildings held for resale.[38]

(s) A breakdown into their main components, where such amounts are important for the purpose of assessing the annual accounts, of the following items: other assets, other liabilities, other operating charges, extraordinary charges, other operating income and extraordinary income.

Explanations of the nature and amounts of these items are also required.[38]

(t) Information on the amounts of interest received on subordinated assets and of interest expended on subordinated liabilities.[38]

3.5 Exemptions from disclosure allowed in respect of banking items

The proposed Directive would apply minimum disclosure requirements. Member states would be permitted to legislate for more onerous requirements but would not

---

[32] Article 39.2
[33] Directive 78/660/EEC, article 43.1
[34] Article 39.3
[35] Article 39.4
[36] Article 39.5
[37] Directive 78/660/EEC, article 15.3
[38] Article 40.2

have the authority to allow banks to avoid any of the disclosure provisions contained in the proposed Directive.[39]

3.6 Hidden reserves

The proposed Directive would permit the creation and maintenance of hidden or prudential reserves by allowing loans and advances to credit institutions and to customers to be included in a bank's accounts at an arbitrarily reduced value. The Fourth Directive would require loans and advances to be stated at the lower of cost, normally face value, and market value, or realisable value. The proposed Directive would permit a bank to reduce these values by up to 5%, without disclosing that such a reduction had been made, where this is necessary in view of the prudence dictated by the particular risks attaching to banking business.[40] The reduced values could then be maintained by the bank as long as it wished, thus enabling it to smooth out variations in its disclosed profits.[41] Any increases or decreases in the amount deducted from loans and advances would appear in the profit and loss account as part of the net charge or income relating to value adjustments to loans and advances. The movement in the reduction will therefore not be apparent, but obscured by movements in provisions for bad and doubtful debts.

3.7 Requirements as to consolidated accounts

EEC legislation on the form, content, publication and audit of consolidated accounts is contained in the Seventh Directive on Company Law. The proposed Bank Accounts Directive makes no reference to the Seventh Directive and contains no other provisions requiring or relating to consolidated accounts. The Seventh Directive itself permits a member state to defer its application to banks which are parent companies and to permit companies to omit from consolidation subsidiaries which are banks, until the member state has implemented the proposed Bank Accounts Directive, although this deferment cannot apply to financial years ending after 1993.[42] It is expected that the proposed Bank Accounts Directive will be amended so as to apply the Seventh Directive to banks with modifications similar to those relating to the Fourth Directive. The effect will be to require banks which are parent companies to prepare consolidated accounts in a format that will correspond as closely as possible to the formats required for the bank's own accounts with similar accounting policies and disclosures.

The Seventh Directive provides, as a general rule, that consolidated accounts are required if any member of the group is a Fourth Directive (limited liability) company, regardless of the legal form of the parent.[43] However, member states may limit the requirement for consolidated accounts to those cases where the parent company is itself a limited liability company.[44] Consolidation is required by the Seventh Directive, subject to exemption on the basis of size, where one undertaking in relation to another undertaking:
(a) Has a majority shareholding, or
(b) Has the right to appoint or to remove a majority of the board members, or

(c) Has the right of management, pursuant to a control contract, or
(d) As a minority shareholder, exercises effective control of the board by means of an agreement with other shareholders.[45]

Consolidation is optional where:
(a) Any undertaking is a shareholder in and has appointed the majority of the board of another undertaking,[45] or
(b) Any undertaking has a participating interest in another undertaking (at least a 20% shareholding unless a member state has specified a lower level) and actually exercises a dominant influence over it or actually manages the undertakings on a unified basis,[46] or
(c) Undertakings, at least one of which is a limited liability company, are managed on a unified basis.[47]

4 ACCOUNTING POLICIES

4.1 Responsibility for laying down accounting policies

The proposed Bank Accounts Directive contains detailed valuation rules or accounting policies which member states of the EEC would be required to incorporate into their national laws. These accounting policies could be subsequently varied by EEC legislation. Member states could themselves legislate for additional accounting policies and such organisations as stock exchanges, securities commissions and professional accountancy bodies could lay down further requirements within the prevailing national laws or practices; such additional requirements could not, however, have the effect of excluding any of the provisions of the proposed Directive.

4.2 Particular accounting policies

4.2.1 Foreign exchange[48]

The proposed Directive requires assets and liabilities denominated in foreign currency to be translated at the spot rate ruling at the balance sheet date. Unmatured forward exchange contracts must also be translated at the spot rate, unless the member state stipulates that the forward rate ruling at the balance sheet date should be used. Any gains or losses arising from these translation rules should be included in the profit and loss account, except that member states may require that, in the case of unmatured forward exchange contracts not covered by specific foreign exchange swaps or by currency assets or liabilities, only losses should be included in the profit and loss account and gains should be deferred. Premiums or discounts arising from swaps or other specially covered

---

[39] Directive 78/660/EEC, article 2.6
[40] Article 37.1
[41] Article 37.2
[42] Directive 83/349/EEC, article 40.2
[43] Directive 83/349/EEC, article 4.1
[44] Directive 83/349/EEC, article 4.2
[45] Directive 83/349/EEC, article 1.1
[46] Directive 83/349/EEC, article 1.2
[47] Directive 83/349/EEC, article 12.1
[48] Article 38

forward exchange contracts should be amortised over the period of the transaction.

4.2.2 Deferred taxation

None.

4.2.3 Specific and general provisions for bad and doubtful debts

Under the general provisions relating to the valuation of current assets, loans and advances must be valued at the lower of cost, normally face value, and market value or realisable value. In making this initial valuation, provisions previously made for the purpose of writing down to market value must be released or adjusted if the reasons for the write-down no longer apply.[49] Having established the value at the lower of cost and market value, banks would be permitted to write down loans and advances by a further amount not exceeding 5% (see Section 3.6 above). The net amount of any new provisions and any releases of provisions should be included in the appropriate profit and loss account items (8 in the vertical layout and A.4 or B.4 in the horizontal layout) and should comprise movements both in provisions required to write down to realisable value and in those required to write down to any lower value selected by the bank within the 5% restriction. The proposed Directive would not require any disclosure of these two components of the profit and loss account figure nor of the amounts of the provisions carried at the balance sheet date; it also contains no requirements as to whether provisions for bad and doubtful debts should be specific or general.

4.2.4 Treatment of provisions in accounts

Provisions for bad and doubtful debts are regarded as value adjustments and are therefore deducted from the appropriate assets. Provisions for charges and other liabilities may not be used to adjust the value of assets[50] and must be included on the liabilities side of the balance sheet under item 7(c).

4.2.5 Premiums and discounts on investments

There are no requirements in the proposed Directive relating directly to premiums and discounts on investments. However, the proposed Directive would require all assets to be shown at cost or less (unless the subject of a revaluation)[51] and thus would appear to prohibit the amortisation of discounts where investments are purchased for less than redemption value, although amortisation of premiums would be permissible.

4.2.6 Offsets

The proposed Directive specifically prohibits set-off between asset and liability items and between income and expenditure items.[52] This provision appears to encompass in its prohibition the set-off commonly adopted by banks when they are in effect doing no more than provide a facility by which one entity lends funds to another. However, for profit and loss account purposes, banks would be permitted to disclose net figures for movements on provisions for bad and doubtful debts[53] and on provisions against securities, participating interests (broadly equivalent to associated companies) and shares in affiliated undertakings (e.g. subsidiaries).[54]

4.2.7 Goodwill

The proposed Directive would require goodwill to be written off within a maximum period of five years,[55] although member states would be allowed to permit banks a longer period of systematic write-off, provided that the period did not exceed the economic life of the asset and was disclosed in the notes on the accounts, together with the supporting reasons.[56]

4.2.8 Consolidation

See Section 3.7 above.

4.2.9 Revaluations of assets

The proposed Directive would allow member states to permit revaluations of fixed assets, including financial fixed assets (see Section 4.2.13).[57] While member states would themselves define the permissible methods of valuation and the rules for their application, the proposed Directive would require disclosure in the notes on the accounts of the method of valuation and of information that would reveal the carrying value of the asset as if no revaluation had taken place. Any surplus or deficiency arising on revaluation must be taken to revaluation reserve. Movements on revaluation reserve would have to be disclosed and the use of the revaluation reserve would be restricted either to capitalisation or to transfer to profit and loss account as the revaluation surplus became realised.

4.2.10 Instalment finance and leasing

None.

4.2.11 Dealing assets and investment assets

The proposed Directive contains no provisions relating to dealing assets and investment assets other than those relating generally to current assets and fixed assets.

4.2.12 Pensions

None.

---

[49] Directive 78/660/EEC, article 2.6
[50] Directive 78/660/EEC, article 20.3
[51] Directive 78/660/EEC, articles 35 and 39
[52] Directive 78/660/EEC, article 7
[53] Article 34.2
[54] Article 35.2
[55] Directive 78/660/EEC, article 34.1
[56] Directive 78/660/EEC, article 37.2
[57] Directive 78/660/EEC, article 33

4.2.13 Fixed assets and depreciation

Fixed assets are defined by the proposed Directive as assets intended for use on a continuing basis in the normal course of the credit institution's affairs[58] and, in addition, will always include formation expenses, costs of research and development carried forward, concessions, patents, licences, trade marks and similar rights, goodwill acquired for valuable consideration, plant and machinery, other fixtures and fittings and tools and equipment.[59] Financial fixed assets would comprise participating interests (broadly equivalent to associated companies), shares in affiliated undertakings (e.g. subsidiary companies) and securities intended for use on a continuing basis in the normal course of the credit institution's activities.[60] Unless the subject of revaluation (see Section 4.2.9), fixed assets must be stated at purchase price less depreciation calculated to write off cost systematically over the assets' useful economic lives. If a fixed asset is believed to have suffered a permanent reduction in value, an appropriate adjustment must be made to its value and financial fixed assets may be written down to the value attributable to them at the balance sheet date if lower than cost; these write-downs must be distinguished in the profit and loss account or in the notes on the accounts from the normal depreciation charge.[61]

4.2.14 Other significant accounting policies

The proposed Directive would adopt a number of fundamental accounting principles contained in the Fourth Directive.[62] These comprise:
(a) The presumption of a going concern.
(b) Consistency of valuation from year to year.
(c) Valuation on a prudent basis, i.e. only realised profits may be recognised, account must be taken of all foreseeable losses and liabilities and of all depreciation.
(d) The accrual of income and charges regardless of the date of receipt or payment.
(e) Separate valuation of the components of asset and liability items.
(f) Correspondence of the opening balance sheet for one year with the closing balance sheet for the preceding year.

Any departure from any of these principles would only be permitted in exceptional cases and would require disclosure in the notes on the accounts.

5 WINDOW DRESSING

The proposed Bank Accounts Directive would require the annual accounts of a bank to give a true and fair view of the bank's assets, liabilities, financial position or profit and loss.[63] This provision, coupled with the requirement to adhere strictly to the specified accounts formats, should be sufficient to eliminate any window dressing of accounts. However, it should be noted that the freedom to maintain a hidden reserve (see Section 3.6 above) and to use this reserve to reduce or eliminate fluctuations in disclosed profits may have a significant effect upon the usefulness of the information provided by the accounts and permit an element of window dressing to be practised.

6 CONCLUSION

The European Economic Community is still in the early stages of creating legal provisions relating to bank accounts. The proposed Bank Accounts Directive has yet to be adopted by the Council of Ministers and a further period of several years may be expected to elapse after adoption before its provisions are brought into force by all member states. The proposed Directive has itself been widely criticised on several different grounds and any Directive would undoubtedly differ in several respects from the proposed Directive as published in 1981.

A number of financial institutions have criticised the proposed Directive for its rigidity and inflexibility. They argue that the variety of undertakings falling within the definition of credit institutions is so wide that one single accounts format cannot adequately provide a proper understanding of the financial position and profit or loss of each of them. These critics would wish that credit institutions were given much greater freedom to draw up their accounts in the manner that they consider most appropriate to their particular operations and circumstances.

One of the most hotly debated aspects of the proposed Directive has been that permitting the understatement, within limits, of loans and advances (see Section 3.6). Some would argue that such a significant freedom given to directors to determine balance sheet values and disclosed profit or loss is in irreconcilable conflict with the requirement that the accounts should give a true and fair view of assets, liabilities, financial position and profit or loss. Others argue that banks must be permitted to make undisclosed adjustments to published profits or losses in order to maintain confidence in the banking system. They contend that depositors would be unduly and unnecessarily alarmed by large fluctuations in a bank's results from year to year. Their opponents argue that depositors have a good understanding of the realities of banking and that confidence is more likely to be engendered by disclosure of the truth than by concealment. Others, while supporting the concept of a hidden reserve, contend that the limitation of the reserve to 5% of loans and advances is inappropriate for many credit institutions whose business is such that their funds are mainly deployed in assets other than loans and advances; such institutions may, they argue, be open to the same risks from movements in interest rates and exchange rates as lending institutions and should be permitted to maintain hidden reserves of a greater amount than would be allowed by reference to the proposed Directive's provisions.

---

[58] Article 36.1
[59] Article 4
[60] Article 36.2
[61] Directive 78/660/EEC, article 35
[62] Directive 78/660/EEC, article 31
[63] Directive 78/660/EEC, article 2

Criticism has also been directed at the prohibition of any set-off between asset and liability items or between income and expenditure items. A bank which has taken a deposit from a customer and at the same time made an advance to the same customer and has some right of set-off between the deposit and the advance may well argue that the two balances should be set off for accounts purposes. It is not clear whether such a set-off would contravene the proposed Directive. Certainly more complicated transactions, involving different customers and different currencies with cross-guarantees, which may previously have been the subject of set-off for accounts purposes, would appear to fall within the scope of the publication. Many bankers would argue that prohibiting set-off in circumstances where banking practice has hitherto permitted it would inflate artificially and misleadingly the balance sheet footings of a bank.

Certain of the criticisms made reflect national prejudices and a natural resistance to change. Others undoubtedly have more substance and it is to be hoped that revisions to the proposed Directive will represent satisfactory responses to the points raised.

7 FUTURE DEVELOPMENTS

7.1 Bank branches

A working party set up by the EEC Commission has prepared proposals for the annual accounts of branches of credit institutions whose head office is situated outside the EEC. Such branches of foreign banks would not be subject to the provisions of the proposed Bank Accounts Directive. The working party recommended that branches of foreign banks should be required to comply, as far as possible, with the provisions of the proposed Directive. To comply with this recommendation a foreign bank, whose head office was situated outside the EEC, would be required to publish sub-accounts, for each member state in which it had branches, relating to the branches in that member state (all the branches within a particular member state being regarded as a single branch) and such sub-accounts would comply with the provisions of the proposed Bank Accounts Directive with minor modifications relating to share capital, branch capital and intra-company accounts.

The proposals made by the working party have been widely attacked by critics both within and outside the banking community. Opponents of the proposals have argued that branch accounts would be of little or no use to any reader, since:

(a) They represent only a part of a single entity and only knowledge of the whole has any benefit.

(b) Publication of branch accounts might mislead some users into believing that branches were separate entities.

(c) Branch accounts are unlikely to give a true and fair view of the branch's position as provisions and reserves relating to a branch may not be held in the branch's books.

(d) The proposals discriminate against foreign banks since EEC banks would not be required to publish branch accounts.

(e) The proposals would discourage foreign banks from opening branches in the EEC to the detriment of the Community's financial centres.

In view of the weight of criticism directed against the working party's proposals it must be assumed that they are unlikely to make any significant progress in the near or medium-term future.

APPENDIX I

Layout of the balance sheet

Assets

1 Cash in hand, balances with central banks and postal cheque offices
2 Treasury bills and similar debt instruments of public bodies
3 Loans and advances to credit institutions
   (a) repayable on demand
   (b) with agreed maturity dates or periods of notice
       (ba) of less than three months
       (bb) of three months or more
4 Bill portfolio
5 Loans and advances to customers
   (a) repayable on demand
   (b) with agreed maturity dates or periods of notice
6 Debt securities held in portfolio
   (a) issued by public bodies
   (b) issued by other borrowers, including own debt securities
7 Subordinated claims and debt securities
8 Shares and other variable-yield securities, including
   – participating interests
   – shares in affiliated undertakings
9 Assets as listed in article 9, Assets B, CI and CII(2), (3) and (4) of Directive 78/660/EEC, including
   – formation expenses
   – goodwill, to the extent that it was acquired for valuable consideration
   – assets listed in article 9, Assets CII(2), (3) and (4) of Directive 78/660/EEC
10 Land and buildings
11 Subscribed capital unpaid
   – called-up capital (unless national law provides for called-up capital to be included under liabilities, in which case capital called but not yet paid up must be included either in item 11 of the assets or in item 14 of the assets)
12 Own shares
   – in addition: nominal/accounting par value
13 Other assets
14 Subscribed capital, called but not paid-up (unless national law provides that called-up capital be shown as an asset under item 11)
15 Accruals and deferred income
16 Loss for the financial year (unless national law provides for its inclusion under item 13 of the liabilities)

Total assets

Liabilities

1 Amounts owed to credit institutions
   (a) repayable on demand
   (b) with agreed maturity dates or periods of notice
       (ba) of less than three months
       (bb) of three months or more
2 Amounts owed to customers other than credit institutions
   (a) repayable on demand
   (b) with agreed maturity dates or periods of notice
   (c) savings deposits and savings bonds
3 Commitments represented by certificates
   (a) debt securities issued
   (b) other
4 Other liabilities
5 Accruals and deferred income
6 Profit for the financial year (unless national law provides for its inclusion under item 13 of the liabilities)
7 Provisions for liabilities and charges
   (a) provisions for pensions and similar obligations
   (b) provisions for taxation
   (c) other provisions
8 Subordinated liabilities
9 Subscribed capital (unless national law provides for called-up capital to be shown under this item. In that case the amounts of subscribed capital and paid-up capital must be shown separately)
10 Share premium account
11 Reserves
12 Profit or loss brought forward
13 Profit or loss for the financial year (unless national law provides for this item to be shown under 'Assets' item 16 or 'Liabilities' item 6)

Total liabilities

Below the line items

1 Contingent liabilities
   (a) endorsements
   (b) guarantees and indemnities
   (c) assets pledged as collateral security for liabilities of third parties

2 Commitments arising from forward transactions
3 Commitments arising from sale and repurchase transactions

APPENDIX II

Vertical layout of the profit and loss account

1   Interest receivable, including that derived from fixed-interest securities

2   (a) Income from shares and other variable-yield securities
    (b) Income from participating interests
    (c) Income from shares in affiliated undertakings

3   Commissions receivable

4   Interest payable

5   Commissions payable

6   Other operating income

7   Staff costs
    (a) wages and salaries
    (b) social security costs, with a separate indication of those relating to pensions

8   Charges for value adjustments in respect of loans and advances to credit institutions and customers and provisions for guarantees in credit transactions with credit institutions and customers. Income from the writing-up of loans and advances to credit institutions and customers and from the writing-back of provisions for guarantees in credit transactions, with credit institutions and customers

9   Charges for value adjustments in respect of securities, participating interests and shares in affiliated undertakings/income from value adjustments in respect of securities

10 Value adjustments in respect of 'Assets' items 9 and 10

11 Other operating charges

12 Tax on profit or loss on ordinary activities

13 Profit or loss on ordinary activities after tax

14 Extraordinary income

15 Extraordinary charges

16 Extraordinary profit or loss

17 Tax on extraordinary profit or loss

18 Other taxes not shown under the above items

19 Profit or loss for the financial year

Horizontal layout of the profit and loss account

A Charges

1 Interest payable
2 Commissions payable
3 Staff costs
   (a) wages and salaries
   (b) social security costs, with a separate indication of those relating to pensions
4 Charges for value adjustments in respect of loans and advances to credit institutions and customers and provisions for guarantees in credit transactions with credit institutions and customers
5 Charges for value adjustments in respect of securities, participating interests, and shares in affiliated institutions
6 Value adjustments in respect of 'Assets' items 9 and 10
7 Other operating charges
8 Tax on profit or loss on ordinary activities
9 Extraordinary charges
10 Tax on extraordinary profit or loss
11 Other taxes not shown under the above items
12 Profit for the financial year

B Income

1 Interest receivable including that derived from fixed interest securities
2 (a) Income from shares and other variable-yield securities
   (b) Income from participating interests
   (c) Income from shares in affiliated undertakings
3 Commissions receivable
4 Income from the writing-up of loans and advances to credit institutions and customers and from the writing-back of provisions for guarantees in credit transactions with credit institutions and customers
5 Income from value adjustments in respect of securities, participating interests, and shares in affiliated undertakings
6 Other operating income
7 Profit or loss on ordinary activities after tax
8 Extraordinary income
9 Loss for the financial year

CHAPTER 4

BELGIUM

LUDD SWOLFS

1 GENERAL INFORMATION

Belgium is a Kingdom with a parliamentary democracy. Although more and more powers are given to the regional governments, the major political decisions are still made on a national level and laws and regulations which organise and control the financial activity are made by the national government and institutions.

The major part of the Belgian banking law finds its origin in the period of economic depression during the 1930s. Until then hardly any control or supervision was exercised over banks and many depositors lost their savings through the bankruptcy of banks, which in turn were caused by the high level of risk taken by certain banks in commercial and industrial companies, not only in the form of credits granted but also as shareholders. The fundamentals of banking law were laid in 1935 and subsequent laws and amendments are mainly refinements to this law or modifications required to keep pace with the rapidly changing financial practice.

The central bank in Belgium is the National Bank of Belgium and it is a mixed institution, i.e. it is partly state-owned and partly owned by private shareholders. The National Bank has an important role in the Belgian monetary system and operates quite independently from the government. The Bank's functions include:
  – Issuing the Belgian franc notes.
  – Intervention on the exchange markets to buy or sell foreign currency to maintain the parity of the Belgian (commercial) franc.
  – Bankers' bank: banks can obtain funds from the central bank through a number of ways, the most common of which are rediscounting of trade notes receivable and overdraft facilities. The discount rate charged by the central bank in this connection is the base rate for all money market interest rates in Belgium and is consequently the main tool for monetary policy.
  – Organisation of the inter-bank clearing system and of the guaranteed call money market.

The Belgian banking scene is very international. In 1983 there were 84 banks in Belgium of which 27 were branches of foreign banks. Of the remaining 57 banks established as a Belgian entity, 21 were affiliated with foreign banks. In total, these banks had some 3,700 establishments in Belgium.

Total assets of all banks at 31 December 1982 amounted to Bfr6,078,540 million, of which approximately 60% was represented by foreign currency.

1.1 Organisations covered by banking regulations

The basic legal framework for banking regulations is found in the following decrees and laws:
  – Royal Decree No. 185 of 9 July 1935 (R.D. 185).
  – Law of 28 December 1973 (chapter I).
  – Law of 30 June 1975.

The Royal Decree No. 185 is applicable only to banks whereas the Law of 1973 is aimed at all credit institutions. The Law of 1975 is applicable to banks and savings companies.

The Banking Commission has supervisory authority for three categories of credit institution:
  – Banks.
  – Private savings associations.
  – Enterprises subject to chapter I of the Law of 10 June 1964 (Companies receiving funds from the public repayable after more than six months).

Banks are defined as follows:[1] 'Enterprises (Belgian or foreign) which receive, usually on demand or on terms with a maximum of two years, repayable deposits with the purpose to use these for banking, credit or investment activities for their own account.'

Exception is made for most of the public credit institutions, such as the National Bank, financial enterprises which only receive liquid assets (i.e. cash) from subsidiaries in order to centralise investments, and savings companies which have separate legislation.

1.2 Summary of major types of bank

Almost all categories of banks can exist in Belgium and one bank can have a variety of activities. For legal and regulatory purposes the type of bank does not make any difference (except for the three categories of credit institutions mentioned in Section 1.1).

Banking law does, however, formally prohibit the existence of 'mixed banks', i.e. enterprises which would combine banking with commercial activities and for that reason banks are in principle not allowed to hold shares in commercial or industrial companies.

1.3 Supervisory authorities

As indicated above the supervision of credit institutions is entrusted to the Banking Commission.

---

[1] Royal Decree No. 185 of 9 July 1935; art. 1

1.4 Status of supervisory authorities

The Banking Commission was set up under art. 35 of the R.D. 185. It is an independent organisation consisting of a president and six members appointed by means of Royal Decree signed *inter alia* by the Minister of Finance and the Minister of Economic Affairs. Two of the members are selected from a list proposed by the representatives of the banks and savings associations; two members are selected from a list proposed by the National Bank of Belgium and of the Institut de Réescompte et de Garantie; Herdisconterings- en Waarborginstituut (Institute for Rediscounting and Guarantee).

1.5 Laws and regulations governing banks

There are a number of laws and regulations governing banks dating back to the Royal Decree No. 185 of 9 July 1935 which itself has been subsequently amended. The Banking Commission prepares manuals which are kept up to date and these contain details of the legislation relating to banks together with details of its own guidelines, pronouncements and recommendations.

1.6 Application of general company law to banks

Banks are subject to general company law.

1.7 Sources of laws and regulations

The specific laws and decrees governing the credit institutions are, as any other laws and decrees, made by parliament or, in the case of decrees, by the government. In addition, the Banking Commission is authorised to issue regulations *inter alia* in connection with solvency and liquidity ratios[2] and to determine the form and content of annual and interim accounts.[3]

1.8 Ability of foreign banks to operate through branches and subsidiaries

Foreign banks are allowed to operate through branches and subsidiaries. However, a foreign bank with one or several branches in Belgium is required to maintain its accounting records in such a way that all the operations carried out in Belgium are recorded separately from the foreign operations.[4]

1.9 Level of supervisory control for branches and subsidiaries of foreign banks

The level of supervisory control is the same for branches and subsidiaries of foreign banks. The capital adequacy requirements are, however, different for branches of foreign banks.

1.10 Methods of incorporation

Banks must be incorporated in the form of commercial companies;[5] these are:

Stock company with limited liability (Société Anonyme; Naamloze Vennootschap)

Private limited liability company (Société de Personnes a Responsabilité Limitée; Personenvennootschap met Beperkte Aansprakelijkheid)

Partnership limited by shares (Société en Commandite par actions; Vennootschap bij wijze van Geldschieting op Aandelen)

Co-operative company (Société Cooperative; Co-operatieve Vennootschap)

Limited partnership with legal personality (Société en Commandite Simple; Vennootschap bij wijze van Eenvoudige Geldschieting)

General partnership with legal personality (Société en Nom Collectif; Vennootschap onder Gemeenschappelijke Naam)

Branches are also accepted as trading entities for foreign banks.

1.11 Areas within the country subject to special laws

None.

2 ACCOUNTING

2.1 Laws and regulations governing accounts

The laws and regulations governing accounts are as follows:
- The Law of 17 July 1975 deals with the bookkeeping and annual accounts of enterprises. This law prescribes the requirement of a bookkeeping system and is applicable to all enterprises. The part of the law dealing with annual accounts is not applicable to banks.
- The Royal Decree No. 185 of 9 July 1935 art. 12 imposes the requirement for banks to prepare and present interim and annual accounts and authorises the Banking Commission to determine the principles governing these accounts (which, as far as annual accounts are concerned, have to be sanctioned by Royal Decree).
- The Royal Decree of 24 November 1937 determines the form and content of interim and annual accounts and other periodical returns to be prepared by banks.
- The regulations and pronouncements of the Banking Commission issued in execution of the Royal Decree of 24 November 1937 and specifying the contents of the accounts.

2.2 Application of general company law

The annual accounts of banks are subject to general company law in so far as their approval by the shareholders and publication is concerned. Specific laws and regulations (see above) deal with the other matters such as form and content.

2.3 Roles of legislature and supervisory authority

The laws and decrees are made by Parliament or government, and the Banking Commission issues

---

[2] Royal Decree No. 185 of 9 July 1935; art. 11
[3] Royal Decree No. 185 of 9 July 1935; art. 12
[4] Royal Decree No. 185 of 9 July 1935; art. 6
[5] Royal Decree No. 185 of 9 July 1935; art. 3

pronouncements and regulations in order to execute the legal provisions.

2.4 Extent to which requirements as to returns and accounts are prescribed by laws and regulations

The requirements for the submission of returns and accounts and the form of the accounts are laid down by law. The regulations of the Banking Commission specify the contents of the accounts.

2.5 Obligations to furnish accounts

Interim and annual accounts must be furnished in the prescribed form to the National Bank of Belgium and to the Banking Commission.[6]

The interim accounts consist of a monthly balance sheet (including contingency accounts) and a quarterly profit and loss account.

Annual accounts have to be made public in accordance with general company law if the bank is established as a stock company with limited liability, private limited liability company, partnership limited by shares, or a co-operative company.[7] This requires that the annual accounts be lodged with the National Bank which files all accounts and makes them available to any interested party. General company law does not provide for the publication of annual accounts of companies incorporated as a limited partnership with legal personality or a general partnership with legal personality. However, banking law requires that the accounts of banks incorporated in one of these forms should also be registered in the same way.[8]

All branches of foreign companies have to register the accounts of the foreign legal entity of which they are a part and this is reinforced in the case of foreign banks by banking law.[8]

2.5.1 Accounting periods and times of furnishing

General company law requires that annual accounts be lodged with the National Bank within one month of their approval by the shareholders.

The accounting period is always one year except for initial accounting periods (which can be shorter) or in the case of a modification of the statutory accounting date.

2.5.2 Form of accounts to be furnished

The form of the annual and interim accounts is laid down by law and the format for the annual accounts is shown in the Appendix. The interim accounts are very similar to these annual accounts, the only difference being that they are more detailed:

(i)   The interim balance sheet includes a geographical breakdown of all balance sheet captions (Belgium and abroad) and a breakdown into amounts denominated in local and foreign currencies.
(ii) Certain captions, such as deposit and current accounts, are broken down by original due date in the interim accounts and summarised in the annual accounts.

2.5.3 Mandatory accounting dates

There are no mandatory accounting dates although most banks close as of 31 December.

2.6 Requirements as to accounts (a) prior to incorporation (b) prior to commencement of trading and (c) in order to continue trading

There is no specific requirement to furnish accounts prior to incorporation or commencement of trading although in order to be listed as a bank by the Banking Commission a questionnaire has to be completed and certain information has to be furnished.[9] In addition, the requirement to furnish accounts on an ongoing basis is laid down by law and consequently is required if the bank continues trading.

2.7 Audit requirements

The shareholders of banks established under one of the following forms have to appoint a Statutory Company Auditor (Commissaire-Reviseur; Commissaris-Revisor):
   Stock company with limited liability;
   Private limited liability company;
   Partnership limited by shares;
   Co-operative company.

Where a bank is incorporated as a limited partnership with legal personality or as a general partnership with legal personality the partners appoint a Company Auditor[10] in accordance with banking law.

The Statutory Company Auditor must be a member of the Institute of Company Auditors (Institut des Reviseurs d'Entreprises; Instituut der Bedrijfsrevisoren) who has passed the institute's special bank auditing examination.

The Statutory Company Auditor reports to the shareholders and the conclusions of his report are registered along with the annual accounts of the bank.

In addition, the Banking Commission appoints one or more Special Bank Auditors (Reviseurs Agréés; Erkende Revisoren) for each bank. These Special Bank Auditors are members of the Institute of Company Auditors who are individually recognised and authorised to act as Special Bank Auditors. They report to the Banking Commission, who pays them, and cannot undertake any other work in respect of the bank to whom they have been appointed. Their duties are generally as follows:[11]

− To verify the fairness and completeness of the bookkeeping, the interim and the annual accounts.

− To verify the observation by the bank of the legal and regulatory requirements.

− To verify the operation of the administrative and accounting organisation and internal controls.

− To monitor the bank's situation with respect to capital adequacy, liquidity and profitability.

Although the duties and responsibilities of the Statutory Company Auditor and of the Special Bank

---

[6] Royal Decree No. 185 of 9 July 1935; art. 12
[7] Co-ordinated Company Law articles 80, 107, 137 and 158
[8] Royal Decree No. 185 of 9 July 1935; art. 12
[9] Memorandum of the Banking Commission dated October 1977
[10] Royal Decree No. 185 of 9 July 1935; art. 20
[11] Royal Decree No. 185 of 9 July 1935; art. 19

Auditor are very similar there is a difference in emphasis and reporting context:

The Statutory Company Auditor reports to the shareholders and expresses an opinion on the annual accounts.

The Special Bank Auditor reports to the Banking Commission and is mainly concerned with the periodic returns submitted to the Banking Commission and the central bank and with the bank's compliance with regulatory and legal requirements.

In the performance of their audits both auditors obviously have to work closely together.

2.8 Acceptability to fiscal authorities of accounts submitted to supervisory authority

The registered accounts of banks are, as for any other company, the same as those used for fiscal purposes. However, the fiscal authorities may not accept certain charges to the profit and loss account and consequently the taxable basis can be different from the accounting profit before tax. The fiscal authorities perform their own verifications and do not rely on the work or reports of the auditors.

2.9 Submission of accounts to any authority other than by requirement of law

No accounts are required to be submitted to any authority other than by requirement of law. Banks whose names are listed on a stock exchange also have to file the annual accounts with the Stock Exchange Commission and inform that Commission of any changes in their statutes.

2.10 Application of laws and regulations to foreign banks operating through branches and subsidiaries

The regulations in connection with the accounts of banks are also applicable to subsidiaries of foreign banks.

Branches of foreign companies normally need only register in Belgium the accounts of the foreign company to which the branch belongs. However, in the case of branches of foreign banks, the accounts of the branch, together with the conclusions of the auditor on the branch accounts and the accounts of the foreign entity, must be registered. This effectively means that there is no difference between the requirements for Belgian banks or subsidiaries and branches of foreign banks. If foreign banks have more than one establishment in Belgium, they must submit one set of accounts covering the activities of all the establishments in Belgium.

The requirements to submit interim accounts with the National Bank and the Banking Commission are also valid for Belgian banks and subsidiaries and branches of foreign banks.

2.11 Availability of accounts for public inspection

All annual company accounts lodged with the National Bank (see Section 2.5) are available to the public on request.

The format of the accounts which are open for public inspection is shown in the Appendix.

3 FORMAT, STYLE AND CONTENTS OF ACCOUNTS

3.1 Extent to which format is laid down by statute, supervisory authority, generally accepted accounting practice or otherwise

The format of the interim and annual accounts is set out in the Royal Decree of 24 November 1937, executing art. 12 of the Royal Decree No. 185 of 9 July 1935. The format for interim and annual accounts to be presented to the National Bank and the Banking Commission (Form A) is basically the same but more detailed than the format of the annual accounts which are available to the public (Form B).

3.2 Description of format

The format for the annual accounts (Form B) is shown in the Appendix.

3.3 Extent to which contents are prescribed by statute, supervisory authority, generally accepted accounting practice or otherwise

The contents of the accounts (interim and annual) are laid down by the Banking Commission.

3.4 Disclosure of specific items required other than those required by general law

The Banking Commission plays an active role in monitoring the disclosures made by banks to the public and will use its influence to persuade banks to make supplementary disclosures to those required by law in their annual accounts, if this is considered necessary for the fair presentation of the information.

3.5 Exemptions from disclosure allowed in respect of banking items

All disclosures in the annual accounts of banks are set out in the Royal Decree of 24 November 1937 and effectively are included either in the balance sheet, profit and loss account or contingency accounts. The contingency accounts in fact provide supplementary information following a clearly defined format. They are quite different from the disclosures required by general law for other companies and *inter alia* the disclosure of accounting principles and other note information is not required.

3.6 Hidden reserves

Banking law does not mention hidden reserves. However, the regulations of the Banking Commission specify *inter alia* that provisions for risks, in so far as they arise in accordance with accounting rules approved by the Banking Commission and to the extent that they are free of any allocation to known risks which would require a special provision, can be considered to be part of the bank's equity for the purpose of verifying the compliance with the capital adequacy requirements.[12] In this case, however, the Banking Commission requires that the 'reserve' be disclosed.

In the case of reserves for risks which would be shown on the 'liabilities and equity' side of the balance sheet, the build-up would be charged to the profit and loss caption 'reserve fund' and use thereof would be disclosed in the caption 'transfers from reserve fund'.

On the other hand it is not uncommon for banks to set up loan-loss reserves and deduct these from the debtors' caption in the balance sheet without disclosure thereof in the accounts presented to the public. These are consequently hidden reserves. The amounts used to build up these reserves will then be included, but not separately disclosed, under the profit and loss caption 'depreciation'. This includes depreciation of tangible and intangible fixed assets as well as provisions against all or part of certain loans. The use of such a reserve would not be disclosed and such a reserve could not be considered to be part of the bank's equity for the purpose of verifying the capital adequacy requirements.

3.7 Requirements as to consolidated accounts

Banks incorporated as stock companies with limited liability, private limited liability companies, partnerships limited by shares or co-operative companies are strictly forbidden to hold shares or any form of participations in other companies except in other banks or savings associations or other credit institutions.[13] Exemptions, mostly of a temporary nature, may be granted by the Banking Commission. This legal constraint reduces considerably the requirement for banks to produce consolidated accounts.

Nevertheless, the Banking Commission has recommended[14] that banks with total assets exceeding Bfr50,000 million should prepare, in addition to their own accounts, consolidated annual accounts.

4 ACCOUNTING POLICIES

4.1 Responsibility for laying down accounting policies

Very few accounting policies have been specified for the annual accounts of banks. The few specific items which are covered are laid down by the Banking Commission and certain concepts such as accrual accounting, prudence and fairness follow generally accepted accounting practice in Belgium. Banks usually do not disclose their accounting policies in their annual accounts.

4.2 Particular accounting policies

4.2.1 Foreign exchange

There are no principles laid down in respect of foreign exchange accounting. However, most banks revalue foreign exchange positions on a periodic basis and take the resulting profits and losses to or against income. With respect to any revaluations on forward contracts a variety of methods is applied. These range from profits being ignored, taking to profit or loss the difference between the original forward rate and the new forward rate for a

contract for the remaining period, to revaluing these contracts at the spot rate and taking the result to income. Swap transactions are usually accounted for by taking the swap result to or against income over the period of the transaction.

4.2.2 Deferred tax

The principle of accounting for deferred tax is not applied in Belgium.

4.2.3 Specific and general provisions for bad and doubtful debts

Again, no principles have been laid down regarding provisions for bad and doubtful debts. In Belgium, generally accepted accounting practice in conformity with the concepts of prudence and good faith would normally require that known bad and doubtful debts be provided for although to what extent is not specified. In connection with general provisions a variety of practices can be noted and it can be assumed that most banks will have such a general provision, although all or part of it may not be disclosed (see also Section 3.6 in this respect).

4.2.4 Treatment of provisions in accounts

Specific provisions for bad and doubtful debts are normally netted off with the related loans. General provisions can be shown separately on the 'liabilities and equity' side of the balance sheet ('reserve fund') or netted off against loans, depending on whether or not they are disclosed.

4.2.5 Premiums and discounts on investments (amortise, write off, etc.)

This is the only area on which the Banking Commission has issued a specific recommendation[15] to the effect that banks are allowed to apply the accretion method. In this connection the Banking Commission also requires that the accounting principle is described in a note to the annual accounts.

4.2.6 Offsets, i.e. to what extent can assets and liabilities be set off against each other (legally or in practice)

Except for some minor specific exceptions it is not allowed to set off assets against liabilities or income against expense.

4.2.7 Goodwill

No specific provisions are foreseen. In view of the limitations placed on banks to acquire participations the problem does not often arise.

---

[12] Pronouncement of the Banking Commission of 13 June 1972
[13] Royal Decree No. 185 of 9 July 1935; art. 14
[14] Circular letter Banking Commission No. B82/2 of 1 March 1982
[15] Circular letter Banking Commission No. B81/2 of 30 January 1981

4.2.8 Consolidation

As stated earlier the Banking Commission has recommended[16] that certain banks must publish consolidated accounts. This recommendation emphasises that such consolidated accounts should reflect clearness, prudence and good faith, while leaving the actual principles applied to the discretion of the board of directors after consultation with the Statutory Company Auditors. It is, however, specified that the consolidated accounts should correspond with the rules laid down by the Institute of Company Auditors.[17]

The recommendation of the Banking Commission also calls for the following disclosures:[16]
(a) A list of companies consolidated and a list of companies accounted for in accordance with the net equity method.
(b) The criteria used to determine which companies are consolidated and for which participations the net equity method is used.
(c) The methods used for the preparation of consolidated accounts.
(d) The conclusions of the report of the Statutory Company Auditor on the consolidated annual accounts.

The standards of the Institute of Company Auditors to which reference is made above do not prescribe any specific basis for translation of accounts of foreign subsidiaries but require that the method and rates used should be disclosed.

4.2.9 Revaluations of assets

According to general company law the revaluation of assets is permitted if a proper basis can be established (e.g. report of independent valuators). No specific provision is expected.

4.2.10 Instalment finance and leasing including basis of recognition of income

No principles are imposed or predominate in the area of recognition of income of instalment finance. Systems applied range from the 'straight line' method to actuarial methods or application of the 'rule of 78'. In banks where this activity is significant it is normal to find an actuarial method. Leasing is not normally carried out by banks but rather through subsidiary or affiliated companies. The general accounting law lays down the principles to be applied in lease accounting. These require that for capital leases an actuarial method is used to recognise income.

4.2.11 Dealing assets

The recommendation of the Banking Commission in connection with fixed yield investments suggests as an acceptable policy:[18]
(a) To value fixed yield investments, which it is anticipated will be disposed of prior to the due date, at acquisition cost and only to record value reductions if repayment on the due date is, in part or in whole, uncertain or unlikely.
(b) To record value reductions on fixed yield investments which it is intended will be disposed of prior to the due

date, if the market value at the balance sheet date is lower than the acquisition cost.

Bonds held as investments may not be accounted for according to a principle which would entail that the carrying value at the due date would exceed the repayment value.

4.2.12 Pensions

No specific accounting policies are laid down in relation to pensions. In Belgium, basic pension liabilities are covered by the social security system and additional pension plans for the employees are often provided by the employer by means of a group insurance plan, whereby all liabilities (including back-service) are covered by the annual insurance premium.

4.2.13 Depreciation

Fixed assets are normally recorded at cost (including ancillary costs) less depreciation. No special rules have been laid down for banks and the depreciation rates applied are, in the majority of cases, those accepted by the fiscal authorities. These rates are intended to relate to the expected useful life of the assets except when advantage is taken of special incentives. It is, however, possible to apply different rates which will necessarily give rise to a difference between accounting income and taxable income. No rules presently exist requiring deferred taxation to be accounted for.

4.2.14 Other

As can be seen from the above list very few specific accounting policies have actually been laid down. However, the Banking Commission plays an active role in monitoring the accounting principles of banks on an individual basis and has established a certain doctrine to avoid improper or imprudent principles being applied.

5 WINDOW DRESSING

Since the contents of each balance sheet heading are defined, at least in general terms, by the Banking Commission the possibilities for window dressing in annual accounts are limited to certain activities on the overnight money market or deposits from certain related parties. It is a well known fact that the inter-bank interest rates for overnight borrowing tend to be very high on 31 December of each year. Incorrect classification as to liquidity of deposits taken or placed is prohibited by the Banking Commission regulations.

---

[16] Circular letter Banking Commission No. B82/2 of 1 March 1982
[17] Standards laid down by the Institute on 30 June 1976
[18] Circular letter Banking Commission No. B81/1 of 30 January 1981

6 AMOUNTS REQUIRED TO BE MAINTAINED BY LAW OR OTHERWISE

6.1 Share capital[19]

The minimum required capital of any bank incorporated as a Belgian company is Bfr50 million. A branch of a foreign bank is required to demonstrate to the Banking Commission that it has available 'own funds' of at least Bfr50 million.[20]

6.2 Reserves

Under general company law all stock companies with limited liability, private limited liability companies or partnerships limited by shares are required to appropriate annually at least 5% of net profits, normally after deduction of losses carried forward, to a non-distributable legal reserve until the amount of that reserve equals 10% of the share capital.

7 KEY RATIOS

Two key ratios are used by the Banking Commission to monitor the progress of banks in Belgium, namely the capital adequacy and liquidity ratios.

7.1 Capital adequacy

A Belgian bank's 'equity'[21] should not be lower than[22] the largest of the following two reference amounts:
(a) The total of:
(i) certain assets and other items to be fully covered by 'equity';[23]
(ii) the sum of various percentages of assets weighted by classification increased by (in most cases) Bfr15 million.
(b) The total amount of certain intangible depreciable fixed assets; known or probable value reductions for which no provision has been made; loans to, deposits with and contingent amounts receivable from companies within the bank's group; all investment type participations in companies and associations and long-term advances to these companies and associations.

The amount mentioned in (a) (ii) above is calculated by using the average over a given period and can be summarised as follows:

5% of: loans, notes receivable and advances; investments other than in state bonds or certain other bonds; participation in other than public credit institutions; guarantees issued for account of third parties; certain letters of credit.

Plus 2.5% of: the assets listed above if the total exposure to one customer or customer group exceeds 20% of the bank's equity.

Plus 1% of: call money granted outside the official call money market, deposits with and advances to other bankers, the bank's parent company and affiliated companies; other short-term accounts receivable; notes receivable held by the bank or rediscounted if signed by another bank, savings association or public credit institution; investment bonds in another bank or savings association; certain letters of credit.

Plus 0.2% of: the total of Belgian francs and foreign currency receivable on forward exchange contracts.

If the bank's equity should become lower than either of the amounts in (a) or (b) above then the Banking Commission shall determine the period within which the equity should be increased in order to re-establish the capital adequacy.

The Banking Commission can ask that the capital adequacy requirement be applied on a consolidated basis.[24]

In the case of branches of foreign banks all assets and liabilities expressed in a foreign currency, and in so far as they relate to assets in or amounts receivable from and liabilities to foreign countries, can be excluded from the ratio mentioned above.

7.2 Liquidity

The monthly returns submitted by banks to the Banking Commission and to the National Bank include the computation of two liquidity ratios:
(a) Special liquidity ratio (only assets and liabilities denominated in Belgian francs are taken into account).

Numerator:

Cash on hand, with the National Bank and Post Office account.
Call money placed.
Due from banks – deposits on demand in Belgium.
Due from parent and 'group' banks – deposits on demand in Belgium.
Certain rediscountable trade notes if a sufficient rediscounting facility is still available with the National Bank.
Certain short-term government bonds and state certificates of deposit available for use as security to obtain funds from the National Bank.

Denominator:

Call money borrowed (not secured).
Due to banks – deposits on demand.
Due to parent and 'group' banks – deposits on demand.
Other short-term liabilities.
Deposits and current accounts on demand.

---

[19] Royal Decree No. 185 of 9 July 1935; articles 9 and 10
[20] The 'own funds' of a branch are defined by the circular letter of the Banking Commission No. B72/4 of 17 August 1972
[21] 'Equity' in this connection is defined as follows: capital, reserves and profits brought forward (as decided by the shareholders and therefore excluding the current year's profit) less losses brought forward and the current year's loss; provisions for risks shown on the 'liabilities and equity' side of the balance sheet in so far as they are not meant to cover specific known risks requiring provision; certain other provisions recorded elsewhere but meeting the same criteria; certain subordinated loans received and drawing lines available (to be approved by the Banking Commission)
[22] Decree of the Banking Commission of 13 June 1972
[23] These assets and other items are: certain intangible depreciable fixed assets; known or probable value reductions for which no provision was set up yet; participations in other banks or companies with a related activity if the participation represents at least 10% of the capital of this bank or company, or if the voting rights attached to the participation represents at least 10% of the total voting rights; participations in other companies in the bank's group; loans to, deposits with and contingent amounts receivable from companies within the bank's group
[24] Circular letter Banking Commission No. B82/1 of 25 February 1982

(b) General liquidity ratio (calculated separately for assets and liabilities denominated in Belgian francs and in foreign currencies and for total assets and liabilities).

Numerator:
Cash on hand, with the National Bank and the Post Office account.
Call money placed.
Due from banks on demand and term deposits.
Due from parent and 'group' banks on demand and term deposits.
Other short-term amounts receivable.
Trade notes.
Certain loans which can be used as security to obtain funds from the National Bank.
Certain government and other bonds.

Denominator:
Preferential creditors.
Call money borrowed (not secured).
Due to banks.
Due to parent and 'group' banks.
Other short-term liabilities.
Creditors for notes in collection.
Deposits and creditors on demand and on terms of up to two years.
Savings accounts.

Note: Specific assets funded by specific liabilities should be excluded from numerator and denominator.

The Banking Commission realises that these liquidity ratios are merely indicators and therefore has not laid down percentages which banks should maintain. It is, however, generally considered adequate if the special liquidity ratio amounts to at least 20%, and the general liquidity ratio to 60%.

If the Banking Commission feels that liquidity is insufficient it will encourage a bank to take corrective action.

7.3 Solvency requirements

The Banking Commission monitors the exposure of banks in the areas of credit, term amounts due from other banks and forward exchange deals. Banks are therefore required to submit the following information on a monthly basis:
– Loans and credit lines granted in excess of 20% of the bank's 'equity'.
– Term amounts due from other banks in excess of 20% of the bank's 'equity'.
– Forward exchange deals in excess of 20% of the bank's 'equity'.
'Equity', in this context, can include certain items which are not normally included therein, for example subordinated advances.

Loans and credit lines will include loans or lines granted but not yet taken out and all loans to one customer or one customer group should be taken together.

The loans, placements and forward exchange deals are classified by the portion of equity they represent as follows: from 20% to 25%; from 25% to 33.3%; from 33.3% to 50%; more than 50%.

In the case of banks incorporated as Belgian companies the Banking Commission considers that loans and credit lines to one customer group should not exceed 50% of 'equity'.

7.4 Foreign currency position

The Banking Commission also monitors the bank's position in foreign currencies by due date. Banks therefore have to submit a quarterly return for each major foreign currency showing the amounts for assets, liabilities and forward contracts by remaining period to due date as follows:

on demand	to less than 3 months
more than 3 months	to less than or equal to 6 months
more than 6 months	to less than or equal to 1 year
more than 1 year	to less than or equal to 2 years
more than 2 years	to less than or equal to 5 years
more than 5 years	to less than or equal to 7 years
more than 7 years	not determined

Should the Banking Commission be of the opinion that the if 'gaps' are too large it will request the bank to take remedial action.

8 ACCOUNTING RETURNS OTHER THAN ACCOUNTS

8.1 By whom required

Requirements relating to accounting and statutory returns to be submitted to the Banking Commission and to the National Bank are laid down by the Banking Commission. The number of returns required varies from time to time but as a general rule returns as detailed below must be submitted.

In addition, a number of statistical returns are made to the Institut Belgo-Luxembourgeois du Change so that the latter can monitor that the exchange control regulations are working correctly (see Section 11.2).

8.2 Nature of requirements

The following is a list of the most important returns to be submitted by banks:

Period	*Purpose*
Weekly or fortnightly	
List of credits granted in excess of Bfrl million and increases/decreases thereof.	To allow the National Bank to prepare the overall borrowing position by company or individual.
Monthly	
Information in connection with the application of the regulation of 13 June 1972 with respect to the capital adequacy requirement.[25]	To verify compliance with the regulation and to obtain the basis for determining the capital requirements for future periods.
Details of government and similar bonds by remaining period to due date.	To determine the amount to be included in the numerator of the liquidity ratio.

[25] Part of this information can also be submitted quarterly

Period	Purpose
Possibilities of state certificates of deposit and short-term government bonds being available for use as security to obtain funds from the National Bank.	To determine the amount to be included in the numerator of the liquidity ratio.
Possibilities of loans being available for use as security to obtain funds from the National Bank.	To determine the amount to be included in the numerator of the liquidity ratio.
Special liquidity computation.	To evaluate liquidity.
General liquidity computation.	To evaluate liquidity.
Lists of loans and credit lines granted in excess of 20% of the bank's 'equity'.	To monitor credit exposure of bank and the concentration of risks.
Lists of term amounts due from other banks in excess of 20% of the bank's 'equity'.	
Lists of forward exchange deals with banks and non-banks in excess of 20% of the bank's 'equity'.	
Movements on savings accounts.	To monitor compliance with the regulation governing withdrawals on savings accounts.
Statistical information on fixed term accounts.	To evaluate concentration and quantify large accounts with higher than normal interest rates.
Information on accounts with parent and group banks and other banks.	Supplementary information.
Information on activity on the call money market.	To verify compliance with the regulations in this connection.
Quarterly	
Position by remaining period to due date in each major foreign currency.	To evaluate the risk of unmatched positions in time.
Loans granted to companies in the steel industry.	In view of the economic difficulties of this industry and the measures taken to support it.
Information on assets, liabilities and contingent accounts with related banks.	To disclose to the Banking Commission accounts with these related parties.
Information on advertising expenses.	To verify compliance with legal provisions in connection with advertising undertaken by banks.
Statistical information on loans and other forms of credit.	To allow the National Bank to prepare overall statistics.
Half-yearly	
Full details of the investment portfolio.	Legal requirements.
Statistical information on savings accounts and fixed term accounts.	To evaluate the concentration and to prepare overall statistical data.

9 TAXATION

9.1 General method of taxation

In principle there is no difference in the method of taxation applicable to banks with that applicable to commercial or industrial corporations.

There are two types of company taxpayers in Belgium:

Residents: all companies, associations, organisations or establishments with legal personality which have their registered offices or main establishments or places of management in Belgium, including subsidiaries of foreign companies established in Belgium as independent legal entities.

Non-residents: companies, associations, institutions or organisations, whether with legal status or not, which do not have their registered offices, main establishments or places of management in Belgium. This category includes Belgian permanent establishments.

For the computation of both a resident and non-resident company's net taxable income, the same method can be used. It should be noted, however, that in respect of resident companies, corporate income tax is assessed on the worldwide income, whatever the source.

The taxable income is the income which has been earned during the taxable period and which is calculated by deducting certain authorised items from the business profits.

In the absence of a tax treaty, Belgium does not unilaterally relieve foreign source income by means of a foreign tax credit available under its national law. However, unilateral regulations and treaties for the avoidance of double taxation have their effect on the amount of tax actually paid. Without prejudice to treaty regulations, the unilateral measures are the following:

– The Belgian tax attributable to the foreign income from real estate and business profits will be reduced by a rate of 75%. (This reduction is not applicable to the special tax rates on certain capital gains, the purchase of own shares, and distribution of open and hidden reserves on liquidation.)

– Dividends received from abroad are exempted, if the receiving corporation has a permanent participation. This exemption only applies to 95% or to 90% of the net dividend increased by a 5% deemed movable prepayment. This deemed movable prepayment is creditable and refundable. If there is no permanent participation, no exemption is granted. Nevertheless, a lump-sum tax credit which equals 15% of the net dividend is available as a credit but is not refundable. This rule is also applicable to interest and royalties from a foreign source.

Tax rates in effect as from tax year 1983 are as follows:

Resident companies
- 45% normal tax rate
- 22.5% on capital gains
- 67.5% on secret commissions (these are amounts paid out by a company without identification of the beneficiary)

Non-resident companies
- 50% basic tax rate
- 45% application of tax treaties (group I)
- 47.75% application of tax treaties with France, Luxembourg and The Netherlands
- 50% application of tax treaties with Great Britain and Ireland
- 50% application of tax treaties with Canada and Tunisia

9.2 Accounts as basis for taxation

The basis for computing the net taxable income is the annual accounts of the company. The Royal Decree which executes the Income Tax Code provides rules to compute minimum profits for foreign companies with activities in Belgium but which do not keep accounting records for these activities. This is, however, not applicable to banks since branches of foreign banks are required to prepare accounts for their activities in Belgium.

9.3 Adjustments permitted or required

The accounting profit shown by the annual accounts is often adjusted for the purpose of determining taxable income because some items are disallowed for tax purposes. These items can be permanent differences (such as the taxes themselves) or timing differences, mainly in the case of disallowed provisions (e.g. for loan loss) or excess depreciation. Deferred tax is, however, not accounted for.

As a general rule expenses or charges can only be allowed by the tax authorities if they have been recorded as such in the annual accounts.

9.4 Effect of tax considerations on presentation of accounts

As all charges deducted from income for the determination of taxable profit have to be recorded in the accounts, taxation considerations sometimes play a role in determining the presentations of these accounts. This is particularly the case where certain incentives are concerned (for instance in certain past periods it was possible to depreciate certain qualifying fixed assets at rates which could be determined by the company or bank, even allowing 100% in the year of acquisition; in order to be acceptable to the tax authorities, however, this depreciation had to be recorded in the annual accounts).

10 INTERPRETATION OF ACCOUNTS

10.1 Adequacy of information as to contents and disclosure

The major criticism that can be made of the published annual accounts of banks is the complete absence of explanatory notes. There are no requirements to disclose accounting principles and since most principles to be followed are not laid down by law or regulation, explanatory notes become essential. Certain banks have taken the initiative to provide additional information in their annual brochure, but this is more the exception than the rule. The Banking Commission does try to encourage banks, on an individual basis, to disclose this information.

The presentation of the prescribed balance sheet, profit and loss account and contingency accounts is somewhat old-fashioned in certain respects and does not always reflect the aspects of modern banking.

A big step forward was made in relation to the annual accounts of companies with the publication of the Royal Decree of 8 October 1976, which effectively introduced into Belgian accounting law the Fourth EEC Directive on company accounts at its proposal stage. However, since banks were exempt from this decree the annual accounts of banks remained unchanged. The Banking Commission nevertheless accepted that the published annual accounts of banks needed reappraisal and several years ago started investigating the various alternatives and prepared proposed modified formats for interim accounts and related returns. However, since the Commission of the EEC had started working on a proposed directive for the annual accounts of banks, it was decided that it would be better to wait for the completion of this directive before making significant changes.

10.2 Audit and reliability of information

As previously explained most banks have in fact two auditors, namely a Statutory Company Auditor, appointed by the shareholders, and a Special Bank Auditor, appointed by the Banking Commission. Both auditors are members of the Institute of Company Auditors. Auditing standards laid down by this institute are comparable to those of the institutes of the countries which are held to apply high standards of auditing. However, it must be mentioned that Belgium is not yet as 'audit-minded' as, for example, the English speaking countries.

10.3 Comparability between different banks on the basis of published accounts or publicly available returns

The format and the contents of most items in the published annual accounts of banks are clearly defined. This should permit some degree of comparability between banks engaged in similar activities. However, considering the fact that in most cases accounting principles are not disclosed, comparisons could be misleading.

11 OTHER RELEVANT INFORMATION

11.1 Foreign exchange

Foreign exchange operations in Belgium and Luxembourg are subject to a rather complicated set of regulations, the correct application of which is monitored by the Institut Belgo-Luxembourgeois du Change; Belgisch-Luxemburgs Instituut voor de Wissel (Belgian-Luxembourg Institute for Foreign Exchange).

Effectively there are two foreign exchange markets (and consequently two types of Belgian francs as far as relations with other countries are concerned):
– The financial franc market, used for all capital movements. This market is also referred to as 'free' market because there is no intervention by the central bank to support or influence the rate of the Belgian franc and transactions do not have to be supported by documentation.
– The commercial franc market, used for all commercial activities, i.e. mainly import and export of goods and services.

The difference between the rates of both types of Belgian francs can be quite substantial (sometimes over 10%) and consequently the controls exercised by the supervisory authority are very tight in order to prevent banks or other parties from taking undue advantage of the situation.

Since banks deal and trade in both markets, the accounting system has to identify the market for each foreign currency asset, liability or contingent amount. Banks also have to ensure that the transactions that they carry out on behalf of their clients are routed through the appropriate market and that these are duly supported where required (in the case of transactions on the commercial market).

11.2 Banking and the fiscal authorities

Banks do not have to disclose details of their relationship with clients to the fiscal authorities, except in cases where a legal proceeding is instituted against a person. Also, the supervisory authorities (Banking Commission and central bank) are not informed of transactions with individual clients (except in unusual, defined circumstances).

Banks are, however, prohibited to have available for their clients any 'special mechanisms' which would facilitate tax evasion. Specific instructions are given to banks in this respect and compliance with these instructions is monitored by the Banking Commission through the appointed bank auditor.

APPENDIX

Form B: Format of annual accounts of banks

I ASSETS

	31 Dec 19x2		31 Dec 19x3	
Cash, National Bank, Post Office account		xxx		xxx
Call money		xxx		xxx
Due from banks		xxx		xxx
Due from parent and 'group' banks		xxx		xxx
Other short-term amounts receivable		xxx		xxx
Bills receivable				
Government bills	xxx		xxx	
Commercial bills	xxx	xxx	xxx	xxx
Customers' liabilities for acceptances		xxx		xxx
Sundry debtors (loans)		xxx		xxx
Securities				
Belgian government bonds	xxx		xxx	
Other securities	xxx		xxx	
Shares	xxx	xxx	xxx	xxx
Securities held for legal reserve		xxx		xxx
Participations				
Subsidiaries	xxx		xxx	
Other participations	xxx	xxx	xxx	xxx
Setting-up costs		xxx		xxx
Buildings		xxx		xxx
Participations in subsidiary property companies		xxx		xxx
Advances to subsidiary property companies		xxx		xxx
Furniture and equipment		xxx		xxx
Other assets		xxx		xxx
Profit and loss account				
Loss brought forward	xxx		xxx	
Loss for the year	xxx	xxx	xxx	xxx
Total assets	xxx	xxx	xxx	xxx

II LIABILITIES AND EQUITY

	31 Dec 19x2		31 Dec 19x3	
Liabilities				
Preferential and secured creditors				
Preferential creditors	xxx		xxx	
Secured creditors	xxx	xxx	xxx	xxx
Call money				
Secured by collateral	xxx		xxx	
Unsecured	xxx	xxx	xxx	xxx
Due to banks		xxx		xxx
Due to parent and 'group' banks		xxx		xxx
Acceptances		xxx		xxx
Other short-term liabilities		xxx		xxx
Creditors for notes in collection		xxx		xxx
Deposits and current accounts				
On demand and at 30 days maximum	xxx		xxx	
At more than 30 days	xxx	xxx	xxx	xxx
Bonds and savings bonds		xxx		xxx
Uncalled amounts on bonds and participations		xxx		xxx
Other liabilities		xxx		xxx
		xxx		xxx
Capital and reserves				
Capital	xxx		xxx	
Non-distributable reserves	xxx		xxx	
Legal reserve	xxx		xxx	
Distributable reserves	xxx		xxx	
Reserve fund	xxx	xxx	xxx	xxx
Profit and loss account				
Profit brought forward	xxx		xxx	
Profit for the year	xxx	xxx	xxx	xxx
Total liabilities and shareholders' funds		xxx		xxx

III CONTINGENCY ACCOUNTS	31 Dec 19x2		31 Dec 19x3	
Assets deposited as collateral				
On behalf of the bank	xxx		xxx	
On behalf of third parties	xxx	xxx	xxx	xxx
Securities deposited as collateral		xxx		xxx
Guarantees issued by third parties on behalf of the bank		xxx		xxx
Guarantees and collateral received		xxx		xxx
Guarantees issued on behalf of third parties		xxx		xxx
Bills rediscounted		xxx		xxx
Forward foreign exchange transactions				
Purchases		xxx		xxx
Sales		xxx		xxx
Forward stock exchange transactions		xxx		xxx
Securities held on behalf of third parties		xxx		xxx
Commitment to participate in the 'extraordinary intervention reserve of the I.R.G.-H.W.I.'		xxx		xxx
Miscellaneous		xxx		xxx

IV PROFIT AND LOSS ACCOUNT
for the year ended 31 Dec 19x3

	19x2		19x3	
Credit				
Interest and commissions earned		xxx		xxx
Income from securities and participations		xxx		xxx
Transfers from 'reserve fund'		xxx		xxx
Other income		xxx		xxx
Loss balance				
Loss brought forward	xxx		xxx	
Loss for the year	xxx	xxx	xxx	xxx
Profit brought forward		xxx		xxx
Total credit		xxx		xxx
Debit				
Interest and commissions paid		xxx		xxx
General expenses				
Operating expenses	xxx		xxx	
Legal and other allowances for employees	xxx		xxx	
Taxes on income and other taxes	xxx		xxx	
Advertising expenses	xxx	xxx	xxx	xxx
Reserve fund — increases		xxx		xxx
Depreciation and amortisation		xxx		xxx
Other expenses		xxx		xxx
Available profit				
Profit brought forward	xxx		xxx	
Profit for the year	xxx	xxx	xxx	xxx
Loss brought forward		xxx		xxx
Total debit		xxx		xxx

CHAPTER 5

FRANCE

CHRISTOPHER JOHNSON

1 GENERAL INFORMATION

The modern French banking profession has its origins in the post-revolutionary period of the early part of the nineteenth century. The Banque de France was created in 1806, followed by the progressive appearance and development throughout the nineteenth century and the beginning of the twentieth century of the institutions which today form the core of the banking sector in France.

Since World War II, the French economy has developed rapidly and vigorously from traditionally high reliance on an essentially agricultural base to a point where France is now recognised as one of the major industrial nations. A rapid expansion of banking activity has accompanied this change; for instance, as recently as 1966 only 30% of the population operated bank checking accounts whereas today the figure is 93%. However, in spite of this expansion, the organisation of the banking sector did not undergo any fundamental structural reform until 1984, the previous significant legislation being the law of 2 December 1945.

In 1979 the government of Raymond Barre commissioned an investigation into the need for reform of the banking sector to enable it to respond to the changing requirements of the economy. The resultant 'Mayoux' report was the foundation stone for the Banking Reform Act of 24 January 1984, which came into effect in July 1984.

The Act constitutes an important contribution to the government's efforts to reform and modernise finance provided to the economy by the banking system. The first step, seen by many as an essentially political gesture, was the nationalisation of 39 banks in February 1982, which brought over 90% of commercial banking activity under state control. The Banque Nationale de Paris Crédit Lyonnais and Société Générale, which together represent 50% of the retail banking sector, had already been nationalised in 1945.

The Act itself, however, is seen as more of an economic than a political expedient, which is consistent with its origins under the previous government.

In addition to the nationalisations and the Banking Reform Act other recent government initiatives include:
− The creation of a framework for banking pools to provide finance to industry.
− An encouragement towards the decentralisation of the banking sector coupled with an effort to deal more flexibly with the problems of companies in financial difficulties.
− The creation of a major investment fund, in which banks and insurance companies are required to participate, for the provision of long-term finance to industry.
− The modernisation of the systems of processing commercial bills of exchange and inter-bank clearing mechanisms.
− The restructuring of certain banking groups.
− The reform of the caisses d'épargne (savings banks).

The caisses d'épargne are controlled by the Caisse des Dépôts et Consignations (central deposit agency) which acts as both an investment depository and a government investment agency. The reform of the caisses d'épargne is designed to improve the circulation of the funds obtained by the caisses with particular emphasis on directing funds towards financing industry. The caisses d'épargne account for 28% of sight deposits in France.

Finally, the existing method of restricting bank lending (encadrement du crédit, see Section 6.2) may be modified to some extent. A criticism of this method of credit regulation, involving lending ceilings for each bank by reference to its past level of lending, is that it is rigid and fails to encourage competition between the banks. The alternatives are seen as either to allow the banking system to act as its own self-regulator with a consequential likelihood of volatile interest rates, or, more probably, for the Banque de France to act outside the financial markets in financing short-funded institutions.

The underlying objective that can be detected in many of these reforms is the creation of a banking system which is able to finance business on a more stable basis than has been the case in the past. The banking sector, impelled by the government's initiative, is now facing the prospect of providing global company finance on a long-term basis which will be considered as part of a company's permanent funds. Since the measures may also result in greater commitments to companies in financial difficulty, considerable strain may be put on the banks' own stability.

French banks' capital bases have been traditionally lower than those of their foreign competitors and the need to strengthen capital bases will be an objective of the government over the next two years. At the present time heavy reliance is placed on bond issues and it is envisaged that non-voting shares may be offered to the public.

The paragraphs which follow describe the reformed structure of the French banking sector resulting from the 1984 Act. In order to provide a clear understanding of the evolution of the structure, prior legislation is referred to where this continues to have a marked influence. The 1984 Act is far-reaching in the reforms decided upon, although it does not specify in detail all the methods and procedures which will be used to carry out the changes. These will most probably become the responsibility of the committee of the Conseil National du Crédit or the Comité de la Réglementation Bancaire. It is also possible that the law will be supplemented by subsequent texts to incorporate further changes.

1.1 Organisations covered by banking regulations

Under the 1984 Act banking institutions are covered by the term credit institution (établissement de crédit). This new definition replaces the former categories of banks and 'établissements financiers' under which only banks were permitted to receive deposits from the public. Under the new definition an établissement de crédit is an institution which carries out, as a regular part of its operations, any of the following:
  – Receiving deposits from the public.
  – Credit operations.
  – Providing clientele with methods of payments.
  – Managing methods of payment.
Credit operations are defined as those whereby, for consideration, sums are made available or promised to be made available to a person, in his interest, including acceptances and guarantees.

Complementary banking operations envisaged by the Act are:
  – Foreign exchange operations.
  – Operations involving precious metals and coins.
  – Investment operations including portfolio management.
  – Investment advisory services.
  – Financial advisory services to companies.
  – Leasing operations.

1.2 Summary of major types of bank

Etablissements de crédit are classified by the Act under the following categories:
  – Banks.
  – Mutual or co-operative banks.
  – Savings banks.
  – Municipal credit institutions.
  – Financial companies.
  – Specialised financial institutions.
Only the first four types of institution are generally entitled to receive deposits from the public repayable at less than two years. Specific authorisation is required for the last two categories to receive such deposits.

Mutual or co-operative banks, savings banks and municipal credit institutions are subject to specific legal and regulatory texts in addition to general banking laws. Financial companies, an expression introduced by the 1984 Act, can only undertake banking operations with specific authorisation.

The specialised financial institutions are subject to the 1984 Act with the exception of the Caisse des Dépôts et Consignations and the Post Office. The Banque de France is also exempted from the requirements of the Act.

1.3 Supervisory authorities

Under the 1984 Act the supervisory roles are to be exercised by the Conseil National du Crédit (CNC), the Comité de la Réglementation Bancaire (CRB), the Comité des Etablissements de Crédit (CEC) and the Commission Bancaire. All établissements de crédit are also required to be members of an appropriate professional association, and each association itself comes under the overall supervision of the Association Française des Etablissements de Crédit (AFEC). The commercial banks are members of the Association Française des Banques (AFB). Historically this association has played an important role in promulgating and supervising the implementation of regulatory requirements of commercial banks and this will probably continue to be the case.

1.4 Status of supervisory authorities

(a) Conseil National du Crédit

The CNC is presided over by the Minister of Finance with the Governor of the Banque de France as vice-president. The members of the CNC are: four representatives of the state, of which one is the Director of the Treasury, two members of the National Assembly and two members of the Senate, one member of the Economic and Social Council, three elected regional representatives, ten representatives from diverse sectors of the economy, thirteen representatives from établissements de crédit including one from the AFEC, and six persons of high standing in the financial and economic field.

The CNC acts as a consultative body, providing guidance and opinions on monetary policy and the functioning of the banking system.

(b) Comité de la Réglementation Bancaire

The CRB is presided over by the Minister of Finance with the Governor of the Banque de France as vice-president. The members of the CRB are: four members co-opted by ministerial decree, one representative of AFEC, one trades union representative and two distinguished personalities with a financial or economic background.

The CRB's reponsibilities cover the definition of banking regulations. The Act stipulates these as:
  – The minimum capital of établissements de crédit and the circumstances under which investments in them may be made or increased.
  – The conditions relating to agency networks.
  – The conditions applying to substantial investments made by établissements de crédit.
  – The operating conditions with which établissements de crédit must comply, with particular reference to customer relations and competition.

– The organisation of common services.

– The standards which must be respected in order to guarantee liquidity, solvency and overall financial soundness.

– The chart of accounts applicable to établissements de crédit, consolidation requirements and the rules for publication of accounting information.

– The rules and instruments governing the application of credit policy.

The CRB does not, however, have jurisdiction over the creation and activities of mutual and co-operative banks, specialised financial institutions or banks which receive public aid.

The CRB is empowered to stipulate different rules according to the legal nature of établissements de crédit, their agency network and their activities. Exceptions and temporary dispositions may be made.

(c) Comité des Etablissements de Crédit

The CEC's responsibility covers the granting of licences to operate and individual dispensations. Its members are the Governor of the Banque de France as president, the Director of the Treasury, four members co-opted by ministerial decree, an AFEC representative, a trades union representative and two competent personalities.

(d) Commission Bancaire

The Commission Bancaire carries out the control function over the banking profession. Formerly the Commission de Contrôle des Banques (CCB), the Commission Bancaire has retained its prior status with increased powers under the 1984 Act.

The membership of the Commission Bancaire comprises: the Governor of the Banque de France as president, the Director of the Treasury and four members co-opted by ministerial decree and consisting of one member of the Council of State, one counsellor of the Cour de Cassation and two banking and financial experts.

The Commission Bancaire carries out inspections of individual banks at its discretion. The inspections are undertaken on the Commission's behalf by representatives from the Banque de France. The inspectors are entitled to have access to all relevant documentation and information, including access to subsidiary companies and, where relevant, to overseas operations. The report of the inspectors is communicated to the bank's board and its statutory auditors.

Where, following an inspection, the Commission Bancaire considers that a bank has failed to comply with the professional regulations, a formal warning may be addressed to the bank. Where a bank's financial situation justifies it, the Commission can require the bank to take the necessary measures to restore or reinforce its financial position within a specified period of time. In extreme cases the Commission can appoint a receiver at the bank's request or at its own initiative.

The disciplinary sanctions available to the Commission Bancaire are as follows, according to the severity of the infractions committed:

– Warning.

– Blame.

– Disallowance of specific operations or limitations on the bank's activity.

– Temporary withdrawal of powers of management to act.

– Permanent dismissal of some or all members of management.

– Withdrawal of banking licence.

Financial sanctions which can be imposed at the discretion of the Commission Bancaire are limited to the relevant institution's minimum required capital. It can also appoint a liquidator to a bank whose licence has been withdrawn or to an enterprise which illegally carries out banking operations.

Persons carrying out controls on behalf of the Commission Bancaire are committed to professional secrecy. The 1984 Act, nevertheless, allows the results of controls to be communicated to supervisory authorities in other countries on the condition of a reciprocal arrangement and providing the same rules of professional secrecy apply in the other country.

1.5 Laws and regulations governing banks

All major changes in the structure and regulation of the banking profession are enacted by parliament. The list set out in Appendix I covers the main laws and their amendments.

1.6 Application of general company law to banks

Etablissements de crédit which exist in the form of companies are subject to general company law as embodied in the Law of 24 July 1966, its related Decree of Application of 23 March 1967 and the Law of 30 December 1981.

'Companies' comprise the following types of entity:

– Société anonyme à capital fixe (limited liability company with a fixed share capital).

– Société à responsabilité limitée (limited liability company with a fixed capital though not represented by share certificates).

– Société en commandite simple (limited partnership).

– Société en commandite par actions (limited partnership with personal liability of directors for partnership debts).

– Société en nom collectif (general partnership).

Practically all établissements de crédit operating as companies in France are incorporated as sociétés anonymes. Banks may not be incorporated as sociétés à responsabilité limitée.

1.7 Sources of laws and regulations

Company law is enacted by parliament. Banking law is also enacted by parliament. Instructions issued by the supervisory authorities are not enacted by parliament but have the force of statutory instrument.

1.8 Ability of foreign banks to operate through branches and subsidiaries

Since the implementation of the EEC Directive of 28 June 1973, dealing with the abolition of restrictions on freedom of establishment and freedom to provide services in respect of banks, there is no discriminatory distinction between French and foreign banks embodied in banking laws and regulations. Foreign banks may operate through subsidiary companies or branches after complying with the registration formalities and obtaining authorisation from the CEC after formal application to the CEC through the Association Française des Banques.

Authorisation will be obtained if the CEC can identify the economic justification for the opening of a branch or subsidiary based on the type of banking to be undertaken and the services to be rendered. To this effect the CEC may require the management to provide a report setting out the general and local needs justifying the bank's creation.

Authorisation is not required for opening second or subsequent branches in France although the CEC must be notified of changes in the branch structure.

Management of banks operating in France (whether French or foreign) can only be carried out by French or other EEC nationals, unless specific permission is obtained from the Ministry of Finance. In this context, management includes those persons involved in the administration of the bank's affairs on a regular basis, including those persons empowered to sign on its behalf. Non-EEC nationals are normally required to obtain a commercial identity card (carte de commerçant) before participating in the management of a bank. The CNC may also assess the professional qualifications of the management before accepting the application.

Approval of the CEC is required for a member of a bank's management to hold a managerial post in an enterprise in which the bank has a participating interest and there are similar restrictions on duality of employment. In practice, however, exceptions are allowed.

Minimum capital requirements are also imposed. These are explained in detail in Section 6.1.

Ministry of Finance approval may also be required for the operation of a French branch or subsidiary by a foreign entity. This falls outside the scope of banking regulations and is identical to the rules applicable to all foreign companies wishing to operate in France.

The procedure for obtaining approval consists of submitting a file comprising the following principal information:

– Details of the nationality of the investing institution or shareholders.

– The identities of the principal shareholders of the investing institution.

– The nature of the operations to be undertaken in France.

– The legal form and title of the French entity and its capital.

– The source of the capital (cash, business assets, etc.).

– The method of financing the capital (borrowings in France, abroad, own available funds, etc.).

– Details of the objectives of the French operation (including the creation of employment, the size of its activities, its area of operation, expected profitability).

The Ministry of Finance would consult the CEC before issuing its approval and can require further information

to be provided before the approval is finally granted.

An important distinction exists between investing entities or shareholders of EEC origin and other nationalities. Initial investments by EEC investors do not require *prior* Ministry of Finance approval. The above information must nevertheless be supplied prior to the investment. Non-EEC investors must obtain approval prior to making the investment. This approval is normally obtained within two months.

Specific requirements of branches of foreign banks comprise the publication in French of the balance sheet of the parent group and the identification of the endowment capital allocated to the branch. The amount of the endowment capital must be at least equal to the minimum required within the relevant category of banks incorporated as companies (see Section 6.1). A complete set of accounting records must also be maintained at the branch's premises.

Foreign banks do not have to register the opening of representative offices. Such offices, however, are prohibited from carrying out any banking activity.

Generally there is no requirement for parent entities to guarantee the debts of their subsidiaries. In exceptional cases the Commission Bancaire can call for such guarantees or alternatively the creation of blocked deposits by the foreign parent.

1.9 Level of supervisory control for branches and subsidiaries of foreign banks

The level of supervisory control for foreign owned banks is identical to that applicable to French domestic institutions.

1.10 Methods of incorporation

Apart from the obligation to obtain authorisation for banking operations (see Section 1.8), a company must be incorporated and both company and branches must be recorded at the commercial registry. As indicated in Section 1.6 above, most banking companies are incorporated as sociétés anonymes.

1.11 Areas within the country subject to special laws

There are no areas within metropolitan France subject to special dispensations or restrictions. The laws also apply to overseas departments and territories.

2 ACCOUNTING

2.1 Laws and regulations governing accounts

Etablissements de crédit are required to keep their accounting records in accordance with a detailed specialised chart of accounts (plan comptable bancaire, see Appendix II). The plan comptable bancaire was substantially revised in 1978 following consultations between the CCB and the Conseil National de la Comptabilité, the principal accounting authority and consultative body in France. Accounting disciplines are imposed upon banks by the various authorities described below.

2.2 Application of general company law

Those banks organised as a company with limited liability have to comply with French company law which is embodied in the Law of 24 July 1966 and its related Decree of Application of 23 March 1967. These texts, however, do not address accounting matters other than in a general way. Accounting practice has developed principally through the recommendations of the Conseil National de la Comptabilité, which is an independent authority on accounting matters, guidance from the professional accounting bodies and the requirements of tax law. Historically, tax law has played a dominant role in defining the accounting practices adopted by companies. The recent French harmonisation with the EEC Fourth Directive, which has been implemented by an accounting law dated 30 April 1983, has revised the standard chart of accounts (plan comptable général) used by French businesses, but banks are not affected by this change and are still required to comply with the plan comptable bancaire as mentioned in Section 2.1.

2.3 Roles of legislature and supervisory authority

The CCB was empowered to issue instructions to the banking profession under the Law of 13 June 1941 and subsequent texts. The instructions issued by the CCB cover mainly specific matters such as the requirements for submission of periodic returns. However, certain general principles are also dealt with, including the requirement to maintain separate records of transactions with non-residents and foreign currency transactions, and the principle of not compensating balances in the accounts.

Under the 1984 Act the CRB has the responsibility for defining regulatory and accounting requirements, although the monitoring of the implementation of these requirements is expected to be delegated to the Commission Bancaire as was previously the case with the CCB.

General accounting matters which may affect banks are covered by the Association Française des Banques. Thus, where pronouncements are made by the Conseil National de la Comptabilité or other competent authorities (including the tax authorities), the AFB issues interpretative instructions to the profession in order to ensure the correct practical application of the requirements.

2.4 Extent to which requirements as to returns and accounts are prescribed by laws and regulations

The banking laws give the supervisory authorities power to issue regulations concerning the form and content of returns and accounts required to be submitted to them.

2.5 Obligations to furnish accounts

2.5.1 Accounting periods and times of furnishing

2.5.2 Form of accounts to be furnished

2.5.3 Mandatory accounting dates

Under general company law, banks are required to submit their annual accounts to their shareholders for approval in a general meeting.

Banks are also required to submit their accounts to the Commission Bancaire who will publish the annual balance sheets, prepared on the standard Form No. 3041, of all banks.

Annual accounts must be made up to 31 December and submitted to the Commission Bancaire within four months, i.e. by 30 April.

Annual accounts presented to the shareholders also have to be filed at the commercial registry.

Where a branch of a foreign bank is operating in France the branch accounts must be filed with the Commission Bancaire by 30 April and, in addition, a certified copy in French of the annual financial statements of the parent entity must be filed by 30 June.

2.6 Requirements as to accounts (a) prior to incorporation (b) prior to commencement of trading and (c) in order to continue trading

A bank which commences operations in France prior to completion of the formalities of incorporation will, by definition, be carrying out a branch activity and will thus be subject to the authorisation and registration procedure described in Section 1.8 before being allowed to undertake any transactions in France. Once authorisation has been obtained, the accounting requirements set out above become immediately applicable regardless of whether or not the branch is subsequently transformed into a company.

A bank incorporated as a company which does not in fact undertake any business for a period of time is not absolved from complying with the reporting requirements already described.

2.7 Auditing requirements

All the returns described in Appendix IV must be certified (certifié conforme) by a member of the management. The annual balance sheet, Return No. 3041, must also be certified in the same way by one or more statutory auditors (commissaires aux comptes).

In the case of a branch only one commissaire aux comptes is required to certify. In the case of a bank incorporated as a company with a share capital (société anonyme or société en commandite par actions) which is in excess of Ffr5 million the signatures of two commissaires aux comptes are required.

Exactly what 'certifié conforme' implies has been the subject of discussion. An interpretation given by the Compagnie Nationale des Commissaires aux Comptes, the professional association of the commissaires aux comptes, indicates that it should be attributed the same meaning as the standard wording prescribed by law for certifying company financial statements, following an examination without scope restriction, and that therefore by implication the expression 'certifié conforme' is the unqualified result of an examination of the financial statements. Etablissements de crédit in the form of companies are in any event subject to company law which, since implementation of the EEC Fourth Directive, requires an 'image fidèle' (true and fair) opinion on their financial statements presented to shareholders.

In addition to the above auditing requirements and the continuous review procedure by the Commission Bancaire, the Commission also carries out periodic examinations of banks' operations at their premises. These tend to take place once every four or five years or more frequently if circumstances require. The examinations are undertaken by executives of the Banque de France and result in the issuance of a written report giving comments and opinions. Where infringements of the Commission's instructions have taken place, disciplinary measures may be taken. These measures are described in Section 1.4.

2.8 Acceptability to fiscal authorities of accounts submitted to supervisory authority

Tax declarations for ordinary trading concerns subject to company taxation are in the form of a pre-printed balance sheet, trading account and profit and loss accounts, which follow the presentation of the plan comptable général. In addition, a pre-printed Schedule (No. 2057), determining taxable income from reported accounting income, must be completed together with certain supplementary analysis schedules. The 2057 Schedule serves to define the taxation liability to be settled. Banks, which are subject to company taxation whether in branch or company form, complete the same documents as ordinary trading concerns.

Since these financial statements follow the plan comptable général, the presentation of the accounts of banks in such a form is not particularly meaningful and needs a reconciliation to indicate the headings under which the accounts of the plan comptable bancaire are included on the tax declaration.

2.9 Submission of accounts to any authority other than by requirement of law

Banks which are quoted on the stock exchange, of which there are very few since 1982, must also comply with the filing requirements of the Commission des Opérations de Bourse (COB) including the submission of annual accounts.

2.10 Application of laws and regulations to foreign banks operating through branches and subsidiaries

Foreign banks operating through branches and subsidiaries have to comply with the same laws and regulations as domestic banks concerning the preparation of their accounts. However, as mentioned in Section 2.7, the balance sheet of a branch need only be certified by one statutory auditor.

2.11 Availability of accounts for public inspection

Accounts submitted to shareholders must also be filed at the commercial registry and are consequently available for public inspection.

The annual balance sheets of all banks are filed with the Commission Bancaire and are included in an annual volume which the Commission issues to all banks. In addition, the balance sheets are published in one of the legal journals.

3 FORMAT, STYLE AND CONTENTS OF ACCOUNTS

3.1 Extent to which format is laid down by statute, supervisory authority, generally accepted accounting practice or otherwise

As mentioned in Section 2.1, banks are currently required to maintain their accounting records and to prepare their annual financial statements in conformity with a standard chart of accounts applicable to banks which was developed by the CCB in 1978. This chart of accounts defines both the account codes for recording each type of transaction as well as providing the format for the presentation of the annual financial statements. The implementation of the EEC Fourth Directive does not cover banks although part of the implementation of the Directive included the revision of the French Commercial Code which is applicable to banks and which requires the preparation of notes to the financial statements and the presentation of a true and fair view (image fidèle). The banking authorities, however, have not yet issued instructions to those banks which have not previously been required to prepare notes to their financial statement submissions to the CCB. It remains to be seen whether instructions will be issued soon, or whether the authorities will choose to wait until French legislation is passed which conforms with the EEC Banking Directive, which is itself presently in draft form.

The main headings of the plan comptable bancaire are set out in Appendix II.

3.2 Description of format

The annual balance sheet (Return No. 3041) and income statement (Return No. 3081) are two of a series of forms which a bank has to submit to the Commission Bancaire; details of the other returns are included in Section 8. It should be noted that the required annual financial statements consist of only a balance sheet and profit and loss account without any footnotes. Examples of a balance sheet and profit and loss account are shown in Appendix III. It should be noted, however, that the profit and loss account submitted to shareholders can differ from the form lodged with the Commission in that certain headings may be combined to show a single figure for the net of:
(i)   Provision for doubtful debts, less previous provision written back.
(ii) Depreciation of investments.
(iii) Other provisions relating to ordinary items less related write-backs.
(iv) Bad debts written off less related provisions.
(v)   Recoveries of bad debts previously written off.

3.3 Extent to which contents are prescribed by statute, supervisory authority, generally accepted accounting practice or otherwise

3.4 Disclosure of specific items required other than those required by general law

3.5 Exemptions from disclosure allowed in respect of banking items

It will be apparent from the above that the content of the accounts are precisely defined by law and regulations. In the case of a bank with a listing on the stock exchange the COB requires additional disclosure with particular reference to consolidated accounts, adequate footnotes and a report by management on the operating results. In this connection it should be noted that those nationalised banks which used to be listed on the stock exchange are still continuing to present their annual reports in the same detail as before.

3.6 Hidden reserves

To the extent that specific provisions deducted from the related assets are not excessive, 'hidden reserves' cannot exist. Obviously excessive general provisions can be in the nature of reserves, but as explained in Section 4.2.3, these are included in liabilities and not 'hidden' as undisclosed deductions from assets.

Land and buildings are frequently undervalued in relation to current market values. The building portion of the property cost is almost always depreciated, as allowed by tax law, which at a time of rising property prices has the effect of creating hidden reserves. This applies not only to banking, however, and in order to redress this tendency towards undervaluation, and consequential apparent under-capitalisation, legal revaluations have been permitted from time to time (see Section 4.2.8).

3.7 Requirements as to consolidated accounts

Quoted institutions are expected by the COB to prepare consolidated financial statements where appropriate and to disclose the basis of consolidation used. Pending implementation of the EEC Seventh Directive there is no legal requirement to prepare consolidated financial statements; institutions which are not quoted do not generally do so. The financial statements of overseas subsidiaries are generally translated at year end rates.

4 ACCOUNTING POLICIES

4.1 Responsibility for laying down accounting policies

General accounting requirements and disclosures have developed in France from the relatively strict and narrowly defined obligations imposed by tax law. Thus, historically, enterprises have tended to apply the accounting policies necessary to comply with the requirements for the preparation of the annual tax declaration.

The interpretations and recommendations published by the Conseil National de la Comptabilité, in addition to prescribing accounting treatment for specific types of transactions and situations, are designed to enable enterprises to reconcile the requirements of tax law with those of accepted accounting practice, as evidenced by the Conseil's own pronouncements or those from the international bodies such as IASC and the EEC Directives. In turn, the AFB applies these requirements to the particular circumstances of the banking profession.

In view of the only very recent implementation of the EEC Fourth Directive there has been significant contrast between the presentation and disclosures of the annual financial statements of quoted and private companies, owing to the requirements imposed by the COB on the former, and the relatively low level of disclosure obligation on the latter. In particular, the COB expects consolidated financial statements to be prepared by quoted companies, whereas this is frequently not done by private groups.

This is also true of quoted and private banks including branch operations. Many major banks have, nevertheless, so far limited their accounting policy disclosures to the principles of consolidation applied and do not give details of the underlying significant accounting policies relating to the group's activity.

The nationalisation in 1982 of virtually all the major French banks means that the stock exchange requirements with regard to reporting to shareholders are no longer applicable to them. Institutions will continue to comply with the requirements of the COB, however, since these are also applicable to companies which make bond issues to the public.

4.2 Particular accounting policies

The following paragraphs set out the accounting policies most frequently applied by banks and financial institutions.

4.2.1 Foreign exchange transactions

All balance sheet accounts denominated in foreign currencies are translated at mid-market year end rates of exchange. The differences arising from this translation are taken to income.

Open forward exchange contracts are translated at year end rates and the profits and losses are taken to profit and loss account on a *pro rata temporis* basis over the period of the contract.

4.2.2 Deferred tax

In most cases deferred tax is not recognised, other than in consolidated accounts of institutions which consider themselves as having an international reporting obligation. To date, the Conseil National de la Comptabilité has not issued any specific recommendations on the matter. Since in practice fixed asset depreciation reported in financial statements usually corresponds to fiscal allowances (which are deemed to be based on useful lives) no timing differences arise from that source. Principal timing differences consist of non-deductible general bad debt and other provisions.

4.2.3 Specific and general provisions for bad and doubtful debts

Management will review the loan portfolio at the end of each accounting period and raise specific provisions against any item considered to be bad or where there is doubt as to the ability of the debtor to meet the repayment terms. It is common practice for management to raise a general provision against unidentified losses which may be present. There are no laid down criteria for the size of this general provision and the amount to be provided must be a matter of management's judgement.

As explained in Section 2.10 above, the accounts submitted to the Commission Bancaire will show the separate components of the charge to profit and loss account. The accounts submitted to shareholders and filed at the commercial registry will have these netted together and shown under the heading of 'Excess of provisions over amount written back'.

4.2.4 Treatment of provisions in accounts

The specific provisions will be deducted from the appropriate assets in the balance sheet but the general provisions will be shown on the liabilities side grouped with other provisions, accruals, etc. under the heading of 'Accruals, provisions and sundry items'.

4.2.5 Premiums and discounts on investments (amortise, write off, etc.)

See Section 4.2.11.

4.2.6 Offsets, i.e. to what extent can assets and liabilities be set off against each other (legally or in practice)

This is not allowed under the requirements of the plan compatable bancaire except in very limited circumstances.

4.2.7 Goodwill

Goodwill arising on consolidation is usually set off against shareholders' funds. Treatment of other goodwill items varies according to the nature of the goodwill, although accounting practice here is frequently subordinated to tax law which does not generally allow goodwill to be written off as a deduction against taxable profits.

4.2.8 Consolidation

As stated in Section 3.7 there is as yet no legal requirement to prepare consolidated financial statements but those banks who do so prepare them on conventional lines, that is to say a single set of consolidated financial statements is produced consolidating all assets and liabilities of the group, and showing a minority interest where ownership of a subsidiary is less than 100%. Accounting policies of the parent and subsidiaries will be the same or else consolidation adjustments will be made to reflect uniform treatment.

4.2.9 Revaluations of assets

The Finance Law of 1976 permitted revaluation of fixed assets in accordance with closely defined criteria for the years to 31 December 1979. Such revaluations were not taxable and many enterprises took advantage of this dispensation. Since 31 December 1979 any fixed asset revaluations are taxable and consequently they would only be undertaken in exceptional circumstances.

4.2.10 Instalment finance and leasing including basis of recognition of income

The practice most commonly adopted is for leasing finance to be accounted for in a similar way to rental contracts. Where banks provide finance for the acquisition of assets by customers on a leasing basis, whereby the assets remain under the ownership of the bank over the period of the lease, such assets are recorded in the accounts of the bank and the leasing revenues are taken directly to income. The distinction between financial leases and operating leases, as currently recognised in an Anglo-Saxon reporting environment, has not been widely taken up in France. Tax law allows for leasing costs to be treated as deductible expenses by the lessee and therefore correspondingly requires the leasing income to be treated as taxable revenue by the lessor. This tax treatment presently determines the prevailing accounting treatment.

4.2.11 Dealing assets

The plan comptable draws a distinction between investments made for resale (titres de placement) and trade and other investments made for retention (titres de participation). Titres de participation are usually investments of between 10% and 50% of the capital of the company concerned, smaller investments thus being considered as titres de placement.

Titres de placement are valued at the lower of cost and market value at the year end. In the case of unquoted investments an estimate of market value is needed at the balance sheet date; for quoted investments the average of the quotations for the previous month is taken. Increases in values above cost should not be recognised.

Titres de participation are retained at their historical cost less provisions for lasting reductions in their values.

While the rules as to valuations of investments are widely respected, the published financial statements of the major institutions show that differing practices may be adopted as to their presentation.

The treatment of premiums paid and discounts obtained on purchases of investments can vary between institutions depending on their significance. The principle of lower of cost and market value, however, when applied annually, ensures that as a minimum the investments are not overstated.

4.2.12 Pensions

Most institutions subscribe to state or otherwise externally funded schemes with the result that special disclosures are rare.

4.2.13 Depreciation

Depreciation of fixed assets almost always corresponds to the fiscally acceptable rates applied to cost or revaluation. The fiscal rates are deemed to correspond to lives of assets in normal use. Accounting policy disclosures for fixed asset depreciation are rare because of the universality of the above method. It is important to note that in order to be considered as tax allowable, depreciation must be effectively booked in the accounting records.

4.2.14 Taxation

The charge for taxation is invariably that arrived at after taking into account tax credits arising on dividend income. Dividend income arising on investments in which the institution holds more than 10% does not give rise to a tax credit but is not taxable in the hands of the recipient (régime des sociétés mères). In order to benefit from this regime, the institution must be a French registered company.

Disclosure of the method of arriving at the charge for taxation is again generally only made by the major institutions.

4.2.15 Conclusions as to accounting policies

As explained earlier, disclosures in the published annual reports of banks vary significantly depending on their size, nature and ownership. Frequently, in addition to accounting policy disclosures, the financial statements of the major banks are accompanied by quite detailed footnote disclosures for significant items. The general, relatively low level of disclosure of accounting policies is partly explained by the obligations, in many instances, to comply with the requirements of the Commission Bancaire and AFB which are of universal application to banks and financial institutions and which provide minimal scope for choice of accounting policy.

While the proposed EEC Bank Accounts Directive is not likely to give rise to major revision in the presentation of the financial statements themselves or in the policies applied in their preparation, the requirement to describe fully the accounting policies adopted will require many institutions to provide more such information than is presently the case.

5   WINDOW DRESSING

The principal motivation for banks to window dress is to seek to improve their liquidity ratio (see Section 7.4) by obtaining finance for a period in excess of three months. This can be done either by discounting existing negotiable instruments held in portfolio with payment dates in excess of three months or by straight financing on the money market. However, because of the prescriptive nature of banking returns and the presentation of accounts, there is very little scope for varying the presentation of these documents within the instructions issued by the CCB. The motivation to increase footings can obviously be answered by money market operations,

although balances on money market transactions are netted off for the purpose of calculating the liquidity ratio.

6   AMOUNTS REQUIRED TO BE MAINTAINED BY LAW OR OTHERWISE

6.1   Minimum capital

The minimum required paid-up capital of banks depends upon the nature of the institution, its balance sheet totals (including off-balance sheet guarantees) and the number of branch operations, as follows:

	Balance sheet total Ffr millions			
	Up to Ffr 600 million		More than Ffr 600 million	
	Branches:		Branches:	
	1 or 2	More than 2	1 or 2	More than 2
Deposit banks and medium- and long-term credit banks				
Companies with share capital	7.5	15	15	30
Other forms	3	6	6	12
Other banks				
Companies with share capital	30	60	60	120
Other forms	15	30	30	60

The above minimum levels were fixed by the Ministry of Economy and Finance on 13 November 1978 and had to be attained by 31 December 1982. The expression 'medium- and long-term credit banks' has disappeared under the 1984 Act although no alteration has yet been made to the above headings. These banks lend as their principal activity for periods in excess of two years.

'Minimum capital' for the purpose of this definition represents paid-up capital plus reserves, less any assets without effective value not already written off (e.g. preliminary expenses), less doubtful debts net of provisions.

6.2   Government credit policy: obligatory reserves with the Banque de France and encadrement du crédit

Direct credit controls are exercised on the banking system by the Banque de France through the requirement for banks to maintain with the Bank unremunerated deposits determined by reference to:

(a) Liabilities represented by French franc sight and short-term deposits (original term less than three years). The amount to be retained on deposit with the Banque de France is currently 4.25% of the sight deposits and 0.50% of other deposits.

(b) Advances to customers (subject to certain exceptions) and capital employed plus bond issues. The required reserve is currently 0.10% of the total of these two figures.

In addition to the obligatory reserves, as a limiting factor on increases of credit within the economy, banks are restricted as to the amount by which their advances can increase (commonly called 'encadrement du crédit').

The allowable increases are fixed by the CNC at six-monthly intervals by reference to the size of the institutions. Where the lending ceilings are exceeded, supplementary reserves (réserves supplémentaires) must be deposited with the Banque de France, and these are calculated on a steeply progressive basis in relation to the amount of the excess. The ceilings are applied selectively to different types of credit.

Increases in capital employed enable banks to increase their advances by a multiple of 1.5 of the increase.

The relevant ratios are calculated on Return No. 3022 submitted either monthly or quarterly (based on the criteria set out in Section 2.5.3) to the CCB.

7 KEY RATIOS

Ratio requirements imposed by the monetary authorities serve either to protect depositors or to act as a means of implementing government credit policy. The application of the existing requirements have been defined by the CCB in instructions issued to banks.

The following paragraphs set out the principal requirements and summarise the methods of calculation. The calculations are in some instances complicated and reference should be made to the relevant instructions of the CCB for detailed explanations.

7.1 Solvency ratio (rapport de couverture des risques)

These rules were instituted by the Decree of 5 July 1979, followed by Instruction No. 79-02 A issued by the CCB on 3 August 1979.

The solvency ratio (rapport de couverture des risques) is determined by calculating the ratio of capital employed (after exclusion of intangible assets, values of investments in other banks and financial institutions unless consolidated – see below) to risk items. Risk items comprise the various categories of advances made plus guarantees given, less guarantees received. In order to weight the risks relating to each individual category of items, percentages of their value are retained (varying from 100% of ordinary customer advances to 2.5% of guarantees given to financial institutions) to arrive at a total net value of risk items for the purpose of the ratio calculation.

Bond issues with a term of at least seven years may be used to improve the ratio for half their value.

The required ratio varies depending upon the actual ratio at 2 January 1979 but all institutions were required to have improved their ratio by 30 June 1982 and now have a target minimun ratio of 5%.

Banks may calculate the ratio on a consolidated basis. The calculation is prepared on Return No. 3002 based on the institution's position at 30 June each year and must be filed at the same time as Return No. 3010, periodic balance sheet (see Section 8).

7.2 Division of risk ratios (rapport de division des risques)

These ratio requirements, also instituted by the Decree of 5 July 1979 and followed by the CCB Instruction No. 79-034 of 3 August 1979, are designed to identify the extent of risk relating to any one entity or group of entities.

Banks may not carry net risks (i.e. after deduction of related provisions) as defined for the solvency ratio (i.e. advances plus guarantees given less guarantees received) in respect of any one beneficiary (a group being deemed as one beneficiary) which exceed in total 75% of the bank's capital employed (also as defined for the solvency ratio) unless the risk relating to the beneficiary is less than 5% of total outstanding risks or less than 50% of the beneficiary's own bank debt.

Additionally, beneficiaries for whom total risks carried represent more than 25% of the bank's capital employed must be identified.

The information is declared on Return No. 3003 which must be filed with the solvency ratio declaration.

7.3 Limitations on specific commitments

The following specific restrictions are applicable to banks:
– Investments in enterprises other than financial institutions by deposit banks and medium- and long-term credit banks may not exceed their own capital employed and investments cannot exceed 20% of the capital of such enterprises.
– Completion guarantees given and guarantees given for sales of buildings must not exceed 20 times the amount of the bank's capital employed and any single guarantee must not exceed 50% of the capital employed.
– Banks are required to supply summaries of sales-type lease operations applied to assets appearing in their balance sheets on an annual basis. The details are supplied solely for information purposes and currently there are no specific obligatory ratios laid down. Similar information must be supplied on a quarterly basis in respect of purchases by customers of capital goods financed by the institution under instalment finance or hire purchase arrangements.

7.4 Liquidity ratio (rapport de liquidité)

CCB Instruction No. 77-02 A of 16 December 1977 sets out the complex method of determining the liquidity ratio based on the periodic balance sheet return (No. 3010).

The basic ratio which must be respected is for liquid assets divided by immediate liabilities to be equal to or greater than 60%. Liquid assets consist of:
– Paper discountable with the Banque de France.
– Treasury bills.
– Quoted investments.
– Amounts receivable from financial institutions at less than three months.

Immediate liabilities consist essentially of all amounts payable at sight or at less than three months.

If foreign currency balances amount to more than 10% of assets or liabilities, separate ratios must be calculated for French franc and foreign currency liquidity. In this case, forward exchange commitments have to be brought into the calculation.

In order to prevent institutions from artificially improving their ratios, by increasing both the numerator and the denominator through treasury or foreign exchange transactions, debit and credit balances with financial institutions are netted, as are foreign exchange commitments given and received.

The results of the ratio calculations are reported on Return No. 3019 which accompanies the periodic balance sheet (No. 3010).

7.5 Coefficient of medium- and long-term operations (coefficient d'opérations à moyen et long terme)

This ratio, which is required by CCB Instruction No. 77-03A of 16 December 1977, is designed to keep the use of funds in medium- and long-term lending in proportion to the related sources of funds.

The ratio is calculated by dividing the total of:
- medium-term advances not discountable with the Banque de France
- long-term advances
- advances to financial institutions with an initial period of over two years,

by the total of:
- capital employed
- savings deposits and term deposits of over three months maturity
- participating loans (emprunts participatifs).

The calculation must not give a ratio greater than three, unless at least 80% of the total advances described above are financed by the sources described above plus loans from other financial institutions repayable at more than two years.

The CCB has allowed the unused portion of standby or refinance facilities with remaining maturity longer than two years to be included in the calculation.

If foreign currency balances represent more than 10% of the institution's total assets or liabilities, separate ratios must be calculated for French franc amounts and consolidated values (French franc and foreign currency amounts translated into French francs).

The ratio calculations must be submitted quarterly on Return No. 3001.

7.6 Minimum medium-term portfolio (portefeuille minimum de créances à moyen terme ou d'obligations)

In order to encourage banks to grant medium-term finance to the economy, the Banque de France has required that at least 5% of customer sight or short-term deposits should be utilised in financing medium-term advances, which are eligible for discounting with it, or alternatively in bond issues with terms of seven years maximum made by companies quoted on the stock exchange. A standard reduction of Ffr200 million of customer deposits is allowed in determining the ratio.

The exact ratio is calculated in accordance with CCB Instruction No. 77-07 of 26 December 1977 which must be submitted monthly or quarterly according to the criteria set out in Section 8.

8 ACCOUNTING RETURNS OTHER THAN ACCOUNTS

Apart from the annual balance sheet (Return No. 3041) and profit and loss account (net income statement Return No. 3081) which were described in Section 3, there are a number of other accounting returns which have to be submitted. Details of these are shown in Appendix IV and they have to be filed as follows:

Returns 3010, 3011, 3030 and 3040: monthly if any of the following are applicable (otherwise quarterly):
- Customer deposits exceed Ffr3,000 million.
- Advances to customers exceed Ffr3,000 million.
- Leasing finance operations exceed Ffr2,500 million.
- Foreign currency balances (assets or liabilities) exceed Ffr5,000 million.

If balance sheet totals do not exceed Ffr100 million, the 3040 Return need only be submitted on a half-yearly basis.

Returns 3012 and 3013: quarterly.

Periodic returns must be submitted within 20 days of the relevant accounting date for banks with less than three branches, within 25 days for banks with three to 100 branches and within 30 days for banks with more than 100 branches.

Provisional returns: The 3082 and 3083 Returns must be submitted by 31 August and 28 February for the two half-year ends at 30 June and 31 December respectively.

Annual returns: The definitive annual returns must be filed by 30 April.

The obligation to submit the various accounting returns set out above is not subject to any form of derogation or special exception. Failure to comply with the requirements will cause the Commission to question the bank's ability to prepare timely information and, in the case of consistent failure, would lead to disciplinary action or even withdrawal of the bank's licence.

9 TAXATION

9.1 General method of taxation

Banks are subject to the following principal taxes:
(a) Direct taxation: profits tax, tax on customer advances (taxe sur les encours de crédit), exceptional taxation and business tax (taxe professionnelle).
(b) Indirect taxation: value added tax (taxe sur la valeur ajoutée).

(a) Direct taxation

Profits tax

As explained in Section 2.8, banks, whether in the form of branches or companies, are subject to company profits tax (impôts sur les sociétés), the determination of which is made on the annual tax declaration to be filed before 30 April each year.

The taxable profit is determined by taking the accounting profit and adjusting it for specific fiscal requirements or allowances. The requirements and allowances are essentially the same as those applicable to business enterprises generally. A specific allowance given by the tax authorities enables banks to provide up to 5% of annual taxable profits against medium- and long-term credits. The total provision in the balance sheet must not exceed 0.5% of the related credits.

The rate of company taxation is 50%.

There are no other special tax regulations applicable to banks which are not applicable to commercial or industrial enterprises.

Tax on customer advances

This tax is levied on the amount of customer advances owing to a bank or financial institution at 31 December each year. Advances on which the tax is calculated include all categories of Franch franc advances except for export financing, advances to finance housing, machinery and equipment purchases by enterprises and advances to finance bond issues. Medium- and long-term advances are to become subject to the tax progressively until their amounts will be retained for their full values as from 1 January 1985.

For institutions which have opted to be subject to VAT the rate of the tax on customer advances is currently 0.13%. For those institutions which have not exercised the VAT option the rate is 0.195%.

Exceptional taxation

From time to time the government may introduce exceptional forms of taxation on banks as economic circumstances may require. For 1981 this took the form of a 0.3% tax on average balances held by customers on current and deposit accounts for the year. For 1982 and 1983 the exceptional tax was based on total annual operating expenses (personnel costs, outside services, travel, entertaining, depreciation and other expenses) and, subject to certain specific adjustments, amounted to 1% thereof.

Business tax (tax professionnelle)

This tax is based on a combination of annual salaries paid and the rental value of tangible fixed assets. All businesses are subject to the tax, the rate of which is fixed annually by the municipality in which the business operates.

(b) Indirect taxation
Value added tax

Banks may opt to apply the VAT regime. Some activities are exempt from VAT unless an option is specifically taken by an institution to apply the regime. These activities comprise the following major areas:
- Lending.
- Supply of guarantees.
- Treasury operations.
- Foreign exchange operations.
- Customer deposit and checking account operations.

Those activities which are automatically subject to VAT consist mainly of general service activities such as client portfolio management, financial advisory services, credit information services, safekeeping and debt recovery services.

Naturally, where the option is not taken no relief is available on input tax borne. Where the option is taken, on the other hand, exemption in respect of activities directly related to exports can be obtained.

9.2 Accounts as basis for taxation

As indicated in Section 2.8 the accounts prepared as a basis for direct taxation are a bank's annual statutory accounts, adjusted for presentation and disclosure requirements as required on the standard tax declaration form and incorporating a tax computation which reconciles accounting profit to taxable profit.

9.3 Adjustments permitted or required

The tax computation incorporates permitted or required adjustments. Permitted adjustments, that is those that can be made at the discretion of the bank, would not normally exist because of the prescriptive nature of the law. In particular, provisions are only considered as deductible by tax law if they are effectively booked in the accounts. This usually results in businesses booking the maximum tax allowable provisions.

A permitted adjustment specific to banks and établissements financiers is the allowance of a provision against medium- and long-term advances. For any one year this must not exceed 5% of accounting profit or 0.5% of such advances. This is in the nature of a general provision allowance in the absence of specific provisions. Where, therefore, specific provisions on such advances, which are themselves treated as deductible, exceed the allowance, which is frequently the case, this discretionary measure is of no tax benefit to the bank.

Required adjustments can be numerous. The most frequent adjustments are for non-deductible provisions. In order to be deductible, provisions must not only be effectively booked but represent known and quantifiable losses to the undertaking. Thus all provisions of a general nature are disallowable (notwithstanding the above exception), as are some items of accrued expenses, such as holiday pay and bonuses, which are deductible only when actually paid or payable. Other adjustments may include capital gains tax treatment for disposals of investments and fixed assets.

9.4 Effect of tax considerations on presentation of accounts

The effect of tax considerations on the preparation and presentation of annual financial statements of a bank do not differ significantly from those relevant to an ordinary business enterprise in France.

Beyond isolated or exceptional areas, which may in particular circumstances require interpretation as to the tax consequences of alternative accounting treatments, the prescriptive aspect of tax law together with the imposed standard annual reporting formats for banks provide minimal scope, legally, for influencing either the presentation of balance sheet amounts or the amounts of reported profit.

10 INTERPRETATION OF ACCOUNTS

10.1 Adequacy of information as to contents and disclosure

As already indicated, the quality of annual financial statements of banks generally available to the public depends to a large extent on the national and international reporting obligations of the entities concerned.

The overall quality of disclosure of information in the annual reports of the major French banks is considered as one of the highest in the world. Managements' reports to shareholders on activities are usually well set out, comprehensive and detailed. However, as pointed out earlier, the disclosure of accounting policies is generally less extensive than that of Anglo-Saxon banks.

This quality of disclosure is not evident throughout the banking system. Some of the lesser known quoted banks (until recent nationalisation) have continued to produce less comprehensive annual reports, which in isolated cases even failed to include consolidated accounts.

10.2 Audit and reliability of information

All banks are audited. The degree of reliability that can be placed on the information provided in financial statements by banks, as with any enterprise, depends upon the quality of the audit and ultimately upon the quality and integrity of the management.

The larger banks in France are usually statutorily audited by commissaires aux comptes of high professional standing and reputation. Although the audit appointments are frequently in the names of individuals, the individuals mostly belong to firms equipped to provide the staff and specialist expertise necessary to carry out an effective audit. However, some of the largest audit assignments include the involvement of international auditing firms, particularly where major consolidations, which are a relatively recent development in France, are undertaken, or where a bank has extensive overseas interests.

10.3 Comparability between different banks on the basis of published accounts or publicly available returns

Comparisons of performance between banks are made by the COB and the AFB; in addition, detailed studies may be undertaken by the Commission Bancaire. Comparisons are facilitated by the standardised reporting format imposed by the plan comptable.

On an international basis France claims the largest bank in the world based on balance sheet totals (Crédit Agricole) and three among the 10 largest banks in the world. Their performance in terms of profitability however, is less impressive, which can be at least partly attributed to their relatively low level of capitalisation. This observation has frequently been made in the financial press.

Comparisons between the major banks can be made on the basis of their published annual financial statements. These tend to be issued rather later than those of Anglo-Saxon banks.

Where banks choose, however, to provide only the minimum required information to the shareholders, amounting to the forms set out in Appendix IV, these obviously do not permit on their own a meaningful assessment of an institution's performance.

APPENDIX I

Principal laws and regulations governing banks

Law No. 2532 of 13 June 1941, on the regulation and organisation of the banking profession.

Law No. 45-015 of 2 December 1945, on the nationalisation of the Banque de France and the major banks, on the organisation of credit and on the creation of the Conseil National du Crédit.

Law No. 46-1071 of 17 May 1946, relating to the organisation of credit in France.

Decree No. 46-1246 of 28 May 1946, setting out the basic rules for the functioning of the nationalised deposit banks.

Decree No. 46-1247 of 28 May 1946, setting out the basic rules for the functioning of the private sector banks.

Decree No. 66-81 of 25 January 1966, changing certain points in the regulation of banks.

Law No. 66-455 of 2 July 1966, relating to undertakings carrying out leasing operations.

Decree No. 72-103 of 4 February 1972, amending Law No. 2532 of 13 June 1941.

Law No. 73-7 of 3 January 1973, on the Banque de France.

Law No. 75-601 of 10 July 1975, modifying the nationality requirements for the banking profession.

Decree of 13 November 1978, on the minimum capital of banks.

Decree No. 79-561 of 5 July 1979, introducing rules for covering and spreading risks.

Law No. 82-155 of 11 February 1982, on the nationalisation of most of the remaining unnationalised banks.

Law No. 84-46 of 24 January 1984, reforming the structure and regulation of the profession.

APPENDIX II

Summary of the plan comptable bancaire

(translation of extract from CCB instructions)

	Balance sheet accounts				Profit and loss accounts			Off balance sheet
Class 1	*Class 2*	*Class 3*	*Class 4*	*Class 5*	*Class 6*	*Class 7*	*Class 8*	*Class 9*
Treasury and inter-bank accounts	*Accounts with customers*	*Other financial accounts*	*Fixed asset accounts*	*Capital accounts*	*Expense accounts*	*Revenue accounts*	*Net result*	*Off balance sheet accounts*
11. Cash	21. Advances to customers	31. Cheques to be cleared	41. Long-term investments and investments in subsidiaries	51. Balances with shareholders	61. Expenses from banking operations	71. Revenue from banking operations	87. Net result	91. Commitments to financial institutions
12. Bank of France, Public Treasury, Post Office	22. Customer deposits	32. Suspense accounts for settlements in progress	42. Endowment capital of branches and participating loans	52. Loan capital	62. Personnel costs	72. Revenue from other operations		92. Commitments from financial institutions
13. Banks and financial institutions	23. Non-productive advances	33. Accounts with branches in France	43. Fixed assets	53. Participating loans	63. Indirect taxes	73. Unallocated		93. Commitments to customers
14. 24 hour deposits made	24. Doubtful debts	34. Sundry debtors and creditors	44. Fixed assets in progress	54. Provisions	64. General expenses	74. Unallocated		94. Foreign currency commitments
15. Term deposits made	25. Certificates of deposit issued	35. Accruals and prepayments	45. Balances on leasing operations	55. Reserves	65. Depreciation expense and provisions	75. Provisions written back		95. Unallocated
16. 24 hour deposits received		36. Investment suspense accounts	46. Balances on rental operations	56. Share capital	66. Other expenses	76. Other income		96. Guarantees given by state bodies
17. Term deposits received		37. Unallocated	47. Preliminary expenses	57. Undistributed profit brought forward	67. Employee profit-sharing expense			97. Other items
18. Treasury and related bills		38. Investment portfolio		58. Unallocated	68. Profits tax			
		39. Liabilities on uncalled capital of investments		59. Net result awaiting appropriation				

99

APPENDIX III

Geographically summarised income statement: Form 3081

DEBIT	Metropolitan France	Overseas Territories	Foreign	Total
Expenses on banking operations	xxx	xxx	xxx	xxx
Expenses on treasury and inter-bank transactions	xxx	xxx	xxx	xxx
Bank of France, Public Treasury, Post Office	xxx	xxx	xxx	xxx
Banks and other financial institutions	xxx	xxx	xxx	xxx
Current accounts	xxx	xxx	xxx	xxx
Loans and term deposits	xxx	xxx	xxx	xxx
Loans received against bills	xxx	xxx	xxx	xxx
Commissions	xxx	xxx	xxx	xxx
Expenses on transactions with customers	xxx	xxx	xxx	xxx
Customer accounts	xxx	xxx	xxx	xxx
Current accounts in credit	xxx	xxx	xxx	xxx
Term deposits	xxx	xxx	xxx	xxx
Savings accounts	xxx	xxx	xxx	xxx
Certificates of deposit	xxx	xxx	xxx	xxx
Expenses on leasing operations	xxx	xxx	xxx	xxx
Expenses on other operations	xxx	xxx	xxx	xxx
Interest on loan stock and participating loans	xxx	xxx	xxx	xxx
Losses on short-term investment disposals	xxx	xxx	xxx	xxx
Personal expenses	xxx	xxx	xxx	xxx
Remuneration of personnel	xxx	xxx	xxx	xxx
Social charges	xxx	xxx	xxx	xxx
Taxes based on employee remuneration	xxx	xxx	xxx	xxx
Indirect taxes	xxx	xxx	xxx	xxx
General expenses	xxx	xxx	xxx	xxx
Outside services and supplies	xxx	xxx	xxx	xxx
Other general expenses	xxx	xxx	xxx	xxx
Allocation of head office expenses		xxx	xxx	
Depreciation and provisions on operations	xxx	xxx	xxx	xxx
Fixed asset depreciation expense	xxx	xxx	xxx	xxx
Bad debts written off not previously provided for	xxx	xxx	xxx	xxx
Provisions on operations	xxx	xxx	xxx	xxx
Provisions on non-productive and doubtful debts (banks, etc.)	xxx	xxx	xxx	xxx
Provisions on non-productive and doubtful debts (customers)	xxx	xxx	xxx	xxx
Provision for depreciation of investments	xxx	xxx	xxx	xxx
Other operating provisions	xxx	xxx	xxx	xxx
Other expenses	xxx	xxx	xxx	xxx
Employee profit sharing costs	xxx	xxx	xxx	xxx
Profits tax	xxx	xxx	xxx	xxx
Net profit for year	xxx	xxx	xxx	xxx
Total debit	xxx	xxx	xxx	xxx

CREDIT	Metropolitan France	Overseas Territories	Foreign	Total
Revenues from banking operations	xxx	xxx	xxx	xxx
Revenues from treasury and inter-bank transactions	xxx	xxx	xxx	xxx
Bank of France, Public Treasury, Post Office	xxx	xxx	xxx	xxx
Banks and other financial institutions	xxx	xxx	xxx	xxx
Current accounts	xxx	xxx	xxx	xxx
Advances and term deposits	xxx	xxx	xxx	xxx
Non-productive and doubtful accounts	xxx	xxx	xxx	xxx
Advances against bills	xxx	xxx	xxx	xxx
Commissions	xxx	xxx	xxx	xxx
Revenues from transactions with customers	xxx	xxx	xxx	xxx
Advances to customers	xxx	xxx	xxx	xxx
Current accounts in debit	xxx	xxx	xxx	xxx
Doubtful accounts	xxx	xxx	xxx	xxx
Commissions	xxx	xxx	xxx	xxx
Revenues from leasing operations	xxx	xxx	xxx	xxx
Revenues from rental operations	xxx	xxx	xxx	xxx
Other operating revenue	xxx	xxx	xxx	xxx
Revenues from investments	xxx	xxx	xxx	xxx
Revenues from investment portfolio	xxx	xxx	xxx	xxx
Gains on disposals of short-term investments	xxx	xxx	xxx	xxx
Revenues from other operations	xxx	xxx	xxx	xxx
Property income	xxx	xxx	xxx	xxx
Other operating income	xxx	xxx	xxx	xxx
Allocation of head office expenses	xxx			
Provisions written back	xxx	xxx	xxx	xxx
Provisions on non-productive and doubtful debts written back (bank, etc.)	xxx	xxx	xxx	xxx
Provisions on non-productive and doubtful debts written back (customers)	xxx	xxx	xxx	xxx
Provisions for depreciation of investments written back	xxx	xxx	xxx	xxx
Other provisions written back	xxx	xxx	xxx	xxx
Other income	xxx	xxx	xxx	xxx
Bad debts recovered	xxx	xxx	xxx	xxx
Other provisions previously utilised recovered	xxx	xxx	xxx	xxx
Sundry	xxx	xxx	xxx	xxx
Loss for year	xxx	xxx	xxx	xxx
Total credit	xxx	xxx	xxx	xxx

APPENDIX III

Balance sheet: Form 3041

Assets		**Liabilities**	
Cash, Bank of France, Public Treasury, Post Office	xxx	Bank of France, Public Treasury, Post Office	xxx
Banks and other financial institutions:		Banks and other financial institutions:	
Current accounts	xxx	Current accounts	xxx
Advances and term deposits	xxx	Loans and term deposits	xxx
Treasury and other bills held	xxx	Bills issued and re-discounted	xxx
Advances to customers:		Customer deposits:	
Commercial advances	xxx	Business: current accounts	xxx
Other short-term advances	xxx	term accounts	xxx
Medium-term advances	xxx	Individuals: current accounts	xxx
Long-term advances	xxx	term accounts	xxx
Other customer debit balances	xxx	Sundry: current accounts	xxx
Cheques and bills in course of settlement	xxx	term accounts	xxx
Sundry debtors and prepayments	xxx	Savings accounts	xxx
		Certificates of deposit	xxx
Investment suspense account	xxx	Settlement suspense accounts	xxx
Short-term investments	xxx		
Long-term investments and investments in		Accruals, provisions and sundry	xxx
subsidiaries	xxx		
Participating loans	xxx	Investment suspense account	xxx
Fixed assets	xxx	Loan stock	xxx
Balances on leasing operations	xxx	Participating loans	xxx
Balances with shareholders	xxx	Revaluation reserves	xxx
Losses brought forward	xxx	....	
Loss for the year	xxx	....	
		Reserves	xxx
		Capital	xxx
		Undistributed profits brought forward	xxx
		Net profit for the year	xxx
Total	xxx	Total	xxx

Off balance sheet		**ANNEXE**	
Acceptances, endorsements and guarantees in favour		**Leasing operations**	
of financial institutions	xxx		
Acceptances, endorsements and guarantees received		Leasing commitments on moveable property	xxx
from financial institutions	xxx	Leasing commitments on land and buildings	xxx
Undrawn credit facilities to customers	xxx		
Acceptances, endorsements and guarantees in favour		**Revaluations**	
of customers	xxx		
Other commitments in favour of customers	xxx	Gains on investment revaluation	xxx
		Gains on fixed asset revaluations	xxx
		Part of share capital resulting from incorporation of	
		revaluation reserves	xxx
		Part of revaluation reserve exceeding surpluses	
		arising from the application of specified indices	xxx

102

APPENDIX IV

Accounting returns

Document reference No.	Title	Content	Document reference No.	Title	Content
Periodic returns			**Periodic returns**		
3030	Situation globale géographique	Balance sheet and detail of off-balance sheet commitments in same form as 3010 indicating balances arising from operations in: France French overseas departments and territories elsewhere	3010	Situation territoriale	Detailed balance sheet and analysis of off-balance sheet commitment by territory indicating: balances with residents and non-residents balances in French francs and foreign currency
3040	Situation globale publiable	Summarised version of 3010	3011	Concours à l'économie	Detailed analysis of advances to clientele by: type of balance: discountable/non-discountable with Banque de France short, medium or long-term object of advance type of client: companies personal businesses individuals other non-residents
Provisional returns					
3082	Compte de résultats territorial provisoire	These are provisional income statements relating to 3080 and 3081 respectively (see below)			
3083	Compte de résultats provisoire global géographique				
Annual returns			3021	Emplois, ressources et engagements selon la durée restant à courir	Analysis of employment and external sources of funds by: type of employment type of source period of unexpired balance left to run: less than 3 months 3 months to 6 months 6 months to 1 year 2 years to 5 years more than 5 years
3041	Bilan	As for 3040, plus summaries of leasing commitments and asset revaluations			
3030	Situation globale géographique de fin d'exercice	This document is simply the annual version of periodic 3030 described above			
3080	Compte de résultats territorial	Detailed income statement by territory[1]	3013	Renseignements divers	Analysis of employment and external sources of funds by original contractual term: less than 1 year, indicating resident/non-resident balances and Ffr/foreign exchange balances 1 year to 2 years more than 2 years
3081	Compte de résultats global géographique	Summarised version of 3080			
3095	Relève de titres en portefeuille	Details of investments and shareholdings			
3095	Fiche annuelle de renseignements	Details of changes in directors, number of branches, shareholders having more than 5% of the bank's capital			

[1] Territory: metropolitan France, French overseas departments and French overseas territories

CHAPTER 6

GERMANY

JOACHIM EPPERLEIN

1 GENERAL INFORMATION

The Federal Republic of Germany is a federation of 10 states and its capital is Bonn.

Among the powers reserved to the federal authorities is the management of the economy. The Federal Bank (Deutsche Bundesbank), which is owned by the federation, is responsible for the day-to-day management of the monetary supply. The Federal Bank's banking operations are conducted from operating centres (Landeszentralbanken) located in the federal states.

The Federal Bank Act[1] defines the nature and mode of the Bank's operations and its relationship with the Federal Government. The Bank has the sole power to issue banknotes and it acts as the government's banker. As well as raising finance for the government in the form of treasury bills it exercises control over the monetary sector by following various discount, credit supply and open market policies and can determine minimum reserve requirements for banks.

The open market policies adopted by the Federal Bank mainly take the form of purchase and sale of treasury bills to the commercial banks. In this way the Bank regulates the liquidity in the economy and deals with large inflows of money from abroad. The Federal Bank also trades in the capital market and in the buying and selling of government stocks: such activities may not, under the terms of the Federal Bank Act, serve to supply the credit requirements of the government, and so the Federal Bank is never a purchaser in the first instance of such stocks. Such trading is to be conducted only in pursuance of the Bank's official duties as defined in the Act.

The Federal Bank also acts as the bankers' bank for the settlement of funds between them but the actual clearance of cheques and other money orders is carried out by the Giro-networks established by the various classes of banks for this purpose.

The Federal Bank Act also defines the role of the Federal Bank *vis-à-vis* the Federal Government, and its function as the government's bank. The Act states that the Bank in carrying out its duties is not subject to direction by the Federal Government. The Federal Bank is obliged to support the general economic policy of the government while performing its functions; the independence of the Federal Bank is guaranteed, however, by provision in the Federal Bank Act that if the requirements of supporting governmental policy conflict with the Bank's primary role (as defined by the Act) then the Bank's legal duties shall have precedence. Furthermore, the Federal Government has no veto over decisions of the Federal Bank (S.13 B Bank G).[2] The co-operation of Federal Bank and Federal Government is ensured by the provision that members of the government may attend and contribute to meetings of the Federal Bank directorate. Conversely the Director of the Federal Bank is invited to government discussions concerning monetary policy. Thus the independence of the Federal Bank to carry out its primary duties is legally guaranteed; such support as the Federal Bank gives to the governmental monetary policy is only given coincidentally to performing the duties as laid down in the Federal Bank Act.

1.1 Organisations covered by banking regulations

All businesses and enterprises that engage in any kind of banking activity are subject to banking regulations.

Banking activities are defined as (S.1 (1) KWG):[3] deposit taking; credit issuance; discounting of cheques and bills; stock exchange transactions; investment broking; factoring; security custody; bonding and guarantee business; clearing and money transfer.

While the various classes of banks (see Section 1.2) have their own general banking laws, organisations such as the central bank have their own particular laws.

Banks must have approval in writing from the Federal Banking Supervisory Agency before they can operate and banks can no longer be owned by a sole proprietor.

1.2 Summary of major types of bank

The major types of West German financial institutions covered by the banking laws and regulations are: universal banks; savings banks (Sparkassen); private mortgage banks (Hypothekenbanken); ship mortgage banks (Schiffshypothekenbanken); building societies (Bausparkassen); investment trusts.

---

[1] Gesetz über die Deutsche Bundesbank was first published in the Federal Gazette on 26 July 1957 (BGBl.I.p.745), the latest amendment dating from 23 May 1975

[2] Gesetz über die Deutsche Bundesbank – see note 1

[3] The Banking Act known as Gesetz über das Kreditwesen (abbreviated as KWG) was first published in the Federal Gazette on 10 July 1961 (BGBl.I.p.881), the latest amendment dating from 14 December 1976

The majority of banks are universal banks, that is to say they engage in all types of banking operations. Three of the largest are Deutsche Bank, Dresdner Bank and Commerzbank. Other large universal banks are the 'Landesbanken' such as Westdeutsche Landesbank. These banks are specially authorised under state law and, besides their other banking activities, act as the central clearing institutions (Girozentralen) of the savings banks.

Savings banks are incorporated under the laws of municipalities or districts and are guaranteed by them. As well as taking in deposits they engage in most of the other activities carried out by universal banks.

Private mortgage banks are limited to making long-term loans secured by mortgage and to the granting of loans to public or municipal organisations. Funds are raised by issuing mortgage bonds or municipal bonds which in turn are secured on the mortgages obtained through their lending activities.

Mortgage banks must take the form of a public company or a public limited partnership and the minimum capital required is DM8,000,000.

Ship mortgage banks are similarly organised as private mortgage banks but they specialise in making secured loans on ships.

Building societies may only take in deposits from their members for the purpose of making loans to other members secured by mortgages for the purchase or construction of private houses, condominiums, the repair of these properties or for the repayment of a loan raised for the same purpose. Building societies may only be formed as public companies, unless they are owned or guaranteed by the states or districts. There is no minimum capital requirement apart from the minimum required for public companies, i.e. DM100,000.

Investment trusts take in money from their customers for investment in stocks and shares, land, etc. and they grant their customers participation certificates in exchange for the deposits received. The deposited funds must be kept separate from their own funds and the trust can only be formed as a public company or a limited liability company and must have a minimum capital of DM500,000.

There are a number of other specialised banks which are subject to the general banking laws. These are:

(i)   Investment credit banks who make short- to medium-term consumer loans which are repayable by equal instalments over the life of the loan. They are generally set up as limited liability companies or partnerships.

(ii)   The Industriebank AG was set up to make medium- to long-term secured loans to small enterprises which have no access to other finance.

(iii)   The Ausfuhr-Kredit GmbH was founded in 1952 by 32 banks to provide medium- and long-term export finance particularly for exports to developing countries.

(iv)   The Deutsche Verkehrs-Kredit-Bank AG is a subsidiary of the German railways (Deutsche Bundesbahn). While its main purpose is to act as the banker for the German railways, it is also empowered to provide a virtually full banking service to the general public and has branches at major railway stations, airports and border crossings.

(v)   The Liquiditäts-Konsortial-Bank GmbH was set up in 1974 after the collapse of the Herstatt Bank. Its purpose is to support German banks suffering from liquidity problems. It has a share capital of DM250,000,000 and can call up a further DM750,000,000 in case of need under certain circumstances. Its shareholders are the central bank and a large majority of the German banks.

(vi)   The Kassenvereine (security deposit banks) who provide giro-transferable collective certificates and security giro transfer of individual certificates and bonds. This service is provided for inter-bank transactions and avoids the physical transfer of the individual certificates.

Two other speciality banks are the Privatdiskont AG and the Kreditanstalt für Wiederaufbau which are mainly concerned with import and export finance.

See Appendix I for a summary of the major types of bank, the business they transact and the laws and regulations under which they operate.

1.3   Supervisory authorities

As already mentioned, the central bank plays an important part in controlling the banking sector. However, the main supervisory authority is the Federal Bank Supervisory Agency (the Bundesaufsichtsamt für das Kreditwesen). The Agency was set up under the authority of the KWG and is an official body of the federation. It is empowered to supervise and control all banking institutions within the Federal Republic of Germany and it is located in West Berlin. There is close co-operation between the Agency and the central bank who provide the Agency with copies of all the statistical information received by it from the banks.

1.4   Status of supervisory authorities

The Agency's principal powers are:

(i)   Issue and withdrawal of banking licences.

(ii)   Authority to require a bank to cease carrying out banking activities not permitted under the KWG.

(iii)   Audit of a bank's accounts and records.

(iv)   Attendance at a bank's shareholders meeting including the power to call such a meeting and to place items on the agenda for consideration at that meeting.

(v)   Monitor and require compliance with requirements on capital and liquidity ratios.

(vi)   Disapproval of a bank director's appointment and thereby preventing him from taking up the appointment.

(vii)   Lay down minimum requirements for the internal organisation of a bank including its internal audit and control procedures.

(viii) Approval of a bank's statutory auditors is required before their appointment can be confirmed.

(ix)   Wide-ranging powers to curtail or stop a bank's activities if the liquidity and capital requirements are not met, or if the bank is in difficulties; these powers include the removal of bank directors and requesting the court to appoint new directors.

State and municipal banks may be subject to additional reporting requirements and supervision under the individual state or municipal laws, i.e. Landesbanken and Sparkassen. Co-operative banks have to be members of an association of co-operative banks following para 54 of the law on co-operative companies.

Otherwise there are no legal institutions or organisations that banking institutions have to report to or by whom they are supervised. However, there is a number of private institutions of which banks normally would be members. The most important associations in this respect are:

− Bundesverband deutscher Banken, Cologne (Federal Association of German Banks)
− Deutscher Sparkassen- und Giroverband, Bonn (German Savings Bank and Giro Association)
− Bundesverband der Deutschen Volksbanken und Raiffeisenbanken, Bonn (Federal Association of German Urban and Agricultural Co-operative Banks)
− Verband öffentlicher Banken, Bonn-Bad Godesberg (Association of Public Banks)
− Bundesverband Deutscher Investmentgesellschaften, Frankfurt (Federal Association of German Investment Companies)

Membership of these associations is voluntary. Usually it is the aim of these associations to improve a bank's operations, and to follow and resolve questions of mutual interest including issues of a promotional nature.

1.5 Laws and regulations governing banks

As already mentioned, the central law governing banking in West Germany is the Kreditwesengesetz (KWG). Other important laws in the banking industry are:

− Hypothekenbankgesetz (Mortgage Bank Act)
− Schiffspfandbriefbankengesetz (Ship Mortgage Bank Act)
− Gesetz über Bausparkassen (Law on Building Societies)
− Gesetz über Kapitalanlagegesellschaften (Investment Company Act)

In addition to these laws, there is a variety of laws that regulate specific banking activities, or that respond to banking activities during specific economic situations. Important among these laws are:

− Depotgesetz (Custody Business Act)
− Börsengesetz (Stock Exchange Act)
− Auslandinvestmentgesetz (Foreign Investment Company Act)
− Stabilitätsgesetz (Law on the improvement of economic stability and growth)
− Aussenwirtschaftsgesetz (Foreign Trade Act)

Based on these laws the Supervisory Agency is entitled to publish directives that the banks have to observe. In addition, the Agency publishes principles relative to certain balance sheet and operating ratios, which will be dealt with in a later section. Interpretations of the law and practice recommendations, which have to be observed by the banks in their day-to-day business, are also issued by the Agency.

1.6 Application of general company law to banks

Banking laws and regulations − in the widest sense − only affect the operating aspect of banking, whereas general company law remains in force for all other aspects of a company's or enterprise's organisational, formal and legal operations. The Banking Act, for instance, makes reference to various paragraphs of the law on public companies (Aktiengesetz) and both expands and restricts the application of this law to banks, even if organised in other legal forms, or to waive their application to banks in the form of a public company. As with banking laws, all applicable general company laws are federal laws.

1.7 Sources of laws and regulations

See preceding sections.

1.8 Ability of foreign banks to operate through branches and subsidiaries

1.9 Level of supervisory control for branches and subsidiaries of foreign banks

The KWG follows the principle that all banking transactions executed within the boundaries of the Federal Republic of Germany are subject to supervision by the 'Bundesaufsichtsamt für das Kreditwesen' if these transactions are made through a commercially fully organised enterprise.[4] This principle is also applicable to branches of foreign banks operating in the Federal Republic. The formation of a representative office of a foreign bank has to be reported to the Supervisory Agency (Bundesaufsichtsamt für das Kreditwesen) and to the Deutsche Bundesbank (para 53a KWG). The same applies for the relocation and closing of a representative office.

The formation of a branch (and any branches opened subsequently) of a foreign bank is subject to the approval of the Supervisory Agency. The approval may be denied if the formation is not desirable from an overall economic point of view (para 52 (2) 1 KWG). The approval may not be denied on the grounds of general economic considerations if bilateral agreements to that effect exist between the Federal Republic and the country of origin.

Banks domiciled in EEC countries only require approval for the first branch they wish to open, based on a directive of the Council of the EEC dated 12 December 1977. The establishment of further branches has to be communicated to the Supervisory Agency, but no approval is required.

Obviously, the approval to operate a branch has to be obtained before any banking activities are undertaken and it would normally be assumed that the branch of a foreign bank would require a commercially fully organised enterprise which would automatically subject the branch to the requirements of the KWG.

For the purposes of control by the Supervisory Agency, both a one-branch operation and a network of

---

[4] German commercial law (Handelsgesetzbuch) distinguishes between fully organised commercial units and commercial units operating at a very low level of insignificant activities (paras 1 and 4). The latter will not qualify for the application of a variety of laws including the KWG

branches will be considered as one credit institution under the KWG (para 53 (1)), in the same way as for domestic German banks. Areas where organisational or formal differences arise from the nature of a branch operation are covered by additional regulations in para 53 KWG. As a result, branches of foreign banks are — in general — treated the same way as domestic institutions.

In contrast to operating through a branch, foreign banks may wish to operate in Western Germany through participating in an existing bank or through formation of a wholly-owned subsidiary. In both cases the foreign bank will be operating through a separate banking institution which is fully subject to the regulations of the KWG by virtue of its own legal identity.

At present no restriction is placed on foreign banks acquiring interests in existing German banks, nor on the formation of subsidiaries by foreign banks. The only limitations could arise from company law, because most German companies require from two to seven shareholders (or partners) to participate in the formation process.

Following a recent change in the law on limited liability companies (Gesellschaft mit beschränkter Haftung), it would be possible to form a 'one' shareholder company with limited liability (para 1 of the law on limited liability companies). A second founding shareholder, who would have to be bought out subsequently if a 100% subsidiary is desired, would no longer be required. Apparently, a 'one' shareholder company would be subject to the same requirements of the Supervisory Agency as any other banking institution.

1.10 Methods of incorporation

The incorporation of banking institutions follows the normal requirements which exist for the main legal forms available for other industries. These include public companies (Aktiengesellschaften), limited liability companies (Gesellschaften mit beschränkter Haftung), limited liability partnerships (Kommanditgesellschaften), partnerships (offene Handelsgesellschaften) and co-operatives (Genossenschaften). Individuals cannot obtain approval to operate a banking institution (para 2a KWG). Banking institutions formed by a state or municipal community are established under the laws of these authorities.

The legal forms of public company and limited liability company require notarised statutes before they are registered in the commercial register, whereas partnership companies would — in theory — not even require written statutes to be submitted before registration. The written approval, however, by the Supervisory Agency to operate as a banking institution has to be presented to the commercial registrar before the entity can be registered (para 43 (1) KWG). The name of the new entity and the use of the word 'bank', or any variation thereof, is subject to the approval of the Chamber of Commerce and, ultimately, of the Supervisory Agency (para 42 KWG).

Another requirement to be fulfilled before the commencement of operations by a new bank is the nomination of two active bank directors, who will be responsible for all the activities of the banking institution under the KWG. These directors have to have a minimum of three years' management experience in a similar institution (para 33 (2) KWG).

The minimum capital requirements under the banking laws for the various types of bank were listed in Appendix I. However, the Supervisory Agency has set up its own requirements for the so-called 'adequate funding' for the various types of bank, which need to be fulfilled before the Agency will issue an approval for the commencement of any banking activities. The Supervisory Agency's present practice, based on para 10 KWG, is to require a total of DM6 million as the minimum level of 'funding' for a universal bank; this is reduced to DM3 million if no deposits are to be taken. These requirements are continuously updated for changing circumstances. The current minimum requirements for each category of banking institution are set out in Appendix I.

The formation of subsidiaries by foreign banks is subject to the same procedures as the formation of domestic banking institutions.

The establishment of branches or representative offices of foreign banks is subject to the same requirements that are applicable for domestic banks, i.e. approval by the Supervisory Agency, nomination of two bank directors who must be resident in the Federal Republic, availability of adequate funding (i.e. DM6 or 3 million) from the bank represented by the branch. Specific accounting and reporting requirements are dealt with in Sections 3, 4 and 8.

For registration with the commercial register, notarised copies of the statutes, translated into German, must be submitted and employees authorised to legally represent and bind the branch (i.e. the company abroad) must be nominated. These employees can be identical with the above-mentioned bank directors.

1.11 Areas within the country subject to special laws

Special laws dealing with specific types of banking transactions have already been discussed above. There are no laws in the Federal Republic which permit offshore banking operations.

2 ACCOUNTING

2.1 Laws and regulations governing accounts

2.2 Application of general company law

2.3 Roles of legislature and supervisory authority

2.4 Extent to which requirements as to returns and accounts are prescribed by laws and regulations

In general, any of the various legal forms of companies available in the Federal Republic may be used for the purposes of banking. With the exception of the law on public companies (Aktiengesetz), the company law applicable to these forms includes only very general directives for accounting rules and for the format and contents of accounts. However, in practice, the German business community — together with the fiscal authorities — have conceived what is normally referred to as principles of orderly bookkeeping, valuation and accounts presentation. There is no codification of these principles which would be binding, except that paras 149 *et seq.* Public Company Law are often interpreted as being applicable to other types of legal entity. This, however, is not accepted entirely throughout the accounting profession, so that accounting rules in practice may differ somewhat between the various legal forms, as far as general accounting is concerned.

In the case of credit institutions, however, directives have been issued laying down the format of the annual accounts. Thus there is a directive[5] for the format of accounts of universal banks and this will apply to such a bank no matter which legal form the bank takes, i.e. not just public companies. Similar directives have been issued for the specialised banks and all these directives have been issued under the authority of the law[6] on the format of the annual accounts.

2.5 Obligations to furnish accounts

2.5.1 Accounting periods and times of furnishing

2.5.2 Form of accounts to be furnished

2.5.3 Mandatory accounting dates

2.6 Requirements as to accounts (a) prior to incorporation (b) prior to commencement of trading and (c) in order to continue trading

The accounts prepared on the above basis are, in fact, the statutory accounts of the respective banking institution. Apart from being submitted to the Supervisory Agency and central bank (para 26 (1) KWG), accounts have to be published and are available to shareholders and partners. They also form the basis for any resolutions taken by shareholders, and others. Companies not operating in the form of a public company have to observe the first part of the law on reporting and accounting by certain enterprises and concerns[7] as determined by para 25a KWG, which mandates certain publication requirements.

Accounts have to be submitted to the Supervisory Agency and central bank within three months of the close of the business year (para 26 KWG), which generally covers a period of twelve months (para 39 (2) Commercial Law).[8] Accounts subsequently approved by a general annual meeting of shareholders or partners also have to be submitted.

The submission of accounts to the Supervisory Agency and central bank has to be accompanied by the institution's management report covering the past business year (if one is prepared), by an explanatory report on the accounts, and by the audit report (see below) including the auditor's opinion (para 26 (1) KWG).

The publication of accounts, in general, will be not later than eight months after the close of the business year because this is the longest timespan allowed by Public Company Law (para 175 (1)) for the annual general meeting to take place. The publication will be immediately thereafter.

The financial year end for the annual accounts of companies is optional. Also, there are no specific requirements for banking institutions to close off on a particular day in the year. However, the normal practice is for a 31 December year end.

For businesses beginning operations during the year, there will be a business year of less than twelve months, i.e. from the day of inception to the first closing day. Business years exceeding twelve months are not allowed (para 39 (2) Commercial Law), but business years of one day would be possible. In the event that the closing date is amended, there could be more than one business year ending in a twelve-month cycle, which is also accepted by the fiscal authorities.

Newly-established credit institutions normally do not have to submit their accounts (opening balance sheet) to any authority, except that the formation of a public company is subject to an audit (para 33 Public Company Law) and, in the case of a limited liability company, the commercial registrar has to ascertain that the funds representing the share capital are at the company managers' disposal (para 8 (2) Law on Limited Liability Companies).

A bank's failure to comply with the submission requirements would lead ultimately to the loss of the approval to operate as a banking institution (para 35 (2) 5 KWG).

2.7 Audit requirements

The annual accounts, the accounting records, the management report if prepared, and the explanatory report are subject to audit by independent auditors. The audits of all private commercial and other banks have to be conducted by public auditors or audit firms (Wirtschaftsprüfer/Wirtschaftsprüfungsgesellschaften); the audits of co-operative banks have to be conducted by auditors of the audit associations of which co-operative banks have to be members (para 54 Law on Co-operatives);[9] the audits of savings banks and giro banks (Girozentralen) have to be conducted by the audit departments of their respective associations. The audits have to be completed within five months of the closing date (para 27 (1) KWG).

The scope of regular audit includes (para 29 KWG):

− An examination of the economic situation of the bank (para 29 (1) KWG).

− Compliance with reporting requirements for so-called large loans and loans exceeding DM1 million (para 13 KWG).

− Adherence to approval procedures to be followed by bank directors for the issuance of loans (para 15 KWG).

− Compliance with reporting requirements for loans granted to bank directors and other employees of the bank exceeding one year's salary and for loans granted to certain other related parties (para 16 KWG).

---

[5] Verordnung über Formblätter für die Gliederung des Jahresabschlusses von Kreditinstituten, first published 20 December 1967 (BGB1.I.p.1300) amended 27 May 1969 (BGB1.I.p.444)

[6] Gesetz über Formblätter für die Gliederung des Jahresabschlusses, first published 11 December 1935 (BGB1.I.p.1432)

[7] Gesetz über die Rechnungslegung von bestimmten Unternehmen und Konzernen (Publizitätsgesetz), first published 15 August 1969 (BGB1.I.p.1189)

[8] Handelsgesetzbuch, first published 10 May 1897 (RGB1.p.219), amended through July 1980

[9] Gesetz betreffend die Erwerbs- und Wirtschaftsgenossenschaften, first published 1 May 1889 (RGB1.p.55)

– Compliance with reporting requirements for the appointment or dismissal of bank directors, acquisition or disposal of investments in other companies exceeding 10% of their capital and changes if they exceed 5% of their capital (para 24 KWG).

– Compliance with disclosure requirements existing in respect of debtors' financial situation (para 18 KWG).

Exceptions observed by the auditors have to be described in the audit report. Any situation that might justify a qualification or disclaimer of the audit opinion, or could endanger the bank's existence, or severely impair its future performance, or constitutes a breach of law or statute, must be reported immediately to the Supervisory Agency by the auditors. At the request of the Supervisory Agency, the auditor in his report must, *inter alia*, communicate any irregularity observed in the execution of the bank's transactions and may, subsequently, be asked by the Agency to comment thereon.

The credit institutions have to report to the Supervisory Agency their nomination for auditors as soon as this has been made. The Agency can reject the nomination if it believes this is necessary to achieve the purpose of the audit, and another auditor has to be nominated (para 28 (1) KWG). This, of course, is not applicable in cases where banking institutions are members of co-operative audit associations, savings banks or giro associations.

In addition to regular year end audits, special audits of security deposit activities and stock exchange transactions are mandatory for all institutions engaging in these activities (paras 6 and 30 KWG). The audit can be conducted by the same auditors as for regular year end audits; however, the auditors in such special situations are engaged directly by the Supervisory Agency (para 30 (2) KWG). Audit reports are submitted to the Supervisory Agency, the central bank and the credit institution. In the event that serious weaknesses are detected when examining security deposit and trading activities, the audit report may not be given to the credit institution; the Supervisory Agency will decide on any further action.

Audit reports that may be prepared in connection with a voluntary audit, conducted by the auditors of a deposit protection fund association of which the bank is a member, also have to be submitted to the Supervisory Agency and the central bank (para 26 (2) KWG).

Apart from external audits by independent public accountants, all banks have to have an internal audit department in line with a directive issued by the Supervisory Agency.[10]

Irregular audits can also be conducted by the Supervisory Agency in the fulfilment of its duties as described above.

2.8 Acceptability to fiscal authorities of accounts submitted to supervisory authority

The audited accounts are also available to the fiscal authorities and normally form the basis for taxation (para 5 Income Tax Law). The tax authorities, however, will conduct their own independent examinations of the underlying accounts. The results of their examinations may differ from the independent auditors' results simply because the tax accounting treatment may legally be different from the accounting treatment adopted for public reporting. The so-called tax balance sheet that would reflect all legal accounting differences between the commercial accounts and the tax basis is normally not available for public inspection, nor is it filed with the Supervisory Agency or any other institution, except for the fiscal authorities.

2.9 Submission of accounts to any authority other than by requirement of law

There are no legal requirements to submit accounts or audit reports to any institutions other than the Supervisory Agency and the central bank. Banking associations with voluntary membership may ask for various accounting-related data or complete accounts from their members, but submission would be on a voluntary basis.

2.10 Application of laws and regulations to foreign banks operating through branches and subsidiaries

Subsidiaries and branches of foreign banks are subject to exactly the same laws and regulations as domestic banks. For audit purposes, branches will be treated like independent credit institutions (para 53 (1) KWG).

2.11 Availability of accounts for public inspection

Banks organised as a public company have to comply with the general law concerning such companies, that is to say, they must file their annual report at the commercial register and publish their accounts in a newspaper.

Banks organised in other legal forms will have to publish their financial statements in a newspaper and also file at the commercial register if the total of their balance sheet after certain adjustments is in excess of DM300 million for three years in succession.

3 FORMAT, STYLE AND CONTENTS OF ACCOUNTS

3.1 Extent to which format is laid down by statute, supervisory authority, generally accepted accounting practice or otherwise

3.2 Description of format

3.3 Extent to which contents are prescribed by statute, supervisory authority, generally accepted accounting practice or otherwise

3.4 Disclosure of specific items required other than those required by general law

3.5 Exemptions from disclosure allowed in respect of banking items

As discussed earlier, the format, style and content of the annual accounts are laid down by law[11] and directives[12]

---

[10] Anforderungen für die Ausgestaltung der Innenrevision, pronouncement by the Federal Supervisory Agency issued to the Federal Associations of Credit Institutions, 28 May 1976 (I4–3)

[11] Gesetz über Formblätter für die Gliederung des Jahresabschlusses, *op. cit.*

[12] Verordnung über Formblätter für die Gliederung des Jahresabschlusses von Kreditinstituten, *op. cit.*

pronounced by the Ministry of Justice in co-operation with the Ministry of Finance. Separate formats are laid down for the following main institutions:

– Universal banks in the form of public companies, partnerships limited by shares, limited liability companies (Aktiengesellschaft, Kommanditgesellschaft auf Aktien, Gesellschaft mit beschränkter Haftung).

– Universal banks in the form of co-operative companies (Genossenschaften).

– Universal banks in the form of individual proprietorships,[13] partnerships and limited liability partnerships (Einzelfirma, offene Handelsgesellschaft, Kommanditgesellschaft).

– Savings banks in the form of entities owned and guaranteed by a state, county, or municipality.

– Mortgage banks in the form of public company or partnership limited by shares (Aktiengesellschaft, Kommanditgesellschaft auf Aktien).

– Ship mortgage banks in the form of public company or partnership limited by shares (Aktiengesellschaft, Kommanditgesellschaft auf Aktien).

– Various types of bank in the form of credit institutions owned and/or guaranteed by the states, counties or municipalities (öffentlich-rechtliche Kreditanstalten).

– Building societies in the form of public companies, limited liability companies owned and/or guaranteed by states, counties or municipalities (Aktiengesellschaft, Gesellschaft mit beschränkter Haftung, öffentlich-rechtliche Bausparkassen).

The format used for universal banks in the form of public companies, public limited liability partnerships and limited liability companies is set out in Appendix II.

In addition to the various asset and liability positions, the balance sheet contains certain contingency, intercompany and indebtedness information.

3.6 Hidden reserves

As a result of various bank collapses after World War I and also in more recent times, there is still considerable sensitivity about the stability of individual banks and the annual results reported by banks in general. Bank managements therefore have a strong incentive to report steady and increasing annual profits which will result in the distribution of reasonable dividends and will maintain the confidence of depositors, although in the case of the latter it must be remembered that there exists both the Liquiditäts-Konsortial-Bank GmbH and the deposit protection fund maintained by the private banking industry as part of their membership of the Federal Association of German Banks (Bundesverband deutscher Banken eV).

It is therefore common practice among German banks to maintain hidden reserves and to report steady or ever-improving profits and use the hidden reserves to smooth out any fluctuations.

These hidden reserves are built up in three different ways:

(i)   The consistent application of codified or generally accepted accounting principles, e.g. the application of historic cost accounting rules in a period of inflation or the adoption of accelerated depreciation rates in order to obtain taxation advantages.

(ii) The adoption by management of valuation options permitted by codified or generally accepted accounting principles, e.g. the adoption of conservative valuation for say investments by writing them down to the lower of cost and market value and not releasing the provision when the market value subsequently rises above cost. Indeed, German company law permits an asset to be written down to a lower future realisable or market value if this is supported by a 'prudent' management estimate.

(iii) Reserves set up by management through low valuations. Examples of this type of hidden reserve are the excessive accrual in respect of liabilities and the creation of a general provision for bad debts in excess of what is reasonably required.

While categories (i) and (ii) are almost certain to be tax deductible it is unlikely that those in category (iii) will be and therefore they will have to be disclosed to the tax authorities.

It should be noted that Public Company Law prohibits the build-up of excessive hidden reserves in the case of ordinary companies but banks are expressly permitted[14] to carry receivables (advances, etc.) and securities (shares, participations, etc.) at a lower value than permitted by paragraph 155 of Public Company Law, if management consider this appropriate in view of the risks prevailing in the banking industry in general.

3.7 Requirements as to consolidated accounts

In the past, consolidated accounts were normally only prepared by banks operated in the form of public companies following paras 329 et seq. Public Company Law. Mandatory consolidation under these paragraphs, however, is limited to subsidiaries located in the Federal Republic of Germany in which the parent company holds a more than 50% interest (para 329 (2) Public Company Law). After the introduction of the law on reporting requirements concerning certain enterprises and concerns,[15] consolidated accounts were also required for banking institutions operated in other legal forms if the balance sheet total plus own drafts in circulation, plus liabilities from the endorsement of discounted bills, plus liabilities from guarantees, bills and cheques guaranteed, and performance warranties exceeds DM300 million in three consecutive years (para 11 (1), (4) and para 1 (3)).[15]

The consolidation practice for these banks is similar to the requirements under Public Company Law and a management report on the consolidated statements has to be prepared. However, the Supervisory Agency found this to be unsatisfactory because consolidation is limited only to banks and other subsidiaries located in the

---

[13] This form will not be accepted by the Supervisory Agency for new banks

[14] Para 26a (1) KWG

[15] Gesetz über die Rechnungslegung von bestimmten Unternehmen und Konzernen (Publizitätsgesetz) first published 15 August 1969 (BGBl.I.p.1189) Publication Law

Federal Republic of Germany and subsidiaries located in other countries, particularly in Luxembourg, were not accessible to the supervisory authorities. Therefore the inherent risks for German parent banks could remain unknown or undetected by the Supervisory Agency. Consequently, negotiations were held between the Supervisory Agency and the leading bank associations to agree on the submission of consolidated accounts including foreign subsidiaries.

Those negotiations resulted in the 'gentlemen's agreement'[16] of 17 August 1981, to which all appropriate banking institutions subscribed, which obliges the banks to include 100% subsidiaries in a consolidated submission to the Supervisory Agency. The latter's major concern in this respect is that the banks can exceed their loan/equity capital ratio (see discussion below on key ratios) as a result of foreign subsidiaries increasing their loan volume but not increasing their equity capital correspondingly.

4 ACCOUNTING POLICIES

4.1 Responsibility for laying down accounting policies

Bank accounting principles in Germany are regulated by a variety of laws, regulations and standards. These include the principles of orderly bookkeeping and accounting which are applicable to all businesses. Accounting rules and regulations, including valuation rules codified in paras 149 *et seq.* Public Company Law, are also deemed — to a certain extent — to form generally accepted accounting principles. For banks, however, a general exception from the application of certain rules is expressed in para 26a KWG (see Section 4.2). More rudimentary references to accounting principles are included in paras 38 *et seq.* Commercial Law which are applicable to all businesses. Pronouncements by the Institute of public accountants (Institut der Wirtschaftsprüfer — the auditors' professional body) also form a source of accounting principles to be observed, generally in the preparation of annual accounts.

Specific bank-related accounting principles are laid down by the Supervisory Agency. These pronouncements extend from the compulsory format to be observed in the presentation of the accounts and their contents and detailed valuation requirements. The pronouncements are issued on a case-by-case basis and deal with very detailed accounting regulations, which are binding for all banks once they have been decreed. The key pronouncements issued by the Agency are the following:
— Guidelines on format and presentation of annual bank accounts.[17]
— Guidelines on the preparation of annual accounts of credit institutions.[18]
— Directives and interpretations of accounting matters.[19]
— Directive on the formation of general bad debt provisions by credit institutions.[20]
There are sixty-five individual guidelines, pronouncements and directives that have to be observed by the various banking institutions. The majority of the

regulations relate to presentation and disclosure of bank assets, liabilities and profit and loss account items, whereas valuation matters are dealt with to a lesser extent, except for the directives on general bad debt provisions.

4.2 Particular accounting policies

Accounting policies generally accepted in the Federal Republic of Germany are based on two main principles:
— The principle of prudence or caution which, e.g. leads to the acceptance of the 'lowest-value' valuation referred to above. This extends to recognition of losses when foreseeable, or at least anticipated, whereas profits are only recognised when *de facto* realised or when realisation is secured beyond doubt.
— The principle of balance sheet continuation, i.e. the closing balance sheet must always correspond — in detail — to the next business year's opening balance sheet. The introduction of the principle is necessary because within limits there exists no principle of consistency between years. Indeed, differing valuation options may be adopted for the same item at successive closing dates. For public companies, however, any material effect of adopting alternative valuation methods has to be disclosed (para 160 (2) sub-section 4 Public Company Law). This disclosure requirement for banks is, however, waived by para 26a (2) KWG for banks in the form of public companies and there are no disclosure requirements for valuation changes for all other legal forms of entities.

In connection with the observations made on hidden reserve accounting, published bank accounts in Germany tend to give an understated picture of a bank's financial position at the year end in good years and an overstated profit in bad years, the disclosure of a bank's 'true' profit during any one business year is relatively unlikely. The individual accounting treatment of various key banking situations is described below.

4.2.1 Foreign exchange

The most comprehensive presentation of foreign

---

[16] Schreiben des Bundesaufsichtsamtes für das Kreditwesen betreffend das Gentlemen's Agreement über die Konsolidierung der Bankausweise von 1 September 1981 — I3-5-12/81
[17] Verordnung über Formblätter für die Gliederung des Jahresabschlusses von Kreditinstituten, *op cit.*
[18] Richtlinien für die Aufstellung des Jahresabschlusses der Kreditinstitute und das Muster für die Anlage zur Jahresbilanz der Kreditinstitute in der Rechtsform der eingetragenen Genossenschaften, ausgenommen Zentralkassen, pronouncement No. 1/68 by the Bundesaufsichtsamt für das Kreditwesen 22 July 1968 (appended to Federal Gazette No. 161) amended through 16 November 1976 (Federal Gazette No. 238)
[19] Directives and interpretations of accounting matters are often issued by the Supervisory Agency in the form of letters to the various Federal Associations of German banking institutions. A complete record in chronological order is contained in Consbruch, Moller, Bahre and Schneider, 'Kreditwesengesetz mit verwandten und zugehörigen Vorschriften', C. H. Beck'sche Verlagsbuchhandlung, Munich, amended through March 1983.
[20] Anordnung über die Bildung von Sammelwertberichtigungen bei Kreditinstituten, pronouncement by the Bundesaufsichtsamt für das Kreditwesen, 17 September 1974 (Federal Gazette No. 180)

exchange accounting is probably included in a pronouncement by the banking committee of the Institut der Wirtschaftsprüfer.[21] The pronouncement differentiates immediate transactions ('Kassageschäfte'), which are closed within two days, and forward transactions, which can include:

– Hedge transactions to eliminate a foreign exchange risk.

– Interest arbitrage in the form of swap deals.

– Holding of open forward positions – the net open forward and swap position allowable for banks is limited under principle Ia (see Section 7).

The mere matching of asset and liability positions for each single currency, without considering the individual due date for each contract, assumes that the bank can prolong or match each contract at the cost of the prevailing swap rates. For the purposes of the pronouncement, closed or open positions are defined more narrowly in that closed positions only exist when asset and liability positions for each currency fall due within the same business year. Foreign currency risks arising from long or short positions (open positions) in one currency cannot be offset against balancing positions in other currencies, but must be accounted for individually. In practice, foreign currency assets and liabilities carried in the balance sheet and forward exchange deals are valued separately, but without reference to the fact that open or closed positions are involved. Unrealised profits generated in this valuation process have to be identified separately by grouping balance sheet assets and liabilities to match forward positions falling due within the same business year.

The valuation of assets and liabilities relating to the three types of foreign exchange transactions identified above is made on the following basis:

– Swap deals matching in amount and due date by currency are valued with the exchange rate prevailing at the acquisition date for the part of the transaction carried in the balance sheet and the contracted rate for the forward part of the transaction. Premiums or discounts are accounted for *pro rata temporis* if they arise from differences in interest rates.

– Foreign currency assets and liabilities carried in the balance sheet are valued at the average buying/selling rate of the closing day. Profits or losses arising from the valuation at the closing rate, compared to the original acquisition cost for each currency, are credited or charged to the profit and loss account except for unrealised profits. Unrealised profits in this context exist when a transaction is not yet completed, i.e. a foreign currency receivable would yield a higher Deutschmark amount at the closing date than the Deutschmark countervalue initially paid out to the debtor, or the repayment of a liability would result in a lower Deutschmark amount than the Deutschmark countervalue initially received from the creditor.

– The potential future profit or loss, inherent in forward sales and purchases of foreign currencies, is determined by comparing the value at contracted rates with the value at the corresponding average forward rates prevailing at the closing date, separately for each future business year. The resulting profit or loss is to be corrected for the valuation of open positions (long or short). Profits still existing, after adjusting for the valuation of open positions, may only be used to offset future losses calculated for the same currency in following years. Profits not set off thereby are disregarded for reporting purposes. Future losses not yet offset by future (unrealised) profits have to be accrued in the balance sheet. Open positions are valued as described above for the determination of unrealised profits included in balance sheet items.

4.2.2 Deferred tax

Deferred tax accounting is generally not practised in Germany. However, para 152 (5) Public Company Law requires disclosure of items included in reserves but not yet subject to income taxes (Sonderposten mit Rücklageanteil). The disclosure of such items is, if at all, also found in the accounts of banks in other legal forms. This relatively rare disclosure reflects the gross reserve amount and gives no indication of the future tax burden it will entail when reflected in income. The formation of such untaxed reserves can only arise from the optional use of tax reliefs under various beneficial income tax or other income-related tax laws.

In the rare case where a company elects to set up an untaxed reserve in its tax accounts only (which is possible, e.g. for reserves against inflationary price increases, Preissteigerungsrücklage) the corresponding future tax charge will have to be included in the statutory accounts. This accrual would represent a deferred tax item which would in practice only be observed in very exceptional circumstances.

4.2.3 Specific and general provisions for bad and doubtful debts

Specific bad debt allowances are set up on a case-by-case basis whereby individual loans or receivables are evaluated as to their future collectability. The allowance may vary from a low percentage such as 5% of the face value to a complete write-off if the loan or receivable is unsecured. Specific allowances are always offset directly against the asset balance:[22] the amount carried in the bank's books will therefore be the estimated net collectable amount. The interest related to written off amounts will no longer be accrued if its future collection is doubtful.

The need to establish specific allowances is a matter of bank management's judgement. A pronouncement by the Institut der Wirtschaftsprüfer[23] proposes specific allowances in cases where, at the date of the audit, the cash-flow necessary for pay-back cannot be generated either from the debtor's operations or from the liquidation of the debtor. A continuous loss situation, including considerable loss of equity, will cause

---

[21] Bilanzierung und Prüfung der Devisengeschäfte der Kreditinstitute: Stellungnahme des Bankenfachausschusses des Instituts der Wirtschaftsprüfer 1/75, published in 'Die Fachgutachten und Stellungnahmen des Instituts der Wirtschaftsprüfer auf dem Gebiete der Rechnungslegung und Prüfung', IdW-Verlag, Dusseldorf, amended through June 1980
[22] Para 3 (3) Formblattverordnung, 20 December 1967
[23] Stellungnahme des Bankenfachausschusses 1/78

considerable doubt as to the collectability of an unsecured loan. Necessary specific allowances need to be set up even if the bank records the prescribed general allowances or if considerable known hidden reserves exist.

Bank management may decide to establish overall allowances for groups of debts which cannot be individually evaluated because no immediate risk situation can be recognised, although a loss is anticipated in the near future. The basis of these allowances is formed by each group of assets after deduction of items already covered by specific allowances. The amount set off will be derived from the bank's loan loss history and the allowance thus created will normally be deducted from the assets concerned.

Whereas the formation of an overall allowance is not compulsory, the formation of a general allowance (Sammelwertberichtigung) is prescribed by the Supervisory Agency. A directive[24] based on paras 6 (1) and 26 KWG and para 40 (2) Commercial Law prescribes the minimum general allowance percentages applicable to various asset captions as follows:

Description of asset	Legal form of credit institution	
	Sole proprietor, partnership, limited liability partnership %	All other legal forms %
Bills of exchange		
– own drafts	1.8	1.05
– all other bills of exchange	0.9	0.525
Receivables, loans and advances to customers with a term of notice of less than four years	1.8	1.05
Contingent receivables from own drafts in circulation and discounted	1.8	1.05
Bills and cheques guaranteed, warranties, liabilities from endorsement of discounted bills	0.9	0.525
Receivables with agreed terms of notice exceeding four years (excluding ship mortgages)		
– secured by mortgage	0.1	0.1
– other	0.5	0.5

Items falling under the following categories need not be included in the computation of the general allowance: (1) Receivables from the federation, state, or community, or other public body, or guaranteed by these institutions. (2) Receivables from foreign states or foreign public bodies. (3) Receivables from other credit institutions. (4) Receivables guaranteed by a body or institution mentioned in Section 1.4. (5) Receivables insured against the risk of loss. (6) Receivables covered by specific allowances.

The basis of the computation is generally the net receivable; interest accrued or overdue is subject to the same rates as the principal. The rates mentioned above are the minimum rates accepted by the Supervisory Agency; bank management may of course choose to increase the rates, thereby creating additional hidden reserves. On the other hand, overall allowances may not be set up where high general allowance rates are adopted.

General allowances, unlike specific and overall allowances, are normally shown as one sum on the liability side of the balance sheet. Alternatively, portions of the allowance identifiable with individual asset captions can be deducted from the assets but any portion of the allowance not identifiable with an asset carried in the balance sheet, i.e. contingent receivables from own drafts in circulation, will have to be shown on the liability side, not in the caption 'compulsory general allowances', but in the accrual caption. In practice, both forms of account presentation are adopted by German banks.

4.2.4 Treatment of provisions in accounts

To the extent that allowances need to be set up for individual asset items such as loans, advances, etc. the allowance will be deducted from the outstanding balance and only the net amount will be carried on the asset side of the balance sheet (see Section 4.2.3).

General allowances for doubtful debts are carried on the liabilities' side of the balance sheet and consequently they are not offset against the corresponding asset balances (see Appendix II for balance sheet format).

There is no other netting of allowances.

4.2.5 Premiums and discounts on investments (amortise, write off, etc.)

It is not normal practice to amortise the premium or discount on investments. The basic principle is to value current assets at the lower of cost and market value and therefore when an investment is purchased at a premium or discount it would be held at cost (or market value, if lower), until redemption, or date of sale, when the total profit would be recognised.

4.2.6 Offsets, i.e. to what extent can assets and liabilities be set off against each other (legally or in practice)

Offsets of assets and liabilities are not allowed under orderly bookkeeping requirements and para 152 (8) Public Company Law specifically confirms this for public companies. Offsets are nonetheless possible under civil law considerations and for accounting purposes if a debtor and creditor are identical, i.e. the same legal person, if the nature of the receivable and liability are identical, and they have matching settlement terms. A guideline has therefore been issued by the Supervisory Agency requiring offsets of assets and liabilities if the

---

[24] Anordnung über die Bildung von Sammelwertberichtigungen bei Kreditinstituten, *op. cit.*

above criteria are met and the currency denomination of receivables and liability are identical.

Legally independent member companies of one group are not considered as one entity for offset purposes, nor are state organisations and public bodies.

Assets and liabilities that can be offset include call money, cash due daily, overdrafts and current account balances, repayable on demand.

Items that qualify for offset have to be carried in the bank's books, i.e. there is no offset for bills receivable and deposits.

Balances that are generated through the so-called 'English accounting method', i.e. commitments and the draw-down are recorded in separate accounts, have to be offset to reflect the net current balance.

Because of the administrative difficulties, compulsory offsets need not be made in minor cases and the same applies when assets and liabilities are recorded in different branches of the bank.

An exception to the general rule was issued by the Supervisory Agency on 26 March 1970, to the effect that balances due daily do not have to be offset if the bank does not treat them as one unit, i.e. if interest calculation and commission payments are different for asset and liability.

Offsets are also possible for term assets and liabilities provided amounts, due dates and interest are identical; if interest rates differ, offset is not absolutely necessary.

Accrued interest receivable and payable for asset and liability items offset for balance sheet purposes may not, however, be offset for income statement purposes, but have to be shown gross as income and expense.

4.2.7 Goodwill

Accounting rules for goodwill are codified in para 153 (5) Public Company Law. By inference these rules are considered part of generally accepted accounting principles and therefore are also largely observed by companies that do not use the legal form of a public company.

In essence, the recording of goodwill is not compulsory and management may exercise the option not to capitalise goodwill at all. If capitalised there is a requirement to write goodwill off over a period not exceeding five years. Should there be proof that goodwill ceased to have any value before the expiry of the five-year period, an appropriate downward adjustment will have to be made at once.

The conditions prerequisite to the recording of goodwill are:

– Purchase of an enterprise or acquisition of all assets and liabilities of an enterprise.

– Purchase price paid is in excess of the fair market value of all assets less all liabilities.

In cases where shares of companies with separate legal identity are purchased there will be no accounting for goodwill, because any consideration paid for goodwill is an integral part of the acquisition cost of the shares acquired and cannot be separated therefrom. Shares representing participations in other companies have to be carried at acquisition cost and revaluations in excess of acquisition cost are not permitted. If, however, possible

continuing loss situations persist then a write-down would be necessary which would also imply indirect write-down of goodwill if paid for as part of the share purchase price.

For tax purposes the accounting treatment is different in that any identifiable goodwill has to be capitalised and amortisation of goodwill is disallowed altogether for tax purposes. Exceptional write-down may be accepted when continuing loss situations exist.

4.2.8 Consolidation

Formal consolidation requirements only exist for public companies and their majority held subsidiaries located in Germany (para 329 (2) Public Company Law). Through paras 11 and 13 (2) of the law on reporting and accounting by certain enterprises and concerns, these regulations are also applicable to other large groups if, in the case of banks, the consolidated balance sheet total exceeds DM300 million. As mentioned in Section 3.7, a voluntary agreement was reached between the banks' federal associations and the Supervisory Agency in 1981 whereby full consolidations including foreign subsidiaries are now prepared and published.

The accounts consolidated have to be prepared in conformity with accounting principles generally accepted in Germany. Except for possible consolidation adjustments, the accounts submitted by the subsidiaries are binding and they will generally be audited.

There are no specific foreign currency translation rules other than those existing for foreign currency translations within domestic accounts. It is therefore common practice to translate the subsidiaries' accounts into Deutschmarks at the average selling/buying closing rates.

Under German consolidation practice the investment in subsidiaries is netted off against the subsidiaries' share capital and undistributed reserves – both pre- and post-acquisition reserves – so that the 'difference on consolidation' (Konsolidierungsausgleichsposten), which appears as a separate balance sheet caption, will change from year to year and will represent the difference between the original investment in subsidiaries and the current net assets of those subsidiaries attributable to the parent company.

This is in contrast to Anglo-Saxon practice and indeed International Accounting Standard No. 3, both of which recommend that consolidated accounts should regard the group as a single entity so that all undistributed profit of the group on a post-acquisition basis would reflect in the group figure for reserves.

It should be noted that any hidden reserves in the subsidiaries will result in a larger debit consolidation difference than would otherwise have been the case.

4.2.9 Revaluations of assets

In principle, all assets acquired by a business are recorded at their original acquisition cost. Depreciation, accelerated write-off or lower valuation may be acceptable under tax or general accounting regulations, which may even lead to understated asset values compared to their current replacement value. Write-backs for over-depreciated or low-valued assets are generally possible, but would have to be disclosed in the management report (see above). Write-backs, however, must never lead to a valuation in excess of original acquisition cost − with depreciation charged on a straight line basis deducted in the case of depreciable items. Any revaluation to reflect a higher current or market value, particularly in the case of land and buildings, is unacceptable for accounting purposes.

4.2.10 Instalment finance and leasing including basis of recognition of income

Instalment credit business is subject to a number of regulations issued by the Supervisory Agency.[25] These include that:
− The term of the financing should not exceed 24 months.
− The customer should have made an appropriate downpayment on the purchase.
− Equal monthly instalment payments are agreed.
− The instalment credit cost and their breakdown are disclosed to the customer.
− Percentages for each cost element are disclosed when percentages enter into the computation of the cost.

Standard types of instalment credit contracts include an administrative fee of 2% or more and monthly interest rates of a relatively wide scale.

Interest income from instalment payments is recognised on a monthly basis, and the administrative fee will generally be taken into income over the life of the loan.

Leasing activities are not normally undertaken by German banks, but some major banks do have subsidiaries exclusively set up to operate as leasing companies. Receivables from leasing activities would normally be classified as customer receivables. To the extent that receivables for future periods are included, an appropriate disclosure is required. Leasing assets and leasing income is reported similarly to normal rental contracts, i.e. the leasing asset is capitalised at its normal acquisition cost and depreciated over its estimated future life, which may be identical with the life of the lease. Leasing payments are recorded as income in the period in which they are due.

A different treatment is adopted for income tax purposes when the life of the lease covers less than 40% or more than 90% of the life of the asset. In these cases, the lessee may have to capitalise the asset and the lease liability under present value considerations, and a corresponding treatment on the lessor's side is required. The tax accounting treatment is normally not followed for public reporting purposes.

4.2.11 Dealing assets

The essential difference in valuation of assets for dealing as opposed to those held for the long-term exists in the strict applicability of the 'lowest valuation principle' (discussed in Section 3.6) to dealing assets. Banks may value their dealing assets even below that value following the express regulation in para 26b (1) KWG, which leads to the creation of hidden reserves. For long-term

investments the lowest value principle is not fully applicable. In principle, these have to be valued at their respective acquisition costs and impairments in value only have to be reflected when they are of a durable nature, i.e. if management considers that a reduction in value will not only be of a short-term nature. Management may, however, opt to write down an asset held for the long-term where there are seasonal fluctuations in its value. When the reason for write-down disappears, there is no need to write up the asset, but the write-up may again be effected at management's discretion. Where the impairment is permanent the long-term investment must be maintained at its lower valuation (paras 153 and 154 Public Company Law).

The accounts format for banks does not differentiate between dealing and long-term. Para 3 (4) Formblattverordnung therefore requires disclosure of the carrying value of investments not valued following the 'lowest value principle' on the face of the balance sheet. This disclosure indicates the volume of assets valued at higher than year end market rates, but does not indicate the amount of the overstatement compared to market.

The asset lines requiring this disclosure, if applicable, are:
− Loans and promissory notes.
− Other securities.

4.2.12 Pensions

Even after the introduction of the law on the improvements of company pension regulations[26] which resulted in the improvement in pension rights, German authoritative literature still takes the view that the accrual of pension liabilities in company accounts is optional. In practice, however, largely as a result of tax legislation, companies offering pensions to their employees have provided for existing pension liabilities. The pension accruals shown in commercial balance sheets will, therefore, reflect the actual tax position in a large number of cases because the accrual has to be included in the commercial balance sheet to be accepted for fiscal purposes.

The basis for the accrual is the future pension entitlement as stipulated in the pension plan. The present value of the pension liability is normally computed for tax purposes on an actuarial basis using a discount factor of 5.5% (6.0% with effect from 1982). This calculation will in general reflect the actual present value of the liability, including past service liabilities. The accrual included in the commercial balance sheet may, however, vary from the tax accrual because management may elect to provide for a larger or smaller liability than that acceptable for tax purposes. However, a larger figure is not tax deductible, and a lower increase may not be 'caught up' in subsequent years for tax purposes.

This flexibility has given rise to confusion and, in order to improve the disclosure situation, public companies are now required to disclose under para 159 of

[25] Regeln für das Teilzahlungsfinanzierungsgeschäft, pronouncement No. 2/64 by the Bundesaufsichtsamt für das Kreditwesen, 24 August 1964

[26] Gesetz zur Verbesserung der betrieblichen Altersversorgung, published 19 December 1974 (BGB1.I.p.3610)

Public Company Law the actual pensions paid during the year and the anticipated pensions payable during the next five years, expressed as a percentage of the pensions paid for the year.

4.2.13 Depreciation

The valuation of fixed assets is essentially determined by the historical cost principle. All fixed asset acquisitions are capitalised, together with any additional cost incurred to put the asset in place and/or operation. Depreciable assets have to be depreciated using a depreciation method acceptable under orderly bookkeeping and accounting provisions which include straight line and declining balance depreciation over reasonably estimated useful lives.

The fiscal authorities have published average useful lives and depreciation rates acceptable for taxation purposes, which are normally deemed to represent reasonable estimates and, for simplicity, they are used for commercial accounting purposes as well, together with other advantages offered by the tax laws. For major asset groups these are as follows:

Description	Straight line rate % p.a.
Land	—
Buildings	2% or accelerated depreciation accepted under new tax legislation
Motor vehicles	25%
Office equipment and furniture	10–20%
Computers	20%

So-called 'small value items' with individual acquisition cost not exceeding DM800 may be written off immediately upon acquisition.

Depreciable assets other than buildings may be charged with a full year's depreciation when acquired during the first half of the year and a half year's depreciation when acquired during the second half. *Pro rata temporis* depreciation is also possible, but has to be charged for newly acquired buildings.

Exceptions from the acquisition cost principles may occur when long-term fixed assets are sold and a substantial gain on disposal is realised, e.g. for the sale of buildings or land. To avoid taxation of this gain it may be offset from the acquisition cost of a similar replacement item. The reduced 'cost' represents the carrying value of the newly-acquired asset and the basis for the computation of depreciation in the case of depreciable items. This income tax regulation (para 6b Income Tax Law) helps to establish type (i) hidden reserves (see Section 3.6) because it has to be followed for public reporting purposes to be accepted for tax purposes.

4.2.14 Other

Apart from the accounting policies described above, there are no policies in relation to bank accounting which are worth mentioning in the context of this report.

5 WINDOW DRESSING

Annual bank accounts in Germany are subject to considerable public attention. Bank management is therefore generally very interested in showing continuous growth, adequate liquidity and stable profit performance. A bank's performance in these respects, below or above average, will be scrutinised closely by the general public.

To a certain extent, all of the goals mentioned above can be influenced by bank management when preparing the annual accounts. Profit performance can be manipulated — to a large extent — by hidden reserve formation and releases, as discussed above. Additional transactions around the year end can, at the same time, influence the reported profit and the bank's liquidity position. These could include the sale of investments, securities, shares, etc. which would result in extra liquidity and possible profits.

Pure window dressing transactions, designed to reflect better liquidity at the year end, would include:[27]

− The increase of the minimum cash reserve balance maintained with the Bundesbank by raising additional call money or time deposits over the year end; the latter would, however, be a relatively costly exercise.

− The raising of extra Lombard loan facilities from the Landeszentralbanken; this option may not always be favoured because of the disclosure required in the management report.

− The rediscounting of finance bills and bills of exchange would, at the same time, result in the disclosure of a corresponding contingent liability.

− The sale of money market papers and the shift of balances due from other credit institutions to the central bank to increase the cash reserve.

− Loans and advances are often issued with agreed terms of just under four years (but with prolongation offered beyond the initial terms, which does not have to be disclosed) to qualify the items as short-term.

− Long-term loans, also in the form of promissory notes, that are due within less than four years from the balance sheet date are paid back before their original due date and new loans with approximately equal terms and due dates are issued to show more short-term receivables.

− Loans and advances authorised for payout will only be paid in the new business year.

− Long-term securities and certain receivables from customers (mainly those documented in promissory notes) are exchanged for treasury bills and interest-free treasury bonds.

− Customer receivables are turned into bills of exchange which are then traded with another bank to be able to show bills of exchange available for discounting[28] with the Bundesbank.

− Bills of exchange on hand not available for discounting with the Bundesbank are discounted at another bank, which has corresponding facilities to offer,

---

[27] Essentially taken from H. Birch and H. Meyer, 'Die Bankbilanz, Handkommentar zum Jahresabschluss der Kreditinstitute', 3. Auflage, Wiesbaden, 1979, pp.vii, 20 *et seq.*

[28] Only bills of exchange bearing three so-called 'good' signatures are discounted by the Bundesbank

providing it does not unduly impair its own liquidity position.

– Customer receivables may at times, with a view to minimum cash reserve requirements, be exchanged for securities.

– In the event that the volume of bills on hand appears excessive, a sale and buy-back agreement (so-called Pensionsgeschäfte) can be negotiated with another bank which would result in higher receivables from banks (Nostroguthaben) or in increased cash reserves; after the year end, the bills are bought back at a predetermined price.

'Pensionsgeschäfte' can be structured two ways: the seller can have a firm obligation to buy back at a predetermined date and a predetermined price, and the buyer may have to sell back or alternatively may have an option not to sell back, if he considers this more advantageous.

Deals of this nature may involve a variety of securities, bills, debt certificates, acceptances, promissory notes, etc. They may also involve third parties, whereby bank A sells to bank B, who in turn resells to bank C after the balance sheet date. The involvement of a third party may be necessary if a sale and buy-back agreement will not remove the item sold from the seller's balance sheet because of the reporting guidelines established by the Supervisory Agency.

Another important aspect in accounts presentation is the balance sheet total because the continuous growth of the balance sheet total is considered to represent similar growth of the bank's transaction volume during the year. Slow growth of this indicator or even a reduction are both therefore deemed to be a negative sign of overall performance and profitability. However, an objective in reducing the balance sheet total would be to avoid the preparation and publication of consolidated accounts if the consolidated balance sheet total exceeds DM300 million in three consecutive years (see Section 3.7).

Some of the window dressing measures described above need not necessarily be aimed at increasing liquidity, but at increasing (or decreasing) the balance sheet total. The raising of extra call money in the market or Lombard facilities over the year end would at the same time increase liquidity and the balance sheet total. An increase in the balance sheet total can also be achieved by three bank transactions involving call or deposit money. The three partners in the transaction will pass on amounts of approximately the same size with equal terms or due dates, which constitutes the cheapest way to realise this objective.

Other measures to achieve better balance sheet relationships would include the sale or acquisition of fixed assets to or by subsidiaries in order to improve the ratio between long-term assets, equity capital (para 12 KWG) and liabilities of an individual bank within the group (see Section 7).

6 AMOUNTS REQUIRED TO BE MAINTAINED BY LAW OR OTHERWISE

Appendix I reflects the various types of bank and the various legal forms in which they can be operated. The amount of share capital required for each form and the minimum funding required by the Supervisory Agency to operate a certain type of bank are also indicated.

The build-up of additional legal reserves is only required for public companies (para 150 (1) Public Company Law) up to 10% (or more if provided for in the company's statutes) of the initial share capital. Similar reserves may be set up for limited liability companies, but they are not compulsory.

There are no legal requirements in this respect for limited liability partnerships and general partnerships. They will consequently be subject to the minimum fund regulations pronounced by the Supervisory Agency, which are also indicated in Appendix I.

Branches of foreign banks do not have a share capital *per se* and they will show the funding made available to them by the parent bank in accordance with para 53 (2) No. 2 KWG as their operating capital. As indicated in Appendix I, the minimum required is DM3 or 6 million depending on the type of banking business operated. In addition, any profits retained by the branch to increase its operating capital have to be disclosed separately on the face of the balance sheet (para 53 (2) No. 2 KWG); they can be viewed as voluntary reserves because there is no legal or similar requirement to build up such reserves.

In general, there is a strong tendency in the German banking industry to regard a capital relationship of 3-5% of the balance sheet total as good financing practice. In this connection, capital is considered to be the total of share capital, reserves and retained profits.

7 KEY RATIOS

In accordance with para 10 (1) sub-section 3 and para 11 sub-section 3 KWG, the Supervisory Agency has published the following key ratios that have to be observed by all affected banks. Before publishing the ratios, the Bundesbank (central bank) and the representatives of the various federal associations were consulted. The ratios are referred to as principles (Grundsätze):

Principle I: Advances and investments held by a bank should not exceed a ratio of 18 times the equity capital. In this context the following items are considered advances:

– Bills on hand and mailed for collection.

– Advances to credit institutions and customers.

– Potential receivables arising from the sale of bills of exchange, from guarantees and warranties.

Of these, the advances to the following customers or debtors will not be rated 100% but at the indicated percentage:

0%: advance to public bodies with the exception of banks guaranteed by states, etc.

20%: advances to domestic banks and domestic branches of foreign banks.

50%: long-term loans for land and buildings secured by first mortgages on land/building (and similarly for ships), advances, guarantees and warranties guaranteed by public bodies and advances to foreign banks.

As a result, the face value of assets less specific allowances, etc. will have to be 'covered' by equity capital by approximately the following ratios:

– Investments and advances rated 100%: 5.5%.
– Loans secured by mortgages, etc. rated 50%: 2.75%.
– Advances to credit institutions, etc. rated 20%: 1.00%.[29]

Principle Ia deals with the foreign exchange exposure of banks (and was introduced in 1974 after the collapse of the Herstatt-Bank):

– The open balances (long/short positions) in foreign currencies and (with effect from 1980) precious metals, including precious metals on hand, are not to exceed 30% of the equity capital.

– Open foreign exchange balances for each single currency falling due within one calendar month shall not exceed 40% of the equity capital.

– The same relationship has to be observed for open foreign exchange balances falling due within one half calendar year.

– All of the above relationships have to be observed on a daily basis.

The application of principle Ia does not in any way affect the volume of foreign exchange transactions or the dealings in precious metals, but only requires that the open position in an individual foreign currency and/or precious metal should not exceed the relationships mentioned in the principle. An actual limitation of the exposure related to foreign currency and precious metals can arise from the observation of principle I.

Principle II deals with liquidity aspects in relation to a bank's long-term assets and liabilities, i.e. in excess of four years.

Long-term assets, comprising fixed assets, investments, unquoted or unlisted securities, and long-term receivables from credit institutions and customers, net of accumulated depreciation and allowances, shall not exceed the total of long-term financing composed of:

– Equity capital.

– Liabilities with agreed terms or period of notice exceeding four years (excluding savings deposits) to banking institutions and other banking creditors.

– 10% of liabilities (excluding savings deposits) to non-banking creditors due daily or with agreed terms of less than four years.

– 60% of savings deposits.

– Promissory notes in circulation or sold with agreed terms of more than four years.

– 60% of pension accruals.

– 20% of liabilities with agreed terms or with terms of notice of a minimum of six months but not exceeding four years to other member banks of the Sparkassen und Giro-associations (which is only applicable to credit institutions organised in this form).

Principle III deals with liquidity aspects in short- and medium-term activities. The total of the following assets:

– 20% of receivables from credit institutions with terms or notice of minimum three months, but less than four years.

– Receivables from customers with agreed terms or notice of less than four years (including trade receivables from trading credit institutions).

– Own drafts charged to customers and bills of exchange issued by customers and on hand and contingent receivables from bills in circulation.

– Quoted securities and investment certificates.

– Other assets (including trading stock for trading credit institutions).

less all applicable allowances shall not exceed the total of the following liabilities:

– 10% of liabilities to credit institutions due daily or with notice of less than three months, excluding loans passed on by customers to third parties.

– 50% of liabilities to credit institutions with terms or notice of more than three months but less than four years excluding loans passed on by customers to third parties.

– 80% of liabilities to credit institutions for loans passed on by customers to third parties.

– 20% of savings deposits.

– 60% of other liabilities to other non-banking creditors due daily or with term or notice of less than four years.

– 80% of trade liabilities and own acceptances and bills of exchange in circulation plus any excess or shortage observed for the application of principle II.

In cases where a credit institution does not maintain adequate equity capital (para 10 (1) No. 1 KWG), or where its financing relationships are not in agreement with the above principles, the Supervisory Agency may prohibit the distribution of profits and/or the issuance of further loans and advances to its clientele. The Supervisory Agency can also prohibit the investment of liquid funds in land, buildings, ships and investments (para 45 (1) KWG). However, these measures may not be taken unless the bank has been given an opportunity to correct differences notified by the Agency (para 45 (2) KWG).

Apart from the observation of the above principles, banks in general have to observe the minimum cash reserve regulations laid down in para 16 Federal Bank Act. The corresponding cash balance has to be maintained with the central bank in a current account which is not interest bearing. The elements for the computation of the minimum reserve are as follows:

– Up to 30% of liabilities due daily to non-banking customers, credit institutions that are not subject to minimum reserve regulations and foreign banks.

– Up to 20% of liabilities with agreed terms of notice.

– Up to 10% of savings deposits.

– Up to 100% of liabilities to non-resident creditors.

The percentages indicated may be varied by the central bank in line with the prevailing economic situation. The detailed computation of the underlying liabilities is relatively complex and is based on monthly averages for the indicated liabilities. The Federal Bank has issued detailed guidelines[30] on the computation of the minimum cash reserve.

In para 1 (2) the guideline describes the credit institutions that are not subject to minimum cash reserve requirements. These are social insurance and similar public bodies which are also exempt from the KWG. Non-compliance with the minimum cash reserve requirements is subject to penalty interest payments to the central bank (para 10 of the guidelines).[30]

[29] Taken from Obst and Hintner, 'Geld, Bank- und Börsenwesen, ein Handbuch', Stuttgart, 1980, p. 184
[30] Anweisung der Deutschen Bundesbank über Mindestreserven (AMR), first published 11 November 1968 (BAwz. 214)

Additional regulations exist for the banks' credit business, which are designed to limit risks particularly inherent in large loans. The lending regulations are described in paras 13 *et seq.* KWG. The most important regulations include the following definitions and provisions:

– The term loan is defined in para 19 KWG and includes a variety of forms of credit extended to a customer, such as guarantees, promissory notes and even equity participation in the debtor, if the participation exceeds 25% of the debtor's capital. The term debtor is defined by the law as one 'borrower' comprising the group's member companies or enterprises.

– Loans exceeding 15% of the equity capital (para 13 (1) KWG) are defined as 'large loans'. The total of the five largest 'large loans' may not exceed three times the equity capital and all 'large loans' together may not exceed eight time the equity capital; commitments do not have to be considered in computing the total (para 13 (3) 2 KWG).

– Any individual 'large loan' may not exceed 75% of the equity capital (para 13 (4) KWG).

Securities held by the bank for such loans and deposits by the borrower with the bank are not deducted in computing the lending limits (para 19 (1) KWG). Loans granted to federal, state, county or similar public bodies, unsecured deposits on call or deposit money with other banks up to three months, bills of exchange purchased from other banks with due dates not in excess of three months and written-off loans are exempt from the computation of 'large loans'.

8 ACCOUNTING RETURNS OTHER THAN ACCOUNTS

8.1 By whom required
8.2 Nature of requirements

In addition to the banks' obligation to submit annual accounts to the Supervisory Agency and the central bank, appropriate monthly returns have to be filed with the Bundesbank. These include monthly returns in respect of the minimum cash reserve requirements, which are subject to review by the Bundesbank (para 11 (4), (5) of the guidelines).

Following para 18 of the Federal Bank Act all banking institutions have to submit ample statistical information on their operations to the central bank. The format of these returns (monthly balance sheet statistics report) very much resembles the format prescribed for the annual accounts, but the data submitted is significantly more detailed than in the annual accounts. There is no cut-off or valuation required. The statistical information also serves as a monthly return to be filed by credit institutions in line with para 25 KWG.

The main contents of the returns are:
– Receivables from and payables to credit institutions, grouped by agreed terms of notice and various debtors and creditors (weekly summary and monthly detail).
– Receivables from and payables to non-banking debtors and creditors, also grouped by terms of notice (weekly summary and monthly detail).
– Savings deposit liabilities towards non-banking customers.

– Details of investments including shares and securities on hand.
– Details of trading activities with branches, subsidiaries and other related parties abroad.
– Details of foreign exchange receivables and payables, gold and other precious metals.
– Statistical data relating to advances, loans and credit lines offered to domestic enterprises and individuals, together with the actual draw-down thereof, will furnish the Bundesbank with an indication of short-term credit demand and changes therein.
– Statistical data relating to debtors is to be submitted quarterly to the central bank including loans, bills discounted and advances to domestic enterprises and individuals grouped by debtors, agreed terms and type of security made available to the bank.
– An annual statistical summary of security depots including the number of depots maintained with the bank and their value, grouped by type of security deposited and depot owners.

The above information is used by the central bank and the Supervisory Agency essentially for two purposes: primarily, to obtain data about economic developments in general, and more particularly, to gain a relatively close insight into the individual bank's day-to-day operations (in particular, to monitor the solvency of the credit institution and to identify any potential bankruptcy at an early stage).

Certain other information submitted by the major universal credit institutions is designed to enable the Bundesbank to monitor foreign currency imports and exports in connection with balance of payments statistics. This important information is submitted on a weekly basis and corroborated monthly.

In conjunction with principles I, Ia, II and III, a monthly report is to be submitted to the Supervisory Agency and the central bank detailing the individual computation. Monthly reports are also required for the computation of the minimum cash reserve to be maintained at the central bank.

In regard to a bank's loan business, bi-monthly reports of large outstanding and new loans in excess of DM1 million or more, including all details, have to be submitted; reports on so-called 'large loans' are required both on draw-down and annually; reports on 'Organkredite'[31] are also required immediately.

Other matters of an organisational nature have to be filed with the Agency when reportable items occur, such as:
– Appointment or dismissal of bank directors.
– Changes in a company's statutes, including changes in share capital registered in the commercial register and changes in the bank's name.
– A loss of 25% or more of the bank's equity capital.
– The extension or termination of non-banking activities within the bank such as leasing.

---

[31] Organkredite are loans granted to employees and directors (Geschäftsleiter) of a bank and to enterprises or companies that hold an interest of at least 25% in the bank's capital or when the bank holds a similar interest in a customer's capital

9 TAXATION

9.1 General method of taxation

9.2 Accounts as basis for taxation

9.3 Adjustments permitted or required

9.4 Effect of tax considerations on presentation of accounts

In essence, there are no differences in the taxation of banks and companies in other industries in Germany. Companies forming separate legal entities, such as public and limited liability companies, are subject to taxes by virtue of their own legal identity for all taxes; limited liability partnerships and general partnerships are subject to the same taxes as corporations. In the case of income tax, however, each partner is assessed separately on his share of the profits.

Para 5 Income Tax Law stipulates that the commercial accounts, i.e. the published accounts, form the basis of taxation for income tax purposes. The published accounts may in turn be influenced by tax considerations when tax options require that they be followed for statutory accounts purposes to be accepted for tax purposes. In addition, there exists a variety of possible adjustments to the commercial balance sheet and profit and loss account until the final tax basis (taxable profits) is calculated. The following major adjustments may have to be made to conform to tax requirements:

– The allowance for doubtful debts including specific, overall and general allowance may be over/understated. In this connection it should be noted that the general allowance prescribed by the Supervisory Agency is accepted for tax purposes through a specific tax ruling.

– Increases/decreases in pension accruals may not be acceptable for tax purposes.

– The valuation of securities/investments may lead to excessive formation of hidden reserves which are unacceptable from a tax point of view.

– Sale/buy-back agreements entered into for window dressing purposes may not be accepted for tax purposes.

– The write-off of goodwill is not accepted for tax purposes unless a permanent impairment of the subsidiary's/investment's profit-earning potential is demonstrated.

Profit elements which are tax exempt on the grounds of double taxation treaties are deducted from the tax basis. Profits earned in countries with which Germany does not have a double taxation treaty are not tax exempt; for German tax purposes, they are recomputed following German tax regulations; this does not apply to dividends from investments organised as a separate legal entity (for foreign tax credits, see below). Income taxes paid on such profit elements can be deducted as an expense from the tax basis, if the tax does not qualify as a foreign tax credit (see below).

Trade tax on income (Gewerbeertragssteuer – a municipal tax) is calculated from the adjusted tax basis – including only income earned in Germany – at rates of between 14% and 20%, depending on the individual levy rates fixed by the various communities. This tax is deductible from its own basis, so that practitioners compute the actual charge at 90% of the statutory tax rate, i.e. 12.6% to 18%.

The income tax basis is reduced by the charge in respect of trade-tax-on-income to form the basis for corporation tax on a worldwide income basis. The tax rate is 56% for undistributed profits and 36% for distributed profits. Various expenses are not deductible for corporation tax purposes, such as the net property tax (see below). Certain entertainment expenses, etc. are taxed at 56% because they are not considered to represent distributed profits.

Foreign tax credits (para 26 (1) Corporation Tax Law) are available in respect of income elements taxed abroad by a tax (including withholding taxes) equivalent to the German corporation tax. The foreign tax credit is calculated on a country-by-country basis; the foreign tax attributable to that profit element is deducted from the corresponding German tax charge attributable to that element. However, the foreign tax credit cannot exceed the German tax charge, so that the income tax attributable to that profit element will always be the higher of the German or foreign tax charge.

Property taxes are levied in the form of trade-tax-on-property and net property tax. Trade-tax-on-property (Gewerbekapitalsteuer) is a municipal tax, whereas the net property tax is a federal tax. Levy rates are 0.5-8.8% and 0.7% respectively, of the underlying tax basis. The basis for both taxes is taxable net worth of the company at 1 January of a business year. The taxable net worth is computed following a number of tax valuation regulations which differ considerably from commercial and income tax valuation rules. Additional adjustments are required in the case of the trade-tax-on-capital basis. One major difference between these property taxes is the deductibility of the trade-tax-on-capital for income tax purposes, whereas the net property tax is not deductible for corporation tax and trade-tax on income purposes.

10 INTERPRETATION OF ACCOUNTS

10.1 Adequacy of information as to contents and disclosure

10.2 Audit and reliability of information

10.3 Comparability between different banks on the basis of published accounts or publicly available returns

Except for so-called private banks, i.e. banks owned by individuals, partnerships and limited liability partnerships, all banks have to prepare a management report together with the annual accounts. Traditionally, the management report includes a report on the bank's performance during the period and, possibly, an outlook on the coming business year and an explanatory report on the annual accounts. This report should discuss important aspects of the accounts and explain significant year-on-year changes in both the balance sheet and profit and loss account. Public companies have to disclose additional items under para 160 (3) Public Company Law. These disclosures include details on 'own shares' held by the bank, disclosures of contingent liabilities not reflected on the face of the balance sheet, and details of certain relationships with related parties.

Public company banks are, however, exempt from certain disclosure requirements regarding the effect of accounting changes, unusual write-offs and depreciation charges resulting from the impairment of asset values (para 26 (2) KWG, para 160 (2) Public Company Law).

Banks' annual reports therefore give ample general data, but detailed information is not required.

Other disclosure requirements deal mainly with the bank's investment activities. The balance sheet discloses the amount of shareholdings in banks, bank-to-bank shareholdings in a controlling company, and the carrying value of all shareholdings.

The fact that annual accounts and management reports are subject to audit by independent accountants ensures that the information submitted is reliable within the framework of legal requirements and that legal requirements *per se* are largely observed by the bank.

However, the following factors prohibit meaningful and valid comparisons of annual accounts between various banks and even between one bank's annual accounts between years:

– Extensive hidden reserve accounting is possible and, to a certain extent, favoured by existing bank legislation.

– There is no requirement for consistency between years; disclosure requirements for the effect of accounting changes between years have been abolished for banks.

– Window dressing transactions are possible around the year end.

A bank's 'true' performance and financial position at a year end could be clouded by such measures. Only the Supervisory Agency has a relatively close insight into a bank's operating situation, due to the extensive and detailed information submitted by banks at very short intervals.

11 OTHER RELEVANT INFORMATION

11.1 Future changes in legal regulations governing the banking sector

Certain changes are planned in the legal regulations governing the banking sector and to this end a draft statute has been published. This statute aims both to amend the existing banking regulations to take account of the changed risk climate in which banks operate, and to implement the EEC Directive concerning supervision of banks on a consolidated basis.

The suggested changes to the law are discussed briefly as follows:

(a) Amendment of the banking regulations to take account of changed risk climate in which banks operate

(i)   By introduction of a new section into the KWG – para 10(a) – the requirement that a bank should maintain sufficient equity capital, as embodied in the current para 10, is to be extended to apply to a group of banks taken together. A subsidiary bank would belong to a group if at least 40% of the share capital is held, directly or indirectly, by another bank, or if the latter were able to exercise a controlling influence over the former. This provision would apply also to companies carrying out 'banking activities' - para 1 KWG – in a foreign country, and to leasing companies, but not to companies solely concerned with safe deposit services or investment business.

The equity capital of the group would be calculated by adding the appropriate proportion of the 'equity capital', as defined in para 10, of the group members to that of the group parent bank. The appropriate proportion is that proportion of the capital held by the group parent. From the sum arrived at, the book value of the shares in the group member and the capital investments of sleeping partners, as far as they relate to the group member, must be deducted.

(ii)   Para 13 KWG, which defines the lending regulations, is to be amended as regards 'large loans'. No 'large loan' would be permitted to exceed 50% (previously 75%) of the equity capital. An additional section – para 13a – is to be added, to apply the requirements of para 13 to groups of banks. For this purpose a group would be composed of a parent and all banks in which the parent holds a 50% shareholding, or can exercise controlling influence. The existence or not of a 'large loan' would be established by calculating the sum of the equity capital of the parent and the appropriate proportion of the group members' share capital, and likewise for the loans extended.

(b) Implementation of EEC Directive concerning supervision of banks on a consolidated basis

The draft statute foresees several changes: under para 8, a new paragraph 3 would allow the Federal Supervisory Agency and the Federal Bank to work in co-operation with their equivalents in foreign countries when supervising on a consolidated basis banks that operate in other EEC countries.

An addition to para 14 would permit the German Federal Bank to pass information on loan activities of banks in Germany to a foreign authority, with the object of informing the bank and authority in the foreign country of the loan activities in Germany.

A further amendment to para 44 would remove any restrictions on the flow of information abroad if (a) the information is required for the supervision of a credit institution on a consolidated basis, and (b) the recipient holds at least 25% of the capital of the German bank. Furthermore, the Federal Supervisory Agency would be able to carry out an examination of the information submitted by a foreign group member for consolidation purposes and bank supervisory purposes in Germany in so far as permitted by the foreign state.

As was indicated at the start, this revision to the laws governing the supervision of banks in Germany is intended to reflect the changing circumstances in the bank sector, both externally (by way of EEC directive) and internally, because of increased international activity of German banks and generally greater risk of exposure. The new law as drafted would come into effect on 1 January 1985, but there would be an interim period allowed for banks to comply with the new legislation.

APPENDIX I

Summary of major types of bank

Type of bank	Applicable law	Minimum legal capital requirement (DM)	Minimum funding requirements[1] (DM)	Legal form
Universal bank (Geschäftsbank)	Banking Act (Kreditwesengesetz)	100,000 (50,000)[2]	6,000,000[3]	Public company, limited liability company, public limited liability partnership, partnership, limited liability partnership, state or community organisation
Savings bank	Banking Act	not specified	6,000,000	Community organisation
Mortgage bank	Mortgage Bank Act	8,000,000	30,000,000	Public company, public limited liability partnership
Ship mortgage bank	Ship Mortgage Bank Act	8,000,000	30,000,000	Public company, public limited liability partnership
Building societies	Law on Building Societies	100,000	10,000,000	Public company, state or community organisation
Investment company	Investment Companies Act	500,000	2,000,000 − 3,500,000	Public company or limited liability company
Co-operative banks	Law on Co-operatives	not specified	6,000,000[4]	Co-operative company

[1] These funding requirements are based on the Supervisory Agency's present practice in conjunction with para 32 (1) KWG
[2] State or community organisation
[3] Reduced to DM3,000,000 if no deposits are taken
[4] When operating as a universal bank, and deposit taking

APPENDIX II

Balance sheet

(Public company and
limited liability company)

Assets	(DM)	(DM)	(DM)
Cash in hand			xxx
Balance with the German Federal Bank			xxx
Balance on post office account			xxx
Cheques, promissory notes due, interest and dividend warrants, and documents for collection			xxx
Bills of exchange of which			
(a) discountable with the Federal Bank	xxx		
(b) financing bills	xxx		
Receivable from banks			
(a) due on demand		xxx	
(b) with a fixed term or repayment notice of			
(ba) less than three months		xxx	
(bb) at least three months, but less than four years		xxx	
(bc) four years or more		xxx	xxx
Treasury bills and interest-free treasury bonds			
(a) federal and state		xxx	
(b) other		xxx	xxx
Loans and promissory notes			
(a) with a fixed term of up to four years			
(aa) federal and state	xxx		
(ab) banks	xxx		
(ac) other	xxx	xxx	
of which: refinanceable with the German Federal Bank	xxx		
(b) with a fixed term of more than four years			
(ba) federal and state	xxx		
(bb) banks	xxx		
(bc) other	xxx	xxx	xxx
of which: refinanceable with the German Federal Bank	xxx		
Other securities			
(a) marketable stocks and shares		xxx	
(b) other securities		xxx	xxx
of which: exceeding 10% of the share capital of a company or of a mining trade union without shares	xxx		
Customer advances with a fixed term or repayment notice of			
(a) less than four years		xxx	
(b) four years or more		xxx	xxx
of which:			
(ba) secured	xxx		
(bb) municipal loans	xxx		
Clearing and reimbursement balances with public bodies			xxx
Clearing accounts (only trustee transactions)			xxx
Shareholdings			xxx
of which: in banks	xxx		
Land and buildings			xxx
Fixtures and fittings			xxx
Outstanding capital contributions (share capital)			xxx
Own shares (business interests)			
Nominal values:	xxx		xxx
Shares in a controlling or holding company			
Nominal value:	xxx		xxx
Own promissory notes			
Nominal value:	xxx		xxx
Other assets			xxx
Prepayments			xxx
Retained earnings deficit			xxx
Total assets			xxx

	(DM)
Included in assets and in recourse receivables arising from recorded liabilities are:	
(a) Receivables from associations	xxx
(b) Receivables from advances under para 15 subsection 1 No. 1, 3 to para 6 subsection 2 KWG, so far as not included under (a)	xxx

Liabilities	(DM)	(DM)	(DM)
Payables to banks			
(a) due on demand		xxx	
(b) with a fixed term or repayment notice of			
(ba) less than three months	xxx		
(bb) at least three months, but less than four years	xxx		
(bc) four years or more	xxx	xxx	
of which: due within four years	xxx		
(c) third party credit lines used by customers		xxx	xxx
Banking liabilities to others			
(a) due on demand		xxx	
(b) with a fixed term or repayment notice of			
(ba) less than three months	xxx		
(bb) at least three months, but less than four years	xxx		
(bc) four years or more	xxx	xxx	
of which: due within four years	xxx		
(c) savings accounts			
(ca) with a statutory repayment notice	xxx		
(cb) other	xxx	xxx	xxx
Promissory notes with a fixed term of			
(a) up to four years		xxx	
(b) more than four years		xxx	xxx
of which: due within four years	xxx		
Own acceptances and bills of exchange in circulation			xxx
Clearing accounts (only trustee transactions)			xxx
Provisions			
(a) pension provisions		xxx	
(b) other provisions		xxx	xxx
Allowances			
(a) specific allowances[1]		xxx	
(b) compulsory general allowances		xxx	xxx
Other liabilities			xxx
Accruals			xxx
Special reserves			xxx
Share capital			xxx
General reserves			
(a) statutory		xxx	
(b) other		xxx	xxx
Retained earnings			xxx
Total liabilities			xxx
Own drafts in circulation			xxx
of which: charged to borrowers	xxx		
Liabilities from endorsement of discounted bills			xxx
Liabilities from guarantees, bills and cheques guaranteed, and performance warranties			xxx
Unrecorded liabilities from the possible repurchase of securities			xxx
Liability from the granting of securities for third party liabilities			xxx
Savings bonuses in accordance with the savings bonus law			xxx
Included in liabilities are payables to associates (including the liabilities under 14 to 18)			xxx

[1] Accumulated depreciation on fixed assets, or specific allowances against other non-current assets may be disclosed here, or may be set off against the value of the asset

Profit and loss account

(Public company and limited liability company bank)

		(DM)	(DM)	(DM)
1	Interest and similar income from banking and money markets		xxx	
2	Current income from			
	(a) fixed interest securities and book debts	xxx		
	(b) other securities	xxx		
	(c) shareholdings	xxx	xxx	
3	Commission and other income from banking services		xxx	
4	Other income, including income from the release of banking provisions		xxx	xxx
5	Interest and similar expense		xxx	
6	Commissions and similar charges for banking services		xxx	
7	Depreciation and allowances on receivables and securities, and additions to banking provisions		xxx	xxx
				xxx
8	Income from profit sharing, profit transfer and partial transfer agreements		xxx	
9	Income from the release of provisions not included under 4		xxx	
10	Income from the release of special reserves		xxx	
11	Income by way of loss transferred		xxx	xxx
				xxx

		(DM)	(DM)	(DM)
12	Wages and salaries		xxx	
13	Social insurance		xxx	
14	Pension contributions		xxx	
15	Banking expenses		xxx	
16	Depreciation and amortisation of land and buildings, fixtures and fittings		xxx	
17	Depreciation and allowances against shareholdings		xxx	
18	Taxes			
	(a) income and property	xxx		
	(b) other	xxx	xxx	
19	Expenditure through loss transfer		xxx	
20	Addition to special reserves		xxx	
21	Other expenditure		xxx	
22	Profits transferred under profit sharing, profit transfer or partial transfer agreements		xxx	xxx
23	Profit (loss) for the year			xxx
24	Retained earnings (deficit) brought forward			xxx
25	Releases from general reserves			
	(a) statutory		xxx	
	(b) other		xxx	xxx
				xxx
26	Additions to general reserves			
	(a) statutory		xxx	
	(b) other		xxx	xxx
27	Retained earnings (deficit) carried forward			xxx

CHAPTER 7

ITALY

RALPH CADOW and GIACOMO BUGNA

1 GENERAL INFORMATION

1.1 Organisations covered by banking regulations

Banking in Italy can trace its origins back to the Renaissance although many banks were founded after Italy became a unified country in 1870.

Today there are over 1,000 banks operating in the country with over 12,000 branches.

The industry is divided into a number of types of institutions all of which are regulated by the Bank of Italy, the Interministry Committee for Economic Planning, the Treasury Ministry and the Interministry Committee for Credit and Savings.

1.2 Summary of major types of bank

(a) Banks of national interest

These banks are organised as corporations and are owned by a government holding company. There are only three such banks, all of which ranked among the top five Italian banks in terms of deposits. These banks all offer full banking services and are allowed to operate in the same manner as ordinary banks.

(b) Public banking institutions

Such banks are not organised as corporations but as entities established by Act of Parliament. The Treasury Minister appoints the top executives of each bank after consulting the Interministry Committee for Credit and Savings, local governmental bodies, and the managing committee of the respective banks. There are only six such banks, five of which ranked among the top ten Italian banks in terms of deposits. These banks all offer full banking services and operate in the same manner as ordinary banks; however, taken as a group these banks tend to have more standardised bank operations than ordinary banks.

(c) Ordinary banks

Ordinary banks can either be organised as corporations, in which all the shareholders have limited responsibility, or as corporations with two classes of shareholders, one of which has limited responsibility and the other which has unlimited responsibility. As a group, ordinary banks are only second to savings banks in the number of banking units in the country.

These banks range in size from small local banks to large banks which cover most of the country. Ordinary banks offer all the banking services that banks in other countries offer with the exception of long-term credit. Unless there is a special approval by the central bank or a special law, these banks cannot lend on repayment terms which exceed 18 months; however, these banks are permitted to invest in banks which are chartered as medium-term or long-term lending institutions. Direct leasing activities by banks are not permitted by the Bank of Italy; however, leasing subsidiaries are permitted subject to Bank of Italy approval.

(d) Community banks

Community banks are organised as co-operatives, the members of which have limited responsibility; for the most part, they are small- to medium-size banks with operations restricted to specific geographic areas. There are a few which have been authorised and do operate throughout the country. These banks offer full banking services and are allowed to operate in the same manner as ordinary banks.

(e) Savings banks

Savings banks are principally organised as foundations or corporations and their charter and the appointment of chief executive officers must be approved by the Treasury Minister. These banks can take medium- and long-term deposits and make medium- and long-term loans in accordance with their charter, as well as operate in the same manner as ordinary banks. Savings banks as a group have the largest number of banking units and have approximately one third of the total deposits in the banking system.

(f) Rural and artisan banks

These banks are organised as co-operatives, with members having limited or unlimited responsibility as defined by the co-operative's charter. Such banks are limited in the extension of credit to entities or individuals who are not members of the co-operative. Rural and artisan banks' activities are restricted to relatively small geographical areas with a principal market of farming and artisan communities. As a group, rural and artisan banks have formed an association to manage liquidity better and for technical and financial assistance.

(g) Foreign banks

Foreign banks present in Italy are generally branches of foreign corporations, whose capitalisation must be approved by the central bank. Generally, these banks obtain their funds in the inter-bank market and their retail banking activities are normally voluntarily restricted. A significant part of these banks' lending activities is in foreign currencies.

The central bank restricts lending to Italian companies to the region in which the branch is located; however, loans to foreign corporations have no geographic restrictions.

(h) Medium- and long-term lending institutions

These banks are principally organised in the same manner as their shareholders, which are mostly other types of banks which are not permitted to operate in the medium- and long-term lending market. Their funding comes mainly from the issuance of medium- and long-term bonds and depositors in the form of certificates of deposit.

The principal types of lending that these institutions engage in are industrial credit, public works, agriculture and construction.

The above summarises the main types of bank in Italy. Other types do exist but have not been discussed because they are not a significant force in the industry or because of similarity to the types of bank already discussed.

1.3   Supervisory authorities

The principal supervisory authorities in the banking industry whose authority rests in the Italian Banking Laws are the Interministry Committee for Economic Planning, the Interministry Committee for Credit and Savings, the Treasury Ministry and the Bank of Italy.

1.4   Status of supervisory authorities

The Interministry Committee for Economic Planning is the body which sets the country's economic policies and assigns the responsibility of carrying out these policies, as they relate to the banking system, to the Interministry Committee for Credit and Savings.

The Interministry Committee for Credit and Savings, which is chaired by the Treasury Minister, is responsible for the control and safeguarding of deposits in the banking system, the control and supervision of the extension of credit within the banking system and the regulations of the banking system's transactions in foreign currencies.

The Treasury Minister is the final authority in determining the monetary policy of the country as well as the appointment of chief executive officers of certain types of bank, approval of charters and modification of charters of certain banking institutions, overseeing of the control activities of the Bank of Italy, determination of the official central bank discount rate, regulation of savings deposits made to the Italian Postal System and management of the daily affairs of the Italian Treasury.

The Bank of Italy executes the directives of the Interministry Committee for Credit and Savings and controls banking institutions to ascertain compliance with such directives. Furthermore, the Bank of Italy can influence the entire banking system because it has the most complete information available on the operations and trends within the banking system. The Bank of Italy also has audit authority to ensure compliance with banking regulations. The Bank of Italy has approval authority for the formation of new banking institutions or the opening of new branches or banking units.

The Bank of Italy along with the Italian Exchange Control Office, which is legally autonomous but organisationally dependent on the Bank of Italy, function as the country's central bank. As such these combined entities serve as the bankers' bank, serve as the Treasury Ministry's bank, manage the foreign currency reserves of the country, and print and circularise bank notes and mint coins.

Apart from banking services to the government and to banks within the banking system, the principal duties of the Bank of Italy are to regulate the money and credit supply, to protect the lira, and to supervise the banking system.

Recently the stated government objective for monetary policy has been to reduce the rate of inflation and regulate the trade deficit within acceptable limits. The Bank of Italy has been given certain powers in order to achieve these objectives. In order to influence the liquidity and the interest rate structure of the economy, the Bank of Italy uses the following techniques:

(i)   Statutory reserves
   Originally a form of deposit protection, these are now a means of monetary control; to this end the banks (with the exception of rural banks) are required to deposit a cash reserve equal to 25% of each month's rise in deposits (excluding deposits between banks) less any increase in capital funds. Statutory reserves bear interest at 5%.

(ii)   The official Bank of Italy discount rate, set by the Treasury Minister. The Bank of Italy lends to other banks at this rate.

(iii)   Last resort lending
   This consists of advances (on current account or fixed-term) guaranteed by securities, and the rediscounting of bills. The former are more often used. Current account advances are utilised by the banks for normal day-to-day liquidity requirements, up to a limit periodically reviewed by the Bank of Italy. Fixed-term advances are for exceptional short-term liquidity requirements and are available as a single payment and at a fixed maturity (eight, fifteen or twenty-two days). The Bank of Italy has discretionary powers in respect of refinancing (reflected, in the case of current account advances, by the limit it sets) which means that it has direct control over the credit it grants to the banks. Indirect control through interest rates is less important; the 'base rates' (official discount rate and the rate for fixed-term advances) are

adjusted according to the frequency with which the banks apply to the Bank of Italy for refinancing.

What is different in Italy, when compared to other countries, is the existence of certain tools of an administrative nature that directly influence the domestic total credit. These devices are commonly referred to as 'vincoli amministrativi' and are transmitted by directives from the Bank of Italy. The principal 'vincolo amministrativo' presently in force is the compulsory investment in bonds, types of which are defined by the Bank of Italy, equal to 5% of the increase in the deposits measured semi-annually.

Up to 1 July 1983, there was a limit placed upon the allowable growth of bank lending portfolios. This limit has now been abolished in order to have a less restricted market situation.

1.5 Laws and regulations governing banks

The powers given to the above principal supervisory authorities stem from the Banking Law of 1936, are wide ranging and can restrict banks and many of their operational functions, such as establishing interest rates on deposits and loans, setting commissions and fees for banking services, defining composition of assets and liabilities, restricting distribution or allocation of earnings, establishing lending limits with regard to the extension of credit to any one customer, directing of lending activities to a particular industry or geographical area, and setting liquidity and reserve requirements.

Banks as a group have organised trade associations, the principal one being the Italian Association of Bankers, which acts as a central agency for the banks to negotiate with the authorities on the interpretation of their regulations and directives and to help the banks in complying with them. It also functions as a lobby to support legislation favourable to the industry. Furthermore, certain types of bank have formed trade associations to promote their own special interests.

1.6 Application of general company law to banks
1.7 Sources of laws and regulations

As well as being required to comply with the directives of the banking industry regulatory bodies, banks must adhere to the Italian Civil Code and the Italian Fiscal Code, both of which are legislated requirements and which respectively represent general company law and tax law. The Civil Code principally deals with corporate organisation and responsibility, commercial law, accounting and reporting for statutory purposes. The Fiscal Code contains the taxation laws, both direct and indirect, which all companies must adhere to and which include certain provisions that apply principally to banks.

1.8 Ability of foreign banks to operate through branches and subsidiaries
1.9 Level of supervisory control for branches and subsidiaries of foreign banks

Foreign banks are allowed to operate through branches and subsidiaries upon approval from the central bank. Most foreign banks are organised as branches because the central bank approval process is less burdensome and time consuming and consequently less costly than that of a subsidiary. Supervisory control is for the most part the same for branches and subsidiaries.

1.10 Methods of incorporation

Before a bank can be set up as a separate corporation in Italy, the Interministry Committee for Credit and Savings must approve the application and fix the minimum capital for the new corporation, which can then be formed either through a private transaction or a public offering.

In either case the procedure laid down in the Civil Code should be followed.

1.11 Areas within the country subject to special laws

At present all areas of the country are subject to the same legislation in connection with banking operations. However, finance companies do not fall under the control of the Bank of Italy to the extent that banks do.

Finance companies are not subject to the same restrictions on the maximum amounts of loans that can be granted to individual borrowers nor do the overall limitations on the extension of credit apply. In addition, finance companies may carry out activities prohibited to banks, such as leasing, factoring, etc. Naturally, finance companies may not accept deposits from the public.

A finance company need not be entered in the official register of finance companies but, in such case, it may not participate in the Bank of Italy's periodic auctions of treasury bonds.

The establishment of a finance company by an Italian bank or the Italian branch of a foreign bank, or the acquisition of an investment in an existing finance company will require the authorisation of the Bank of Italy, which will examine matters such as the scope of activities, the appropriateness of the name, the appointment of bank management as directors, etc.

2 ACCOUNTING
2.1 Laws and regulations governing accounts
2.2 Application of general company law
2.3 Roles of legislature and supervisory authority
2.4 Extent to which requirements as to returns and accounts are prescribed by laws and regulations

Banks prepare their statutory accounts in accordance with the Civil Code which applies to all companies. The Civil Code lays down the general accounting policies to be adopted and the items to be included in the balance sheet. However, a separate decree prescribes the form and content of the profit and loss account.

The banking laws empower the Bank of Italy to make regulations prescribing the form and content of returns it requires for supervisory purposes. Other accounting regulations have been issued by Presidential or Ministerial decree.

2.5 Obligations to furnish accounts

2.5.1 Accounting periods and times of furnishing

2.5.2 Form of accounts to be furnished

2.5.3 Mandatory accounting dates

The statutory accounts consist of a balance sheet, profit and loss account – together with an appendix detailing foreign exchange and securities trading volumes, gains and losses, and directors' report, which among other matters must comment on the operating result of the bank.

A listing of the controlled and related companies must be included indicating the par value and the carrying value in the accounts. This listing should be accompanied by accounts of the controlled companies and key financial data of related companies.

The statutory accounts must be presented to the statutory auditors 30 days prior to the presentation of the accounts to the shareholders for approval.

A copy of the statutory accounts, inclusive of the board of directors' and statutory auditors' reports, must be made available at the bank's legal headquarters for inspection by the shareholders for 15 days prior to the shareholders' meeting.

The shareholders' meeting to approve the statutory accounts must be scheduled by the board of directors within four months of the year end. The supervisory authorities normally require all banks to close their accounts on 31 December and therefore approval of the accounts by the shareholders must be given by 30 April, unless the bank's charter specifies time requirements which in any case cannot exceed six months after the year end or 30 June.

A copy of the approved accounts, inclusive of the board of directors' and statutory auditors' reports and the minutes of the shareholders' meeting approving the accounts, must be deposited with the corporate registry office within 30 days of the shareholders' meeting approving the accounts. The accounts then become public information and copies can be obtained from the registry office on payment of a nominal fee.

The supervisory authorities also require the submission of returns and accounts. This information which is considered secret and confidential is protected by the bank secrecy laws. The information required is generally in a format prescribed by the regulatory authorities and the frequency of submission varies, depending on the type of information.

On an annual basis, banks are required to furnish to the regulatory authorities, in addition to the returns and accounts filed for control purposes, the statutory accounts and detailed schedules as shown in Appendix I.

2.6 Requirements as to accounts (a) prior to incorporation (b) prior to commencement of trading and (c) in order to continue trading

Prior to incorporation or trading no financial information is required, other than details of the share capital etc. of the new company being formed in accordance with the procedure mentioned in Section 1.10.

For a bank to continue trading it must comply with the statutory and regulatory reporting requirements as well as the banking laws and regulations.

2.7 Audit requirements

The accounts are audited by statutory auditors who are normally appointed at an annual shareholders' meeting, generally for a period of three years. The statutory auditors do not conduct an audit as it is known in the Anglo-Saxon context, but merely review accounts for compliance with the Italian Civil Code, the Italian Fiscal Code and the directives of the regulatory authorities. They may or may not review valuation criteria used by bank management in preparing the accounts and comment on such as they deem appropriate.

2.8 Acceptability to fiscal authorities of accounts submitted to supervisory authority

The statutory accounts or those submitted to the supervisory authorities are not accepted by the fiscal authorities, principally because the Fiscal Code has requirements which differ from those of the Civil Code or supervisory authorities. The bank is required to submit its statutory accounts with its tax declaration, which includes a reconciliation between statutory net income and taxable income.

2.9 Submission of accounts to any authority other than by requirement of law

None.

2.10 Application of laws and regulations to foreign banks operating through branches and subsidiaries

Foreign banks operating through subsidiaries or branches are required to comply with the same regulations as Italian banks, that is the Civil Code, Fiscal Code and banking laws.

2.11 Availability of accounts for public inspection

Italian banks, including branches of foreign banks, are required by law to prepare annual accounts which must be filed with the Bank of Italy. Furthermore, annual accounts prepared in accordance with the Italian Civil Code must be deposited annually with the local registry office. These accounts are available for public inspection.

All banks whose shares are quoted on one of the recognised Italian stock exchanges will be required to publish audited financial statements commencing with the year ending 31 December 1985. For the most part such banks presently publish unaudited financial statements.

3 FORMAT, STYLE AND CONTENTS OF ACCOUNTS

3.1 Extent to which format is laid down by statute, supervisory authority, generally accepted accounting practice or otherwise

3.2 Description of format

3.3 Extent to which contents are prescribed by statute, supervisory authority, generally accepted accounting practice or otherwise

3.4 Disclosure of specific items required other than those required by general law

3.5 Exemptions from disclosure allowed in respect of banking items

As mentioned in Section 2, accounts of banks are drawn up in accordance with the requirements of the Civil Code but modified by decree in respect of the profit and loss account.

The Civil Code prescribes the minimum headings which must be included in a balance sheet. However, there is a degree of flexibility and banks have expanded and adapted the layout to suit their circumstances. An example of a typical balance sheet is shown in Appendix II.

The format and content of the profit and loss account is, however, prescribed by decree and an example is shown in Appendix III.

It should be noted that the accounts of banks quoted on a stock exchange are expected to be drawn up in accordance with international accounting standards. The supervisory authority requires the balance sheet of a bank to be submitted to it in considerable detail and the form to be completed runs to 37 pages. Key items on this balance sheet are shown in Appendix IV. The profit and loss account to be submitted to them is also detailed but is not as long as the balance sheet; the layout is included in Appendix V.

3.6 Hidden reserves

Officially, banks are not allowed to maintain hidden reserves. The Civil Code, however, does require banks to observe the prudence concept and it is generally accepted that banks take advantage of this to create hidden reserves. Areas which lend themselves to the creation of these reserves are:
- Carrying value of equity investments.
- Loan loss reserve provisions.
- Reserves for taxes.
- Reserves for other banking risks.
- Reserves for market fluctuations in regard to foreign currencies and securities.

3.7 Requirements as to consolidated accounts

Consolidated accounts are not required and are not normally prepared. However, the accounts of directly controlled subsidiaries must be included as an appendix to the statutory accounts. These may be in summary form.

4 ACCOUNTING POLICIES

4.1 Responsibility for laying down accounting policies

The Civil Code sets out the general principles to be observed when preparing the financial statements of all companies including banks, and directors and the statutory auditors would have to explain and justify any departures from the Civil Code.

More detailed principles have been evolved by the banking industry to cater for their requirements and sometimes these follow the rules adopted by the tax authorities. It is implicit in the Civil Code that the general concepts of going concern basis, accruals convention, consistency and prudence are followed.

4.2 Particular accounting policies

4.2.1 Foreign exchange

Assets and liabilities in foreign currency are usually translated at year end rates.

Profits and losses on forward contracts open at the year end are not brought into the profit and loss account, mainly for tax reasons but the profits and losses on swap deals are normally accrued over the life of the contract.

4.2.2 Deferred tax

In Italy banks do not normally account for deferred taxes.

4.2.3 Specific and general provisions for bad and doubtful debts

Banks usually make three different provisions for doubtful loans:
(a) An ordinary provision as allowed by fiscal laws, which can never exceed 5% of loans made to customers.
Annual additions can be made to this reserve at the rate of 0.5% of loans made to customers, until the reserve equals 2% of loans made to customers.
Subsequent annual additions are restricted to 0.2% of loans made to customers, until the reserve reaches the maximum permitted.
(b) A supplementary reserve, for amounts over and above those permitted by fiscal laws to the extent determined necessary by bank management, to adequately provide for the bank's loan risk.
(c) A specified provision, to cover the obligatory accrual of interest income on non-performing loans. This provision is fully deductible for fiscal purposes.

4.2.4 Treatment of provisions in accounts

The provision for bad and doubtful debts is not deducted from the assets but is included on the liabilities side of the balance sheet.

Bad debts are not written off until the inability of the debtor to repay has been proved.

131

4.2.5 Premiums and discounts on investments (amortise, write off, etc.)

Discount and premiums arising on the purchase of new bond issues can be amortised each year, in accordance with the amortisation schedule of the bond issue, or over the period for which the bond is held in portfolio.

4.2.6 Offsets, i.e. to what extent can assets and liabilities be set off against each other (legally or in practice)

Provisions cannot be netted off in the accounts because offsets of this nature are specifically prohibited by the Civil Code. The Civil Code prohibits offsets between assets and liabilities and profit and loss accounts.

4.2.7 Goodwill

Goodwill can be recorded as an asset in the balance sheet only if a specific amount has been paid toward the same on acquisition of a firm and it must be booked at an amount not greater than the amount paid for it. Goodwill must be amortised over its economic life as determined by the directors on a prudent basis.

4.2.8 Consolidation

Consolidation of banks' financial statements is not required by law in Italy and it is not a common accounting practice (but see Section 3.7).

4.2.9 Revaluations of assets

Fixed assets (real estate, furniture, equipment, installations, etc.) are to be recorded at cost and can only be revalued when permitted by a special law, when the surplus is taken to a revaluation reserve.

4.2.10 Instalment finance and leasing including basis of recognition of income

Recognition of income on instalment financing is generally recognised on an accelerated basis, as opposed to a straight line basis. Instalment loans are recorded at full repayment value inclusive of interest and a liability is set up for unearned interest income. The unearned portion is then taken into income as payments come due.

4.2.11 Dealing assets

Dealing assets are not recognised as a separate category and the valuation of securities is to be determined by the directors, according to their prudent appraisal and taking into account fluctuations in market value during the last quarter of the financial year. The criteria followed in this evaluation are usually approved by the statutory auditors in their report to the shareholders.

4.2.12 Pensions

If pension plans exist, the liabilities for such must be actuarially determined and recorded, based on an actuarial report. The staff leaving indemnity fund must be calculated in accordance with the national labour contracts and laws.

4.2.13 Depreciation

Fixed assets are depreciated on the straight line basis and maximum rates are fixed by the tax authorities (see Appendix VI).

However, for fiscal purposes depreciation may be anticipated at the rate of 15% annually for three years, starting from the year of purchase or the year the asset was placed in service.

Generally, depreciation in the year of acquisition or the year the asset is placed in service is either calculated on one half-year basis or the actual number of months from the above-mentioned dates to the financial year end.

Depreciation is shown as a provision on the liabilities side and not deducted from the asset.

4.2.14 Other

Intangible assets

Intangible assets are to be recorded at cost. Such cost should be amortised each year by charges to income based on the estimated useful life of the asset. In case of loss value these should be written off when such loss of value becomes apparent.

Investments in subsidiaries

The investments in subsidiaries must be valued at an amount not greater than the net equity resulting from the most current balance sheet of the subsidiary.

Deferred charges

Deferred charges subject to approval of the statutory auditors can be amortised over a period not longer than five years. In case of loss of value these should be written off when such loss of value becomes apparent.

5 WINDOW DRESSING

Some window dressing is practised by Italian banks, mainly by taking in short-term deposits and making short-term loans. This is done to increase balance sheet totals which is the main indication of the size or ranking of banks in Italy. However, the Bank of Italy does endeavour to restrict this practice.

6 AMOUNTS REQUIRED TO BE MAINTAINED BY LAW OR OTHERWISE

The Bank of Italy establishes the capitalisation requirements for all banking entities on a case-by-case basis when the initial application is made for the formation of the banking entity. The Civil Code requires a minimum capitalisation of L200,000,000 for limited liability corporations. Banks not organised as corporations have minimum capitalisation requirements which are specified in the banking laws. These minima arc extremely low and Bank of Italy approval without capital significantly exceeding these minima is not likely. Indeed, in a recent case L6 billion was required. Increases in capital or changes in the entity's charter must also be approved by the Bank of Italy.

The banking laws require corporations to allocate at least 10% of the annual net income to a legal (ordinary) reserve, until such reserve equals 40% of capital. For banks not organised as corporations, the allocation of net income to the various reserves is either specified by the banking laws and/or the entities' charter. The legal (ordinary) reserves are not normally distributable. The allocation of net income to reserves not covered by law or charter must be approved by the board of directors, members and/or shareholders.

Banks are required to maintain a minimum deposit reserve and currently this is set at 15.75% of net non-bank deposits (certain deductions are allowed in calculating this figure). It is monitored by the Bank of Italy on a monthly basis and the deposit reserve has to be held at the Bank of Italy in the form of interest-earning deposits at the rate of 5 % p.a.

In the case of savings banks the deposit reserve is held at the Credit Institute of the Savings Banks. Rural and artisan banks are exempt from this requirement, as are certain other categories of bank.

7 KEY RATIOS

In addition to the minimum capital, legal reserve and deposit reserve requirements which were described in Section 6, all banks, with the exception of rural and artisan banks and medium- and long-term credit institutions, are required to follow certain prudential ratios. These ratios are monitored by the Bank of Italy from the various statistical returns submitted.

The principal prudential ratios are:

(i)   Own funds/liabilities ratio
      While the Bank of Italy is empowered to fix the ratios between own funds and liabilities, in practice it monitors the ratios between own funds and deposits from non-banks and funds managed by the bank. Own funds include paid-up share capital, ordinary and extraordinary reserve risks and losses fund, and fixed asset revaluation fund.

(ii) Own funds/fixed assets ratio
      Banks are not allowed to own land and property (other than for bank use) or shares in non-banks except as a consequence of a default of a borrower. The total of fixed assets and shares and participations in other banks should not exceed 100%.

(iii) Own funds/individual large loans ratio
      Without permission from the Bank of Italy a bank cannot lend more than 20% of its own funds to a single borrower.
      However, this can be increased up to 100% of own funds if the deposit/large loan ratio is not exceeded (see below). In both cases a group is considered as a single borrower.
      A branch of a foreign bank can lend up to 60% of the own funds of the branch to a single customer,

provided that the parent bank has given an undertaking to be liable in full for the liabilities of the branch.

(iv) Deposits/total large loan ratio
      The total of large loans must not exceed a percentage of the total deposits from non-banks and funds from third parties. This percentage is on a sliding scale of 25% to 40% depending upon the own funds/liabilities ratio mentioned in (i) above.

(v)   Total loan/deposits ratio
      Total loans must not exceed a percentage of total deposits without permission from the Bank of Italy.

8 ACCOUNTING RETURNS OTHER THAN ACCOUNTS

8.1 By whom required

8.2 Nature of requirements

Besides requiring annual accounts, the supervisory authorities require a significant amount of additional information to be furnished in a standard format, for the purpose of assisting the supervisory authorities in monitoring the activities of the banks individually and the entire banking system. A brief description of the requirements is as follows:

Form number	Description	Frequency of submission
Magnetic tape	Standard analytical accounts (balance sheet only)	Monthly
Magnetic tape	Standard analytical accounts (income statement only)	Quarterly
81 VIG	General balance sheet information on domestic assets and liabilities	Monthly
83 VIG	Purchase of shares and securities on international markets	Quarterly
84 VIG	Purchase of equity investments	Upon purchase
85 VIG	Changes in equity investments previously reported on 84 VIG	Upon occurrence
86 VIG	Detail balance sheet broken down into lire and foreign currency and resident and non-resident	Monthly
87 VIG	Banking relationship with each credit institution	Monthly
88 VIG	Details of correspondent bank balances (due from accounts)	Monthly
89 VIG	Details of correspondent bank balances (due to accounts)	Monthly
90 VIG	Deposit and loan information in lire and foreign currencies for resident customers broken down by business activity	Quarterly
91 VIG	Details of securities held for investment purposes	Annually

Form number	Description	Frequency of submission
92 VIG	General balance sheet information on a country-by-country basis	Monthly
93 VIG	General balance sheet information on foreign assets and liabilities	Monthly
94 VIG	Deposit and loan information in lire and foreign currency by banking unit for resident clients	Annually
95 VIG	Savings accounts and demand accounts in an overdraft position with resident customers	Annually
109 VIG	Determination of reserve requirements	Monthly
112 VIG	Profit and loss account	Annually
113 VIG	Analytical profit and loss account	Quarterly
122 VIG	Reporting of borrowers who are not in compliance with lending arrangements or supervisory authority requirements	Upon occurrence
365/6A VIG	Agricultural lending by province	Quarterly

The above requirements are either eliminated or the frequency of submission lengthened for very small banks. Furthermore, depending on the size or type of bank there are other reporting requirements instead of or in addition to the above. Specifically, there are different forms in varying degrees for savings banks, rural and artisan banks, medium- and long-term lending institutions and special medium-term lending institutions.

9 TAXATION

9.1 General method of taxation

Banks are taxed in much the same manner as commercial companies as specified in the Italian Fiscal Code. There are principally two types of income tax, a corporate income tax (IRPEG) and local trade taxes (ILOR). The corporate income tax is presently 36% of taxable income and the local taxes are 16.2% of taxable income. Local income taxes are deductible from taxable income for corporate tax purposes. The effective combined rate of corporation and local taxes is therefore 46.4%.

If income produced abroad is included in taxable income, taxes paid upon such income should be recognised as credits against corporate income tax, in the same manner that the foreign taxing country grants a tax credit for income of the same nature earned in Italy. The amount of the allowed tax credit, however, shall not exceed that part of the Italian tax which is proportional to the ratio between foreign source income and total income. If the foreign country does not grant a tax credit, a credit shall be allowed not exceeding 90% of the proportion previously discussed with respect to business income and 50% of the same proportion with respect to other income.

There is a loss carry forward provision whereby losses for corporate income tax purposes may be carried forward to the five tax periods subsequent to the tax period in which a loss is declared. There are no loss carry back provisions.

Value added taxes on goods and services purchased by banks are additional expenses because the banks cannot recover these under current legislation.

There are also a number of taxes or duties on various bank transactions which the banks usually charge customers and pay to the government. The bank principally acts as a collection agency and usually does not bear such costs.

9.2 Accounts as basis for taxation
9.3 Adjustments permitted or required

Because of the complexities in the taxation process in Italy, the statutory accounts of banks prepared in accordance with the Italian Civil Code will, more often than not, be significantly different from those presented for tax purposes. Numerous adjustments are made, most of which are required and some of which are permitted, to arrive at taxable income from book income.

Because banks are required to withhold 21.6% of interest paid on deposits, including inter-bank deposits, most banks at the end of the year find themselves in an overpayment position. This is difficult to manage because the withholding is mandatory and because correspondent relationships cannot easily be maintained in a manner to achieve tax objectives. The problem is further aggravated by the fact that it can normally take up to five years or longer to obtain a refund. Banks are entitled to interest at the legal rate of 6%, compounded semi-annually on such overpayments, which is significantly lower than the prime rate.

The statute of limitations for tax audit purposes runs for five years from the date the tax return is filed. All banks are required by the central bank to close their accounts as of 31 December. Banks are required to file their tax returns within 30 days after the approval of the statutory accounts, no later than 31 May.

9.4 Effect of tax considerations on presentation of accounts

Certain items have to be put through the books before they can be claimed as a deduction, e.g. provision for bad and doubtful debts. Apart from this, tax considerations have little effect on the way accounts are presented.

10 INTERPRETATION OF ACCOUNTS

10.1 Adequacy of information as to contents and disclosure

Bank accounts are generally quite detailed and give a comprehensive presentation of the affairs of the bank. Footnote disclosure, especially in terms of accounting

policies, is not sufficiently developed to give a clear understanding of the underlying amounts included in the balance sheet and the profit and loss account. Attachments to the accounts such as:
 — supplementary information on securities trading activities,
 — supplementary information on foreign exchange trading activities,
 — summarised accounts of controlled companies and entities, and
 — key operating data of related companies
give the reader additional information concerning the operations of the bank and the underlying value of some of the assets of the bank.

10.2 Audit and reliability of information

The accounts are subject to audit by the statutory auditors who do not perform what is considered an audit by Anglo-Saxon standards. The statutory auditors primarily review the accounts and records of the bank to ascertain compliance with legal requirements (Civil Code, banking laws and Fiscal Code) and comment on such in their report. They may or may not comment on valuation judgements made by management in the preparation of accounts, especially in areas where regulations permit valuation judgements.

10.3 Comparability between different banks on the basis of published accounts or publicly available returns

Comparisons can be made between different banks on the basis of published accounts. However, because of the potential for significant differences in accounting policies and the significant amount of subjective valuation judgement permitted to management, it is difficult to make conclusive comparisons. In general, bank managers tend to be conservative but the degree of conservatism varies. This is another element which complicates the comparison process, as would ownership influence and the type of bank activity. For example, a government-owned bank may be subject to political influence, a private bank to private investor influence and a foreign bank to parent company influence and require- ments. Then again, a medium-term lending institution's operations are obviously different from those of an ordinary bank or a foreign bank and this will also affect comparability. Therefore, without a good knowledge of

the banking industry and banking practices, meaningful comparisons are difficult to make.

11 OTHER RELEVANT INFORMATION

11.1 Bank secrecy laws

By law, all data and information concerning banking transactions which are subject to the control of the central bank (Bank of Italy) are covered by the bank secrecy laws and as a result banks are required to maintain the confidentiality of such information. The secrecy law also covers government agencies or representatives such as the tax authorities.

Only for court cases, cases of tax evasion or other special reasons are banks required to release client information if requested by a magistrate or a tax officer. Visits to the bank's premises to inspect or examine documents are restricted to magistrates only.

To fight tax evasion, parliament is presently considering new legislation which would allow police officers and tax auditors to visit and examine documentation of banking transactions.

11.2 Foreign exchange control office

The Foreign Exchange Control Office regulates foreign currency transactions which are effected through banks authorised for this purpose.

In general, authorised banks are permitted to conduct spot transactions in any currency, whereas forward transactions are restricted to major convertible currencies and externally convertible currencies as follows:
 — Up to 360 days for Italian residents.
 — Up to 360 days with non-resident banks.
 — Up to 180 days with non-resident customers other than banks.
 Forward cover is allowed as follows:
 — Freely for commercial transactions.
 — Only with approval for financial transactions.

All settlements of foreign currency transactions must be made in convertible currencies or in lira on foreign accounts, unless specific authorisation is obtained.

The Foreign Exchange Control Office also has supervisory authority over:
 — Loans between residents and non-residents.
 — Foreign trade financing.
 — Inward and outward movements of capital of residents.

APPENDIX I

Accounts and schedules to be filled with supervisory authorities on an annual basis

A copy of the statutory accounts inclusive of the board of directors' and statutory auditors' reports and the minutes of the shareholders' meeting approving the accounts.

A detailed listing of bank-owned securities, indicating par value and carrying value included in the accounts.

A detailed listing of doubtful loans.

A detailed description of the components of other assets and other liabilities.

A detailed listing of bank buildings with the carrying value included in the accounts and the approximate current value, distinguishing between buildings used for banking and non-banking purposes and the relevant authorisation for non-banking premises.

A detailed listing of borrowers who are not in compliance with the approved lending arrangements and the relative authorisation for non-compliance.

A detailed listing of borrowers who have exceeded the authorised lending limits, with the relative authorisation of the regulatory authorities.

Reconciliation between the statutory accounts and the accounts submitted in the prescribed format of the regulatory authorities.

Detailed analysis of profit and loss account and the destination of net income.

Detailed analysis of the bank's income tax position.

Detailed analysis and movements in staff leaving indemnity.

The names of the board members, statutory auditors, chief executive officers, with an indication of appointments or positions held with other companies and the accounts each has with the bank, inclusive of a declaration that restrictions of the regulatory authorities on loans to board members and statutory auditors have been complied with.

APPENDIX II

Balance sheet: typical format for statutory purposes

Assets				Liabilities			
Cash and cash items		xxx		Due to customers:			
Due from the Bank of Italy		xxx		Current accounts		xxx	
Due from banks:				Savings accounts		xxx	xxx
− Domestic	xxx						
− Foreign	xxx	xxx		Due to banks:			
				Domestic correspondent bank accounts		xxx	
Treasury bills	xxx			Foreign correspondent bank accounts		xxx	xxx
Treasury bonds, other government or							
government guaranteed bonds	xxx			Due to controlled companies and entities		xxx	
Ordinary bonds	xxx			Due to related companies and entities		xxx	xxx
Mortgage bonds	xxx						
Treasury bonds	xxx			Outstanding cashiers cheques			xxx
Other shares	xxx	xxx					xxx
Equity investments		xxx		Guaranteed advances from the Bank of Italy			xxx
Loans to customers:				Bills of exchange presented for collection			xxx
Discounted bills of exchange	xxx			Other creditors			xxx
Overdrafts and advances	xxx			Allowance for depreciation:			
Advances on marketable securities	xxx			Real estate		xxx	
Loans with mortgage guarantees and other				Furniture		xxx	
advances	xxx	xxx		Equipment		xxx	
				Bank premises		xxx	xxx
Loans to controlled companies and entities	xxx						
Loans to related companies and entities	xxx	xxx		Reserve for taxes			xxx
				Allowance for staff severance indemnity			xxx
				Reserve for risks			xxx
Bills of exchange for collection		xxx		Accrued liabilities			xxx
INA − Staff severance indemnity fund		xxx		Unearned discount			xxx
Other debtors		xxx		Reserves for possible loan losses:			
Real estate	xxx			Ordinary reserve		xxx	
Furniture	xxx			Reserve for interest on past due loans		xxx	
Equipment	xxx			Additional reserve		xxx	xxx
Bank premises	xxx						
Deferred costs	xxx	xxx		Total liabilities			xxx
Accrued interest income	xxx			Equity capital			
Prepaid expenses	xxx	xxx		Capital stock (xxx shares, par value Lxxx)		xxx	
				Legal reserve		xxx	
Total assets		xxx		Extraordinary reserve		xxx	
				Taxed reserve		xxx	
Bank's commitments				Monetary revaluations reserve		xxx	
Customers' liability for acceptances	xxx			Reserve for purchase of treasury stock		xxx	
Customers' liability for guarantees and				Profits invested in treasury stock		xxx	
counter guarantees	xxx			Taxed reserve for reinvestment of profit on			
Customers' liability for commercial letters				sales of real estate and other properties		xxx	
of credit	xxx					xxx	
Commitment for deferred payment on				Net profit for the year			xxx
equity investments	xxx						
Customers' liability for stock repurchase				Total liabilities and capital account			xxx
agreements	xxx						
Stock to be received	xxx			Contingent liabilities per contra			
Customers' liability for forward FX				Acceptances		xxx	
contracts	xxx			Guarantees and counter guarantees		xxx	
Foreign currency to be received	xxx			Commercial letters of credit		xxx	
Customers' liability for other commitments				Equity investments to be remitted		xxx	
and risks	xxx	xxx		Stock repurchase agreements		xxx	
				Stock to be delivered		xxx	
Contra accounts				Forward FX contracts		xxx	
Assets of third parties held in deposit:				Foreign currency to be delivered		xxx	
Directors' statutory bonds	xxx			Other commitments and risks		xxx	xxx
Real guarantees	xxx						
Safekeeping	xxx			Contra accounts			
Securities on deposit with third parties	xxx	xxx		Assets of third parties:			
				Directors' statutory bonds		xxx	
				Real guarantees		xxx	
				Safekeeping		xxx	
				Securities on deposit with third parties		xxx	xxx
Grand total		xxx		Grand Total			xxx

APPENDIX III

Format of profit and loss account for statutory purposes

Income

1 Interest from customers

    Ordinary customers
Discounts	xxx	
Overdrafts and advances	xxx	
Stock repurchase agreements	xxx	
Loans and other transactions	xxx	
	xxx	

    Controlled companies and entities
Discounts	xxx	
Overdrafts and advances	xxx	
Stock repurchase agreements	xxx	
Loans and other transactions	xxx	
	xxx	

    Related companies and entities
Discounts	xxx	
Overdrafts and advances	xxx	
Stock repurchase agreements	xxx	
Loans and other transactions	xxx	
	xxx	xxx

2 Interest from banking institutions

Bank of Italy	xxx	

    Controlled banking institutions
Deposits and current accounts	xxx	
Stock repurchase agreements	xxx	
Other transactions	xxx	
	xxx	

    Other banking institutions
Deposits and current accounts	xxx	
Stock repurchase agreements	xxx	
Other transactions	xxx	
	xxx	xxx

3 Interest from current accounts with the Treasury, Deposit and Loan Bank and Postal Service   xxx

4 Interest from the Italian Exchange Control Office   xxx

5 Interest from bonds and certificates of deposit   xxx

6 Interest, premiums, dividends and income on
Fixed income securities	xxx	
Investments not represented by securities of controlled companies or entities	xxx	
Related companies or entities	xxx	
Other entities	xxx	
Other securities	xxx	xxx

7 Profits from securities transactions (as determined in detailed statement attached)   xxx

8 Profits from foreign currency transactions (as determined in detailed statement attached)   xxx

9 Commissions, fees and other income from
Loans	xxx	
Deposits and overdrafts	xxx	
Guarantees issued	xxx	
Bills collection	xxx	
Securities transactions	xxx	
Other banking services	xxx	xxx

10 Other income
Rental income	xxx	
Tax collection fees	xxx	
Other banking services	xxx	xxx

11 Gains on disposal of
Land or buildings	xxx	
Other fixed assets	xxx	xxx

12 Non-operating income, to be detailed   xxx

13 Utilisation of reserves
Reserve for possible loan losses	xxx
Reserve for taxes	xxx
Reserve for staff severance indemnity	xxx
Other, to be detailed	xxx

14 Prior period adjustments   xxx

    Total revenues   xxx

15 Net loss   xxx

    Total   xxx

Expenses

1 Interest to customers

    Ordinary customers
on deposits and current accounts	xxx	
on stock repurchase agreements	xxx	
on other transactions	xxx	
	xxx	

    Controlled companies and entities
on deposits and current accounts	xxx	
on stock repurchase agreements	xxx	
on other transactions	xxx	
	xxx	

    Related companies and entities
on deposits	xxx	
on stock repurchase agreements	xxx	
on other transactions	xxx	
	xxx	xxx

Expenses

2 Interest to banking institutions

Bank of Italy	xxx	
Controlled banking institutions		
on deposits and current accounts	xxx	
on stock repurchase agreements	xxx	
on other transactions	xxx	
	xxx	
Related banking institutions		
on deposits and current accounts	xxx	
on stock repurchase agreements	xxx	
on other transactions	xxx	
	xxx	
Other banking institutions		
on deposits and current accounts	xxx	
on stock repurchase agreements	xxx	
on other transactions	xxx	
	xxx	xxx

3 Interest to the Italian Exchange Control Office — xxx

4 Interest on bonds and certificates of deposit — xxx

5 Interest on obligations and bonds — xxx

6 Amortisation of the costs of issuing obligations — xxx

7 Losses from securities transactions (as determined in detailed statement attached) — xxx

8 Losses from foreign currency transactions (as determined in detailed statement attached) — xxx

9 Personnel costs:

(a) Banking activities:

salaries and social contributions	xxx	
payment of staff severance indemnity	xxx	
accrual for staff severance indemnity	xxx	
accrual for staff pension	xxx	
	xxx	

(b) Tax collection activities:

salaries and social contributions	xxx	
payment of staff severance indemnity	xxx	
accrual for staff severance indemnity	xxx	
accrual for staff pension	xxx	
	xxx	xxx

10 Taxes:

Current year	xxx	
Prior year	xxx	xxx

11 Commissions, fees and other expenses on:

Loans	xxx	
Guarantees received	xxx	
Bills collection	xxx	
Securities transactions	xxx	
Other banking services	xxx	xxx

12 Other expenses:

(a) Banking activities:

Professional services and fees	xxx	
Insurance	xxx	
Advertising	xxx	
Charitable contributions	xxx	
Equipment rental	xxx	
Other	xxx	
	xxx	

(b) Tax collection activities:

Equipment rental	xxx	
Office rental	xxx	
Other	xxx	
	xxx	xxx

13 Loan losses:

Ordinary customers	xxx	
Controlled companies and entities	xxx	
Related companies and entities	xxx	xxx

14 Losses on the disposal of:

Land or buildings	xxx	
Other fixed assets	xxx	xxx

15 Non-operating losses or expenses, to be detailed — xxx

16 Depreciation expenses:

Buildings	xxx	
Banking machinery and equipment	xxx	
Tax collection machinery and equipment	xxx	
Other	xxx	xxx

17 Accruals:

Reserve for possible loan losses	xxx	
Reserve for taxes	xxx	
	xxx	
Other – to be detailed	xxx	xxx

18 Prior period adjustments — xxx

Total expenses — xxx

19 Net profit — xxx

Total — xxx

Profit (losses) from securities transactions and foreign exchange transactions

Cost of securities transactions

(a) Beginning balances in portfolio:

Shares
Quoted on stock exchange	xxx
Not quoted	xxx

Fixed income securities
Quoted on stock exchange	xxx
Not quoted	xxx
Other securities	xxx
Investments not in the form of securities	xxx
Total (a)	xxx

(b) Purchases of securities:

Shares quoted on stock exchange
Controlled companies	xxx
Related companies	xxx
Other companies	xxx

Shares not quoted
Controlled companies	xxx
Related companies	xxx
Other companies	xxx

Fixed income securities quoted on stock exchange
Controlled companies and entities	xxx
Related companies and entities	xxx
Other issuers	xxx

Fixed income securities not quoted
Controlled companies and entities	xxx
Related companies and entities	xxx
Other issuers	xxx
Other securities	xxx
Investments not in the form of securities	xxx
Total (b)	xxx

(c) Total costs of security transactions (a+b) — xxx

Revenues from securities transactions

(a) Sale of securities:

Shares quoted on stock exchange
Controlled companies	xxx
Related companies	xxx
Other companies	xxx

Shares not quoted
Controlled companies	xxx
Related companies	xxx
Other companies	xxx

Fixed income securities quoted on stock exchange
Controlled companies and entities	xxx
Related companies and entities	xxx
Other issuers	xxx

Fixed income securities not quoted
Controlled companies and entities	xxx
Related companies and entities	xxx
Other issuers	xxx
Other securities	xxx
Investments not in the form of securities	xxx
Total (a)	xxx

(b) Ending balances in portfolio:

Shares
Quoted on stock exchange	xxx
Not quoted	xxx

Fixed income securities
Quoted on stock exchange	xxx
Not quoted	xxx
Other securities	xxx
Investments not in the form of securities	xxx
Total (b)	xxx

(c) Total revenues from securities transactions (a+b) — xxx

(d) Total costs of securities per above — xxx

(e) Net income from securities transactions (c−d) — xxx

Cost of foreign exchange transactions

(a) Beginning foreign currency position — xxx

(b) Purchases of foreign currencies — xxx

(c) Total costs (a+b) — xxx

Revenues from foreign currency transactions

(a) Sales of foreign currencies — xxx

(b) Ending foreign currency position — xxx

(c) Total revenues (a+b) — xxx

(d) Total costs of foreign currencies per above — xxx

(e) Net income from foreign currency transactions (c−d) — xxx

APPENDIX IV

Balance sheet submitted to supervisory authorities
Key headings

Assets

1	Cash
2	Cash items
3	Deposits with the Treasury, Postal and Deposit and Loan Agencies
4	Deposits with banking institutions
5	Due from correspondent banks
6	Due from Italian Exchange Control Office
7.1	Trading account securities
7.2	Investment account securities
8	Equity investments
9	Financing extended to banking institutions
10	Bills and other instruments of credit
11	Advances on stock repurchase agreements (ordinary customers)
12	Advances (ordinary customers)
13	Overdrafts (ordinary customers)
14	Collateralised loans
15	Instalment loans (repayable from salary)
16	Mortgaged loans (ordinary customers)
17	Discounted instruments of credit
18	Other types of loans
19	Transactions in suspense
20	Inter-branch − in transit
21	Machinery and equipment
22	Land and buildings
23	Tax collection account (contributors account)
24	Receivable from shareholders (capital remittance)
25	Bills of exchange and other credit instruments (credited with future value dates)
26	Bills of exchange and other instruments for collection
27	Other assets
28	Prepaid expenses and accrued interest income
29	Prior period expenses and losses brought forward
30	Current period expenses and losses
31	Prior period charges adjustments
	Total assets
32	Credit guarantees given
33	Other commitments and risks
34	Contra accounts

Liabilities

35	Savings deposits (ordinary customers)
36	Current accounts (ordinary customers)
37	Deposits of banking institutions
38	Due to correspondent banks
39	Due to Italian Exchange Control Office
40	Current accounts
41	Third party funds managed by the bank
42	Outstanding cashiers and bank cheques
43	Financing from financial institutions
44	Financing from ordinary customers
45	Inter-branch − in transit
46	Tax collection account (taxation authority)
47	Bills of exchange and other credit instruments credited to memo accounts
48	Bills of exchange and other credit instruments collected not yet credited to customers
49	Staff severance indemnity accrual
50	Pension fund accrual
51	Accumulated depreciation
52	Other liabilities and accruals
53	Net equity
54	Accrued interest expense and unearned discount
55	Prior period revenue and profits brought forward
56	Current period revenue and profits
57	Prior period income adjustments
	Total liabilities

Supplementary information − Balance sheet

58	Bank-owned trading securities (nominal value)
59	Loss in value of bank-owned trading securities (nominal value)
60	Securities to be delivered for completed transactions (nominal value)
61	Securities to be received for completed transactions (nominal value)
62	Bank-owned investment securities (nominal value) not used for reserve requirements
63	Bank-owned investment securities (nominal value) used to meet reserve requirements
64	Bank-owned investment securities (nominal value) used to meet deposit requirements on cashiers cheques
65	Bank-owned investment securities (nominal value) used to meet deposit requirements on bank cheques and guarantees
66	Bank-owned investment securities (nominal value) used to meet cheque deposit requirements of other banking institutions
67	Bank-owned investment securities (nominal value) used to guarantee advances and extended repayment terms from the Bank of Italy
68	Bank-owned investment securities (nominal value) restricted for other purposes
69	Bank-owned investment securities (nominal value) assigned to staff severance indemnity
70	Bank-owned investment securities (nominal value) assigned to pension fund
71	Stocks purchased to cover future sales with the same person or entity (two separate transactions)

72 Bank-owned investment securities (carrying value) treasury bills and obligations of public entities

73 Bank-owned investment securities (nominal value) treasury bills and obligations of public entities

74 Bank-owned investment securities (deposit value) restricted for reserve, deposit and guarantee purposes

75 Equity investments (nominal value)

76 Equity investments on which capital has been subscribed but not fully paid up

77 Equity investments to be underwritten or purchased

78 Financing to real estate companies in which the bank has a controlling interest

79 The amount of liens or mortgages on the bank's buildings

80 Commitments for the purchase of buildings which have been approved by the authorities

81 Classification of loan risk by type of customer

82 Classification of loan risk by customer activity and terms of loan

83 Discounted bills and other instruments of credit by type of discount operation

84 Past due mortgage loans

85 Loans secured by a personal guarantee

86 Loans secured partially by guarantee and the pledging of assets

87 Revaluations made during the period (securities investments, etc.)

88 Devaluations made during the period (securities investments, etc.)

89 Share capital number of shares or quotas and the respective nominal value

90 Amount of loan guarantees which expired during the year

91 Movements in the number of cashiers' cheques issued during the year

92 Movements in the number of bank cheques issued during the year

93 Funds committed to treasury operations and not available for other purposes

94 Movements in savings accounts, ordinary customers (resident only)

95 Movements in current accounts, ordinary customers (resident only)

96 Amounts credited to ordinary customers for bills of exchange and other instruments of credit, which are not available for the customers use until collected by the bank

97 A breakdown of financing extended to ordinary customers by type of customer

98 A breakdown of ordinary customer current account balances by type of customer

99 Liquid balances in correspondent bank accounts

100 Securities to be delivered on stock repurchase agreements

101 Securities to be received on stock repurchase agreements

102 Open financing extended to ordinary customers

103 Open financing extended to credit institutions

104 Open financing received from credit institutions
(a) Bank-owned investment securities issued by the Deposit and Loan Agency (carrying value)
(b) Bank-owned investment securities issued by the Deposit and Loan Agency (nominal value)
(c) Bank-owned trading securities issued by the Deposit and Loan Agency (nominal value)

105 Loans in lire and foreign currencies by province for ordinary customers (resident only)

106 Deposits in lire and foreign currencies by province for ordinary customers (resident only)

107 Omitted in Mod 86 VIG

108 Details of financing extended to banking institutions

109 Details of other commitments and risks relative to banking institutions

110 Details of banking institutions' deposits

111 Details of financing received from credit institutions

112 Details and classifications of the risk on the collection of bills obtained from credit institutions

113 Details of due from correspondent bank accounts

114 Details of due to correspondent bank accounts
(a) Details of deposits with other credit institutions

115 Continuation of line 58

116 Continuation of line 59

117 Continuation of line 60

118 Continuation of line 61

119 Continuation of line 72

120 Continuation of line 73

121 Investment securities (at carrying value) details of EFIM (government holding company) obligations

122 Investment securities (at nominal value) details of EFIM obligations

123 Trading securities (at nominal value) details of EFIM obligations

The information shown in the standard balance sheet and supplementary information is required to be disclosed where applicable as follows:
− resident relationships in lire
− resident relationships in foreign currencies
− non-resident relationships in lire
− non-resident relationships in foreign currencies

APPENDIX V

Layout of detailed profit and loss account submitted to supervisory authority

EXPENSES

A Costs of Italian operations

1 Interest charges on
   Ordinary customers' savings deposits ... xxx
   Ordinary customers' current accounts ... xxx
   Banking institutions' deposits ... xxx
   Correspondent banks' accounts ... xxx
   Funds managed on behalf of others ... xxx
   Financing from
     ordinary customers ... xxx
     banking institutions
       Bank of Italy ... xxx
       other banking institutions ... xxx
   Transactions with Italian Exchange
   Control Office ... xxx

2 Losses from securities and foreign exchange
   trading:
   Stock repurchase agreements ... xxx
   Other securities transactions ... xxx
   Foreign exchange transactions ... xxx

3 Commissions, fees and other expenses on
   Correspondent banking relationships ... xxx
   Financing from
     ordinary customers ... xxx
     banking institutions ... xxx
   Securities and foreign exchange trading
     stock repurchase agreements ... xxx
     other securities transactions ... xxx
     foreign exchange transactions ... xxx
   Other banking operations inclusive of
   transactions with the Italian Exchange
   Control Office ... xxx

4 Commissions and other expenses on
   Acceptances, guarantees and counter
   guarantees ... xxx
   Collection of bills, other instruments of
   credit and interest coupons ... xxx
   Other services ... xxx

5 Personnel costs
   Compensation ... xxx
   Social contributions ... xxx
   Severance pay indemnity
     current year ... xxx
     other years ... xxx
   Other personnel costs ... xxx
   Fringe benefits ... xxx

6 Rental expense and ordinary maintenance
   Rental expense ... xxx
   Ordinary maintenance ... xxx

7 Taxes
   Indirect taxes
     Value added taxes
       current year ... xxx
       other years ... xxx
     Other indirect taxes
       current year ... xxx
       other years ... xxx
   Income taxes
     current year ... xxx
     other years ... xxx
   Taxes which relate to years prior to 1974
     indirect taxes (exclusive of value added
     taxes) ... xxx
     income taxes ... xxx

8 Insurance expense
   Damages (inclusive of fire and theft) ... xxx
   Customer insurance ... xxx

9 Depreciation and accrued expenses
   Depreciation of buildings
     extraordinary maintenance costs ... xxx
     other depreciation ... xxx
   Depreciation of other fixed assets
     extraordinary maintenance costs ... xxx
     other depreciation ... xxx
   Provision for loan losses ... xxx
   Provision for valuation losses – securities ... xxx
   Provision for valuation losses – equity
   investments ... xxx
   Other depreciation and provisions ... xxx
   Other accrued expenses ... xxx

10 Other expenses
    Purchase of other assets and non-
    professional services ... xxx
    Professional services ... xxx
    Miscellaneous expense ... xxx
    Charitable contributions ... xxx
    Other contributions and donations ... xxx

11 Prior period costs ... xxx

   Total costs of Italian operations ... xxx

B Costs of foreign banking operations

12 Personnel costs ... xxx

13 Other costs ... xxx

   Total costs of foreign operations ... xxx

   Total costs **A+B** ... xxx

C Net income for the period ... xxx

   Total **(A+B+C)** ... xxx

143

REVENUES

A Revenues from Italian operations

14 Interest income from (inclusive of fees)

Treasury, Postal and Deposit and Loan Agency deposits	xxx
Deposits with	
Bank of Italy	xxx
other banking institutions	xxx
Correspondent bank accounts	xxx
Discount activities for	
ordinary customers	xxx
banking institutions	xxx
Non-current account advances to	
ordinary customers	xxx
banking institutions	xxx
Current account (overdrafts) of	
ordinary customers	xxx
banking institutions	xxx
Other financing extended to	
ordinary customers	xxx
banking institutions	xxx
Transactions with Italian Exchange Control Office	xxx

15 Interest and dividend income from

Investment securities	
with short-term maturities	xxx
obligations	
Italian government	xxx
other	xxx
certificates of common investment funds	xxx
Equity investments	xxx

16 Profits from securities and foreign exchange trading

Stock repurchase agreements	xxx
Other securities transactions	xxx
Foreign exchange transactions	xxx

17 Commissions, fees and other income from

Correspondent banking relationships	xxx
Current accounts (overdrafts)	
ordinary customers	xxx
banking institutions	xxx
Financing of	
ordinary customers	xxx
banking institutions	xxx
Securities and foreign exchange trading	
stock repurchase agreements	xxx
other securities transactions	xxx
foreign exchange transactions	xxx
Other banking operations inclusive of transactions with the Italian Exchange Control Office	xxx

18 Commissions and other income from

Acceptances, guarantees and counter guarantees	xxx
Security deposits made on behalf of third parties	xxx
Collection of bills, other instruments of credit and interest coupons	xxx
Custody and management securities for third parties	xxx
Placement of securities on original issue	xxx
Calculation of tax payments	xxx
Other services	xxx

19 Rental and other income

Rental income	
from land	xxx
from other sources	xxx
Implied rental income	xxx
Duties on legal documents	xxx

20 Recovery of expenses incurred on behalf of third parties

Customer insurance	xxx
Expenses related to savings accounts, current accounts, deposits of banking institutions, and funds managed on behalf of third parties	xxx

21 Prior period revenues	xxx
Total revenues from Italian operations	xxx

B Revenues from foreign operations	xxx
Total revenues (**A + B**)	xxx

C Net loss for the period

Total (**A + B + C**)	xxx

The information shown in the expenses and revenue statements is required to be disclosed where applicable as follows:
- — Resident relationships in lire
- — Resident relationships in foreign currencies
- — Non-resident relationships (lire and foreign currencies)

OTHER PROFIT AND LOSS INFORMATION

22 Contributions to interest charged on
    subsidised loans to

    Shareholders or members   xxx
    Board members   xxx

23 Allocation of statutory net income relative
    to the prior year and unallocated net income
    of other years

    To ordinary reserves   xxx
    For charitable purposes   xxx
    For other contributions and donations   xxx
    Other allocations   xxx
    To carry forward to future years   xxx

24 Purchases of new property, plant and
    equipment

    Residential property   xxx
    Buildings   xxx
    Automobiles   xxx
    Furniture, machinery and equipment   xxx
    Land   xxx

25 Purchase of used property, plant and
    equipment

    Residential property   xxx
    Buildings   xxx
    Automobiles   xxx
    Furniture, machinery and equipment   xxx

27 Personnel costs (tax collection employees)   xxx

28 Data processing costs

    Personnel costs   xxx
    Purchase of buildings and installations   xxx
    Purchase of machinery and equipment   xxx
    Rental of buildings and installations   xxx
    Rental of machinery and equipment   xxx
    Ordinary maintenance   xxx
    Extraordinary maintenance   xxx

29 Purchase of data processing services from
    third parties   xxx

30 Sale of data processing services to third
    parties   xxx

31 Payments received from insurance
    companies for damages or losses during the
    year   xxx

32 Taxes paid during the year

    Income taxes   xxx
    Other taxes   xxx

33 Number of employees

    Data processing department
      executives   xxx
      managers   xxx
      salaried employees   xxx
      other   xxx
    Tax collection department
      executives   xxx
      managers   xxx
      salaried employees   xxx
      other   xxx
    Other departments
      executives   xxx
      managers   xxx
      salaried employees   xxx
      other   xxx

There is no breakdown requirement for the other information as
there is for expenses and revenues.

APPENDIX VI

Maximum depreciation rates for fixed assets as agreed by tax authorities

Buildings	3%
Building improvements	10%
Machinery and equipment	15%
Furniture	15%
Bullet-proof counters and windows	20%
Burglary alarm equipment	30%
Internal communications equipment	25%
Office furniture and fixtures	12%
Electronic machinery and equipment	18%
Automobiles	20%
Lift installation and scales	7%

CHAPTER 8

LUXEMBOURG

KENNETH HAY

1 GENERAL INFORMATION

Centrally located in Europe, the Grand Duchy of Luxembourg is a constitutional monarchy with, in recent years, coalition governments generally formed between two of the three traditional parties; all three parties are committed to the development of the financial centre. Although a small country with a population of about 360,000, Luxembourg is a full member of the United Nations, the International Monetary Fund, the World Bank, the European Economic Community and NATO.

The banking tradition in Luxembourg goes back to 1856, when the two oldest credit institutions were founded. In 1922 Luxembourg entered with Belgium into the Union Economique Belgo-Luxembourgeoise (UEBL) to which it belongs to this day. One of the main features of the UEBL is the close monetary co-operation between the two countries, involving common exchange regulations, characterised by the two-tier market described below in more detail.

The Luxembourg stock exchange was set up in 1929 and the enactment of the law on holding companies with its favourable taxation provisions together with the development of the Eurobond business has made Luxembourg an attractive centre for multinational organisations. In 1945 the Banking Control Law was enacted and there are now 113 banks, the vast majority being foreign owned, and approximately 6,000 holding companies.

Under the terms of a Grand Ducal Decree issued in accordance with the Law of 15 March 1979 on monetary status, the Luxembourg franc is at parity with the Belgian franc. The Belgian franc is used by both partners of the UEBL for international transactions and its exchange rate is supported by exchange reserves held by the National Bank of Belgium, although Luxembourg retains control over other external reserves (gold, IMF positions, SDRs and ECUs).

Within the framework of the negotiations for the renewal of the economic union with Belgium, which was renewed for another 10 year term beginning in 1982, an understanding was reached which included a strengthening of Luxembourg autonomy in monetary matters and provided also for the creation of a Monetary Institute, to take over the management of external reserves and monetary policy. The Luxembourg Monetary Institute, which was created on 1 June 1983, also took over the powers and functions of the former Luxembourg Banking Commissioner.

Exchange transactions are regulated by the Institut Belgo-Luxembourgeois du Change (IBLC), a joint body established by Belgium and Luxembourg for exchange regulation.

The exchange regulations are characterised by the existence of a two-tier market. In general terms the commercial franc is used for foreign trade and it is supported by the National Bank of Belgium while the financial rate is used for other transactions. This rate is allowed to float and does not therefore have any impact on the official exchange reserves. In practice, foreign exchange rates have not differed markedly for extended periods on the two markets but the system has provided an escape valve in times of tension. The existence of this free market has permitted an unhampered development of international transactions and thus created a favourable climate for international banking.

1.1 Organisations covered by banking regulations

Luxembourg banking regulations apply to all 'credit institutions' incorporated or otherwise established in the Grand Duchy. A 'credit institution' is defined as an establishment the business of which consists of accepting deposits or other repayable funds with a view to using them for its own account in credit or investment operations.

The law defines certain leasing and factoring operations as credit operations.

'Leasing operations' are deemed as credit operations when they consist of renting equipment, tooling and office equipment or other types of fixed assets bought specially for this purpose by the establishment which remains the owner, and either the rental period fixed within the contract corresponds to the presumed economic useful life of the goods, or the contract gives the tenant the right to acquire the property of all or part of the rented goods during or at the end of the lease for a price fixed in the contract.

'Factoring operations' are deemed as credit operations when the establishment acquires commercial debts, recovers these for its own account and bears any possible losses arising from insolvent debtors.

1.2 Summary of major types of bank

The law identifies three categories of credit institution:
(a) Banks and savings institutions which may accept sight

or short-term deposits. Such institutions may carry out all types of banking business, although in practice many banks established in Luxembourg are selective in their areas of activity, according to the requirements of their parent or associated companies and to the expertise which they have available.

(b) Agricultural or co-operative savings banks, which may also accept sight or short-term deposits.

(c) Non-banking financial institutions, which are not permitted to accept deposits for a period of less than two years except from other credit institutions or from associated companies. A Grand Ducal Decree may define 'associated companies'.

1.3 Supervisory authorities

(a) Luxembourg Monetary Institute (Institut Monétaire Luxembourgeois)

The function of Banking Control Commissioner, the individual with responsibility for the supervision of the financial sector, was created by the Act of 17 October 1945. Under the terms of the Law of 20 May 1983, which created the Luxembourg Monetary Institute (the Monetary Institute or the LMI) with effect from 1 June 1983, the powers and responsibilities of the Commissioner for supervision of the financial sector were transferred to the Monetary Institute.

The objectives of the Monetary Institute are defined by the law as:

(1) The issue of bank notes and management of their circulation.

(2) The promotion of the stability of the currency and in this context the supervision of the satisfactory operation of the financial markets.

(3) The exercise of commitments and of rights arising from international monetary and financial agreements.

(4) The supervision of the financial sector.

The capital of the Monetary Institute, which is wholly-owned by the state, is fixed at Luxfr500 million.

The Monetary Institute is responsible for the supervision of credit institutions, collective investment entities (formerly 'investments funds'), fiduciary representatives, professional depositaries of securities, persons authorised to buy and sell foreign currencies and the public offer or sale of securities.

The Monetary Institute's supervisory responsibility encompasses:

– The application of laws, decrees and regulations concerning credit institutions and their operations.

– The issue, with the approval of the Minister of Treasury, of regulations relating to the periodic submission and publication of financial statements as well as the layout in which they are drawn up.

– The screening of requests for a banking licence.

The Institute also has the power to scrutinise periodic reports submitted by the credit institutions and to carry out regular annual inspections in each bank.

The duties of the Monetary Institute do not extend to the supervision of holding companies which may be associated with banking groups, except in the context of their relationship to a credit institution operating in Luxembourg. If, for example, a Luxembourg holding company is a major shareholder in a Luxembourg bank, the Institute may make such enquiries as are considered necessary to enable it to be satisfied as to the professional repute of that holding company as a shareholder which is in a position to exercise a significant influence on the management of the bank. These enquiries may be extended to an audit of the financial statements of the holding company.

(b) Consultative Committee of the Luxembourg Monetary Institute (Comité consultatif de l'Institut Monétaire Luxembourgeois)

The Committee was established under the Ministerial Regulation of 12 January 1984; although consultative, its objective is to assist the Monetary Institute.

The 11 members of the Committee consist of three managers of the Monetary Institute, four members of the Association of Banks and Bankers of Luxembourg (ABBL), the chairman of the Luxembourg State Savings Bank (the Caisse d'Epargne de l'Etat) and three other members nominated by the above eight members. The function of the Committee is to advise the Monetary Institute on matters of concept and practice relating to the supervision of the financial sector.

1.4 Status of supervisory authorities

The Monetary Institute is governed by a board of seven directors, appointed by the government, of whom three are nominated by the Minister with direct responsibility for the Institute and two by the Minister of the Economy. In the present government the Prime Minister has retained direct responsibility for matters related to international banking and he is assisted by a Minister delegated to the Treasury.

The management of the Institute, comprising a General Manager (Directeur Général) and two other managers, is nominated by the Grand Duke, on the advice of the government, for a period of six years. The appointments may be renewed on the expiry of that period. The government may request the Grand Duke to revoke his nomination of all three members of the management team in the case of fundamental disagreement between the government and management.

1.5 Laws and regulations governing banks

The basic laws and decrees governing credit institutions can be allocated to the following four main headings:

– General company law (see Section 1.6).

– Establishment.

– Supervision.

– Others.

(a) Establishment of a credit institution

Law of 23 April 1981 (implementing the First EEC Directive on credit institutions).

Grand Ducal Regulations of 22 October 1981 (fixing the level of tax applicable to requests for authorisation) and 16 August 1982 (fixing limits for minimum capital requirements).

(b) Supervision of credit institutions

Grand Ducal Decrees of 17 October 1945 (creating the supervisory authority), 1 October 1948 (concerning appeals against decisions of the supervisory authority) and 19 June 1965, amended by the Law of 23 April 1981 (setting operational ratios).

Law of 10 August 1982 (powers of suspension, etc. of the supervisory authority).

Grand Ducal Regulation of 16 August 1982 (fixing limits for credit reporting).

Law of 20 May 1983 (creating Luxembourg Monetary Institute).

Ministerial Regulation of 31 October 1983 (approving LMI Regulation No. 1 of 14 October 1983) (format and publication of the financial statements of credit institutions).

Ministerial Regulation of 12 January 1984 (creating the Consultative Committee of the Luxembourg Monetary Institute).

(c) Others

Law of 30 November 1978 article 7, amended by Grand Ducal Regulation of 16 July 1980 (exemption of certificates of deposit from stamp duty).

Grand Ducal Regulation of 20 January 1968, amended by Grand Ducal Regulation of 23 December 1978 (tax exemption for interest on savings accounts).

Law of 17 August 1935 (regulating interest).

Grand Ducal regulation of 14 October 1963.

Law of 22 April 1984.

Law of 19 July 1983 (fiduciary contracts).

Law of 23 July 1983 (taxation of unrealised foreign exchange gains).

1.6 Application of general company law to banks

In addition to the above laws and regulations, banks are also subject to general company law.

1.7 Sources of laws and regulations

The commercial law of Luxembourg is passed by parliament and approved by the Grand Duke, after consultation at the draft stage with the appropriate professional bodies represented by the Chamber of Commerce and with the Council of State (Conseil d'Etat). Certain definitions and details of the law may be established by Grand Ducal Decree or by Ministerial Decree issued by the appropriate Cabinet Minister. This structure permits the detailed regulations to be amended within the framework of the law without recourse to the formal and time-consuming process of parliamentary approval.

In the case of banking regulations a further tier is added to the formation process through the regulatory powers of the Monetary Institute, for example in defining the format of report to be submitted to it and/or published by credit institutions.

In this way, the Luxembourg supervisory system, characterised by flexibility and minimal bureaucracy, grants the Monetary Institute extensive powers of initiative and appreciation within the framework of the law.

1.8 Ability of foreign banks to operate through branches and subsidiaries

The authorisation procedure for the establishment of a credit institution in Luxembourg permits the Monetary Institute to exercise control over the entry of foreign credit institutions to the Luxembourg market. Foreign banks may operate either through a subsidiary or through a Luxembourg branch of a foreign company. Once authorised to operate through a Luxembourg branch, foreign credit institutions have the same rights and obligations as domestic banks. (See Section 1.10 below for details of authorisation procedure.)

As regards operation through a Luxembourg subsidiary, there are no restrictions on the nationality of shareholders, directors or personnel and the application for authorisation is assessed in the same way as for domestic credit institutions.

There are no restrictions on the business which may be undertaken by authorised branches or subsidiaries of foreign credit institutions.

There are no restrictions in the banking legislation on the establishment in Luxembourg of representative offices of foreign credit institutions. In practice, however, the establishment of a representative office is subject to a series of conditions. It must be called a 'bureau d'information'; it is not allowed to transact any business or even to serve as an intermediary between credit institution and local customers, and its role is limited to collecting and issuing information.

1.9 Level of supervisory control for branches and subsidiaries of foreign banks

The financial statements of branches of foreign banks are required to be submitted for inspection by the Monetary Institute, but there is no requirement for these to be published. However, foreign banks with branch operations in Luxembourg are required to publish annually in the Official Gazette (Mémorial) their world-wide financial statements in the format required in the country of incorporation of the bank, subject to the approval of the publication by the LMI.

As regards operations through a Luxembourg subsidiary, the level of supervision, reporting and publication requirements is identical to that applied to domestic banks.

1.10 Methods of incorporation

(a) Outline of the system

Under the Law of 23 April 1981, no natural or legal Luxembourg or foreign person can accept deposits or other repayable funds with a view to using them for their own account in credit or investment operations, without written authorisation from the Minister for the Middle Classes (Ministre des Classes Moyennes). Each branch and agency of the institution in Luxembourg and abroad must be individually authorised. Authorisations may be granted by the Minister for the Middle Classes only with the approval of the Minister of Finance, and after the application has been examined by the Monetary Institute.

Those credit institutions which were already authorised before the law came into force are deemed to be authorised under the new provisions and were given three years from the coming into force of the legislation to conform with the new management and audit requirements.

Institutions must be notified of the Minister's decision within six months of their application, provided that all the necessary information was supplied. Where this was not the case, a decision must be reached within six months of receipt of the additional information or within 12 months of the original application, whichever is earlier. Failure to reach a decision within these time limits may be treated by the applicant as a refusal. All rejections of applications may be appealed to the Comité du Contentieux du Conseil d'Etat within three months of the notification of the decision.

Authorisation is granted for an unlimited period. The authorisation can be revoked if use is not made of it within 12 months of the date of issue, or if the institution voluntarily stops trading for more than six months.

It can be revoked on the grounds of fraud or on grounds which, if present at the time of the original application, would then have justified a refusal, or if it appears that the institution can no longer fulfil its obligations towards its creditors.

Changes or extensions to the objects of the institution to which the authorisation was granted as well as to its name or form, or the transfer from one place to another or the establishment of subsidiaries, branches or representative offices are subject to the same requirement for authorisation.

(b) Criteria for authorisation

Legal form

A credit institution incorporated in Luxembourg must take one of the following forms:
(a) Etablissement de droit public (state company).
(b) Société anonyme (limited company).
(c) Société en commandite par actions (partnership limited by shares).
(d) Société cooperative (co-operative company).
(e) Association agricole (agricultural association).

Of the 113 credit institutions in Luxembourg, 91 are limited liability companies incorporated in Luxembourg, 19 are companies incorporated under foreign law, two are Luxembourg state companies and one is a co-operative company.

Other criteria

In order to be granted the authorisation to do business as a credit institution in Luxembourg, the bank must meet the following criteria:
(a) The responsibility for effective management and the determination of policy must reside with at least two persons of satisfactory professional repute who have the experience necessary to carry out their duties.
(b) The requirement for satisfactory professional repute extends to the directors, the supervisory bodies and those shareholders or partners who by virtue of their shareholding or contributed capital are in a position to exercise a significant influence on the management of the bank.
(c) An annual audit of the financial statements of the credit institution is to be carried out by one or several external auditors of satisfactory professional repute who have the experience necessary to carry out their duties. Alternatively, audit examination may be carried out by the statutory auditor(s) (considered to be an internal supervisory body of the bank and therefore not independent) provided that he/they has/have the experience necessary to report in accordance with the standards fixed by the Monetary Institute (see Section 2.7).
(d) The institution is required to have sufficient assets to safeguard the interests of its creditors. The current minimal capital requirement for a Luxembourg bank is Luxfr350 million of which at least Luxfr250 million must be paid-up. The minimum designated capital for a Luxembourg branch of a foreign bank is Luxfr250 million, while for a non-banking financial institution it is fixed at Luxfr25 million (fully paid-up).
(e) The establishment must be able to demonstrate that it carries creditworthiness in the financial community, commensurate with the activities which it intends to carry out.
(f) All such other information as may be required for an appreciation of the application for an authorisation is to be provided; an applicant seeking authorisation as a credit institution must disclose its management plans; in particular, details must be given of the type and volume of the intended operations, together with information about the organisational structure of the credit institution.

1.11 Areas within the country subject to special laws

There are no major areas of banking in Luxembourg which are subject to special laws or privileges, nor are there any major restrictions as to the banking activities which an authorised credit institution may undertake. There are, however, some minor areas of banking activities which may require specific authorisation (i.e. shareholdings, mergers, transmission of information to parent companies, utilisation of Luxembourg franc by banks, etc.). Only banks authorised by the Institut Belgo-Luxembourgeois du Change (IBLC) are authorised to operate in the official foreign exchange market, where mainly commercial transactions are settled. The free market is used mainly for capital transactions and is not subject to exchange control regulations.

Since 25 January 1974 a ceiling has been applied to the net foreign currency position on the official market of each bank in Luxembourg and in Belgium.

2 ACCOUNTING

2.1 Laws and regulations governing accounts

The basic Law of 10 August 1915 (modified on 24 April 1983) concerning commercial companies in Luxembourg used to form the framework for the preparation and publication of the annual accounts of all commercial companies, including banks. The requirements of this law were minimal and the existing law has been amended relatively little since it was passed in 1915, except to incorporate the First and Second EEC Directives on company law.

The Fourth EEC Directive on company law has now been embodied in Luxembourg legislation by the Law of 4 May 1984; however, article 204 of this Law, which will in most respects be applicable to financial years commencing after 31 December 1984, does not apply to credit institutions or to insurance companies.

The financial statements of credit institutions will therefore, for LMI purposes, continue to be established following the layout required by the Monetary Institute, until the present draft EEC Directive on the financial statements of credit institutions is embodied in Luxembourg legislation.

For publication purposes, Luxembourg credit institutions must comply with the conditions and layout described in the Ministerial Regulation of 31 October 1983 (see Section 3).

2.2 Application of general company law

In addition to the law, regulations, acts and decrees applicable to them, banks are also subject to general company law.

2.3 Roles of legislature and supervisory authority

See Section 1.3.

2.4 Extent to which requirements as to returns and accounts are prescribed by laws and regulations

The Monetary Institute is empowered under the Act of 17 October 1945 to issue, with the agreement of the Minister of Treasury, regulations governing the form, content and publication of financial statements and of such other returns as it may require to be submitted to it.

2.5 Obligations to furnish accounts

In accordance with the requirements of the basic law on commercial companies, annual financial statements must be presented to the shareholders at least two weeks prior to the annual general meeting of the company. In the case of credit institutions, these financial statements must be in the format prescribed by Regulation No. 1 of 14 October 1983. The prescribed format is one of a standard balance sheet and profit and loss account, but does not include any provision for notes to the financial statements; before publication the financial statements must be approved by the LMI.

Subsidiaries of credit institutions incorporated under foreign law are exempt from the prescribed format and they may prepare their accounts in conformity with the laws and regulations of the country of their parent company.

2.5.1 Accounting periods and times of furnishing

Credit institutions are required to publish their annual financial statements in the Official Gazette (Mémorial) within six months of the end of their financial year or 14 days after the shareholders' general meeting if earlier. There is no mandatory accounting year end. Financial statements may not be published prior to the issue of the Monetary Institute's *nihil obstat* or visa. However, no mention may be made in the financial statements of their approval by the Monetary Institute.

2.5.2 Form of accounts to be furnished

The form of the accounts published in the Official Gazette is laid down by the Monetary Institute and consists of a balance sheet and profit and loss account without any footnote (see Appendix I).

2.5.3 Mandatory accounting dates

There is no mandatory accounting year end for Luxembourg banks, although the majority of banks have a 31 December year end.

2.6 Requirements as to accounts (a) prior to incorporation (b) prior to commencement of trading and (c) in order to continue trading

An applicant seeking authorisation as a credit institution must disclose its management plans; in particular, details must be given of the type and volume of intended operations, together with information about the organisational structure of the credit institution.

For a bank to continue trading it must comply with all laws and regulations. This clearly requires furnishing and publication of the financial statements described in Section 2.5 above.

2.7 Audit requirements

Since the Law of 4 May 1984 (which implements the Fourth EEC Directive) does not apply to credit institutions, the basic Law of 10 August 1915 still applies, which requires that all Luxembourg companies appoint a statutory auditor. The Luxembourg Monetary Institute has the power to prescribe the nature of the statutory auditor's report, and hence the nature of the audit.

The Law of 23 April 1981, which embodied in Luxembourg legislation the First EEC Directive on credit institutions, requires that credit institutions submit their annual accounts to the control of one or more *independent* experts or, alternatively, that their internal supervisory bodies including the statutory auditors (commissaire(s) aux comptes) should, under certain conditions, carry out this examination. A period of three years to comply with this law was granted. In its Circular No. 84/16 of 2 April 1984, the LMI reminded credit institutions that the transitory period of three years was due to expire on 27 April 1984 and defined its requirements for audit.

A clear distinction was drawn in that circular between credit institutions whose annual accounts are subject to the control of an independent expert, and those for whom the audit is carried out by the internal supervisory bodies. The appointment of the independent expert is subject to the approval of the appropriate Ministry, acting upon the advice of the LMI.

(a) Credit institutions audited by independent expert

The law states that the expert must be capable and independent, and lays down the standards of professional respectability, experience and independence.

The supervision of the above standards is under the control of the Minister concerned based on advice from the LMI.

The role of the independent expert is complementary to that of the statutory auditor, who carries broader supervisory powers than the independent auditor. The external audit should not be carried out by the statutory auditor of a credit institution, nor by an audit firm in which the statutory auditor is a partner.

The external auditor, whether an individual person or a firm, should be appointed by the shareholders and reports to them.

(b) Credit institutions not audited by an independent expert

The LMI recommends that credit institutions should appoint as auditor an independent expert; if they decide otherwise, they must leave the examination of their annual accounts to their internal supervisory bodies under the following conditions:
(i)   The supervisory body should have adequate experience.
(ii) The supervisory body should write its report in accordance with standards established by the Luxembourg Monetary Institute. These standards are as follows:
(a) For Luxembourg credit institutions which are subsidiaries of foreign banks, the report should comply with the rules required for external auditors' reports relating to the parent establishment, if clear regulations on this matter exist in its country of origin (e.g. Switzerland, Federal Republic of Germany, etc.).
(b) For Luxembourg credit institutions which do not fulfil the above criterion, the statutory auditor should establish a detailed report on his examination. This report should have the following characteristics:
− It should describe the legal form of the institution and its authorised activities and supply an analysis of its organisation, management and internal control function.
− It should analyse the structure and evolution of the annual accounts and supply explanatory comments about the various lines of the balance sheet, contingent accounts, and profit and loss account.
− It should comment on the institution's solvency, liquidity and profitability, analyse the various banking risks and comment on the bank's covering of those risks, and also describe the significant accounting policies.
− It should certify that the accounts are accurate and complete.

In its form and content the report should be equivalent to the reports required in Switzerland and Germany.

In both cases before the report on the financial statements is issued an audit should have been carried out in accordance with generally accepted international auditing standards, with a view to verifying the application of Luxembourg regulations and the concepts of prudence and consistency in the preparation of the financial statements.

In addition the Monetary Institute is empowered to carry out such audit procedures as are considered necessary prior to the issue of the *nihil obstat* on the annual accounts of the bank.

2.8   Acceptability to fiscal authorities of accounts submitted to supervisory authority

The capital of a Luxembourg company may be denominated in a currency other than the Luxembourg franc and, in consequence, companies may choose the currency in which their capital is denominated and their financial statement expressed. However, Luxembourg fiscal law requires that the tax return should be submitted in Luxembourg francs.

With the introduction in 1983 of legislation retroactive to January 1982, dealing with the taxation of foreign currency gains/losses, it is anticipated that taxable profits/losses will equate with the book figure expressed in the reporting currency.

The commercial accounts, as submitted to the supervisory authority and approved by the shareholders, therefore form the basis for the submission to the fiscal authorities and in broad terms will be acceptable to them. Hence allowances, provisions or deductions which are not recorded in the commercial financial statements will not normally be accepted by the fiscal authorities.

2.9   Submission of accounts to any authority other than by requirement of law

No accounts are required to be submitted to any authority other than by requirement of law. The fiscal authorities may request copies of financial statements or reports that must be submitted to other public authorities.

2.10   Application of laws and regulations to foreign banks operating through branches and subsidiaries

Duly authorised foreign credit institutions have the same rights and obligations as national credit institutions.

No matter what their legal form, all foreign-incorporated credit institutions or banks must publish annually in the Official Gazette their worldwide balance sheet and profit and loss account. The balance sheet of the Luxembourg branch alone is submitted for inspection to the Monetary Institute. It does not at present have to be published in the Official Gazette.

2.11   Availability of accounts for public inspection

Only such financial statements as are published in the Official Gazette are available for public inspection.

3 FORMAT, STYLE AND CONTENTS OF ACCOUNTS

3.1 Extent to which format is laid down by statute, supervisory authority, generally accepted accounting practice or otherwise

By application of the Ministerial Decree of 31 October 1983, the balance sheet and the profit and loss account published by credit institutions and after approval by the LMI, must be laid out in a standard format (Appendix I).

3.2 Description of format

The standard format used for publication in the Official Gazette includes a balance sheet and a profit and loss account (see Appendix I) but makes no provision for notes to the financial statements.

3.3 Extent to which contents are prescribed by statute, supervisory authority, generally accepted accounting practice or otherwise

The format and the contents of the accounts have been established by the Monetary Institute and incorporated in the law by Ministerial Decree.

The annual publication must, under the terms of general commercial law, include:
(a) Name and registered place of business.
(b) Publication date of the statutes and modifications thereto in the Official Gazette.
(c) Balance sheet, profit and loss account and contingent accounts.
(d) Schedule of distribution of net profits according to the decision of the annual general meeting.
(e) Name, profession and domicile of directors and auditors.
(f) The situation of the company's capital, according to article 48 of the Law of 10 August 1915, indicating the list of the shareholders who have not yet fully paid up their shares, as well as the amounts due.

3.4 Disclosure of specific items required other than those required by general law

3.5 Exemptions from disclosure allowed in respect of banking items

None.

3.6 Hidden reserves

Credit institutions in Luxembourg are permitted to maintain hidden reserves by means of the methods described below. These reserves may be included in the total on the face of the balance sheet under the heading 'Provisions' (Appendix I, Liabilities C.15) but the reader is unable to identify either the nature or the amount of the component parts of the total provisions, or the extent to which the provisions are in excess of specifically identified risks.

Alternatively, under the terms of LMI Circular No. 84/14 of 29 March 1984, such reserves may be deducted directly from the assets to which they relate, without separate disclosure, e.g. a general provision for loan losses may now be offset against the total gross loans. Hidden reserves may be established in the following ways:

(a) Investment in subsidiaries and associated companies (participations)

Investments in associated or subsidiary companies are generally carried at acquisition cost (or market value if lower) in the financial statements of Luxembourg companies, with income from the investments being accounted for only on a dividends received basis. Hence hidden reserves may be created to the extent of the Luxembourg parent company's shares of post-acquisition reserves in the subsidiary or associated company, which might otherwise have been accounted for if consolidation or the equity method had been adopted.

(b) Investment in securities

All investments in securities are required to be carried at the lower of acquisition cost and market value at the balance sheet date. The balance sheet date valuation is required to be made on the basis of individual securities, and no distinction is drawn between the dealing portfolio and investments which are to be held to maturity. Hidden reserves may therefore be created under this heading as follows:

(i)   There is no requirement to write up to current market value dealing portfolio investments or investments which were previously written down to a value lower than acquisition cost.

(ii) As all investments which are known by management to be intended to be held to maturity must be carried at the lower of cost and market value at the balance sheet date, those investments may therefore be carried at a value considerably lower than their redemption value.

(c) Loan portfolio

A general loan loss provision calculated as a fixed percentage (at present at rates fixed between 1% and 1.5%) of unsecured loans against which no specific provision has been made is allowable for Luxembourg tax purposes. Such a provision may be in excess of actual requirements. (See Section 4.2.3 below.)

In addition to the above, management may set aside such additional general provisions for loan losses as it may consider appropriate, although these may be in excess of computed requirements and will not be allowable for tax purposes.

3.7 Requirements as to consolidated accounts

As mentioned in Section 3.6, investments in subsidiary and affiliated companies are generally carried at acquisition cost in the official published accounts of credit institutions. There is at present no legal requirement for groups of companies to prepare consolidated financial statements. However, in the case of some international banking groups whose ultimate parent company is incorporated in Luxembourg, consolidated financial statements are prepared in international format, together with explanatory notes thereto, and included in the group's annual report.

The regulations concerning the supervision of credit institutions on a consolidated basis were set out in the LMI Circular No. 84/7 of 17 January 1984. Such supervision is intended to apply to all credit institutions in which a Luxembourg credit institution has a majority shareholding held either directly or indirectly (e.g. via an intermediate holding company).

Some banking groups may be structured in such a way so as to normally exclude supervision on a group basis, e.g. the parent company may not be a credit institution, and within the group there may be credit institutions in different countries. Under these circumstances the various supervisory authorities would agree among themselves which authority would supervise the group on a consolidated basis. In this way, with the consent of the group, the LMI may be appointed as the supervisory authority responsible for a banking group whose ultimate parent company is not a Luxembourg credit institution.

Where the LMI is supervising on a group basis, certain information, including the group's balance sheet and profit and loss account prepared in the format prescribed for Luxembourg credit institutions, has to be submitted on a quarterly basis. This information is required in addition to the returns submitted to the LMI on an unconsolidated basis. In the case of Luxembourg credit institutions which are themselves subsidiaries of a group subject to control on a consolidated basis by a supervisory authority other than the LMI, the information mentioned above is to be submitted to the LMI in the format transmitted to the parent company for consolidation purposes.

The above consolidated financial statements do not require to be audited, however, the LMI recommends that credit institutions should publish in their annual reports, together with their individual financial statements, their consolidated financial statements accompanied by an explanatory statement as to the method(s) of consolidation adopted.

4 ACCOUNTING POLICIES

4.1 Responsibility for laying down accounting policies

Accounting policies adopted by Luxembourg banks tend to follow either the guidelines laid down by the supervisory authority, i.e. the Monetary Institute, or the requirements of the fiscal authorities. There is no requirement for the disclosure in financial statements of accounting policies.

4.2 Particular accounting policies

Details of the main accounting policies generally adopted by Luxembourg banks are set out below. In this connection, definitions used in the LMI financial reporting guidelines are set out in Appendix III.

4.2.1 Foreign exchange

Assets and liabilities denominated in currencies other than the reporting currency are translated into the reporting currency at the rates applicable at the close of business on the balance sheet date. Income and expense account items are translated generally at the actual rate ruling on the date of the transaction or at the month end rate during which the transaction took place.

In line with the overriding principle of prudence applied to bank accounting in Luxembourg, unrealised gains on the translation of foreign currency items are not recognised in income. This principle is extended in the case where the capital of the credit institution has been contributed in foreign currency and converted into Luxembourg francs. Exchange gains arising on such capital as a result of maintaining an open position on capital and shareholders' funds denominated in Luxembourg francs may be 'neutralised' by the creation of a provision for the neutralisation of exchange gains. All losses, realised and unrealised, on translation must be recognised in the profit and loss account. Outright forward foreign exchange contracts are valued at the lower of spot rate at the balance sheet date or the forward rate at that date for the remaining period of the contract. Gains arising on the balance sheet date revaluation are deferred, whereas any losses arising in this way are recognised in the profit and loss account.

In the case of swap transactions, gains or losses arising as a result of the above revaluation policy at the balance sheet date are neutralised, as gains or losses arising as a result of the swap transactions themselves are to be taken to interest income/amortised over the period of the contracts.

Forward positions which are not covered by spot transactions are to be valued according to the daily net positions of each currency. Positive valuation results (i.e. translation gains) are not taken into account, but negative valuation results must be provided for and charged to the profit and loss account. However, it is permitted to deduct future certain profits from losses which would require the creation of a provision, if both the following conditions are fulfilled:

− The profit must be used to neutralise the losses in the same currency only.

− The profit must be realised prior to the losses which are to be neutralised, i.e. the maturity of items which create the profit must be closer to the closing date than the maturity of item(s) which create the loss(es) for which a provision would be necessary. Thus, the expected certain profit may only be deducted from subsequent losses and at most up to this amount; a possible profit surplus must not be accounted for.

4.2.2 Deferred tax

As the commercial accounts of a company form the basis of its tax return, deferred taxation is not common.

4.2.3 Specific and general provisions for bad and doubtful debts

The common accounting policy in this area is to provide for specific identified risks as at the balance sheet date, and to create a general provision in line with the amount allowable for tax purposes, on the basis of a formula applied to unsecured lending of the bank. In this context, 'secured lending' is deemed to include loans secured by personal or corporate guarantee or any other form of security.

More specifically, the fiscal authorities will recognise as tax deductible a general provision, covering risks existing but not identified as at the balance sheet date, calculated under the following guidelines:

(1) Assets for which a determined and identifiable risk has been established (even partly) must be subject to a separate valuation and must not be taken to make up the general provision.

(2) The rates to be applied and recorded in the commercial balance sheet are:

(a) A rate of 1.5% for the following balance sheet items: marketable financial bills, financial bills (i.e. not negotiable), debtors in current accounts (i.e. overdrafts) and unsecured advances at sight, and unsecured term loans and advances.

(b) A rate of 1% for the following balance sheet items: rediscounted bills of exchange, acceptances of the bank, other bills, and instalment credits, except the credits secured by mortgages.

(c) A rate of 1% for credits and ship mortgages. However, the amount of the provision made up for these credits cannot exceed 20% of the total amount of the general provision.

The above rates may not be applied to amounts due from banks or to state or quasi-state lending.

A directive from the Monetary Institute issued in March 1983 distinguishes doubtful debts against which a provision should be created and irrecoverable debts which should be written off.

Assets acquired from other banks in the period of four months prior to the bank's accounting year end may, in certain circumstances, not be eligible for inclusion in the calculation of the general loan loss provision.

As mentioned in Section 3.6 above, management may set aside such additional general provisions as it considers appropriate.

4.2.4 Treatment of provisions in accounts

Provisions established for possible loss in value of assets are not normally separately disclosed. They may be included in aggregate under the heading 'Provisions' in the shareholders' funds section of the balance sheet or offset against the asset to which they relate. However, if the loss is irrecoverable it will be written off and the provision reduced accordingly.

4.2.5 Premiums and discounts on investments (amortise, write off, etc.)

Investments are carried at the lower of acquisition cost and market value at the balance sheet date. No distinction is drawn in this respect between the dealing portfolio and investments intended to be held to maturity. Hence any premium paid or discount allowed on the acquisition of an investment is accounted for as part of the acquisition cost, which is then compared with its market value on succeeding balance sheet dates. On the other hand, prudence dictates that the amortisation of any premium paid would be considered as an acceptable accounting policy.

4.2.6 Offsets, i.e. to what extent can assets and liabilities be set off against each other (legally or in practice)

The compensation in the balance sheet of assets and liabilities towards different counterparties, or towards the same counterparty, is not permitted under the Monetary Institute's guidelines. Agreements on the merging of accounts, compensation or pledging of accounts do not permit deviations from these rules.

A compensated balance is to be reported only if a transfer, sub-participation or realisation of guarantees has taken place.

The compensation of balances between different units of the bank (branch offices, agencies, etc.) is, however, compulsory in the balance sheet which consolidates these units.

4.2.7 Goodwill

As a general rule, investments in subsidiaries and associated companies are carried in the official accounts of the parent company at cost, less provision for any diminution in value which may have occurred subsequent to acquisition, and the income therefrom is accounted for only on a dividend received basis. The treatment of goodwill in this case, i.e. the excess of cost over the net asset value of the investment on acquisition, falls under the basic law governing the accounts of commercial companies, which states that 'all necessary depreciation' must be made in the accounts which are submitted to the shareholders. Hence where investments are carried at cost it would not be considered a common accounting policy to amortise goodwill created on the acquisition over a fixed period, but in the case of any permanent diminution in the value of the investment, normal policy would be to provide for such a diminution.

4.2.8 Consolidation

See Sections 3.7 and 4.2.1.

4.2.9 Revaluations of assets

The revaluation of fixed assets is permissible, but is normally practised only to the limited extent to which the revaluation is tax free. Such a revaluation adjustment is carried directly to a tax free reserve without passing through the profit and loss account.

4.2.10 Instalment finance and leasing including basis of recognition of income

Leasing operations by Luxembourg banks (see Section 1.1) are, at present, relatively limited in size. However, leased assets are required to be disclosed separately in the financial statements together with details of the depreciation thereof and the related income.

4.2.11 Dealing assets

No differentiation is drawn in Luxembourg between assets purchased for dealing purposes and those purchased to hold. Investments are carried at the lower of acquisition cost and market value at the balance sheet date, on the basis of individual securities and not on a portfolio basis. Acquisition cost includes the charges of acquisition, but excludes, in the case of interest-bearing securities, interest accrued but not matured. Any premium paid or discount allowed on the acquisition of the investment is accounted for as part of the acquisition cost and the investment is then revalued at its market value on succeeding balance sheet dates. Securities denominated in currency other than the reporting currency are translated, for the purpose of arriving at market value, at the rate of exchange applicable at the balance sheet date.

The revaluation to the lower of cost and market value of such assets is effected on a provision account, and only when a definitive assessment of a value loss is arrived at, is the cost of the investment reduced by write-off.

4.2.12 Pensions

It is normal practice for a bank to enter into a contract with an insurance company in order to secure pensions for its staff. The cost of the premiums payable to the insurance company is not disclosed.

4.2.13 Depreciation

Fixed assets are carried at cost, net of such amounts set aside for depreciation as are calculated to amortise fully the assets over their estimated useful lives. In most cases, fixed assets (including buildings) are depreciated in line with the amounts allowable under fiscal legislation.

5 WINDOW DRESSING

Neither the law nor banking regulations contain any provision on the question of window dressing. However, regular monthly reporting of a bank's balance sheet in standard format to the Monetary Institute ensures that significant fluctuations from one period to another will be identified and explanation thereof may be required by the Monetary Institute.

6 AMOUNTS REQUIRED TO BE MAINTAINED BY LAW OR OTHERWISE

Under current requirements a bank setting up in Luxembourg is required to have a minimum capital of Luxfr350 million, of which Luxfr250 million have to be paid-up. The Luxembourg branch of a foreign bank also needs a minimum designated capital of Luxfr250 million.

In common with all Luxembourg companies, banks are required to appropriate to a 'legal reserve' 5% of annual net income, until the reserve equals 10% of the nominal value of issued share capital. The legal reserve may not be distributed in the form of cash dividends or otherwise during the life of the company.

There are no requirements for Luxembourg credit institutions to maintain deposits with the State Savings Bank (Caisse d'Epargne de l'Etat), the Monetary Institute or any other central agency.

7 KEY RATIOS

7.1 Solvency ratio (coefficient de solvabilité)

Current liabilities must not exceed $33\frac{1}{3}$ times own funds, that is to say own funds must be not less than 3% of current liabilities.

For the purpose of this ratio, own funds are defined (in article 6 of the 1965 Decree) as capital reserves, subordinated loan capital (within limits and under certain conditions, see below), legally drawn up calculations of appreciation in the value of assets, provisions (see below), profits, less losses brought forward (excluding the profits of the current year).

A second version of the solvency ratio which includes the results (profit or loss) of the current financial year is also calculated for comparative purposes only, outside the terms of article 6 of the 1965 Decree.

The only provisions included in the definition of own funds are those for general risks pertaining to banking activities, and therefore exclude provisions relating to depreciation in the value of assets. Any provision for the neutralisation of exchange gains (see Section 4.2.1) is excluded from own funds in this context.

Subordinated loan stock issued by a bank and maturing within one year from the date of calculation of the ratio is included in the total of current liabilities. For such stock maturing in more than one year, the decision is taken on a case-by-case basis, whether the subordinated debt may be considered as capital or not. The debt must fulfil certain conditions of form and duration, and cannot be repayable without the agreement of the Monetary Institute. If these conditions are met, the loan stock may be taken into account as own funds, up to a maximum of 50% of paid-up capital and reserves.

Current liabilities are defined as all liabilities to third parties.

7.2 Fixed assets ratio (coefficient de couverture d'immobilisé)

The fixed assets, which must not in total exceed the value of a bank's own funds (as defined above), are defined as property (less depreciation), furniture and equipment (less depreciation), participations in subsidiaries and affiliates, claims on affiliated non-banking companies, legal and similar costs of establishing and continuing the bank, plus other fixed assets (e.g. equipment distrained on by the bank to satisfy bad debts).

This ratio is calculated monthly on the basis of own funds as set out above.

7.3 Cash ratio (coefficient de trésorerie)

For the purpose of this ratio, cash is defined to include the following assets: notes and coins, postal cheques, sight balances at the State Savings Bank and monetary reserve assets (réserve monétaire) at central banks.

The short-term liabilities against which cash must be held are defined as those liabilities, not exceeding one month on sundry coupon and similar accounts, plus sight liabilities to banks, term liabilities to banks, current accounts, sight deposits, monetary notes issued, 20% of liabilities on savings books, and sundry sight liabilities (including trade creditors).

There is no longer a fixed minimum for this ratio. The Monetary Institute now expects each bank to maintain an appropriate ratio in the light of its own particular circumstances.

7.4 Liquidity ratio (recommandation de liquidité)

The numerator of this ratio includes cash assets as defined above, plus assets in course of collection, term claims (i.e. over one month) on banks, certain short-term advances, public sector securities eligible for rediscounting with the Banque Nationale de Belgique or with similar institutions, negotiable financial paper, and rediscountable commercial paper.

The denominator includes the liabilities in the cash ratio above, except that all liabilities on savings accounts are included, plus liabilities to privileged or guaranteed creditors (including taxes and excise duties), plus term deposits, certificates of deposit, bonds issued by banks, sundry term liabilities, and the contingent liability on partly paid securities.

The Monetary Institute recommends that banks maintain a minimum coefficient of 30% for this liquidity ratio.

8 ACCOUNTING RETURNS OTHER THAN ACCOUNTS

8.1 By whom required

By application of article 2 of the Grand Ducal Decree of 17 October 1945 relative to banking control, all banking and savings institutions established in the Grand Duchy of Luxembourg must send to the Luxembourg Monetary Institute all information listed below within a specified period of time and according to a standard format.

8.2 Nature of requirements

The schedules must bear the bank's seal and the signature of at least one member of the board of directors or their delegated officer.

(a) Banks with no branches abroad

The form and detail of certain of these returns are specified in the instructions issued by the Monetary Institute and are at present as follows (numbering corresponds to LMI reference numbers):

Monthly
1.1 Statement of assets and liabilities
1.2a Foreign currency positions — free market

1.2b Analysis of outright forward foreign currency contracts
1.3 Loans granted to companies domiciled in Belgium
1.4 Loans for consumer goods granted to Luxembourg residents
1.5 Statement of assets and liabilities in Luxembourg francs, Belgian francs and foreign currencies.
In addition copies of the following IBLC schedules:
(i) Assets and liabilities in foreign currencies (official market: Statement A).
(ii) Assets and liabilities in foreign currencies (free market: Statement B).
(iii) Detailed statement of the foreign exchange position.

Quarterly
2.1 Profit and loss account
2.2a Maturity structure of assets and liabilities in foreign currencies
2.2b Maturity structure of assets and liabilities in francs
2.3 Information concerning important credits
2.4 Analysis of securities portfolio and participations
2.5 Statement of assets and liabilities towards Luxembourg residents
2.6 Statement of assets and liabilities towards Belgium residents
2.7 Liquid or semi-liquid bank deposits of non-banking Luxembourg residents
2.8 Loans granted for real estate located in Luxembourg
2.9 Indexed savings
2.10 Assets and liabilities with holding companies
2.11 Certificates of deposit in circulation
2.12 Sales and repurchases of shares in investment companies and trusts
In addition copies of the following IBLC schedules:
(i) Assets and liabilities in Belgian or Luxembourg francs towards foreign countries.
(ii) Analysis per country of assets and liabilities in foreign currencies (official and free market).

Semi-annually
3.2 Staff numbers
3.3 Analysis of assets and liabilities according to currencies, countries and maturities
3.4 Calculation of the basis of VAT: gold and securities dealings

Annually
4.1 Final statement of assets and liabilities
4.2 Final profit and loss account
4.3 Accounts to be published
4.4 Statement of number of branches and representative offices

On an 'ad hoc' basis
5.1 Results of subscriptions and placings of securities

Important credits, details of which have to be reported quarterly, are defined as all advances to a single customer of the equivalent of Luxfr50 million or more, or, if the shareholders' funds are less than Luxfr500 million, such advances amounting to 10% or more of shareholders' funds. For the purpose of this definition advances include the total facilities available (rather than the amount drawn) in the form of loans, acceptances, guarantees, etc. The intention is to consider under the term 'one customer' different legal personae who may be considered to form the same risk.

(b) Banks with branches abroad

These banks must give three different versions of the required information: figures of each branch separately, figures of the head office, net aggregate figures for the bank. This requirement concerns the following schedules:

1.1 Statement of assets and liabilities (Appendix II)
1.2a Foreign currencies position — free market
1.2b Analysis, according to foreign currencies, of outright forward contracts
2.1 Profit and loss account
2.2a Maturity structure of assets and liabilities in foreign currencies
2.2b Maturity structure of assets and liabilities in francs
2.3 Statement of loans exceeding Luxfr50 million
2.4 Distribution of securities portfolio and participations
3.2 Staff
4.1 Final statement of assets and liabilities (Appendix II)
4.2 Final profit and loss account (Appendix II)

For all other schedules, including IBLC schedules, banks with branches abroad only give figures concerning their head office in Luxembourg, except for schedules 4.3 and 4.4.

Credit institutions with a capital expressed in a currency other than Belgian or Luxembourg francs are required to complete two monthly statements of assets and liabilities, model A, the first expressed in the currency of the capital, the second in Luxembourg francs. All items are converted at the exchange rate of the day from the currency of the bank's capital into Luxembourg francs. The reference rate will be the average of the buying and selling rates of the free market, or of the official market if appropriate.

9 TAXATION

9.1 General method of taxation

(a) Corporate income tax

Banks, in common with other commercial companies in Luxembourg, are subject to income taxes which are computed in two parts:
(i) Corporation tax (impôt sur le revenue des collectivités) which is due to the state at the rate of 41.6% of profits.
(ii) Municipal business tax (impôt commercial) which is due to the commune in which the company is situated, currently at a rate of approximately 10% although the rate may vary from one commune to another.

As municipal business tax on income is an allowable expense in the computation of corporation tax, the effective rate of income tax currently stands at around 47.4%. Other taxes payable, including for example municipal business tax on capital, raise the effective tax rate to around 50% of profits.

(b) Registration duty

A registration duty of 1% is levied on initial capital (which includes the designated capital for branches of foreign banks) and on subsequent capital increases.

(c) Interest/dividend income

Dividends and interest received from associated companies in which the bank has an investment of at least 25% are tax exempt in Luxembourg, if the investee company is subject, in its country of residence, to an income tax similar in nature to that of Luxembourg corporate income tax.

(d) Profits from foreign branches

Foreign countries can be classified into three categories:
− Countries which have signed a double tax agreement with Luxembourg exempting income arising in those countries.
− Countries which have signed a double tax agreement permitting the imputation of foreign taxes paid against taxes due in the home country (convention d'imputation).
− Countries which have not signed a double tax agreement.

The profits originating from the first category countries are wholly exempted in the computation of Luxembourg tax due. For the countries falling under categories two and three above, the tax paid on income can be deducted from Luxembourg income tax payable for a percentage up to the tax rate which would have been applied on that income had it arisen in Luxembourg.

Losses arising in a foreign country may only be offset against future profits arising within the subsequent period of five years in that same country.

9.2 Accounts as basis for taxation

The 'commercial' or published financial statements of all Luxembourg companies, including banks, form the basis of their tax return (see Section 2.8 above).

9.3 Adjustments permitted or required

Although certain items recorded in the accounts may be disallowed for tax purposes, benefits sought by the tax payer, e.g. accelerated depreciation of fixed assets, must first be recorded in the 'commercial' financial statements before they can be accepted for tax purposes.

9.4 Effect of tax considerations on presentation of accounts

The effect of tax considerations on the presentation of accounts is minimal, as the presentation of accounts is determined by the Luxembourg Monetary Institute.

10 INTERPRETATION OF ACCOUNTS

10.1 Adequacy of information as to contents and disclosure

Annual reports, available at the banks' offices as well as the annual accounts published in the Official Gazette, are in the layout prescribed by the LMI as shown in Appendix I.

Most annual reports include comparative figures for the previous year, the report of the board of directors to the Ordinary General Meeting and the statutory auditors' report, although none of these are required to be published. Few banks include notes on the accounts as part of the annual report.

10.2 Audit and reliability of information

An annual audit of the financial statements of the credit institution must be carried out by one or several independent auditors of satisfactory professional repute, who have the experience necessary to carry out their duties. Alternatively, the statutory auditor (or commissaire(s) aux comptes) who is considered to be an internal supervisory body of the bank and therefore not independent, may carry out this examination provided that he or they have the experience necessary to report in accordance with the standards fixed by the LMI (see Section 2.7).

In accordance with the Law of 23 April 1981 and the LMI Circular No. 84/16 the LMI requires an external auditor to be appointed and that he should be independent and qualified. The control of the external auditor should complement the control of the commissaire.

However, credit institutions which at 27 April 1984 are not yet audited by an external auditor and do not wish to appoint one may leave the external control to the commissaire(s) aux comptes, provided that he has the necessary experience and that he presents a long form audit report which must cover the requirements of the LMI, that is to say, he has complied with 'generally accepted auditing standards' and the accounts have been prepared on a prudent and a going concern basis and that the accounts comply with the Luxembourg regulations.

10.3 Comparability between different banks on the basis of published accounts or publicly available returns

The use of a standard format (Appendix I) for published accounts does to some extent facilitate certain broad comparisons of the performance of different banks. However, the task of comparison remains, as in other countries, a very difficult one indeed, as banks do retain a degree of flexibility in the accounting bases which they adopt within the framework of the regulations, and notes to the accounts are generally not published. Also, the existence of hidden reserves and the combination of certain disclosed figures such as interest *and* commission or income *and* other taxes makes the analyst's task an unenviable one.

11 OTHER RELEVANT INFORMATION

11.1 Secrecy

It should be noted that the interests of the customer in Luxembourg are protected by banking secrecy law. It is a criminal offence to provide to a third party information concerning a customer and his account other than under circumstances permitted by the law, e.g. certain defined information may be released to a foreign parent company or the supervisory authorities to enable the bank's activities to be properly supervised. A third party would have to obtain a Luxembourg Court Order before details of a customer and his account could be released by the bank.

APPENDIX I

Prescribed format for publication of annual accounts

BALANCE SHEET

I. ASSETS

A Current assets

1 Liquid assets
   (a) Cash, postal cheque accounts, central banks;
   (b) Due from banks at sight
2 Assets receivable at short notice
3 Due from banks – term
4 Bills
5 Miscellaneous debtors
6 Hire purchase operations
7 Investments
   (a) Luxembourg public bonds
   (b) Foreign public bonds
   (c) Other fixed interest securities
   (d) Shares and other securities with variable return
8 Miscellaneous

B Fixed assets

9 Formation expenses
10 Investment participations
11 Due from non-banking affiliates
12 Premises
    Less depreciation
    Premises–(net)
13 Furniture and equipment

C Profit and loss

   (a) Loss carried forward
   (b) Loss for the year

TOTAL ASSETS

II. LIABILITIES

A Current liabilities

1 Privileged or secured creditors
2 Short-term liabilities
3 Due to banks at sight
4 Due to banks – term
5 Deposits and current accounts
   (a) Sight
   (b) Term
6 Debentures
7 Savings accounts
8 Miscellaneous creditors
9 Other liabilities

B Borrowed capital

10 Subordinated debts

C Non-current liabilities

11 Subscribed capital
    Less unpaid capital
    Paid-up capital
12 Legal reserve
13 Reserves – unavailable
14 Free reserves
15 Provisions

D Profit and loss

   (a) Profit carried forward
   (b) Profit for the year

TOTAL LIABILITIES

III. CONTINGENT ACCOUNTS

1 Amounts to be paid up on securities and participations
2 Commitments and acceptances
3 Guarantees given on own account and on behalf of third parties

TOTAL CONTINGENT ACCOUNTS

PROFIT AND LOSS ACCOUNT

I. DEBIT

1   Interest and commissions
2   General expenses
    (a)   Salaries and personnel expenses
    (b)   Taxes
    (c)   Operating expenses
3   Provisions
4   Depreciation
5   Miscellaneous expenses
6   Expenses and extraordinary charges
7   Net profit

TOTAL DEBIT

II. CREDIT

1   Interest and commissions
2   Other income
3   Transfers from provision accounts
4   Extraordinary revenue
5   Loss for the year

TOTAL CREDIT

161

APPENDIX II

Balance sheet LMI return format (summary form)

ASSETS

*Compared to balance sheet total

	C/Value of foreign currencies	Lux/Belgian Francs	TOTALS	* %
A. Liquid assets				
Cash				
Due from banks at sight	11			
B. Other current assets				
Other assets realisable at short notice	123			
Due from banks – term	125			
Bills	131			
Advances	133+135+137+139+141			
Securities	143			
Other assets	145			
Fiduciary accounts	147			
C. Fixed assets				
Pre-operating expenses	151			
Participations	153			
Subordinated debt on participations	154			
Debts on non-banking affiliates	155			
Premises	1571+1591			
% depreciation	1572+1592			
Net value	157+159			
Furniture and equipment	161			
Other fixed assets	163+165			
D. Profit and loss account	171			
TOTAL ASSETS	18			

LIABILITIES

*Compared to balance sheet total

	C/Value of foreign currencies	Lux/Belgian Francs	TOTALS	* %
A. Current liabilities				
Privileged or secured creditors tax	2111+2112+213			
Due to banks at sight	215			
Due to banks – term	217			
Current accounts	221			
Sight deposits	223			
Term deposits	225			
Certificates of deposit	227			
Bonds	229			
Savings accounts	233			
Sundry creditors	235			
Sundry	239			
Fiduciary accounts	241			
B. Borrowed capital				
Subordinated loans	251			
C.				
Paid-up capital	261			
Share premium	263			
Reserves	265			
Neutralised translation gains	266			
Provisions	267			
D. Profit and loss account	269			
TOTAL LIABILITIES	28			

CONTRA ACCOUNTS

		AMOUNTS		
		C/Value of foreign currencies	Lux/Belgian Francs	PARTIAL TOTALS

A. Future commitments of the bank

Forward transactions (in gross terms)	313			
(a) Foreign currencies	3131			
(b) Securities	3132			
(c) Precious metals	3133			
(d) Future transactions	3134			
REPURCHASE OR RESALE COMMITMENTS	314			
COMMITMENTS RESULTING FROM PURCHASE AND SALE OPTIONS	315			
AMOUNTS TO BE PAID UP ON INVESTMENT SECURITIES AND PARTICIPATIONS	316			
COMMITMENTS AND ACCEPTANCES	317			
GUARANTEES PLEDGED ON OWN ACCOUNT	318			
GUARANTEES GIVEN FOR THIRD PARTIES	319			
(a) Endorsements	3191			
(b) Other	3192			
OTHERS	320			

B. Assets held by the bank for third parties

FIDUCIARY OPERATIONS	331			
SECURITIES DEPOSITS	332			
PRECIOUS METALS DEPOSITS	333			
DEPOSITS – OTHER	334			
ASSETS HELD FOR COLLECTION	335			
TOTAL CONTRA ACCOUNTS	38			
NUMBER OF CREDIT CARDS IN ISSUE				

163

APPENDIX III

Definitions used in the
Luxembourg Monetary Institute's financial reporting guidelines

(1) At sight (à vue)

The words 'at sight' always mean 'at sight and less than one month', based on the remaining period of the contracted term.

If the final maturity of an operation were to fall at the end of a month coinciding with a holiday and were thus to be extended to the following working day, the operation *may* be considered at sight, even if the remaining running period exceeds a calendar month.

(2) At term (à terme)

The expression 'at term' always means at a final maturity over one month, based on the remaining period of the contracted term.

(3) Remaining running period

The classification of assets and liabilities according to their liquidity or their maturity date always refers to the remaining running period as at the balance sheet date; it does not refer to the period initially contracted between parties.

(4) Rollover

For rollover credits it is necessary to refer to the final remaining running period and not to the running period remaining until the next 'rollover' date. Payments coming to a final maturity within the month following the balance sheet date must be classified 'at sight'.

(5) Accrued and matured interest

Accrued and matured interest is the interest payable or receivable which has actually matured before the balance sheet date but paid after that date. Accrued and matured interest must be classified with the item of the individual account to which they relate.

(6) Interest accrued but not matured

Interest accrued but not matured is the interest calculated *pro rata temporis* prior to the maturity date. The interest accrued but not matured is classified under the account heading of Miscellaneous – Transitory accounts.

(7) Instalment credit charges

Notwithstanding the above, instalment credits must be shown at the total value, that is to say a value including the principal claim, the total interest covering the whole renewing period of the credit and all related charges and commission fees. The non-accrued part of the interest must be classified under the account heading of Miscellaneous – Transitory accounts.

(8) Affiliated companies, affiliated banks

A company is defined as being 'affiliated' to another company when
  – a dominant influence can be directly or indirectly exerted;
  – they form a group;
  – a financial relationship is established, identified by a consortium contract, or a pooling of results or activities.

(9) Dominant influence

A dominant influence is assumed when a company
  – either holds 25% of the affiliated company's subscribed capital;
  – or holds 25% of the votes in the affiliated company;
  – or can nominate 25% of the affiliated management or board of directors.

(10) Group

A company which exerts a dominant influence and one or more affiliated companies form a group when all companies are exclusively managed by the company exerting the dominant influence. Each one of these companies is an enterprise of the group.

CHAPTER 9

THE NETHERLANDS

JAN VAN DER BEEK and ROBERT RUIJTER

1 GENERAL INFORMATION

The Netherlands are a constitutional monarchy, where the responsibility for government lies with the two houses of parliament, called First and Second Chamber. The First Chamber is elected by the provincial governments, which in turn are elected by the people of The Netherlands. The Second Chamber is elected directly by the people of The Netherlands on a proportional representation basis.

Banking and finance are important service industries in The Netherlands, providing funds for international as well as domestic trade. As a result, finance of all kinds for industry and commerce is readily available. There is a well-organised and efficient credit market, and the Dutch guilder is a stable and easily convertible currency. The guilder was one of the leading currencies in the former European currency link known as 'the snake', and now forms an important part of the new EEC European Monetary System.

De Nederlandsche Bank NV or The Netherlands Bank, which has its main office in Amsterdam, is the country's central bank. It is the sole issuer of currency and the regulator of the credit system. The Bank can impose its requirements on the other banks and financial institutions as part of its regulating function, in order to contain the growth of credit. In particular, it can prescribe lending ceilings and is authorised to set minimum liquidity ratios for the commercial banks in proportion to the demand deposits they hold. Interest rates charged by the commercial banks are influenced by the discount rates of the Netherlands Bank as well as by market pressures.

The Bank is the licensing authority for foreign exchange transactions, but authorises the commercial banks and other institutions to act as intermediaries in handling international payments. As a consequence of Dutch membership of the EEC's European Monetary System, the Bank regularly publishes buying and selling rates for the other currencies involved.

It also supervises the issue of securities on the internal market through a 'gentlemen's agreement' with the other banks.

The Netherlands Bank does not normally engage in commercial business itself.

Banks in The Netherlands have an excellent reputation for the range and quality of their services. Many have networks of branches spread throughout the country and the three leading Dutch banks rank among the world's 40 largest.

Most of the commercial banks have well-established foreign connections, either through their own branches in other countries or as members of well-known European and worldwide consortia. In addition, about 25 foreign banks have established offices in The Netherlands, among them leading institutions from North America, Europe and Japan.

The commercial banks have broadened their range of services in recent years, although there is still a certain amount of specialisation in that they tend to concentrate on short-term lending. They have, however, also entered the savings deposit market and as a result several have established their own medium-term credit subsidiaries. Moreover, they have diversified into such areas as merchant banking, housing finance, leasing and factoring. They also act as intermediaries with more specialised institutions, including the stock exchange, and manage mutual funds and other investment vehicles.

Because of the efficient direct transfer systems, cheques are seldom used in settlement of debts.

As a result of banking being an important industry, there are a number of laws governing banking in The Netherlands, the most important one of which is the Act on the Supervision of the Credit System, which was issued by the government on 13 April 1978.

1.1 Organisations covered by banking regulations

1.2 Summary of major types of bank

The Act on the Supervision of the Credit System applies to credit institutions which are defined as legal entities and partnerships which, and individuals who, make it their business to obtain funds, withdrawable daily or at less than two year's notice, whether or not in the form of savings, and to grant credits and make investments on their own account. The law then recognises four major types of credit institution:

(a) Commercial banks, also called general or universal banks.

(b) Banks organised on a co-operative basis.

(c) Security credit institutions, which mainly act as intermediaries in security transactions on the stock exchange.

(d) Savings banks.

The law further recognises of course the central bank and puts the Post Office Savings Bank and the postal cheque and giro services, which are both effectively operated under the auspices of the government, in a separate position in that these are mentioned separately throughout the law rather than being referred to as credit institutions. This also applies to banks which specialise in taking mortgages and other capital institutions for which, in article 30 of the law, special rules are laid down; which, however, result in similar supervision by the central bank as for credit institutions.

Only registered credit institutions are allowed to solicit from the public on a commercial basis deposit of less than Dfl100,000, or to act as intermediary in any way to obtain such deposits. Exemptions to this rule may be granted but could be coupled with special requirements or be made subject to restrictions.[1]

No unregistered entity may use the word 'bank' in its name unless it is clear from the context that an operation whereby funds are accepted, and credits granted, is not the object of the entity. This can be for example the case in the insurance industry, which, as in other Western European countries, uses the generally accepted expression 'insurance banks'.

1.3 Supervisory authorities
1.4 Status of supervisory authorities

By law, supervisory and other powers are granted to the Minister of Finance and/or the central bank. One of the tasks of the central bank is to safeguard the value of the guilder. For that purpose, and also in the interest of their solvency and liquidity, the Bank supervises credit institutions. The central bank is entitled to demand from credit institutions any information it deems necessary for carrying out its task. For that purpose credit institutions must submit monthly returns and annual accounts, which are discussed in further detail in the relative section of this chapter. At this stage it should be mentioned that the central bank has issued an English version of the Manual for the Credit System Supervision, which has been prepared for the convenience of foreign bankers operating in The Netherlands. The Dutch version, however, contains the official text.

1.5 Laws and regulations governing banks
1.6 Application of general company law to banks
1.7 Sources of laws and regulations

Credit institutions in The Netherlands are subject to both the general company laws included in Civil Code[2] as well as all the banking laws. These laws are all made by parliament, although it should be noted that the detailed regulations are made by the central bank under powers delegated to it.

1.8 Ability of foreign banks to operate through branches and subsidiaries

Foreign banks are allowed to operate in The Netherlands both through subsidiaries incorporated in The Netherlands and branches. The methods of incorporation and supervision are discussed below.

1.9 Level of supervisory control for branches and subsidiaries of foreign banks

There are three main areas to which the supervision of the central bank is directed: monetary supervision, operational supervision and structural supervision. Each of these main areas is discussed below.

(a) Monetary supervision

The central bank may issue general regulations in respect of:
(a) The minimum of funds a credit institution must maintain with the Bank in relation to funds received by it.
(b) The extent of foreign assets that must be maintained in relation to foreign liabilities.

In the framework of its task to safeguard the value of the guilder the central bank may, in consultation with the Bankers Association,[3] issue general guidelines or, where such guidelines are not followed, specific instructions to individual credit institutions. If the consultations with the Bankers Association are not successful the central bank may issue general instructions which may only contain:

(i)   Regulations dealing with the minimum of liquid funds to be maintained in relation to assets and liabilities.
(ii) Regulations dealing with the maximum credit facilities.
(iii) Prohibitions or restrictions in respect of specific types of advance.
(iv) Regulations dealing with interest and other conditions of foreign liabilities.

(b) Operational supervision

The central bank can issue directives to credit institutions, in consultation with the Bankers Association, dealing with operational matters in the area of solvency and liquidity.

The directives may only contain:
(a) Rules covering the minimum liquid funds in relation to:
(i)   Funds deposited with the bank.
(ii) Individual creditors' funds in so far as they exceed a percentage of the total funds deposited.
(b) Rules covering the minimum own equity to be maintained in relation to:
(i)   Credits granted or investments.
(ii) Risk carrying obligations.
(iii) Uncovered foreign exchange positions.
(iv) Separate items of the above in so far as they exceed a certain percentage of the bank's own equity.
(v)   The liabilities of the bank.
(c) Prohibition, restrictions or regulations for:
(i)   Granting certain types or the size of credits.
(ii) Engaging in certain types or the size of investments.

---

[1] Act on the Supervision of the Credit System dated 13 April 1978, article 42
[2] Book II, titles 2, 6, and with effect from 1984 title 8
[3] The Bankers Association is a joint consultative committee of the commercial banks, excluding, however, one major commercial bank which is organised on a co-operative basis

(iii) Taking on certain types of risk or the size thereof.

(iv) Accepting uncovered foreign exchange positions or the size thereof.

So far the central bank has issued detailed solvency and liquidity directives, the compliance with which is embodied in the reporting requirements formalised in the monthly returns to be submitted to the central bank. The directives issued stipulate that:

– Assets must be classified according to their equity claim. They range from so-called solvency exempt to fully covered assets.

– Overdrafts may not be granted to one customer in excess of 25% of the bank's own equity without approval of the central bank.

– Overdrafts to one or more directors, in excess of respectively 1% and 2% of the bank's own equity, are not allowed without approval from the central bank.

– Assets must be classified according to their liquidity and compared with liabilities which are classified according to their liquidity requirements.

– Cash and similar liquid assets are to be set against short-term liabilities.

(c) Structural supervision

Credit institutions need prior approval from the Minister of Finance, in consultation with the central bank, for:

– Repayment of capital and capital reserves.

– Participations in excess of 5% in other companies.

– Taking over assets and liabilities of other companies.

– Mergers with other companies.

– Internal financial reorganisations.

– Admitting another partner in the case of partnerships.

The shareholder of a credit institution who controls 5% or more of the votes may not exercise his control without prior approval from the Minister of Finance, in consultation with the central bank. The Minister, who must obtain the advice of the central bank, gives his approval unless:

– The central bank feels that the transaction would be contrary to sound banking policy or could lead to undesirable developments in the banking industry.

– The Minister feels that the transaction could lead to undesirable developments in the credit system or that it could be contrary to other matters of public interest.

Other matters dealing with supervision relate to situations where the central bank becomes aware of developments in a credit institution which could endanger its solvency or liquidity; a notification thereof, which may be accompanied by directives, is given to the credit institution. If the central bank feels that such directives are not properly followed, it may designate persons for a period of two years to whom the management of the credit institution must submit all its proposed actions and without whose prior approval the management may not operate. Further, in addition to the normal bankruptcy law the central bank has extensive powers in the areas of appointment of receivers and liquidation in cases where the solvency and liquidity of a credit institution show dangerous developments. The Law of 1978 also provides a guarantee arrangement for claims on credit institutions by private individuals, societies and foundations. This arrangement is made between the various representative organisations of credit institutions and the central bank. The central bank, as executive body of the parties to the arrangements, pays to the above-mentioned creditors of credit institutions which have failed for claims registered in the name of those creditors, excluding subordinated claims, a maximum amount of Dfl30,000. This amount is reconsidered annually.

The amounts so paid by the central bank will be recovered by it from all registered credit institutions, basically on a pro-rata basis to the funds deposited by private individuals with each credit institution. This deposit insurance system first came into operation in 1981 when creditors of the failing bank each received a maximum of Dfl30,000.

Entities which are involved in 'near banking' activities can be subjected to similar supervision by the central bank as credit institutions. Such enterprises and institutions shall be deemed by the central bank to be credit institutions (and therefore subject to supervision) if they have short-term deposits not less than Dfl10 million and not more than Dfl50 million providing these deposits were not obtained from credit institutions.

1.10 Methods of incorporation

All new businesses, whether Dutch or foreign-owned, must comply with registration rules and meet environmental requirements. Each new business entity must be entered in the Commercial or Trade Register kept by the Chamber of Commerce of the district in which the business has its registered address or legal domicile. The information to be filed in the register varies with the type of enterprise – company, partnership, branch or other – and broadly includes:

(1) A copy in the Dutch language of the constitution document of the enterprise, showing its name (and trade name if different), purpose and registered address.

(2) A statement of authorised, issued and paid-in share capital. If any issued shares have not been fully paid, each shareholder's name, address, number of shares and the amount paid must be listed annually until all issued shares have been fully paid in. It should be noted that with effect from 1 January 1982 the minimum equity requirement for credit institutions has been established at Dfl5 million, except for security credit institutions, for which the minimum equity requirement has been established at Dfl1 million.

(3) A list of the names, addresses, nationality and other personal particulars of each supervisory and managing director.

(4) Similar information as in (3), concerning each partner in a general partnership and each general or managing partner in a limited partnership, together with capital contributions concerning each limited partner.

(5) A definition of each managing director's authority to represent and bind the enterprise in dealings with third parties; for example, if there are two or more of such directors, whether one may act alone or only in combination with another:

Each change in the information filed must be reported to the Chamber of Commerce and entered in the register. Each new enterprise must register with the local offices of direct taxation, indirect taxation and social security.

The principal forms of commercial enterprise for banks are:

(1) Private company (Besloten Vennootschap met beperkte aansprakelijkheid or BV). For practical purposes, this is the equivalent of a British private limited company, a German GmbH or a French Sarl. The liability of shareholders is limited to the capital subscriptions; the company is an independent legal entity which can enter in contracts and sue and be sued and shares can be transferred (subject to certain restrictions) without affecting the continued existence of the company, although they may not be offered for public subscription or trading.

(2) Public company (Naamloze Vennootschap or NV). This is the commonest form of incorporation for banks in The Netherlands, partly because this is the form adopted by entities which wish to raise capital publicly, whether listed on the stock exchange or not. It corresponds closely to the Public Company or Corporation form in most other countries. There is normally no restriction in the issue or transfer of an NV's shares or notes although the NV's own constitution documents may introduce restrictions if so desired.

(3) General partnership (Vennootschap Onder Firma or VOF). This is the usual form of commercial partnership, in which all partners are jointly and severally liable for all its debts and obligations. Partnerships are not legal entities separate from the individuals who compose them.

(4) Co-operative society (Cooperatieve Vereniging or CV). This is an association of persons which allows for the free entry and withdrawal of members. The name must contain the word co-operative and give an indication of its objectives as well as certain initials to indicate the liability of its members: WA (unlimited liability), BA (limited liability) or UA (no liability).

(5) Branch of a foreign organisation (Bijkantoor or Filiaal). This is not a separate legal entity but is an establishment of its parent body, in whatever form that body carries out its business. Branches of foreign banks must maintain books and records in The Netherlands.

As indicated, a credit institution must have a licence from the central bank, which is granted upon request, unless:

— Daily management is not by at least two or more persons.

— The credit institution operates as a public or limited corporation (NV or BV) and it does not have at least three or more supervisory directors.

— It does not have the minimum required own equity for corporate entities as indicated above or, in the case of a branch of a foreign bank, the amount reflected in the books of the branch as capital and reserves, less amounts due by the foreign bank to the branch to the extent that they exceed funds deposited by the branch with the foreign bank on behalf of third parties.

— If operating as a branch, its net assets employed in The Netherlands are less than the equity of the branch.

— A foreign entity operating as a branch does not have a licence to operate as a credit institution in its home country.

— One or more of the persons in charge of the day-to-day running of the bank do not have adequate expertise in banking.

— One or more persons who can determine the policies of the bank are in the opinion of the central bank of a character which may jeopardise the position of the creditors of the bank.

A licence can be withdrawn if:

— The entity ceases to be a credit institution.

— The credit institution no longer complies with the requirements as to double management, supervisory directors and minimum equity.

— The credit institution does not comply with the filing and auditing requirements, as discussed later in this chapter.

— The central bank has objections to the professional or moral qualities of one or more persons in the bank's management.

— The foreign entity operating as a branch no longer has a licence to operate as a credit institution in its home country.

Special licensing conditions may be imposed on foreign companies resident in non-EEC countries which wish to operate a credit institution as a branch.

If there exists a relationship whereby one credit institution is liable for another credit institution the latter one may be exempted from complying with the management, supervisory board, filing and auditing requirements.

1.11 Areas within the country subject to special laws

None.

2 ACCOUNTING

2.1 Laws and regulations governing accounts

2.2 Application of general company law

2.3 Roles of legislature and supervisory authority

2.4 Extent to which requirements as to returns and accounts are prescribed by laws and regulations

Accounts of credit institutions are, as a general rule, also subject to general company law as laid down in the Civil Code Book II. In addition, as indicated before, the banking regulations derived from the law by the central bank lay down requirements for the submission of the accounts and prescribe their form and contents. The latter also applies to the monthly returns which have to be furnished to the central bank by all credit institutions. Forms and specifications need to be submitted as soon as possible after the month end, but definitely before the 16th working day following the due date. Some forms are due twice a month, others on a quarterly basis; details are given in the Manual of Credit System Supervision. This manual also includes examples of the returns. The central bank also issued the Model Annual Accounts for Credit Institutions, which contains instructions for the contents of the annual accounts of general banks, co-operative banks, and savings banks.

2.5 Obligations to furnish accounts

2.5.1 Accounting periods and times of furnishing

2.5.2 Form of accounts to be furnished

2.5.3 Mandatory accounting dates

Each credit institution must file its annual accounts, as approved or adopted by the authorised body in its organisation, with the central bank and, in accordance with the Civil Code, with the Commercial Trade Register, within six months of the end of the financial year. The end of the financial year has by law been established for credit institutions as being 31 December. The fact that the annual accounts have been filed with the Commercial Trade Register must be published in the local press.

2.6 Requirements as to accounts (a) prior to incorporation (b) prior to commencement of trading and (c) in order to continue trading

As indicated in the section on methods of incorporation, accounts need to be filed in order to be able to continue trading. Accounts are, however, not required prior to incorporation or commencement of trading.

2.7 Audit requirements

The annual accounts must be audited by a public 'register accountant' or a public accountant with a foreign qualification who has been granted a licence by the Minister of Economic Affairs to practise in The Netherlands. The auditor must be authorised by the credit institution to supply the central bank with information. In certain instances the filing and auditing requirements for a credit institution may be relaxed by the central bank, which can be the case with branches of foreign banks who are allowed to file the accounts of the ultimate holding company. It is mandatory for a monthly return to be audited and reported on to the central bank. This applies both to credit institutions incorporated in The Netherlands as well as to branches of foreign banks. It is the auditor's responsibility to select the monthly return he will report on.

2.8 Acceptability to fiscal authorities of accounts submitted to supervisory authority

Section 9 deals with the taxation laws affecting banks. It should be stressed here that the normal tax regime applies to credit institutions and, therefore, the annual accounts as published or returns submitted to the central bank are not accepted by the fiscal authorities as the accounts for tax purposes.

2.9 Submission of accounts to any authority other than by requirement of law

None.

2.10 Application of laws and regulations to foreign banks operating through branches and subsidiaries

All regulations applying to Dutch banks apply to foreign banks operating in The Netherlands through either subsidiaries or branches. In this context it should also be emphasised that foreign entities operating as branches of credit institutions in The Netherlands fall under the Act only to the extent that they operate in The Netherlands. However, the central bank may decide that all or some transactions entered into with foreign entities outside their branch operation may also form part of such operations.

A special regulation exists in that the own equity of a branch of a foreign bank is considered to be the amount reflected in the books of the branch as capital and reserves, less amounts due by the foreign bank to the branch to the extent that they exceed funds deposited by the branch with the foreign bank on behalf of third parties. An amount equal to this equity must consist of assets held within The Netherlands. In respect of these assets the creditors are preferred in case of failure of the foreign bank.

2.11 Availability of accounts for public inspection

Accounts filed with the Commercial Trade Registers are available for public inspection. The returns provided to the central bank are, however, not available for public inspection and are for use by the central bank only.

3 FORMAT, STYLE AND CONTENTS OF ACCOUNTS

3.1 Extent to which format is laid down by statute, supervisory authority, generally accepted accounting practice or otherwise

3.2 Description of format

3.3 Extent to which contents are prescribed by statute, supervisory authority, generally accepted accounting practice or otherwise

3.4 Disclosure of specific items required other than those required by general law

3.5 Exemptions from disclosure allowed in respect of banking items

In May 1981 the central bank issued the Model Annual Accounts for Credit Institutions in accordance with section 11 of the Act on the Supervision of the Credit System. The Model contains instructions for the contents of the annual accounts of general banks, co-operative banks and savings banks. The Model is shown in Appendix I. A Model for security credit institutions is still under discussion at the present time. The Model in certain instances overlaps the Civil Code. The following observations are taken from, or based on, the central bank's explanatory notes to the Model as well as from the Civil Code.

Subject to the authority of the central bank to grant exceptions, all general banks must file their annual audited accounts with the Commercial Trade Register and with the central bank. Irrespective of the legal structure of a general bank, the annual accounts must comply with the Model. The captions contained in the Model may be combined if a respective balance sheet caption does not exceed the lower of 1% of the balance sheet total or 10% of the respective section, or if the respective profit and loss caption is less than 1% of the total of interest, commission and other income. It is, however, not permitted to add captions to those of the Model. Both the horizontal and vertical forms of presentation are acceptable.

Due to the fact that this special Model for annual accounts is in existence for credit institutions there are certain exemptions from disclosure as required by the Civil Code, for example the industrial segment information for debtors required in the notes may be confined to ratios and smaller banks may omit this information if such information would disclose the activities of an individual client. However, in general the Model requires more detailed information than the Civil Code would require.

Within this context it also needs to be mentioned that the Model Annual Accounts for Credit Institutions, as it stands presently, does not take into account the requirements of the proposed EEC Directive for the accounts of credit institutions. This Directive requires more detailed disclosures than the present Model, and it may therefore be anticipated that in the next few years the Model will be adapted, if necessary, to the final Directive.

3.6 Hidden reserves

Hidden reserves are not allowed to be maintained in The Netherlands. A loss contingency reserve can however be maintained as described in Section 4.2.3.

3.7 Requirements as to consolidated accounts

The Model applies to a credit institution's own accounts and to the consolidated accounts. However, similar to the exception in the Civil Code, to the extent the consolidated profit and loss account gives the required detailed information, the credit institution's own profit and loss account need not give such information. For consolidation purposes, participations are defined as direct or indirect investments of a permanent nature through which management can be influenced. Investments of more than 25% are always considered participations. Other financial institutions in which a participation of more than 50% of the outstanding share capital exists must be fully consolidated, showing minority interests where applicable. A 50% participation is proportionally consolidated. The remaining participations are not consolidated, however, if a bank does not have a majority holding in another financial institution but nevertheless controls it, the participation should be treated as a majority holding and should be consolidated.

4 ACCOUNTING POLICIES

4.1 Responsibility for laying down accounting policies

The Model Annual Accounts for Credit Institutions as

issued by the central bank shows certain accounting principles which have to be adhered to. The general rule for annual accounts of credit institutions, however, is that accounting principles generally acceptable in The Netherlands must be used.[4] These are similar to those in the United States although there are some minor differences.

4.2 Particular accounting policies

4.2.1 Foreign exchange

Assets and liabilities in foreign currencies are translated into Dutch guilders at rates prevailing at the balance sheet date. Unexpired forward exchange contracts due within two working days after the year end are treated as having expired during the year.

Foreign exchange open positions are subject to accounting principles that are considered generally acceptable in The Netherlands, which, being governed by prudence, require the accrual of anticipated losses, whereas profits are not recognised until realised.

Exchange differences, including those on loans to participations and on other investments, must be disclosed in the accounts and, therefore, may not be recorded in the provision for contingencies; however, positive exchange differences may be credited to the valuation differences reserve account. To the extent that negative exchange differences cannot be absorbed by this reserve account, they must be charged to income. Only exceptional exchange differences may be recorded against the provision for contingencies.

4.2.2 Deferred tax

Provision is made for all tax payable on the income earned to the date of the accounts. Differences in accounting principles used for fiscal purposes from generally accepted principles are dealt with through a deferred tax account, using the full liability method. This account is also used to record the notional tax liability on any revaluation surpluses arising from the adoption of replacement value accounting.

4.2.3 Specific and general provision for bad and doubtful debts

In accordance with the Act on the Supervision of the Credit System, general banks are permitted to classify the provision for contingencies under creditors and to show in the profit and loss account only transfers to and releases from the provision. In the explanatory notes to the Model it is confirmed that the provision is created to cover the general risks which a credit institution has, either directly or indirectly through participations, in connection with the granting of credit or other banking activities and that charges for such risks do not have to be disclosed. The provision is meant to cover losses on debtors and extraordinary losses not foreseeable in

---

[4] The main source of generally accepted accounting principles is the Civil Code Book II title 8. In addition there are Richtlijnen (standards) now issued by the Raad voor de Zaarverslaggeving (Accounting Standards Board)

principle and therefore not quantifiable as charges. Examples of such extraordinary losses are large frauds and nationalisations. Transfers to the provision must be made on a consistent basis and a provision should be maintained at a reasonable minimum in relation to the risks it is intended to cover.

The transfers to the provision for contingencies are not tax deductible. In order to compute the tax charge, profit before deducting transfers to the provision must be taken into account. The tax on the transfers to the provision must be charged to the provision and it is therefore assumed that the taxes claimed because of charges to the provision will be credited to the provision. Specific provisions, such as the loan loss reserve, are deducted from the assets they relate to in accordance with accounting principles that are considered generally acceptable in The Netherlands.

4.2.4 Treatment of provisions in accounts

The general provision is included in creditors and is not separately disclosed, while the specific provision is deducted from those assets where the loss is anticipated to arise.

4.2.5 Premiums and discounts on investments (amortise, write off, etc.)

Normal practice is for debentures and other dated investments held in portfolio for investment purposes to be carried in the balance sheet at redemption value, less any provision. The difference between cost and redemption value is included under debtors or creditors and is amortised over the life of the relevant debenture.

4.2.6 Offsets, i.e. to what extent can assets and liabilities be set off against each other (legally or in practice)

Dutch company law does allow offsetting in those cases where a legal right of set-off exists. However, it is normal practice not to offset debit and credit balances even if the items are for the same customer.

4.2.7 Goodwill

Goodwill purchased in connection with participations (which have to be consolidated) may not be deducted from the provision for contingencies. It may be charged to the general reserve or to the valuation differences reserve. If a material increase in profitability is expected, goodwill may be capitalised and included under other investments or, if not in connection with a participation, under other assets and amortised over a period not exceeding five years. The Civil Code presently does not state a period but an amendment to this Code, which is presently under discussion, also states a period of five years but leaves the possibility to adopt a period of 10 years in certain cases. This option will, however, not be open to credit institutions. Negative goodwill may be credited to the general reserve or to the valuation differences reserve. If the negative goodwill is the result of material under-profitability of the enterprise taken over, it may be shown under other liabilities and amortised over a period not exceeding five years.

4.2.8 Consolidation

As mentioned in Section 3.7, consolidated accounts are required and these should be prepared on the basis set out in that section.

4.2.9 Revaluations of assets

Credit institutions' premises and rental property are valued at current cost, which represents the lower of replacement and sales value. In principle this also applies to foreclosed properties, unused bank buildings and buildings under construction. As a result, the depreciation shown in the income statement therefore is also based on this revalued amount. Revaluation as well as devaluation differences are credited or debited to a reserve account in the balance sheet, or, if no such reserve exists, debited to profit and loss account.

4.2.10 Instalment finance and leasing including basis of recognition of income

Unearned interest on instalment loans is taken into income over the lifetime of the loan. Similar to this the unearned income element on direct financing leases is taken to income based on an implicit interest rate. Accounting for leases in general is again very similar to current practice in the United States.

4.2.11 Dealing assets

Investments held for trading purposes are normally valued at market value, which in the case of listed investments is the market quotation and in the case of unlisted investments at the directors' estimate. Where necessary, provisions are raised to cover any expected decline in value.

4.2.12 Pensions

Pension rights of employees are typically either reinsured with a third party insurance company or with an own pension fund, which is then subject to the same laws and funding regulations as the insurance companies. All benefits are normally fully vested through annual premium payments. Backservice typically is fully provided for.

4.2.13 Depreciation

Depreciation is typically accounted for on a straight line basis over the economic life of the relative assets.

171

5 WINDOW DRESSING

The use of window dressing is made difficult due to the detailed reporting requirements applicable in The Netherlands. In addition, the audit requirements make significant window dressing very difficult. However, there is a tendency for banks to make short-term borrowings and placings at the year end in order to inflate balance sheet totals.

6 AMOUNTS REQUIRED TO BE MAINTAINED BY LAW OR OTHERWISE

6.1 Introduction

In the section on Methods of incorporation general requirements which credit institutions must adhere to have been discussed. In addition there are very detailed solvency and liquidity requirements which must be met by credit institutions. Details of these are set out below.

6.2 Solvency directives

Solvency directives apply to commercial banks, banks organised on a co-operative basis and security credit institutions. The basic principle of these solvency directives is that the own resources (capital, reserves and subordinated loans) of a credit institution must be sufficient to cover the risks involved in the conduct of its business. In this connection a distinction is made between assets exempt from and assets subject to solvency requirements, the latter being subject to various percentages. In addition, among other things, solvency requirements are imposed on irrevocable credits, guarantees, etc. and also in respect of 'large items' which are detailed below. The implementation of the solvency requirements, and the way to calculate these, are detailed in the Manual of Credit System Supervision. The calculation is based on the 'net' monthly returns, i.e. after the set-off of balances and after deductions of items under lien and provisions. The solvency rules are also applied to the assets of branches outside The Netherlands of Dutch credit institutions and to the consolidated assets pro rata of the participation of financial institutions in which the reporting institution has an interest of over 10%.

The solvency rules are also designed to promote the spreading of risks by imposing restrictions on 'large items'. Net credit facilities and other items subject to solvency requirements and relating to one single debtor or a group of interconnected debtors together – after the set-off of balances and after deduction of provisions – may not exceed 25% of the credit institutions's capital, reserves and subordinated loans without the central bank's prior approval. In addition, participations in non-financial institutions, investments in objects, as well as homogeneous goods and homogeneous precious metals, which exceed 25% of the equity of the credit institution, are only allowed after approval from the Bank. For the purpose of determining this upper limit these items, in so far as they are covered by guarantees of foreign credit institutions, need only be included for one half. Secondly, if the total of the above items subject to solvency requirements and relating to one single debtor or a group of interconnected debtors represents more than 15% of the credit institution's capital, reserves and subordinated loans, then these items are subject to extra solvency requirements.

Fixed assets (immobilia) are tested separately against capital, reserves and subordinated loans. The amount of these assets, such as business premises and participations in non-financial institutions, may not exceed the reporting institution's capital, reserves and subordinated loans.

In addition to the above requirements the following must be taken into account:

(1) Credit facilities to individual directors or other senior officers of credit institutions are permitted only up to a maximum of 1% of the institution's capital, reserves and subordinated loans, while the total of these facilities may not exceed 2% of that figure. For the purpose of this regulation, directors and other senior officers are generally understood to be: members of the board of management or of the management, partners, members of the supervisory board, as well as their spouses and their relatives in the first and second degree. The maxima mentioned above may only be exceeded with the central bank's prior consent. Such consent is, in principle, only given in so far as the part of the credits in excess of the percentages stated above is adequately covered by normal bankable collateral, such as quoted securities or mortgages with sufficient excess value.

(2) In the event of capital, reserves or subordinated loans being returned to shareholders and/or investors directly or indirectly, the central bank reserves the right to take the amounts returned into account in the solvency test for the determination of actual capital, reserves and subordinated loans of the credit institution.

It should be noted that special solvency and liquidity directives have been issued for savings banks. However, as the traditional distinctions between the various types of credit institutions are increasingly fading, the savings banks are also allowed to opt for the directives applicable to general banks.

6.3 Liquidity directives

The basic principle of the liquidity directives, which also apply to commercial banks, banks organised on a co-operative basis, and security credit institutions, is that liquid assets have to be held against certain liabilities of a credit institution so that it may be assumed that the liabilities can be met on the due date or on demand, as the case may be. In addition to this aim of the liquidity directives, resulting in rules on liquidity in the 'broad' sense, rules have also been laid down for 'narrow' liquidity (comprising only assets with the highest liquidity). The object of the latter rules – which are not yet operative – is to guard against excessive reliance by credit institutions on money market financing.

The components of actual liquidity and the liquidity requirements are detailed in the Manual of Credit System Supervision. A calculation is made on the basis of the 'net' monthly returns which the credit institution has to prepare, i.e. after set-off of balances and after deduction of items under lien and provisions.

A maturity schedule has to be compiled mainly for lending to the public sector, deposit business and moneys borrowed, before the liquidity directives are applied. Depending on the remaining period to maturity, repayments to be made can be offset against money to be received in the same period. The liquidity directives are applicable only to the 'net' items, that is those which can only be offset via the maturity schedule. The 'net' repayments to be made within 24 months are subject to a liquidity requirement of 20%, with the exception of 'net' repayments to be made within one month (remaining period to maturity) to mainly domestic and foreign credit institutions, and to other foreign creditors (in so far as these are above the lowest balance in the past 12 months), for which the liquidity requirement is 100%. Specific rules have been laid down for the inclusion in the maturity schedule of loans on a rollover basis; moreover, a limited amount of credit to the private sector may be included in the maturity schedule.

As liquidity is sensitive to the calling in of large items a 'large item rule' is included in the liquidity directives just as in the solvency directives. Under this arrangement, items which (a) each individually amount to 1-2% and together to 15% or over; (b) each individually amount to 2% or over of total liabilities are subject, after offsetting in the maturity schedule, to extra liquidity requirements.

Furthermore, account is taken of the financing of international and domestic trade; this is reflected in the 'special facility' which means that, within the framework of the 'broad' liquidity test, it is permissible (the arrangement is thus optional) to include in the maturity schedule advances against warehouse warrants and bills of lading − provided that the original period to maturity of these advances is less than three months − for 60% of the value of the goods in question.

Lastly, account is taken in the directives of the refinancing − primarily of importance for security credit institutions − of advances against securities. For this purpose, advances against certain securities obtained do not have to be included as an item to be deducted from actual liquidity within the framework of the rules on 'narrow' liquidity.

In addition to the 'broad' liquidity directives mentioned above, mortgage banks are subject to the following special directives:
(a) The maturity schedule can include:
− All contractual redemptions on fixed advances to the private sector, including rollovers, as well as extra redemptions on these advances.
− Commitments relating to fixed advances, investments and participations as well as the relating redemptions and sales.
− Commitments relating to unused lines of credit from third parties and the relating redemptions.
(b) Mortgage banks can only obtain short money from credit institutions.
(c) Credit facilities which are not or not entirely used may, for the unused portion, under certain circumstances be considered for the 'broad' liquidity.

The amount that mortgage banks can borrow on a short-term basis is subject to certain limitations. If these limits are repeatedly exceeded the central bank can designate the mortgage bank as a credit institution.

7 KEY RATIOS

The key ratios that are relevant for banking in The Netherlands have been discussed in the previous section.

8 ACCOUNTING RETURNS OTHER THAN ACCOUNTS
8.1 By whom required
8.2 Nature of requirements

General banks, banks organised on a co-operative basis and security credit institutions are required to file monthly returns; mortgage banks are required to file these returns on a quarterly basis. These statements − including any appendices − provide the information required by the central bank for the performance of its duties under the Act on the Supervision of the Credit System, namely monetary supervision and operational supervision of the credit system. In view of these special objectives of the reporting system, the revaluation of assets and liabilities cannot always be based on principles which are regarded as acceptable in businesses on a going concern basis. In general it may be stated that in the valuation of assets and liabilities for the monthly return allowance must be made for a break in continuity. Among other things, this means that the value of foreign assets and liabilities expressed in foreign currencies must be converted into guilders at the rates prevailing on the date of the monthly return and that intangible assets must be written down to zero.

On the basis of the above general principles, certain assets are subject to very stringent rules which are detailed in the explanatory notes provided by the central bank together with the statements and forms of the monthly returns. These rules mainly apply to securities and real estate. Securities officially quoted on the stock exchange are to be valued at the latest known quotation as of the date of the monthly return. Securities which are not officially quoted are to be valued at the closest possible approximation to the current value at the date of the monthly return. Real estate is to be valued according to very stringent rules. These rules include mandatory valuation at amounts per cubic metre outside measurements at which commercial buildings are to be capitalised in the monthly return and which amounts are established by the Bank. Depreciation of real estate is also to be applied under very stringent rules, ranging from 5% for non-saleability items to the normal percentage of 1½%, applied on a straight line basis and applying from the date of the asset being taken into use as a commercial building. Further, the amounts can differ substantially per region of the country.

If it appears from the monthly return that circumstances occur which could affect the solvency or liquidity of the credit institution the central bank, by law, must follow certain procedures. As a first step, the central bank must point out the unsatisfactory development to the credit institution. This can be accompanied by instructions for corrective action which will have to be followed by the credit institution. If these instructions are not acted upon satisfactorily the central bank can undertake the following:

(1) Establish a silent guardianship, which means that the central bank will designate persons who will effectively carry out the management of the credit institution. This measure will not be published in order to avoid depositors withdrawing all their funds from the credit institution. To third parties, therefore, the credit institution will still appear to have full legal status. This procedure could be of help in cases of injudicious or unco-operative management of the credit institution.

(2) Publication of the guardianship. The fact that this is a possibility acts as a powerful deterrent.

(3) Discussions with the Bankers Association. Based on such discussions, arrangements for support could possibly be made with other credit institutions or a take-over by a financially sound institution could be achieved.

(4) File a request to apply the so-called emergency ruling. This effectively means that a bank will enter into bankruptcy, and that a liquidator will be appointed to limit losses for the creditors as far as possible.

It should be noted that the central bank has developed rules whereby the public accountants of the credit institutions are requested to report on one of the monthly returns (see Section 2.7).

9 TAXATION

9.1 General method of taxation
9.2 Accounts as basis for taxation
9.3 Adjustments permitted or required

Taxation rules applicable to credit institutions are the same as for all other forms of business organisation within The Netherlands. Therefore, although the annual accounts form the basis for taxation, generally certain adjustments are required to the accounts to arrive at taxable income. This implies, therefore, that taxation considerations in general do not affect the presentation of the annual accounts other than relating to deferred taxes.

The principal taxes in The Netherlands are corporate and personal taxes on income and value added tax. A brief discussion of the principal taxes which apply to the corporate structures most common to banks follows.

(a) Corporate income tax

The most important Dutch corporate entities subject to corporate tax are the BV and the NV. Co-operative mutual insurance and banking associations and certain public enterprises are also subject to this tax.

Resident corporations, both NVs and BVs, are taxed on worldwide income. In calculating taxable income, deductions are permitted for necessary operating expenses, management fees, interest paid, royalties paid, licence fees paid, all domestic taxes except the corporate income tax, contributions to pension funds, insurance premiums, depreciation of fixed assets, contributions to bona fide charities, and amortisation of intangibles.

The income of foreign branches and subsidiaries of Dutch corporations is not ordinarily subject to Dutch income tax.

Returns must be filed for the annual tax within six months after the end of the company's fiscal year, and final payment (the current year's tax less the provisional tax paid) must be paid within one month after receipt of the final tax bill, which is issued after the return has been filed.

(b) Corporate tax rates

The current rate of corporate tax is 43%. A provisional tax of 85% of the prior year's tax is payable annually, unless it can be shown that the current year's income will be less than that of the prior year.

(c) Withholding taxes and taxes on dividends

There is a withholding tax of 25% on dividends. Dividends paid to stockholders in countries with which The Netherlands has double tax treaties are either exempt or subject to a reduced withholding rate, as are dividends paid to a qualified investment company. There are no withholding taxes on interest, royalties, or technical assistance fees. Dividends received by a corporate tax payer owning 5% or more of the capital stock of the paying company are tax exempt.

(d) Exchange fluctuations

Foreign currency assets and liabilities must, for tax purposes, be valued in Dutch currency. Liquid assets, such as cash, which have a definable foreign currency value must be translated at the exchange rate ruling at the balance sheet date. Current receivables and payables are usually translated at rates ruling at the balance sheet date. Fixed assets must be translated at historical rates, while portfolio investments may be translated at either current or historical rates. Long-term lendings and borrowings in foreign currency should be valued at the balance sheet date at the amount estimated to be payable at redemption in Dutch guilders. However, it is permissible for lendings and borrowings to be translated at exchange rates ruling at the balance sheet date or at historical rates, unless there is a substantial and permanent difference between the two. If there is, the rate at balance sheet date prevails. The assets and liabilities of foreign permanent establishments must be valued individually, not as a whole.

(e) Treatment of losses

Carry forward and carry back. Losses incurred may be carried back to the two preceding years, or carried forward for offset against profits of the following eight years. Losses must be utilised in the order in which they are incurred, so that earlier losses must always be utilised in preference to the losses of later years.

To prevent the purchase of shares in tax-loss corporations, in certain cases the law prohibits the carry forward of losses by a corporation whose trade has ceased, almost or completely, at the time the transfer of shares took place. This rule does not apply if at least 70% of the ownership of shares in such a corporation remains in the hands of the same ultimate individual shareholders, or if the change of shareholders is due to either inheritance or marriage.

(f) Branch income tax

Branches of foreign corporations are taxed as corporations but only on their Netherlands source income. There is no withholding tax on remittances to home offices.

(g) Partnership tax

General partnership. A general partnership is not a taxable entity; each partner is taxed on his share of the partnership profits (whether or not distributed).

Limited partnership. A limited partnership, in which the interest of a limited partner may be transferred without consent of other partners, is taxed as a corporation and partnership distributions are considered dividends. If such a transfer does require the consent of other partners, the partnership is treated as a general partnership for tax purposes.

10 INTERPRETATION OF ACCOUNTS

10.1 Adequacy of information as to contents and disclosure

10.2 Audit and reliability of information

10.3 Comparability between different banks on the basis of published accounts or publicly available returns

Annual accounts of credit institutions, which as indicated before are subject to audit, generally provide reliable information on the activities and results of the credit institution. Due to the fact that the annual accounts have to adhere to the Model as set by the central bank it is possible to compare the annual accounts of credit institutions, although information on interest and commissions earned is difficult to compare and movements in the provision for contingencies cannot at all be derived from the information provided. To the extent that a comparison is possible, this is made easier by the so-

called 'Bankenboekje' (Banks book) which is issued every year by the Nederlands Instituut voor het Bank and Effecten Bedrijf (The Netherlands Institute for the Bank and Security Industry). In this booklet the annual accounts of De Nederlandsche Bank, the commercial banks, the banks organised on a co-operative basis, savings banks, security credit institutions, and mortgage banks are summarised, giving such information as addresses, names of management, names of subsidiaries, number of branches, number of staff, and a brief overview of the balance sheets and profit and loss accounts. The booklet also provides further information on institutions which are related to the banking industries, not being credit institutions themselves. As indicated, this booklet compares the published annual accounts of credit institutions and not the monthly returns, because the returns which have to be filed with the Bank are not available for public inspection. The information derived therefrom is only used by the central bank in its own annual accounts, but in those accounts information is only provided by type of credit institution and in totals.

11 OTHER RELEVANT INFORMATION

Dutch banks provide extensive services. They can offer short- and medium-term loans to industry and provide international links, either through their own overseas branches or in co-operation with foreign banks. In addition, more than 25 foreign banks have established offices in The Netherlands, among them leading institutions from North America, Europe and Japan. The combination of domestic and foreign banking expertise gives the businessmen operating in and from The Netherlands a wide range of options. A virtual absence of exchange controls is an important factor for foreign companies operating in The Netherlands. The guilder is a strong currency which is freely convertible. There are no restrictions imposed on the repatriation or transfer of earnings, capital, royalties or loan interest. Such payments may be made in guilders or in any other currency. Currency transactions related to imports and exports do not require any special licence. These operations are embedded in a solid reporting and disclosure framework as a monitoring device to meet the central bank's as well as banking clients' and creditors' informational needs.

APPENDIX

Example of annual accounts of banks

Example Bank NV
Balance Sheet
31 December 19x2
with comparative figures for 19x1

Assets	19x2	19x1	Liabilities	19x2	19x1
Cash in hand, with Central Bank, and money at call	xxx	xxx	Capital Issued	xxx	xxx
Treasury paper	xxx	xxx	Still to be paid-up	xxx	xxx
Domestic and foreign banks	xxx	xxx			
Securities and syndicates	xxx	xxx	Paid-up	xxx	xxx
Advances against treasury paper and/or securities	xxx	xxx	Reserves	xxx	xxx
Bills receivable	xxx	xxx	Shareholders' funds	xxx	xxx
Debts from or guaranteed by public authorities	xxx	xxx	Subordinated loans	xxx	xxx
Debtors	xxx	xxx	Guarantee equity	xxx	xxx
			Minority interests[1]	xxx	xxx
Participations, including advances	xxx	xxx	Capital and reserves of associated foundation[1]	xxx	xxx
Property and equipment	xxx	xxx	Documents of value and other loans	xxx	xxx
Other assets	xxx	xxx	Savings deposits	xxx	xxx
			Deposits	xxx	xxx
			Creditors	xxx	xxx
			Domestic and foreign bankers	xxx	xxx
			Funds accepted	xxx	xxx
			Other liabilities	xxx	xxx
Total	xxx	xxx	Total	xxx	xxx
			Commitments in respect of guarantees	xxx	xxx
			Commitments in respect of irrevocable letters of credit	xxx	xxx
			Recourse obligations from discounted bills	xxx	xxx

[1] Only in the case of consolidated or combined accounts

Example Bank NV

Profit and loss account

for the year ended 31 December 19x2
with comparative figures for 19x1

		19x2	*19x1*
Interest	XXX		XXX
Commission	XXX		XXX
Other income	XXX		XXX
		XXX	XXX
Salaries, pensions and other social charges	XXX		XXX
Other charges	XXX		XXX
Depreciation fixed assets	XXX		XXX
		XXX	XXX
Gross operating income		XXX	XXX
Transfer to/release from provision for contingencies	XXX		XXX
Extraordinary income and charges	XXX		XXX
		XXX	XXX
Profit/loss before taxation		XXX	XXX
Taxation		XXX	XXX
		XXX	XXX
Undistributable profit/loss of associated foundation	XXX		XXX
Minority interest	XXX		XXX
		XXX	XXX
Net profit/loss		XXX	XXX
Unappropriated profit per 31 December, last year		XXX	XXX
Distributable profit/deficit		XXX	XXX
Profit appropriation			
Transfer to reserves		XXX	XXX
Dividend		XXX	XXX
Profit shares, bonuses		XXX	XXX
....		XXX	XXX
....		XXX	XXX
Undistributed profits		XXX	XXX
		XXX	XXX

Example Bank NV

Notes to the Accounts

31 December 19x2

A ACCOUNTING PRINCIPLES

Consolidation

All financial institution subsidiaries, in which a majority interest of more than 50% is held or where the bank has effective control over management, are fully consolidated.

Investments of 50% in financial institutions are proportionally consolidated. The remaining investments are not consolidated.

Netherlands treasury paper

Netherlands treasury paper is valued at face value, including interest accrued.

Securities

(a) Debentures held in portfolio are valued at redemption value less provisions. The difference between cost and redemption value is included under debtors or creditors and is amortised over the life of the relative debenture.

(b) Debentures held for trading are valued at the latest quoted value, less a provision for debentures traded infrequently.

(c) Quoted shares are valued at the latest quoted market price, less a provision for shares traded infrequently. Unquoted shares are valued at the value of the estimated proceeds.

Participations

Participations are valued at equity on the basis of accounting principles adopted by the bank. The equity value includes purchased goodwill in cases where a materially higher profitability is expected. Goodwill is amortised over five years.

Property

(a) Bank premises and rental property are valued at current cost which represents the lower of replacement value and proceeds value. Periodically, independent valuations are made whereas in interim periods the value is established by means of building indices. Depreciation on current cost is based on the estimated useful life of the premises.

(b) Foreclosed properties and unused bank buildings are valued at independent sales valuation. Foreclosed properties are recorded as such as soon as the bank acquires the economic ownership.

(c) Buildings under construction are valued at the lower of cost and market value based on an independent valuation.

Foreign currencies

Assets and liabilities in foreign currencies are translated into Dutch guilders at rates prevailing at the balance sheet date. Unexpired forward exchange contracts due within two working days after year end are treated as having expired during the year.

Assets sold under written repurchase agreements are shown under their relative heading. Funds received in connection therewith are recorded under Funds Accepted. Assets purchased under written resale agreements are not included under asset headings. The funds disbursed are included under Debtors.

Provisions

Provisions relating to the valuation of specific assets are deducted from the relative assets. The provision for contingencies recorded for the general risks encountered by a bank in its granting of credits and its other banking activities has been included under Creditors. An amount is transferred to or from earnings on an annual basis. The provision is used to record losses on debtors and also extraordinary losses which in principle are not foreseeable or quantifiable. The provision for deferred taxation is also recorded under Creditors.

B BALANCE SHEET

	19x2	19x1
Cash in hand, with central bank and money at call	xxx	xxx

Included herein are the accounts with the Nederlandsche Bank and with foreign central banks by offices abroad. Money at call includes only call money with banks and public authorities or with others if secured by treasury paper or securities

	19x2	19x1
Treasury paper		
Domestic, including interest accrued	xxx	xxx
Foreign, including interest accrued	xxx	xxx
	xxx	xxx

Domestic and foreign banks
Included herein are accounts with central banks except those maintained by offices abroad. Also included are advances not on the basis of money at call

	19x2	19x1
Balances on demand	xxx	xxx
Other	xxx	xxx
	xxx	xxx

Securities and syndicates	19x2	19x1
Debentures of domestic public authorities		
Quoted	xxx	xxx
Unquoted	xxx	xxx
Debentures guaranteed by domestic public authorities		
Quoted	xxx	xxx
Unquoted	xxx	xxx
Other securities and syndicates		
Quoted	xxx	xxx
Unquoted	xxx	xxx
	xxx	xxx

	19x2	19x1
Borrowed securities and syndicates	xxx	xxx
Trading securities and syndicates	xxx	xxx
Portfolio securities and syndicates	xxx	xxx
	xxx	xxx

	19x2	19x1
Advances against treasury paper and/or securities	xxx	xxx

Included herein are non-call money advances against treasury paper

	19x2	19x1
Debts from or guaranteed by public authorities	xxx	xxx

Included herein are current account and mortgage loans guaranteed by public authorities and also advances to the Bank voor Nederlandse Gemeenten and the Nederlandse Waterschapsbank

	19x2	19x1
Debts from or guaranteed by domestic public authorities	xxx	xxx
Debts from or guaranteed by foreign public authorities	xxx	xxx
	xxx	xxx

	19x2	19x1
Debtors	xxx	xxx

Included herein are accrued interest and prepayments. Amounts due by executive and supervisory directors not in the ordinary course of banking are Flxxx (19x1: Flxxx)

Debtors can be segregated as follows:	19x2	19x1
Securities		
− mortgages	xxx	xxx
− guaranteed by banks	xxx	xxx
− acceptance credits	xxx	xxx
− other	xxx	xxx
Total	xxx	xxx

Terms, according to average original terms	19x2	19x1
− less than two years	xxx	xxx
− more than two years	xxx	xxx
Total	xxx	xxx

Industry	19x2	19x1
− agricultural, etc.	xxx	xxx
− manufacturing	xxx	xxx
− service	xxx	xxx
− financial	xxx	xxx
Total	xxx	xxx

Participations, including advances	19x2	19x1
Participations not consolidated	xxx	xxx
Advances to unconsolidated participations	xxx	xxx
Total per consolidated balance sheet	xxx	xxx
Consolidated participations	xxx	xxx
Advances to consolidated participations	xxx	xxx
Total per bank balance sheet	xxx	xxx

The total amount of goodwill included herein is Flxxx (19x1: Flxxx)

Property and equipment	19x2	19x1
Bank premises	xxx	xxx
Other property	xxx	xxx
Equipment	xxx	xxx
	xxx	xxx

	19x2	19x1
Other assets	xxx	xxx

Included herein are precious metals and coins not used as currency made from precious metals, and also goodwill not connected with participations

Reserves	19x2	19x1
Revaluation reserve	xxx	xxx
Valuation difference reserve	xxx	xxx
....	xxx	xxx
....	xxx	xxx
Other	xxx	xxx
	xxx	xxx

	19x2	*19x1*
Movements in the reserves during the year were as follows:		
Subordinated loans		
The consolidated accounts include subordinated loans to subsidiaries amounting to Flxxx (19x1: Flxxx). Also included are loans due after one year to shareholders Flxxx (19x1: Flxxx) and to participations Flxxx (19x1: Flxxx)		
Loans due within one year	xxx	xxx
Other loans	xxx	xxx
	xxx	xxx
Savings deposits		
Included are deposits due after one year from shareholders Flxxx (19x1: Flxxx) and from participations Flxxx (19x1: Flxxx)		
Due within one year	xxx	xxx
Other	xxx	xxx
	xxx	xxx
Deposits		
Included herein are all deposits by non-banking institutions, unless they are considered savings deposits. Deposits by shareholders due after one year amounted to Flxxx (19x1: Flxxx) and by participations Flxxx (19x1: Flxxx)		
Due within one year	xxx	xxx
Other	xxx	xxx
	xxx	xxx
Creditors	xxx	xxx
Included herein are the provisions for contingencies and deferred taxation as well as the following provisions:		
....	xxx	xxx
....	xxx	xxx
Other	xxx	xxx
Balances due to shareholders after one year	xxx	xxx
Balances due to participations after one year	xxx	xxx
Due within one year	xxx	xxx
Other	xxx	xxx
	xxx	xxx
Domestic and foreign banks		
Included herein are all accounts with foreign central banks and with general banks except money at call		
Balances on demand	xxx	xxx
Other	xxx	xxx
	xxx	xxx
Funds accepted		
Due within one year	xxx	xxx
Other	xxx	xxx
	xxx	xxx
Other liabilities		
Due within one year	xxx	xxx
Other	xxx	xxx
	xxx	xxx

C PROFIT AND LOSS ACCOUNT

Interest

Included herein is the net amount of interest received and paid, net results of interest dealings, commission on the granting of credits and interest on open foreign exchange positions.

Commission

This includes commission on term contracts, foreign currency sales and purchase commission and commission on transfers abroad.

Other income

This includes all foreign exchange and securities differences, income from consolidated participations, non-banking and non-investment income and revaluation income from non-consolidated participations arising from undistributed profit.

Extraordinary income and charges

This includes all items resulting from actions on instances of an incidental nature outside the normal course of banking and also outside the control of management.

CHAPTER 10

SPAIN

IAN ANGUS and SUSANA ANTOLINEZ

1 GENERAL INFORMATION

The banking industry is central to the Spanish economy. Firstly, direct influence is exercised by the banks over a great number of Spanish businesses through equity participation. Secondly, because of the relative under-capitalisation of much of Spanish industry, it is unduly dependent on short-term bank finance, which gives the banks an extraordinarily large influence over wide areas of the economy.

A major factor in bolstering the importance of the banks is the weakness of the stockmarket as a means of raising venture capital. Institutional investors (which dominate stockmarkets elsewhere) such as insurance companies, investment trusts and pension funds, which have a stabilising influence on security markets, are either controlled by the banks themselves (insurance companies) or are not large enough to exercise significant influence (investment trusts and pension funds).

A number of bank mergers have recently taken place or are being negotiated which have the effect of eliminating small and unprofitable banks, giving way to larger and more competitive units. According to the latest available statistics, between 1947 and 1982 more than 90 banks have been absorbed by 20 larger banks and of these acquisitions, 60 have been made by only five banks.

The Bank of Spain is the main instrument through which the government's monetary policy is implemented. By establishing the key ratios which must be maintained by private and savings banks, setting the rediscount rate and operations on the open market, the Bank of Spain directly intervenes in regulating monetary supply.

In addition, the Bank of Spain acts as banker for the treasury by servicing the national debt and short-term treasury bonds and granting loans and advances to the treasury.

1.1 Organisations covered by banking regulations

The principal elements of the Spanish banking system are as follows:

— Bank of Spain (Banco de España): nationalised central bank which serves as one of the instruments of government monetary policy.

— Official credit institutions (Instituciones de Crédito Oficial): official banks, nationalised in 1962, which are responsible for the management of official loans and are supervised by the Official Credit Institute (Instituto de Crédito Oficial — ICO).

— Savings banks (Cajas de Ahorro, also referred to as Cajas de Ahorro y Montes de Piedad): non-profit financial institutions which grant loans for projects held to be in the public interest and to the agricultural sector.

— Private banks (Bancos privados): profit-orientated financial institutions, authorised to carry out all types of banking transactions.

There are also non-banking financial institutions (investment funds, leasing companies, financial entities and insurance companies) which are not covered by banking legislation.

1.2 Summary of major types of bank

Law 2/1962 of 14 April, which sets forth the basic principles for the regulation of credit and banking, requires private banks, as a fundamental element of banking reform, to limit their activities to one or the other of the following:

(a) Commercial or deposit banking

Carrying out short-term operations, mainly for the financing of commercial transactions.

(b) Industrial or merchant banking

Financing medium- and long-term operations such as the promotion of new businesses and financing of fixed asset investments.

However, only the industrial banks can be considered as fully complying with these requirements, given that some commercial banks act also as industrial banks. Furthermore, the most recent regulations tend to suppress the specialisation which the 1962 Law sought to impose.

Banks can also be classified as national, regional or local according to their geographical branch coverage. The right to open new branches varies with the type of bank. This geographical categorisation of each bank is laid down by the Bank of Spain.

By September 1983, 133 banks were operating in Spain in the following categories:

National banks	13
Merchant banks	25
Regional banks	13
Local banks	48
Foreign banks	34
	133

1.3 Supervisory authorities

These organisations are supervised by the following authorities:

The Bank of Spain, which is directly responsible to the government, through the Ministry of Finance, the Economy and Commerce. Following government directives, the Bank of Spain is responsible for the inspection of private banks. It is also in charge of the co-ordination and inspection of savings banks as well as of formulating overall policy for these institutions.

The Higher Banking Council (Consejo Superior Bancario) is a legal entity, created by Law of 31 December 1946, to serve as consultative body to the Bank of Spain, representing the banking industry. Its organisation and functions are defined by the Decree of 16 October 1950. It is formed by representatives of the Bank of Spain and those of official, private and foreign banks operating in Spain. It issues non-binding regulations which purport to govern relationships between its member banks, as well as acting as arbitrator in disputes among them.

The Official Credit Institute is the permanent liaison body between the administration and the official banks, which it co-ordinates, controls and inspects, providing them with the necessary financial resources.

1.4 Status of supervisory authorities

The functions of the Bank of Spain are set forth in Law 2/1962, which contains the basic principles for the regulation of credit and banking and in the Third Additional Disposition of the Law of 19 June 1971. This law, which deals with the organisation of and guidelines for loans granted by the official banks, also establishes the functions of the Official Credit Institute.

1.5 Laws and regulations governing banks

The basic laws that regulate banking are:
- Law of 31 December 1946 on banking regulation.
- Law 2/1962 of 14 April, on the basic principles for the regulation of credit and banking.
- Law of 19 June 1971 on organisation of and guidelines for official credit.

The following should also be taken into consideration:
(a) Relating to commercial banks: Decree 63/1972 of 13 January, which was partially modified by Decree 2246/1974 of 9 August.
(b) Relating to industrial banks: Decree-Law 53/1962 of 29 November in addition to those mentioned in (a).
(c) Relating to foreign banks: Decree 1388/1978 of 23 June.

A large number of enabling regulations, some of them of great importance, also exist.

1.6 Application of general company law to banks

Savings banks are non-profit institutions, with their own special regulations. Official banks, although established as limited liability companies, are subject to the laws governing state-owned enterprises with respect to their budgeting and control. In other respects they are subject to general company law.

On the other hand, private banks are regulated by the Ley de Régimen Jurídico de las Sociedades Anónimas of 17 July 1951 (general company law) and various specific regulations relating to the legal reserve and the obligation to maintain, *inter alia*, capital, liquidity and cash ratios (see Section 7).

1.7 Sources of laws and regulations

Laws are made by the Cortes (parliament), although the administration establishes the enabling regulations.

1.8 Ability of foreign banks to operate through branches and subsidiaries

Foreign banks may operate in Spain in one of the following forms:
(a) Representative offices, the activities of which are limited to public relations: they may not carry out credit, deposit or other banking transactions. They must be authorised by the Ministry of Finance, at the instance of the Bank of Spain.
(b) Subsidiaries of foreign banks, incorporated as Spanish legal entities, wholly-owned by foreign banks: they must be authorised by the Council of Ministers at the instance of the Ministry of Finance. They are incorporated as limited companies with a minimum capital of Ptas2,000 million, which must be issued at a 100% share premium and 100% paid-up. There exist some limitations with respect to deposit-taking.
(c) Branches of foreign banks, authorised to carry out banking transactions: they must maintain a branch capital of at least Ptas2,000 million, which must be at least 50% paid-up and the remainder must be paid up in a maximum period of one year. They must be authorised by the Council of Ministers at the instance of the Ministry of Finance.

1.9 Level of supervisory control for branches and subsidiaries of foreign banks

Control and supervision of these three types of foreign bank is the same and does not vary from that applicable to banking entities in general.

1.10 Method of incorporation

Decree 2246/1974, of 9 August regulates the establishment of new private banks.

The establishment of a new private bank must be authorised by the Ministry of Finance, at the instance of the Bank of Spain. The request must be accompanied by a report from the Higher Banking Council and the Consultative Committee of Official Credit (Junta Consultiva de Crédito Oficial).

Banks must be incorporated as limited liability companies (Sociedades Anónimas), with a minimum share capital of Ptas750 million if they operate in Madrid or Barcelona or Ptas500 million if they are based in any other city. These limits as set forth above are different for foreign banks. The share capital must be at least 50% paid-up at the date of incorporation and the remainder must be paid up in a maximum period of two years thereafter.

The shares must be issued with a premium of 100%, which must be accounted for in a special account and may not be disposed of without prior authorisation by the Ministry of Finance.

The shareholders must be private investors and participation by foreigners is limited to 15% of the share capital. During the first five years after incorporation, shares may not be traded without a special authorisation granted by the Ministry of Finance and all new shares issued must be subscribed by the existing shareholders.

After incorporation and in order to enable them to commence operations, banks must be registered at the Registry of Banks and Bankers (Registro de Bancos y Banqueros) at the Bank of Spain and the Mercantile Registry (Registro Mercantil).

Foreign banks, as mentioned above, may be established as representative offices, branches and limited liability companies. In the latter case, the restrictions concerning the shareholders are not applicable since they may be wholly-owned by foreign banks.

1.11 Areas within the country subject to special laws

At present all areas of the country are subject to the same legislation in connection with banking operations, except for the share capital requirement discussed under Section 1.10 above.

The differences in legislation depend not upon the area of the country where the bank operates but upon the type of activity it carries out. In this manner, specific legislation exists for each of the major types of bank (i.e. official, foreign, commercial, merchant and savings banks).

2 ACCOUNTING

2.1 Laws and regulations governing accounts

Banking institutions are subject to the Code of Commerce and to general company law with regard to their accounting requirements.

In addition, they must prepare and publish financial statements in the format laid down by an Order of the Ministry of Finance of 28 June 1950 (as modified by subsequent regulations).

2.2 Application of general company law

Bank financial statements are subject to general company law, except for those of savings banks which have their own legislation.

2.3 Roles of legislature and supervisory authority

Laws are made by parliament although the administration establishes the enabling regulations.

2.4 Extent to which requirements as to returns and accounts are prescribed by laws and regulations

Laws and regulations lay down the requirements for the submission of returns and accounts and prescribe their form and content.

Two sets of financial statements must be prepared:
(a) 'Public Balance Sheet and Profit and Loss Account'. These must be made public by the banks on a monthly basis (balance sheet) or on a yearly basis (profit and loss account).

Their format and content are outlined in an Order of the Ministry of Finance dated 16 July 1982.

The Bank of Spain has subsequently issued more detailed specifications as to the exact content of each account and the applicable valuation rules.
(b) 'Confidential Balance Sheet and Profit and Loss Account'. These documents must be submitted to the Bank of Spain, which is prohibited from publishing or exhibiting them.

Circular 16/1982 issued by the Bank of Spain on 11 August 1982 establishes the contents and new format for this set of financial statements.

Apart from these basic financial statements, banks must present other information to the Bank of Spain, to the Higher Banking Council and the National Institute of Statistics (see Appendix I).

2.5 Obligations to furnish accounts

2.5.1 Accounting periods and times of furnishing

The 'Confidential Balance Sheet' must be furnished monthly to the Bank of Spain and quarterly to the Higher Banking Council.

The 'Confidential Profit and Loss Account' must be furnished quarterly (in the months of April, July, October and January) to the Bank of Spain and to the Higher Banking Council.

In compliance with general company law, banks must also present to the shareholders' meeting their annual (public) balance sheet and profit and loss account.

The public balance sheet must be sent monthly to the Bank of Spain.

A great number of additional reports must be submitted; Appendix I contains a list of the documents which must be presented, the bodies to which they must be sent and the periods which they must cover.

2.5.2 Form of accounts to be furnished

The format of the balance sheet and profit and loss account can be seen in Appendix II.

2.5.3 Mandatory accounting dates

The financial year end is 31 December for all banks operating in Spain.

2.6 Requirements as to accounts (a) prior to incorporation (b) prior to commencement of trading and (c) in order to continue trading

No accounts need be furnished prior to incorporation. The filing requirements described in Section 2.5 above must be complied with, both prior to commencement of trading and in order to continue trading.

2.7 Audit requirements

No regulation establishes that accounts must be audited but the Bank of Spain carries out inspections of private banks on a random basis or when special problems arise.

In a widely commented Circular (No. 1/1982) of 26 January, known as the 'Superpastoral', the Bank of Spain 'recommended' that certain banks be audited, in view of a rash of irregularities and bankruptcies. While many banks have followed the recommendation, there is resistance in several quarters.

2.8 Acceptability to fiscal authorities of accounts submitted to supervisory authority

The tax authorities are not bound to accept accounts from a bank merely because they agree with accounts filed with the Bank of Spain, nor is there any evidence that in practice such accounts are regarded as more reliable by them. The fiscal authorities have the right to inspect banks' declarations in the same way as those of other taxpayers.

2.9 Submission of accounts to any authority other than by requirement of law

No such submission is required.

2.10 Application of laws and regulations to foreign banks operating through branches and subsidiaries

The regulations for filing, etc. are the same for foreign banks (operating through branches or subsidiaries) as for national banks.

2.11 Availability of accounts for public inspection

The accounts available for public inspection are the annual and monthly public balance sheets and the annual public profit and loss accounts.

3 FORMAT, STYLE AND CONTENTS OF ACCOUNTS

3.1 Extent to which format is laid down by statute, supervisory authority, generally accepted accounting practice or otherwise

The annual information which private banks must present to their shareholders includes the balance sheet, before and after profit appropriation, the profit and loss account and the proposal for distribution of profits, as well as the names of the members of the board of directors.

There is no obligation to disclose any additional information in notes to the financial statements, although this practice is frequent.

The format of the financial statements which may be published by private banks was last established by an Order of the Ministry of Finance dated 16 July 1982, the implementation of which has been enforced by the Bank of Spain as of 31 December 1982.

The format is essentially the same as that required for Bank of Spain filings, although less detailed information is required.

3.2 Description of format

The format of the balance sheet and profit and loss account can be seen in Appendix II.

3.3 Extent to which contents are prescribed by statute, supervisory authority, generally accepted accounting practice or otherwise

As mentioned above, contents of the accounts are laid down, by way of amplification of the requirements incorporated in general company law, by the Ministry of Finance. All banks operating in Spain must comply with this regulation.

3.4 Disclosure of specific items required other than those required by general law

None.

3.5 Exemptions from disclosure allowed in respect of banking items

None.

3.6 Hidden reserves

Banks are not permitted to maintain hidden reserves.

3.7 Requirements as to consolidated accounts

Consolidated accounts are not required and, therefore, are generally not prepared.

4 ACCOUNTING POLICIES

4.1 Responsibility for laying down accounting policies

The accounting policies are set by the Bank of Spain, as supervisory body, through its Circulars, and are in most cases in agreement with accounting principles set out in the Spanish General Accounting Plan.

In some cases, discrepancies from tax legislation occur as some of the Bank of Spain's accounting policies are not acceptable for tax purposes. An attempt at harmonisation is now being made.

In practice, there is no effective requirement to disclose major accounting policies by way of note or otherwise.

4.2 Particular accounting policies

The following are some specific mandatory policies:

4.2.1 Foreign exchange

Profits and losses from foreign exchange transactions are recognised as follows:

– Forward transactions: assets and liabilities are evaluated at month end by using the forward exchange rate on that date, corresponding to the maturity date of the particular transaction. Differences between monthly valuations are recognised as profits or losses in the profit and loss account for the period in question.

– Other transactions: assets and liabilities are converted into pesetas at month end by using the rate prevailing on that date. Differences arising on monthly valuations are recognised in the profit and loss account for the period in question.

4.2.2 Deferred tax

Deferred taxes are not accounted for in Spain.

4.2.3 Specific and general provisions for bad and doubtful debts

4.2.4 Treatment of provisions in accounts

The regulations for doubtful debt provisions are contained in Circular No. 1 of 1982 (the 'Superpastoral'). The minimum amount of the provision is determined by applying specified minimum percentages to the overdue balances. The resulting provision must be at least 1.5% of the year end total of unsecured loans, bills of exchange discounted, documentary credits and guarantees given (i.e. total of credit investments and 'signature' risks, excluding secured loans).

Banks can choose to reach this minimum either by making the appropriate charges to their profit and loss account or by transferring the necessary amounts from their revaluation reserves (see Section 4.2.9).

The Circular confers on the Bank of Spain the power to require an external audit of those banks failing to record provisions at least equal to the minimum percentage mentioned above.

The provision for doubtful debts appears on the credit side of the balance sheet and may not be deducted from the receivables to which it relates.

4.2.5 Premiums and discounts on investments (amortise, write off, etc.)

No specific policy has been laid down regarding this matter. Normal practice is to value investments at acquisition cost and any profit or loss arising from sale or redemption (in the case of bonds or debentures) is accounted for on the date this transaction takes place.

In the case of premiums or discounts due to the issuance of bonds or debentures, these are normally amortised over the period to redemption.

4.2.6 Offsets, i.e. to what extent can assets and liabilities be set off against each other (legally or in practice)

The offsetting of assets against liabilities is prohibited by the Bank of Spain.

4.2.7 Goodwill

Goodwill may not be accounted for unless it arises from a merger. In this case there is no provision as to the period over which goodwill must be written off.

The depreciation of goodwill, if and where it occurs, must be accounted for as an extraordinary item in the profit and loss account.

4.2.8 Consolidation

As there is no obligation (or prevalent practice) to consolidate, there is no specific policy on this matter.

A Ministerial Order of 15 July 1982 establishes the basis and principle of consolidation without, however, imposing any obligation to consolidate.

4.2.9 Revaluations of assets

Revaluation of fixed assets is authorised, and indeed encouraged, by law on a sporadic basis in order to bring companies' accounts more closely into line with the 'actual' value of fixed assets. Reserves that result from a revaluation process must be shown separately on the balance sheet. Revaluation is calculated by multiplying the acquisition cost (and the provision for depreciation) by coefficients which vary according to the year of acquisition (and the year in which the depreciation was provided) of each specific asset, as set out in the revaluation law in question.

Revaluations are subject to inspection by the Ministry of Finance.

The most recent revaluation law is applicable to the first balance sheet established on or after 31 December 1983.

4.2.10 Instalment finance and leasing including basis of recognition of income

There are no specific accounting norms regarding instalment finance.

From a tax point of view, income arising from instalment sales may be recognised on a cash basis.

As for leasing operations, there is an adaptation of the General Chart of Accounts (Plan General de Contabilidad) for leasing firms, published in June 1976.

This Chart of Accounts regulates the accounting of leasing transactions from the lessor point of view.

Income from leasing contracts is recognised on the basis of the periodic lease payments which fall due over the duration of the contract.

Depreciation of leased equipment may be calculated following the straight line or declining balance methods.

4.2.11 Dealing assets

Quoted investments are valued at the lower of cost or average market value over the last quarter. The difference between cost and this valuation is normally shown in a separate account.

4.2.12 Pensions

No accounting policy is laid down to deal with the liability arising from pension plans, although nearly all banks are obliged to pay pensions under the collective wage agreements, which are regulated by the Ministry of Labour.

Given that the tax authorities generally challenge or disallow transfers to provisions for pensions, most banks account for this liability on a cash basis.

4.2.13 Depreciation

Depreciation of fixed assets must effectively be based on percentages or coefficients within the minimum and maximum rates established by the Ministry of Finance.

Depreciation percentages can vary from year to year within this range and the depreciation method may be either straight line or reducing balance.

Minimum and maximum fiscal rates vary according to the nature of the asset being depreciated.

5 WINDOW DRESSING

Window dressing is not a question which has been specifically addressed by legislation or industry regulations but it is thought to be a common practice.

6 AMOUNTS REQUIRED TO BE MAINTAINED BY LAW OR OTHERWISE

The minimum share capital permitted is Ptas500 million (Ptas750 million if established in Madrid or Barcelona). Shares issued must be totally subscribed and paid-up to a minimum of 50% on the date of formation. The remaining 50% must be fully paid-in a maximum of two years afterwards.

The minimum capital for foreign banks has been set at Ptas2,000 million, issued with 100% share premium, starting in April 1983.

The creation of a bank requires the approval of the Higher Banking Council and of the Consultative Committee of Official Credit. Before commencing operations, banks must be entered in the Official Register of Banks and Bankers maintained by the Bank of Spain.

There exist some other initial limitations with regard to the transactions which may be effected, profit distribution, opening of branches, etc.

Concerning the reserves, the only limitation relates to the legal reserve, which must be built up out of profits to an amount equivalent to at least 50% of the share capital.

Whenever gross profits exceed 4% of the share capital, a transfer must be made to the legal reserve of at least 10% of profits until the 50% minimum level is reached.

7 KEY RATIOS

The primary instruments of bank control are the key ratios, which must be maintained, including the following:

7.1 Capital ratio

Definition: Minimum ratio between own and external financing

The calculation is based on month end balances and is carried out by the Bank of Spain using the confidential balance sheet submitted by banks (see Section 2.4).

If in any given month the ratio is not achieved, the Bank of Spain may grant a period of grace of six months (which may be extended to 18 months) if the achieved ratio is not more than 1% less than the minimum required.

Minimum coefficient: Commercial banks: 8% (the Bank of Spain is empowered to vary the ratio required between 7 and 10%). Industrial banks: 10%

Calculation: Paid-up share capital *plus* reserves *divided by* creditors (pesetas plus foreign currency)

For the purpose of this calculation, industrial banks must include the nominal value of their issued and outstanding short-term bonds and debentures as creditors.

7.2 Cash ratio

This new formula for the cash ratio was effective from 17 January 1984.

Definition: Minimum ratio between liquid assets and creditor balances

Coefficient: 18%

This coefficient must be calculated daily and is declared to the Bank of Spain every ten days. The ten-day average must be of at least 18%. The Bank of Spain pays interest, at the rate of 13.5%, on that part of the qualifying assets which exceeds 5% of the liabilities entering into the computation.

The assets of any particular day are divided by the liabilities registered two days before.

Computation: Cash *plus* Bank of Spain current account *plus* unused credit facility from the Bank of Spain *divided by* creditors (foreign currency plus convertible pesetas) *plus* short-term bonds and debentures issued by the bank *plus* guarantees granted on bonds issued by other companies *plus* rediscounted or endorsed bills of exchange

7.3 Investment ratio

Definition: Minimum ratio which must be maintained between mandatory investments and creditor balances

Coefficient: Commercial banks: maximum, 25%; minimum, 21%. Industrial banks: 18%

Determination: The mandatory investments must be held in the following proportions:

(a) minimum of 13.5% in unpledged government stock

(b) minimum of 3% in export financing

(c) minimum of 5% in internal financing

(d) minimum of 3.5% in treasury notes

The assets of one month are divided by the liabilities of the previous month.

Any shortfall in the holding of government stock in one month must be covered by the 15th of the following month.

Any deficit in export financing must be covered by special cash deposits in the Bank of Spain.

A reform of the entire financial sector is planned by the government. For the time being only the cash ratio has been substantially modified. If and when the reform is completed, both the values of the aforementioned ratios as well as their method of computation might suffer quite radical changes.

8 ACCOUNTING RETURNS OTHER THAN ACCOUNTS

8.1 By whom required

8.2 Nature

Appendix I contains a detailed list of all the information which must be furnished by banks operating in Spain to the different authorities, indicating the authority with whom the information must be filed and the nature of the information.

9 TAXATION

9.1 General method of taxation

Private banks are subject to Spanish company tax (impuesto sobre sociedades) in the same way as commercial companies and at the same rate of 35%. Savings banks are subject to the same tax at the special rate of 26%.

9.2 Accounts as basis for taxation

Corporate tax law establishes that tax declarations must be in agreement with the accounting records maintained by the company which, in turn, must comply with the accounting regulations contained in the Code of Commerce and other applicable regulations. With respect to banks, specific regulations have already been mentioned.

9.3 Adjustments permitted or required

The fact that accounts form the basis for taxation does not mean that accounting policies acceptable for fiscal purposes always agree with accounting policies laid down by the Bank of Spain. A distinction must be made between the taxable profit and the book profit, since some expenses from the tax point of view and some criteria of income recognition differ from those contained in tax legislation.

The above comment is true for all Spanish companies but is specially relevant for banks since there are two tax regulations that conflict with the accounting policies laid down by the Bank of Spain. These are:

(a) Foreign exchange gains and losses: from a tax point of view, foreign exchange gains and losses may be recognised when debts are paid or credits recovered, i.e. only realised gains and losses are acceptable.

(b) Transfers to the doubtful debts provision: tax regulations are much more strict with respect to provisions for doubtful debts and are in conflict with the conservative criteria set forth by the Bank of Spain and mentioned above (see Section 4).

The conflict between these regulations has, however, been in large part resolved by two Orders of 22 March 1983 dealing with two specific questions: the treatment of exchange differences arising from foreign currency dealings and provisions for bad debts. In both cases the tax authorities have effectively accepted the rules laid down by the Bank of Spain.

9.4 Effect of tax considerations on presentation of accounts

Exceptionally, in the case of banks, taxation considerations do not influence the presentation of accounts to any great extent because the format and content of banks' accounts is so closely regulated by the Bank of Spain. The above-mentioned adjustments, which are necessary from a tax point of view, do not affect the presentation of the published accounts. The revaluations of assets explained in Section 4.2.9 above, which are primarily of a fiscal nature, do of course have considerable impact on accounts presentation.

10 INTERPRETATION OF ACCOUNTS

10.1 Adequacy of information as to contents and disclosure

Most bank accounts only show the bare legal minimum information and this restricts the information which can be extracted from the accounts. Investments are invariably accounted for at cost and no information is generally given as to their current worth.

The major banks are now disclosing additional information by way of footnotes and this trend is endorsed by the Bank of Spain which is also encouraging them to have their financial statements audited.

10.2 Audit and reliability of information

Generally, financial information published by Spanish banks is not subject to independent audit (although the situation is rapidly changing) and its reliability suffers in consequence. However, within the Spanish context, banking is the industry most closely controlled by government and a significant degree of uniformity has been achieved.

10.3 Comparability between different banks on the basis of published accounts or publicly available returns

All bank financial statements comply at least as to format with Bank of Spain regulations, facilitating comparison between banks. An increasing volume of prescriptive regulation will ensure that certain fundamental accounting policies are consistently observed.

The permissive nature of the Leyes de Actualización (Laws enabling revaluation of assets) means that some banks will have revalued assets and others not. As the surpluses on revaluation are frequently significant, distortion may arise on comparison in such cases.

Finally, until the requirement to consolidate material subsidiaries and disclose other related party items is imposed, the ability to make valid comparisons will be impaired.

APPENDIX I

Bank filing requirements

Spanish banks must comply with the following filing requirements:

(1) Bank of Spain

Daily

Where the following types of transaction arise, they must be reported at the close of business:

– Detailed list of inter-bank deposits taken or given by telephone.

– Detailed list of sales of foreign currency to customers for tourist or business purposes.

– Notification of changes to the official register of senior officers.

– Similarly, where authorisation is sought for the following operations it must be filed immediately:
(a) Inclusion of short-term export loans or loans for financing of equipment on the domestic market in the investment ratio.
(b) Granting of loans or guarantees to the bank's own senior officers.

Every ten days

Demonstration of compliance with cash ratio requirements.

Report movements and balances on their depositors' convertible peseta accounts.

Monthly

Confidential balance sheet: this is a detailed statement of financial condition at month end and comprises:

– Detailed balance sheet in accordance with the format laid down in Circular 16/1982, issued by the Bank of Spain.

– Condensed balance sheet showing totals for each type of currency (ordinary pesetas, convertible pesetas and foreign currency).

– Analysis of issued bonds and debentures.

Quarterly

Profit and loss account:

– Debtor accounts classified by date of maturity and by type of credit.

– Creditor and debtor accounts classified by province.

– Classification of contingent liabilities in the following categories: acceptances, underwritings and documentary credits.

– Reconciliation of the Bank of Spain current account.

Other quarterly information

Demonstration of compliance with the investment ratio.

Movements of the investment portfolio.

Investments and accounts held by non-residents, classified by country.

Doubtful debtors and special insolvency provisions.

Report of balances held by Spanish banks with their branches outside Spain.

Justification of balances of foreign exchange transactions.

Demonstration of compliance with capital ratio. This report is submitted together with every third ten-daily report on the cash ratios.

Summary of time deposits, showing maturity dates.

Actual interest rate charged or given by the bank for deposits and asset operations for transactions at long term.

Activity report to reflect demand inter-bank borrowings of Ptas50 million or more, excluding those from banks outside Spain and from correspondent banks.

Report of loans to customers at month end in excess or Ptas4 million and list of customers which have gone into bankruptcy, insolvency or suspension of payments.

Half yearly

(i) List of individual customers in respect of which the bank's exposure exceeds 2% of its resources with a description of the type of risk (loans, guarantees, etc.).

(ii) Report for each subsidiary company (company in which the bank owns, directly or indirectly at least 20% of the capital) of the bank's exposure with a description of the type of risk.

Summaries of these two lists must also be prepared.

Annually

Detailed profit and loss account.

Analysis of the bank's security portfolio as at 31 December, showing movements during the year.

The profit and loss statement to be included in the bank's annual report.

Schedule of loans and guarantees to the bank's own senior management outstanding as at 31 December.

List of the bank's senior officers to be recorded in the official register maintained by the Bank of Spain.

(2) National Institute of Statistics

Monthly

A condensed balance sheet summarised from the confidential balance sheet.

Report analysed by province of the total number of customer accounts, opened or closed during the month.

(3) Higher Banking Council

Monthly

Certain balance sheet figures.

'Public' balance sheet. (The 'public' balance sheet represents a reclassification in special format of the confidential balance sheet.)

Quarterly

Summary of the loans outstanding by economic sector.

Other reports required for which there are no official forms

Annual report.

Notice of dividends to be distributed.

Notice of opening new branches.

(4) Ministry of Finance

Yearly

For turnover tax purposes, the bank must file a schedule detailing the total volume of income from or amounts paid to customers and suppliers where such volume exceeds Ptas500,000 during the year.

(5) Ministry of Commerce* (branches of foreign banks only)

In January of each year the Ministry of Commerce should be notified of the balance of the inter-company account with the parent bank as of 31 December, of the preceding year. The format in which this information should be submitted is as follows:

		Amount in Spanish pesetas
(a)	Capital assigned to the branch	xxx
(b)	Amounts received from the parent bank and not repatriable	xxx
(c)	Reserves	xxx
(d)	Loans granted by the parent and repatriable	xxx
(e)	Prior years profits not yet remitted (detailed by year)	xxx
(f)	Proportional part of the parent's expenses allocated to the Spanish branch, not yet paid (detailed by year)	xxx
(g)	Other amounts due to the parent not yet remitted (detailed by year)	xxx
	Total due to parent	xxx
(h)	Prior year losses (detailed by year)	xxx
(i)	Other amounts due to the branch by the parent (detailed by year)	xxx
	Total due by the parent	xxx

* The Ministries of Finance, the Economy and Commerce were merged after the October 1982 elections.

Format of balance sheet and profit and loss account

Spanish Bank

Balance sheet

Assets				**Liabilities**			
1	Cash and credit institutions			1	Capital		xxx
1.1	Cash and Bank of Spain	xxx		2	Reserves		
1.2	Other credit institutions			2.1	Legal reserve (art. 53 Banking Law)	xxx	
1.2.1	Peseta operations	xxx		2.2	Regularisation reserves	xxx	
1.2.2	Foreign currency operations	xxx		2.3	Other reserves	xxx	
1.3	Monetary assets	xxx					xxx
1.4	Foreign currency notes and coins	xxx					
			xxx	3	Credit institutions		
				3.1	Peseta operations	xxx	
2	Credit investments			3.2	Foreign currency operations	xxx	
2.1	Commercial bills of exchange	xxx					xxx
2.2	Accommodation bills	xxx					
2.3	Secured loans	xxx		4	Creditors		
2.4	Fixed term loans (unsecured)	xxx		4.1	Current accounts	xxx	
2.5	Overdrafts and other debtors	xxx		4.2	Savings accounts	xxx	
2.6	Foreign currency loans and bills	xxx		4.3	Time deposits	xxx	
			xxx	4.4	Other accounts	xxx	
							xxx
3	Securities portfolio						
3.1	Government stock	xxx		5	Short-term bonds and other debentures		xxx
3.2	Other securities	xxx					
			xxx	6	Foreign currency creditors		xxx
4	Underwritings, guarantees and endorsed bills			7	Bills and other accounts payable		xxx
4.1	Underwritings and other guarantees	xxx		8	Underwritings, guarantees and endorsed bills		xxx
4.2	Documentary credits	xxx		9	Sundry accounts		
4.3	Rediscounted and endorsed bills	xxx		9.1	Unappropriated profit from previous years	xxx	
			xxx	9.2	Current year's profit (December only)	xxx	
5	Shareholders (for uncalled capital) and shares in portfolio (own shares not subscribed)		xxx	9.3	Other accounts	xxx	
							xxx
6	Fixed assets						
6.1	Furniture and fittings	xxx					
6.2	Buildings	xxx					
			xxx				
7	Sundry accounts						
7.1	Previous year's losses	xxx					
7.2	Current year losses (only in December)	xxx					
7.3	Other accounts	xxx					
			xxx				
	Total Assets		xxx		Total liabilities		xxx

Memorandum items

1	Face value of loans and credits	xxx
2	Other	xxx
	Nominal value of shares held in deposit	xxx

191

Profit and loss account

<table>
<tr><td colspan="3">

Debit

1	Financial costs	
1.1	Creditors	xxx
1.2	Short-term bonds and debentures	xxx
1.3	Financing from credit institutions	xxx
1.4	Other interest and commissions	xxx
		xxx
2	Operating costs	
2.1	Personnel expenses	xxx
2.2	General expenses	xxx
2.3	Building expenses	xxx
2.4	Depreciated expenses	
2.4.1	Tangible assets	xxx
2.4.2	Other	xxx
2.5	Taxes	xxx
		xxx
3	Bad debts	
3.1	Bad debts written off	xxx
3.2	Transfer to the bad debts provision	xxx
		xxx
4	Disposals	
4.1	Losses on sales of securities	xxx
4.2	Losses on disposal of fixed assets	xxx
		xxx
5	Provision for loss in value of securities portfolio	xxx
6	Contribution to the Deposit Guarantee Fund	xxx
7	Other items	xxx
8	Credit balance or net profit	xxx

</td><td colspan="3">

Credit

1	Income from financial activity	
1.1	Bank of Spain and monetary assets	xxx
1.2	Financing to credit institutions	xxx
1.3	Credit investments	xxx
1.4	Securities portfolio	
1.4.1	Government stock	xxx
1.4.2	Other securities	xxx
1.5	Commissions from underwritings and other guarantees and from other financial and banking services	xxx
		xxx
2	Special funds now available	xxx
3	Disposals	
3.1	Gains on sales of securities	xxx
3.2	Gains on disposal of fixed assets	xxx
		xxx
4	Other income	
4.1	Recovery of suspense accounts and other previous years income	
4.2	Other items	xxx
		xxx
5	Debit balance or net loss	xxx

</td></tr>
</table>

CHAPTER 11

SWITZERLAND

HAROLD WILKINSON and FRANCIS ZOLLER

1 GENERAL INFORMATION

Switzerland was originally formed in the thirteenth and fourteenth centuries by an association of small states and the addition of other states since then has brought Switzerland to its present size. Switzerland is a federation of 26 cantons which are sovereign within the limits of the federal constitution which dates from 1874. In all matters not specifically reserved to the federal government, i.e. foreign affairs, defence, communications and some fields of political economy, the cantons can legislate autonomously. This two-tier system of legislation, federal and cantonal, affects business mainly in the field of taxes as the cantons, and to some extent also the communes, are autonomous in legislation concerning the tax system and rate of taxation levied.

Switzerland enjoys a tradition of government stability and political calm which is in part attributable to the fact that the seven-member Federal Council, which governs the country, comprises representatives of all four major political parties. The opposition is made up of the people at large who can accept or reject proposed legislation under a system of referendum. As all Acts of Parliament or any important issue are subject to a popular referendum, changes in legislation are slowed down considerably, but once adopted are likely to be of a more permanent nature.

Switzerland has one of the best-developed banking systems in the world and the reputation of Swiss banks and their influence in Switzerland's business community is perhaps unrivalled.

1.1 Organisations covered by banking regulations

The Swiss Federal Banking Law of 1934, amended in 1971, is the main regulation which covers the banking sector. All banks, private bankers and savings banks, as well as financial institutions which publicly recommend themselves for the acceptance of deposits (article 1, paras 1 & 2) are subject to the law. Specific exemptions from the law are stock exchange agents and stock exchange firms, which merely trade in securities and conduct operations directly related to such trading but do not engage in regular banking transactions, and trustees, notaries and business agents who only manage their customers' funds and do not engage in regular banking transactions (article 1, para. 3). The Banking Law is applicable irrespective of the corporate form of the bank or financial institution.

1.2 Summary of major types of bank

Banks in Switzerland can be divided into the following main categories:

(a) The major banks (1983: 5 banks)

These consist of Swiss Bank Corporation, Union Bank of Switzerland, Swiss Credit Bank, Swiss Volksbank and Bank Leu, of which the first three are by far the largest and dominate the banking sector in Switzerland, as well as having extensive international networks. These banks are active in all aspects of banking, both local and international, and effectively control stock and bond issues.

(b) The cantonal banks (1983: 29 banks)

These banks were established under the relative cantonal legislation to supply local financial needs, particularly mortgage financing, and as such are subject to certain supervision by the cantonal authorities; furthermore, liabilities to customers are guaranteed by the cantons who own all or a majority of the capital. Because of their exceptional nature the cantonal banks are partially exempted from the provisions of the Federal Banking Law.

(c) Local and saving banks (1983: 218 banks)

The main activity of these generally old-established banks is the provision of mortgage financing and general services on a very local basis.

(d) Private bankers (1983: 25 banks)

These, the oldest form of banking in Switzerland, are partnerships with personal liability by the partners. They are subject to the Federal Banking Law with certain exemptions. Their main activity is portfolio management.

(e) Other banks (1983: 196 banks)

This group includes foreign-owned banks (95), most of which obtain or transact a large part of their business with their international network of banks, and Swiss-owned banks (101). The Swiss-owned banks include commercial banks, banks specialising in stock exchange transactions and portfolio management, banks specialising in hire purchase, personal loans, etc. and others.

(f) Financial institutions

This includes those financial institutions which though not constituted as banks do accept deposits from third parties. These are further split into bank-like and other institutions; both are subject to the Banking Law but certain exemptions apply to the latter.

1.3 Supervisory authorities

1.4 Status of supervisory authorities

The main supervisory body for banks is the Federal Bank Commission. The Bank Commission consists of seven to nine members elected by the Federal Council and a permanent secretariat located in Berne. Its function is to monitor compliance by banks with the Federal Banking Law. In its role as a supervisory body, the Bank Commission does not generally carry out audit or control functions at banks itself but delegates such work to recognised audit firms with whom it co-operates closely. Its responsibilities accordingly include:
- The granting and withdrawing of licences to operate as banks.
- The recognition of audit firms to act as bank auditors.
- The issue of pronouncements concerning bank audit practice and reporting.
- The critical review of all bank audit reports.
- The follow-up of violations of law or other irregularities.
- The review of applications for exceeding lending and other limits.

A separate federal law governs the establishment of the Swiss National Bank whose main functions are the supply of money and controls over foreign exchange and balances of payments. It requires the collection of extensive statistical information from all banks.

1.5 Laws and regulations governing banks

1.6 Application of general company law to banks

1.7 Sources of laws and regulations

Current Swiss legislation for the banking sector derives from article 31 of the federal constitution. Under this article the federal government is authorised to issue regulations affecting the banking sector. New laws or changes in the existing law can be proposed by parliament but are subject to a popular referendum. The Banking Law provides for the supervisory authorities (Banking Commission) to make regulations and issue instructions. The most important laws passed based on this clause are:
- The Federal Law Relating to Banks and Savings Banks of 8 November 1934/ 11 March 1971.

- The Implementing Ordinance of 17 May 1972, for the Federal Law Relating to Banks and Savings Banks.

The above laws relate specifically to banking; additionally, all banks formed as corporations are subject to Swiss corporate law and, whatever their legal form, all banking institutions to the relevant federal and cantonal tax laws.

The Federal Banking Law governs in broad terms the following main subjects:
- Scope of the law (articles 1 and 2).
- Approval to conduct business operations (article 3).
- Required financial resources and liquidity (articles 4 and 5).
- Financial statements (article 6).
- Relationship to National Bank (articles 7-10).
- Control and audit (articles 18-22).
- The Federal Banking Commission (articles 23 and 24).
- Bankruptcy and arrangements with creditors (articles 29-37).
- Responsibilities and penalties (articles 38-51).

The Implementing Ordinance provides more detailed regulations to supplement the Federal Banking Law in certain sections.

Swiss corporate law is laid down in the Swiss Code of Obligations (Obligationenrecht), which covers contract law as well as corporate, partnership, etc. law. The Code has been valid for many years and it is generally recognised that improvements are required, especially in the area of financial reporting. Work has been continuing for several years on the draft of a new corporate law, which is likely to include requirements for consolidation, accounting policies footnotes, disclosure of movements on hidden reserves and other disclosures. There is, however, no definite date set for the finalisation of this new law.

As well as changes to the corporate law, a reform of the Federal Banking Law is also proposed, to consolidate existing law and subsequent developments, especially relating to the Bank Commission. Again, no date has been set for the finalisation of the new law. It is possible that in the final version more finance companies will be affected by the bank law than has hitherto been the case.

1.8 Ability of foreign banks to operate through branches and subsidiaries

1.9 Level of supervisory control for branches and subsidiaries of foreign banks

Banks controlled directly or indirectly by foreigners must, in addition to the normal requirements for the approval to conduct business, also:
- Prove that reciprocity is granted to Swiss banks in the country where the founders are domiciled.
- Select a name which does not indicate a Swiss character of the bank or allow such a conclusion to be drawn.
- Give the National Bank assurances concerning the protection of Swiss credit and monetary policies.

Branches of foreign banks in Switzerland are also subject to the Ordinance Relating to Branches of Foreign Banks in Switzerland of 1973 (amended in 1984). This basically submits branches of foreign banks to the same requirements as banks formed as companies as regards approvals, key ratios, management, financial statement presentation, audit, etc.

The major amendments in 1984 were the relief of capital requirements and lending limits.

In all other respects branches and subsidiaries of foreign banks are subject to the same controls as Swiss-owned banks.

1.10 Methods of incorporation

Banks may operate in the form of a stock company, a limited liability company, a partnership or a branch of a foreign bank. However, before a bank may start operations it must obtain a licence to conduct business operations from the Bank Commission. Before granting such a licence, the Bank Commission must be satisfied that:

– The bank states precisely the scope of its business operations in its statutes and provides for an administrative organisation (management, supervision, control) that is adequate for its activities.

– The bank has a capital of at least SF2 million.

– The persons charged with the administration and management of the bank enjoy a good reputation and thereby assure the proper conduct of the business.

– A majority of the persons managing the bank live in Switzerland. Such persons living abroad may only sign jointly with members of management living in Switzerland.

If the licence is obtained, formation of the bank is similar to the normal formation of any other corporate entity in Switzerland and includes, among other matters, approval of the name, proof of share capital paid in, registration in the trade register, etc.

1.11 Areas within the country subject to special laws

While banks may be subject to any particular laws of cantons in which they operate, there are no special laws relating to, for example, offshore banking as exist in certain countries.

2 ACCOUNTING

2.1 Laws and regulations governing accounts

2.2 Application of general company law

As regards the preparation and publication of financial statements, banks in Switzerland are subject to the provisions of Swiss corporate law (included in the Swiss Code of Obligations) and the Federal Law Relating to Banks and Savings Banks. The requirements of the Federal Banking Law are far more strict and detailed than those of the Code of Obligations. Further details are given in Section 4.1.

2.3 Roles of legislature and supervisory authority

2.4 Extent to which requirements as to returns and accounts are prescribed by laws and regulations

2.5 Obligations to furnish accounts

2.5.1 Accounting periods and times of furnishing

2.5.2 Form of accounts to be furnished

2.5.3 Mandatory accounting dates

Under Swiss Federal Banking Law (article 6) all banks, whatever their corporate form, must prepare annual financial statements consisting of a balance sheet and profit and loss account. Furthermore, banks with a balance sheet total of over SF50 million must prepare half-yearly interim balance sheets and those with a total of over SF200 million, quarterly balance sheets. Both annual financial statements and interim balance sheets must be published in the Swiss Commercial Gazette or in a Swiss newspaper or in a business report available to the public. The Implementing Ordinance lays down that publication of the annual financial statements must be within four months of the financial year end and that of the interim balance sheets within six weeks of the period end. Copies of all published information must be sent to the National Bank. There is no fixed requirement for the financial year end but the overwhelming majority of banks end their business year on 31 December.

In principle the financial statements must be drawn up in accordance with general company law as defined in the Code of Obligations. However, the Implementing Ordinance defines in detail (articles 23-25 and appendix II) the form and content of financial statements.

2.6 Requirements as to accounts (a) prior to incorporation (b) prior to commencement of trading and (c) in order to continue trading

The only accounting requirement prior to incorporation is that the capital must be deposited with a recognised bank which must confirm this deposit before incorporation is allowed by the trade registry. For tax purposes an opening balance sheet, generally showing cash and capital, must be prepared. There are no other requirements prior to incorporation or commencement of trading.

For a bank to continue trading it must comply with all the existing legal and tax requirements, i.e. principally: preparation and publication of annual accounts (Section 2.5), the audit of those accounts and the submission of the audit report (Section 2.7) and the preparation and filing of the tax returns (Section 9).

2.7 Audit requirements

Under Swiss corporate law all corporations must appoint a statutory auditor who reports to the general meeting of shareholders as to whether the financial statements are in agreement with the books, the books have been properly kept, and the financial statements have been prepared in accordance with the law and the provisions of the statutes. The auditor may be an individual, a group of individuals or an audit firm. The statutory audit report, which in practice contains minimum disclosures, need only be distributed to directors and shareholders. Banks which operate in the form of partnerships or branches of foreign banks do not fall under these provisions.

Articles 18-22 of the Federal Banking Law stipulate, however, that all banks must be audited annually by an independent audit firm that is recognised by the Bank Commission; the only exception to this is that cantonal banks with their own qualified audit department are exempt from external audit. Articles 43-49 of the Implementing Ordinance give further details as to specific points on which the audit firm must comment in its report, apart from the general requirement to give an opinion on the correct preparation and presentation of the financial statements. These include, in particular:

— Summary of all risks and related reserves.
— Treatment of interest on doubtful accounts.
— Coverage and risks on contingent liabilities (guarantees, letters of credit, etc.).
— Risks on fixed forward exchange transactions.
— Extent and correct treatment of fiduciary (trust) operations.
— Any breaches of legal lending limits.
— Summary of assets located abroad, and restrictions thereon.
— Efficiency and performance of the bank's internal organisation and controls over its business activities.
— Efficiency and reliability of controls over customer securities.
— Foreign exchange position of the bank.

The Bank Commission, in a statement dated September 1978, spelt out in greater detail the required form and content of the audit report. Summarised, this consists of:

1 Index
2 Summarised results of audit
3 Instructions for and performance of audit
4 Detailed comments on balance sheet positions
5 Detailed comments on profit and loss account positions
6 Analysis of financial position
7 Comments to articles 43, 44, 45 of the Implementing Ordinance
8 Confirmations relating to articles 46 and 48
9 Conclusions
10 Appendices

The audit report must be submitted to the Bank Commission within one year of the balance sheet date or at an earlier date if requested by the Bank Commission. In practice, because of the diminished value of reports submitted 12 months after the year end, the Bank Commission is setting much earlier due dates. The audit report must also be submitted to the directors or partners of the bank who must indicate by signing a copy of the report that they have taken notice of the contents. The report, due to the confidential nature of customer names, etc. may not be given to third parties except for restricted purposes by agreement with the directors, and may not be taken out of Switzerland. Audit reports are read critically by the Bank Commission, who frequently raise specific questions of the auditors regarding points which they consider as potentially risky, unclear or incomplete.

This audit report required by the Bank Commission is supplementary to the statutory audit report required for stock companies under Swiss corporate law.

2.8 Acceptability to fiscal authorities of accounts submitted to supervisory authority

For tax purposes banks must submit with their tax returns financial statements without any form of audit report. These financial statements do not need to be in identical form to those published or included in the audit report; however, both must be in agreement with the books. The fiscal authorities review the financial statements of banks from a completely different point of view and would not normally have access to the statutory or Bank Commission reports.

2.9 Submission of accounts to any authority other than by requirement of law

None.

2.10 Application of laws and regulations to foreign banks operating through branches and subsidiaries

Subsidiaries, if formed as corporations, are subject to all applicable laws and regulations. Branches of foreign banks are subject to all aspects of the Federal Banking Law but not to all aspects of corporate law; for example, there is no statutory audit requirement, but publication and Bank Commission audit requirements still apply.

2.11 Availability of accounts for public inspection

Annual financial statements, and interim balance sheets for banks above a certain size (see Sections 2.3-2.5) must be published and are therefore available for public inspection.

3 FORMAT, STYLE AND CONTENTS OF ACCOUNTS

3.1 Extent to which format is laid down by statute, supervisory authority, generally accepted accounting practice or otherwise

3.2 Description of format

3.3 Extent to which contents are prescribed by statute, supervisory authority, generally accepted accounting practice or otherwise

3.4 Disclosure of specific items required other than those required by general law

The format, style and content of published bank accounts is detailed in articles 23-25 of the Implementing Ordinance for the Federal Law Relating to Banks and Savings Banks, supplemented by appendix II. The form is given in articles 23-25, while the appendix describes in some detail the contents of individual balance sheet and profit and loss account items. These classifications, which are to be considered as minimum disclosure requirements, are given in full below. These disclosures exceed by far any disclosures required by Swiss corporate law. (See Appendix to this chapter.)

3.5 Exemptions from disclosure allowed in respect of banking items

Exemption from disclosure of specified items may be applied for but is seldom, if ever, granted. One feature of the rules relating to contents is that the offsetting of items is generally not allowed. Hidden or undisclosed reserves by way of conservative provisions should, as specified in the Appendix, be included under Other liabilities.

3.6 Hidden reserves

The establishment of hidden reserves is specifically permitted by the Swiss Code of Obligations. Banks set up hidden reserves principally through excess provisions for bad debts, foreign exchange fluctuations and securities, and also through undervaluations of securities, foreign currencies, properties and fixed assets generally. It is not permitted to create fictitious liabilities or omit material assets from the balance sheet.

The purpose of establishing hidden reserves is to even out reported earnings and dividends, to defer taxes and, perhaps most importantly, to cover unforeseen major losses. Management is required to inform auditors of the existence of hidden reserves and the auditors are required to summarise movements on hidden reserves in their long-form report to the Bank Commission.

3.7 Requirements as to consolidated accounts

There is no requirement under Swiss law to publish consolidated accounts, however, there is a recent requirement of the Bank Commission to submit to them details of the consolidated equity in connection with the control of lending limits. The Implementing Ordinance does not give any guidelines for the preparation of consolidated accounts.

4 ACCOUNTING POLICIES

4.1 Responsibility for laying down accounting policies

The Swiss Federal Banking Law stipulates (article 6.2) that the balance sheet must be drawn up in accordance with the requirements of the Swiss Code of Obligations relating to stock corporations. The Implementing Ordinance specifies in detail the form and content of financial statements but does not specify the accounting policies to be followed. The Swiss Code of Obligations gives in articles 662-670 and 957-961 broad guidelines as to the accounting policies to be followed by corporations. Briefly, these are as follows:

− Financial statements should be prepared in accordance with generally accepted business principles and shall be complete, clear and easy to refer to in order to enable interested parties to inform themselves as accurately as possible of the economic situation of the business (article 959).

− Assets shall not be valued higher than their value to the business on the date of the balance sheet (article 960).

− An undervaluation of the assets of the company in the balance sheet and the creation of other undisclosed reserves by the management is permissible to the extent necessary to ensure the continued prosperity of the company, or to distribute as equal a dividend as possible (article 663).

− Fixed assets must be valued no higher than cost less adequate depreciation (article 665).

− Inventory and other items intended for sale must not be valued higher than market (article 666).

− Quoted securities must not be valued at a price higher than their average stock exchange price during the month prior to the balance sheet date (article 667).

− Unquoted securities may not be valued higher than cost, with appropriate consideration being given to current yield and any decrease in value (article 667).

− Bond liabilities shall be shown at their full value; costs may be amortised over the period to maturity (article 669).

− Provision should be made for foreseeable losses on contingent liabilities or commitments (article 670).

In spite of article 959, these articles generally allow for conservative accounting which is widely practised by companies in Switzerland and especially by banks. It is commonly recognised that the general nature of the accounting principles set out in the Swiss Code of Obligations is inadequate and not always applicable for the specialised business of banking. The Commentary on the Federal Banking Law ('Kommentar zum schweizerischen Bankengesetz', Bodmer, Kleiner and Lutz) gives in chapter 4 more detailed advice on the accounting policies to be followed by banks.

4.2 Particular accounting policies

4.2.1 Foreign exchange

Contrary to the normal Swiss practice of not recognising unrealised foreign exchange profits, balances in foreign currencies should be translated at year end rates. This recognises the special situation of banks and the practical impossibility of distinguishing realised and unrealised profits.

Under normal Swiss practice, gains on open forward exchange transactions should not be booked, whereas accrual should be made for losses. Again, however, in recognition of the special situation of banks the Commentary suggests that the appropriate year end rates be used, i.e. that both profits and losses be recognised. There are, however, differences of opinion and practice on the matter.

4.2.2 Deferred tax

The Commentary does not include any reference to the accounting treatment of taxation in banks since this is no different to Swiss corporate practice. It is common for Swiss companies to book only taxes paid or assessed and not all taxes accruing based on the results of the financial year. Since most taxes are on a prior year or years assessment basis, this can lead to material under-statements of liabilities by comparison to international accounting practice. It is also most unusual to account for any deferred tax on timing differences.

4.2.3 Specific and general provisions for bad and doubtful debts

Generally, customer receivables should be valued in accordance with article 960 of the Code of Obligations, i.e. at their value to the business at the date of the balance sheet. This means that the collectability of individual receivables, which in the case of private individuals may depend on securities given, must be reviewed. Both specific and general provisions are recommended, and indeed the formation of conservative or excess reserves against receivables is common practice.

4.2.4 Treatment of provisions in accounts

The offset of provisions for bad debts against the related receivables is permitted but not required until the receivable is actually lost. Generally such provisions are included in Other liabilities in the balance sheet.

4.2.5 Premiums and discounts on investments (amortise, write off, etc.)

Quoted securities may not be valued above their market value (Code of Obligations, article 667). This permits in practice the valuation at market or at cost if lower. Unless major fluctuations in value occur, the practice of amortising premiums and discounts over the maturity of the security will have no material effect on the valuation and will therefore be acceptable. For non-quoted securities, consideration should be given to the yield, to the bank's intention to hold or sell and to the economic situation of the borrower.

4.2.6 Offsets, i.e. to what extent can assets and liabilities be set off against each other (legally or in practice)

Generally, under Swiss accounting practice the offsetting of assets and liabilities is not permitted unless the offset is really justified by the circumstances. For example, amounts due from and due to the same bank under the same terms and currency must be offset (appendix II of Implementing Ordinance), as a counter to window dressing. The Implementing Ordinance also requires the offset of own bills discounted and borrowings on indirectly owned property, i.e. owned through a property company. It is also suggested in the Commentary that offsets are required in the case of material repurchases of bonds or cash bonds issued and branch/head office or branch/branch balances.

4.2.7 Goodwill

There are no clearly defined rules for treatment of purchased goodwill. Whereas a conservative company with available profits would expense such goodwill immediately, other companies would defer the cost and write it off over the estimated useful life. Where no better indications of useful life exist, five years is a period commonly taken since this is the recommended period for the write-off of a company's formation expenses.

4.2.8 Consolidation

Neither the Code of Obligations nor the Implementing Ordinance require consolidation and the published financial statements of banks are therefore on an unconsolidated basis. Consolidated balance sheets are, however, required to be submitted to the Bank Commission principally for the purpose of determining the consolidated equity. The Consolidation Guidelines issued by the Bank Commission include advice as to the inclusion of companies, eliminations, treatment of consolidation differences, etc. Consolidation goodwill, whether positive or negative, is required to be shown as a separate item in the consolidated balance sheet but is not required to be written off. Accounts of foreign subsidiaries would normally be translated at year end rates.

4.2.9 Revaluations of assets

In general, a revaluation of assets above their original cost is not permitted under the Code of Obligations. Exceptions to this rule are that securities may be valued at market value (Section 4.2.5), assets and liabilities in foreign currencies should be, for banks only, valued at year end rates (Section 4.2.1) and fixed assets may be revalued under exceptional circumstances (Section 4.2.13).

4.2.10 Instalment finance and leasing including basis of recognition of income

There are no clearly defined principles for the accounting treatment of lease financing. The Commentary recognises the possibility of capitalising the object leased or the discounted instalment receivables and recommends the former. Recognition of income would then be made by any reasonable method over the period of the lease.

4.2.11 Dealing assets

Although the Code of Obligations (article 666) stipulates that inventories should be valued at the lower of cost and market value, the Commentary recognises that, in the case of banks, precious metals should be considered more as foreign currencies and therefore valued at current rates, current being in this case the average of the month before the year end. Again the Commentary suggests that forward transactions in precious metals be treated in the same way as foreign currencies, i.e. valued at the respective forward rate.

4.2.12 Pensions

In Switzerland it is common practice for companies and banks to form pension funds which are separate legal entities. Normally the employee and the employer are contibuting equally to the fund. As a consequence a bank normally has no legal commitments except to make its regular contributions according to the agreement in force. Pension expense has to be disclosed in the profit and loss account.

4.2.13 *Depreciation*

Fixed assets should be valued at cost less depreciation (article 665, Code of Obligations). In practice, many banks expense the smaller items of fixed assets, otherwise any reasonable depreciation method is generally acceptable. A revaluation of property is not permitted except under exceptional circumstances and for the elimination of losses, or to reverse excessive depreciation previously taken.

5 WINDOW DRESSING

The practice of using hidden reserves to regulate published earnings is known and accepted (see Section 3.6). As regards window dressing of the balance sheet, although amounts due to and from the same bank under the same terms must be offset (Implementing Ordinance, appendix II C), there are no other regulations to prevent it. Any such manipulations would become obvious to the Bank Commission through the details given in the audit reports, although not to members of the public or minority shareholders.

6 AMOUNTS REQUIRED TO BE MAINTAINED BY LAW OR OTHERWISE

The equity or own resources required to be maintained by banks, which has a direct effect on the bank's lending limits, is covered by two sections of the Banking Law.

(i)   The Implementing Ordinance lays down that the share capital of a bank must be at least SF2 million (article 4). Branches of foreign banks are also currently required to have capital (so-called 'Dotations-Kapital').

(ii) A bank must set up a legal reserve in accordance with the provisions of Swiss corporate law comprising 5% of net profit until the reserve has reached 20% of the share capital; share premiums, less related costs; and 10% of dividends which exceed 5% of share capital.

These legal reserve provisions do not apply to cantonal banks or to certain private bankers.

The legal reserve provisions are derived from the Swiss Code of Obligations (article 671) but are repeated in the Federal Banking Law (article 5). The Ordinance concerning branches of foreign banks in Switzerland provides that branches should also allocate 5% of net earnings to the legal reserve, unlike branches of non-banks.

7 KEY RATIOS

Key ratios required to be maintained or affecting the operations of banks fall under four main headings:
- Own resources.
- Liquidity.
- Lending limits.
- Foreign exchange position.

The ratios required related to *own resources* are regulated by the Amendment to the Implementing Ordinance dated 1 December 1980. Under this Amendment the bank's own resources, meaning in principle equity, taxed hidden reserves and subordinated debts, must at least equal certain given percentages of particular assets, contingent liabilities and open positions of the bank.

The required *liquidity* ratios are given in articles 15-19 of the Implementing Ordinance. Under these articles a bank must maintain the total of its liquid assets and easily marketable assets, at a given percentage of its short-term liabilities in accordance with the following criteria:

(a) Liquid assets must normally amount to:
- 6% of short-term liabilities if below 15% of total liabilities.
- 12% of short-term liabilities if between 15 and 25% of total liabilities.
- 24% of short-term liabilities if between 25 and 35% of total liabilities.
- 36% of short-term liabilities if over 35% of total liabilities.

(b) Liquid assets and easily marketable assets must amount to at least:
- 35% of short-term liabilities if below 15% of total liabilities.
- 52% of short-term liabilities if between 15 and 25% of total liabilities.
- 70% of short-term liabilities if over 35% of total liabilities.

Lending limits are defined in article 21 of the Implementing Ordinance. Under this article banks must inform the Bank Commission if their lendings to a single customer, or group, exceed certain percentages of their own resources. The percentages are:
- 160% for Swiss public authorities, cantonal banks or certain Swiss mortgages.
- 50% for other banks (or double for short-term deposits up to one year).
- 40% for other secured lendings.
- 20% for unsecured lendings.

The Bank Commission can require that lendings be lowered below these limits.

Limits on *foreign exchange positions* are determined by the Bank Commission's circular of 19 December 1974 under which the foreign exchange position by currency must be established at each month end. The total of long and short positions in individual foreign currencies should normally not exceed 40% of the bank's own resources.

All of these ratios should be maintained at all times and reviewed by banks at least monthly. Any infringements must be reported to the Bank Commission.

8 ACCOUNTING RETURNS OTHER THAN ACCOUNTS

8.1 By whom required

8.2 Nature of requirements

The majority of accounting returns other than annual accounts relate to the requirements of the Swiss National Bank. The National Bank is empowered, under article 7 paras 3 and 4 of the Federal Banking Law to demand any information it may require for the purpose of carrying out its function.

The National Bank requires annually within four months of the year end, in addition to copies of the published financial statements, various analyses of balance sheet items, including the split between assets and liabilities in Swiss francs and other currencies in Switzerland and abroad and between cantons. Further detailed information is required on loans to Swiss public authorities, building credits, mortgage credits, savings accounts and bonds, and liquidity ratios. A new requirement in 1983 was a return concerning the split of risks between sovereign countries.

Also required on a regular basis from certain banks are interest conditions (half-yearly), status of building credits (quarterly), new building credits (monthly), Eurocurrency statistics (quarterly), forward exchange transactions (monthly) and Swiss franc holdings of other countries' currency authorities (monthly).

The key ratios required to be maintained by banks on own resources, liquidity and foreign exchange positions require to be reported only on an exception basis and then to the Bank Commission.

9 TAXATION

9.1 General method of taxation

In principle, banks in Switzerland, whether they operate as limited companies or branches, are subject to the same tax regulations as other legal entities.

The Swiss tax system is a reflection of the country's federal structure. Each of the 26 cantons and half-cantons has its own tax laws in addition to those of the Confederation. Municipalities also charge taxes, mostly in the form of annually determined surcharges to the cantonal taxes. Therefore a Swiss bank pays taxes to at least three different public bodies, the Confederation, the canton and the municipality where it is domiciled. In cases where a bank operates in more than one canton, for example through a branch, its taxable income and net assets would be split between the relevant cantons based on the actual figures or on a basis agreed between the cantonal tax authorities.

A bank in Switzerland is liable to tax on its income and its capital; for this purpose capital means capital and retained earnings, or net worth. Tax rates and the determination of taxable income vary widely between cantons and between the cantonal and federal systems. These differences include the base period, the deductibility of taxes paid and loss carry forward periods.

Federal income taxes are payable on income and capital. The rate of federal income tax depends on the relationship between taxable income and taxable capital and is graduated from 3.63% (minimum) to 9.8% (maximum); the maximum rate is reached only when taxable income exceeds 23.15% of taxable capital. Federal net worth tax is levied at 0.825% on taxable capital (net assets). Assessments for federal taxes are made on the average income of the preceding two-year period, starting with an odd year. All taxes paid are

deductible for federal income tax purposes. Cantonal basic tax rates are normally established by the cantonal tax authorities which are then multiplied by a factor determined annually by the cantonal and municipal authorities. As with the federal tax, cantonal and municipal taxes are generally graduated depending on the relationship of taxable income to taxable capital. The approximate maximum effective cantonal and municipal tax rates, i.e. taking into account the deductibility of taxes paid, are as follows:

Basel (Basel-Stadt)	21%
Berne	23%
Fribourg	20%
Geneva	25%
Graubünden	25%
Lucerne	24%
Vaud	22%
Zug	16%
Zürich	26%

9.2 Accounts as basis for taxation

9.3 Adjustments permitted or required

Generally the published accounts of a bank, which by law must be in agreement with the books, form the basis also for taxation. The tax authorities can challenge or audit the accounts of a bank which could result in disallowance of excess reserves or write-offs and the establishment of a basis of valuation differing from the books for future years. In practice, however, the tax authorities permit the adoption by banks of generally conservative policies.

9.4 Effect of tax considerations on presentation of accounts

Since the presentation of accounts is governed by the Federal Banking Law, it is not generally affected by tax considerations. The deferral of tax liabilities and the maintenance of income tax rates below the maximum is one important factor leading to the common practice of establishing substantial hidden reserves which are partially tax deductible.

10 INTERPRETATION OF ACCOUNTS

10.1 Adequacy of information as to contents and disclosure

The required publication by banks of annual and quarterly financial information in a prescribed format does permit financial analysts, and the general public, valuable insight into the size and activities of banks. However, the published information is not accompanied by explanatory information in footnote form or otherwise, and results are likely to be influenced by the adoption of conservative accounting principles and the creation or release of hidden reserves.

10.2 Audit and reliability of information

The published financial information is not audited and the annual financial statements may indeed be published before the audit is complete. If, however, major adjustments arose on audit it is likely that the Bank Commission would investigate and institute tighter controls on the bank before future publication. Many banks do issue audited financial statements as a separate exercise for public relations purposes; however, in accordance with Swiss practice such financial statements do not generally provide any information in addition to that in the published statements.

10.3 Comparability between different banks on the basis of published accounts or publicly available returns

Although the published information is not accompanied by explanatory information in footnote form or otherwise, and results may be influenced by the adoption of conservative accounting principles, certain basic information, for example total assets, interest spread, total personnel costs, is available to enable some comparison to be made between the size and activity of banks.

11 OTHER RELEVANT INFORMATION

11.1 Bank secrecy and numbered accounts

One of the most well-known and discussed features of Swiss banking is the concept of bank secrecy. The Federal Banking Law, article 47, imposes penalties on bank officers, etc. who disclose confidential information. Furthermore, Swiss Criminal Law (para. 273) makes it a punishable offence to divulge anything to the disadvantage of the Swiss state to representatives of a foreign country, and is occasionally invoked in connection with banking transactions.

In practice, the consequences of bank secrecy are that there is no widespread system of credit information available as exists in other countries, and that tax and exchange control authorities, whether Swiss or foreign, do not have the right to obtain any information from the banks. There are, however, some limitations to bank secrecy, specifically in criminal cases, bankruptcy and debt collection. Tax evasion, however, is not considered a crime under Swiss law. There has been general criticism, particularly from the United States, on bank secrecy as a result of which there is now increased co-operation between Swiss and foreign authorities, specifically to combat organised crime. Swiss banks must also satisfy themselves on the bona fide nature of funds before accepting funds from new clients.

Numbered accounts are client accounts designated by a code number or name rather than the client's name. This merely provides additional confidentiality to the client in relation to the clerical staff at the bank, since the bank is obliged to keep complete data on the identity of the client somewhere on file. Use of such numbered accounts is, however, widespread.

11.2 Portfolio management and trustee deposits

The traditional security of Swiss banks, coupled with bank secrecy and the strength of the Swiss franc, have contributed to large amounts of funds being deposited with Swiss banks both by foreigners and Swiss citizens. Consequently, Swiss banks are likely to have larger portfolio management or investment departments than banks in many other countries.

One specific form of investment not common in other countries is the trustee deposit. Trustee deposits are clients' funds deposited by a bank with another foreign bank, often an affiliate, in the bank's name but for the client's account. Such deposits have the advantage of avoiding withholding taxes on interest which would arise if the deposit remained with the bank. Trustee deposits are not included in a bank's financial statements.

APPENDIX

Instructions for the balance sheet accounting provisions for articles 23–25 of the Implementing Ordinance

A

The annual balance sheet and the interim balance sheets must be itemised at least as follows:

1 ASSETS

1.1 Cash on hand, giro account deposits with the National Bank and the Post Office

Swiss coins and bank notes;
foreign currencies in as far as they are freely convertible into Swiss francs;
deposits with the Swiss postal checking system;
giro account deposits with the Swiss National Bank;
giro account deposits with a central office recognised by the Banking Commission;
sight deposits with a foreign central bank up to the amount of liabilities in the same currency;
clearing balances of foreign branch offices with a recognised clearing bank of that country up to the amount of the liabilities incurred by the branch office in the same currency.

1.2 Balances with other banks on sight

Call money granted with notice of no more than 48 hours;
immediately available deposits with domestic and foreign banks;
postal checking balances with foreign postal systems.
Considered as banks are:
In Switzerland: the institutions and central mortgage institutions subject to the law within the meaning of article 1, para. 1.
Abroad: (a) institutions that are considered banks or savings banks according to the legislation of the country in question; (b) recognised or organised brokers that in pursuit of their profession accept funds from third parties.

1.3 Balances with other banks on time

Secured or unsecured advances limited in time;
claims with notice periods agreed in writing;
all other investments limited in time, with the exception of claims arising out of securities;
balances with foreign banks subject to foreign exchange restrictions;
blocked balances, especially margin and similar accounts.
For the definition of the term 'bank' see heading 1.2 above.

1.3.1 of these with maturities up to 90 days

1.4 Bills and money market paper

In particular:
Swiss and foreign trade bills and acceptances;
'Reskriptionen' and treasury notes of Swiss and foreign public authorities;
bills to the order of the bank, bills that have only been

received as collateral are not to be taken into consideration;
cheques;
money market paper maturing within 180 days such as BIS notes, bankers acceptances, commercial paper, certificates of deposit.
The bank's own discounted acceptances must be offset.

1.4.1 of these 'Reskriptionen' and treasury notes

1.5 Unsecured current account loans

To be included under this heading:
unsecured loans from acceptance credits (customers and banks);
unsecured portions of secured credits;
current account loans to general and limited partnerships ('Kollektiv-und Kommanditgesellschaften') which are guaranteed by only one partner liable without limitation;
current account loans to safekeeping customers who have not signed a contract of pledge.

1.6 Secured current account loans

To be included under this heading:
loans with personal sureties (guarantees, joint and several liability, etc.);
loans to co-operative companies with unlimited joint liability or with an unlimited assessment liability of the co-operative members;
secured loans resulting from acceptance credits (customers and banks).
Not considered as security are wage and salary assignments, objects having only sentimental value, contingent rights, promissory notes of the debtor, claims that are contested in judicial proceedings, shares of one's own bank that are not traded officially or over-the-counter, equity paper of the debtor company and a company financially affiliated with it within the meaning of article 21, para. 5, assignments of future claims.

1.6.1 of these secured by mortgages

To be included:
credits advanced against pledge of mortgage title. If other security is furnished in addition to mortgages, the former must be in the nature of accessory security.

1.7 Unsecured fixed loans and advances without the character of current account loans, in so far as they do not belong to headings 1.4 and 1.9

To be included:
loans, in particular small loans, in the form of instruments similar to bills. Furthermore, the general rules mentioned under headings 1.5 and 1.6 on loans to be reported as unsecured also apply to this heading.

1.8 Secured fixed loans and advances

Loans without the character of current account loans, in so far as they do not belong to headings 1.4, 1.9 and 1.10.

To be included:

loans and advances with personal sureties (guarantees, joint and several liability, etc.);

advances against the mortgaging of ships and aircraft;

call loans;

advances on and purchase of claims, including those arising out of instalment contracts, where the assignor has guaranteed collection or with reservation of ownership.

Furthermore, the general rules mentioned under headings 1.5 and 1.6 on loans to be reported as secured apply analogously.

1.8.1 of these secured by mortgages

To be included:

credits advanced against pledge of mortgage title (indirect mortgage business). If other security is furnished in addition to mortgages, the former must be in the nature of accessory security.

1.9 Current account loans and advances to public authorities

Loans to domestic and foreign public authorities and their commercial enterprises. In Switzerland these public authorities are the Confederation, the cantons, communities and districts (political, civic, religious and school). Semi-public enterprises as well as enterprises of the public authorities subject to private law do not fall under the present position.

Not to be included under this heading are claims against such public authorities arising out of mortgages, from bills or from securities.

1.10 Mortgages

Claims arising from mortgages taken firmly, those against public authorities included.

1.11 Securities

To be included under this heading:

participations in limited partnerships, co-operative companies and limited liability companies;

paid-in shares, participation certificates and bonds, even if the titles have not yet been issued;

registered debt certificates;

investment trust certificates;

money market paper, in so far as it is not reported under heading 1.4.

1.12 Permanent participations

Shares and other equity paper acquired as a permanent investment for the purpose of holding an interest or exercising control. Indirect real estate ownership is listed in the balance sheet under headings 1.13 or 1.14.

1.13 Bank premises

Real estate used entirely or predominantly by the bank itself;

balances resulting from construction and alteration costs;

indirect real estate holdings (participations in and claims against real estate companies).

1.14 Other real estate holdings

All kinds of building lots that are not or only to a small extent used by the bank itself;

balances resulting from construction and alteration costs;

indirect real estate holdings (participations in and claims against real estate companies).

1.15 Other assets

In particular:

transitory assets;

interest due and accrued interest;

life insurance policies;

coupons;

furniture, furnishings and installations;

balance resulting from transactions between the head office and the branches;

depreciable surplus from establishment costs, issue costs, interest margin and cost repayments on mortgage bond loans and loans granted by the central issue institutions, goodwill and similar assets;

precious metals;

foreign currencies in so far as they are not shown under heading 1.1.

1.16 Capital not yet paid in

1.17 Balance of the profit and loss statement subdivided into balance carried forward from previous year and result for the current year

1.18 Balance sheet total

2 LIABILITIES

2.1 Balances of other banks on sight

To be included:

call money received with a notice term of no more than 48 hours;

collateral loans and accounts of correspondents of the Swiss National Bank;

accounts of other banks without a written term of notice.

For the definition of the term 'bank' see heading 1.2.

2.2 Balances of other banks on time

To be included:

all advances and deposits of banks at fixed term;

drafts drawn by customers directly for account of banks on third banks and accepted by the latter banks;

loans of the central mortgage institutions to non-member banks against pledges.

For the definition of the term 'bank' see heading 1.2.

2.2.1 of these with maturities up to 90 days

2.3 Sight deposits

For customers, not including banks.

To be included:

cheques and items due within short periods.

2.4 Time deposits

For customers, not including banks.

To be included:

funds received and repayable on fixed dates;

deposits with a written term of notice, with the exception of actual deposit accounts (heading 2.6);

liabilities arising from call loans;

all types of blocked accounts;

liabilities in respect to central issuing institutions resulting from orders;

certificates of deposit.

2.4.1 of these with maturities up to 90 days

2.5 Savings deposits

Books and accounts that contain the expression 'savings' in any combination of words whatsoever.

2.6 Deposit books

To be included:
  deposit accounts, investment savings accounts and similar accounts which may not be freely withdrawn or otherwise disposed of on demand.

2.7 Medium-term notes and cash bonds

2.8 Bond issues

Bonds that are issued in debenture form with uniform terms and conditions (interest rate and due dates);
issues with warrants for the purchase of shares.

2.8.1 of these convertible bond issues

2.9 Mortgage bond loans

To be included:
  loans of the central mortgage institutions granted to member banks against pledges.

2.10 Acceptances and promissory notes

Only the amount of the bills in circulation.

2.11 Mortgages on own real estate holdings

Concerns balance sheet headings 1.13 and 1.14 with the exception of indirect real estate holdings.

2.12 Other liabilities

In particular:
  transitory liabilities;
  interest due and accrued interest;
  coupons;
  bank-owned funds without legal personality, such as welfare funds, benefit funds and construction funds;
  balance resulting from transactions between the head office and the branches;
  provisions of all kinds;
  undisclosed reserves.

2.13 Capital

Nominal capital, including the portion not paid in, as well as dotation capital. Guarantee capital not paid in must be listed under supplementary statements (article 24, para. 2.2).

2.14 Statutory reserves

2.15 Other reserves

2.16 Balance of the Profit and Loss Statement subdivided into surplus carried forward from previous year and result for the current year

2.17 Balance sheet total

B

The profit and loss statement must be itemised at least as follows:

1 INCOME

1.1 Interest receivable

To be included:
  net income from call loans.
Not to be included:
  interest whose collection is doubtful.

1.2 Income from bills and money market paper

To be included:
  income from collection of bills.

1.3 Commission income

Commission income of all kinds, including:
  safe deposit fees;
  safe deposit box rental fees;
  brokerage;
  income from the securities issuing business.

1.4 Income from trading in foreign exchange and precious metals

Foreign exchange profits;
income from foreign bank note and coin trading;
income from trading in precious metals;
exchange rate losses and write-offs must be deducted.

1.5 Income from securities

Interest and dividends, proceeds from the sale of rights, plus market profits and less market losses and depreciation.
To be included:
  realised capital gains from promissory note trading.

1.6 Income from permanent participations

1.7 Miscellaneous

To be included:
  income from coupon accounts;
  rental income after deduction of maintenance costs, including capital gains from the sale of real estate holdings, less capital losses.

1.8 Net loss

Only result of the current year without balance carried forward.

1.9 Total

2 EXPENDITURE

2.1 Interest payable

Not to be included:
  interest paid on dotation and co-operative company capital;
  interest paid on reserves (see heading 2.8).

2.2 Commission expense

Commission expense may be offset against commission income only to the extent that it concerns retrocessions agreed upon in advance.

2.3 Bank directors and staff

Attendance fees and fixed emoluments for bank officers;
salaries, allowances, per diem compensation, social security, disability and other statutory contributions.

2.4 Contributions to staff welfare funds

Premiums and voluntary contributions to pension and other funds, as well as to bank-owned funds established for the same purposes but without legal personality, provided they are not resolved to be paid out of net profits;
premiums for life and annuity insurances.

2.5 Office expenses

In particular:
rents and maintenance for office premises;
real estate expenses not covered by real estate income;
office equipment and supplies, printed matter, telephone, telegraph, telex, postage and other mailing costs;
machinery and furniture (including vehicles), purchases not reported as assets, and maintenance;
travel compensation;
premiums for property and accident insurance;
advertising expenses, including free savings books;
legal and collecting costs, register of commerce and land register fees;
auditing expenses;
issuing costs including stamp taxes, in so far as they are not included among the assets, as well as the related provisions;
donations not deducted from net profit.

2.6 Taxes

Including allocations to provisions for taxes.

2.7 Losses, write-offs and provisions

In particular:
loan losses;
net loss from trading in foreign exchange, foreign bank notes and coins as well as precious metals;
write-offs on building lots, furniture, installation costs and other assets that must be depreciated;
amortisation of securities, in so far as this is not deducted directly from securities income.

CHAPTER 12

AUSTRALIA

CLYDE DICKENS and ROGER BURRITT

1 GENERAL INFORMATION

A federation, known as the Commonwealth of Australia, was formed in 1901 by written constitution. It now comprises six states (New South Wales, Queensland, South Australia, Tasmania, Victoria and Western Australia), two territories on the mainland (the Australian Capital Territory and the Northern Territory) and a small number of external territories.

Australia is a member of the British Commonwealth of Nations and the head of state of the Commonwealth of Australia, Queen Elizabeth II, is represented in Australia by the Governor-General and the state governors.

The constitution provides for legislative power to be vested in a parliamentary system similar to that of the United Kingdom. The Australian Commonwealth and each of the states have their own constitution, parliament and courts of law. There is a division of powers between the Commonwealth and the states broadly along the lines that the Commonwealth legislates over defence, foreign affairs, income and sales tax, customs and excise, tariffs, social services, overseas trade, postal services and communications, banking, currency, copyrights, patents and trademarks. The residual powers of education, justice, railways, roads, housing, etc. are vested in the states, but there is considerable overlapping.

The High Court of Australia acts as arbiter in matters involving the interpretation of the constitution and in determining the validity, under the constitution, of laws enacted by the federal and state parliaments.

The existing Australian banking system is the product of over 160 years of development. Until 1941 the industry was regulated only by the relevant company legislation in each state. A number of domestically incorporated banks operated side-by-side with banks formed overseas. Since 1941, however, it has been necessary to hold an authority from the federal government to carry on a banking business in Australia.

1.1 Organisations covered by banking regulations

The Australian constitution confers powers on the federal government and the various state governments to regulate the operation of the financial system. Banking other than state banking, state banking extending beyond the limits of the state concerned, the incorporation of banks and the issue of paper money are all the responsibility of the federal government.[1]

The Australian financial system clearly distinguishes banks from other financial institutions. The Banking Act 1959,[2] which is the main federal legislation applicable to all banks other than state government-owned banks (which are subject to the legislative control of the states which have created them) provides that, subject to the Act, only a body corporate may carry on banking business in Australia (s7) and then only when in possession of an appropriate authority (s8). Appropriate sections of the Act confer such authority on existing banks. Any other body corporate which seeks authority to carry on banking business may apply to the federal Treasurer (s9(2)). The granting of such an authority is discretionary (s9(3)) and may be varied, revoked or additional conditions may be imposed (s9(5)). In addition, the word 'bank' cannot be used in a name or in relation to a business without the written consent of the Treasurer (s66).

1.2 Summary of major types of bank

The Australian banking system, like that of many other countries, is dominated by a few large banks with a wide network of branches. A central bank, the Reserve Bank of Australia, established in its present form under the Reserve Bank Act 1959, is responsible for the administration and regulation of the monetary and banking system, as well as providing a specialist banking business for government financial institutions and other banks. The banking industry in Australia can be classified into three main types: trading banks, savings banks, and special purpose banks.

The Banking Act places trading and savings banks in separate schedules and also refers to three small trading banks as 'prescribed banks'. This latter distinction owes more to a historical grouping for purposes of Statutory Reserve Deposit determination than to any philosophical approach to establishing separate classes of banks.

(a) Trading banks

Currently 11 trading banks operate in Australia, with four banks, which operate nationally, holding some 85% of all trading bank assets. Trading banks have established over 5,000 branches and nearly 1,000 agencies in

---

[1] Commonwealth of Australia Constitution Act 1900, s51
[2] As amended, hereafter referred to as the Banking Act

Australia, as well as operating branch networks in some other countries − principally the United Kingdom, New Zealand and the Pacific Islands. Their dominant position derives from their control over the domestic and international payments systems. Until August 1984 only trading banks were allowed to offer cheque account facilities to their customers and deal in foreign exchange, but now savings banks can also offer cheque facilities on all accounts.

The traditional function of the trading banks has been the acceptance of money from lenders on current and deposit accounts. The banks make loans to all sections of the economy in the form of overdrafts, fully drawn advances, term loans and personal loans. The trading banks have the authority to deal with practically all overseas commercial and trade transactions, and also offer certain nominee and trustee services to clients.

(b) Savings banks

Currently ten savings banks operate in Australia. Each of the four major national banking groups conducts a savings bank operation (as a wholly-owned subsidiary of the trading bank) and these banks hold almost 74% of all savings bank assets in Australia. Savings bank facilities, frequently operating in conjunction with associated trading banks, are available at over 5,000 branches and 12,000 agencies throughout Australia.

The role of savings banks has traditionally been directed towards collection of household savings and the provision of long-term finance on the security of residential property. Savings banks draw their funds principally from individuals but also accept deposits from socially orientated non-profit organisations. The great bulk of savings banks' deposits are held in low interest-bearing passbook savings accounts repayable on demand, and savings investment accounts which attract higher interest rates but have minimum term requirements.

As mentioned above, savings banks can now provide cheque account facilities to all account holders.

(c) Special purpose banks

(i) The Commonwealth Development Bank of Australia was established under the Commonwealth Banks Act 1959 and is a member bank of the Commonwealth Banking Corporation.

(ii) The Australian Resources Development Bank was established in 1967 to facilitate the medium- to long-term financing of large-scale projects of national importance, particularly those involving the development of natural resources and associated infrastructure.

(iii) The Primary Industry Bank of Australia (originally named the Australian Rural Bank Limited) commenced operation in 1978; it was established to augment the existing long-term rural lending capacity of banks and other lenders.

1.3 Supervisory authorities

The Banking Act provides for the supervision of all the banking business conducted nationally in Australia.

Some of these responsibilities are vested in the federal government, and some are delegated to the Reserve Bank and the federal Auditor-General. The state government-owned banks, which are not subject to the Banking Act, are directed by Commissioners or Trustees appointed by the respective state governments.

The Reserve Bank of Australia was established as the country's central bank in 1959. Although it is autonomous it has a close relationship with the Treasury. Indeed, provisions in the Banking Act ensure close liaison between the two. The major function of the Reserve Bank is to assist the government with the regulation of the monetary and banking system. But it does have other specialist functions including the provision of banking services to the federal government, some state governments and semi-government authorities. Apart from managing the note and coin issue it helps manage the government debt, acts as lender of last resort to authorised short-term money market dealers and provides some liquidity support for the trading and savings banks. In addition, the Reserve Bank is responsible for monitoring the affairs of financial institutions, a role which may expand in scope as banks diversify into other activities and as deregulation of the financial sector continues.

Although the state government-owned banks are not subject to the regulations of the Banking Act, they co-operate with the Reserve Bank in the implementation of its banking policies. These banks are kept informed of, and are required to take into account, the lending policies applying to the banks under the Banking Act. In practical terms the interest rates charged by the state government-owned banks follow the levels applying to other banks.

1.4 Status of supervisory authorities

The authorities referred to above are all established by law.

Self-regulation is provided by The Australian Bankers' Association which is the main banking association within the retail banking industry. Membership comprises the major private trading banks and their savings bank subsidiaries. The Association consults with the Commonwealth Bank group.

1.5 Laws and regulations governing banks

The current banking legislation enacted by the federal government comprises three Acts: the Reserve Bank Act 1959, the Commonwealth Banks Act 1959 and the Banking Act 1959, all of which came into force on 14 January 1960. These Acts extend to all the territories of the Australian Commonwealth with the exception of any external territory excluded from the operations of the Acts by declaration of the federal Treasurer. The Acts and the Regulations are intended to provide a comprehensive scheme for the regulation and control of all banks other than state banks.[3]

---

[3] State legislation sets out requirements which regulate the business activities of the state banks, including such items as the holding of reserves, liquidity requirements, the maximum interest rate which may be paid on certain borrowings and charged on certain loans, the maximum term of deposits and requirements concerning accounts and audits. These requirements vary between the states

There is also the Banks (Shareholdings) Act which came into force on 11 May 1972. The basic provision of the Act (s10) is aimed at ensuring that no person (including a corporation) shall, without the federal Treasurer's consent, acquire directly or indirectly a holding of 10% or more in the voting shares of any bank incorporated in Australia and authorised to carry on banking business in terms of s9 of the Banking Act.

The Reserve Bank is authorised under the Banking Act to regulate banks' liquidity, lending and interest rate policies (s20, s36 and s50 respectively).

1.6 Application of general company law to banks

The main component of company law in Australia is the Companies Act 1981, enacted in July 1982. This applies as such only in the Australian Capital Territory. The individual states have adopted this legislation with some local modifications and the resultant modified legislation is referred to as a code, for example, Companies (New South Wales) Code. The Companies Act 1981 and the State Companies Codes are complemented by the Companies Regulations which form an integral part of the legislation, and are also identified by the state to which they relate.

Private banks are subject to the general provisions of the Companies Code of the state where they were incorporated.[4] However, there are specific provisions in the Companies Code relating to banking corporations.

The Companies Code in each of the states provides that a banking corporation:
(a) Is not required to issue a prospectus in connection with any invitation to the public to deposit money (ss97(6), (7)).
(b) Is deemed to comply with the provisions of the Code relating to accounts, provided that under a law of the Commonwealth relating to banking it is required to prepare accounts annually and accounts of the corporation comply with the provisions of that law (s288(3)).
(c) Is not required to attach a directors' report to the balance sheet (s288(4)).
(d) If a foreign company, is not obliged to state
(i)   its name, whether it is limited, or its place of incorporation in all its notices, business letters and other official publications (s517(1));
(ii) its name, whether it is limited, or its place of incorporation outside its registered office and every place of business within the state (s517(4)).

In addition, the Ministerial Council for Companies and Securities, which oversees the companies securities markets, has established an Accounting Standards Review Board which aims to give approval to accounting standards developed by appropriate accounting bodies. This development will lead to a set of generally accepted accounting standards being backed by the force of law, except where departures are endorsed by a company's auditors.

1.7 Sources of laws and regulations

The Banking Act and the Regulations made pursuant to that Act are made by the federal parliament. The supervisory authority, the Reserve Bank, has wide powers in relation to determining the lending and investment policies of banks and may make regulations under section 50 (interest rate controls) of the Banking Act, but in practice control is exercised in a non-statutory manner.

The legislation governing the state banks is that of the individual state parliaments.

Company laws and regulations are made by the federal parliament; however, state parliaments may make modifications to these laws. The supervisory authority, the National Companies and Securities Commission (NCSC), has responsibility for the administration of company legislation. The NCSC is responsible to the Ministerial Council (comprising the federal and state Ministers responsible for company law) which approves proposed amendments prior to their being tabled in the federal parliament. Any subsequent changes to the Companies Act 1981 passed by the federal parliament automatically apply to each state code. Changes to Companies Regulations are made in a similar way. However, in this case, once a change to the Companies Regulations has been agreed by the Ministerial Council, the change is effected merely by proclamation by the Governor-General.

1.8 Ability of foreign banks to operate through branches and subsidiaries

There are only two foreign-owned banks still licensed under the Banking Act to carry on banking activities in Australia, namely the Bank of New Zealand and the Banque Nationale de Paris, which have been operating in Australia for over 100 years.

The participation of foreign banks in the Australian financial system is limited by the federal government. However, overseas banks are permitted to establish representative offices to conduct liaison activities but not to engage in financial transactions.

In addition, foreign banks are very active in Australia through partly or wholly-owned subsidiaries (until late 1973 foreign banks were not restricted as ownership participants in the non-bank sector). These subsidiaries, such as merchant banks and finance companies, while not 'banks', offer a wide range of banking-type services.

Following the recommendation of an Inquiry into the Australian Financial System (the Campbell Committee), the federal government indicated its willingness to allow up to 10 new foreign banks to commence operations in Australia. But a change of government in March 1983 has made the prospect of foreign bank entry uncertain. However, early in 1984 a Report of the Review Group on the Australian Financial System (the Martin Report) provided an appraisal of the earlier Campbell report for the new government. The Martin Report gave broad support to continuing deregulation of the financial system and the entry of some new foreign banks into Australia. The government is presently considering the Martin Report's recommendations.

1.9 Level of supervisory control for branches and subsidiaries of foreign banks

Most provisions of the Banking Act apply to both foreign

---

[4] Westpac Banking Corporation was established by Charter and is not subject to the Companies Code

and domestic banks. However, controls exercised by the Reserve Bank under the Banking Act apply less rigidly to prescribed banks, which include the foreign banks.

1.10   Methods of incorporation

Some of the older banks were incorporated by Special Act or Charter, but most banks are incorporated under the Companies Code of the various states.

All savings banks shown in part II of the first schedule of the Banking Act were incorporated in or since 1956 and are wholly-owned subsidiaries of the respective trading banks of similar name.

The Commonwealth Banks Act 1959 established the Commonwealth Banking Corporation, and provided for the continuation of the Commonwealth Trading Bank of Australia and the Commonwealth Savings Bank of Australia, established under the Commonwealth Bank Act 1911-43 and continued under the Commonwealth Bank Act 1945-53, notwithstanding the repeal of these latter Acts. The Commonwealth Development Bank was created under s71 of the Act. In April 1984 the federal government announced that the Commonwealth Trading Bank of Australia would be renamed the 'Commonwealth Bank of Australia'. Also, to make the Commonwealth Banking Group of banks more effective the Commonwealth Savings Bank is to become a wholly-owned subsidiary of the Commonwealth Bank of Australia.

The Primary Industry Bank of Australia was established in terms of the Primary Industry Bank Act 1977. The bank was incorporated under the New South Wales Companies Act on 28 July 1978 and was granted a banking authority by the Governor-General in Council on 21 September 1978.

1.11   Areas within the country subject to special laws

State government-owned banks operating within a single state are subject to the laws of the states which created them, otherwise banking laws apply uniformly throughout the country.

2   ACCOUNTING

2.1   Laws and regulations governing accounts

The Banking Act (part VI) requires that trading and savings banks prepare and deliver annually to the Reserve Bank and the Australian Statistician a balance sheet, a profit and loss statement, and a statement of income and expenditure in respect of Australian business. A statement of liabilities and assets within Australia is required to be lodged weekly with the above bodies and the Secretary to the Department of the Treasury. All returns must be verified by a statutory declaration made by a senior officer of the bank.

The state government-owned banks voluntarily comply with these requirements, in addition to submitting accounting returns in accordance with the statutory requirements of their state legislation.

2.2   Application of general company law

Over the years the reporting practices of Australian banking companies have been governed by regulations from a variety of sources. Initially, disclosures by the pioneering institutions were subject to the terms of the Deeds of Settlement or the specific statutes which established them. State-owned banks were established and regulated by state legislation. Private banks incorporated in terms of the general company law were subject to the provisions of those statutes. Currently, however, the major source of rules governing reporting by non-state-owned banks is federal legislation. Even though most private banks are incorporated in terms of state laws, the state Companies Codes specify that banking corporations which meet federal disclosure requirements are also deemed to satisfy state requirements (see Section 1.6 for details).

The extent of the disclosure made by banks has recently been largely brought into line with the statutory requirements for other Australian companies, as set out in the state Companies Codes (see later Sections, particularly 4.1 and 4.2).

2.3   Roles of legislature and supervisory authority

The federal parliament through the Banking Act and the Banking (Statistics) Regulations promulgates the laws governing accounts for those banks authorised under the Act. State government-owned banks are only subject to the statutory requirements of the Acts establishing them.

Under the Banking Act (s55(1)) accounting returns must be prepared in accordance with the directions specified in the prescribed forms contained in the second schedule of the Banking Act.

These forms and the directions specified in the forms may be varied by regulation provided that no change is made to their essential nature (Banking Act s56). Substantial changes would require amendment to the Act. In practice the supervisory authority, the Reserve Bank, has met new data requirements by reaching agreement with the banks on non-statutory collection of information.

Laws and regulations relating to the accounting provisions of the Companies Code are made by parliament and the supervisory authority, the National Companies and Securities Commission.

2.4   Extent to which requirements as to returns and accounts are prescribed by laws and regulations

2.5   Obligations to furnish accounts

2.5.1   Accounting periods and times of furnishing

2.5.2   Form of accounts to be furnished

2.5.3   Mandatory accounting dates

The Banking Act lays down requirements for the submission of returns and accounts and prescribes their form and content for those banks subject to the Banking Act. Forms required to be lodged by banks pursuant to the Banking Act are:[5]

---

[5] Returns other than accounts which are required under the Banking Act are discussed in Section 8

(a) Forms to be lodged annually

These forms must be lodged with the Australian Statistician and the Reserve Bank within six months of the annual reporting date.

(i) Trading banks[6]
     Form A   Balance sheet
     Form B   Statement of profit and loss
     Form C   Statement of income and expenditure
               in respect of Australian business
(ii) Savings banks
     Form G   Balance sheet
     Form B   Statement of profit and loss
     Form H   Statement of income and expenditure
               in respect of Australian business

(b) Forms to be lodged weekly

These forms must be lodged with the Australian Statistician, the Reserve Bank and the Secretary to the Department of the Treasury within the time periods shown below.

(i) Trading banks (within 14 days of date to which prepared)
     Form D   Statement of liabilities and assets
               within Australia
(ii) Savings banks (within 21 days of date to which prepared)
     Form I   Statement of liabilities and assets
               within Australia

The above forms must be prepared in accordance with the directions specified in the prescribed form of balance sheet and income statement and in accordance with such instructions (not inconsistent with those directions) as are given by the Reserve Bank (Banking Act s55(1)).

2.6 Requirements as to accounts (a) prior to incorporation (b) prior to commencement of trading and (c) in order to continue trading

Accounts do not have to be furnished prior to incorporation or commencement of trading. Requirements relating to the continuance of trading are dealt with in Section 2.4.

2.7 Audit requirements

Under the Banking Act (s61), the federal Auditor-General is required to investigate periodically the books, accounts and transactions of those banks subject to the Act and to furnish a report to the federal Treasurer and the Reserve Bank. In practice this investigation is carried out on an annual basis. The federal Treasurer may, on the recommendation of the Reserve Bank, direct the Auditor-General to make an investigation of any bank's books, accounts and transactions at any time.

In addition, under the Companies Codes of the states private banking companies are required to have an annual audit by independent registered company auditors. The Commonwealth Banks Act 1959 provides for the annual audit of the Commonwealth Banking Corporation by the federal Auditor-General.

Most state banking legislation requires that accounts be audited by the state Auditor-General. In the case of the State Bank of Victoria and the Savings Bank of South Australia there are provisions for the appointment of auditors by the state governor, with the proviso that accounts and transactions may be audited at any time by the state Auditor-General.

2.8 Acceptability to fiscal authorities of accounts submitted to supervisory authority

Accounting profit is not the same as profit for taxation purposes and adjustments are made to the accounting profit for such items as doubtful debts (which are not deductible for tax purposes), profits on securities (which may be of a capital nature for other companies and a revenue item for banks), long service leave provisions, and investment allowances (e.g. on leased equipment) (see Section 9).

2.9 Submission of accounts to any authority other than by requirement of law

Banks which are listed on the Australian Associated Stock Exchanges (AASE) have to comply with the terms of the official listing agreement. This provides for the issue of an audited annual report, profit and loss statement and balance sheet within four months of the end of the financial year. The stock exchange also requires data from an interim report, but there is no requirement that interim data be audited.

Legislative support for the listing requirements has been provided through the Securities Industry Act 1981, part III, section 38.

While the AASE has not laid down too many policies for the preparation of accounts, the following points are taken into account by most listed banks:

(i)   The annual audited accounts must be in consolidated form.
(ii) Trading banks do not have to disclose details of the classification of receivables to reflect the various types of business financed.
(iii) A statement of sources and applications of funds is required, with comparative figures for the previous year.
(iv) The names of major shareholders and the number of shares in which they have an interest should be shown.
(v)   A statement of the percentage of the total holding of the 20 largest shareholders of each class of equity security and a distribution schedule, according to the number of shares owned, must be shown.

2.10 Application of laws and regulations to foreign banks operating through branches and subsidiaries

As noted, only two foreign banks, the Banque Nationale de Paris and the Bank of New Zealand, operate branches

---

[6] For the purposes of statistical returns, 'trading bank' includes the special purpose banks

in Australia at the present time. They must comply with the accounts provisions of the Banking Act in the same way as domestic banks.

The Companies Codes of the states require foreign companies carrying on business in Australia to lodge annual accounts with the Registrar of Companies within three months of their year end. The accounts to be lodged must comply with company legislation in the country of origin of the company. Where no such legislation exists, the accounts to be lodged must comply with relevant Australian company law requirements. If the documents lodged do not, in the opinion of the Corporate Affairs Commission, sufficiently disclose the company's financial position, such additional information as would be required of a public company incorporated under the code may be requested.

There is no local statutory requirement for branch audits, but the accounts of the two foreign banks operating in Australia are audited to satisfy foreign statutory and head office requirements.

2.11 Availability of accounts for public inspection

The Banking Act (s58) requires that certain accounts, for each bank, be published in the Australian Gazette. They are:

(i) The balance sheet, in accordance with Form A (trading banks) or Form G (savings banks).

(ii) The statement of profit and loss, in accordance with Form B (trading and savings banks).

(iii) The statement of liabilities and assets within Australia, in accordance with Form D (trading banks) or Form I (savings banks). The Australian Gazette also publishes this information for the state government-owned banks, which voluntarily supply the accounts.

The accounts of the government-owned banks, drawn up according to the statutory requirements of the Acts which created them, are also available to the public through Parliamentary Papers.

3 FORMAT, STYLE AND CONTENTS OF ACCOUNTS

3.1 Extent to which format is laid down by statute, supervisory authority, generally accepted accounting practice or otherwise

3.2 Description of format

3.3 Extent to which contents are prescribed by statute, supervisory authority, generally accepted accounting practice or otherwise

3.4 Disclosure of specific items required other than those required by general law

The Banking Act prescribes the format of the accounts which have to be filed with the Reserve Bank and the Australian Statistician (see Section 2.5).

While accounts prepared in accordance with the Banking Act are deemed to satisfy the requirements of the Companies Code, many banks depart from the Banking Act format when publishing accounts in their annual report and provide additional information not required by the Banking Act. In particular, the banks

have voluntarily agreed to disclose their bad debt provisions including the movements thereon, thus bringing them in line with the requirements of the Companies Code. Banks listed on the Australian Associated Stock Exchanges will have to comply with the requirements of the listing agreement (see Section 2.9 for further details of disclosure).

The balance sheet and profit and loss account of a typical bank are given in Appendix I.

3.5 Exemptions from disclosure allowed in respect of banking items

Compared with the disclosure requirements of the Companies Code the format of accounts prescribed by the Banking Act does provide exemption from disclosure of certain items, with particular reference to bad debt provisions. However, as pointed out earlier, banks have made a voluntary agreement to disclose items such as bad debt provisions so that the statutory exemptions are not so significant in practice as they used to be.

3.6 Hidden reserves

Up to 1978 banks maintained inner contingency reserves, a practice which of course was permitted by law, but in September of that year the Federal Treasurer announced that he had obtained the voluntary agreement of banks to disclose their inner reserves. Although bad debt provisions were specifically excluded from this agreement, the banks, as indicated in Section 3.5, are now disclosing this information and the published accounts of most banks reveal almost the same amount of information as other listed Australian companies.

3.7 Requirements as to consolidated accounts

The Banking Act accounting requirements only apply to individual banks and, as accounts prepared in accordance with that Act are deemed to comply with the Companies Code, there is no statutory requirement to prepare group accounts in respect of any bank subject to the Banking Act.

However, the listing agreement of the Australian Associated Stock Exchanges requires annual accounts to be published in consolidated form and all listed banking groups prepare group accounts.

As yet, no Australian Accounting Standard on consolidated accounts has been published but the International Accounting Standard No. 3 is regarded as laying down the minimum standard acceptable in Australia.

4 ACCOUNTING POLICIES

4.1 Responsibility for laying down accounting policies

The accounting policies for banks are not rigidly defined by law although certain matters are dealt with under the Banking Act. It is the responsibility of the directors to decide what policies are appropriate for their bank but in reaching their decision they must take the following points into consideration:

(a) The requirements of the Banking Act

The Banking Act is mainly concerned with the prescriptive format of the accounts and has little effect on accounting policies. However, occasionally notes on the forms which have to be completed will require a certain policy to be adopted, e.g. foreign assets and liabilities should be translated into Australian dollars at the exchange rate current at the date of the balance sheet.

(b) The requirements of company law

Although banks which are subject to the Banking Act are legally exempt from certain disclosure requirements of the Companies Act, since 1978 they have agreed to bring their accounts broadly in line with the requirements of the Companies Act. These requirements, particularly Schedule Seven of the Regulations regarding disclosure, are presently under review by the National Companies and Securities Commission.

(c) The status of the bank and its shareholders

The attitudes and objectives of a state bank might well be different from those of a trading bank.

(d) Requirements of the supervisory authority

On occasion the Reserve Bank will issue a directive or, more frequently, advice concerning the treatment of a particular item.

(e) Obligation to follow generally accepted accounting practice

Broadly speaking, listed banks would be expected to follow generally accepted accounting practice (GAAP), which in Australia is codified in the Australian Accounting Standards, and the directors would have to explain the circumstance which in their opinion made it necessary to depart from GAAP.

(f) Requirements of the Associated Australian Stock Exchanges

In the case of a listed company the accounting and disclosure requirements set out in the listing agreement must be considered (see Section 2.9).

(g) The circumstances of a particular bank and the need to present fairly the financial position and results of the entity

The requirement to present fairly the financial position and results of a bank should be paramount and therefore the circumstances of a particular bank might be such as to require it to adopt a certain accounting policy for a fair presentation of the results.

4.2   Particular accounting policies

It follows from Section 4.1 that there will be differences between banks in the policies adopted. Nevertheless, it is possible to detect a majority view in most of the policies adopted.

4.2.1 Foreign exchange

Banks subject to the Banking Act are required to translate their assets and liabilities denominated in a foreign currency into Australian dollars at the rate of exchange current at the balance sheet date.

Greater freedom is given to the profit and loss account where any rate current during the period may be used.

Normal practice is for dealing profits and losses matured during the year to be taken to the profit and loss account at the actual rate and forward contracts open at the balance sheet date to be valued at the appropriate rate at the balance sheet date. Some banks will take unrealised gains and losses to profit and loss, while others will take them to reserves or a contingency account.

4.2.2 Deferred tax

State government-owned banks do not pay federal income tax and therefore are not concerned with deferred tax.

With regard to the other banks, GAAP requires that the tax charge in the accounts should be directly related to the profit shown in the profit and loss account. This 'tax effect' accounting gives rise to deferred tax and banks generally do reflect this in their accounts.

Although deferred tax asset accounts are seen most banks would adopt a prudent course and only recognise those cases where realisation of the future benefit is beyond doubt.

4.2.3 Specific and general provisions for bad and doubtful debts

Banks subject to the Banking Act do not have to disclose the total amount of the provisions outstanding, but they do have to disclose the amount of bad debts written off in respect of their Australian business on Forms C and H, together with total of recoveries.

Following the voluntary agreement on disclosure, most banks now give in their notes to the accounts details of the movements on their bad and doubtful provisions.

Most banks subject to the Banking Act split the provisions between general and specific, although state banks show a combined figure.

4.2.4 Treatment of provisions in accounts

All banks deduct their provisions from the appropriate asset and only bring the net figure into their balance sheet.

4.2.5 Premiums and discounts on investments (amortise, write off, etc.)

It is normal practice for the premium and discount on fixed interest rate investments with a fixed redemption rate to be amortised over the life of the investment.

4.2.6 Offsets, i.e. to what extent can assets and liabilities be set off against each other (legally or in practice)

Australian banks follow customary practice when setting off related deposits and loans in their financial reports. This may occur when a legal right of set-off exists, when the same entity is involved in both the loan and deposit and when the deposit can be held until the loan is paid back.

4.2.7 Goodwill

Purchased goodwill does not feature in the accounts of Australian banks.

4.2.8 Consolidation

As mentioned in Section 3.7 the Banking Act does not require the production of consolidated accounts. However, the listing agreement of the Australian Associated Stock Exchanges requires companies listed on the stock exchange to prepare audited annual accounts on a consolidated basis and banks are no exception to this rule.

There is, as yet, no Australian accounting standard on consolidated accounts but the requirements of the International Accounting Standard No. 3 are generally regarded as the minimum acceptable in Australia.

4.2.9 Revaluations of assets

Both the Banking Act and the Companies Act permit banks to revalue their fixed assets and several banks have taken advantage of this to carry fixed assets at current value rather than historical cost. The revaluation is not carried out every year but at intervals of several years.

4.2.10 Instalment finance and leasing including basis of recognition of income

Although instalment finance and leasing are assuming increasingly larger proportions of total lending, they are not shown as separate items in the balance sheet, but are included in the total for loans, advances, etc.

Income is released to profit and loss account over the life of the contract, in relation to the outstanding balance.

4.2.11 Dealing assets

Dealing assets do not feature as a separate item in an Australian bank's balance sheet and it is not easy to quantify the amount of investment held for dealing purposes, as opposed to holding to final maturity.

It is noted, however, that certain banks show their investments at the lower of cost and market value, so it is clear that where investments are held for dealing purposes profits are not being recognised until the investments are sold.

4.2.12 Pensions

In general, payments are made to pension funds to cover the future cost of pensions to present employees, based upon actuarial consideration.

4.2.13 Depreciation

The Banking Act only requires the amount of depreciation written off bank premises to be disclosed in the profit and loss account. Fixed assets, net of depreciation, may be stated as a single figure in the balance sheet but the basis of valuation must be disclosed.

Under company law the aggregate cost or valuation of each class of fixed asset, together with its accumulated depreciation, must be shown but there does not appear to be a requirement to show the annual depreciation charge.

Disclosure practice among the banks is varied but best practice would be to provide an analysis of cost (or valuation) and accumulated depreciation for each class of fixed asset and a similar analysis of the charge against profits for depreciation. Where assets are revalued it will of course be necessary to revise the depreciation charge.

Details of the estimated lives of assets or depreciation rates should also be disclosed.

4.2.14 Other

Inflation accounting

Australia's first Statement of Accounting Practice, SAP1, on Current Cost Accounting, was issued in November 1983. It represents a revised version of Provisional Accounting Standards 1.1 and 1.2. SAP1 recommends that all entities present current cost accounting supplementary statements in addition to their conventional financial statements. Entities are also encouraged to present CCA statements as prime statements. Banks have, in the past, indicated that they would make no move on inflation accounting until the profession makes firm recommendations. Now that these recommendations have been published, the banks can give the matter additional consideration. Any change in practice will first be observed in their 1984 financial reports.

5 WINDOW DRESSING

Window dressing of financial reports is not a practice that is condoned in Australia. Whether it exists in the accounts of banks is largely a matter for the banks' auditors to decide. If window dressing is discovered, auditors would need to qualify their opinion in their report.

6 AMOUNTS REQUIRED TO BE MAINTAINED BY LAW OR OTHERWISE

The Reserve Bank has indicated that it has no specific statutory powers to prescribe capital requirements for banks, although the central bank does consult with each bank about its capital position.

Banks are given the main responsibility for prudent management of their own affairs. The Reserve Bank's prudential system of control relies upon co-operation, not formal specification. Although the Inquiry into the

Australian Financial System favoured adoption of the USA's 'camel' ratio approach to assessment of capital adequacy, this suggestion was not supported by the 1984 Review Group. Hence it seems unlikely that formal control of capital ratios will be invoked in Australia in the near future.

Yet, in its non-statutory role, the Reserve Bank does keep trends in a number of capital ratios under review for banks and for their consolidated groups.

7 KEY RATIOS

Laws and regulations governing certain financial ratios of Australian trading and savings banks are summarised below and it should be noted that the average LGS and SRD ratios for 1983/1984 were 19% and 7%.

7.1 Trading banks

(a) Loans below A$100,000 are subject to interest rate ceilings (14.5% in June 1984).

(b) Each trading bank must maintain a Statutory Reserve Deposit (SRD) account with the Reserve Bank. The amount in this account is determined as a percentage of the trading bank's current level of Australian deposits. The ratio is uniform for all trading banks and can be increased with one day's notice provided that the revised ratio does not exceed 25% of total deposits. A ratio of more than 25% may be prescribed with 45 days notice. The prescribed ratio in June 1984 was 7%. Section 25 of the Banking Act provides that a 'prescribed bank' shall not have imposed on it a statutory reserve deposit ratio greater than that of a non-prescribed bank, but the ratio could be less.

(c) Each bank ensures that its liquid asset and government securities (LGS) ratio, being the ratio of notes and coins, cash with the Reserve Bank, treasury notes and other government securities to total deposits, does not fall below an agreed minimum. This minimum is a uniform rate for all major trading banks and in June 1984 was 18%. This liquidity restriction does not have a statutory basis. It was established by the LGS Convention, agreed between the banks and the Reserve Bank in 1956.

7.2 Savings banks

The Banking (Savings Banks) Regulations made pursuant to s71 and div. 6 of pt. 11 (ss37 and 38) of the Banking Act contain the following provisions:

(a) Savings banks, under the Banking Act, must maintain in prescribed assets an amount equal to their deposits in Australia. The prescribed assets are:
(i)   Cash on hand in Australia.
(ii)   Deposits with the Reserve Bank.
(iii) Deposits with, and loans to, other banks.
(iv)   Federal and state government securities.
(v)   Securities issued or guaranteed by a federal or state government authority.
(vi)   Loans to authorised dealers in the short-term money market.

(vii) Loans to Australian Banks Export Re-Finance Corporation Limited.
(viii) Government guaranteed loans.
(ix)   Loans for other purposes on the security of land in Australia.
(x)   Other investments, not including fixed assets (e.g. bills). An amount not exceeding 6% of deposits may be held in this 'free choice' category.

Each savings bank is required to hold at least 15% of its depositors' funds in categories (i), (ii) and, from 1 August 1984, (vi) above, provided that the loans in category (vi) are secured by federal securities (Regulation 5(3)).[7]

(b) A savings bank shall not have on deposit with trading banks in Australia an amount exceeding the sum of A$4 million plus 2.5% of its Australian depositors' balances (Regulation 5(5)).

In addition, the Reserve Bank does monitor the capital gearing (ratio of capital employed to total liabilities) of all banks subject to the Banking Act. Although it has no specific powers to determine benchmarks or guidelines for the adequacy of banks' capital resources, either absolutely or relative to the liability that they underpin or might be called on to underpin, it does discuss this ratio with them and also the implications for their own capital positions of their equity investments in, and other financial relationships with, associated institutions.

8 ACCOUNTING RETURNS OTHER THAN ACCOUNTS

8.1 By whom required

Under the Banking Act (s52 to s54) banks supply the Reserve Bank, the Treasurer and the Australian Statistician with a wide range of statistics on their operations. The format in which much of this information is to be supplied is laid down in the second schedule of the Banking Act.

In addition to the prescribed returns, the Reserve Bank requests statistical data on such matters as lending, interest rates and foreign exchange operations. Information received by the Reserve Bank, in the course of regular consultations with the banks, supplements the statistical collections.

8.2 Nature of requirements

The returns required to be lodged weekly, pursuant to the Banking Act are:

(i)   Trading banks (within 14 days of date to which prepared)
       Form E   Statement of debits to customers' accounts
       Form F   Statement of foreign currency position

---

[7] The Banking (Savings Banks) Regulations were revised on 26 August 1983. The federal government announced that it would remove existing asset requirements for savings banks which serve to limit lending for housing. A minimum liquidity requirement of 15% was introduced in place of a 40% prescribed assets ratio and a 7.5% ratio for Treasury notes and deposits with the Reserve Bank

(ii) Savings banks (within 21 days of date to which prepared)
   Form J   Statement relating to depositors' accounts in each state and territory in which the bank carries on business

In addition, banks are required to provide a statement of loans, advances and bills discounted, and a statement of deposits as specified by the Reserve Bank.

9 TAXATION

9.1 General method of taxation

There is no special method of taxation applicable to banks which would be different from the taxation of any other company. It may be useful to point out some basic features of Australian income tax, which is at present levied only by the federal government.

(i)   There is no capital gains tax as such, but some profits which may be regarded as capital in accounting or business parlance are treated as assessable income and taxed at ordinary rates of 46%. (See also Sections 9.2 and 9.3.)

(ii) Dividends received by Australian resident companies are subject to tax rebate at the company tax rate of 46%. In effect there is no tax payable on dividends, hence no credit is allowed for foreign tax on dividends.

(iii) Except in the case of dividends, interest and royalties income earned outside Australia and subject to foreign income tax is exempt from Australian income tax. Thus the significance of foreign tax credits is limited to interest and royalties. In this case the credit is limited to the lesser of the Australian or foreign tax on the amount of interest or royalties.

(iv) There is no provision for the carry back of losses, although a deduction is allowed for the carry forward of losses for up to seven years. However, there are restrictions on this carry forward deduction where there has been a change in more than 50% of the shareholding of a company. This restriction may also preclude a deduction of a loss incurred in the current year.

(v)   A withholding tax is levied at rates of 30% on dividends paid to residents of countries with which there is no double tax treaty with Australia, and 15% on dividends to residents of Treaty countries. The rate of withholding tax on interest paid to non-residents is 10%.
   Where withholding tax has been paid, there is no further tax payable by the non-resident.

(vi) There has been a considerable volume of anti-avoidance legislation during the past four years, both concerning specific provisions of the Income Tax Assessment Act and general anti-avoidance provisions.
   This legislation is also designed to deal with transfer pricing. Consequently it is desirable to look at income tax liability on a case-by-case basis.

(vii) Government savings banks are exempt from tax.

9.2 Accounts as basis for taxation

Taxable income is primarily determined on net profit for accounting purposes but subject to adjustments to satisfy the income tax law. (See Sections 9.3 and 4.2.2.)

9.3 Adjustments permitted or required

There are some adjustments which apply to all corporations and some which may have particular application to banks. Generally, no deduction is allowed for accrued liabilities or provisions so these are required to be added to net profit to arrive at taxable income. Again, where depreciation rates charged in the accounts differ from income tax rates the appropriate adjustment has to be made. There is presently an investment allowance deduction of 18% of the cost of new plant. This applies in addition to ordinary depreciation and may be allowed to banks where they 'lease' plant for a period of not less than four years. It should be noted that although there is no capital gains tax as such, some businesses such as banks may be taxed at ordinary rates on profits from the sale of land and securities where these are purchased and sold in the course of the business. All taxpayers are taxed on profits of such assets where the assets are sold within 12 months of acquisition.

9.4 Effect of tax considerations on presentation of accounts

Although the income tax computation is based on the net profit disclosed by the accounts, nevertheless adjustments as required by taxation law are made in the computation, and taxation aspects have little or no effect on the presentation of the accounts.

9.5 Other taxes

There are other taxes payable in Australia. These include in the case of the Commonwealth government, customs and excise and sales tax. The latter is payable on the wholesale value of goods and as such would not be of much direct consequence to banks.

The several state governments impose land taxes, payroll taxes and stamp duties on documents. Payroll tax imposed on salaries and wages paid to all employees is at the rate of 5%. In the case of New South Wales and Victoria the rates are generally 6%.

On 1 January 1983 the federal government introduced a Bank Account Debits (BAD) tax on certain bank transactions. The tax applies to all debits to accounts with banks that are subject to operation by cheque or like instrument. The rate rises from 10 cents for a debit of less than A$100 to A$1 for a debit in excess of A$5,000.

In addition, all states, with the exception of Queensland and Tasmania, introduced a tax on financial institutions, including banks. This Financial Institutions Duty (FID) tax is at a rate of 0.03% per A$100 on receipts of all financial institutions to a maximum of A$300 per transaction. Other taxes such as loan instrument duties have been abolished.

10 INTERPRETATION OF ACCOUNTS

10.1 Adequacy of information as to contents and disclosure

Since the voluntary disclosure agreement of 1978 there has been an improvement in the standard of disclosure, particularly in the case of the trading banks. However, there is less disclosure compared to US banks and the clearing banks in the UK. In this respect the format of the accounts prescribed by the Banking Act has been an inhibiting factor in the development of more meaningful accounts.

10.2 Audit and reliability of information

The banks operate in a closely supervised environment and the accounts are subject to audit by professional auditors with high standards. Therefore the accounts can be considered as reliable, and they will present fairly the financial position and results of a bank in accordance with Australian accounting standards.

10.3 Comparability between different banks on the basis of published accounts or publicly available returns

Comparisons between different banks on the basis of published accounts may not be valid for a number of reasons:

(i) Several trading and savings banks are interrelated, and (a) transfer prices may be used to improve the results of one bank at the expense of another (e.g. through the charges for management expenses and interest on loans); (b) some published accounts of savings banks are consolidated accounts (e.g. Westpac Savings Bank and its subsidiary company Westpac Savings Bank (NZ) Limited). The problem can be overcome by obtaining a copy of unabridged accounts for each bank from the Corporate Affairs Commission in the state of the bank's incorporation.

(ii) Different valuation rules are used by different banks for similar items. Hence ratio analysis may not be justified for certain items. In addition, no adjustments are made for the distorting effects of inflation. For example, cost, appraisal, lower of cost and market value, cost amortised for premiums and discounts and other techniques are used to derive balance sheet figures for investments.

(iii) Capital composition differs between private and government banks making direct comparison difficult.

(iv) Different classifications are used by banks for the same item.

See also Sections 10.1 and 10.2.

Typical balance sheet and profit and loss account

X Banking Group Limited and its subsidiaries

Balance sheet as at 30 September 19x2

	19x2 ($000)	19x1 ($000)		19x2 ($000)	19x1 ($000)
Authorised capital: xxx ordinary shares of one dollar each	xxx	xxx			
Shareholders' funds			Liquid assets		
Issued and paid-up capital (xxx ordinary shares of one dollar each fully paid)	xxx	xxx	Coins, notes and cash at bank	xxx	xxx
			Loans to authorised dealers in Australian short-term money market	xxx	xxx
Reserves	xxx	xxx	Money at short call overseas	xxx	xxx
Retained profits	xxx	xxx	Bills receivable and remittances in transit	xxx	xxx
			Cheques in course of collection and balances with other banks	xxx	xxx
Share capital and reserves applicable to shareholders of X Banking Group Limited	xxx	xxx	Investments other than trade investments	xxx	xxx
Minority shareholders' interest in subsidiaries	xxx	xxx	Regulatory deposits with central and other banks		
Customers' accounts, etc.			Reserve Bank of Australia	xxx	xxx
Deposits	xxx	xxx	Overseas	xxx	xxx
Borrowings by borrowing corporation subsidiaries	xxx	xxx	Customers' accounts, etc.		
Bank acceptances of customers (see contra)	xxx	xxx	Loans, advances and net receivables	xxx	xxx
			Customers' liability for acceptances (see contra)	xxx	xxx
Due to other banks	xxx	xxx	Trade investments	xxx	xxx
Bills payable and other liabilities	xxx	xxx	Premises and equipment	xxx	xxx
Provisions			All other assets	xxx	xxx
Proposed final dividend	xxx	xxx			
Provision for income tax	xxx	xxx			
Other provisions	xxx	xxx			
	xxx	xxx		xxx	xxx

Profit and loss statement for year ended
30 September 19x2

	19x2 ($000)	19x1 ($000)
Gross income, discount and interest earned net exchange commission and other items	xxx	xxx
Less expenses of management and interest paid	xxx	xxx
Operating profit before income tax	xxx	xxx
Less income tax expense	xxx	xxx
Operating profit after tax	xxx	xxx
Less interests of minority shareholders	xxx	xxx
Operating profit applicable to shareholders of X Banking Group Limited	xxx	xxx
Extraordinary items	xxx	xxx
Less interests of minority shareholders in extraordinary items	xxx	xxx
Operating profit and extraordinary items applicable to shareholders of X Banking Group Limited	xxx	xxx
Retained profits at beginning of year	xxx	xxx
Total available for appropriation	xxx	xxx
Less appropriations		
Transfers to reserves		
General	xxx	xxx
Contingencies	xxx	xxx
Capital	xxx	xxx
Dividends		
Interim	xxx	xxx
Proposed final payable	xxx	xxx
Retained profits at end of year	xxx	xxx

Note: Consolidated and holding company accounts are usually provided for the current and previous year

APPENDIX II

Australian accounting standards

Accounting standards

AAS1   Profit and loss statements

AAS2   Valuation and presentation of inventories in the context of the historical cost system

AAS3   Accounting for company income tax (tax-effect accounting)

AAS4   Depreciation of non-current assets

AAS5   Materiality in financial statements

AAS6   Accounting policies: determination, application and disclosure

AAS7   Accounting for the extractive industries

AAS8   Events occurring after balance date

AAS9   Expenditure carried forward to subsequent accounting periods

AAS10   Accounting for the revaluation of non-current assets

AAS11   Accounting for construction contracts

AAS12   Statement of sources and applications of funds

AAS13   Accounting for research and development costs

AAS14   Equity method of accounting

AAS15   Disclosure of revenue

AAS16   Financial reporting by segments

AAS17   Accounting for leases

AAS18   Accounting for goodwill

Statement of accounting practice

SAP1   Current cost accounting/guidance notes on current cost accounting

CHAPTER 13

CANADA

JOHN HOWARD

1 GENERAL INFORMATION

Canada is a federal democracy with responsibility for government shared between ten provincial governments elected by the eligible citizens of each province and a federal government elected by the people of Canada. The allocation of responsibility between governments can be difficult to interpret but has evolved from the Act incorporating Canada, The British North America Act, up to the 1982 Canadian constitution.

While incorporation of corporate entities is regulated at both provincial and federal levels, banks may only be chartered under federal jurisdiction and in recent years the Canadian government has steered an increasingly nationalistic course.

Under the Foreign Investment Review Act of 1974 the Canadian government has reserved the right to grant approval for the acquisition of Canadian business enterprises by non-Canadian individuals and corporations. Since 1975 it has also required that it grant approval for the establishment of new businesses in Canada by non-Canadian persons or by persons controlled by non-Canadian persons. To obtain such approval, non-Canadian investors must convince the Foreign Investment Review Agency (FIRA) that their proposals will be 'of significant benefit to Canada'. Therefore, particularly in acquisition situations, non-Canadian investors must convince the Agency that their investments will do more than maintain the status quo – they must provide a significant incremental benefit to Canada. Additionally, the Act also requires that any change in foreign ownership requires approval by FIRA.

Although Canadian banking legislation specifically excludes foreign banks which may wish to establish in Canada from review by FIRA,[1] knowledge of this background attitude is important in evaluating an investment in Canada.

While wishing to pursue a nationalistic course the Canadian government has recognised that foreign capital will continue to play an important role in the country's economic growth in the 1980s and beyond, and this has been shown by the Banks and the Banking Law Revision Act, 1980 (Bank Act) which has opened the Canadian banking industry to the outside world.

Monetary policy is determined by Canada's central bank, the Bank of Canada, which was established in 1934 by the Bank of Canada Act. It is entirely owned by the Government of Canada and its mandate is to exercise overall control of Canada's monetary system by regulating credit and the money supply.

The Bank of Canada implements government monetary policy through its influence of interest rates. Each week it establishes the rate of interest charged to the chartered banks on advances from the Bank of Canada. This rate is set at the average yield rate for 90-day Government of Canada treasury bills plus ¼%. Adjustments to this rate are influenced by the supply of treasury bills which the Bank of Canada controls.

1.1 Organisations covered by banking regulations

Only banks are covered by the banking regulations set out or empowered by the Bank Act. The 'near bank' activities of Trust and Mortgage Loan companies, Credit Unions and Caisses Populaires are governed by separate legislation, which can be either federal or provincial. At this time, legislation and regulation governing the operation of Trust companies is being redrafted and documents released by the federal government suggest that many of the principles underlying the Bank Act will also be made applicable to Trust companies. The activities and legislation, present or proposed, of these other entities is not covered by this text.

To provide a feeling of the relative magnitude at the end of the third quarter of 1983, the relative size of these industries in terms of assets was as follows:

Chartered banks: $369 billion[2]

Credit Unions and Caisses Populaires: $37 billion[3]

Trust and Mortgage Loan Companies: $89 billion[4]

Of the non-bank assets, some 50% of the Credit Union and 70% of Trust and Mortgage assets were in the form of mortgage loans.

1.2 Summary of major types of bank

The Bank Act creates two major classes of banks,[5] schedule A and schedule B banks.

Schedule A banks presently consist of the eleven Canadian chartered banks which were in existence when the Bank Act was passed and two formed since that date.

---

[1] Section 307
[2] Bank of Canada Review April 1984, s.35
[3] Bank of Canada Review April 1984, s.93
[4] Bank of Canada Review April 1984, s.95
[5] Sections 5 and 174 (2) (3)

No more than 10% of such of the issued shares of these banks as have voting rights may be held by any one shareholder.

A bank will be considered to be a schedule B bank if more than 10% of such of the issued shares of the bank as have voting rights exercisable in all circumstances attached thereto are held by any one resident or non-resident shareholder and his associates. Schedule B banks may be further categorised as domestic banks or foreign bank subsidiaries (see Section 1.8). There are presently 58 which are foreign controlled and one which is Canadian controlled.

If a bank is incorporated as a schedule A bank, and control of more than 10% of the issued shares of the bank as have voting rights pass into the control of one share-holder, the bank becomes a schedule B bank and the schedules to the Act are amended accordingly. Conversely, a schedule B bank which becomes widely held will be reclassified as a schedule A bank.[6]

1.3 Supervisory authorities

1.4 Status of supervisory authorities

Banks are supervised by the Inspector General of Banks, who in turn makes demands on the external auditors (see Section 11.4).

The Bank Act is administered by the Inspector General of Banks, who is appointed by the federal cabinet on recommendation of the Minister of Finance, to whom he reports. The primary duty of the Inspector is to ensure that all banks are prudently managed in the interests of bank depositors, creditors and shareholders. His other responsibilities include advising the Minister of Finance on matters of government banking policy, reviewing applications for new bank charters including the licensing of foreign bank subsidiaries, overseeing the issuance of shares and other bank securities and general administration of the Bank Act.

To this end the Inspector General of Banks is required to examine the business and affairs of each bank and report his findings to the Minister of Finance not less than once each year.[7] The purpose of this examination is to satisfy himself that each bank is in a sound financial position and that it has complied with the various provisions of the Bank Act.

For an explanation of the function provided by the external auditor, see Sections 2.7 and 11.5.

1.5 Laws and regulations governing banks

1.6 Application of general company law to banks

1.7 Sources of laws and regulations

Canadian banking law is unique in federal legislation because it expires every ten years, with new legislation or extension of the existing legislation only possible by an Act of Parliament. The latest Bank Act was the result of revision to the 1967 Bank Act and is entitled Banks and the Banking Law Revision Act, 1980. The revision of the 1967 Act was delayed by a number of matters including a federal election which resulted in a short-lived change in government in 1979.

This Act is the primary instrument through which the federal government regulates and supervises all banks in Canada. Included in the comprehensive legislation are provisions dealing with the types of bank that can operate, their respective powers and the prohibitions and limitations to their activities. The legislation also details specific requirements for reserves, financial reporting and the incorporation of new banks. Since the Act was designed to be the overall authority for bank operations, it incorporates many of the requirements of the Canada Business Corporations Act, which is the legislative authority for incorporation of limited liability corporations under federal law.

Effectively for the first time in Canadian banking history, foreign banks are permitted to operate their banking business through foreign bank subsidiaries. Previously, foreign banks wishing to carry on business activities in Canada had to do so through finance companies incorporated under corporate legislation, either federal or provincial, rather than banking legislation. There were benefits and drawbacks to this practice which, for example, required no reserves to be maintained. The Bank Act now contains detailed provisions specific to foreign bank subsidiaries.

The 'spirit of the legislation' is the overriding factor in the administration of the Act, rules and regulations, and will be used to control any attempt to make use of legislative loopholes. Constraints on all banking activities come in the form of the Act, the regulations and the rules issued by the Inspector General of Banks.

(a) Bank powers

The business powers of a bank, including some specific prohibitions, are set down in part V of the Bank Act. Generally, these powers and restrictions apply to schedule A and B banks, although a number which apply only to foreign bank subsidiaries are covered under Section 1.8.

The Bank Act provides that a bank may engage in, and carry on, such business generally as appertains to the business of banking.[8] In addition to this general power, specific activities are expressly sanctioned, which allow the bank to:

(a) Open branches (note, however, schedule B banks may not open any branches outside Canada, nor may they open more than one head office and one branch without the permission of the Minister of Finance).[9]

(b) Borrow money.

(c) Lend money with or without security.

(d) Act through a subsidiary as a factor and collection agent for receivables.

(e) Guarantee the payment or repayment of money, subject to regulations prescribing the terms and conditions under which guarantees must be made.

(f) Engage through a subsidiary in financial leasing, subject to regulations made pursuant to the Act. These regulations include a number of restrictions including the prohibition on banks leasing automobiles.

(g) Issue credit and charge cards.

(h) Sell transit and government sponsored lottery tickets as well as other tickets of a non-profit nature.

---

[6] Section 22 (5)   [8] Section 173 (1)
[7.] Section 246 (2)   [9] Section 173 (2)

(i) Sell savings, retirement and home ownership savings plans, as well as certain savings plans that qualify for registration under the Income Tax Act of Canada.

(j) Act as adviser to, or administrator of, real estate investment trusts, mortgage investment companies or mortgage-based mutual funds.

In general, banks are prohibited from making significant equity investments.[10] They may not own more than 10% of the voting shares of any Canadian company, except:[11]

(a) A bank service corporation. This is a wholly-owned subsidiary which holds, leases or maintains real property on behalf of the bank.

(b) The Export Finance Corporation of Canada Limited or any other Canadian corporation, the sole objective and activity of which is to engage in and promote the financing of exports from Canada.

(c) A mortgage loan corporation if it is a subsidiary of the bank and owns no shares of any other corporation.

(d) A venture capital corporation if it is a subsidiary of the bank and does not hold more than 10% of the voting shares of a trust or loan company or a company that accepts deposits from the public.

(e) A corporation whose activities are limited solely to assisting in the establishment or operation of a real estate investment trust or mortgage investment company. If less than 100% of the shares are held by the bank, the other shareholders must be 'Financial Corporations', defined as Canadian corporations, other than those carrying on an insurance business, 80% of the assets of which are made up of debt securities and loans receivable.

(f) A factoring or leasing corporation that is a subsidiary of the bank.

No limit is placed on the number of shares in foreign corporations which a schedule A bank may own, provided the 10% limit on ownership of voting stock in Canadian corporations is not exceeded by virtue of a combination of the direct holding through the schedule A bank and the foreign corporation's shareholdings in any Canadian corporations.[12] Schedule B banks, on the other hand, are specifically prohibited from owning more than 10% of the voting shares of any foreign corporation.[13]

If the 10% limit is exceeded as a result of shares obtaining voting rights after acquisition, as a result of shares acquired through realisation of security or due to certain temporary investments, the excess shares must be disposed of within two years.[14]

If such excess investments existed at the time the Act came into force, then disposition of the excess shares had to be within two years for a data processing corporation and within five years (or any such longer period as the Minister might allow) for any other non-financial corporation.[15]

(b) Real estate

The Bank Act permits banks to acquire and hold real property for their own use and occupation,[16] subject to a limitation imposed on schedule B banks, more fully set out in Section 1.8. If the bank ceases to have a need for the use of the real property, it is allowed a grace period of seven years to dispose of the property. Note also that the

bank must have a controlling interest (i.e. greater than 50%) in such property.

For property received or acquired through a mortgage or hypothec securing a loan or advance made by the bank,[17] the bank is allowed a 12-year disposition period.[18]

(c) Loans

Division B of the Bank Act defines the types of loans that banks may make and the security that they may take. The procedures to be followed for registration of the securities are prescribed in the regulations. On loans to most borrowers, banks are permitted to take security in the form of floating or specific charges on accounts receivable and inventories.

With regard to most loans made on the security of real property the amount of the loan, together with amounts outstanding on prior and equal ranking mortgages or hypothecs, cannot exceed 75% of the value of the property, unless the loan is guaranteed under the National Housing Act, or is insured. Furthermore, the total value of residential mortgages may not exceed 10% of the aggregate of the bank's Canadian dollar deposit liabilities and outstanding debentures.[19] The latter restriction does not apply to mortgage lending subsidiaries, nor to mortgage loans guaranteed by federal law.

In 1982 the Inspector General announced a further limitation on the size of an individual loan. The maximum amount a foreign bank subsidiary can lend to a borrower or group of borrowers with a common management is limited to 100% of the aggregate of the bank's shareholders' equity and reserves. However, the Inspector General expects that the normal practice of the bank will be to limit the size of loans to one borrower to no more than 50% of shareholders' equity and reserves. Where a foreign bank subsidiary, as a participant in a major financing, believes it necessary to make a loan in excess of the 100% limit, the foreign bank parent may take up the excess over the 100% limit. However, such shared arrangements need to be approved in advance by the Inspector General. This move was necessitated by the dramatic asset growth in 1981 when Canadian corporations ventured out to acquire important holdings of foreign-owned oil companies, financed by significant loans from the banking system. This debt resulted in a relative weakening of corporate balance sheets and 1982 saw a dramatic rescheduling of debt repayment by the corporate sector.

(d) Funding of Canadian dollar assets

The Inspector General has further indicated that he expects that at least 50% of the total Canadian dollar assets of foreign bank subsidiaries should be funded by Canadian dollar liabilities. This guideline was introduced following a tendency of certain foreign bank subsidiaries

---

[10] Section 193 (2)
[11] Section 193 (5) and (6)
[12] Section 193 (3)
[13] Section 193 (4)
[14] Section 193 (10) to (12)
[15] Section 196
[16] Section 199 (1)
[17] Section 185 (1)
[18] Section 199 (2) (6)
[19] Section 176

to fund an increasing portion of their Canadian dollar business with foreign currency liabilities. The Inspector General felt that while these liabilities were fully hedged they might, over a period of time, represent a funding risk.

(e) Dealing in securities[20]

A bank may act either as principal or agent in dealing in real property mortgages, bonds and debentures and may act as principal in buying and selling equity securities for its investment portfolio. The services of a registered broker must be used for all other dealings in equity securities. Furthermore, banks may not act as underwriters of securities except in respect of bonds, debentures and other evidences of indebtedness:
(a) Of the bank.
(b) Of or guaranteed by the Government of Canada or a province or municipal corporation.
(c) Of a public utility.
(d) Of an international agency of which Canada is a member.
(e) Where the bank is acting as a member of a selling group in connection with an underwriting of securities issued by a corporation other than a bank.

Banks, their officers, employees and controlled corporations are restricted from managing mutual funds in Canada.[21]

(f) Limitations and restrictions placed on banks

The Bank Act prohibits all banks from engaging in certain specific activities including, among others, the following:[22]
(a) Dealing in goods or merchandise or engaging in any business other than banking.
(b) Engaging in fiduciary activities (this is a significant function provided by trust companies).
(c) Engaging in portfolio management or investment counselling.
(d) Lending to a director or to a corporation in which a director or officer of the bank has a significant interest, outside of the ordinary course of business. If the loan exceeds 2% of paid-up capital and contributed surplus, it requires authorisation by two thirds of the loan committee or the board of directors.
(e) Lending to officers or employees of the bank or corporations controlled by the bank, unless the loan is secured by the borrower's residence or is less than the greater of Can$25,000 or the borrower's annual salary.
(f) Contributing to a bank guarantee or pension fund where any part of the fund is invested in shares of a Canadian corporation in which the bank is authorised, under the Act, to own more than 10% of the voting shares, or where more than 10% of the fund has been invested in shares of the bank.
(g) Acquiring, dealing in or lending more than Can$50,000 on security of shares or debentures of the bank or any other bank, except under certain conditions.
(h) Investing in partnerships or limited partnerships.
(i) Engaging in data processing services, other than banking related data processing services prescribed by the regulations to the Bank Act.
(j) Making loans, within a bank's first two financial years, to a director who is not also a full-time officer or employee of the bank.[23]

1.8 Ability of foreign banks to operate through branches and subsidiaries

At present, foreign banks are prohibited from directly carrying on the business of banking or maintaining a branch for any purpose in Canada, but are permitted to:[24]
(a) Maintain representative offices in Canada for the purpose of promoting their services. They may not, however, carry on any banking business in Canada from these offices. The government has proposed detailed regulations governing the establishment and operation of representative offices.
(b) Locate their head offices in Canada and from these offices do all things necessary to the conduct of their business *outside* Canada.
(c) Carry on the business of banking in Canada through a 'Foreign Bank Subsidiary'. This is a bank incorporated in Canada, under the provisions of the Bank Act, as a schedule B bank.
(d) Establish a non-bank affiliate of a foreign bank. This is a corporation, other than a bank, which is incorporated and carrying on business in Canada, 10% or more of the voting stock of which is owned by the foreign bank or its associates. A non-bank affiliate of a foreign bank shall not:[25]
(i)   Engage in the business of both lending money and accepting deposit liabilities transferable by cheque or other instrument;
      or
(ii) engage in the business of lending money at any particular time when another non-bank affiliate of the foreign bank is engaged in the business of accepting deposit liabilities transferable by cheque or other instrument.
      In addition,[26] unless the consent in writing of the Minister is first obtained, a non-bank affiliate of a foreign bank that carries on as part of its business any aspect of the business of banking shall not:
(iii) borrow money by way of loan, deposit or otherwise, or
(iv) issue debentures, bonds and other securities evidencing any such borrowing of money
      if it is represented by or on behalf of the non-bank affiliate in any document related to the borrowing or to the issue of debentures, bonds or other securities that the repayment of money so borrowed or received or the payment of any interest thereon is guaranteed, directly or indirectly, by the foreign bank or any corporation associated with the foreign bank. The intent of these restrictions is to encourage foreign banks to carry on banking business in Canada through foreign bank subsidiaries, thereby bringing their activities within the framework of the Bank Act.

---

[20] Section 190
[21] Section 191 (1)
[22] Section 174 (2)
[23] Section 174 (10)

[24] Section 302 (1)
[25] Section 303 (5)
[26] Section 303 (8)

The general powers and limitation of foreign bank subsidiaries parallel those set out in Sections 1.5, 1.6 and 1.7. In addition, however, the following limitations and restrictions pertain to foreign bank subsidiaries and other schedule B banks. Some of the more notable restrictions are listed below:

(a) Assets in Canada

A foreign bank subsidiary must maintain assets in Canada at least equal to the sum of its paid-in capital and its total liabilities to Canadian residents.[27]

(b) Maximum asset holdings

Along with the minimum asset provisions, a schedule B bank, which includes all foreign bank subsidiaries, may not have domestic assets exceeding twenty times its deemed authorised capital. In addition to this restriction, the total domestic assets of all foreign bank subsidiaries combined is limited to 8% of total domestic assets of all banks in Canada. These restrictions are designed to allow the government to control the overall size of schedule B banks in Canada without limiting the growth of their foreign operations.[28] In the summer of 1984 a law was passed which increased the ceiling of domestic assets for foreign bank subsidiaries to 16%.

(c) Branches

Foreign bank subsidiaries (as schedule B banks) are allowed to open a head office and one branch office in Canada. Additional branches may be opened only with the prior approval of the Minister of Finance. Moreover, while no branches may be opened outside Canada there is no similar restriction regarding representative offices.[29]

(d) Capital

Authorised capital must be at least Can$5,000,000, for a schedule B bank, of which one-half (Can$2,500,000) must be issued and fully paid.[30]

(e) Licence

The foreign bank subsidiary may only commence the business of banking once a licence allowing it to carry on business has been issued by the Minister of Finance.[31] This licence may carry with it such restrictions and conditions on the carrying on of the business of banking as deemed expedient by the Minister of Finance. The licence may be renewed for periods of up to one year for the first five years and thereafter for periods of up to three years.[32] It is important to note that renewal of the licence is entirely within the discretion of the Minister and may be made with such conditions and restrictions as he deems expedient. The intent of this provision is to use licensing as a means of ensuring that foreign bank subsidiaries continue to make a contribution to competitive banking in Canada and that Canadian banks continue to receive reciprocal treatment in the foreign jurisdiction.

(f) Property and equipment

A schedule B bank's investment in real property and equipment, either directly or through a bank service corporation, may not exceed 50% of the aggregate of the paid-in capital, contributed surplus, retained earnings and general reserves of the bank.[33]

1.9 Level of supervisory control for branches and subsidiaries of foreign banks

Supervisory control is maintained at the same level for all banks in Canada.

1.10 Methods of incorporation

(a) General

The Inspector General is responsible for reviewing each application for incorporation as a bank. The Minister of Finance, through an Order in Council, has the ultimate responsibility for approving such applications.

Under the Bank Act,[34] a bank may be incorporated in one of the three following ways:
(a) Special Act of Parliament.[35]
(b) Letters Patent issued by the Minister of Finance[36] (establishing a bank de novo).
(c) Conversion of an existing non-bank affiliate or amalgamation with other existing financial institutions and the issuance of Letters Patent by the Minister of Finance.[37]

(b) Publication of application to incorporate

Before an application for incorporation of a foreign bank subsidiary by Letters Patent can be accepted, a notice of intention must be published in the Canada Gazette and in a newspaper, local to the proposed head office, at least once a week for a period of four consecutive weeks.[38]

The notice must contain the following information:
(a) The name of the bank, which may be either English or French, or a combined English and French form.
(b) The location of the head office of the bank.
(c) The names, residential addresses, citizenship and occupations of the first directors of the bank.
(d) The authorised capital sought, in terms of the number and par value of each class of shares.

(c) Incorporation of a foreign bank subsidiary

Where the bank to be incorporated is a foreign bank subsidiary, Letters Patent will not be issued unless the Minister of Finance is satisfied that the bank has the potential to make a contribution to competitive banking in Canada and that equally favourable reciprocal arrangements for Canadian banks exist or will be arranged in the foreign jurisdiction.[39]

---

27 Section 175 (2)
28 Section 174
29 Section 173 (2)
30 Section 116 (1)
31 Section 28 (1) and (5)
32 Section 28 (6)
33 Section 200

34 Sections 7 and 11
35 Schedule C to the Act
36 Schedule D to the Act
37 Schedule E to the Act
38 Sections 12 and 259
39 Section 8

The office of the Inspector General of Banks has suggested the following basic criteria which may be considered in determining whether to grant Letters Patent to a foreign bank subsidiary:

(a) The applicant must be a 'foreign bank' within the definition of the Act.[40] This definition is fairly wide and would include almost all foreign banking institutions as generally understood.

(b) The applicant should be of sufficient asset size to support a foreign bank subsidiary in Canada.

(c) The applicant should have international banking expertise.

(d) The applicant should have had a favourable earnings record over the last five years.

(e) Shares of the applicant should be widely held. This reflects the government's preference for widely-held ownership where no one shareholder (and those associated with him) effectively control the bank. An exception to this policy is where the applicant bank is owned or controlled by a foreign government.

(f) The home jurisdiction should report favourably on the applicant. The applicant should submit a certificate of good standing from its home jurisdiction attesting that the applicant is authorised to carry on the business of banking in the home jurisdiction, is carrying on business in accordance with applicable law, is financially sound, disclosing any legal action that may affect the financial condition of the applicant, and that the applicant is authorised (or does not require authorisation) to own the shares of a foreign bank subsidiary in Canada.

(g) The applicant should be well-supervised in its home jurisdiction.

(h) The applicant must demonstrate that Canadian banks receive or will receive similar competitive opportunity in the home jurisdiction. This would, ideally, involve producing a letter from the official responsible for the licensing of banks in the home jurisdiction, to the effect that Canadian banks are eligible to conduct banking business on essentially the same terms and conditions as apply to banks indigenous to the home jurisdiction.

(i) The applicant must be able to demonstrate a potential to make a contribution to competitive banking in Canada.

(j) Comfort letter. The applicant (the foreign bank) is expected to provide a letter to the effect that it has ultimate responsibility for the operation of the foreign bank subsidiary and that it undertakes to ensure that this foreign bank subsidiary meets its obligation under Canadian law.

To assist the preparation of an application to form a foreign bank subsidiary in Canada, a 'Guide for Foreign Banks',[41] which details specific information which must be provided to the Office of the Inspector General with the application, has been made available. The following are some of the principal requirements:

(a) Details concerning the parent bank.

(b) The shareholders of the parent bank, including the names and addresses of corporations in which any shareholder owns an equity of greater than 10%. In cases where governments own shares, an overview of their involvement in the bank's operations.

(c) Existing Canadian business, including details of parent bank's direct or indirect shareholdings of Canadian companies in excess of 10%.

(d) A five-year business plan comprising market analysis, capital requirements and pro forma financial statements in the format prescribed by the Act.

(e) Names of two independent audit firms to be appointed for the proposed subsidiary.

(f) Any other information which may be required by the office of the Inspector General.

(d) Commencement of business of a new bank

For banks created by conversion or amalgamation, the approval to commence business occurs when the Letters Patent are issued by the Minister of Finance.[42] On or after the date the bank comes into existence the first directors of the bank must meet[43] and may:

(a) Make by-laws.

(b) Adopt forms of share certificate and incorporation records.

(c) Appoint officers.

(d) Appoint two auditors to hold office until the first meeting of shareholders of the bank.

(e) Transact any other business necessary to organise the bank.

Where banks have been created *de novo*, the above meeting of directors is still required and in addition the directors are permitted to authorise the issue of shares of the bank and make banking arrangements.[44] However, the *de novo* banks cannot commence business until they have met a number of further requirements. These include the first meeting of shareholders after at least Can$2.5 million has been received from the issue of shares[45] (or in certain cases a lesser amount),[46] and the approval from the Governor in Council to commence business.

Newly incorporated banks by conversion or amalgamation do not escape the requirement to have a shareholders' first meeting; they are required by the Act to call such a meeting within three months of the date the bank came into existence.[47]

For all newly incorporated banks under the Act the purpose of the first meeting of shareholders is to ratify or amend the by-laws, to elect the auditors for the financial year and to elect the directors.

1.11 Areas within the country subject to special laws

At present, all areas of the country are subject to the same legislation in connection with banking operations. However, there is no restriction on the operations of Canadian banks offshore, other than the opening of offshore branches by schedule B banks and the fact that on consolidation they must meet the various informal guidelines as decreed by the Inspector General of Banks. Such guidelines would, among other things, include the limitation on the size of loans issued.

---

[40] Section 2 (1)
[41] Available from the Office of the Inspector General of Banks
[42] Section 265
[43] Section 266
[44] Section 26
[45] Section 27
[46] Section 29
[47] Section 267

The Inspector General has indicated a preference for centres other than Toronto for new foreign bank subsidiaries to set up a head office.

2 ACCOUNTING

2.1 Laws and regulations governing accounts

The Bank Act, with its schedules and regulations, rather than the Business Corporations Acts, stipulates the form of financial statements for all banks and they also establish the minimum financial information to be disclosed. The Inspector General issues annually detailed instructions to provide guidance and assistance in interpreting these requirements.

2.2 Application of general company law

As indicated in Section 2.1 all banks are subject to the provisions of the Bank Act, rather than the provision contained in the federal and provincial Business Corporations Acts which govern other corporate entities.

2.3 Roles of legislature and supervisory authority

Legislature and supervisory authority provide the backbone of bank accounting regulations. These regulations are drawn up after discussion with the chartered banks and form the basis for the preparation of the annual accounts and other returns required to be completed throughout the year.

2.4 Extent to which requirements as to returns and accounts are prescribed by laws and regulations

All returns and accounts are prescribed by the Bank Act and regulations thereto.

2.5 Obligations to furnish accounts

At each annual meeting of the shareholders the bank's directors are required to present financial statements to the shareholders, which must be prepared in a comparative form.[48] In addition, the legislation provides that all banks must disclose their affairs to the Inspector General and the Bank of Canada through the presentation of weekly, monthly, quarterly and annual statements in conformity with the schedules to the Act. Contents of the monthly balance sheet returns are published every month for every individual bank in the Canada Gazette.

2.5.1 Accounting periods and times of furnishing

All banks in Canada have the same financial year end, which is stipulated by the Act to be 31 October.[49] However, if approval to commence business as a bank is obtained after 1 May in any year, the first financial year will end on 31 October of the following calendar year. All banks must publish their annual results in a daily newspaper in every province in which the bank has a branch within 65 days of the year end.[50] In addition, the quarterly consolidated statement of income is also required to be published, within 45 days of the quarter end, in the form specified in the schedules to the Act (schedule 0).

2.5.2 Form of accounts to be furnished

Below are some of the more notable reporting requirements:

Annually

(1) An 'annual statement', containing:
(a) a statement of assets and liabilities (schedule K);[51]
(b) an income statement (schedule L);[52]
(c) a statement of appropriations for contingencies (schedule M);[53]
(d) a statement of changes in shareholders' equity (schedule N);[54]
(e) financial statements for factoring, leasing, mortgage loan and venture capital subsidiaries of the bank;
(f) a list of corporations in which the bank owns more than 10% of the voting shares, disclosing: (i) the name and address of each corporation's head office; (ii) the book value of the shares owned by the bank; (iii) the percentage ownership represented by the shares owned;
(g) such other information as may be required by regulation.
(2) Supplemental information, including financial statements (as required under the Bank Act) of subsidiaries of the bank, information on the total value of deposits held and loans made by the bank, information on the distribution of such deposits and loans by account size, type, currency and geographic area, information on the aggregate of the outstanding balances owing to the bank in respect of loans made by the bank as part of a consortium of lenders, charts showing the organisation of the bank, its subsidiaries and their relationship with the bank and information disclosing the criteria for selecting directors, the aggregate amount of loans to directors and the functions and activities of each committee of directors.

Quarterly

All banks must publish quarterly consolidated statements of income in the form specified in the schedules to the Act (schedule 0).[55]

Monthly

Part VII of the Bank Act requires that banks file monthly returns on their financial positions, in specified form (schedule J),[56] with the Minister of Finance and the Bank of Canada. Banks are also required to file monthly returns, for use in the determination of reserve requirements, of their assets and liabilities valued or payable in foreign currencies and of their total domestic assets for the month.

Weekly

A statement of assets and liabilities in prescribed form shall be submitted to the Inspector General.[57]

---

[48] Section 215 (2)
[49] Section 215 (1)
[50] Section 217 (1)
[51] Reproduced in Appendix I
[52] Reproduced in Appendix II
[53] Reproduced in Appendix III
[54] Reproduced in Appendix IV
[55] Appendix V
[56] Appendix VI
[57] Section 229 (1)

227

2.5.3 *Mandatory accounting dates*

As previously mentioned, all banks in Canada are required to have the same financial year end which is stipulated to be 31 October.

2.6 Requirements as to accounts (a) prior to incorporation (b) prior to commencement of trading and (c) in order to continue trading

For a *de novo* bank, no financial statements are required prior to incorporation or trading, other than the five-year plan referred to earlier. For converted finance companies, however, financial statements at the date of incorporation and commencement of trading are required.

For a bank to continue trading it must comply with all laws and regulations as set out in the Act and regulations. This clearly requires furnishing of financial statements to continue trading.

2.7 Audit requirements

The Act stipulates that every bank should have two auditors.[58] It requires the shareholders to appoint two firms as auditors at their first meeting and each annual meeting thereafter. A firm of accountants is qualified to audit a bank[59] if two or more of the members thereof are accountants who:

(a) Are members in good standing of an institute or association of accountants incorporated by or under an Act of the legislature of a province.

(b) Are ordinarily resident in Canada and are Canadian citizens.

(c) Have practised the accounting profession in Canada continuously during the six consecutive years immediately preceding the appointment of the firm as auditor of the bank.

(d) Are independent of the bank and of any corporation the financial statements of which are consolidated with the financial statements of the bank.

In addition, to ensure objectivity of the auditors, the same two firms may not be appointed for more than two consecutive years.[60] After two years, one auditor must be replaced by another firm for at least two years. The Act will permit all three firms to rotate, or alternatively, allow one firm to act as auditor continuously, while the remaining two firms rotate. If the bank has any subsidiaries, the Act stipulates that the same auditors must be appointed to those companies.

2.8 Acceptability to fiscal authorities of accounts submitted to supervisory authority

The Bank Act stipulates those returns which are required to be filed, either with the Inspector General of Banks or with the Bank of Canada. These returns provide detailed information and analysis on the banks' financial position. The annual financial statements required to be filed with the fiscal authorities follow the format as prescribed in the Bank Act and regulations. However, they provide significantly less detail than the financial information submitted to the regulatory authorities.

2.9 Submission of accounts to any authority other than by requirement of law

No accounts are required to be submitted to any authority other than by requirement of law but banks whose shares are listed on a Canadian stock exchange are required to file financial statements with that stock exchange in accordance with the relative securities legislation.

2.10 Application of laws and regulations to foreign banks operating through branches and subsidiaries

Foreign banks are not allowed to operate through branches in Canada and the reporting requirements of foreign bank subsidiaries parallels that of Canadian domestic banks.

2.11 Availability of accounts for public inspection

As can be deduced from the above comments, a significant amount of financial information concerning banks is public knowledge.

3 FORMAT, STYLE AND CONTENTS OF ACCOUNTS

3.1 Extent to which format is laid down by statute, supervisory authority, generally accepted accounting practice or otherwise

As indicated in Section 2.1 the Bank Act, schedules and regulations stipulate the format of the accounts. Where these sources give no ruling on a particular matter, generally accepted accounting principles would apply.

3.2 Description of format

Appendices I to IV provide a description of the format of the accounts.

3.3 Extent to which contents are prescribed by statute, supervisory authority, generally accepted accounting practice or otherwise

The contents of the accounts follow in a similar manner to the format of the accounts, in that statute and supervisory authority stipulate the contents, which are supplemented by generally accepted accounting principles where statute and supervisory authority are given no ruling.

3.4 Disclosure of specific items required other than those required by general law

None.

3.5 Exemptions from disclosure allowed in respect of banking items

None.

---

[58] Section 237 (1)
[59] Section 238 (1)
[60] Section 238 (2)

3.6 Hidden reserves

Loan loss reserves[61] account for the majority of the reserves which are maintained on the books of Canadian banks. In this connection the Bank Act and regulations provide for two types of loss reserves, specific and general.

Specific reserves are related to individual assets. As part of the annual audit, the joint auditors are required to report to the Inspector General of Banks in respect of loans owing to the bank by any person the aggregate amount of which exceeds one half of 1% of the total of the paid-in capital, contributed surplus and retained earnings accounts of the bank, in respect of which, in their opinion, loss to the bank is likely to occur.[62]

General reserves are maintained essentially via the 'Appropriations for Contingencies' account. The bank's charge against income for loan losses in any one year is determined by applying the bank's five-year loan loss average to the eligible loans outstanding. This policy is consistent with the posture of 'smoothing' the income statement effect of significant fluctuations in loan losses. Any differences between the statutory charge and the provision for loan losses is recorded in the Appropriation for Contingencies account. In addition, further transfers can be made directly from retained earnings to Appropriation for Contingencies within certain limits.

As a result of the above, 'hidden' reserves do not play a role in the operations of the Canadian banking system. Indeed, in the current economic climate more concern has been expressed about the inadequacy of bank loan loss reserves as opposed to the use of hidden reserves.

3.7 Requirements as to consolidated accounts

The Bank Act requires that subsidiaries of the bank be consolidated for reporting purposes where the bank owns more than 50% of the voting shares and that equity accounting be followed for investments in other corporations of which the bank owns between 20% and 50% of the voting shares.[63] Although Canadian generally accepted accounting principles allow some discretion on whether or not an investment requires equity accounting, this is not the case for banks. Bank reporting regulations require specific treatment, as indicated above.

Equity accounting must also be used for subsidiaries whose financial statement components are largely dissimilar to those of the bank.

4 ACCOUNTING POLICIES

4.1 Responsibility for laying down accounting policies

All banks in Canada are required to follow the accounting policies and principles as laid down in the Bank Act and regulations. Where the Bank Act gives no ruling on a given matter, then generally accepted accounting principles will apply.

4.2 Particular accounting policies

4.2.1 Foreign exchange

For those assets and liabilities recorded in foreign currencies which are not covered by a forward contract, translation into Canadian currency is to be made at the balance sheet date using the spot rate as provided by the Bank of Canada. Translation of the income statement is to be made at the average rate for the period, with gains or losses recorded in the income statement. For those assets and liabilities covered by a forward exchange contract, translation is to be made using the amortised forward rate.

4.2.2 Deferred tax

Rules for calculating deferred taxes follow Canadian generally accepted accounting principles, which may be briefly defined as the amount by which the current tax provision differs from the amount of taxes currently payable and is considered to represent the deferring to future periods of a benefit obtained or expenditure incurred currently. It is accordingly computed at current tax rates without subsequent adjustment of the accumulated tax allocation debit or credit balance to reflect changes in tax rates. Since the fixed assets of a bank are traditionally those classes of assets whose tax depreciation rates approximate the rates of depreciation for accounting purposes, deferred taxation is not usually considered a significant item. In calculating the amount of deferred taxation, this deferral method is used.[64]

In addition, following generally accepted accounting principles, the deferred tax debits in respect of the benefit of tax losses carried forward will not be recorded unless the conditions of 'virtual certainty' exist. Virtual certainty exists where:[65]

(i) The loss results from an identifiable and non-recurring cause.

(ii) A record of profitability has been established over a long period by the corporation, or a predecessor business, with any occasional losses being more than offset by income in subsequent years.

(iii) There is assurance beyond any reasonable doubt that future taxable income will be sufficient to offset the loss carry forward and will be earned during the carry forward period prescribed by the tax laws.

4.2.3 Specific and general loan loss reserves[66] for bad and doubtful debts

4.2.4 Treatment of loan loss reserves[66] in accounts

As mentioned earlier, bank reporting requires that the charge against income in respect of loan losses is calculated on the basis of the bank's five-year loss history. This five-year average loss history calculation is also applicable to the bank's subsidiary companies. However, only the consolidated financial statements of the bank reflect the five-year average loss history charge.

---

[61] See page xi of Introduction
[62] Section 242 (3) (b)
[63] Section 216 (1)
[64] CICA Handbook 3470.17
[65] CICA Handbook 3470.40
[66] See page xi of Introduction

The individual financial statements of bank subsidiaries reflect loan losses based upon generally accepted accounting principles.

On a periodic basis the loan portfolio is reviewed for specific bad accounts which must be written off and accounts which are considered to be doubtful to some extent. The total of their 'actual loan loss' experience is credited or deducted from the balance sheet value of the asset and debited or charged to the Appropriation for Contingencies account. Thus a differential between actual loss experience and that charged by way of the five-year average to the income statement builds up in this account. In the event that any appropriation for unforeseen contingencies is required, this may be made from the retained earnings account to the Appropriation for Contingencies account. This account is shown as a separate item in the balance sheet and movements on this account are disclosed in a separate statement forming part of the annual accounts.

4.2.5 Premiums and discounts on investments (amortise, write off, etc.)

Premiums and discounts on the purchase of investments will generally be amortised over the remaining term to maturity. Gains and losses on the sale of investments with a fixed maturity are deferred and amortised over a five-year period. This follows the general concept of 'smoothing' the impact on the income statement of significant fluctuations arising from gains or losses on the sale or purchase of investments.

4.2.6 Offsets, i.e. to what extent can assets and liabilities be set off against each other (legally or in practice)

In general, balances with the same entity are required to be disclosed separately. However, where the balances of an operating or demand loan account and a deposit account (other than fixed term) of the same entity may be partially or wholly offset by legal set-off or by a written customer agreement and the offsetting balances are in the same currency and bear the same or no rate of interest, then the account balances may be reported net. Otherwise, loan and deposit accounts must be reported separately.

4.2.7 Goodwill

Goodwill arising on a business combination, which represents the difference between cost and the acquiring company's interest in the identifiable net assets, is recorded at cost and amortised to income by the straight line method over the estimated life of such goodwill. Forty years is the maximum allowable life for goodwill. This accounting principle is applicable to goodwill arising subsequent to 1 April 1974, prior to which date there was no requirement to amortise goodwill. Obviously it is necessary to consider the on-going value of goodwill each year to ensure that there has been no impairment relative to the carrying value.

4.2.8 Consolidation

Under the Bank Act all banks are required to prepare consolidated financial statements in respect of subsidiaries. The 1967 Act permitted consolidation of only wholly-owned banking operations. A result of this change is that financial statements prepared under the new Act include a bank's real estate, leasing and mortgage activities conducted through subsidiaries, together with its banking or trust operations conducted through wholly- or partly-owned foreign subsidiaries.

4.2.9 Revaluations of assets

Currently there are no pronouncements issued by the Inspector General's office in connection with the revaluation of assets and therefore generally accepted accounting principles will apply.

Revaluation of assets may be considered applicable primarily to fixed assets. Under Canadian GAAP,[67] fixed assets are normally accounted for on the basis of their historical cost and the writing up of fixed asset values should not occur in ordinary circumstances. However, in a reorganisation it may be appropriate to reflect fixed assets at appraised values. When this occurs, the date of the appraisal should be stated. In addition, if the appraisal was made within five years preceding the date of the balance sheet, the name of the appraiser, the basis of valuation and the disposition of the appraisal adjustment should be disclosed.

The excess of the appraised value of fixed assets over cost should be shown as a separate item in shareholders' equity and should either remain indefinitely or be transferred to retained earnings in amounts not exceeding the realisation of appreciation through sale or depreciation provisions.

4.2.10 Instalment finance and leasing including basis of recognition of income

Recognition of income for instalment financing and leasing follows generally accepted accounting principles. Income is recognised on the 'interest earned' basis. The Inspector General of Banks has indicated, however, that for leases and instalment financing with periods of less than five years the 'rule of 78' may be used, as this method of income recognition approximates closely the 'interest earned' basis.

4.2.11 Dealing assets

Investments in securities held for trading purposes are revalued to market at each reporting date with the resulting gain or loss being reflected in income. Investments in other securities will be carried at cost in the statement of assets and liabilities, subject to any requirement to write down their value to reflect permanent impairment.

---

[67] CICA Handbook 3060.01

4.2.12 Pensions

The Inspector General of Banks requires no specific disclosure on pensions and therefore generally accepted accounting principles will apply. Under current Canadian GAAP,[68] pension costs are considered to be an element of employees' remuneration and therefore need not be shown separately in the income statement. However, the following principles and disclosures are considered appropriate:

(i)   Past service costs should be charged to operations over a reasonable period of years which may or may not coincide with the period over which any related funding payments are made.

(ii) The present value of vested past service benefits, to the extent that it has not been charged to operations, should be recognised in the financial statements as a deferred charge offset by a liability.

(iii) A material adjustment, brought about by an actuarial revaluation, should be shown separately in the income statement.

(iv) The amount of past service costs remaining to be charged to operations and the rate at which such costs are being absorbed, should be shown in a note to the financial statements, as should the effect of any new plan or of any significant changes in an existing plan.

4.2.13 Depreciation

Fixed assets are required to be recorded at cost. Depreciation is provided at a rate which is designed to write off the asset over its estimated useful life and may be on either the straight line or declining balance basis. Note also that depreciation is not an eligible expense for the purpose of calculating taxable income (see Section 9).

5   WINDOW DRESSING

The use of window dressing, while not impossible, is made more difficult due to the requirements for significant detailed reports which must be made to the Inspector General and the public on a regular basis. Added to these, the requirement for an annual external audit conducted by two firms of auditors makes the use of significant window dressing difficult.

6   AMOUNTS REQUIRED TO BE MAINTAINED BY LAW OR OTHERWISE

The Act requires that a bank shall maintain adequate capital and adequate and appropriate forms of liquidity.[69] The Inspector General has recently issued certain guidelines regarding capital adequacy. Capital is distinguished as being either primary or secondary, depending upon its permanence, its being free of mandatory fixed charges against earnings and its subordinated legal position to the rights of depositors and other creditors. Examples of primary capital would include:

(1) Common shareholders' equity, comprising:
(a) paid-up common shares;
(b) contributed surplus;
(c) general reserve; and
(d) retained earnings.
(2) Certain 'permanent' preferred shares.
(3) Certain long-term convertible preferred shares.
(4) Appropriations for contingencies.

Secondary capital is composed of residual financial instruments which carry certain attributes of capital and which are subject to a number of general limitations, the most significant being that the aggregate amount of such capital may not exceed ten times primary capital. The Inspector General does not presently intend to impose specific limits for the components of primary capital for measuring capital adequacy for regulatory purposes. Rather, bank managements are expected to independently ensure that the common shareholders' equity components of primary capital remain predominant and at a prudent level. In addition, the Inspector General has indicated that the determination of appropriate capital ratios will continue to be a matter for discussion between his office and each bank individually.

Schedule A banks must have an authorised capital of not less than Can$2,000,000 of which one half must be issued and fully paid. Note, however, that recent discussions with the Inspector General indicate that it is highly unlikely that a new schedule A bank would in fact be granted a charter with so small a capital base. Schedule B banks require an authorised capital of not less than Can$5,000,000 of which one half also must be issued and fully paid.

Apart from these requirements for capital maintenance, banks in Canada are required to maintain specified liquidity levels, which are enforced by the requirement to maintain cash or treasury bills. The extent of this enforced liquidity is dependent on the deposit liabilities due by the bank to its depositors from time to time, and are called primary and secondary reserves. In other words, a portion of the deposit liabilities must be set aside for immediate availability should the depositors seek to withdraw funds.

(a) Primary reserves[70]

These reserves are required (as set out below) in accordance with the Act, and consist of non-interest bearing reserves in the form of coins, Bank of Canada notes, or deposits in Canadian currency with the Bank of Canada, as follows:
(a) 10% of Canadian currency demand deposits.
(b) 2% of Canadian currency notice deposits up to Can$500 million and 3% over Can$500 million.
(c) 3% of foreign currency deposits of Canadian residents with branches of the bank in Canada or with offices in Canada of subsidiaries of the bank.

Deposit liabilities do not include Canadian currency deposits of non-residents with branches of the bank outside Canada or with offices of subsidiaries of the bank

---

[68] CICA Handbook 3460   [70] Section 208 (1)
[69] Section 175 (1)

231

outside Canada. Foreign currency deposits by non-residents are also exempted from reserve requirements.

(b) Secondary reserves[71]

These reserves, which are required to be held by all banks to the extent deemed appropriate by the Bank of Canada, in addition to the primary reserves which are specifically mandated by the Bank Act, are held in the form of coins, Bank of Canada notes, Canadian currency deposits with the Bank of Canada, treasury bills of Canada and day loans to authorised investment dealers. The actual amount of the reserve will be equal to a prescribed monthly average percentage (set by the Bank of Canada) of the bank's Canadian currency deposits and foreign currency deposits of Canadian residents. The secondary reserve is currently (1984) fixed at 4%.

7 KEY RATIOS

As mentioned previously, Canadian banks have historically been controlled and monitored on an informal basis. Following passage of the 1980 Bank Act, certain key factors are now placed into statute. However, monitoring and direction by the authorities is on the basis of moral suasion rather than formal penalties.

7.1 Assets in Canada

For a foreign bank subsidiary the ratio of assets in Canada[72] to paid-in capital and liabilities to residents of Canada shall equal or exceed one to one.[73] This requirement, which is not mandated for Canadian banks, has been enshrined in statute to provide a legislative umbrella to Canadian depositors and creditors of banks which are not controlled in Canada. The decline in the value of the Canadian dollar versus the US dollar of more than 20% since 1972 has resulted in significant concern by fiscal and political authorities. Perhaps as an offshoot of this concern, as well as prudent banking, there is a requirement that foreign bank subsidiaries established in Canada provide a net foreign capital inflow rather than an outflow.

7.2 Gearing ratio

There is no statutory limit to the extent to which assets may exceed authorised capital for schedule A banks. In 1982, however, the Inspector General issued a guideline to limit the asset size of all banks, by specifying the maximum gearing ratios as a multiple of their capital and reserves. These gearing ratios are thirty times for the largest banks, twenty-five times for the medium-sized banks and twenty times for the small banks. In the case of foreign bank subsidiaries this guideline is over and above the limit on domestic assets relative to deemed authorised capital as detailed previously. At 31 October 1983 schedule A banks reflected a 26.2 times ratio.

For the schedule B banks, however, there is a statutory limit on the allowed gearing of domestic assets of twenty times its deemed authorised capital.[74] During any three-month period, a schedule B bank may not have average outstanding domestic assets of more than twenty times its authorised capital, which shall not be less than Can$5,000,000.[75] Note that for the twenty times test, the authorised capital may be deemed to be less than the actual authorised capital.[76] No such limitation is placed on foreign assets, but the overriding limits recommended by the Inspector General would come into play. It is not yet clear whether, as the new schedule B banks prove themselves, the gearing ratio will be increased to allow them to become more competitive with schedule A banks. For fiscal 1983 the B bank ratios were 15.8.

7.3 Domestic asset limitation

Aggregate average domestic assets of all foreign bank subsidiaries may not exceed 8% of the aggregate domestic assets of all banks in Canada as set out in the return of domestic assets.[77] This return at 29 February 1984 reflected total domestic assets of all chartered banks of Can$243,773 million.[78] The statutory 8% allows a ceiling of schedule B banks of Can$19,502 million of which they had used Can$18,793 million.

7.4 Loan loss experience

In Canada, banks are required to charge the income account in any fiscal year with the average loan loss experience of the bank over a five-year period. Accordingly, in any one year, the charge to income in respect of loan losses may be more or less than the actual loss incurred. In 1983 the average five-year loan loss provision for the banking system was 0.329% of eligible assets. Note, however, that for purposes of calculating income for taxation purposes, other allowances are made (see Section 9).

8 ACCOUNTING RETURNS OTHER THAN ACCOUNTS

8.1 By whom required
8.2 Nature of requirements

In addition to reporting requirements mentioned in Sections 2.4 and 2.5, the following returns of financial information must also be made:

(a) A consolidated return of revenue, expense and changes in capital and reserves, to be filed with the Minister of Finance before the end of each calendar year.[79]

(b) A return of non-current loans outstanding, once each year at such time and in such form as prescribed by the Minister of Finance.[80]

(c) A return of deposit liabilities, once each year at such time and in such form as prescribed by the Minister of Finance.

(d) A return of unclaimed deposits, within 30 days after the end of each calendar year, in such form as prescribed by the Minister of Finance.[81]

---

[71] Section 208 (7)
[72] Section 175 (3)
[73] Section 175 (2)
[74] Section 174 (2) (d)
[75] Section 116 (1)
[76] Section 174 (6)
[77] Section 302 (7)
[78] Canada Gazette part I, 21 April 1984
[79] Schedule P to the Act, see Appendix VII
[80] Section 58 (3)
[81] Section 226

(e) A return of real property held by the bank and not required for its own use, once each year at such time and in such form as prescribed by the Minister of Finance.[82]
(f) A return of information as to directors and executive officers of the bank, within 30 days after each annual meeting.
(g) A return of shareholders by calendar year end.
(h) PAR Package to be filed by 30 November each year (see Section 9).
(i) Such further information at such time and in such form as the Bank of Canada may require.

9 TAXATION

The following comments are based on Canadian tax laws in effect on 14 September 1984.

9.1 General method of taxation

The Canadian Income Tax Act subjects the worldwide income of corporations to Canadian tax, if they are incorporated under Canadian law, as if they are resident in Canada (residence being based on mind and management). Each corporation is rated separately on its own income since there is no concept of consolidated tax returns. Losses realised by a corporation for taxation years ending after 31 December 1983 may for tax purposes be carried back three years and forward seven years.

(a) Corporate income tax

The federal government levies corporate tax on most corporations, including banks, at the rate of 36% on their taxable income. With the exception of a number of specific provisions such as depreciation and loan loss reserves, taxable income is based on accounting income.

Each province also levies an income tax on corporate taxable income ranging from 5.5% to 16% depending on the province in question. For the most part, provincial and federal taxable income is calculated in the same manner.

(b) Interest income

Banks and other corporations whose principal business is the making of loans, or who borrow money from the public in the course of carrying on business the principal purpose of which is the making of loans, must recognise interest income on the accrual basis. They cannot report interest on the received or receivable basis.

(c) Dividend income

In general, dividend income received by a taxable Canadian corporation is exempt from normal income tax, which is termed Part I tax. However, dividends received by private corporations, including banks, from other Canadian corporations in which the recipient owns 10% or less of the voting shares and from certain foreign affiliates, are subject to Part IV tax of 25% on the dividends received. This Part IV tax is recoverable when the private corporation in turn pays dividends to its shareholders. For every $4 of dividends paid, $1 of Part IV tax is refunded.

It is important to note that public corporations (i.e. corporations listed on a Canadian stock exchange), as distinguished from private ones, are not subject to either Part I or Part IV tax on dividend income from Canadian corporations.

(d) Trading profits

Securities purchased by a bank can have two different tax treatments, depending on the reasons that the bank holds them. Stocks and bonds held for long-term purposes (portfolio investments) can have resulting gains or losses taxed on a capital basis. Half of capital gains, net of half of capital losses, are subject to ordinary tax rates. On the other hand, where securities are purchased for trading purposes, income treatment will prevail.

(e) Foreign tax credits

The Income Tax Act allows in section 126 deductions for foreign taxes, ordinarily known as foreign tax credits. There are two types, one applicable in respect of foreign non-business income and one in respect of income from business carried on in a foreign country.

(f) Non-business income tax credit

Most foreign bank subsidiaries operating in Canada and making loans outside the country fall under the non-business tax credit rules. Non-business income tax represents foreign tax paid by a Canadian company in respect of foreign income other than income from business carried on in the foreign country. Non-business income tax is defined to be income or profits taxes (other than business income taxes) paid to the government of a foreign country or to the government of a state, province or other political subdivision of that country.

Foreign tax credits for non-business income must be calculated separately from amounts applicable to business income, on a country-by-country basis. Foreign taxes paid to several countries may not be grouped together. The formula is as follows:
(1) Determine the proportion that the taxpayer's income (other than business income) for the year from sources in a particular foreign country is of its net income for the year (from all sources).
(2) Calculate income tax otherwise payable to the federal government for the year.
(3) The foreign tax credit in respect of non-business income from that particular country is the lesser of (i) the proportion (determined in 1) of the income tax otherwise payable (determined in 2), or (ii) the foreign non-business income tax paid in respect of that foreign income.

If the foreign non-business income tax paid for a year exceeds the credit available (e.g. because the foreign rate

---

[82] Section 227

233

is higher than the Canadian overall tax rate or because the taxpayer has an overall loss in that year), the excess cannot be carried over but may be taken as a deduction from income rather than as a credit against rates.

(g) Business income tax credit

Where a resident of Canada carries out business in a foreign country, the foreign tax credit rules are slightly different. The main difference is that foreign 'business income' tax which is not absorbed as a foreign tax credit in the year may be carried forward up to five years to be claimed in the future.

(h) Capital taxes

In addition to income tax, six of the ten Canadian provinces levy annual taxes on corporate capital. The provinces which levy capital tax are British Columbia, Manitoba, Newfoundland, Ontario, Quebec and Saskatchewan. Essentially, the taxable paid-up capital of a bank will include its:
- Paid-up capital stock.
- Retained earnings and other surplus.
- All reserves, whether created from income or otherwise unless such reserves are deductible for income tax purposes.

While most corporations must include certain liabilities in the calculation of paid-up capital, banks are exempt from this requirement.

Liability for capital tax arises where the bank has a permanent establishment in a taxing province. Where the bank has permanent establishments in more than one province, its taxable paid-up capital will be allocated among the respective provinces in the same manner as is taxable income.

(i) Income tax rates (1983)

Federal (with at least one provisional permanent establishment)	36%
Provinces (in addition to federal):	
Newfoundland	16%
Prince Edward Island	10%
Nova Scotia	15%
New Brunswick	14%
Quebec	5.5%
Ontario	15%
Manitoba	16%
Saskatchewan	14%
Alberta	11%
British Columbia	16%
North West Territories	10%
Yukon	10%

(j) Capital tax rates

In view of their special basis of computing taxable paid-up capital, banks are subject to rates of capital tax which differ from those applicable to other corporations. The current rates are as follows:

British Columbia	0.8%*
Manitoba	1.9%
Newfoundland	1.5%
Ontario	0.8%
Quebec	0.9%
Saskatchewan	0.8%

* Banks with taxable paid-up capital in excess of $500 million: 2%

9.2 Accounts as basis for taxation

Generally speaking the Income Tax Act levies a tax on a company's profit and, unless there are specific provisions in the Act, profit is determined using generally accepted accounting principles. Therefore, on a general basis, accounts do form the basis for taxation.

There are, however, a number of exceptions. The most important deal with loan loss reserves and depreciation.

9.3 Adjustments permitted or required

(a) Non-bank lenders

Corporate taxpayers which are not chartered banks have two sections of the Income Tax Act (the Act) applicable to them. The first and more general is paragraph 20 (1) (1) which permits a reasonable reserve for bad debts.

Alternatively, in lieu of a paragraph 20 (1) (1) deduction, a non-bank whose business includes the lending of money on the security of a mortgage, hypothec or agreement of sale of real estate property may claim a subsection 33 (1) reserve.

Under subsection 33 (1), the maximum reserve is equal to 1½% of the first Can$2 billion of the total amount of qualifying securities and 1% of any excess. The amount which the taxpayer may deduct is limited to the amount deducted in the preceding year plus one third of the maximum reserve calculated for the current year. The effect of this alternative minimum provision is that this reserve is not permitted to build up at a rate exceeding one half of 1% of the computed aggregate for the current year and it cannot exceed a maximum of 1½% of the computed aggregate. Thus, any sudden choice to deduct a reserve under this provision, or any sudden increase in outstanding mortgage obligations will not lead to an increase in the reserve of more than one third of the computed aggregate for the year.

Loan companies which are not chartered banks must decide which loan loss provision to apply to their mortgage loans. On non-mortgage loans, only a 20 (1) (1) deduction is available. Hence, it is possible to have both a 33 (1) and 20 (1) (1) deduction in the same year.

(b) Chartered banks

For chartered banks, neither paragraph 20 (1) (1) nor subsection 33 (1) are applicable. They must use section 26 of the Act, which allows a bank falling under the Bank Act to deduct general appropriations by way of write-downs of assets, appropriation to contingency reserves, bad or doubtful debts and depreciation in the value of assets, other than depreciable property of the bank, as is, in the opinion of the Minister of Finance, not in excess of the reasonable requirements of the bank. The rules for determining the permissible appropriations are issued each year by the Minister of Finance.

It is also important to note that newly-chartered banks are treated somewhat differently during the first year than are existing banks.

(c) Newly-chartered banks

For the first financial year of a new bank (other than one formed by amalgamation or conversion) present rules state that the tax-deductible loan loss provision will be the actual loss experience for that financial year.

For new banks in their second, third and fourth financial years following inception, the loan loss provision is to be calculated largely in accordance with the method as described for existing banks except on the basis of two, three or four years experience as the case may be.

(d) Existing chartered banks

Tax-deductible loan loss reserves consist of both the annual provision for loan losses (charged to operations on the basis of a five-year average of actual loan loss experience) and further contingency appropriations made at the directors' discretion out of retained earnings. These amounts are deductible for tax purposes to the extent that they are booked in a special reserve account that does not exceed a prescribed limit, termed 'PAR' (Permitted Aggregate Reserve), determined by the Inspector General of Banks.

PAR is 1½% of the aggregate book value of 'Eligible assets' up to two billion dollars plus 1% of the remaining book value of such assets at the end of the financial year. The eligible assets include loans, letters of credit, acceptances and guarantees other than those guaranteed by Canada, the US, the UK, or a province, those guaranteed by other banks and treasury bills, notes and similar evidence of indebtedness and certain other specified loans.

As mentioned in Section 4.2.3, for accounting purposes a bank makes an annual charge to income of a provision for losses based on its five-year average loss experience. (Except, as set out earlier, where it does not have five years of history.) This amount may be higher or lower than its actual loss experience for the year and is designed to prevent large fluctuations in reported income. The offset to the expense on the income statement is a credit in the statement of accumulated appropriations for losses, the balance of which appears as a capital fund account on the balance sheet.

The amount of the five-year average loan loss experience is deductible for tax purposes even though it might increase the balance of general appropriations (i.e. the tax deductible portion of total appropriations) beyond the Permitted Aggregate Reserve (PAR) level.

The bank must then reduce (i.e. debit) the appropriations account by the actual loss experience for the year on loans (net new reserves for losses on loans less recoveries of loans previously written off). The credit is booked to the loans receivable account and does not impact the balance of revenue.

The balance in the general appropriations may be increased further (and still be deductible for tax purposes) to an amount not in excess of PAR. This must, however, be reduced by specific provisions in respect of those eligible assets. There is a further limitation on this increase to PAR in that it may not exceed the lesser of the booked income of the bank and one third of PAR.

If the directors of the bank determine that an additional provision in excess of the five-year average is required, a charge will be made to the income statement below the balance of revenue after provision for income taxes. The offsetting credit is booked to the accumulated appropriation account. If PAR is greater than the five-year average figure, then the additional discretionary reserve is even larger than the five-year average and the PAR increment, so that the excess would be treated as a tax paid (a non-deductible) appropriation.

(e) Depreciation

The accounting depreciation of fixed assets is not allowed as a deduction for tax purposes. Instead, the Income Tax Act allows the cost of fixed assets to be amortised at prescribed rates which vary with the class of asset. These rates are set out in section 1100 of the regulations to the Income Tax Act and the classes are prescribed in the schedule to the regulation. The amount allowed for income tax purposes is a maximum and any amount up to the maximum can be claimed in a particular taxation year.

The three classes most relevant to a bank are:
– Class 3 for buildings: maximum annual allowance 5% on declining balance basis.
– Class 8 for furniture and equipment: maximum annual allowance 20% on declining balance basis.
– Class 13 for leasehold improvements: maximum annual allowance one fifth of cost improvements.

9.4 Effect of tax considerations on presentation of accounts

Financial statement presentation is governed by the Bank Act and therefore income tax considerations do not affect the presentation.

10 INTERPRETATION OF ACCOUNTS

10.1 Adequacy of information as to contents and disclosure

10.2 Audit and reliability of information

The introduction of the 1980 Bank Act has resulted in the preparation of audited financial statements which, to a significant extent, follow generally accepted accounting principles. The major deviation from Canadian GAAP is in the area of accounting for loan losses addressed earlier. Therefore the adequacy of information provided, whether in content or disclosure, is a reflection of Canadian GAAP.

To the extent that formalised accounting rules for specific items have not as yet been established in Canada, accountants look to exposure drafts or other countries (primarily the US and the UK) for guidance. However,

Canadian GAAP has addressed or is in the process of addressing all the major accounting issues and both the contents and disclosure in the financial statements which are subject to external independent audit reflect this.

10.3 Comparability between different banks on the basis of published accounts or publicly available returns

All banks are required to report in the format prescribed in the Bank Act and regulations and therefore valid comparisons can be made between different banks. However, comparisons may be of limited value due to the difference between the banks themselves.

The large schedule A banks form the nucleus of the banking community, since many of these banks have been in operation since the early nineteenth century. Most provide a full range of banking services with, in most instances, branch networks across the country.

The schedule B banks, which are primarily the foreign bank subsidiaries, have only officially existed as banks since July 1981. While many of these foreign banks had operations in Canada prior to July 1981, they were not previously subject to the provisions of the Bank Act. Accordingly, at present they do not provide a full range of banking services. In particular, the majority find it impractical and uneconomical to compete with the schedule A banks for customer deposits in the form of personal checking accounts or savings accounts. In addition, the five major schedule A banks are attached to a major credit card organisation (VISA or Master Card) and have a significant capability in personal banking through automated tellers. These activities, with the exception of some retail banking, do not currently exist with the schedule B banks other than through their parent banks and none have introduced a Canadian charge card.

Thus a clear distinction needs to be made between the schedule A and B banks in terms of comparability of financial information. Furthermore, valid comparisons of the schedule A banks need to be subdivided into the five major banks (Bank of Montreal, Bank of Nova Scotia, Canadian Imperial Bank of Commerce, Royal Bank of Canada and Toronto-Dominion Bank) which provide facilities across the country and which have been in operation for more than a century, and the other seven banks, most of which have only been in operation for the last 30 years at most (the exception being the National Bank of Canada which first operated in 1861).

11 OTHER RELEVANT INFORMATION

11.1 Canadian Bankers' Association

Formed in 1887, this is a true industry association. Having lost in 1924 its responsibility for supervision of ailing banks (with the establishment that year of the office of Inspector General of Banks) the CBA today has become a significant mouthpiece for Canadian banks.

Through a series of committees elected by the banks, members of the association discuss and make known the concerns and feelings of the banking community to the appropriate authorities.

This association is concerned with legislation, public relations, education, production of publications and exchange of bank-related information, research, co-ordination of foreign exchange, inter-bank clearing and bank security.

11.2 Cheque clearing

Canadian chartered banks clear more than 1.5 billion cheques through more than 7,000 branches in the space of a year. To accomplish this they have developed an effective system of cheque clearing where a cheque deposited at one end of the country one day will receive same day credit, even though the cheque was drawn on a competing bank at the other end of the country. The amount of the cheque will be charged against the account of the drawer of the cheque the next day.

This significant achievement is accomplished through ten clearing centres in major Canadian cities. The Bank of Canada will debit or credit the account of each of the chartered banks each day in accordance with the results of that day's clearings.

A standardised magnetic encoding on each cheque automatically summarises the majority of transactions, so that almost all transactions are posted before the next business day commences.

This program has historically been run by the Canadian Bankers' Association. With passage of the 1980 Bank Act, however, a new corporation entitled the Canadian Payments Association has been established, which has recently assumed responsibility for the clearing of cheques.

11.3 Canada Deposit Insurance Corporation

This is a Crown Corporation (owned by the people of Canada through a government agency) established in 1967 by an Act of the parliament of Canada. The purpose of the corporation is to provide, for the benefit of persons having deposits with member institutions, insurance against the loss of all or a part of such deposits because of the insolvency of the member institution.

All banks must be members and pay an annual fee to the corporation, based on insurable deposits. In return, depositors are effectively insured up to Can\$60,000 for a deposit with a term of up to five years with any one member institution.

11.4 Relationship between the Inspector General of Banks and external auditors

In June 1983 the Inspector General met with representatives of the banks' external auditing firms to discuss among other things the relationship between the Inspector General and the banks' external auditors. This meeting highlighted the following items:

(1) The Inspector General does not expect the external auditors to ensure that the banks have complied with all the provisions of the Bank Act. Rather, he does expect external auditors to be aware of the provisions of the Bank Act and to report to him any violations of the provisions. Areas of specific concern include:

(a) Leasing being carried on by the bank's legal entity, rather than a separate subsidiary.

(b) Loans secured by mortgages which are in excess of 75% of the value of the property.

(c) Liquidity ceilings on domestic assets.

(2) It is expected that external auditors will exercise their statutory right[83] to attend audit committee meetings. The Inspector General believes that audit committees are an important part of banks in Canada for the following reasons:

(a) The smaller schedule B banks generally do not have their own internal audit department, in which case they have to rely upon internal inspections by their head office staff who may not be familiar with Canadian statutory and bank issues. Due to the relatively small size of their Canadian subsidiaries, these inspections may also be infrequent. During the time between inspections the audit committee can play a key role in resolving any problems that might arise.

(b) Schedule B banks are all subject to policies dictated by their respective parents. Behaviour which may be appropriate in the home country may not be appropriate in Canada – audit committees may act as a check on such behaviour.

(c) Audit committees assist non-executive Directors in discharging their legal duties.

(3) As part of the annual inspection of each Canadian bank by the Inspector General of Banks (which is a requirement under the Bank Act), a meeting is held with the external auditors. The Inspector General considers external auditors to be complementary to his function and thus, rather than creating a government department to monitor banks' operations, the Inspector General works closely with the external auditors. He relies on the external auditors to inform him of the accuracy of the books of account and, in addition, to comment on other areas of interest. Such areas would include:

(a) Evaluation of management.

(b) Adequacy and effectiveness of the bank's management information system.

(c) Evaluation of the bank's internal control systems.

(d) Effectiveness of the internal audit department.

(e) Adequacy of allowances for doubtful loans.

(f) Calibre and quality of accounting personnel.

(g) Effectiveness of the audit committee.

Many of the above matters are considered confidential by the external auditors and thus this causes concern in terms of discussion of these matters with non-client personnel. A significant degree of trust and co-operation is therefore necessary for the external auditors to effectively fulfil their responsibilities to both the client bank and the Inspector General.

---

[83] Bank Act section 243

APPENDIX I

Banks and the Banking Law Revision Act, 1980
Schedule K
(Paragraph 215(3)(a))

Example Bank

Consolidated statement of assets and liabilities
as at 31 October 19x2
(in thousands of dollars)

Assets		*19x2*	*19x1*	Liabilities		*19x2*	*19x1*
Cash Resources				**Deposits**			
1	Cash and deposits with Bank of Canada	$	$	1	Payable on demand	$	$
2	Deposits with other banks			2	Payable after notice		
3	Cheques and other items in transit, net			3	Payable on a fixed date		
		$	$			$	$
Securities				**Other**			
4	Issued or guaranteed by Canada	$	$	4	Cheques and other items in transit, net	$	$
5	Issued or guaranteed by provinces and municipal or school corporations			5	Advances from Bank of Canada		
6	Other securities			6	Acceptances		
		$	$	7	Liabilities of subsidiaries, other than deposits		
				8	Other liabilities		
				9	Minority interests in subsidiaries		
						$	$
Loans				**Subordinated Debt**			
7	Day, call and short loans to investment dealers and brokers, secured	$	$	10	Bank debentures	$	$
8	Loans to banks					$	$
9	Mortgage loans						
10	Other loans			**Capital and Reserves**			
		$	$	11	Appropriations for contingencies	$	$
Other					Shareholders' equity		
11	Customers' liability under acceptances	$	$	12	Capital stock: (separately by class) Authorised: ....shares with par value of $........ each; .... shares without par value. (Issued and fully paid: ....shares)		
12	Land, buildings and equipment			13	Contributed surplus		
13	Other assets			14	General reserve		
		$	$	15	Retained earnings		
						$	$
		$	$			$	$

* Note: Titles may be deleted where there are no material amounts to be reported

Banks and the Banking Law Revision Act, 1980
Schedule L
(Paragraph 215(3)(b))

Example Bank

Consolidated statement of income
for the year ended 31 October 19x2
(in thousands of dollars)

		19x2	19x1			19x2	19x1
	Interest Income				Non-interest Expenses		
1	Income from loans, excluding leases	$	$	15	Salaries	$	$
2	Income from lease financing			16	Pension contributions and other staff benefits		
3	Income from securities			17	Premises and equipment expenses, including depreciation		
4	Income from deposits with banks			18	Other expenses		
5	Total interest income, including dividends	$	$	19	Total non-interest expenses	$	$
	Interest Expense			20	Net income before provision for income taxes	$	$
6	Interest on deposits	$	$	21	Provision for income taxes		
7	Interest on bank debentures						
8	Interest on liabilities other than deposits			22	Net income before minority interests in subsidiaries and extraordinary items	$	$
9	Total interest expense	$	$	23	Minority interest in subsidiaries		
10	Net interest income	$	$	24	Net income before extraordinary items	$	$
11	Provision for loan losses			25	Extraordinary items (net of income taxes of $.............)		
12	Net interest income after loan loss provision	$	$	26	Net income for the year	$	$
13	Other income						
14	Net interest and other income	$	$	27	Average number of shares outstanding		
				28	Net income per share before extraordinary items	$	$
				29	Net income per share after extraordinary items	$	$

APPENDIX III

Banks and the Banking Law Revision Act, 1980
Schedule M
(Paragraph 215(3)(c))

Example Bank

Consolidated statement of appropriations for contingencies
for the year ended 31 October 19x2
(in thousands of dollars)

		19x2	*19x1*
1	Balance at beginning of year (including tax-paid appropriations of $............)	$	$
2	Loss experience on loans less provision for loan losses included in the Consolidated Statement of Income		
3	Other losses (specify)		
4	Transfer to (from) retained earnings		
5	Balance at end of year (including tax-paid appropriations of $.........)	⎯⎯⎯	⎯⎯⎯
		$	$

APPENDIX IV

Banks and the Banking Law Revision Act, 1980
Schedule N
(Paragraph 215(3)(d))

Example Bank

Consolidated statement of changes in shareholders' equity
for the year ended 31 October 19x2
(in thousands of dollars)

		19x2	*19x1*
Capital Stock			
1	Balances at beginning of year (Details for each class of shares)	$	$
2	Add: Increases during the year		
3	Deduct: Redemptions during the year		
4	Balances at end of year	$	$
Contributed Surplus			
5	Balance at beginning of year	$	$
6	Additions from capital stock issues		
7	Less reductions during the year		
8	Balance at end of year	$	$
General Reserve			
9	Balance at beginning of year	$	$
10	Transfer to (from) retained earnings		
11	Balance at end of year	$	$
Retained Earnings			
12	Balance at beginning of year	$	$
13	Prior period adjustments (net of income taxes of $............)		
14	Net income for the year		
15	Dividends		
16	Transfer to (from) appropriations for contingencies		
17	Income taxes related to the above transfer		
18	Transfer to (from) general reserve		
19	Balance at end of year	$	$

Banks and the Banking Law Revision Act, 1980
Schedule O
(Subsection 217(2))

Example Bank

Consolidated interim statement of income

(in thousands of dollars)

		Three months ended				Three months ended	
		19x2 (current year)	19x1 (prior year)			19x2 (current year)	19x1 (prior year)
Interest Income				Non-interest Expenses			
1	Income from loans, excluding leases	$	$	15	Salaries	$	$
2	Income from lease financing			16	Pension contributions and other staff benefits		
3	Income from securities			17	Premises and equipment expenses, including depreciation		
4	Income from deposits with banks	___	___	18	Other expenses	___	___
5	Total interest income, including dividends	$	$	19	Total non-interest expenses	$	$
Interest Expense				20	Net income before provision for income taxes	$	$
6	Interest on deposits	$	$	21	Provision for income taxes	___	___
7	Interest on bank debentures						
8	Interest on liabilities other than deposits	___	___	22	Net income before minority interests in subsidiaries and extraordinary items	$	$
9	Total interest expense	$	$	23	Minority interest in subsidiaries	___	___
10	Net interest income	$	$	24	Net income before extraordinary items	$	$
11	Provision for loan losses	___	___	25	Extraordinary items (net of income taxes of $............)	___	___
12	Net interest income after loan loss provision	$	$	26	Net income	$	$
13	Other income	___	___				
14	Net interest and other income	$	$	27	Average number of shares outstanding		
				28	Net income per share before extraordinary items	$	$
				29	Net income per share after extraordinary items	$	$

APPENDIX VI

Banks and the Banking Law Revision Act, 1980
Schedule J
(Subsection 219(1))

Example Bank

Consolidated return of assets and liabilities
as at .... 19 ...... (in thousands of dollars)

	Foreign currency	Total		Foreign currency	Total
Assets			**Liabilities**		
1 Gold coin and gold and silver bullion	$	$	1 Deposits payable on demand to	$	$
2 Other coin			(a) Canada		
3 Bank notes			(b) Provinces		
4 Deposits with Bank of Canada			(c) Banks		
5 Deposits with other banks			(d) Individuals		
(a) Operating balances			(e) Others		
(b) Other balances			2 Deposits payable after notice to		
6 Cheques and other items in transit, net			(a) Canada		
7 Securities issued or guaranteed by Canada, at amortised value			(b) Provinces		
(a) Treasury Bills			(c) Banks		
(b) Other securities maturing within three years			(d) Individuals		
(c) Other securities			(i) Checkable		
8 Securities issued or guaranteed by provinces, at amortised value			(ii) Non-checkable		
9 Securities issued or guaranteed by municipal or school corporations in Canada, at amortised value			(e) Others		
			3 Deposits payable on a fixed date to		
10 Other securities			(a) Canada		
(a) Shares, at cost			(b) Provinces		
(b) Other, at amortised value			(c) Banks		
11 Securities of associated corporations			(d) Individuals		
(a) Shares, valued on the equity method			(e) Others		
(b) Other, at amortised value			4 Cheques and other items in transit, net		
12 Loans, less provision for losses			5 Advances from Bank of Canada		
(a) Day, call and short to investment dealers and brokers, secured			6 Acceptances		
(b) To banks			7 Liabilities of subsidiaries, other than deposits		
(c) To provinces			(a) Secured		
(d) To municipal or school corporations in Canada			(b) Unsecured		
(e) To associated corporations			8 Other liabilities		
(f) Lease receivables			9 Minority interests in subsidiaries		
(g) To others			10 Bank debentures issued and outstanding		
13 Mortgages, less provision for losses			11 Appropriations for contingencies		
(a) Residential			(a) Tax allowable appropriations	—	
(i) Insured under the National Housing Act			(b) Tax paid appropriations	—	
(ii) Conventional			12 Shareholders' equity		
(b) Non-residential			(a) Capital stock, issued and fully paid		
14 Customers' liability under acceptances			(i) Preferred	—	
15 Land, buildings and equipment, less accumulated depreciation	—		(ii) Common	—	
			(b) Contributed surplus	—	
16 Other assets	—		(c) General reserve	—	
			(d) Retained earnings	—	
Total Assets	—	$	Total liabilities	—	$

243

Supplementary information

Aggregate amount of loans to directors, firms of which they are members and loans for which they are guarantors: $ ....

Returns of branches or subsidiaries antedating the last day of the month used in the preparation of this return:

Branch or Subsidiary   Date of Return

Subsidiaries whose assets and liabilities are included in this return:

Subsidiary   Bank's Holding of Voting Shares (%)

Investments in corporations accounted for on the equity basis:

Corporation   Bank's Holding of Voting Shares (%)

Banks and the Banking Law Revision Act, 1980
Schedule P
(Section 222)

Example Bank

Consolidated return of revenue, expenses and changes in capital and reserves

for the financial year ended 31 October 19......
(in thousands of dollars)

	Foreign currency	Total
Interest Income		
1 Income from loans, excluding leases	$	$
2 Income from lease financing		
3 Income from securities		
4 Income from deposits with banks	_____	_____
5 Total interest income, including dividends	$	$
Interest Expense		
6 Interest on deposits	$	$
7 Interest on bank debentures		
8 Interest on liabilities other than deposits	_____	_____
9 Total interest expense	$	$
10 Net interest income	$	$
11 Provision for loan losses	—	_____
12 Net interest income after loan loss provision	—	$
13 Other income	—	_____
14 Net interest and other income	—	$
Non-Interest Expenses		
15 Salaries	—	$
16 Pension contributions and other staff benefits	—	
17 Premises and equipment expenses, including depreciation	—	
18 Other expenses	—	_____
19 Total non-interest expenses	—	$
20 Net income before provision for income taxes	—	$
21 Provision for income taxes	—	_____

	Foreign currency	Total
22 Net income before minority interests in subsidiaries and extraordinary items	—	$
23 Minority interest in subsidiaries	—	_____
24 Net income before extraordinary items	—	$
25 Extraordinary items (net of income taxes of $ ....)	—	_____
26 Net income for the year	—	$
27 Average number of shares outstanding		
28 Net income per share before extraordinary items		$
29 Net income per share after extraordinary items		$
Capital and Reserve Changes		
30 Net income for the year		$
31 Prior period adjustments (net of income taxes of $...........)		
32 Dividends		
33 Loss experience on loans less provision for losses – Item 11		
34 *Other losses*		
35 Capital contributions from shareholders		
36 *Redemption of capital stock*		
37 Income taxes relating to transfer to (from) appropriations for contingencies		_____
		$
Allocation of Changes		
38 *Appropriations for contingencies*		$
39 *Capital stock*		
40 Contributed surplus		
41 *General reserve*		
42 Retained earnings		_____
		$

CHAPTER 14

HONG KONG

JOHN CRAWFORD and ANTHONY WU

1 GENERAL INFORMATION

Hong Kong is located centrally in the South East Asia area and is viewed as the gateway to China. It possesses a highly professional and skilful work force. Its low rates of taxation and financial stability, together with its well developed internationally linked commercial and banking infrastructure, attract overseas investment activity. It is the third largest financial centre in the world after New York and London in terms of the number of banks represented.

It is expected that there will be an ever-increasing Chinese involvement in this international business centre through to 1997 when the British lease on the territories expires.

1.1 Organisations covered by banking regulations

Hong Kong has a three tier banking system. Licensed banks, licensed deposit-taking companies and registered deposit-taking companies together form the basis of this system. For the purpose of this book, deposit-taking companies have not been included since the relevant law excludes them from using 'Bank' in their title. It should, however, be noted that most banks have one or more deposit-taking subsidiaries to attract deposits (as deposit-taking companies can offer any rate of interest on deposits whereas banks are subject to the overall Interest Rates Agreement of the Hong Kong Association of Banks, except for deposits which are HK$500,000 or above and mature within three months) and to carry on certain specific functions like merchant banking and corporate finance.

Banks are regulated by the Banking Ordinance which is applicable to all banks which have a physical presence in Hong Kong, irrespective of their place of incorporation. Banks are defined in the Ordinance as companies carrying out the business of banking which is further defined as:
(a) Receiving from the general public money on current, deposit, savings or other similar accounts repayable on demand or within less than three months or at call or notice of less than three months; and/or
(b) The paying and collecting of cheques drawn by or paid in by customers.

1.2 Summary of major types of bank

The word 'bank' is only permitted to be used in Hong Kong by an entity which has been granted a licence under the Banking Ordinance. Section 67 of the Banking Ordinance also allows the word 'bank' to be used by a bank incorporated outside Hong Kong which is recognised by the central bank of the country or place in which it is incorporated, or a local representative office maintained in accordance with the Banking Ordinance. The Banking Ordinance prohibits merchant banks or deposit-taking companies from using the word 'Bank' in their title. The functions of merchant banks are usually carried out by deposit-taking companies.

There are currently two types of banking licence in Hong Kong, i.e. those having a single branch licence and those having a multiple branch licence. As the terms indicate, the former allows only a single outlet through which banking business can be conducted, whereas the latter allows a number of outlets. The single branch licence is subject to the condition that the bank may maintain offices to which customers have access for the purpose of any business, including banking business, in only one building.

There is one more type of banking licence which has been issued in the past to an unincorporated person or body of persons who or which, at commencement of the Banking Ordinance, held a valid licence issued under the Banking Ordinance 1948, now repealed. There are three such unincorporated banks in Hong Kong, but the banking business conducted by them is minimal by virtue of the restrictions imposed upon them under part VI of the Banking Ordinance.

1.3 Supervisory authorities

Hong Kong does not have a central bank similar to those found in other countries. The normal functions of a central bank are carried out by the Monetary Affairs Branch of the Government Secretariat which is under the direction of the Financial Secretary. Certain other functions are also carried out on an agency basis by the two largest banks in Hong Kong, namely, the Hongkong & Shanghai Banking Corporation and The Chartered Bank.

Banking supervision and the administering of the Banking Ordinance are mainly the responsibility of the Commissioner of Banking who acts within the guidelines laid down by the Monetary Affairs Branch. In addition, the Commissioner of Banking shall, in the exercise or performance of his respective powers, functions and duties under the Banking Ordinance, comply with any directions given by the Governor under section 4B of the Banking Ordinance.

The Hong Kong Association of Banks is responsible for prescribing a uniform deposit rate structure for all the licensed banks through an Interest Rates Agreement. It also reviews the operating environment of banks with respect to competition in the banking industry, the scope of their operations and the cost of bank services.

1.4 Status of supervisory authorities

The Commissioner of Banking is appointed by the Governor and is a public officer. The Hong Kong Association of Banks is incorporated under the Hong Kong Association of Banks Ordinance of 1980.

1.5 Laws and regulations governing banks

The major statutes governing the banking industry in Hong Kong are the following:
(a) The Banking Ordinance.
(b) The Monetary Statistic Ordinance.
(c) The Hong Kong Association of Banks Ordinance.

1.6 Application of general company law to banks

All licensed banks in Hong Kong are also subject to the regulations of the Hong Kong Companies Ordinance, with the exception of those incorporated overseas (i.e. operating through branches in Hong Kong) and the three unincorporated banks referred to above.

1.7 Sources of laws and regulations

All Ordinances in Hong Kong are enacted by the Legislative Council. Major provisions of the Hong Kong Companies Ordinance closely follow the 1948 Companies Act of the United Kingdom.

1.8 Ability of foreign banks to operate through branches and subsidiaries

Foreign banks operate in Hong Kong either through a subsidiary or a branch office, most taking the latter form.

1.9 Level of supervisory control for branches and subsidiaries of foreign banks

All licensed banks in Hong Kong, irrespective of their place of incorporation, are subject to the same regulatory controls as banks incorporated locally.

1.10 Methods of incorporation

It is very easy and relatively inexpensive to incorporate a company in Hong Kong. However, a company cannot trade as a bank until it has received a licence and here the procedure is significantly more difficult.

There is no standard form of application for a banking licence but the documents required to be attached to the application include a copy of the certificate or document of incorporation of the company and such other documents that will assist the licensing authority in their consideration of the proposed application.

The office of the Commissioner of Banking has indicated that the following matters should be taken into consideration in respect of any proposed application for a banking licence by an overseas bank:
(a) That the applicant bank be incorporated in a country whose monetary authorities exercise effective supervision and that the application must be accompanied by a letter of approval from the principal monetary authority in the bank's country or state of incorporation.
(b) That the application must be accompanied by a certified copy of the latest audited balance sheet of the bank to confirm that the total assets (after deducting contra items) are in excess of the equivalent of US$12 billion (this minimum asset criterion is subject to review annually).
(c) Independent evidence must be provided to confirm that some form of reciprocity is available to Hong Kong banks in the bank's country or state of incorporation.

If an overseas bank which meets all the requirements submits an application for a banking licence with all the required documentation, it is reasonable to expect that a banking licence will be granted within two months from the date of application. The number of banks incorporated in the applicant's country of origin which already hold a licence in Hong Kong and the present and future levels of bilateral trade and other commercial relations between Hong Kong and that country will be taken into consideration in reviewing the application.

It should, however, be noted that meeting all the requirements does not entitle the applicant to have a bank licence. The licensing authority retains the discretion to refuse any application even though all criteria appear to be satisfied.

The procedures for obtaining a banking licence are set out in part III of the Banking Ordinance and the main provisions are summarised below:
(a) No banking business is allowed to be transacted in Hong Kong except by a company (local or foreign) which is in possession of a valid licence issued by the Governor in Council authorising it to transact such business in Hong Kong.
(b) Applications for a licence must be made to the Governor via the Commissioner of Banking.
(c) An application for a licence must be accompanied by the data/information outlined above. The Commissioner of Banking or the Governor have powers to request any other documents they desire.
(d) After receiving and considering an application for a licence, the Governor may either:
(i)   Grant an unconditional licence.
(ii)   Grant a licence subject to certain conditions.
(iii) Refuse to grant a licence without giving any reason.
(e) It is a condition attached to the licence held by a bank incorporated in Hong Kong that the bank shall not establish or maintain any branch or representative office thereof outside Hong Kong without the approval of the Commissioner of Banking. Permission is also required from the Commissioner before one or more branches may be established in Hong Kong by licensed banks incorporated in Hong Kong or incorporated outside

Hong Kong. (Section 12A and 12F of Banking Ordinance.)

(f) A banking licence will not be granted to a Hong Kong company unless its issued and paid-up capital is not less than HK$100 million after deducting any debit balance on the profit and loss account.

(g) A banking licence may be revoked by the Governor:

(i)   If he is satisfied that the holder has ceased to transact banking business in Hong Kong.

(ii) If the holder proposes to make or has made any composition or arrangement with creditors, has gone into liquidation or has been wound up or otherwise dissolved.

(iii) If it is considered to be in the public interest.

(h) Every bank must pay an annual licence fee of HK$200,000 or such other sum as may from time to time be specified by the Governor. The fee is payable on the date the licence is granted and thereafter on the anniversary of the granting of the licence.

1.11 Areas within the country subject to special laws

None.

2 ACCOUNTING

2.1 Laws and regulations governing accounts

The accounts of banks are governed by the Companies Ordinance. They should also comply with the Statements of Standard Accounting Practice (SSAPs) issued by the Hong Kong Society of Accountants.

2.2 Application of general company law

Accounts of banks are subject to the same Company Ordinance rules/reporting requirements as other companies although certain exemptions are granted under section III of the tenth schedule to the Ordinance. Reference should be made to Section 10 of this chapter for mandatory disclosure requirements for banks.

2.3 Roles of legislature and supervisory authority

The Companies Ordinance was enacted by the Legislative Council while the SSAPs are issued by the Hong Kong Society of Accountants. The Commissioner of Banking has not issued any specific pronouncements on the reporting requirements for accounts of banks.

2.4 Extent to which requirements as to returns and accounts are prescribed by laws and regulations

The Banking Ordinance requires all banks to submit monthly and quarterly returns to the Commissioner of Banking, but such information is not made available to the general public because accounting information in relation to each individual licensed bank in Hong Kong is not permitted to be disclosed to anyone under section 53 of the Banking Ordinance. However, aggregate banking statistics are available to the general public on a monthly basis as released by the Monetary Affairs Branch.

2.5 Obligations to furnish accounts

2.5.1 Accounting periods and times of furnishing

2.5.2 Form of accounts to be furnished

2.5.3 Mandatory accounting dates

The Banking Ordinance requires all licensed banks to publish their audited accounts within six months of their year end in one Chinese and one English daily newspaper. The accounts together with additional information in respect of the full and correct names of all persons who are directors or managers of the bank and the names of all subsidiary companies for the time being should be exhibited in each of its offices and branches in Hong Kong in accordance with section 37(1) of the Banking Ordinance.

The accounts should first be sent to the office of the Commissioner of Banking for approval prior to being published and exhibited.

Banks incorporated outside Hong Kong may be exempted from publishing and exhibiting their accounts if the Commissioner of Banking is satisfied that the group accounts of the parent bank are audited and a copy (including the auditors' report) is sent to him. If all the requirements have been met, a letter of exemption may be issued. This exemption will normally be granted to branches of foreign banks only.

Accounts of Hong Kong incorporated banks, in general, include at least the following:

− Consolidated balance sheet and profit and loss account.

− Bank's balance sheet and profit and loss account.

− Notes to the accounts.

− Directors' report.

− Auditors' report.

− Chairman's statement.

After publishing the accounts in the daily newspaper and exhibiting them in the offices and branches, there are no further accounts filing requirements except for banks that are 'public' in nature where they have to submit a copy of their audited accounts to the Companies Registry together with their annual return. However, in practice, the Company Registry requests all banks, whether private or public, to submit a copy of their audited accounts.

2.6 Requirements as to accounts (a) prior to incorporation (b) prior to commencement of trading and (c) in order to continue trading

Foreign banks wishing to establish in Hong Kong should furnish a copy of their latest audited accounts to the Commissioner of Banking with their application for a licence.

Accounts need not be furnished prior to the commencement of trading unless it is a public company in which case it will have to file a copy of its accounts with the Companies Registry.

To continue trading, accounts must be furnished in accordance with Sections 2.4 and 2.5 above.

2.7 Audit requirements

Accounts must be audited by qualified auditors. Only members of the Hong Kong Society of Accountants who possess practising certificates are qualified to sign audit reports.

The Commissioner of Banking is also empowered to request that the monthly returns submitted by banks be accompanied by an auditor's certificate.

At present, the Commissioner has only requested such a certificate in respect of the return for the last month of a bank's financial year.

2.8 Acceptability to fiscal authorities of accounts submitted to supervisory authority

Audited accounts are normally acceptable to the Banking Commissioner and the Inland Revenue Department.

2.9 Submission of accounts to any authority other than by requirement of law

None.

2.10 Application of laws and regulations to foreign banks operating through branches and subsidiaries

Subsidiaries and branches of foreign banks are required by the Banking Ordinance to publish and exhibit their audited accounts although the latter generally get exemption from this requirement as discussed in Section 2.4 above. Moreover, branches of foreign banks do not need to be audited.

2.11 Availability of accounts for public inspection

Accounts published in the daily newspaper and accounts of public companies filed with the Companies Registry are available for public inspection. Normally, copies of such audited accounts can be obtained by writing to the banks.

3 FORMAT, STYLE AND CONTENTS OF ACCOUNTS

3.1 Extent to which format is laid down by statute, supervisory authority, generally accepted accounting practice or otherwise

The format of the accounts of banks are not governed by any statutes although it should be such that it presents a 'true and fair view' of the bank's financial position and complies with the Companies Ordinance disclosure requirements.

3.2 Description of format

Typical balance sheet and profit and loss account of a bank is as follows:

BALANCE SHEET

Share capital	x	Cash and short-term	
Reserves	x	funds	x
Retained earnings	x	Bills receivable	x
		Advances	x
		Other accounts	x
	x		x
Current, deposit and other accounts	x	Investments	x
Proposed dividends	x	Fixed assets	x
Customers' engagements	x	Customers' engagements	x
	x		x

PROFIT AND LOSS ACCOUNT

Profit after taxation		x
Transfers to reserves	x	
Dividends	x	x
		x
Retained earnings at beginning of year		x
Retained earnings at end of year		x

Some banks do show the pre-tax profit and tax charge for the year. Comparative figures are provided as a generally accepted accounting principle and some banks distinguish their assets between current and non-current. The vast majority of banks which distinguish their assets treat all loans as current assets.

3.3 Extent to which contents are prescribed by statute, supervisory authority, generally accepted accounting practice or otherwise

Contents of accounts of banks are governed by the Companies Ordinance.

3.4 Disclosure of specific items required other than those required by general law

There are no specific items that need to be disclosed other than as specified in the Companies Ordinance.

3.5 Exemptions from disclosure allowed in respect of banking items
3.6 Hidden reserves

Banks are permitted to maintain hidden reserves. The reserves are created by transferring an amount from the profit and loss account every year. The amount transferred is determined by the board of directors.

3.7 Requirements as to consolidated accounts

Consolidated accounts are required and are generally prepared by banks where applicable.

4 ACCOUNTING POLICIES

4.1 Responsibility for laying down accounting policies

Banks in Hong Kong enjoy significant flexibility in determining their accounting policies provided that they are in compliance with the Companies Ordinance and the Statements of Standard Accounting Practice (SSAPs) issued by the Hong Kong Society of Accountants.

There are no regulations laid down by the Commissioner of Banking nor are there any statutes in Hong Kong which require banks to disclose their accounting policies. The Companies Ordinance, however, requires that the accounts of companies, including banks, present a true and fair view of the financial position of the reporting entity. It is a generally accepted concept in Hong Kong that a 'true and fair view' will be impaired if the major accounting policies are not disclosed. The Hong Kong Society of Accountants has issued a statement to this effect.

Banks in Hong Kong generally disclose their major accounting policies although some smaller, closely controlled banks do adopt a 'minimum disclosure' approach.

4.2 Particular accounting policies

4.2.1 Foreign exchange

Assets and liabilities denominated in foreign currencies are usually translated at the exchange rate ruling at the balance sheet date. Profits and/or losses arising therefrom are taken to the profit and loss account without separate disclosure unless the amounts are material.

In so far as forward contracts are concerned, there are principally three ways of accounting for unexpired contracts outstanding at the balance sheet date:
(a) Forward contracts are revalued at the spot/forward rate ruling on the balance sheet date and any resulting profits/losses are taken to the profit and loss account without separate disclosure.
(b) Forward contracts are revalued at the spot/forward rate ruling on the balance sheet date and the resulting gains/losses are apportioned over the term of the contracts and taken to income without separate disclosure.
(c) Forward contracts are not revalued at the balance sheet date.

Banks usually do not disclose their accounting policies on forward contracts on the grounds that the amounts involved are normally immaterial in the context of their accounts.

4.2.2 Deferred tax

Banks in Hong Kong do not provide for deferred taxation in so far as the tax rate is only 18.5% and the incident of timing differences renders such deferral not material. However, if banks have a foreign subsidiary which provides for deferred taxation, it will generally be consolidated without any tax adjustment. Deferred taxation in respect of foreign subsidiaries is normally grouped under the heading of 'Other accounts' in the balance sheet.

4.2.3 Specific and general provisions for bad and doubtful debts

4.2.4 Treatment of provisions in accounts

It is customary in Hong Kong for banks to set up a loan loss provision to provide for identified loan losses. Specific provision is made based on management's judgement of recoverability on individual loans. It is also normal to set up a general provision for contingency losses based on a bank's policies and past experience.

It is a requirement of section 19A of the Banking Ordinance that every bank shall maintain a provision for its bad and doubtful debts and shall ensure that such provision is adequate before any profit and loss is declared. Banking inspectors will also review the adequacy of loan loss provisions during their audit examination and advise the banks of their recommended minimum requirements.

The mechanics for setting up a loan loss provision are in line with US/UK practices, i.e. the debit is to an expense account and the credit entry is to the loan loss provision account which is netted off against the loans outstanding in the balance sheet.

When an actual loss is suffered, the credit is to the loans account and the debit to the loan loss provision account. In no circumstances should the loss be charged directly to retained earnings.

As far as disclosure is concerned, there is no requirement in Hong Kong to disclose the aggregate amount of the loan loss provision nor the amount charged to the profit and loss account during the year.

4.2.5 Premiums and discounts on investments (amortise, write off, etc.)

Short-term investments acquired at a premium or discount are stated at the lower of cost and market value.

Long-term investments so acquired are stated at cost or cost adjusted for the amortisation of premium or accretion of discounts. The amortisation and accretion are calculated on a straight line basis over the life of the investment. The yield method is allowable but is not commonly used in Hong Kong.

4.2.6 Offsets, i.e. to what extent can assets and liabilities be set off against each other (legally or in practice)

Legally, banks can only offset assets and liabilities against each other if a contractual right to do so exists. In practice, banks are inclined to minimise such set-offs even if they have the legal right to do so.

4.2.7 Goodwill

There is no significant difference between the treatment of goodwill specifically purchased and goodwill arising as part of the purchase consideration. Under the Hong Kong Companies Ordinance, the amount of goodwill so far as it is not written off must be shown as a separate item in the financial statements.

Where goodwill is considered to be consistently maintained by the normal operations of a business the amount is not amortised unless there is a permanent impairment in value, in which case the write-off will be treated as an extraordinary item in the profit and loss account.

Where goodwill is considered no different from other capital assets, it is amortised over its estimated useful life. In those circumstances where there is a planned write-off on the basis of a consistently applied accounting policy it would be normal to treat the write-off as an ordinary item in the profit and loss account. The method and period of providing amortisation and the amount provided would normally be disclosed in the accounts. Where there is an impairment in the value of goodwill any additional write-off will be treated as an extraordinary item.

4.2.8 Consolidation

Banks are required under the Companies Ordinance and SSAP 126 to provide group accounts. Equity accounting for associated companies is not mandatory although some banks have elected to do so on a voluntary basis. It is expected that a SSAP will be issued on this subject in the future.

Most banks in Hong Kong acquired their subsidiaries at incorporation, i.e. set them up, and, accordingly, goodwill and capital reserves on consolidation seldom arise.

The closing rate method is normally used for the translation of foreign subsidiaries at the year end. Any resulting foreign exchange gains or losses arising therefrom are taken to the profit and loss account or adjusted through the inner reserve account.

4.2.9 Revaluations of assets

Revaluation of assets is allowed in Hong Kong. There is no requirement for banks to disclose the date and basis of such revaluations although some banks do elect to do so voluntarily.

Revaluations, if made, most often apply to land and buildings owned by banks. In the Commissioner's opinion, only 70% of the amount of a revaluation conducted by a qualified valuer can be taken into account by debiting the asset account and crediting the revaluation reserve or capital reserve account.

4.2.10 Instalment finance and leasing including basis of recognition of income

Both instalment finance and leasing are in an infant stage in Hong Kong. There are currently no accounting pronouncements on these subjects. Banks enjoy significant flexibility in these areas as far as accounting is concerned.

4.2.11 Dealing assets

Dealing assets are stated at the lower of cost and market value. Investment assets are normally stated at cost less any provision for permanent diminution in value. Certain banks do, however, state their 'quoted' investment assets at the lower of cost and market value.

4.2.12 Pensions

There are currently no accounting pronouncements on this subject in Hong Kong. Most banks only charge their actual contributions during the year to the profit and loss account without any adjustment for amortisation of past or prior service costs.

4.2.13 Depreciation

Fixed assets are stated at cost or valuation less depreciation. Detailed movements in fixed assets are not normally disclosed in the accounts.

Freehold land and land held on leases with more than 50 years to expiry are usually not depreciated. Most banks depreciate their buildings over 50 years.

There is no statutory requirement to disclose the amount of depreciation charged during the year.

Although the lease with China which expires in 1997 has been a controversial topic in Hong Kong, no accounting pronouncements have yet been issued on this subject. It is, however, the general practice in Hong Kong that land and buildings held on leases expiring in 1997 are being amortised over the periods of the leases.

4.2.14 Other

Inner reserves

Banks in Hong Kong are allowed to maintain inner reserves. The aggregate amount of the reserves and the amount transferred to/from such reserves each year are not required to be disclosed. However, the financial statements should state clearly that profit is arrived at after transferring an amount to/from the inner reserve and the heading it is grouped under in the balance sheet.

Inner reserves are normally used to provide for contingencies. Some banks also transfer their foreign currency adjustments to/from this reserve.

It is implied in the Companies Ordinance (tenth schedule, part III section 26) that the existence of such reserves and the exemption of banks from certain disclosure requirements does not impair a 'true and fair' view of the accounts.

Customers' engagements

It is common practice in Hong Kong to show customers' engagements which include, *inter alia*, bills sent for collection, confirmed credits, acceptances and guarantees on the face of the balance sheet. Some banks also include forward contracts as customers' engagements.

5 WINDOW DRESSING

As mentioned in Section 4.2.8, banks in Hong Kong are inclined to minimise their set-offs in the balance sheet. This policy extends not only to customer accounts but also to intra-group balances. It is a common practice among international banks in Hong Kong to place deposits with their offshore subsidiaries, branches or group companies and in return borrow or accept back-to-back deposits from these companies at identical or low spread interest rates. The intention of such transactions is to increase a bank's business capabilities by providing a larger liquid asset base.

The present legislation requires the minimum holding of specified liquid assets to be maintained by a bank in any calendar month to be not less than 25% of the deposit liabilities of the bank during that month. Specified liquid assets are arrived at after the deduction of a bank's aggregate liabilities to other banks in Hong Kong. In addition, the formula for arriving at net specified liquid assets specifically requires the exclusion of non-local bank liabilities. Banks are therefore in compliance with the legislation in this respect and the desired result of a larger liquid asset base is achieved.

6 AMOUNTS REQUIRED TO BE MAINTAINED BY LAW OR OTHERWISE

7 KEY RATIOS

The legislation governing the operation of banks in Hong Kong is contained in the Banking Ordinance (1964) as amended. A bank incorporated in Hong Kong is required to have a minimum paid-up capital less accumulated losses of not less than HK$100 million.

A bank incorporated in Hong Kong is required to appropriate not less than one third of its reported profit each year to published reserves prior to the declaration of a dividend until such time as the aggregate amount of paid-up share capital and published reserves is not less than HK$200 million. Branches of foreign banks are exempted from this requirement for obvious reasons.

Section 18 of the Banking Ordinance requires all banks to have a minimum holding of specified liquid assets of not less than 25% of their deposit liabilities.

Balances payable on demand and money at call or short notice due to other banks and deposit-taking companies are excluded from the total deposit liabilities for the purposes of calculating minimum specified liquid assets.

At least three fifths of the specified liquid assets mentioned above, i.e. covering not less than 15% of the deposit liabilities, must be in cash, bullion, certain authorised certificates of deposit and demand balances and money at call with other banks and deposit-taking companies (which are freely remitted into Hong Kong).

Section 27 disallows a bank to hold shares in a company or companies to an aggregate value in excess of 25% of its paid-up capital and reserves.

Under section 28, a bank is not permitted to hold interest in land, other than its own business premises or staff quarters, in excess of 25% of its paid-up capital and reserves.

In accordance with section 24 of the Banking Ordinance, the aggregate amount of unsecured advances to directors and their relatives cannot exceed 10% of the bank's paid-up capital and reserves.

The aggregate amount of holdings in the last three paragraphs cannot exceed 55% of the bank's paid-up capital and reserves and 80% if it includes the bank's own business premises and staff quarters.

The price/earnings ratio and the yield ratio are the two major ratios employed in measuring a bank's performance. Liquidity and capital ratios are on the other hand seldom used.

8 ACCOUNTING RETURNS OTHER THAN ACCOUNTS

8.1 By whom required

8.2 Nature of requirements

Every bank is required to submit the following information to the Commissioner of Banking:

(a) Within 14 days of each month end, a statement of Assets and Liabilities as at the end of the previous month.
(b) Within 14 days of the last day of March, June, September and December, a quarterly statement of External Liabilities and Claims outstanding at the end of the quarter.

Under the Monetary Statistics Ordinance 1980, a return of assets and liabilities in respect of the last business day of each calendar month must be forwarded by each bank to the Secretary for Monetary Affairs within 14 days of the date to which it refers. The Secretary also requires the undermentioned to be submitted and may require further statistical information by giving notice in writing to any bank.

Within 14 days of each quarter end, a Quarterly Analysis of Loans and Advances (which analyses the loans and advances by country) outstanding at the end of the quarter.

Within seven days of every Wednesday, a weekly return on certain assets and liabilities outstanding at the close of business as of the previous Wednesday.

9 TAXATION

9.1 General method of taxation

A bank carrying on business in Hong Kong is assessable to Profits Tax in respect of its profits which arise in or derive from Hong Kong. The current tax rate is 18.5%. Banks are no longer required to withhold tax on any interest payments made by them.

(a) Sources of income other than interest

The legislation does not categorically define when income is regarded as having arisen in or been derived from Hong Kong. As a consequence, judicial precedents by way of decisions in court cases have to be looked at for guidance as to precise interpretation. The current view is that for income other than interest, the operations test is applicable, i.e. the source of income is considered to be located where the operations giving rise to the income do, in substance, take place.

Since the legislation has not provided a definitive basis to apportion particular income into onshore and offshore, the income is normally either deemed to be onshore or wholly exempt from tax. The apportionment basis is not acceptable to the tax authorities.

In applying the tests to determine the locality and, hence, source of income in the nature of fees and commissions in respect of services, the Inland Revenue Department have been seen to place particular emphasis on where the contract for the provision of the services was signed and where the particular service was actually performed. With respect to income from the sale of securities, bills of exchange, etc., the place where the sale was negotiated and concluded and where the contract of sale was signed are considered to be of particular importance.

In this connection it is worthwhile to note that gains from negotiable bills of exchange and certificates of deposits on redemption or presentation to the original drawer and/or issuer are deemed to be interest, to which different source criteria apply.

(b) Sources of interest income

Interest income received by or accrued to a bank is generally regarded as sourced in Hong Kong if the funding and/or the credit is made available to the borrower in Hong Kong. Where the availability of funds and/or credit is made elsewhere, interest income derived therefrom might still be deemed to have a source in Hong Kong if it arises through or from the carrying on of a bank's business in Hong Kong.

There is as yet no legislative or judicial interpretation as to when interest arises through or from a business in Hong Kong, although the Department Interpretation and Practice Notes No. 13 issued by the IRD do give a certain amount of guidance as to the IRD views. The view of the IRD, however, is that all the activities relating to the generation of income have to be looked at on a situation-by-situation basis. If a substantial portion of activities are carried out in Hong Kong, then the interest income falls into the taxable category and vice versa. In this regard the IRD have been seen to have paid particular attention to the following activities:

(a) The initiation of a business contact either by the customer or the bank.
(b) Negotiation of the terms of a loan.
(c) Evaluation and monitoring of credit risk.
(d) Approval and decision to grant a loan.
(e) Signing of loan documentation.
(f) Source and arrangement of funding.
(g) Administration of the loan, e.g. drawdown, rollover and collection of interest.

The weight which the IRD places on each of the above criteria varies according to the type of loan and involvement of the bank therein. Presently, the place where the funding of the loan was arranged has been given considerable importance in ascertaining the taxability of interest from syndicated loan participations and sub-participations.

It must, however, be emphasised that the IRD's practice has not yet been tested in any court of law and, accordingly, the outcome of a situation is dependent to a large extent on future decisions of the Board of Review and higher court of law rulings on the issue.

(c) Exempt income

Income which is specifically exempt from Profits Tax irrespective of its source in Hong Kong includes dividends and capital gains, i.e. gains derived from the realisation of long-term investments.

(d) Foreign exchange gains/losses

Foreign exchange gains/losses arising on the repayment of loans and deposits on revenue account, on the realisation of trade debtors and creditors, etc. are considered to be taxable/allowable, depending on the nature of the revenue/expense of the originating transaction.

Unrealised gains/losses created on revaluation of such deposits, loans, trade debtors and creditors at year end are also regarded by the IRD as taxable/allowable. This practice has no legal support in Hong Kong but is deemed to be expedient and administratively convenient for both the IRD and the taxpayer.

(e) Expenses

Expenses are allowable as deductions against income if they are:
(a) Reasonable in amount.
(b) Incurred in the production of income chargeable to Profits Tax.

Where an expense is not yet paid but a provision is made in the accounts, the provision will qualify as a deduction if it is in respect of a definite liability, the amount of which is ascertainable with reasonable accuracy. However, a general provision for an expense item such as a general reserve for claims/losses would normally not be accepted as an allowable deduction.

On the basis that capital gains are not subject to tax, expenditures and/or losses of a capital nature are not allowable.

(f) Bad and doubtful debts

Bad debts which are written off are accepted as allowable deductions if:
(a) The IRD are satisfied that they are uncollectable.
(b) Either the debts have previously been included as trading receipts or they represent money lent by the bank in the normal course of business.

Provision for specific doubtful debts made in the accounts might also be admissible if the two conditions above are satisfied.

Subsequent recovery of debts written off or provided as bad would, of course, be regarded as a taxable receipt.

9.2 Accounts as basis for taxation

There is no statutory definition of the word 'profit' but it is the practice of the IRD to accept profit as the surplus of income over expenditure, both of which are recognised on an accrual basis and accounted for in accordance with the Statements of Standard Accounting Practice issued by the Hong Kong Society of Accountants. In other words, a bank's tax liability is computed on the basis of profit reflected in the accounts with adjustments made to comply with specific requirements of the Inland Revenue Ordinance.

9.3 Adjustments permitted or required

Adjustments to the accounting profit are permitted if they are in compliance with the Inland Revenue Ordinance. The following is a list of items normally requiring adjustment in tax computations:
(a) Offshore income and expenses.
(b) Depreciation/tax capital allowances.
(c) General bad debt provisions.
(d) Expenditures of a capital nature.

9.4 Effect of tax considerations on presentation of accounts

Taxation considerations do not normally affect the presentation of accounts provided that they are prepared on a consistent basis from year to year. Exceptions might, however, be found in cases where investments are deliberately classified as long-term assets to assist in any claim for non-taxability of gains on subsequent disposal. The gains are then of a capital nature and the classification is a demonstration of initial intention regarding the asset. It strengthens the case against the IRD if the audited accounts classify such assets as long-term.

10 INTERPRETATION OF ACCOUNTS

10.1 Adequacy of information as to contents and disclosure

Under the Companies Ordinance, banks have to provide the following information in annual reports:
 − Consolidated Balance Sheet and Profit and Loss Account.
 − Bank's own Balance Sheet and Profit and Loss Account.
 − Notes to the Accounts.
Directors' reports are normally included in banks' annual reports. Most banks also provide a Chairman's Statement which summarises the operations for the year under review and the outlook for the following year. Some major banks also provide financial highlights for previous years.

Apart from disclosing accounting policies, the following disclosure requirements are mandatory:
 − Directors' emoluments.
 − Rental income.
 − Dividends from subsidiaries and associated companies.
 − Tax rate used and method of providing for taxes.
 − Balances with related companies.
 − Analysis of investments into quoted and unquoted.
 − Detailed movements in share capital.
 − Capital commitments.
 − Contingent liabilities.
 − Ultimate holding company.
 − Name, country and percentage holding of subsidiaries and associated companies.
 − Earnings per share if it is quoted and the basis of the computation.
 − Auditors' remuneration.

10.2 Audit and reliability of information

The balance sheet, profit and loss account and notes to the accounts are subject to audit and should therefore be reliable.

10.3 Comparability between different banks on the basis of published accounts or publicly available returns

Although banks in Hong Kong enjoy substantial flexibility in determining their accounting policies, reasonable comparisons can still be made between banks in terms of earnings and yields, so long as the reader is aware that the results are not conclusive due to the different mix of businesses comparable banks are engaged in and the existence of inner reserves in bank accounts.

It is not possible to compare the liquidity and certain other key financial measures between banks as such information is often not available.

CHAPTER 15

JAPAN

TERRY ICHIKAWA

1 GENERAL INFORMATION

1.1 Organisations covered by banking regulations

The Bank of Japan, founded in 1882, derives its legal authority from the Bank of Japan Law. It is the central bank of Japan and forms the core of the financial system in Japan. There are ordinary banks (which include city banks and regional banks), specialised foreign exchange banks, long-term credit banks and trust banks – all of which are private financial institutions. Medium-size and small businesses have private financial operations known as mutual banks, credit associations and credit co-operatives. The Central Bank for Commercial and Industrial Co-operatives, established under a special law and partially funded by the government, is concerned with them. There are specialised financial institutions for companies involved in agriculture, forestry and fisheries, for which the Central Co-operative Bank for Agriculture and Forestry is the pivotal institution. As for other private financial institutions, there are short-term credit companies, securities finance corporations, securities companies, and insurance companies. There are government financial institutions to supplement the functions of these private financial institutions. Furthermore, there were 74 foreign banks with 102 branches, and 104 foreign bank representative offices in Japan as of May 1983.

Ordinary banks correspond to commercial banks in most other countries. Generally, commercial banks provide short-term financing as their main business. Specialised foreign exchange banks and foreign banks in Japan, in addition to ordinary banks, would all fall under the category of commercial banks. Ordinary banks in Japan provide not only short-term financing but also medium- and long-term financing. They are established under the Banking Law (enacted in 1927 and fully revised in May 1981).

Long-term credit banks and trust banks are private financial institutions for long-term financing. Long-term credit banks are established under the Long-term Credit Bank Law of 1952 and include the Industrial Bank of Japan, the Long-term Credit Bank, and the Nippon Credit Bank. Trust banks are those ordinary banks authorised under the Banking Law which are concurrently engaged in trust business under the Law Concerning Ordinary Banks' Concurrent Management of Saving Bank or Trust Bank Operations (enacted in 1943). In practice, however, trust-type transactions are mainly handled by those banks which originally began business in the pre-war period as trust companies. Legally, there is no separate classification for trust banks.

Mutual banks, credit associations, credit co-operatives, and financial institutions other than those mentioned above are authorised under special laws applicable to them.

Foreign exchange is conducted by authorised foreign exchange banks under the Foreign Exchange and Foreign Trade Control Law (enacted in 1949 and fully revised in 1979). There are 186 authorised foreign exchange banks, including the Bank of Tokyo (a specialised foreign exchange bank), ordinary banks (city banks and regional banks), long-term credit banks, mutual banks, and foreign banks in Japan.

1.2 Summary of major types of bank

Financial institutions in Japan have evolved with their own history and are difficult to classify into strict legal or functional categories. The chart provided in Appendix I attempts a general classification.

1.3 Supervisory authorities
1.4 Status of supervisory authorities

The legal authority, the supervisory body and the accounting system explained in the following sections apply only to ordinary banks, foreign exchange banks and foreign banks in Japan, unless otherwise stated. Foreign banks generally will engage in ordinary banking and foreign exchange business when they start operations in Japan. Supervision and control of banks in Japan is exercised fairly strictly by the Ministry of Finance and the Bank of Japan under the authority of the Banking Law and other pertinent laws.

The Ministry of Finance has been given authority under the Banking Law to supervise banks individually for sound management of banking operations. The supervisory authority of the Ministry of Finance is divided into three sections covering investigation, inspection and suspension of financial institutions.

In addition, banking operations are regulated through 'administrative guidance' by the Minister of Finance (mostly through the Director of the Banking Bureau).

'Administrative guidance' is generally interpreted to mean that the administrative body encourages and guides individuals and organisations to co-operate voluntarily in matters under its jurisdiction.

Administrative guidance in the area of banking operations has been exercised frequently, generally in the form of circulars or communiques issued in the name of the Director of the Banking Bureau of the Ministry of Finance. They are classified into (a) recommendations, advice, or requests according to the degree of legal authority involved, or (b) by content into matters relating to (1) management policy, (2) operations and (3) accounting.

The Bank of Japan handles deposits and loans, discounts bills, and trades in securities with ordinary banks and other banks. Through these transactions, the Bank of Japan implements such monetary policies as lending, open market operations and reserve deposit requirements for banks under the reserve deposit system. Guidance (e.g. recommended limits on loans to certain customers) is employed as a supplementary means to enforce these policies.

Based on a contractual agreement with the Bank of Japan, ordinary banks and other banks are subject to inspection by the Bank of Japan. Such operational inspections include guidance for the improvement of business and management. Operational inspections further monetary policies.

1.5   Laws and regulations governing banks

Major laws and regulations governing banking operations are the Banking Law, Ministerial Ordinances of the Banking Law, and the Foreign Exchange and Foreign Trade Control Law.

1.6   Application of general company law to banks

Ordinary banks and foreign exchange banks in Japan must be joint stock companies (article 5, item 1 of the Banking Law; article 3, item 1 of the Foreign Exchange Bank Law) which are subject to the provisions of the Commercial Code. Branches of foreign banks in Japan are subject to the provisions of the Commercial Code in certain areas of company law relating to accounts.

1.7   Sources of laws and regulations

All laws are legislated by the Diet, cabinet orders which establish guidelines and procedures for implementation of laws are formulated by the cabinet, and ministerial ordinances which provide further rules to follow are issued by the minister in charge. Accordingly, the Banking Law, and the Foreign Exchange and Foreign Trade Control Law are legislated by the Diet, and the Ministerial Ordinances of the Banking Law are issued by the Minister of Finance.

1.8   Ability of foreign banks to operate through branches and subsidiaries

While foreign banks are allowed to operate through either branches or subsidiaries, all foreign banks in Japan, which numbered 74 as of May 1983, operate through branches. The foreign banks usually open a representative office before establishing a branch. In order for a foreign bank to operate as a subsidiary or a joint venture, approval is required by the appropriate government authorities under the Anti-Monopoly Law, the Banking Law, and the Foreign Exchange and Foreign Trade Control Law. Under present circumstances, it is said to be next to impossible to obtain approval under all these laws.

1.9   Level of supervisory control for branches and subsidiaries of foreign banks

There are presently no subsidiary operations of foreign banks in Japan.

Certain matters are treated differently when applied to branches of foreign banks.

(a)   Establishment of branches

Previously, foreign banks were allowed to operate through only one branch and they were not permitted to open additional branches. Recently, however, requirements for applications for establishing additional branches have become less restrictive and now 74 foreign banks have a total of 102 branches in Japan.

(b)   Merger and acquisition of financial institutions in Japan

The Anti-Monopoly Law prohibits either Japanese or foreign financial institutions from acquiring 5% or more of the stock of other financial institutions or companies in Japan. Acquisition of a branch of an existing bank requires approval by the majority of depositors of the branch, which makes it difficult for foreign banks to acquire or take over Japanese financial institutions.

(c)   Call, bills, and Gensaki transactions (securities purchased or sold under resale or repurchase agreements)

There are no restrictions for either Japanese banks or branches of foreign banks.

(d)   Certificates of deposit (CDs)

Banks are allowed to issue yen-denominated certificates of deposit with a minimum face value of ¥100 million, with maturity from one to six months. Japanese banks are allowed to issue CDs up to 75% of capital stock; foreign banks are allowed to issue CDs up to 30% of their yen loans and securities, which is said to be rather favourable treatment for foreign banks.

(e)   Limit on conversion of foreign currency into yen

To procure funds required for expansion of business, branches of foreign banks which are less capable than Japanese banks in attracting yen deposits rely to a large extent on issuance of CDs, call, bill, Gensaki and conversion of foreign currencies into yen. The limit on the convertible amount is gradually being increased and this limit was finally abolished in June 1984.

(f) Foreign currency loans (impact loans)

Foreign currency loans have become more frequent since revision of the Foreign Exchange Control Law in December 1980, which liberalised restrictions in foreign currency financing. Foreign currency loans which were formerly available only from foreign banks operating in Japan are now available from Japanese banks as well.

1.10 Methods of incorporation

Japanese companies are incorporated in accordance with the procedures laid down in the Commercial Code. As it is practically impossible for a foreign bank to set up a Japanese subsidiary, the procedures for obtaining a bank licence are dealt with in this section.

(a) Licence for branch of foreign bank

When a foreign bank engages in banking through a branch or an agent in Japan, a licence from the Minister of Finance (article 47 of the Banking Law) is required.

(b) Matters for consideration in granting a licence

The following matters will be considered in determining whether to grant a licence:
(a) Financial strength, credit status, and size of the bank (particularly the ranking in the home country).
(b) Economic relations between Japan and the home country of the applicant bank.
(c) Whether Japanese banks are allowed to operate in the home country of the applicant bank (i.e. on a reciprocal basis).
(d) The period of time for which the bank has had a representative office in Japan (in order to judge the familiarity with Japanese laws and practices).
(e) The time when the bank indicated its intention to establish a branch, so that the impact of the new branch on Japanese financial institutions can be judged.

(c) Application for a branch licence

When a foreign bank intends to obtain a licence to conduct business through a branch or an agent, it must submit to the Minister of Finance an application signed by the bank's officer having representative power, accompanied by the following documents (article 28 of the Ministerial Ordinance of the Banking Law):
(i) A statement of the reasons for establishment of the proposed branch.
(ii) The Articles of Incorporation of the bank, or equivalent.
(iii) A certified copy of the registration of the bank, or equivalent.
(iv) A certified copy of the registration of the bank's officer who has representative power, or equivalent.
(v) A three-year projection of the proposed branch's operations.
(vi) A personal history of the representative of the proposed branch.

(vii) A document listing the names, addresses, nationalities, and occupations or businesses of major stockholders of the bank and the number of shares held by them.
(viii) The latest balance sheet, income statement and statement of appropriation of profits of the bank.
(ix) The permission of the home country government for establishment of the branch, if such permission is required in the home country.
(x) Any other information which the Minister of Finance considers necessary.

(d) Provisional review of application

A foreign bank intending to apply for a branch licence pursuant to the provisions of article 47, item 1 of the Banking Law, may submit the application document prescribed in article 28 of the Ministerial Ordinance of the Banking Law to the Minister of Finance for a provisional review.

1.11 Areas within the country subject to special laws

At present, Japan does not have an offshore market; however, the Ministry of Finance is reviewing specific plans for an offshore market as part of internationalisation of the Tokyo money market, although what form it would take is yet to be decided.

2 ACCOUNTING

2.1 Laws and regulations governing accounts

Accounting is very closely regulated in Japan and the following are the laws and regulations governing bank accounting:
(1) The Banking Law.
(2) Ministerial Ordinance of the Banking Law.
(3) Bank Accounting Standards.
(4) Financial Accounting Standards for Business Enterprises.
(5) Regulations concerning Terminology, Forms and Methods of Preparation of Financial Statements, etc. (hereinafter referred to as Financial Statement Regulations of the Securities and Exchange Law).
(6) The Commercial Code.
(7) Regulations concerning Balance Sheet, Income Statement, Business Report and Supporting Schedules of Joint Stock Corporations (hereinafter referred to as Financial Document Regulations of the Commercial Code).

The Financial Accounting Standards for Business Enterprises summarises generally accepted accounting practices and sets forth the standards that corporations should observe in the treatment of accounts. Financial Statement Regulations of the Securities and Exchange Law set forth terminology, forms and methods of presentation of corporate accounts. These standards and regulations provide accounting treatment and presentation applicable to ordinary corporations.

Bank Accounting Standards, which are included in Basic Circular for Ordinary Banks originally issued on 1 April 1982 (Kuragin No. 901), stipulate accounting

259

standards for banking businesses together with the Banking Law and Ministerial Ordinances of the Banking Law.

Article 1, item 2 of the Financial Statement Regulations of the Securities and Exchange Law provides that bank accounting standards must be applied in preference to financial statement regulations for ordinary banks.

Bank accounting is treated in accordance with Bank Accounting Standards, the Banking Law, and Ministerial Ordinances of the Banking Law. Financial Accounting Standards for Business Enterprises and Financial Statement Regulations of the Securities and Exchange Law apply to those items for which accounting treatment is not stipulated in Bank Accounting Standards, Banking Law and Ministerial Ordinances of the Banking Law.

Pursuant to the provisions of the Commercial Code, Japanese banks must prepare financial documents which include the balance sheet, income statement, statement of appropriation of profits, supporting schedules and a business report for approval by the shareholders' meeting, and they must be located at the head office for public inspection (articles 281, item 1, 282, item 1, and 283, item 1 of the Commercial Code). While ordinary corporations must prepare these financial documents in accordance with Financial Document Regulations of the Commercial Code (article 1), banks may prepare financial statements in accordance with the Ministerial Ordinance of the Banking Law, pursuant to article 2 of the Ministerial Ordinance relating to Special Treatment of the Balance Sheet, Income Statement, and Supporting Schedules of Joint Stock Corporations (Ministerial Ordinance, Ministry of Justice No. 99, 30 March 1963).

Item 1-(1) of the Bank Accounting Standards provides that bank accounts must be treated in accordance with the provisions of the Commercial Code and other laws and regulations, and thus they do not necessarily supersede all the provisions of the Commercial Code.

The Japanese Institute of Certified Public Accountants states in 'Handling of Bank Accounting Standards and format of financial statement for audit' that financial statements prepared in accordance with the format of financial statements for banks are considered to meet the requirements of article 2 of the Financial Document Regulations of the Commercial Code.

Japanese banks must, when preparing financial statements, follow the provisions of the Banking Law, Ministerial Ordinances of the Banking Law, and Bank Accounting Standards, and for items which are not covered by the above they must follow the provisions of the Financial Accounting Standards for Business Enterprises, Financial Statement Regulations of the Securities and Exchange Law, and the Commercial Code.

2.2 Application of general company law

Since branches of foreign banks in Japan are required to submit a business report to the Minister of Finance pursuant to the provision of article 19, item 1 of the Banking Law, they must prepare financial statements in accordance with Bank Accounting Standards, the Banking Law, and the Ministerial Ordinances.

For reporting purposes to the home office, branches of foreign banks generally record transactions in the general ledger using the same accounting system as the home office. This is allowed if appropriate reclassification can be made in preparing a business report.

2.3 Roles of legislature and supervisory authority

As has already been mentioned in Section 2.1 above, accounting is very closely regulated in Japan and the bodies responsible for the various laws and regulations are shown in Appendix II.

2.4 Extent to which requirements as to returns and accounts are prescribed by laws and regulations

2.5 Obligations to furnish accounts

2.5.1 Accounting periods and times of furnishing

2.5.2 Form of accounts to be furnished

2.5.3 Mandatory accounting dates

Besides their obligation under the Commercial Code to prepare financial documents for approval by shareholders, banks are required by law to submit accounts and business reports to the Minister of Finance. Details of these requirements are shown in Appendix III.

In Japan the bank accounting year begins 1 April and ends 31 March.

Annual accounts are required to be made public within a three-month period after the end of the business year.

2.6 Requirements as to accounts (a) prior to incorporation (b) prior to commencement of trading and (c) in order to continue trading

Foreign banks must submit the documents referred to in Section 1.10(3) when applying for a branch licence; items (v) and (viii) pertain to accounts.

Foreign banks in Japan are required to submit accounting documents mentioned in Sections 2.4. to 2.5.3 in order to carry on business. See the chart in Appendix III.

2.7 Audit requirements

Japanese banks are subject to the following audits, in addition to inspection by the Ministry of Finance and review by the Bank of Japan:
(a) Banks capitalised at ¥1,000 million or more whose stock is *not* listed on the stock exchange: audit by statutory auditor under the Commercial Code and audit by independent auditor under the Commercial Code.
(b) Banks capitalised at ¥1,000 million or more whose stock *is* listed on the stock exchange: audit by statutory auditor under the Commercial Code, audit by independent auditor under the Commercial Code *and* audit by independent auditor under the Securities and Exchange Law.

Foreign banks in Japan are not subject to audits under Japanese laws, other than inspection by the Ministry of Finance and review by the Bank of Japan. However, there are cases in which branches are subject to audit or review based on laws of the bank's home country, if the bank is audited in its home country, and if the branch operation is material to the financial statements of the home office.

2.8 Acceptability to fiscal authorities of accounts submitted to supervisory authority

The tax authorities do not necessarily accept accounting documents approved by the inspection carried out by the Ministry of Finance, or by the review carried out by the Bank of Japan, or by an independent auditor.

2.9 Submission of accounts to any authority other than by requirement of law

Other than by requirement of law, submission of accounting documents to the Bank of Japan is required based on contractual agreement with the Bank.

2.10 Application of laws and regulations to foreign banks operating through branches and subsidiaries

Since foreign banks in Japan presently operate only through branches, comparisons between branch operations and subsidiary operations are not applicable. However, it should be noted that branches have to comply with Japanese accounting laws and regulations.

2.11 Availability of accounts for public inspection

Banks must prepare the balance sheet and income statement for each accounting period pursuant to the provisions of the Ministerial Ordinance of the Ministry of Finance (Ministerial Ordinance No. 10, 31 March 1982), and make them public within three months of the end of the accounting period (article 20 of the Banking Law).

Banks must prepare, for each accounting period, supporting documents which explain their business and financial position, and make them available for public inspection at their main offices. However, banks are not obliged to disclose those matters which might impair financial stability, confidentiality of depositors and customers, or matters which might be disadvantageous to banks or which might incur undue extraordinary expense in preparation (article 21 of the Banking Law).

The above applies to both Japanese banks and foreign banks in Japan.

Article 23 of the Banking Law provides that the shareholders' right to inspect accounting records (article 293-8 of the Commercial Code) does not apply to the accounting records and documents of Japanese banks.

3 FORMAT, STYLE AND CONTENTS OF ACCOUNTS

3.1 Extent to which format is laid down by statute, supervisory authority, generally accepted accounting practice or otherwise

The format of an interim business report is provided in article 18, item 1 and the format of an annual business report is provided in article 18, item 2 of the Ministerial Ordinance of the Banking Law.

3.2 Description of format

3.3 Extent to which contents are prescribed by statute, supervisory authority, generally accepted accounting practice or otherwise

The format of a business report applicable to branches of foreign banks is provided in article 18, item 2. The format of the balance sheet and income statement is shown in Appendix IV.

Even the method of closing the books of account for banking businesses is prescribed in the Banking Law and Bank Accounting Standards.

3.4 Disclosure of specific items required other than those required by general law

None.

3.5 Exemptions from disclosure allowed in respect of banking items

None.

3.6 Hidden reserves

In the past the Ministry of Finance's administrative guidance for bank accounting was to restrict over-statement of profits, but to permit banks to maintain more reserves (additional depreciation not deductible for tax purposes, and additional provisions for loan loss reserves) than allowed for ordinary corporations.

However, the Ministry of Finance, in its administrative circular of September 1967 regarding bank accounting standards, provided that income and expenses be recorded accurately on an accrual basis and that depreciation and provision for loan loss reserves be accounted for uniformly by all banks, and not be accounted for by the bank's own judgement.

3.7 Requirements as to consolidated accounts

On 30 October 1976 the Ministerial Ordinance amending part of the ordinance regarding subscription or placement of securities (Ministerial Ordinance No. 30) was promulgated, whereby all companies whose stock is listed on the stock exchange were required to prepare consolidated financial statements, starting with the accounting year beginning on or after 1 April 1977, and to attach them to the registration statement or the securities report.

Companies which are required to submit consolidated financial statements must, in principle, include all subsidiaries in which 50% or more of the voting power is owned by the parent company(ies) or the parent(s) and subsidiaries in consolidation (article 8, item 3 of the Financial Statement Regulations of the Securities and Exchange Law) (article 5, item 1 of the Consolidated Financial Statement Regulations). In practice, however, there are few banks which prepare consolidated financial statements, the reason being that subsidiaries are immaterial.

Branches of foreign banks in Japan are not required to prepare consolidated financial statements.

4 ACCOUNTING POLICIES

4.1 Responsibility for laying down accounting policies

Major accounting policies for banking are laid down by the Banking Law, Ministerial Ordinances of the Banking Law, Bank Accounting Standards, and other circulars issued by the Director of the Banking Bureau of the Ministry of Finance.

4.2 Particular accounting policies

4.2.1 Foreign exchange

The circular 'Accounting Policy of Assets, etc. in Foreign Currencies of Authorised Exchange Banks' provides two accounting methods for foreign exchange: (1) the total net position method including forward contracts, and (2) the separate position method (net spot position). These accounting policies differ from those of foreign banks in Japan, which adopt their own methods. The methods employed in Japan (apart from the two methods formally provided by the Ministry of Finance) are acceptable for tax purposes if application is made and approved by the Director of the Regional Tax Bureau (article 139-4, Enforcement Order of Corporation Tax Law). The two methods provided by the Ministry of Finance are summarised below:

(1) The total net position method (spot and forward)

Under this method, the yen equivalent of assets, etc. in foreign currencies is calculated by adopting prescribed exchange rates. The prescribed exchange rate used is the telegraphic transfer buying rate (TTB) where at the closing date the total net position is long, or the telegraphic transfer selling rate (TTS) at the closing date where the total net position is short.

Valuation gain or loss of assets, etc. can be computed as follows:

Total net position in foreign currency (including forward contracts) (say)	$xxx
Exchange rate (TTB/TTS at the closing date)	x @ ¥ /$
Yen equivalent of total net foreign currencies (including forward contracts)	¥xxx
Total net position of assets, etc. in yen (either historical rate or rate at last valuation date) per books of account	less ¥xxx
Unearned interest equivalent on export bills in foreign currencies purchased against yen (when not included in net book position)	less ¥xxx
Valuation gain or loss	¥xxx

See chart in Appendix V.

(2) The separate position method

Under this method, valuation gain or loss of assets, etc. can be computed as follows:

Total net position in foreign currency (excluding forward exchange contracts)	$xxx
Exchange rate (TTB/TTS at the closing date)	x @ ¥ /$
Yen equivalent of total assets in foreign currencies (excluding forward exchange contracts)	¥xxx
Total net position of assets, etc. in yen (excluding forward exchange contracts) per books of account	less ¥xxx
Unearned interest equivalent on export bills in foreign currencies purchased against yen	less ¥xxx
Translation gain (or loss) related to net spot position	subtotal ¥xxx (A)
Translation gain (or loss) related to net forward position (where (B) is greater than (A), the amount shown as (B) must be limited to (A))	plus ¥xxx (B)
Valuation gain or loss	¥xxx

The difference between these two methods is that the whole amount of translation gain (or loss) to be booked is limited to the amount of translation gain (or loss) related to the net spot position in case of the separate position method.

4.2.2 Deferred tax

Tax effect accounting is not practised in Japan and, accordingly, no legislative requirements exist for it to be adopted.

However, when preparing consolidated financial statements the tax charge would be adjusted if it were necessary to eliminate inter-company profit.

Japanese branches of foreign banks who practise tax effect accounting have the choice of keeping their accounting records in accordance with Japanese GAAP and making adjustments in their return to head office, or keeping their records in accordance with their head office systems and reclassifying certain items for reporting purposes in Japan. However, if the latter method is adopted they run the risk of losing certain deductions for tax purposes, as they have to be booked before the tax authorities will permit them to be classified as allowable deductions.

4.2.3 Specific and general provisions for bad and doubtful debts

(1) The write-off of bad debts (item 2-(1) of Bank Accounting Standards)

Bad debts judged as uncollectable, and/or bad debts of

which ultimate collections are significantly difficult and expected to cause losses at year end, must be written off.

The write-off of bad debts, even though non-deductible for tax purposes, can be allowed if the necessary descriptive documents are filed with the banking authority (Zaimukyoku) in advance.

(2) The write-off of other bad debts (item 2-(2) of Bank Accounting Standards)

Other bad debts include due from foreign banks, foreign bills purchased, import bills receivable and accrued income, and must be written off in the same manner as described above.

(3) Allowance for doubtful accounts (item 3-(1)-(a) of Bank Accounting Standards)

The maximum amount allowed to be provided for tax purposes is regulated and is calculated by multiplying the outstanding loan balance at year end by 3/1000 (article 97-(1)-3 of Enforcement Order of Corporate Tax Law).

(4) Special bad debts reserve (item 3-(1)-(b) of Bank Accounting Standards)

A special bad debts reserve must be provided in accordance with tax law. Overprovision, which is non-deductible for tax purposes, can be allowed if the necessary descriptive documents are filed with the banking authority (Zaimukyoku).

The provision of a special bad debts reserve is specified by Tax Law Basic Circulars 9-6-4 and 9-6-5. According to 9-6-5, when a debtor declares his intent to commence reorganisation or special liquidation in accordance with the Commercial Code, or to declare bankruptcy in accordance with the Bankruptcy Act, 50% or less of the debts owed by the said debtor can be provided as a special bad debts reserve for tax purposes.

(5) Reserve for special foreign loans (item 3-(1)-(c) of Bank Accounting Standards)

A reserve for special foreign loans is a reserve for special risks involving loans to certain countries.

The amount to be provided is from 10/1000 to 50/1000 of the outstanding loan balance to foreign governments, their agents, or corporations therein at year end, the ultimate collection of which is significantly difficult because of the political and economic situation in the countries involved.

This provision is non-deductible for tax purposes. The necessary descriptive documents must be filed with the banking authority in advance.

4.2.4 Treatment of provisions in accounts

An allowance for doubtful debts must be disclosed separately on the liability side of the balance sheet, and its provision shall be separately disclosed in the operating expenses of the income statements.

Bad debts to be written off must be written out of the balance sheet, and the amount written off must be separately disclosed in the operating expenses of the income statements.

The special bad debts reserve is included with the allowance for doubtful accounts on the balance sheet.

4.2.5 Premiums and discounts on investments (amortise, write off, etc.)

Banks hold securities, such as portfolio investments, for liquidity purposes or as a long-term investment in subsidiaries and associates. Portfolio investments are held to earn interest and/or dividends, rather than to earn capital gains.

Securities include national bonds, local bonds, corporate debentures, stocks, other securities and loaned securities on the balance sheet.

In calculating the cost of securities, accompanying expenses (e.g. commissions, etc.) must be added to the purchase price, and where there are purchases and sales of a particular security then methods such as the average-cost method or moving-average cost must be applied to calculate the acquisition cost (Financial Accounting Standards for Business Enterprises, B/S principle 5B).

If securities have been acquired at a premium or discount on their face value then the premium or discount may periodically be amortised on a consistent basis to income over the remaining lives of the bonds (note 22 of Financial Accounting Standards for Business Enterprises, article 285-5-(1) of the Commercial Code).

Valuation of securities listed on the Stock Exchange (item 2-(3) Bank Accounting Standards):
(i) National bonds and other bonds (excluding convertible bonds) . . . At, the bank's option, either cost or the lower of cost and market value.
(ii) Securities other than those stated in (a) (excluding shares in affiliated companies) . . . At the lower of cost and market value.

There are no rules in the Bank Accounting Standards for the valuation of shares of affiliated companies and unlisted securities but the Commercial Code requires them to be valued at cost or a lower valuation if the underlying financial condition of the companies concerned has deteriorated.

Capital gains or losses, or redemption gains or losses of securities, must not be netted off but separately disclosed on the income statements. (Financial Accounting Standards for Business Enterprises also requires that income and expenses shall be stated in total.)

4.2.6 Offsets, i.e. to what extent can assets and liabilities be set off against each other (legally or in practice)

Offsetting is voluntary, but banks have entered into special written contracts with their customers for offsets in accordance with the Civil Code.

In order to offset, the required condition is that two opposing credits exist having the same maturity. A declaration of intention against the counter party is required in order to offset (article 506 of the Civil Code).

The standard bank trading contract (common contract which is entered into between a bank and its customer when starting transactions) includes an article about 'Balancing' (article 7). 'Balancing' is a generic name for

263

offsets and assignment (the bank takes the debtor's deposit and assigns it to its outstanding loans), which is a more extensive concept than an offset under the Civil Code.

Balancing is done so that the bank can offset its credit against the customer's deposit at any time and, as an agent of the customer, take the deposit and appropriate it to the debt when the customer does not make payments on time. The offset can only be reflected in the balance sheet after the bank has exercised its right to offset.

The related interest, discounts, and losses on such loans must be recognised separately up to the date of the balancing, and the foreign exchange rate at the date of the balancing must be adopted for foreign currency items.

4.2.7 Goodwill

Goodwill is recognised in the balance sheet only when purchased or acquired through merger and must be amortised every year on the straight line basis (note 25 of Financial Accounting Standards for Business Enterprises). Article 285-7 of the Commercial Code provides that it must be amortised within five years.

4.2.8 Consolidation

As stated in Section 3.7, consolidated financial statements are not always prepared by Japanese banks.

On 26 June 1979 the Financial Accounting Board issued 'Foreign Currency Transaction Principles' which stipulates that overseas subsidiaries' financial statements must be translated using the closing rate for cash and short-term monetary claims or debts and the historical rate for long-term monetary claims and debts, securities, inventories and tangible fixed assets and deposits received and unearned income. For income and expense items the average rate for the year is used but net income and retained income for the year is translated at the closing rate, while the difference on translation is carried as an asset or liability in the balance sheet.

4.2.9 Revaluations of assets

Write-offs of bad debts, provision for doubtful accounts, valuation loss on securities, etc. are allowed as previously stated. However, valuation gains are not allowed.

4.2.10 Instalment finance and leasing including basis of recognition of income

The Bank Law does not allow banks to engage in leasing operations (article 10 of the Bank Law).

Banks carry out instalment financing in the form of secured loans for capital investments, loans to municipal corporations, commercial loans and housing loans. According to 'Concerning Revision of Accounting of Accrued Interest Income on Loans, etc. and the Related Amendment of the Reports' (Kuragin No. 1638, 16 December 1966; latest revision, Kuragin No. 960, 31 March 1969), the interest income on loans and securities must be recognised on the 'interest earned' basis, related to the outstanding principal. This is the same as for instalment financing.

4.2.11 Dealing assets

Valuation of portfolio securities was covered in Section 4.2.5. Since June 1984 the authorities permit banks to engage in underwriting national bonds, local bonds and government-guaranteed debentures and offering for subscription the bonds underwritten.

In April 1984 the Ministry of Finance issued a circular requiring a bank to segregate dealing securities from portfolio securities for accounting purposes. Once segregated, no transfers are allowed from one category to another.

There are no regulations at present as to valuation of dealing securities and accordingly they would be valued in the same manner as portfolio securities.

4.2.12 Pensions

Item 3-(4) of Bank Accounting Standards regulates retirement allowance as follows:

Retirement allowance (including pensions) must be provided in full for the liability to employees at the year end in accordance with the retirement allowance regulations, on the assumption that all qualified employees voluntarily retire at the year end. Only 40% of this voluntary liability can be deductible for tax purposes (article 106-(1) of Enforcement Order of Corporation Tax Law).

4.2.13 Depreciation

Item 2-(4) of Bank Accounting Standards provides that banks should depreciate movable assets in accordance with tax laws and regulations, and depreciate real estate by 160% of the depreciation amount based on tax laws and regulations. Tax laws and regulations as to fixed assets are as follows:

(1) Acquisition cost

Determined by adding related expenses to purchase price (article 54-(1) of Enforcement Order of Corporation Tax Law).

(2) Useful lives

Useful lives are determined, in accordance with business, size, type, structure, use, etc. Tax laws, however, specify the useful lives to be used and examples are shown in Appendix VI (article 56 of Enforcement Order of Corporation Tax Law).

(3) Scrap value

The scrap value of tangible fixed assets is deemed to be 10% of the acquisition cost and that of intangible fixed assets is taken as zero. When the book value reaches 10% of the acquisition cost, an additional 5% can be depreciated for tangible fixed assets.

(4) Depreciation methods

Depreciation is based on the useful life of the asset or determined by the Ministry of Finance. Depreciation for tax purposes must be that used for accounting purposes.

Common methods of computation are the straight line method and the declining balance method.

See chart in Appendix VI.

4.2.14 Other

(1) National bonds price fluctuation reserve (item 3-(3) of Bank Accounting Standards)

A reserve equal to 10% of the book value of national bonds at the year end must be established.

(2) Other reserves (item 3-(5) of Bank Accounting Standards)

Reserves other than those stipulated by the Commercial Code and by the banking authority cannot be provided. However, if tax laws and regulations include provision for any reserves, such reserves must be provided for bank accounting purposes.

5 WINDOW DRESSING

Window dressing by banks is not allowed by the Ministry of Finance. The Ministry of Finance performs periodical inspections and watches out for window dressing. Such transactions are also subject to independent audits. Generally, these audits and inspections are very strict, which makes it very difficult for banks to indulge in any window dressing.

6 AMOUNTS REQUIRED TO BE MAINTAINED BY LAW OR OTHERWISE

6.1 Capital

Capital of Japanese banks must be not less than one billion yen (¥1,000,000,000) (article 5, item 2 of the Banking Law). There are no provisions for the capital amount of the bank's home office when foreign banks apply for a branch licence in Japan, although the size of a foreign bank will be one of the major factors taken into consideration in granting a licence.

6.2 Legal earned reserve

At the end of each accounting period, banks must set aside as a legal earned reserve not less than one fifth of cash dividends paid, until the reserve is equal to the amount of capital stock (article 18 of the Banking Law).

The requirements of a legal earned reserve are applied to foreign banks, with certain adjustments. A branch of a foreign bank must set aside at least 10% of its annual net income as the legal earned reserve until the reserve reaches ¥1 billion. However, a foreign bank with more than one branch in Japan will be permitted to provide an aggregate reserve of only up to ¥1 billion, with the Minister of Finance's approval. (Article 9 of Cabinet Order No. 40.)

7 KEY RATIOS

Standards for key ratios to be observed are determined by the Ministry of Finance's administrative guidance and details of these are shown in Appendix VII.

8 ACCOUNTING RETURNS OTHER THAN ACCOUNTS

There are no financial documents other than those discussed in previous sections which must be disclosed by statute or supervisory authority.

9 TAXATION

9.1 General method of taxation

9.2 Accounts as basis for taxation

9.3 Adjustments permitted or required

9.4 Effect of tax considerations on presentation of accounts

9.4.1 Corporate Income Tax

Japanese corporations are taxed on their worldwide income, while foreign corporations are subject to corporate income tax on their Japanese-source income (article 9 of Corporation Tax Law).

The corporate income tax rate depends on the amount of dividends expected to be paid from current earnings, as follows:

For corporations capitalised at less than ¥100 million:

(i)   for taxable income up to ¥8 million:
24% (25%*) on distributed profits
30% (31%*) on undistributed profits

(ii) for taxable income over ¥8 million:
32% (33.3%*) on distributed profits
42% (43.3%*) on undistributed profits

For corporations capitalised at ¥100 million or more:
32% (33.3%*) on distributed profits
42% (43.3%*) on undistributed profits

Income for each accounting period is computed after making adjustments for tax purposes to corporate profits of that year calculated in accordance with corporate accounting principles. Special preparation of the balance sheet and income statement for tax purposes only is not required.

Adjustments required by tax laws are as follows:

(1) Items to be excluded from gross revenue

(a) Dividends received from Japanese corporations (article 142, CTL).

(b) Refund of corporation tax, etc. (article 25, CTL).

(2) Items to be excluded from expenses

(a) Depreciation of depreciable assets and amortisation of deferred charges which exceed certain limits (articles 31 and 32, CTL).

(b) Bonuses, extraordinary compensation and retirement allowances paid to directors (articles 34 to 36, CTL).

---

* These rates shall apply for the two accounting years ending 1 April 1984 or after as a temporary measure.

(c) Contributions and entertainment expenses paid to directors which exceed certain limits (article 37, CTL and article 62, Special Tax Measures Law).
(d) Corporation tax, penalties, etc. (article 38, CTL).
(e) Allowances and reserves which exceed deductible limits (articles 52 to 56-2, CTL and articles 53 to 57-5, STML).

(3) Items to be included in gross revenue

Reserve for retirement allowance and reserve for special repairs which should be deducted in the current year of payment (articles 55(3) and 56(3), CTL).

(4) Items to be included in expenses

(a) Allowances and reserves within deductible limit (articles 52 to 56-2, CTL and articles 53 to 57-5, STML).
(b) Tax loss carry forward (articles 57 to 59, CTL).

Adjustments of certain items must be made at the time of closing the books, while others are allowed to be adjusted on tax returns. Items to be adjusted on the books include the following:
(1) Items which are not deductible for tax purposes unless accounted for as expenses on the books:
(a) Depreciation of depreciable assets (article 31, CTL).
(b) Amortisation of deferred charges (article 32, CTL).
(c) Employee portion of bonus paid to employee-director (article 42, CTL).
(d) Allowances (article 52, CTL, etc.).
(e) Special bad debt reserve (Basic Circulars 9-6-4 and 9-6-5, CTL).
(2) Items which are deductible for tax purposes if accounted for on the books as expenses or as disposition of profit or surplus:
(a) Special depreciation reserve (article 52-4(1), STML).
(b) Reserves (article 53, etc., CTL).
(3) Items which are not deductible for tax purposes if accounted for as disposition of profit:
(a) Employees' bonus (article 35(3), CTL).
(b) Contributions (article 37(1), CTL).

Items which are allowed to be adjusted on tax returns include the following:
(a) Exclusion from gross revenue of dividends received from Japanese corporations (article 142, CTL).
(b) Withholding (except that on dividends received from Japanese corporations) (article 144, CTL).

If corporations want to deduct items listed under (1) above for tax purposes, they must be recorded on the books. If the home office's chart of accounts does not have accounts applicable to these items, the branch must record them on the branch's books at the time of closing the books.

Major items which are allowed or require adjustments by tax laws are explained below:
(1) Directors' compensation, bonus and retirement allowances: That amount of directors' compensation which is considered unreasonably high is not deductible (article 34(1), CTL). Bonuses paid to directors are considered a distribution of profit and are not deductible (article 35(1), CTL). Of the retirement allowances paid to directors, that amount which is considered unreasonably large is not deductible (article 36, CTL).
(2) Entertainment expenses in excess of statutory limits are not deductible. The statutory limit is ¥4 million for corporations capitalised at ¥10 million or less. It is ¥3 million for corporations capitalised at ¥10 million or more but less than ¥50 million. For corporations capitalised at ¥50 million or more, no amount of entertainment expenses is deductible for tax purposes.
(3) Taxes paid: Non-deductible taxes: (i) i.e. corporation tax, and penalties (for understatement, non-filing and fraud), etc.; (ii) i.e. inhabitant tax; (iii) i.e. miscellaneous others. Deductible taxes: (i) enterprise tax paid for the preceding tax year and paid on interim tax return for the current tax year; (ii) fixed property tax, city planning tax, business office tax, automobile tax, etc.; (iii) miscellaneous others.

Tax losses

Tax loss may be carried back to the preceding year (one year's carry back shall be suspended for the two accounting years ending 1 April 1984 or after as a temporary measure) or carried forward to the five succeeding years.

Income tax credit

In order to avoid the double tax burden of corporation tax and income tax, income tax assessed on interest on public bonds, corporate debentures, and savings and deposits, and also distributions of earnings of joint operation trusts and public and corporate bond investment trusts can be credited to corporation tax due for the taxable year (article 68(1), CTL). Excess credit will be refunded (article 79, CTL).

Foreign tax credit

Foreign tax credit is not applicable to foreign corporations; however, corporation tax, enterprise tax and inhabitant tax assessed on the income of Japanese branches of foreign corporations can often be deducted from the amount of tax payable in the country of its head office.

A Japanese corporation may credit against its Japanese corporation tax any foreign taxes levied on its foreign source income, up to a maximum calculated as follows:

$$\text{Japanese corporation tax} \times \frac{\text{total foreign-source income}}{\text{total worldwide income}}$$

(Enforcement Orders 142 and 143, CTL).

Foreign taxes eligible for foreign tax credit are those taxes levied by national or local government on income which corresponds to Japanese corporation tax (Enforcement Order 141, CTL).

Filing and payment

A corporation with an accounting period of longer than six months must file an interim tax return, covering the first six-month period, within two months after the end of the six-month period. Computation of corporation tax on an interim return may be done by either of the following methods:

(a) $\text{Corporation tax for the preceding tax year} \times \dfrac{6}{\text{number of months for the preceding tax year}}$

(b) Tax computed on provisional closing of accounts for the first six-month period of the current tax year.

The amount of tax reported on an interim return must be paid before the filing due date.

A corporation is required to file a final tax return within two months after the end of each accounting period. Computation of income and corporation tax due on the final tax return is based on financial statements. Tax prepaid on an interim return is credited against tax due on the final return.

9.4.2 Enterprise tax

The enterprise tax is levied on taxable income at rates ranging from 12% to 13.2%, depending on the prefecture in which the business is located. For national tax purposes, a deduction is allowed on a cash basis for enterprise taxes paid.

9.4.3 Inhabitant tax (prefecture and city or ward tax)

The inhabitant tax is computed as a percentage of the corporation income tax at rates ranging from 17.3% to 20.7%. An assessment for per capita taxes, which range from ¥20,000 to ¥1,500,000 per annum, is included in the inhabitant tax return. The per capita tax is based on the company's capitalisation and the number of employees.

Effective tax rate

The effective tax rates are calculated as follows:

(i)	Corporation tax	42.00%
		(43.3%*)
(ii)	Enterprise tax	13.20%
(iii)	Inhabitant tax 42% (43.3%)×20.7%	8.69%
		(8.96%*)
		63.89%
		(65.46%*)

Considering that the enterprise tax is deductible from national and inhabitant taxes in the following fiscal period, the effective tax rate (excluding the per capita levy) is calculated as follows:

$$\frac{63.89\% \ (65.46\%*)}{(1+0.132)} = 56\% \ (57.80\%*)$$

10 INTERPRETATION OF ACCOUNTS

10.1 Adequacy of information as to contents and disclosure

As stated previously, banks in Japan are subject to close supervision by the Ministry of Finance; inspection by the Ministry of Finance and review by the Bank of Japan are conducted every two to three years. In the light of this, the contents and disclosure of financial information prepared by banks are considered to be adequate for use by investors and analysts.

10.2 Audit and reliability of information

All ordinary banks in Japan are subject to statutory audits which are made to examine whether the bank's financial statements are prepared in accordance with generally accepted accounting practice. Therefore, financial statements with the independent auditors' opinion on the fair presentation of the bank's financial condition are considered reliable.

10.3 Comparability between different banks on the basis of published accounts or publicly available returns

Japanese accounting standards give companies options to elect accounting treatment for certain accounts, e.g. straight line or declining balance method for depreciation. Therefore, financial statements of each company are not necessarily prepared on the same basis. It is possible, however, to determine which accounting principles have been used, since major accounting policies must be disclosed.

Since banks are required to apply bank accounting standards to their accounts, and the format of bank financial statements is provided in the Ministerial Ordinances of the Banking Law, it would be possible to make valid comparisons to a considerable extent. It is important to compare footnotes in such cases.

---

* These rates shall apply for the two accounting years ending 1 April 1984 or after as a temporary measure.

APPENDIX 1

Chart of principal financial institutions (as of December 1981)

Central Bank —————— The Bank of Japan

Private financial institutions

- Ordinary (Commercial) Banks (75)
  - City banks (12)
  - Regional banks (63)
  - Foreign banks (71)

- Specialised financial institutions
  - Financial institutions for international finance
    - Specialised foreign exchange bank (1)
  - Financial institutions for long-term credit
    - Long-term credit banks (3)
    - Trust banks (7)
  - Financial institutions for small business
    - Sogo (mutual) banks (71)
    - Credit associations (456)
    - Credit co-operatives (473)
    - Shoko Chukin Bank (central bank for commercial and industrial co-operatives) (1)
  - Financial institutions for agriculture, forestry and fishery
    - Norinchukin Bank (central co-operative bank for agriculture and forestry) (1)
    - Credit federations of agricultural co-operatives (47)
    - Agricultural co-operatives (4,501)

- Other financial institutions
  - Insurance companies
    - Life insurance companies (21)
    - Non-life insurance companies (22)
  - Securities companies (230)
  - Housing finance companies (8)

Government financial institutions
- Banks (2)
- Corporations (10) (including Shoko Chukin Bank)
- Others
  - Post Office (approximately 22,300 branch offices)
  - Trust Fund Bureau (1)

Note: The number of institutions appears in parentheses
Source: Generally, the Federation of Bankers Association of Japan

APPENDIX II

Details of laws and regulations concerning banks

Law or Regulation	Legislative Body	Description
The Banking Law	The Diet	Law No. 59, 1 June 1981
Ministerial Ordinance of the the Banking Law	The Ministry of Finance	Ordinance of the Ministry of Finance No. 10, 31 March 1982
Bank Accounting Standards	The Director of the Banking Bureau of the Ministry of Finance	Kuragin No. 901, 1 April 1982 Final amendment: Kuragin No. 801, 8 April 1983
Financial Accounting Standards for Business Enterprises	The Financial Accounting Deliberation Council	9 July 1949 Final amendment: 20 April 1982
Financial Statement Regulations of the Securities and Exchange Law	The Ministry of Finance	Ordinance of the Ministry of Finance No. 59, 27 November 1963 Final amendment: Ordinance of the Ministry of Finance No. 46, 21 September 1982
The Commercial Code	The National Diet	Law No. 48, 9 March 1899 Final amendment: Law No. 74, 9 June 1981
Regulations concerning balance sheet, income statement, business report and supporting schedules of joint stock corporations	The Ministry of Justice	Ordinance of the Ministry of Justice No. 31, 30 March 1963 Final amendment: Ordinance of the Ministry of Justice No. 25, 24 April 1982

Note: Kuragin is one of the administrative circulars for Banking issued by the Ministry of Finance

APPENDIX III

Details of accounts and other reports to be submitted by banks

Contents of submission or disclosure	Authority	Submit to	Period – Term	Form of report	Due date for submission
Interim business report	Article 19, Banking Law	The Minister of Finance	1 April– 30 September	General interim business report, Interim balance sheet, Interim income statement	Within a three-month period after the end of each interim period
Final business report	Article 19, Banking Law	The Minister of Finance	Each business year (1 April– 31 March)	General business report, Balance sheet, Income statement	Within a three-month period after the end of each business year
Public notice of balance sheet, etc.	Article 20, Banking Law	—	Each interim period and each business year	Balance sheet, Income statement	Within a three-month period after the end of each interim period and each business year
Submission of materials by foreign bank's branches	Article 48, Banking Law	The Minister of Finance	—	Books, documents, and other materials in a consolidated form to cover all of them, for those matters designated by Ministerial Ordinance	As demanded by the Minister of Finance
Statement of condition (Nikkei-Hyo)	Kuragin No. 901, 1 April 1982	The Minister of Finance	The end of each month	Daily accounts (daily balance)	The 20th of the following month
Interim business accounts (Chukan-Kessan-Jokyo-Hyo)	Kuragin No. 901, 1 April 1982	The Minister of Finance	1 April– 30 September	Balance sheet, Income statement, etc.	Within a three-month period after the end of each interim period (within 40 days for some of the documents)
Business accounts (Kessan-Jokyo-Hyo)	Kuragin No. 901, 1 April 1982	The Minister of Finance	Each business year	Balance sheet, Income statement, etc.	Within a three-month period after the end of each business year (within 40 days for some of the documents)

Note: In applying the Banking Law, branches of foreign banks, which are regarded as independent banks must, as a rule, prepare account books, documents and other materials for each branch

Format of accounts for banks

Balance Sheet as of ....

Account	Amount		Account	Amount	
Cash on hand and due from banks			Deposits		
Cash on hand	xxx		Demand deposits	xxx	
Deposits with banks	xxx	xxx	Ordinary deposits	xxx	
Call loans		xxx	Notice deposits	xxx	
Bills purchased		xxx	Time deposits	xxx	
Securities			Time deposits of an instalment type	xxx	
Government bonds	xxx		Other deposits	xxx	xxx
Municipal bonds	xxx		Negotiable certificates of deposit		xxx
Corporation bonds	xxx		Call money		xxx
Stocks	xxx		Bills sold		xxx
Other securities	xxx		Borrowed money		
Loaned securities	xxx	xxx	Bills rediscounted	xxx	
Loans and discounts			Borrowed money	xxx	xxx
Commercial bills discounted	xxx		Foreign exchange		
Loans on bills	xxx		Due to foreign banks	xxx	
Loans on deeds and securities	xxx		Borrowings from foreign banks	xxx	
Overdrafts	xxx	xxx	Foreign currency bills sold	xxx	
Foreign exchange			Foreign currency bills payable	xxx	xxx
Due from foreign banks	xxx		Other liabilities		
Loans to foreign banks	xxx		Domestic exchange settlement Cr.	xxx	
Foreign currency bills purchased	xxx		Accrued income tax	xxx	
Foreign currency bills receivable	xxx	xxx	Accrued expenses	xxx	
Other assets			Unearned income	xxx	
Domestic exchange settlement Dr.	xxx		Employees' deposits	xxx	
Prepaid expenses	xxx		Other liabilities	xxx	xxx
Accrued income	xxx		Reserve for loan losses		xxx
Other assets	xxx	xxx	Reserve for employees' severance and retirement		xxx
Bank premises and equipment			Reserves for special purposes		
Land, building and equipment	xxx		National bonds price fluctuation reserve (Note)		xxx
Construction in progress	xxx				
Lease deposits	xxx	xxx			
Customers' liability under guarantees and acceptances		xxx	Bank's liability under guarantees and acceptances		xxx
Head office and branches			Head office and branches		
Head office	xxx		Head office	xxx	
Branches in Japan	xxx		Branches in Japan	xxx	
Branches abroad	xxx	xxx	Branches abroad	xxx	
			Sub-total		xxx
			Legal earned reserve		xxx
			Unappropriated retained earnings (Undisposed deficit)		xxx
			Income for the current year		xxx
			(Deficit for the current year)		
Total		xxx	Total		xxx

Note: The national bonds price fluctuation reserve is computed by multiplying the outstanding book value of the national bonds at the year end by $^{10}/_{1000}$, in accordance with regualtions issued by the Minister of Finance

The above format is applied to foreign banks in Japan. The format for Japanese banks is the same as above except for the section on 'Shareholders' Equity'

Instructions for preparation of the balance sheet

1 The following items shall be discussed in the footnotes:
   (1) The fact, if such is the case, that securities are stated at the lower of cost and market value, or are stated at acquisition cost when the market price is considered to have been markedly lower than the acquisition cost.
   (2) The accumulated depreciation of bank premises and equipment.
   (3) Translation method of foreign currency assets, etc.
   (4) Accounting method of recording reserve for loan losses and reserve for employees' severance and retirement.
   (5) Other significant accounting policy.
   (6) The fact and the effect of any changes in valuation methods and other accounting policies, except those which are immaterial.
   (7) The fact of any changes of useful lives or scrap values of fixed assets, except those which are immaterial.
   (8) Accumulated depreciation of bank premises and equipment.
   (9) The total amount of receivables from bank representatives.
   (10) The total amount of payables to branch representatives.
   (11) Contingent liabilities related to material disputes.
   (12) Other items which are necessary to judge financial positions.

2 The fact that national bonds price fluctuation reserve is recorded in accordance with article 26 of Banking Law.

3 If there are cases in which certain items are to be disclosed which are not indicated in this sample format, they shall be disclosed with appropriate account titles in the balance sheet.

4 If there are any items with balances in excess of 1% of the total asset amount in other assets and/or other liabilities, they shall be disclosed with the appropriate account title.

Statement of earnings

From (date)
To (date)

Account	Amount (¥ million)	
Operating income		xxx
Interest on loans	xxx	
Interest and dividends on securities	xxx	
Other interest income		
Interest on call loans	xxx	
Interest on bills purchased	xxx	
Interest on foreign currency	xxx	
Interest on accounts with head office and branches	xxx	
Other interest	xxx	
Other operating income		
Commission on foreign exchange	xxx	
Other commissions	xxx	
Profit on foreign exchange transactions	xxx	
Profit on sales of securities	xxx	
Profit on redemption of securities	xxx	
Other income	xxx	

Account	Amount (¥ million)	
Operating expenses		xxx
Interest on deposits	xxx	
Other interest paid		
Interest on negotiable certificates of deposit	xxx	
Interest on call money	xxx	
Interest on bills sold	xxx	
Interest on borrowed money	xxx	
Interest on foreign currency	xxx	
Interest on accounts with head office and branches	xxx	
Other interest	xxx	
Administrative expenses	xxx	
Other operating expenses		
Commission on foreign exchange	xxx	
Other commissions	xxx	
Loss on foreign exchange transactions	xxx	
Provision for bad debts	xxx	
Bad debts written off	xxx	
Loss on sales of securities	xxx	
Loss on redemption of securities	xxx	
Write-off of securities	xxx	
Other expenses	xxx	
Ordinary income		xxx
Extraordinary profits		xxx
Profit on disposal of premises and equipment	xxx	
Recovery of receivables written off	xxx	
Reversal of national bonds price fluctuation reserve	xxx	
Other extraordinary profits	xxx	
Extraordinary losses		xxx
Losses on disposal of premises and equipment	xxx	
Provision for national bonds price fluctuation reserve	xxx	
Other extraordinary losses	xxx	
Net income before taxes		xxx
Corporate and inhabitant (prefecture and city or ward) taxes		xxx
Net income for the current year		xxx
Retained earnings brought forward (Retained deficit brought forward)		xxx
Transfer to legal earned reserve		xxx
Remittances to (from) head office		xxx
Unappropriated earnings carried forward		xxx

Note: The difference between 'operating income less profit on sales and redemption of securities' and 'operating expenses less loss on sales and redemption of securities' is ¥xxx million

The above format is applied to foreign banks in Japan. The format for Japanese banks is the same as above except for the 'Dividends' section

Instructions for preparation of the income statement

1   Items which are necessary to judge operation results.

2   Expenses allocated by the head office shall be disclosed in the footnotes. The items comprising these expenses shall be divided as follows:
    (1) Direct expenses (expatriates' remuneration, etc.).
    (2) Indirect expenses allocated to branches.

3   In the sections 'Other extraordinary profit' or 'Other extraordinary loss' adjustments of profit or loss for the previous period and other unusual profits or losses shall be included.
    However, they can be stated instead in the sections 'Operating profit' or 'Operating expenses' when the total of these items does not have a material effect.

4   If there are cases in which certain items are to be disclosed which are not indicated in this sample format, they shall be disclosed with appropriate account titles in the income statement.

APPENDIX V

Calculation of foreign exchange profits and losses

Schedule of assets, etc. in foreign currency   Currency_____

Assets

Account	Amount in foreign currency	Amount in yen		Adjustment		Adjusted yen equivalent	
		Per unit	Amount	Per unit	Amount	Per unit	Amount
Cash on hand							
Due from banks							
Loans							
Call loans							
Stocks and bonds							
Loans on promissory notes							
Loans on agreements							
Foreign bills purchased							
Foreign bills receivable							
Loans corresponding to overseas borrowings							
Due to head office and other branches							
Other							
Subtotal	(A)						(A′)
(A) is greater than (B) Net spot position − long	(A)−(B)=(C)						(C′)
Forward exchange contract purchases	(E)						(E′)
(E) is greater than (F) Net forward position − long	(E)−(F)=(G)						(G′)
Grand total	(A)+(E)=(I)						(F′)
(I) is greater than (J) Total net position − long	(I)−(J)=(K)						(K′)

(Note) TTB rate or TTS rate at the closing date_____

The total net position method

Valuation gain or loss

¥ _____

274

Liabilities

Account	Amount in foreign currency	Amount in yen		Adjustment		Adjusted yen equivalent	
		Per unit	Amount	Per unit	Amount	Per unit	Amount
Deposits							
Borrowings from banks							
Due from banks							
Call money							
Bills sold							
Bills payable							
Overseas borrowings							
Due to head office and other branches							
Other							
Subtotal	(B)						(B')
(A) is less than (B) Net spot position − short	(B)−(A)=(D)						(D')
Forward exchange contract sales	(F)						(F')
(E) is less than (F) Net forward position − short	(F)−(E)=(H)						(H')
Grand total	(B)+(F)=(J)						(J')
(I) is less than (J) Total net position − short	(J)−(I)=(L)						(L')

The separate position method

Evaluation profit or loss of net spot position	Translation profit or loss of net spot position	Translation profit or loss of net forward position
¥	¥	¥

APPENDIX VI

Table of depreciation rate for fixed assets as approved by the authorities

Depreciation of Assets	Useful life (years)	Depreciation percentage	
		Straight line method	Declining balance method
Buildings (built of concrete and for office use)	65	0.016 (0.0256)*	0.035 (0.056)*
Buildings (built of concrete and for shop use)	60	0.017 (0.0272)*	0.038 (0.0608)*
Leasehold improvements (movable partitions but durable)	15	0.066 (0.1056)*	0.142 (0.2272)*
Automobiles (for general use)	6	0.166	0.319
Desks, chairs, cabinets	15	0.066	0.142
Sofas (not for the hotel or restaurant business)	8	0.125	0.250
Carpet (not for the hotel or restaurant business)	6	0.166	0.319
Typewriters (not for printing business)	5	0.200	0.369
Calculators, air conditioners, heaters and electric refrigerators	6	0.166	0.319
Forklifts	4	0.250	0.438

* These rates apply only to bank business

APPENDIX VII

Key ratios for banks

Items	*Standard ratio*	*Authority*
1 Loans/deposits ratio		
Target ratio of average balance	Average balance of loans *divided by* average balance of deposits, negotiable deposits and bonds *equal to* not more than 80%	Kuragin No. 901 1 April 1982
2 Current assets ratio		
(a) Target ratio of average balance	Average balance of current assets (including stocks) *divided by* average balance of deposits and negotiable deposits *equal to* not less than 30%	Kuragin No. 901 1 April 1982
(b) Guidance ratio at end of the year (applicable if ratio in 2(a) above is less than 30%)	Increase of current assets for the year (excluding postage and notes) *divided by* increase of deposits and negotiable deposits for the year *equal to* not less than 30%	Kuragin No. 901 1 April 1982
3 Comparing expenses to operating income		Kuragin No. 218 2 March 1959 Partial amendment: Kuragin No. 683 31 March 1979
Guidance	Expenses (excluding taxes) *divided by* operating income to be diminishing	
4 Premises and equipment ratio		
(a) Standard ratio	Premises and equipment used in operations *divided by* net worth (shareholders' equity) *equal to* not more than 50%	Kuragin No. 901 1 April 1982
(b) Target ratio	Premises and equipment used in operations *divided by* net worth (shareholders' equity) *equal to* not more than 40%	Kuragin No. 901 1 April 1982
(c) Marginal premises and equipment ratio	$A-(B+C)$ *divided by* increase of net worth for the prior year and the year before that *equal to* not more than 50%	Kuragin No. 901 1 April 1982
	A: The value of premises and equipment used in operations which are acquired in the current and preceding years (excluding head office)	
	B: Total of depreciation of premises and equipment used in operations for the prior two years	
	C: The value of premises and equipment used in operations which are sold in the current and preceding years	
5 Dividend ratio		
Ordinary dividend ratio	The maximum dividend for each business year	Kuragin No. 901 1 April 1982

	Per value	*Maximum dividend p.a.*
	¥50	¥7.5 per share
	¥500	¥75 per share

Dividend *divided by* net income after tax *equal to* not more than 40%

6 Net worth ratio	Net worth (shareholders' equity plus reserves) *divided by* balance of deposits and negotiable deposits at end of the year *equal to* not less than 10%	Kuragin No. 901 1 April 1982

Items	Standard ratio	Authority
7 Official reserve requirement Central bank reserve ratio	Reserve to be deposited in central bank is calculated as follows: A: For banks whose balance of deposits exceeds ¥2,500 billion: (a) Time deposits balance×1.625% (b) Negotiable deposits balance×1.625% (c) Other deposits balance×2.50% B: For banks whose balance of deposits exceeds ¥800 billion and are not more than ¥2,500 billion at the end of the prior year: (a) Time deposits balance×0.625% (b) Negotiable deposits balance×0.625% (c) Other deposits balance×1.25% C: For banks whose balance of deposits is no more than ¥800 billion at the end of the prior year: (a) Time deposits balance×0.125% (b) Negotiable deposits balance×0.125% (c) Other deposits balance×0.25%	Law concerning Reserve Deposit requirement system (Law No. 135 27 May 1957) Enforcement Order Reserve Deposit Requirement System (Final amendment: Cabinet Order No. 260, 1980)

CHAPTER 16

THE MIDDLE EAST

DAVID YOUNGMAN and ROBERT HUGHES

INTRODUCTION

For the purposes of this book a number of countries have been grouped together in a single chapter on the Middle East. The layout of this chapter is different from the standard layout in that banking in the Middle East is discussed in general terms and this is followed by a detailed review of four of the countries in that area.

1 GENERAL INFORMATION

The geographical boundaries of the Middle East are not clearly defined. Space prevents a consideration of banking in every Arab or Middle East country. This section deals with accounting by commercial banks in Bahrain, Jordan, Kuwait, Lebanon, Oman, Qatar, Saudi Arabia and the United Arab Emirates. The term 'Middle East' will be used to refer collectively to these eight countries and there may be instances where what is said is inapplicable to banks of other states in the region. In the four sections that follow, more detailed consideration will be given to banking in Bahrain, Kuwait, Saudi Arabia and the United Arab Emirates.

Many Middle East banks produce two different sets of audited financial statements; one for the central bank and the other for shareholders and third parties. The central bank statements are prepared in accordance with a laid down format. They provide full details and disclosures of all significant matters, in particular the amounts of items such as inner reserves and loan loss provisions. They are used by the central bank for regulatory and statistical purposes but, since they are not available publicly, have little relevance for third parties. Shareholders and others who wish to review the circumstances of a Middle East bank will only have access to the published financial statements and, for this reason, it is the form and practices of the published statements that will be considered in this section.

Banking in the Middle East has seen enormous changes in its nature and scale over the past 20 years. The description of banks and bank accounting in this chapter may leave the reader with the impression that Middle East banking is unsophisticated; such a conclusion would fail to recognise the massive achievements of the past and the considerable further changes that will take place in the near future. To write of Middle East banking at this stage in its development is to describe a partly completed building, with scaffolding and unpainted walls but a large and solid foundation, which on completion will be fit for comparison with the long-established structures in Europe and North America.

Until comparatively recently, the Middle East had little need for a full range of banking services. Such wealth as existed was usually held in the form of tangible assets. There was little trade between the Middle East and the rest of the world and the limited requirements of currency for travellers (especially pilgrims) were satisfied by moneychangers. Such trading and manufacturing operations that existed were small and most requirements for finance could be met by personal contacts; there was no need for institutional lending. Only a few foreign banks operated in the area.

The first signs of change took place in the 1920s following the collapse of the Ottoman Empire. An influx of Europeans led to greater trade which was accelerated by early discoveries of oil. With the increased trade came a much greater need for banks which was met from two sources. European banks began to set up branches in key trading centres and the local moneychangers expanded their activities.

Branches of British banks were formed in the Gulf states and in Jordan while French bankers established operations in Lebanon. In Saudi Arabia, apart from the operations of a Dutch bank, local moneychangers catered for the main customer requirements. While the first major service provided by banks was to facilitate trade by issuing letters of credit or confirming bills of exchange, the concept of interest-bearing deposits was soon introduced by the Europeans.

The second stage of development in Middle East banking came with the formation of central banks and the increase in wealth from oil revenues. During the 1960s and 1970s banks greatly increased their deposits and, as a result, developed their lending and investment functions. In order to protect these increasing deposits, central banks were given greater regulatory powers. The accumulating wealth led to the formation of locally-owned banks which was supported in some countries by legislation requiring banks to be majority-owned by nationals.

At the end of 1983, the number of Arab banking institutions among the 500 largest in the world had reached 32.[1] For several years the total assets of the Arab banks have risen by considerably more than those

---

[1] *Euromoney*, June 1984, 'Top 500'

of the top 500 banks generally. If the faster growth of Arab banks continues for only a few more years, their importance will soon match the major European, American and Japanese institutions.

While the Middle East central banks have been given increased powers and resources to supervise local banks, the regulations have so far tended to concentrate on registration, monitoring of activities and the reporting of financial information to the central bank, rather than on financial reporting to third parties. As a result, there is a wide range of different standards of financial reporting between Middle East countries and there are also significant variations within each country. In many cases the form of financial reporting dates back to the origins of the banks themselves and the influence of early British and French accounting remains strong. Even in those countries where the central bank lays down standards of external financial reporting, these standards correspond more closely to those followed by European banks 20 years ago rather than to their current practice.

2 TYPES OF MIDDLE EAST BANKS

Banks in the Middle East can be categorised as central banks, commercial or clearing banks, offshore banks, and investment and development banks.

2.1 Central banks

The most influential central bank in the Middle East is the Saudi Arabian Monetary Agency (SAMA), formed in 1957. Not only does it carry out the normal central banking functions (including management of the currency, banker to government departments and commercial banks and the regulation of the banking system), but it is also responsible for the maintenance and management of the government's foreign currency reserves and overseas investments. In terms of the volume of its assets it is one of the most significant banking institutions in the world.

Some other Middle East countries established monetary agencies at this time or soon after, but originally these tended not to perform supervisory functions. Central banks were established in Lebanon (1963) and Jordan (1964) and subsequently in the Arabian Gulf states: Kuwait (1968), Bahrain, Qatar and the United Arab Emirates (1973) and Oman (1974). Outside Saudi Arabia, the central banks or monetary agencies do not usually carry out extensive investment or lending functions. Accordingly, their own accounting methods are of limited interest to international bankers and, for this reason, will not be considered.

2.2 Commercial or clearing banks

In each Middle East commercial centre there are banks taking deposits from the general public and carrying out a full range of banking services. With the rapid accumulation in recent years of wealth from oil, the deposit base of the commercial banks has increased dramatically. With the increase in deposits, these banks have needed to develop increasingly sophisticated means of investing or lending their funds.

Many of the largest commercial banks in the area covered by this section are in Saudi Arabia and Kuwait. In terms of assets the first five in these territories rank as follows:

Bank		Country	Assets (excluding contra accounts) 31 December 1983 (US$ billion)
National Commercial Bank	84	Saudi Arabia	14.68
National Bank of Kuwait	124	Kuwait	9.05
Riyadh Bank	82	Saudi Arabia	7.99
Gulf Bank	143	Kuwait	7.09
Commercial Bank of Kuwait	180	Kuwait	6.55

(*Euromoney*, June 1984)

Local requirements for bank finance in Saudi Arabia and Kuwait generally fall short of the available funds of the banking sector so that some commercial banks in these countries must place a significant proportion of their funds in overseas loans and investments or with offshore banks; as a result commercial banks have become increasingly international in their outlook.

Elsewhere in the Middle East the commercial banks, while some carry out significant international business, tend to place most of their funds locally to satisfy the loan requirements in their home countries. The largest commercial banks (in terms of assets) in other Middle East countries which rank in the top 500 in the world are:

Bank		Country	Assets (excluding contra accounts) 31 December 1983 (US$ billion)
Arab Bank	158	Jordan	10.33
Arab Banking Corporation	67	Bahrain	8.76
National Bank of Abu Dhabi	132	United Arab Emirates	6.13

(*Euromoney*, June 1984)

The fundamental purpose of most Middle East commercial banks is to satisfy the banking requirements of people and businesses in their home country. As a result, for the most part they have not sought to develop a multinational network of branches, except in so far as it has been considered helpful to their customers to offer overseas facilities, for example in London and New York.

Many of the smaller commercial banks do not have a wide range of different types of asset. They place funds with borrowers and other banks but, in the absence of sophisticated stock markets in their home country and with no need to seek overseas investment opportunities, their balance sheets do not include the wide range of investment assets common to banks elsewhere. Furthermore, many countries have legislation which prevents or limits equity investments by banks.

Because Middle East commercial banks tend to operate in only one country and largely to serve the people of that country, their financial statements are not designed primarily for international use. Nevertheless, these financial statements are widely distributed to banks and other readers overseas and it is to the accounting methods of these banks that the greater part of this chapter is devoted.

2.3 Offshore banks

The offshore banking centre for the Middle East is Bahrain where licences have been granted for over 70 Offshore Banking Units (OBUs). In addition there are about 45 representative offices of foreign banks. It is in Bahrain that the major international banks can operate without the restrictions that are applied elsewhere in the Middle East to foreign-owned companies. The offshore banks are not permitted to carry on business with the Bahrain domestic private sector and, as a result, are not subject to any reserve requirements. Most OBUs are branches, subsidiaries or consortia of major international and Arab banks.

The accounting policies and form of financial statements of OBUs reflect their parentage. An examination of their financial statements depicts the full range of international accounting methods. They are considered in further detail in the section on Bahrain.

2.4 Investment and development banks

Throughout the Middle East are institutions whose names include the word 'bank' but which do not carry out banking business in the conventional sense. Investment and development banks are usually government-funded bodies which lend money to assist local industries or developing countries. The loans may be at favourable rates of interest.

The accounting practices of these banks will vary according to their activities and, since most of these institutions are wholly or majority-owned by governments, their financial statements are unlikely to be critical to a credit decision by third parties. Accordingly, the accounting practices of these banks are not considered in detail in this section.

3 EXTENT OF DISCLOSURE IN FINANCIAL STATEMENTS

In the Middle East there is little legislation on the subject of disclosures in corporate financial reporting. Such legislation as exists tends to focus on the requirements for information which must be reported to regulatory and taxation authorities and, on the whole, these needs are met by financial statements or returns that are not publicly available. There is no strong pressure from the public for greater disclosure in financial reporting. Major local shareholders are either represented on the boards of companies or can obtain information by word of mouth in the comparatively small financial communities in the region. Creditors find that they can judge credit risks better by considering a company's ownership and pedigree than by reviewing its financial data. There are few organisations such as pressure groups or trade unions which, in Western countries, claim a right to information on corporate activities and performance. As a result the requirements for external financial reporting by banks, while sometimes covered by more onerous legislation than for other companies, are generally undemanding.

Apart from legislation there are no accounting standards laid down by accountancy bodies or others in Middle Eastern countries. Countries in the region are not members of international bodies setting accounting standards.

There have been comparatively few liquidity problems among Middle East banks in recent years involving losses to depositors. Depositors generally feel that their money is safe and do not press for the protection of more detailed financial reporting. Middle Eastern banks have also avoided much of the pressure for disclosure from international users of the banks' financial statements. This is because they are usually net lenders of funds to the London, New York and other money markets; accordingly they do not feel it necessary to provide greater information merely to extend their credit lines with international banks.

We therefore see that there are few external pressures on Middle East banks to disclose more than the minimum financial information. The form of financial reporting in much of the region bears a strong resemblance to that followed by the non-disclosure banks in the United Kingdom.

Changes in external financial reporting for Middle East banks during the past 15 years have taken place through a process of evolution. Bankers have, consciously or subconsciously, developed their reporting along lines similar to each other. This process, which has been assisted by auditors and the central banks, has led to a number of general practices being developed for Middle Eastern banks which are examined in the remainder of this section. It is important to appreciate that this section can only seek to indicate the general trend for accounting policies among Middle East banks. In the absence of legislation or laid down standards, banks are free to adopt different accounting policies for their individual purposes. Furthermore, the general trend may not be followed in all countries and certain different policies are referred to in the sections dealing with Bahrain, Kuwait, Saudi Arabia and the United Arab Emirates.

3.1 Inner reserves

The most important single feature of accounting by Middle East banks is the extensive use of inner, or secret, reserves. These reserves are normal practice in Kuwait and will also be found in the United Arab Emirates and elsewhere. When considering the financial statements of a Middle East bank, the reader should establish from the outset whether inner reserves are being maintained. His interpretation of any ratios or balances should take this into account.

The inner reserves are created, or may be reduced, by annual unquantified transfers which are made before arriving at the disclosed profit for the year. The accumulated balance of these reserves, again un-quantified, is usually included within the heading of deposits on the balance sheet. In most cases, though not invariably, there will be an accounting policy or other note to the financial statements which indicates that inner reserves exist. There will sometimes also be a statement on the face of the profit and loss account to show that the annual transfer to or from inner reserves has been made before arriving at the disclosed profit. This latter disclosure is achieved by describing the profit for the year in terms such as 'profit for the year after transfer to inner reserves'.

The existence of inner reserves can seriously detract from financial statements as a measure of performance. A creditor or depositor might feel unconcerned. He can reason that the true equity of the bank is no less than the amount shown in the balance sheet so that, if he makes his decision on the basis of what is disclosed, he knows that the true wealth of the bank can only be greater than he has assumed.

For other users of financial statements, the complications can be considerable. The profit trends shown by banks with inner reserves may well be smoother than the true trends and a bank with such reserves can conceal, or at least mitigate, the impact of a bad year's trading or sudden substantial loan losses. Banks may hint at the real trend of profits by indicating whether the disclosed profit has been increased or reduced by inner reserve transfers. In the United Kingdom, many non-disclosure banks follow a code whereby the disclosed profit would always move in the same direction from year to year as the movement in actual profit. Users of financial statements should not assume that this code is necessarily followed by banks in the Middle East.

It is unlikely that the financial statements will give any indications of the scale of inner reserves which might vary from modest sums, that could be viewed as equivalent to general provisions against loans, to massive amounts in relation to the disclosed equity of the bank. A small shareholder, without access to the full information available to directors or major shareholders, could find it difficult to assess the value of his holding although, in any event, it is unlikely that the market value of his shares will be related to net asset values as disclosed in the published balance sheet.

The existence of inner reserves is the single most important bank accounting topic for consideration by auditors in the region. As a result of their professional training, auditors tend to have reservations with regard to inner reserves or any other methods for distorting the actual profit or state of affairs. However, they cannot ignore the convention in some Arabian Gulf countries where a considerable number of banks have these reserves. In certain countries it is quite clear that inner reserves form part of normal bank accounting practice so that, as measured in terms of that country's accounting methods, it can be argued that inner reserves need not detract from the truth or fairness of financial statements. As measured by internationally accepted accounting standards, inner reserves distort financial statements and may even render them misleading. The auditor's dilemma is to decide whether 'truth and fairness' is a universal concept which should be imposed regardless of local custom or whether it is a concept that varies according to the commercial environment in which he is working. Both views are evident in auditors' reports on Middle East banks.

Inner reserves can also lead to the need for other non-disclosures. In those countries where banks pay taxation on their actual profits, there is a reluctance to disclose the precise amount of the tax charge from which the transfer to inner reserves could be estimated. In addition, those banks with large inner reserves may be reluctant to provide any detailed analysis of their deposits and other liabilities since, if they do, it may be easier for a reader to estimate the approximate amount of accumulated inner reserves which are included within that balance sheet heading. A meaningful statement of source and application of funds cannot be produced when there are material movements on inner reserves.

3.2 Window dressing

While window dressing undoubtedly takes place, there is no evidence to suggest that it is more extensive in the Middle East than elsewhere. There are no regulations designed specifically to cope with window dressing but most Middle East countries have legislation requiring that the financial statements of banks be drawn up at 31 December. Where all banks are producing their statements at the same date, the scope for window dressing is perhaps less than it might otherwise be. While banks may attempt to adjust liquidity ratios or the percentages of different categories of asset through window dressing, the area which receives the greatest attention appears to be balance sheet totals. Middle East banks, many of which are young and growing, vie with each other as to size, which tends to be measured in terms of balance sheet totals. There is a general desire among management to build up totals to as high a figure as is commensurate with their bank's equity. Quite apart from window dressing, this desire has led to the widespread practice of including guarantees, acceptances and other contra items in balance sheet totals.

4 GENERALLY ACCEPTED ACCOUNTING POLICIES

As has been stated earlier, it is difficult to summarise the accounting policies of all Middle East banks in one section. There are differences both between and within countries. What follows is a description of policies that appear to be followed by a majority of banks:

4.1 Foreign exchange

Balances in foreign currency are almost invariably translated at market rates ruling at the balance sheet date. There are variations in accounting for forward currency contracts. Some banks will book all profits and losses arising on revaluations of such contracts at forward rates while others will only recognise losses. There are also examples of banks which amortise profits and/or losses over the period of the forward currency contract. For swap or arbitrage transactions, the premium or discount is usually amortised evenly over the term of the transactions.

4.2 Deferred tax

It is unusual to find any reference to deferred tax in the financial statements of Middle East banks. If deferred tax balances exist, they are likely to be immaterial. Many states do not levy any tax on the profits of banks so that the question of deferred tax does not arise. In some other countries the impact is reduced because rates of tax are comparatively low and the taxation rules, being un-sophisticated, will not involve large timing differences between the accounting and taxable profits. Finally, in those countries where taxation rates are high and timing differences exist, the taxation rules tend to defer rather than accelerate reliefs. For example, in Jordan loan losses are only allowable for tax when it can be proved that the amounts are definitely irrecoverable and a bank may not receive tax relief on a loan loss provision for several years while a liquidation is in progress. The result is that deferred tax amounts, were they to be accounted for, would be debit balances. There is no evidence to suggest that significant debit balances are being carried forward by banks as assets.

4.3 Loan loss and other provisions

Middle East banks make specific provisions against loans and other credit risks on the basis of an estimate of the amounts recoverable. Where specific losses are foreseen, the write-off or provision is recognised immediately as a charge against profit. Banks do not normally amortise foreseeable loan losses over future accounting periods.

Many, though not all, banks make general provisions against latent loan losses and credit risks. These general provisions, often expressed as a percentage of the loan portfolio, vary widely but certain observations can be made. The tax authorities of some countries (including Oman and Lebanon) tend to disallow as a taxable expense general provisions against loans but will allow relief on specific provisions. Not surprisingly, bankers in these countries try to allocate their provisions to specific loans wherever possible.

Some banks will include provisions against loans within 'deposits and other accounts' on the balance sheet. Others show provisions as a deduction from loans. There may be no indication in the financial statements as to the treatment that has been adopted.

Where loans are categorised as doubtful, it is common practice for interest to be accounted for on a cash rather than an accruals basis. However, because there is no standard definition of what constitutes a doubtful loan, the effect of 'reserved interest' on profits of different banks will vary. The subject of interest on doubtful loans is of special significance in certain states. In several countries, civil and religious courts operate in parallel. The latter, called Sharia Courts, place considerable emphasis on the prohibition by the Quran of usury and there have been several judgements, notably in the United Arab Emirates, which have ruled that any charging of interest is illegal. In these circumstances

banks in the United Arab Emirates sometimes consider it necessary to make provision against unpaid interest more quickly than commercial considerations alone would require. Modern Quranic jurisprudence draws a distinction between interest and usury, the latter involving the charging of exorbitant rates of interest. In line with this view interest is permitted by most courts in the Middle East but there are often restrictions on the rates that they consider acceptable; maxima, where set, are established at around 10% p.a. These restrictions can cause problems for banks at times of high international interest rates. It should be emphasised that difficulties in collecting interest can only arise if a case comes to court; the vast majority of loans are made and repaid without disagreement and on these banks earn market rates.

Disclosure of loan loss provisions varies between countries. In Jordan, Lebanon and Qatar it is common for banks to quantify both the provision made in the year and the accumulated provision at the balance sheet date. In most other countries a quantification of provisions is unusual and the financial statements are unlikely to disclose more than an accounting policy indicating that provisions have been made.

Other provisions tend to be made in the financial statements of Middle East banks only in respect of known or anticipated liabilities. For those banks with inner reserves there is little temptation to establish unnecessary provisions for purposes of profit equalisation.

4.4 Premiums and discounts on investments

There is no standard method of accounting for the premiums or discounts on investments being held to maturity. Most banks will amortise the premium or take credit for the discount in equal instalments over the period to maturity, but others will defer either or both premiums and discounts until the maturity date or the date of sale. Investments on which premiums or discounts arise are not held in large volume by Middle East banks and it is unlikely that their accounting treatment could affect profit materially. Where significant, the accounting policy adopted is likely to be disclosed in the financial statements.

4.5 Offsets

The general practice is not to offset loans to and deposits from the same party, even where the deposit is blocked to secure a loan of equal amount in the same currency. There are a few exceptions to this but, because the accounting treatment for offsets is not usually disclosed in financial statements, a user of the statements is unlikely to discover whether offsetting has taken place within a particular bank.

4.6 Goodwill

Because each Middle East commercial bank largely operates in a single country, it usually functions on a branch basis without the need for subsidiary companies. Some commercial banks have subsidiaries which may carry on a banking business in another country or a non-banking business in the same country but, where they exist, subsidiaries tend to be small in relation to the bank itself. Furthermore, such subsidiaries tend to be set up by the bank rather than being acquired from third parties, in which case goodwill does not arise.

The result is that material amounts of goodwill are not a regular feature in accounts of Middle East banks. Small balances of goodwill may be included within 'other assets' or, more likely, written off at the time of acquisition.

Apart from goodwill, the comparatively recent beginnings and rapid development of Middle East banks has involved them in greater pre-operational costs in recent years than banks generally. Although some central banks require that such costs are written off immediately in financial statements, banks which are allowed to do so will sometimes amortise these costs over periods of up to five years. The deferred costs being carried forward are viewed as a form of goodwill and, if material, are likely to be disclosed separately in the financial statements; where applicable the accounting policy will usually be stated.

4.7   Consolidation and year ends

The majority of Middle East banks are required by law to draw up financial statements to 31 December each year; the main exceptions are Saudi Arabia and Qatar. Banks in the area tend not to have large numbers of material subsidiaries or associated companies; their main operations both at home and overseas are generally carried on through a branch network. Accordingly, consolidated financial statements are rarely important and are not common. However, for those banks with significant subsidiaries, consolidated accounts are normally produced under the equity method so as to include the attributable results of subsidiary and associated companies drawn up to the same accounting date.

4.8   Revaluations

Revaluations of fixed assets and investments are usually permitted although in practice they are rare. Middle East commercial banks do not normally hold sufficient amounts of fixed assets or equity investments to justify a revaluation and in some countries a revaluation may lead to a tax charge. Either because of local laws, the constitution of the bank itself, or convention, surpluses arising on any revaluations are taken direct to reserves and are not considered as available for distribution.

4.9   Instalment financing/leasing

Instalment financing and leasing are not major forms of funding in the Middle East. Instalment financing is sometimes offered to personal customers for purchases of such assets as vehicles but, because corporate customers mainly obtain funds for asset purchases through overdraft or loan arrangements, the proportion of a bank's loan portfolio in the form of instalment credit is likely to be low. Leasing is very rare. There are no taxation advantages with this form of credit so that the cost of administration is less easy to justify than in

countries where banks can obtain tax allowances on fixed assets. Interest on instalment financing is taken over the term of the transaction by one of the recognised methods for matching income and costs, most usually the 'rule of 78'.

4.10   Investments

Most Middle East banks do not distinguish dealing from investment securities and will either show all investments under a single heading or under the headings of quoted and unquoted investments.

Some banks disclose the market value of their investments but this is not a standard practice. Accordingly, a reader needs to take into account the possibility that the market value of investments might be higher or lower than the book amount.

Although financial statements will sometimes distinguish between investments in equities, interest-bearing securities and shareholdings in or balances with affiliates, it is rare, except in respect of major subsidiary or associated companies, for the name or nature of the investment to be specified.

4.11   Pensions and leaving payments

The type of staff benefits offered by Middle East banks varies between the banks and the countries in which they operate; most countries have legislation laying down minimum scales for pensions or leaving payments and some banks will offer arrangements more generous than this minimum.

In the Gulf states the principal form of benefit is the leaving payment or gratuity which is payable to members of staff when they leave the bank's employment (there may be rare exceptions where benefits are not due if staff leave for special reasons). The payment varies according to salary and length of service. For the most part these liabilities and their amounts are certain; all that is in doubt are the dates on which staff will leave when the liability will crystallise. Leaving payments, if material, are shown as a long-term liability, although in most cases the amount is comparatively small and the balance is included within 'other liabilities'.

In certain other countries (e.g. Lebanon) pension arrangements exist. Under the legislation pensions, which may be internally or externally funded, are not automatically payable to all staff. Rules might involve no payment to those staff who leave the bank on their own initiative before retirement age and there is often no requirement to transfer accrued pension benefits to the new employer. Banks tend to fund pensions internally by making full provision for the accrued benefits on the assumption that all members of staff will remain in their employment until retirement. The resulting provisions will therefore be higher than necessary, although this conservatism is unlikely to be material to the financial statements as a whole.

Banks may also operate externally funded pension plans for senior staff. The most common accounting treatment is to charge against profit the amount of the annual payment that has been made in accordance with actuarial advice.

4.12 Fixed assets

A number of Middle East banks expense fixed assets at the time of acquisition; this particularly applies to the offshore banks in Bahrain and others which do not have many branches. Those banks with a branch network are likely to have more substantial investments in land and buildings which, often being material, are more likely to be depreciated in the normal way.

Depreciation is generally charged in respect of all depreciable fixed assets (i.e. everything except freehold land).

4.13 Fees

Strict Islamic doctrine prohibits interest on borrowed funds. Certain banks, known as Islamic banks, conduct their business in accordance with these rules and neither pay nor receive interest. Other banks adapt their practices for the requirements of particular customers.

Banking or investment transactions in accordance with strict Islamic doctrine involve the payment of fees or the sharing of profits and banks generally account for income or expense of this type over the term of the transaction. Some other banks charge less than the market interest rate on their loans but include a fee in the arrangements. These fees can cause practical accounting difficulties; for a loan or overdraft facility which has been granted on payment of a fee, it may not be easy to predict the period over which it will run or the future variation of the drawn down balance. Accordingly, the proportion of the fee that should be taken to income in any year can only be calculated on the basis of assumptions about repayment dates and future draw-downs.

Other fees are normally accounted for on an accruals basis if they relate to services being provided over a period (e.g. commitment fees on undrawn overdraft facilities) or on a cash basis if they relate to a one-off service. Examples of fees that are normally taken direct to profit are brokerage on foreign exchange transactions and front end fees covering the administration costs of setting up a loan, guarantee or other credit arrangement.

4.14 Asset and liability headings on the balance sheet

There are no standard rules for determining the location in the balance sheet of certain assets and individual financial statements will often give no indication of the treatment adopted in their case. 'Cash at hand and with bankers' may include foreign currency current accounts with correspondent banks or, alternatively, these balances may be incorporated within 'deposits with other banks'. Banks will almost invariably have an asset heading of 'Money at call and short notice' but the definition of 'short notice' is rarely disclosed.

It is not usual for Middle East banks to give any indication of the repayment schedules of 'deposits with other banks' or 'loans to customers'. As a result it is rare to see a quantification of assets maturing, realisable or repayable within one year. In practice a quantification might be misleading because many Middle East banks grant annually reviewable overdraft facilities to customers to meet long-term financial requirements; many of these overdrafts are not, in practice, likely to be repaid within twelve months.

Financial statements rarely disclose the geographical spread of 'loans to customers' or 'deposits with other banks' or the industry categories of 'loans to customers'.

The majority of banks will distinguish either on the balance sheet or in a note to the financial statements between 'deposits from customers' and 'deposits from other banks'. Apart from this, detailed information about deposits is rare and, in particular, it is most unusual to find any indication of their maturity dates.

4.15 Contra accounts

Contingent liabilities in respect of guarantees, letters of credit and acceptances form a major part of the customer operations of most Middle East commercial banks. They arise mainly through the financing of international trade. These contingent liabilities can amount to as much as 50% of the total of all other liabilities of a bank. As mentioned earlier, it is a common practice for Middle East banks to show these contingencies, and the corresponding claim on customers, as assets and liabilities on the face of the balance sheet and to include them in the balance sheet totals. Any comparison of balance sheet ratios of Middle East banks with those elsewhere could be misleading unless due allowance is made for contra items.

4.16 Related party transactions

Transactions between commercial banks and their directors, shareholders, staff, or companies associated with these persons, are common in some countries. The regulation by central banks of such loans is being performed with varying success. There are a few instances of large lending taking place; commercial banks are sometimes controlled by groups of companies and the loans by these banks to other businesses in the group sometimes exceeds the bank's total equity. Neither the existence nor the terms of such loans are necessarily disclosed in financial statements.

5 CONCLUSION

Because there are few standard accounting policies adopted by all banks in any Middle Eastern country, it is of the utmost importance that an international user of financial statements should study the accounting policies and notes before analysing the financial statements of a Middle East bank. In most cases the notes will give an indication of any unusual accounting policies that have been followed although this is not invariably the case. It is regrettable that a minority of banks continue to provide sparse information which could be misleading to a user who is unaware of local practices.

STATE OF BAHRAIN

1 GENERAL INFORMATION

Bahrain, an island in the Arabian Gulf, with an area of 622 square kilometres and a population of approximately 350,000 including expatriate workers, has been independent since 15 August 1971. Bahrain has now 18 commercial banks (with 48 branches in total), 70 offshore banking units, 10 investment banks, and some 45 representative offices. In addition there are six money brokers.

The island had been a major trading centre within the Gulf for centuries. Oil was first produced in Bahrain in 1936. The currency of trade up to the introduction of the Bahrain dinar had been the Indian rupee, which had simplified transactions within the Gulf and with India since this currency was accepted throughout the region.

With the introduction of the Bahrain dinar in 1964, under the provisions of the Bahrain Currency Decree (No. 6 of 1964), trade became more concerned with foreign exchange and other banking services.

1.1 Organisations covered by banking regulations

The increase in the number of commercial banks made the establishment of a centralised control essential and the Bahrain Currency Board was established in 1964 for this purpose, and to control the issue of currency. In 1973 the Bahrain Monetary Agency was formed by Law No. 23 of 1973 to take over the functions of the Currency Board and increase the control aspect to that of a central bank.

Article 3 of the Bahrain Monetary Agency Law states:
'The objects of the Agency are to:

A   Organise the issue and circulation of the currency of the State of Bahrain as well as the foreign exchange operations.

B   Maintain the value of the currency of Bahrain and endeavour to ensure monetary stability.

C   Organise the banking business and control the banking system.

D   Control and direct bank credit so as to realise the objectives of the economic policy of the state.

E   Participate in the creation of a developed money and financial market.'

Article 56 of the Agency Law states 'any company, firm, agent or representative who wishes to practice the banking profession in the State of Bahrain must file with the Agency an application to this effect . . .'.

However, nowhere in the law is there a definition of a bank. Without first obtaining a licence from the Agency and a commercial registration number from the Ministry of Commerce and Agriculture, which administers Company Law, no operations of any kind will be permitted.

1.2 Summary of major types of bank

Banks are categorised by the type of licence under which they operate. The licences presently available are: (a) commercial bank; (b) offshore banking unit; (c) investment bank.

In addition to these licensed banks there are also representative offices which are not permitted to undertake banking operations. Offshore Banking Units (OBUs) were first established under the terms of a circular issued in 1975 which set out the specific rules governing their operation. The text of the circular is given in Appendix I. Similarly, investment banks are allowed by a circular in 1977, which was amended by No. 81/2 of 25 March 1981, and is given as Appendix II.

The main restrictions on the OBUs activities relate to dealings with residents of Bahrain and the provision of Bahrain dinar cheque accounts. Investment banks cannot offer current account services, nor may they issue cheque books. In addition, liquidity and gearing ratios are more stringent than for commercial banks. Advances to residents of Bahrain may only be made with the prior approval of the Agency.

1.3 Supervisory authorities

1.4 Status of supervisory authorities

The Bahrain Monetary Agency is charged with the task of supervising the activities of banks within the State of Bahrain. Article 14 (para D) of the Agency Law states 'The Board shall in particular lay down the special regulation required for the application of the provisions of this law as regards the organisation of the banking business and the strict control over banks and other financial firms.' This article gives the Board of the Agency the wide powers necessary to enable it to control the banking sector.

Article 41 brings financial and investment firms and companies within the purview of the Agency Law, to the same extent that banking firms are governed.

The local banking community has established the Bahrain Bankers' Society, which meets periodically to discuss and present collective representation on matters to be agreed, generally with the Bahrain Monetary Agency.

1.5 Laws and regulations governing banks
1.6 Application of general company law to banks
1.7 Sources of laws and regulations

In addition to the Bahrain Monetary Agency Law which sets out specific banking control regulations there is also a Commercial Law which must be complied with by those banks which are also Bahraini companies (including Exempt Companies established under the terms of a Ministry of Commerce and Agriculture circular dated 17 October 1977 which also obtained offshore banking licences).

However, the Commercial Law is not particularly onerous and does not contain any specific provisions which are not also in the Monetary Agency Law, with the exception of a prohibition (article 189 of the 1975 Company Law) on the distribution of capital profits and the need for the establishment of a legal reserve (see following paragraphs).

(a) Laws and regulations: commercial banks

The procedure and requirements for obtaining a commercial bank licence are not embodied within the Monetary Agency Law, and as such preliminary discussions should be held with the Agency at an early stage. In addition, the Agency's requirements are amended from time to time and again early consultation is essential.

Should the Agency refuse to grant a licence, article 68 provides for appeal to the Minister of Finance.

With the exception of branches of foreign banks, all commercial banks operating in Bahrain must be corporations organised in accordance with the laws of the State of Bahrain (article 56). The minimum paid-in capital for any banking organisation is BD500,000. Article 72 sets out provisions requiring a reserve account to be established with 20% of annual profits being transferred, until such time that the reserve plus share capital amounts to 5% of the value of deposits and other similar liabilities. However, Company Commercial Law (article 189) requires the establishment of a legal reserve with 10% of profits transferred thereto, until the reserve is equal to not less than 25% of share capital. In practice only one reserve is created which serves as the legal reserve and also maintains the 5% ratio.

The prior approval of the Agency is required for any modification of share capital, changes to Memorandum of Association or bylaws, or any merger or combination with another company (article 65A). Rules and formalities to be followed when merging or combining shall be laid down by the Agency's Board of Directors (article 65B).

A bank may have its licence cancelled under the following circumstances (article 66).

A If it has not started to operate within six months of being granted the licence.

B If it acts in contravention of the conditions of the licence or fails to follow the formalities prescribed in article 65.

C If it repeatedly violates any of the provisions of the Bahrain Monetary Agency Law.

D If it suspends operations in the State of Bahrain.

Prior to cancellation of a licence the Agency will give notice to the bank of its intention to cancel the licence and the bank may then, within a reasonable time, object to the cancellation, stating the grounds for the objection. The Agency, with the approval of the Minister of Finance, then notifies the bank of its decision on the subject. There is no laid-down appeal procedure once this decision has been made.

Article 76 sets out detailed provisions regarding restrictions of certain classes of lending, e.g. loans to directors, loans against its own shares, etc. Article 76 is set out in Appendix III.

The Agency has power to make instructions to commercial banks (individually and collectively) and in particular, articles 35 to 38 mention specific areas where the Agency may issue instructions to the banks. These areas include:

(a) Percentage cash reserve against deposits, the actual percentage being notified by the Agency.

(b) Method of calculating liquidity reserve ratios, with the potential to apply different percentages to different classes of deposit.

(c) Purposes for which credit may be granted and maximum limits. Periods of maturity and minimum securities to be obtained from customers.

(d) Minimum percentage of assets to be maintained in Bahrain dinars.

(e) Maximum limit of operating balances allowed in one or several specified foreign currencies.

Contravention of these decisions render a bank liable to fines of up to BD1,000 per day.

Articles 82 to 84 allow the Agency to appoint bank inspectors to examine the affairs of a particular bank, which must allow the inspectors access to all documents and information they request, and to issue instructions to the bank to correct any contraventions of the law.

Articles 92 to 107 deal with the administration of banking firms by the Agency and their forced liquidation.

(b) Laws and regulations: Offshore Banking Units (OBUs)

The specific regulations governing the operation of all OBUs are set out in Appendix 1. In addition to branches of foreign banks it is also possible to obtain OBU licences for Bahrain Exempt Companies, and for commercial banks already operating in Bahrain either as corporations or branches of overseas banks.

Those OBUs which are set up as Exempt Companies are subject to all the commercial and Monetary Agency laws. As the business which is undertaken by OBUs is significantly different from commercial banks there are no liquidity ratio requirements, but for Exempt Companies there would need to be a substantial capital to obtain the approval of the Agency to issue an OBU licence. This capital requirement has not been defined anywhere but is currently believed to be US$50 million, of which at least 50% must be paid-up. Again, early consultation with the Agency is advisable for anyone contemplating forming this type of bank.

(c) Laws and regulations: investment banks

The specific rules governing investment banks are set out

in Appendix II. Investment banks are also controlled by the Bahrain Monetary Agency Law.

As with OBUs, investment banks may be branches of overseas banks, Bahraini companies or Exempt Companies.

(d) Laws and regulations: other financial institutions and investment firms and companies

There is no definition of either a financial institution or an investment firm within the Agency Law. Specific rules for investment banks have been issued, but as far as other financial institutions are concerned the Agency has yet to take any significant action. Regulations covering dealers and brokers in precious metals and commodities were introduced in July 1981 under article 41 of the Agency Law.

(e) Other types of bank

Islamic Banking: One commercial bank (the Bahrain Islamic Bank) and one OBU (Mosraf Faisal Al-Islami) have been licensed. The Bahrain Islamic Investment Company has also been licensed as an investment bank. The Housing Bank, a government-owned institution, was established by a special charter. It provides finance for housing under the auspices of the Ministry of Housing.

Although not regarded as banks, the many currency exchanges traditionally have much of the local exchange business. This is true not only of note exchange in the market but also of expatriate remittances. The business being largely based on trust, the currency exchanges will issue drafts drawn on banks in the country destined to receive the remittance. This makes the remittance by post a much safer proposition and, with the large number of exchanges, very fine exchange rates can be obtained due to the competition to attract business. The currency exchanges also have a thriving travellers' cheque business. All aspects of banking in Bahrain are dominated by the freedom to convert currencies and to remit any currency to anywhere in the world.

1.8 Ability of foreign banks to operate through branches and subsidiaries

As can be seen from the table in Section 1.10, a foreign bank which is considering operating in Bahrain has several options as to how to set up, providing of course that the Monetary Agency is willing to grant the necessary permission. Because of the establishment of Exempt Company regulations it is now possible to have an OBU as either a branch of a foreign bank or a subsidiary with an Exempt Company status.

1.9 Level of supervisory control for branches and subsidiaries of foreign banks

The level of supervision and control exercised by the Monetary Agency over branches and subsidiaries of foreign banks is primarily governed by the 1974 Basle Concordat, coupled with the subjective judgement of Agency officials regarding levels of control being exercised by head office supervisory authorities.

Commercial banks and investment banks, whether local companies or branches of foreign banks, are controlled much more rigorously than OBUs which have no liquidity or capital ratio requirements. Only in specific circumstances are OBUs permitted to transact business with residents of Bahrain.

1.10 Methods of incorporation

	Commercial bank	OBU	Investment bank
Local company	x		x
Branch of local company		x	x
Exempt company		x	x
Branch of overseas company	x	x	x

Locally incorporated companies must have at least a 51% local shareholding. The options available for the operation of the various types of bank are shown above. In addition some special charter companies have been formed which need not necessarily fit this standard pattern, but these are normally on a government-to-government basis and each one is subject to the requirements of the Amiri Decree under which it was established. Such banks are subject to all the prudential requirements and supervision of the Agency.

It is possible for a local company or an overseas bank to have branches with both commercial and OBU licences. However, these branches must maintain independent accounting records and submit separate returns to the Agency.

1.11 Areas within the country subject to special laws

The major area with special laws is that concerning Exempt Companies (ECs) and Offshore Banking Units. Both of these categories of operation are restricted in that they cannot deal with residents of Bahrain. However, for the purpose of defining residents, other OBUs, ECs and commercial banks are not considered to be prohibited. Where the national interest is deemed to be concerned, permission can be obtained to deal with Bahrain residents.

The exemption referred to in the title of ECs is to the general requirement for locally incorporated companies to have a 51% Bahraini shareholding. ECs are allowed to register with no local participation, but thereafter cannot deal with residents of Bahrain.

2 ACCOUNTING

2.1 Laws and regulations governing accounts

Article 77 of the Agency Law sets out that the accounting year shall be the same as the calendar year and also that audited accounts shall be submitted to the Agency within three months of the year end. The form and manner of the accounts is to be as specified by the Agency. This law applies to all banks licensed in Bahrain, regardless of the type of licence issued.

2.2 Application of general company law

Those banks which operate as corporations within Bahrain, rather than as branches of foreign banks, must also comply with company law when producing annual accounts.

2.3 Roles of legislature and supervisory authority

2.4 Extent to which requirements as to returns and accounts are prescribed by laws and regulations

Under powers conferred on it in article 78 of the Agency Law, the Agency requires all banks to submit monthly and quarterly returns within 21 days of the month end in a format specified from time to time by the Agency. This format varies depending on the type of licence, but is not affected by the nature of the entity, i.e. Corporation, Exempt Company or branch.

Of particular interest to the Agency are currencies, maturities, industry sectors being serviced and geographic spread.

2.5 Obligations to furnish accounts

2.5.1 Accounting periods and times of furnishing

2.5.2 Form of accounts to be furnished

2.5.3 Mandatory accounting dates

Depending upon the type of bank licence and the nature of the entity, annual audited accounts of the Bahrain operations have to be provided to various authorities and individuals as laid down by article 77 as follows:

Local incorporated commercial banks, investment banks, Exempt Companies:

Bahrain Monetary Agency

Shareholders (either by individual circularisation, or publication in the national press), including any OBU figures

Ministry of Commerce and Agriculture

Branch of locally incorporated bank, holding offshore banking licence:

Bahrain Monetary Agency: separate audited accounts for the OBU and the commercial bank

Shareholders: incorporated within the annual accounts

Ministry of Commerce and Agriculture: incorporated within the annual accounts

Branch of an overseas company, holding a commercial bank licence:

Bahrain Monetary Agency

Head Office

In addition, these branches must display in their Bahrain offices an abbreviated balance sheet and profit and loss account covering Bahrain operations.

Branch of an overseas company, holding an offshore banking licence:

Bahrain Monetary Agency

Head Office

Accounts must be prepared on a calendar year basis and be submitted to the Agency within three months of the end of the year.

The format to be adopted for audited accounts being submitted to the Agency is specified by the Agency on an annual basis. The format of accounts being published is not defined, except for the normal requirement of showing a true and fair view as defined by Company Law in article 186.

2.6 Requirements as to accounts (a) prior to incorporation (b) prior to commencement of trading and (c) in order to continue trading

There is no requirement to submit either audited or unaudited accounts prior to incorporation or trading of a company which will hold a bank licence.

Failure to provide accounts will eventually result in the bank's operation being suspended. Temporary delays in submission of accounts, with prior approval of the BMA, do not generally represent a problem. However, the BMA exercises its discretion in these matters.

2.7 Audit requirements

All annual accounts being submitted to the Agency must (article 79) be audited by a 'technically qualified auditor acceptable to the Agency'. There is no list of auditors who are acceptable to the Agency.

2.8 Acceptability to fiscal authorities of accounts submitted to supervisory authority

2.9 Submission of accounts to any authority other than by requirement of law

At the time of writing there are no taxes imposed on the profits of banks, whether locally incorporated or branches of overseas banks, nor on the emoluments of staff employed in Bahrain. Accordingly, accounts do not need to be submitted to the tax or any other authorities except for the Agency.

2.10 Application of laws and regulations to foreign banks operating through branches and subsidiaries

All laws and regulations relating to banks are applied by the Bahrain Monetary Agency in a manner which relates to the type of operation, rather than the nature of the legal entity. As such, branches and subsidiaries of foreign banks are subject to the regulations and laws concerning the particular licensed operation.

2.11 Availability of accounts for public inspection

There is no facility at the Monetary Agency to allow public inspection of annual audited accounts. Article 290 of the Bahrain Commercial Law provides for interested parties to have access to the filed annual audited accounts. This will relate to those banks which are also Bahraini companies.

Commercial banks must publish their annual accounts, but this is generally done by way of an abstract of the balance sheet and profit and loss account being displayed in the bank's main offices or by advertisement in the local press.

3 FORMAT, STYLE AND CONTENTS OF ACCOUNTS

3.1 Extent to which format is laid down by statute, supervisory authority, generally accepted accounting practice or otherwise

3.2 Description of format

(a) The format of annual accounts prepared for submission to the Agency is defined on an annual basis by the Agency, for both commercial banks and OBUs under article 77 of the Agency Law. The formats laid down by the Agency for 1982 are shown at Appendix IV.

Accounting policies are required by the Agency to be disclosed in conformity with International Accounting Standard No. 1 and detailed breakdowns of such items as Capital and Reserves are also required.

(b) The format and contents of accounts for publication, i.e. the accounts of Bahraini companies with banking licences, is dictated more by the use to which they will be put, rather than any other factor. These accounts are used to obtain or improve lines with correspondents, as advertisements for the banks with potential customers and to keep shareholders informed of the bank's progress. As such they tend to contain considerably more information than the accounts submitted to the Agency. However, the format and content varies from bank to bank and, provided that all necessary disclosure is made to give a 'fair view', the format and content can be a matter for agreement between bank and auditor.

3.3 Disclosures

Specific disclosure of bad and doubtful debt provisions is required in the accounts submitted to the Agency. Otherwise the accounts have to disclose all necessary information to give a true and fair view (article 79).

There are no legal requirements to disclose specific items in the published accounts of banks.

3.4 Inner reserves

The Agency Law includes no provision for the setting up of inner reserves and it would appear that no such reserves are maintained by banks in Bahrain.

3.5 Consolidated accounts

There is no specific requirement, in either the Agency Law or the Commercial Law, to prepare consolidated accounts. However, to give a true and fair view of the bank's position it is considered by the Agency that it would be necessary to prepare and submit audited consolidated accounts in addition to submitting returns covering the Bahrain operations.

4 AMOUNTS REQUIRED TO BE MAINTAINED BY LAW

4.1 Capital and reserves: commercial banks

The minimum share capital of any banking firm specified in article 70 of the Agency Law is BD500,000. If the bank is the branch of a foreign bank, BD500,000 is the minimum amount to be set aside for its operations in Bahrain.

Article 71 gives the Agency the authority to set the capital requirement for any particular bank, provided that it is not less than BD500,000. A reserve account established by transfers from the profit and loss account of up to 20% of the profit, when added to the share capital, must amount to not less than 5% of the value of deposits and other similar liabilities (article 72). In practice the Agency makes certain deductions (for fixed assets, goodwill, investments in subsidiaries, etc.) in assessing the capital adequacy of banks. However, the Company Law requires a legal reserve to be set up by transfers of 10% p.a. of net profits, until this reserve is equal to not less than 25% of the share capital, and in practice this is the transfer which is made in banks' accounts.

4.2 Capital and reserves: Offshore Banking Units

There are no capital or reserve requirements for OBUs which are branches of foreign or Bahrain commercial banks.

OBUs which are established under Exempt Company rules are subject to the same minimum capital requirements as commercial banks, but in practice their capital is set considerably higher than BD500,000. The 10% legal reserve transfer is still required under the Company Law, but there is no requirement in law to meet any ratio of capital and reserves to deposits. In practice, for Bahrain based OBUs the Agency requires shareholders' funds (less deductions for fixed assets, goodwill, investment in subsidiaries) to be not less than 5% of total deposit liabilities.

4.3 Capital and reserves: investment banks

The minimum capital of investment banks which are Bahrain registered companies is BD500,000. In this case the minimum transfer of 10% of profit to legal reserve also applies as with other Bahraini companies.

Deposits are then restricted to ten times the capital and reserves of the company (less the deductions mentioned above).

For investment banking branches of foreign banks there are no defined capital or reserve requirements, but the Agency will agree the amount of deposits which may be accepted.

4.4 Cash reserve against deposits

As specified in article 35, the Agency has the right to specify the percentage of cash reserve which commercial banks will maintain interest free with the agency. At present this is 5% of Bahrain dinar deposits and 1% of foreign currency deposits. Both these ratios are calculated net of inter-bank deposits (see Appendix V).

5 KEY RATIOS

5.1 Capital and reserves

For commercial banks the capital plus reserves to total deposit liabilities is the most significant ratio, as this effectively limits the growth of the bank to twenty times its equity. Hence, to increase balance sheet footings significantly, additional equity has to be provided either by an injection of capital or a retention of profits.

Although no official regulations have been made it is the Agency's practice, in assessing a bank's capital for the purposes of the ratio, to deduct certain assets such as premises, equipment investment in subsidiary companies and goodwill (including all intangible assets). Subordinated unsecured loan stock with an initial maturity of five years or more may be acceptable as part of a bank's capital base on terms and conditions to be agreed by the agency.

This ratio of 5% is applicable both to locally registered banks and to branches of foreign banks which have commercial banking licences. For branches of foreign banks the capital amount, or BD500,000, whichever is the greater, has to be recorded as due from head office in an account titled 'Capital Account', not be repayable within 12 months and not bear any interest. Any deposits with head office with a maturity of greater than six months have to be deducted from the Capital Account amount in computing required levels of capital (Agency Circular 76/22 dated 7 November 1976). Offshore Banking Units are not restricted by any capital and reserve ratio, and indeed those OBUs which are branches of banks (both foreign and Bahraini registered) have no capital requirements whatsoever. As a result of this situation and the practice of transferring profits to head office on an annual basis, there are many OBUs with substantial balance sheet footings but without any designated capital account. In all these situations the OBUs are of course supported by head offices which are fully committed to their branches.

Investment banks are restricted by a capital and reserve ratio which stipulates that the total deposit liabilities may not exceed ten times capital and reserves for a Bahraini registered company, or a figure to be agreed by the Agency for a branch of a foreign company (see Appendix II for detailed instructions for investment banks).

All the above capital and reserve ratio requirements are strictly enforced by the Agency.

5.2 Liquidity ratios

Liquidity ratio requirements for commercial banks are set out in general terms in the Agency Law at article 35, and are notified to the banks specifically on a monthly basis by the Agency. For an indication of the method used in calculating the cash reserve see Appendix V.

As can be seen, the cash reserve requirement is computed at different rates for Bahrain dinar and foreign currency liabilities and allowance is made for capital, inter-bank deposits and residents' foreign currency deposits, CDs and certain government approved financing.

At the present time the liquidity requirement is 5% on Bahrain dinar and 1% on foreign currencies, but this can be varied by the Agency (article 35).

Any shortfall in cash reserves is penalised by an interest charge made by the Agency, based on the daily shortfall, at rates up to 5% over the maximum rate for other Agency transactions.

The Agency offers swap facilities to commercial banks, depending upon the bank's dinar position and requirements to finance commercial assets in BD. The amount of the swap availability is calculated monthly in arrears and is used extensively by the commercial banks.

OBUs are not yet subjected to any formal liquidity requirements as such, although detailed maturity by currency schedules are required by the Agency as part of monthly returns so that the Agency can monitor the bank's management of its funds, especially the mismatched position up to one month.

Investment banks are required to maintain liquid assets (which include bank deposits maturing within one month) of at least 25% of deposit liabilities (see Appendix II for precise wording).

Again, the liquidity ratio requirements as set out above are strictly enforced by the Agency.

5.3 Other key ratios

It is understood that the Agency monitors closely the foreign exchange positions of OBUs and investment banks, both spot and forward, and the geographical spread of lending, although no ratios have been formally set.

6 ACCOUNTING RETURNS OTHER THAN ACCOUNTS

6.1 Requirement

Article 78 of the Agency Law empowers the Agency to require banking firms to provide such statements, particulars or information regarding their operations as it sees fit. These requirements are generally met by the completion of a pro forma monthly return which the banks have to submit within 21 days of the month end.

6.2 Information required: commercial banks

The monthly return for commercial banks is an analysis into Bahrain dinar and other currencies by residents, non-residents and government, of each of the following headings:

Assets	Liabilities
1 Notes and coins	1 Capital and reserves
2 Other offices outside Bahrain	2 Other offices outside Bahrain
At sight or demand	At sight or demand
Up to 1 month	Up to 1 month
Over 1 month	Over 1 month
3 Banks	3 Banks
At sight or demand	At sight or demand
Up to 1 month	Up to 1 month
Over 1 month	Over 1 month
4 Certificates of deposit held	4 Non-banks
At sight or demand	At sight or demand
Under 1 year	Up to 1 month
Over 1 year	Over 1 month
	Savings account

Assets	Liabilities
5 Quoted securities and treasury bills	5 Certificate of deposit issue
6 Advances	Under 1 year
7 Discounts	Over 1 year
8 Fixed assets premises	6 Other liabilities
9 Other assets	7 Total (excl. contra)
10 Total (excl. contra)	8 Contra items
11 Contra items	Letters of credit
Letters of credit	Guarantees
Guarantees	Acceptances
Acceptances	Other
Other	9 Total (incl. contra)
12 Total (incl. contra)	10 Of which US$
13 Of which US$	Stg. pounds
Stg. pounds	Others
Others	

A quarterly return is also required. It is an analysis of advances and discounts by industry sector to residents and non-residents, and showing amounts in foreign currencies. Again, this return is due 21 days after the quarter end and must agree in total with the monthly return.

The Agency also operates a confidential Credit Risk Unit, for which monthly returns showing agreed facilities exceeding BD100,000 have to be made. The Agency then returns a copy of this risk statement showing the total of all banks' exposure to the customer.

6.3 Information required: Offshore Banking Units

The monthly returns for OBUs, which must be submitted in US$000, give the following analyses:

(a) Liabilities: schedule 1

By currency, and divided geographically inside and outside Bahrain, showing class of customer; i.e. government, banks, non-banks, OBUs, head office and branches, investments and other. Currencies are then totalled and again divided into the country of origin and other countries.

(b) Assets: schedule 1

The detailed analysis of assets is on the same basis as the analysis of liabilities.

(c) Liabilities: schedule 2

This requires the figures in schedule 1 to be analysed geographically in two classes: banks and others. The form is divided into individual Arab countries, offshore centres, North America, Europe (being split into the United Kingdom and others), Eastern Europe, Africa, Iran, Japan and other. The overall totals, and the amounts for Bahrain, have to agree with figures shown on schedule 1.

(d) Assets: schedule 2

The detail required on this form is the same as for the liabilities schedule 2 analysis.

(e) Sources of funds (classification by currency and maturity): liabilities

This schedule analyses the bank's liabilities into major currencies (being US dollar, Deutschmark, Swiss franc, Sterling, Kuwaiti dinar, Saudi riyal, Qatari riyal, UAE dirham, Bahrain dinar, and others) and then spreads these totals over the remaining periods to maturity, e.g. up to seven days; over seven days to one month, one to three months, etc.; up to items maturing in excess of three years' time.

This schedule requires Negotiable Certificates of Deposit to be identified separately and also carries details of forward sales by currency.

(f) Uses of funds (classification by currency and maturity): assets

This schedule shows the same kind of detail as the liability analysis above, except of course that forward purchases are analysed.

6.4 Dissemination of information

Although detailed specific information regarding individual banks cannot be disclosed by the Agency, it has power (article 78B) to publish the information which it obtains on a total basis. This is done quarterly, when statistics are issued giving aggregate figures for banks in Bahrain, analysing currency and country of origin, maturities of the Bahrain bank and OBU balance sheets. In addition, aggregate forward exchange deals outstanding are analysed into the broad categories of US dollar, regional currencies and other currencies.

7 TAXATION

As detailed in section 2.9 above, banks in Bahrain are not subject to any form of taxation on their profits and there is no personal taxation on the emoluments of employees.

8 INTERPRETATION OF ACCOUNTS

Only banks which are incorporated in Bahrain produce accounts for public record and the content of these accounts is not governed by any specific rules or regulations, other than the general requirement of the Commercial Law (article 186) that they shall show a true and fair view.

The accounts themselves are audited, but any other ancillary information is not necessarily examined by auditors to ensure reliability.

With the increasing need of the banks to market themselves, the accounts which they produce and distribute to shareholders, correspondents and others are tending to take on a more professional look with greater disclosure of significant facts and details.

However, until a standard is adopted which can be relied upon to group like items in the same balance sheet heading, regardless of which bank is concerned, attempts at making comparisons will be fruitless.

APPENDIX I

Bahrain Monetary Agency Circular, 1975
Offshore banking units

(1) Offshore banking units (OBUs) established in Bahrain must be full branches of the parent bank or must satisfy the Bahrain Monetary Agency (BMA) of the commitment of the parent bank to its office.

(2) OBUs must be fully staffed operational branches whose staff are actively engaged in the business which is written in the books of the branch. Permission will not be given for brass plate operations in which the business is written elsewhere and booked into Bahrain solely as an accounting device.

(3) OBUs will not be allowed to deal in any way with residents of Bahrain except for the government, its agencies, the fully licensed banks and to participate in the financing of development projects approved by the BMA.

(4) OBUs will not be allowed to offer BD cheque account services but will otherwise be free to offer all banking services to non-residents of Bahrain of all classes, governments, banks and non-banks.

(5) OBUs will not be required to maintain any reserves with the BMA or observe any formal liquidity ratios.

(6) OBUs will be required to supply regular monthly statistical information including a balance sheet to the BMA and to satisfy the BMA if called upon to do so of their ability to meet their obligations as they fall due.

(7) OBUs will be required to submit to the BMA a balance sheet and profit and loss account of their OBU operation, audited by auditors approved by the BMA, within 90 days of the year end and in due course file a copy of their group's published accounts.

(8) An annual licence fee of US$25,000 is payable to the BMA for an OBU licence, no taxation on OBU profits is at present planned or proposed by the Government of Bahrain.

(9) Existing fully licensed banks may apply for an OBU licence for their non-resident business. The BMA will wish to be satisfied that adequate arrangements are made for separate accounting records.

APPENDIX II

Bahrain Monetary Agency Circular 81/2
Investment bank licences

The Agency has been reviewing the conditions of the investment bank licences and these will be revised as follows:

Investment banks

(1) May maintain fully staffed operational offices in Bahrain for all forms of securities business including underwriting, placing and trading in securities and for advisory operations on investments and capital raising.

(2) May accept deposits from other banks in Bahrain or outside, including OBUs, in any currency and at call or on fixed deposit.

(3) May accept deposits from non-banks outside Bahrain at call or on fixed deposit with a minimum value of US$50,000 (or equivalent in other currencies) per deposit.

(4) May not issue cheque books or offer current account services.

(5) Deposit liabilities may not exceed ten times the capital and reserves of a Bahrain registered company or such figure as the Agency may agree in the case of a branch of a foreign company or bank.

(6) May make loans and advances to non-residents on mutually agreed terms provided such facility is not in the form of an overdraft. Loans to residents of Bahrain require the prior permission of the Monetary Agency.

(7) Must maintain liquid assets (defined to include bank deposits maturing within one month and certain other short-term marketable investments) equal to 25% of deposits received and generally be able to satisfy the Agency of its ability to meet its liabilities as they fall due.

(8) Must submit a monthly report within 21 days of the month end in a form required by the Agency.

(9) Must submit audited accounts within three months of the end of each financial year.

(10) Must pay an annual licence fee of BD6,000 to the Agency.

(11) Will be classified in Banking Statistics as a non-resident bank. Holders of existing investment bank licences will be required to comply with the new licence conditions. However, where the Agency has agreed special conditions with an individual licence holder, these conditions will override the requirements of this circular.

APPENDIX III

Bahrain Monetary Agency Law
Article 76

A banking firm shall not, without the approval of the Agency and except upon the terms and conditions the Agency shall determine:

(a) Grant loans or credit facilities, or give a guarantee or securities, or assume any other financial obligation in favour of any natural or juristic person, in amounts exceeding in the aggregate such percentage of the banking firm's own funds as shall be determined by the Agency.

(b) Grant loans for the purchase or acquisition of real property or for any other investment in real estate in excess of a percentage of the institution's deposits and other similar liabilities to be determined by the Agency, or allow the aggregate value of accrued loans for such purposes to exceed such limit.

(c) Grant loans upon the security of its own shares of capital stock.

(d) Allow the aggregate value of accrued unsecured loans to exceed the following limits, or grant unsecured loans in excess of such limits:

(1) The maximum to be set by the general meeting for any member of the board of directors, whether such loans are granted to the directors jointly or individually.

(2) Ten per cent of the total of its irreducible capital and the reserve account, for any other firm in which one of its directors has an interest as a director, partner or part-owner or manager of such a firm, or in any other form.

(e) Allow the value of accrued unsecured loans granted to any of its officials or employees to exceed in the aggregate the annual salary of such official or employee, or grant unsecured loans to such an official or employee in excess of such limit.

(f) Engage in trade, except so far as may be temporarily necessary for the conduct of its business or to recover debts due to it.

(g) Purchase, acquire or lease real property, except so far as is necessary for the conduct of its business, taking into consideration future needs, and for housing its officials and employees, provided that:

(1) As regards real property acquired or leased by the banking firm before the coming into force of this Law and for a purpose not included in those mentioned above, the firm shall be granted a grace period of three years to conform to the provisions of this paragraph.

(2) A banking firm may accept real or other property or assets as a security for its loans and, in case of non-payment, the banking firm may acquire such assets provided that it disposes of them within the period to be fixed by the Agency. Every banking firm which may have, prior to the coming into force of the provisions of this Law, carried out any operations that are inconsistent with the provisions of this Article, must report such operations to the Agency and liquidate all such operations within the period to be fixed by the Agency.

Bahrain Monetary Agency format for
annual audited accounts of commercial banks and OBUs

Bal

Ass

Du
Du
Tra
Inv
Loa
Oth

To

Profit and loss account

	Current year (BD/US$)	Prior year (BD/US$)
Interest income	xxx	xxx
Interest expense	xxx	xxx
Net interest income	xxx	xxx
F.X. trading profit/loss	xxx	xxx
Commissions	xxx	xxx
Fees	xxx	xxx
Other income	xxx	xxx
Total income	xxx	xxx
Provision for bad and doubtful debts	xxx	xxx
Total income after provisions	xxx	xxx
Staff costs including housing	xxx	xxx
Premises and equipment costs	xxx	xxx
Head office charges – where applicable	xxx	xxx
Other costs	xxx	xxx
Total operating costs	xxx	xxx
Operating profit	xxx	xxx
Other items incl. – share of profits of associated companies (where applicable)	xxx	xxx
– interest on loan capital (where applicable)	xxx	xxx
Net profit for the year	xxx	xxx

Bahrain Monetary Agency format for
balance sheet of commercial banks which are branches of foreign banks

Assets	Current year (BD)	Prior year (BD)	Liabilities	Current year (BD)	Prior year (BD)
Cash and balance with BMA	xxx	xxx	Capital and reserves	xxx	xxx
Deposits with other offices	xxx	xxx	Due to other offices of bank	xxx	xxx
Deposits with other banks	xxx	xxx	Due to other banks	xxx	xxx
Trading securities	xxx	xxx	Other deposits (non-banks)	xxx	xxx
Investment securities	xxx	xxx	Other liabilities	xxx	xxx
Loans, advances, discounts	xxx	xxx			
Fixed assets	xxx	xxx			
Other assets	xxx	xxx			
Total assets	xxx	xxx	Total liabilities	xxx	xxx

Contra accounts

	Current year (BD)	Prior year (BD)
Letters of credit	xxx	xxx
Guarantees and indemnities	xxx	xxx
Acceptances	xxx	xxx
Total contra accounts	xxx	xxx

The accounts should cover any other contingent liabilities not already reported in the contra accounts including:

Irrevocable undrawn loan commitments.

Forward and unmatured exchange transactions.

Irrevocable commitments to buy or issue CDs, FRNs.

Bullion, commodity, financial futures or other dealing commitments.

Liability on endorsements.

APPENDIX V

Bahrain Monetary Agency format for reserve ratios work sheet

Name of bank

Balance sheet as at............

		BD	F.C.	Total
1	Reported liabilities (excluding contra)			
2	Allowable items			
(a)	5% of capital			
(b)	Inter-bank			
(c)	Residents F.C. deposits			
(d)	Certificates of deposit			
3	Balance			
4	Reserve			
5	Less Alba Financing (where applicable)			
6	Less Government Bonds (where applicable)			
7	Less Banoco Financing (where applicable)			
9	MINIMUM CASH BALANCE FOR			

STATE OF KUWAIT

1 GENERAL INFORMATION

1.1 Organisations covered by banking regulations

The activities of banks in Kuwait are subject to regulation by the Central Bank, which was established by Law No. 32 of 1968. This law was substantially amended and updated by Law No. 130 of 1977. Central Bank supervision applies to banks (defined in article 54) and also to specialist banks (article 76) although possibly to a reduced extent.

The organisation of banking business is covered in articles 54 to 85 of the law. Articles 72 and 73 give the Central Bank power to issue regulations concerning liquidity, maximum rates of interest, maximum lending to one person, etc., all of which have been the subject of various instructions and regulations issued since 1968. The rights of the Central Bank to carry out inspections of banks and other institutions subject to its supervision are covered by article 78.

Accounts and financial statements are dealt with in articles 81 to 84 from which relevant extracts are as follows:
(a) The financial year end of banks shall be 31 December.
(b) The balance sheets and profit and loss accounts of the banks shall be submitted to the Central Bank by 31 March following.
(c) Banks must submit to the Central Bank such other information and statistical data as it requests.

The accounts submitted to the Central Bank are in a specified form which differs considerably from the published accounts. The information thus submitted by each bank remains confidential, although some of it may be published in consolidated statistics.

1.2 Summary of major types of bank

The number of banks operating in Kuwait is relatively small and in 1984 consisted of seven commercial banks and four specialist banks.

The contents of this chapter relate primarily to the seven commercial banks, all of which are of substantial size and were included in the world 'Top 500' list published by *Euromoney* in June 1984.

1.3 Laws and regulations governing banks

With the exception of the Kuwait branch of the Bank of Bahrain and Kuwait, the commercial banks are all share companies formed under the Law of Commercial Companies (No. 15 of 1960) and are therefore subject to the provisions of that law.

1.4 Ability of foreign banks to operate through branches and subsidiaries

Article 68 of Law 15 requires the ownership of banks to be 100% Kuwaiti and foreign banks cannot therefore operate either through branches or subsidiary companies (Bank of Bahrain and Kuwait was a special case in this respect).

The only general exception to this rule is that various foreign banking institutions own minority shareholdings in certain financial companies which are not recognised as banks by the Central Bank; the activities of these companies are normally more of the nature of merchant (rather than commercial) banking.

2 ACCOUNTING

2.1 Laws and regulations governing accounts

Share companies are required by Law 15 to lay audited accounts before their shareholders in a general meeting at least once each year. There is no mandatory accounting date for companies generally, but, as mentioned above, the Central Bank requires banks to produce accounts at 31 December.

Law 15 does not contain any specific requirements relating to the content of the published accounts of banks.

2.2 Audit requirements

Auditors of share companies including banks must be registered with the Ministry of Commerce; in terms of Kuwait law the practice of professional accounting is considered to be personal and auditors' reports are therefore signed in the names of individuals. Under article 164 of Law 15 the auditor of a share company is required (*inter alia*) to report whether its accounts give a true and fair view.

3 FORMAT, STYLE AND CONTENTS OF ACCOUNTS

In the absence of specific legal requirements the commercial banks have considerable discretion as to the form and content of their published accounts. In these circumstances it is not surprising that there are variations between the format of accounts of individual banks, but the pro forma examples set out in Appendix I give an idea of the trend generally followed.

3.1 Inner (hidden) reserves

The maintenance of inner reserves is still accepted banking practice in Kuwait and the accounts of the majority of banks include a note drawing attention to the existence of such reserves and to the fact that they are included under the heading of deposits and other accounts. The amounts of the reserve balances and of actual transfers to or from profit and loss account are not disclosed.

4 ACCOUNTING POLICIES

4.1 Particular accounting policies

A review of the financial statements of the Kuwait commercial banks shows the following accounting policies and practices.

4.1.1 Foreign exchange

Although the treatment of forward contracts is not clearly specified in all cases, the majority of Kuwait banks appear to follow standard practice in this and other respects, that is to say, the contracts are translated at the appropriate closing rates on the balance sheet date and the appropriate profits and losses are included in the year's results.

4.1.2 Specific and general provisions for bad and doubtful debts

The accounts of most (but not all) banks include a note setting out policy in this respect but no figures are given. It appears probable that both specific and general provisions are maintained.

A note to the accounts of the majority of banks reports that the provisions are not netted off but are included under the heading of deposits and other accounts.

4.1.3 Premiums and discounts on investments

Although few notes on this subject are included, and there may well be some variations in practice, it would appear that the majority of banks treat these items in a conventional manner, i.e. the investment is carried at cost and the premium or discount is amortised on a straight line basis over the life of the investment.

4.1.4 Offsets

There is no legal requirement for set-off and it would seem unlikely that it occurs other than in cases involving special circumstances and large amounts.

4.1.5 Goodwill

This is not generally of relevance since the banks seldom acquire other banks or entities already in existence; it is more customary to participate in the formation of new entities.

4.1.6 Consolidation

Consolidated accounts have not yet been prepared by the banks due to the absence of any legal requirement and the immateriality of amounts so far invested in subsidiaries.

4.1.7 Revaluations of assets

None.

4.1.8 Instalment finance and leasing

None.

4.1.9 Dealing and investment securities

This delineation is not observed by the majority of Kuwait banks, distinction being made between quoted and unquoted securities instead.

4.1.10 Pensions

Provision is generally made for amounts payable under the Kuwait Labour Law on the basis of employees' accumulated periods of service.

4.1.11 Fixed assets/depreciation

Accounting policies vary between banks and are generally disclosed by note. Certain banks write off all fixed assets in the year of acquisition.

5 AMOUNTS REQUIRED TO BE MAINTAINED BY LAW OR OTHERWISE

Banks, in common with other share companies, are required by Law 15 of 1960 to transfer 10% of profit to statutory reserve. Local practice is to include under this balance sheet heading share premium account balances (which may be very substantial) but to disclose their amount separately.

6 KEY RATIOS

There are no formal ratio requirements nor have any guidelines been published, but these matters are kept under review by the Central Bank.

7 ACCOUNTING RETURNS OTHER THAN ACCOUNTS

No returns are required other than those submitted to the Central Bank and the published accounts sent to shareholders.

8 TAXATION

The profits of Kuwait banks arising within the State of Kuwait are not subject to income tax.

9 INTERPRETATION OF ACCOUNTS

In endeavouring to analyse the accounts of Kuwait banks difficulties may well be encountered due to:

(a) the relative lack of detailed supporting figures and information;

(b) the inner reserve practices outlined above.

APPENDIX

Kuwait commercial banks: typical balance sheet

Assets		**Liabilities**	
Cash and balances with banks	xxx	Demand, time deposits and other accounts including contingencies	xxx
Money at call and short notice	xxx		
Negotiable certificates of deposit	xxx	Proposed dividend	xxx
Quoted investments	xxx		
Deposits with banks	xxx	Total liabilities	xxx
Loans and discounts	xxx		
Unquoted investments	xxx	Shareholders' equity	
Land, premises and equipment	xxx	Capital	
Other assets	xxx	Reserves − Statutory	xxx
		− General	xxx
Total assets	xxx	− Undistributed profits	xxx
Liability of customers for letters of credit, acceptances and guarantees	xxx	Total shareholders' equity	xxx
		Total liabilities and shareholders' equity	xxx
		Letters of credit, acceptances and guarantees on behalf of customers	xxx
	xxx		xxx

Kuwait commercial banks: typical profit and loss account

Undistributed profit brought forward	xxx
Profit after charging expenses and writing down assets	xxx
	xxx
Proposed appropriations:	
Statutory reserve	xxx
General reserve	xxx
Proposed dividend	xxx
	xxx
Undistributed profit carried forward	xxx

Note: No details of income and expenditure are disclosed

SAUDI ARABIA

1 GENERAL INFORMATION

Saudi Arabia is a kingdom governed by the King and his appointed Council of Ministers. Laws are enacted either directly by Royal Decree, or by Council of Ministers' Resolutions which have received Royal Assent. Royal Decrees and Council of Ministers' Resolutions may then be codified to form laws. For example article 19 of the Council of Ministers Resolution given Royal Assent on 22.10.1317 (10 May 1958) and article 179 of the Resolution given Royal Assent on 5.2.1386 (11 February 1966) form the basis for the group of pronouncements now embodied in the Banking Control Law. The Banking Control Law was approved by Royal Decree on 11 June 1966.

In the early stages of banking in Saudi Arabia the industry was served by local banks and moneychangers, and branches and representative offices of foreign banks. Banking activity was limited due to the lack of demand and the lack of a significant amount of currency in circulation.

Although two local banks, National Commercial Bank and Riyadh Bank, were established in 1938 and 1957 respectively, little significant banking development took place until the 1970s when the oil price increases and the construction boom provided spectacular opportunities.

Overall control of the banking environment rests with the Saudi Arabian Monetary Agency (SAMA) which is the government's banker. SAMA was given its current form by Royal Decree 23 of 23.5.1377 (15 December 1957) which took account of Decrees 30 and 7 of 25.7. and 17.9.1374 respectively, and Council of Ministers Resolution 103 of 20.5.1377. Article 1 of Decree 23 states the objectives of SAMA as (a) issue and strengthen the Saudi currency and to stabilise its internal and external value; (b) to deal with the banking affairs of the government; (c) to regulate commercial banks and exchange dealers.

SAMA's main instrument of control has traditionally been policy directives and it has not in the past intervened directly in the local currency market by issuing its own paper, but it has been able to influence local banks by virtue of the size and attractiveness of its deposit business. Recently, however, SAMA has introduced a new instrument by offering to banks the opportunity to place funds in Bankers Security Deposit Accounts which are fixed interest short-term borrowings denominated in Saudi riyals. These accounts are similar in concept to treasury bills but involve book entries, not the issue of paper, and are not marketable. Control is therefore now exercised both by influence and direct intervention in the money market. Saudi-isation of foreign based banking operations also transferred control of Saudi banking operations to institutions within the Kingdom.

The Kingdom also set up by Royal Decree semi-government organisations governed by their own charters to provide the finance needed for development. The Saudi Industrial Development Fund, the Real Estate Development Fund and the Saudi Arabian Agricultural Bank among others provide low-cost long-term finance to aid in the development of the Saudi infrastructure generally and the development of specific projects considered to be in the national interest. Specialised banks were also established to promote medium-term investment, e.g. the Saudi Investment Banking Corporation.

In the early stages, while the Saudi banking environment was less able to cater for the demand for corporate financing, 'suitcase bankers' operating mainly out of Bahrain filled the gaps. In 1977, however, foreign syndications denominated in Saudi Riyals were limited at SAMA's request and more recently, in January 1983, SAMA published a circular specifying that prior permission is required before offshore banks may participate in Saudi riyal syndications.

A significant part has also been played by moneychangers who, although principally dealers in foreign exchange, also accepted deposits, advanced credit and conducted other commercial banking operations. SAMA has informed moneychangers that these banking activities will no longer be permitted and gave a period of grace for their discontinuance. In July 1983 a significant moneychanger, the Al Rajhi Company for Exchange and Commerce, was given permission by Royal Decree to form a joint stock bank.

1.1 Organisations covered by banking regulations
1.2 Summary of major types of bank

The principal banking regulations in force are the provisions of the Banking Control Law and directives, circulars or general rules issued from time to time by SAMA under article 16 of the Law. The Banking Control Law refers to banks as 'any natural or juristic person practising any banking business in the Kingdom'. In order to carry out banking business it is necessary to be licensed in accordance with the law. Thus the principal banking regulations cover all banks licensed to operate. This would exclude in theory licensed moneychangers since article 2b of the Law allows moneychangers to practise exchange of currency but prohibits all other banking business. In practice, moneychangers have traditionally carried out other banking practices outside the Banking Control Law and outside the control of

SAMA. Also excluded would be the government agency form of financial institution, for example the Saudi Industrial Development Fund, since they were established by Royal Decree to be governed by their own charters.

When the Banking Control Law was published in 1966, two indigenous banks (the National Commercial Bank and Riyadh Bank) were in existence, as were branches of a number of foreign banks. After publication of the Banking Control Law it was envisaged that no further banking licences would be issued except to Saudi joint stock companies (article 3).

It was also envisaged that existing branches of foreign banks would form Saudi joint stock companies, by issue of shares to the Saudi public and by retention of a minority share of usually around 40% for themselves. With the formation of the United Saudi Commercial Bank, the last of the Saudi branches of foreign banks have, along with Saudi International Bank and the Saudi public, formed a joint stock company.

In summary, therefore, the organisations covered by banking regulations are the commercial banks, being two indigenous banks and nine Saudi joint stock companies with foreign bank participation. Specialised development banks are governed by their own charters. Money-changers are prohibited from carrying out banking business except currency exchange. SAMA has reminded moneychangers of this prohibition and introduced a minimum capital base and the need to file accounts with SAMA. Thus moneychangers will fall increasingly within the control of SAMA either by observance of the prohibition or by formation of joint stock banks.

One anomaly exists in that a number of foreign commercial banks have retained liaison offices in the Kingdom. In general these liaison offices, while existing with the full knowledge of SAMA, do not fall within the traditional banking regulations and do not carry on commercial banking business in the Kingdom.

These liaison offices in general represent nations trading with Saudi Arabia who do not have a share in a Saudi joint stock bank.

1.3 Supervisory authorities

1.4 Status of supervisory authorities

Supervision of banking activities covered by the Banking Control Law is carried out by SAMA which in turn is responsible to the Minister of Finance and National Economy.

SAMA administers the provisions of the Banking Control Law by monitoring monthly statements of financial position which banks are required to submit, and by carrying out periodic inspections. SAMA maintains close contact with the management of banks operating within the Kingdom and will inform bankers of SAMA's view on fiscal policy and expect compliance without the need to resort to direct intervention. Nevertheless, the Banking Control Law gives the Agency broad regulatory as well as supervisory powers which include: appointing advisers to a bank; ordering the supervision or removal of directors or officers; limiting or suspending the granting of credits or acceptance of

deposits and requiring a bank to effect whatever remedial action the Agency considers necessary. The Banking Control Law provides for the regulation of banks by stipulating cash margin requirements, maximum deposit levels, maximum credit limits and statutory deposit levels. The Agency has the responsibility for enforcing observance of the limits and also for varying the limits should it see fit. The Agency has the status of a government department and its pronouncements can be given the force of law if need be through the Minister of Finance and National Economy and the Council of Ministers.

1.5 Laws and regulations governing banks

1.6 Application of general company law to banks

1.7 Sources of laws and regulations

The Law covering banks is the Banking Control Law of 1966.

The Law is supplemented by SAMA directives which are circulated to banks from time to time. Since in practice the majority of banks in the Kingdom are joint stock companies, the banks are subject also to the provisions of the commercial laws of Saudi Arabia that are pertinent to joint stock companies.

The Law provides definitions of banks and banking business and includes under banking business the following: receive money on current or fixed deposit accounts; open current accounts; open letters of credit; issue letters of guarantee; pay and collect cheques, orders or payment orders and similar other papers of value; discounting of bills, promissory notes and other commercial paper; foreign exchange business; other banking business.

The Law also makes specific reference to limits and proscriptions on certain types of business. The following activities for example are forbidden:

(a) Engaging in the wholesale or retail trade including import and export.

(b) Purchasing without SAMA's approval stocks and shares of any bank conducting business in the Kingdom.

(c) Ownership of stock in any other joint stock company in excess of 10% of that company's paid-up capital and the value of which exceeds 20% of the banks paid-up capital and reserves.

(d) Ownership or lease of property except as is necessary for conducting banking business and housing employees. (Exception is made in the case of acquisition in satisfaction of debts due to the banks.)

Banks are also prohibited from extending credit facilities on the security of their own shares, or granting any credit facilities without security to directors or auditors, or any non-joint stock company in which a director or auditor has an interest.

The Law limits the risk to a bank from the failure of a single obligor by limiting the amount of credit facilities or guarantees available to a single natural or juristic person to 25% of a bank's paid-up capital and reserves. Transactions with banks, however, are not included in the above limitation.

Provisions of the Companies Law affecting banks which are joint stock companies do not significantly extend the provisions of the Banking Control Law. For example, the Companies Law extends the Banking Law's financial statement reporting requirements to publication in a national newspaper. The Companies Law provides for a minimum capital for joint stock companies of SR10,000,000. Joint stock companies are required to file financial statements with the Companies Department of the Ministry of Commerce within six and a half months of their year end.

1.8 Ability of foreign banks to operate through branches and subsidiaries

1.9 Level of supervisory control for branches and subsidiaries of foreign banks

Article 3 of the Banking Control Law provides that banking operations in Saudi Arabia are subject to the granting of a licence by SAMA and the Ministry of Finance and National Economy.

The licence for a national bank shall stipulate that it shall be a Saudi joint stock company. Should a bank wish to set up a branch, the grant of a licence shall be subject to such conditions as the Council of Ministers may stipulate upon the suggestion of the Ministry of Finance.

In practice it is no longer the intention of SAMA and the Ministry of Finance to grant licences for branch operations.

1.10 Methods of incorporation

Apart from one partnership, licensed banks in Saudi Arabia are Saudi joint stock companies. There is therefore, in practice, only one method of incorporation. Application is made to SAMA and the Minister of Finance and National Economy who pass on their recommendations to the Council of Ministers. The licence may be granted by Royal Assent to a Resolution of the Council of Ministers or by Royal Decree. A joint stock bank may then be formed and registered. The minimum share capital allowed is SR10,000,000.

1.11 Areas within the country subject to special laws

The banking regulations referred to in previous paragraphs apply equally throughout the Kingdom.

2 ACCOUNTING

2.1 Laws and regulations governing accounts

2.2 Application of general company law

2.3 Roles of legislature and supervisory authority

2.4 Extent to which requirements as to returns and accounts are prescribed by laws and regulations

The Banking Control Law, Companies Law and SAMA all provide for certain accounting requirements. In addition, SAMA may at any time require[1] a bank to provide any information that it deems necessary for ensuring the realisation of the purposes of the law. Thus the basic requirements of the Banking Control Law and the Companies Law can be expanded at any time by SAMA directives.

2.5 Obligations to furnish accounts

2.5.1 Accounting periods and times of furnishing

2.5.2 Form of accounts to be furnished

2.5.3 Mandatory accounting dates

In common with other joint stock companies, banks are required under company law to publish their balance sheet, profit and loss account and audit report in a national newspaper and they must file a copy of their accounts with the Ministry of Commerce within six and a half months of their year end.

Any accounting year end (either Gregorian or Hejira) may be selected, although for fiscal purposes it is necessary to seek permission for year end dates other than 31 December. Financial statements should be provided annually except for the first accounting period which may be shorter or longer than one year, depending on the provisions of the Articles of Association and the appropriate permission of the fiscal authorities.

The financial statements, audit report and annual report of the bank's management must be approved in general meeting and copies sent to SAMA within six months of its year end.[2]

In addition, a bank must furnish SAMA within six months of its year end a copy of its balance sheet and profit and loss account prepared in the prescribed format and covered by a report from its auditors.[3]

Also, by the end of each month a bank shall furnish SAMA with a consolidated statement of its financial position relating to the previous month, again in the form prescribed by SAMA.

The latter requirement allows SAMA to monitor on a regular basis the key ratios prescribed by law or its own directives and it therefore plays a major part in SAMA's regulation of banking operations.

2.6 Requirements as to accounts (a) prior to incorporation (b) prior to commencement of trading and (c) in order to continue trading

The laws make no mention of these matters with the exception that failure to provide financial statements and other information constitutes a breach of the Banking Control Law. SAMA is empowered,[4] among other things, to recommend suspension of a bank's licence if a bank persistently fails to comply with the provisions of the Law.

2.7 Audit requirements

The Banking Control Law requires[5] that every bank shall appoint annually two joint auditors from the approved list of auditors.

2.8 Acceptability to fiscal authorities of accounts submitted to supervisory authority

The accounts normally submitted to the fiscal authorities are the published financial statements which may differ

---

[1] BCL art. 17
[2] BCL art. 14 and 15
[3] BCL art. 15
[4] BCL art. 22
[5] BCL art. 14

in format from those submitted to SAMA. The SAMA returns would contain information allowing specific legal ratios to be calculated which a bank may not wish to be known to the world at large and which are of no particular interest to the fiscal authorities. The fiscal authorities, however, require considerable additional detail to be submitted along with the published financial statements. For example, withholding tax is levied on certain payments to organisations resident outside Saudi Arabia and therefore detailed analysis of the profit and loss account is required to establish this and a number of other matters.

2.9 Submission of accounts to any authority other than by requirement of law

None.

2.10 Application of laws and regulations to branches and subsidiaries

As mentioned above, branch and subsidiary operations of foreign banks have ceased.

2.11 Availability of accounts for public inspection

A joint stock company's financial statements are published in a national newspaper, and its accounts are therefore available for public inspection.

3 FORMAT AND STYLE OF ACCOUNTS

3.1 Extent to which format is laid down by statute, supervisory authority, generally accepted accounting practice or otherwise

3.2 Description of format

3.3 Extent to which contents are prescribed by statute, supervisory authority, generally accepted accounting practice or otherwise

3.4 Disclosure of specific items required other than those required by general law

3.5 Exemptions from disclosure allowed in respect of banking items

As discussed in the general chapter on Middle East bank accounting there are no regulations dealing with the above. The supervisory authority requires accounts and monthly returns in a particular format, but this format need not at present be applied to the published financial statements.

However, it is apparent that SAMA may not accept this in the future. The format does not extend to recommendations on disclosure or accounting policies. The year end return to SAMA should be accompanied by a certificate from the bank's management, countersigned by the auditors, representing that the Banking Control Law and related circulars have been complied with, that all necessary reserves for loan losses and doubtful loans have been made and that the profit and loss account presents a fair view of the profit for the year.

An example of the SAMA format is shown in Appendix I.

3.6 Hidden reserves

In general, bank results in Saudi Arabia have shown continual strong growth. Therefore there has usually been no need to maintain hidden reserves in order to smooth out anomalies in annual results. Furthermore, a bank's capacity for growth is limited by the requirement to limit deposit obligations to 15 times capital and reserves. The incentive therefore is to transfer the maximum possible to statutory and general reserves which are shown on the face of the balance sheet.

3.7 Requirements as to consolidated accounts

There are no specific requirements. In practice the Saudi banks have operated solely in Saudi Arabia and do not hold controlling interests in other banks or companies.

4 ACCOUNTING POLICIES

4.1 Responsibility for laying down accounting policies

Accounting policies are not laid down by statute or by the supervisory authority. The accounting policies adopted depend on the outlook of the individual bank and the attitude of its auditors.

4.2 Particular accounting policies

Descriptions of accounting policies and extent of disclosure vary considerably in detail and precision. Examples based on a review of selected published financial statements are as follows:

4.2.1 Foreign exchange

(a) No disclosure.
(b) Foreign currencies have been expressed in Saudi riyals at rates ruling at the balance sheet date.
(c) Assets and liabilities in foreign currencies are translated into Saudi riyals at exchange rates prevailing at the year end. The foreign exchange position including spot and forward contracts is revalued at month end to prevailing market rates. The premium or discount on forward contracts is amortised on a straight line basis over the life of the contract.

4.2.2 Deferred tax

Banks in Saudi Arabia do not make provisions for deferred taxation. Provision is not appropriate since there are no material tax timing differences.

4.2.3 General and specific provisions for loan losses

The accounting policy notes reviewed refer to provisions being based on management judgement without reference to specific criteria.

4.2.4 Netting of provisions for loan losses

The provision is netted off against loans and advances without separate disclosure of the amount.

In some cases the charge for the year is separately disclosed in the profit and loss account, but in other cases appears as a component of other provisions, or is included in service charges.

4.2.5 Investments

Investments are usually stated at cost less provisions to reduce cost to market value. However, the accounts of one bank disclosed that domestic investments had been revalued at the request of SAMA and the resultant surplus reflected in reserves. Investments are not frequently traded.

4.2.6 Offsets

There are no laid down rules governing offsets of debit and credit balances relating to the same customer or group of customers or where a deposit is 'blocked' to secure a loan. Nor is the accounting policy normally disclosed. Practices of banks can therefore differ but, for the most part, Saudi banks will not offset related balances.

4.2.7 Goodwill

None of the Saudi banks recorded goodwill on the acquisition of the predecessor foreign bank branch assets and liabilities.

4.2.8 Consolidation

Consolidation in Saudi Arabia is usually limited to inclusion of all branch results. It would be unusual for a Saudi bank to have foreign subsidiaries. Participation in non-banking entities is recorded as investment and income is generally recorded on receipt of dividend.

4.2.9 Fixed assets

Fixed assets disclosure is fairly standard, although some banks do not disclose movements or the depreciation charge for the year. Fixed assets have in the past been revalued. Although there is no specific instruction regarding accounting treatment, in one case the surplus was taken to reserves. It does not, however, appear to be common policy to revalue assets and the Ministry of Commerce recently issued a declaration that revaluations are no longer acceptable.

4.2.10 Instalment financing and leasing

No banks in Saudi Arabia currently undertake such activities to any material extent.

4.2.11 Pensions

In general, provision is made solely for staff terminal benefits on a contractual basis, or in accordance with Saudi Labour Law.

4.2.12 Depreciation

Banks normally depreciate their fixed assets over estimated lives by the straight line method.

4.2.13 Related party transactions

Where such disclosure exists it is limited to a statement that transactions take place with affiliates. The extent of such transactions is not quantified.

5 WINDOW DRESSING

The general opinion is that there is no large-scale window dressing. SAMA requires that a bank's deposit obligations should not exceed 15 times capital and reserves. In order to maximise profits a bank will normally maintain deposits up to this limit. With specific SAMA permission the limit may be exceeded. A balance sheet is submitted to SAMA monthly. Thus short-term manipulation of liquidity ratios is relatively impractical. Furthermore, up to now banks have not generally encountered difficulties in maintaining key ratios at the expected levels.

6 AMOUNTS REQUIRED TO BE MAINTAINED BY LAW

The Banking Control Law[6] states that a bank's paid-up capital should be not less than SR2,500,000. However, almost all banks would now be joint stock companies with a minimum capital of SR10,000,000.

Each year 25% of a bank's net profits before appropriation should be transferred to a non-distributable reserve until such time as that reserve is equal to the paid-up capital.

7 KEY RATIOS

Key ratios are required to be maintained by law. A bank's obligations in deposits shall not exceed 15 times its total reserves and paid-up capital. Should deposits exceed such an amount, the bank's capital and reserves must be increased, or 50% of the excess deposited with SAMA, within one month of the date of submission of the monthly return showing the increase.[7]

Each bank must maintain a statutory deposit with SAMA amounting to 15% of its deposit liabilities[8] although SAMA has, with the permission of the Ministry of Finance and National Economy, reduced the percentage to 7% for demand deposits and 2% for time deposits. This demonstrates the flexibility within the law given to SAMA to regulate banking activities.

In addition to the statutory deposits each bank must maintain a liquid asset level of 15% of deposit liabilities.[8] Liquid assets are defined as cash, gold, or assets which can be converted into cash within 30 days.

---

[6] BCL art. 3 (2)
[7] BCL art. 6
[8] BCL art. 7

8 ACCOUNTING RETURNS OTHER THAN ACCOUNTS

As stated in Section 2.5 above, in addition to the annual accounts each bank must submit monthly returns to SAMA showing the financial position for the previous month.

9 TAXATION

9.1 General methods of taxation

There are various types of taxation. Saudi nationals pay Zakat (a tax, the proceeds of which are distributed to the needy) at 2.5% of, basically, net worth after deducting fixed assets. This tax is often deducted from dividend at source. Foreigners pay tax at various rates on their taxable profits. The rates are given in Appendix II.

Payments of interest or commissions to foreign banks are subject to withholding tax based on the concept that 15% of the payments are deemed to be profits arising in Saudi Arabia and taxed accordingly. Each foreign bank receiving payments is taxed separately.

Taxable profits are normally based on net profit after adding back various items, the principal ones being contingency or provision related. Provisions for contingencies, terminal benefits and loan losses are not permitted. Loan losses can only be charged against taxable income when they have been actually written off. The Minister of Finance and National Economy has, however, recently made a major concession available specifically to banks. All banks' articles require that gross profit before distributions or appropriations must be shared in the ratio of shareholdings, and each portion would be taxed by the general methods described above. The foreigners' share would be taxed at a higher rate than the Saudi share. After deduction of tax distribution and transfer to reserves could be made, but by this time the amounts attributable to the two sets of shareholders would not allow the proper ratios and intended transfers to reserves to be maintained. Therefore, the Minister directed that tax on the foreigners' share would be applied to the dividend paid and not to gross profit.

The provisions of the Foreign Capital Investment Code provide that non-Saudi shareholders are exempt from income tax for five years from the date of commencement of the bank's activities.

9.2 Accounts as basis for taxation

The financial statements are generally filed with the Department of Zakat and Income Tax as a basis for the tax declaration. However, as mentioned in Section 2.8 above, the tax authorities require much more detailed information. The amount of detail required varies to some extent but is generally considerable. The form of accounts is therefore of little significance compared with the total amount of information eventually required.

9.3 Adjustments permitted or required

Many items quite properly charged against a bank's profits are not tax allowable, or are subject to withholding tax, or, as in the case of depreciation, are allowable only at specified rates. Thus the result as shown by the published accounts is often changed considerably by adjustment to arrive at taxable profit. However, since tax is now to be levied only on dividends paid, these processes may become largely redundant. How the process of maintaining records of taxable profits develops remains to be seen.

9.4 Effect of tax considerations on presentation of accounts

It is not necessary to take into account tax considerations when drawing up the accounts as the tax authorities make their own adjustments to the accounts when compiling the taxation liability.

10 INTERPRETATION OF ACCOUNTS

As mentioned in the Middle East chapter and in the sections on specific areas in the Middle East, the lack of specific rules and regulations on accounting and auditing, and the wide variety of interpretation applied to balance sheet classifications, do not permit meaningful detailed interpretation of accounts. Appendix III shows the various ratios derived from a selection of five banks. The wide variety of ratios and percentages does not necessarily indicate a wide divergence in portfolios or in maintenance of operating ratios.

It may be useful to bear in mind the following when reading Saudi Arabian bank financial statements.

Because of Islamic attitudes to payment and receipt of interest and commission all banks hold, to a greater or smaller extent, free money. The amounts of non-commission bearing deposits are often equal to or greater than amounts of commission bearing deposits. The relationship between commission bearing and non-commission bearing deposits is not disclosed and therefore comparable measures of performance cannot readily be drawn from figures extracted from the published financial statements.

Bank profit and loss accounts seldom provide a detailed statement of the sources of income, combining commission with fees, other income and income from foreign exchange trading.

The growth period in Saudi banking was coupled with an expanding economy where profits were generally high and the value of underlying security given for loans, generally increasing. Unlike other countries, overdraft financing was not noticeably more expensive than other forms of financing and therefore loan portfolios often include a large number of evergreen overdrafts. Loans were made and overdraft facilities granted, based more frequently on reputation than on financial statements or similar financial data. All the above factors combine to make portfolio risk evaluation a more difficult task than in other countries. It should be borne in mind that provisions made in the past for potential loan losses would not be comparable with banks in other countries. Only recently have the risks attached to loan portfolios been recognised and specific loan loss provisions been built up. However, the necessity to expand reserves in order to maintain growth has resulted in considerable sums being set aside in general reserves.

It has been pointed out by SAMA that guarantees often form a large part of the contingencies shown in bank balance sheets in the Kingdom and that, in the current economic climate, this is an increasingly high risk area.

APPENDIX I

Information to be disclosed in accounts submitted to Saudi Arabian Monetary Agency

PROFIT AND LOSS ACCOUNT

A Expenses

1 Employees' salaries and other expenses
2 Board of directors' remuneration
3 Expenses paid for services
4 Cash deposits for covering depreciation, etc.
   (a) Depreciation of real estate, furniture, etc.
   (b) Other deposits
5 Other expenses
   (a) Building rentals
   (b) Others
6 Net income (divided as follows)
   (a) Taxes
   (b) Statutory reserve
   (c) Net profit for fiscal year
   (Note: In case of loss the balance should be shown as the last item of the revenues account)
7 Total expenses including:
   Expenses abroad

B Revenues

8 Income from foreign exchange operations and other services
9 Charges for services
10 Interests and commission on investments
11 Other revenues
12 Total revenue including:
   (a) Capital loss
   (b) Income from abroad

BALANCE SHEET

Assets	Liabilities

Assets

Cash funds

1 Cash in hand
2 Regular deposits with SAMA
3 Other deposits with SAMA

Deposits with banks

1 In the Kingdom
2 Overseas

Investments
(at the market price or cost price whichever is the lower)

1 Shares and securities:
   (a) Firms inside the Kingdom
   (b) Overseas
2 Other investments

Loans and advances . . . etc.
(after setting aside the reserve for bad and doubtful debts)

1 Loans and advances extended to:
   (a) Private sector
   (b) Banks
   (c) Others
2 Bills purchased and discounted

Fixed assets (after depreciation)

1 Bank premises and estate property
2 Office furniture, installations and equipment

Other assets

1 Customer's undertakings against acceptances
2 Other assets
   Contra accounts
   Customer's liabilities for letters of guarantee
   Documentary credits and other engagements

Liabilities

Capital

Authorised capital (of ....shares ....each)
Paid-up capital
(Note: Foreign banks should state the invested capital only)

Reserves

Statutory reserve
Other reserves

Deposits

1 Customer's (call, time and saving) deposits
2 Bank deposits
   (a) In the Kingdom
   (b) Overseas
3 Other deposits (deposits for letters of credit and guarantees accepted and transfers, etc.)

Borrowed funds

1 From banks
   (a) In the Kingdom
   (b) Head office and branches abroad
   (c) Overseas
2 Other sources

Profit and loss

1 Profit posted from last year
2 Net profits for the year (when a loss is sustained the balance shall be shown as a separate item under 'Other assets')

Other liabilities

1 Customer's acceptances
2 Other liabilities

Contra accounts

Engagements on behalf of customer's acceptances, documentary credits, guarantees . . . etc.

APPENDIX II

Saudi Arabian income tax
Rates of taxation/zakat

A   Taxation applicable to non-Saudis

Limited companies and other corporate entities:

On the first	SR100,000	25%
On the next	SR400,000	35%
On the next	SR500,000	40%
On profits exceeding	SR1,000,000	45%

B   Zakat applicable to Saudis (including deemed Saudis*)

Saudi corporation   2½%

Tax must be paid in Saudi Riyals

* For the purposes of Saudi Arabian tax/zakat regulations Kuwaitis, Bahrainis and Qataris are deemed to be Saudis

APPENDIX III

Bank ratios

Bank	A	B	C	D	E
Cash/Deposits	1:14 (7%)	1:13 (8%)	1:14 (7%)	1:4.7 (21%)	1:4.4 (23%)
Loans and advances/Deposits	1:2 (50%)	1:1.6 (63%)	1.1:1 (105%)*	1:2.3 (44%)	1:2 (49%)
Deposits/Capital and reserves	10:1	11:1	12.7:1	8:1	16:1
Loans and advances/Total assets	1:2.3 (43%)	1:1.9 (53%)	1:2.2 (85%)*	1:2.7 (37%)	1:2.6 (38%)
Return on capital	38%	93%	92%	145%	1890%
Return on opening capital and reserves	31%	75%	67%	80%	36%

* Includes placings with banks abroad

UNITED ARAB EMIRATES

1 GENERAL INFORMATION

1.1 Background

The United Arab Emirates was established in 1971 as a federation of seven Emirates at the South Eastern end of the Arabian Gulf. Before that date these Emirates (Abu Dhabi, Ajman, Dubai, Fujairah, Ras Al Khaimah, Sharjah and Umm Al Quwain) were known as the Trucial States; each was responsible for its own internal affairs, although for foreign policy and defence they were protected by defence treaties with the United Kingdom.

At the time of federation, oil had already been discovered in several Emirates, most significantly in Abu Dhabi (although revenues from oil were at that time modest), and several towns, notably Dubai, had established reputations as major trading ports in the Arabian Gulf area. The conditions which led to the subsequent economic development of the UAE were thus already present in 1971. However, formal legislation and central supervision over economic activity were lacking. In 1971 the UAE did not have its own currency. The need for a local currency had led to the development and general acceptance of two unofficial currencies: the Indian (Gulf) rupee and the Qatar Dubai riyal. Most bank accounts were denominated and financial transactions carried out in these currencies although other foreign currencies and gold and silver coins were also used as mediums of exchange.

The formation of a central banking authority was a major priority for the newly formed UAE. The Currency Board was set up in 1973 to issue currency notes and coins in the Emirates and to license banks and other financial institutions. By naming the central banking authority the 'Currency Board' the law indicated that the initial emphasis lay in creating and controlling the newly established UAE currency (the UAE dirham) and that the supervision of the banking sector was, at that time, a secondary objective.

Having successfully achieved its main task, the role of the central banking authority was changed in 1980, and greater emphasis was placed on the supervision of the activities of financial institutions. The authority was renamed the 'Central Bank of the United Arab Emirates'.

1.2 Summary of major types of bank

The Central Bank recognises five categories within the banking and financial sector: (a) commercial banks; (b) investment banks; (c) financial institutions; (d) financial and monetary intermediaries; (e) representative offices.

Commercial banks are the most important banks in the UAE. They are clearing banks taking deposits from the general public, in most cases from a chain of branches in various locations within the country. There are over 50 licensed commercial banks in the UAE of which about half are locally owned; the remainder are branches of foreign banks. Together they operate over 300 bank branches.

Investment banks are characterised as 'merchant, investment, development, medium-term, or long-term banks which do not accept deposits for less than two years'.

Financial institutions are defined as 'institutions whose principal functions are to extend credit, to carry out financial transactions, to take part in the financing of existing or planned projects, to invest in movable properties, and such other functions as may be specified by the Central Bank'.

Financial or monetary intermediaries are 'any physical or juridical person, other than financial institutions who:
(a) Practise the profession of foreign exchange dealer based on purchase and sale of currencies, currency notes, coins of all kinds and travellers' cheques.
(b) Act as stockbroker or agent and sell and purchase domestic as well as foreign stocks and bonds, in a local capacity, or as agent of foreign institutions.'

Representative offices are 'offices representing foreign banks and financial institutions in the United Arab Emirates'.

The following organisations are specifically excluded from supervisory control by the Central Bank:
(a) Public credit institutions set up by law, other than commercial banks.
(b) Government investment institutions and agencies.
(c) Governmental development funds.
(d) Private savings and pension funds.
(e) Insurance and reinsurance companies and agencies.

1.3 The Central Bank

The Central Bank is the only supervisory authority over the banking sector in the UAE. Its initial capital was established at Dh300 million all of which is owned by the UAE government. The seven board members of the Central Bank are appointed for a four year term by Union decree; appointees may not normally be directors of any UAE commercial bank. The specific duties of the Central Bank are to:
(a) Be the sole issuer of currency in the UAE.
(b) Endeavour to support the currency, maintain its stability and ensure its free convertibility into foreign currencies.
(c) Direct credit policy so as to help achieve a steady growth of the UAE economy.

317

(d) Organise and promote banking and supervise the effectiveness of the banking system.

(e) Act as the bank of the government.

(f) Advise the government on financial and monetary matters.

(g) Maintain the government's reserve of gold and foreign currency.

(h) Act as the bank for banks operating in the UAE.

(i) Act as the representative of the UAE in all dealings with the International Monetary Fund, the International Bank for Reconstruction and Development and other such international and Arab organisations.

Apart from its capital, the Central Bank holds all government dirham funds on interest-free deposits and holds a permanent government foreign currency deposit, also interest free, of no less than the equivalent of US$2,000 million. This structure ensures that the Central Bank is very soundly based.

Included in the powers of the Central Bank is the general power to issue to banks instructions and recommendations as appropriate, so as to ensure that its monetary or credit policies are achieved, and take any measures necessary to ensure the sound functioning of the banking system.

The Central Bank therefore can make wide-ranging directives to banks, collectively or individually. These directives are issued in the form of circulars of which approximately 50 are produced each year. Many of the circulars deal with routine matters such as instructions for banks to close on national holidays but others are more important. Circulars apply equally to local banks and branches of foreign banks.

1.4 The UAE Bankers' Association

The local banking industry established the UAE Bankers' Association in 1974. It meets periodically to discuss matters of general interest and to agree on areas where it is considered that collective representation should be made to the Central Bank. Although a useful forum for discussion, the association has few powers and does not seek to control the activities of its members.

1.5 Laws and regulations: general

The laws and regulations governing the activities of the banking industry in the UAE consists of Union Law 10 of 1980 together with circulars issued by the Central Bank and its predecessor, the Currency Board. The law and the circulars are all written in Arabic and, although an English translation is usually provided, the Arabic version takes precedence. Accordingly, it is important that where there is any ambiguity in the English wording reference is made to the Arabic original.

A law on trading companies (Law 8 of 1984) was enacted in March 1984. We believe that this law will not apply to banks since its provisions are generally less onerous than those already applying to banks.

Any organisation falling within the definitions in Section 1.2 above is required to obtain a licence from the Central Bank before it can carry out any trade in the UAE. In the case of a commercial bank the requirements before a licence will be issued are laid down in some detail. For other organisations there is greater discretion vested in the Central Bank. The requirements for each category of organisation are dealt with in the following paragraphs, except that the subject of accounting is covered below in a separate section.

1.6 Laws and regulations: commercial banks

The Central Bank is empowered to establish the requirements to be met and the procedures to be followed in an application for a licence to trade as a commercial bank, whether as a local company or as a branch of a foreign bank. Because these requirements and procedures are not all laid down in the legislation, anyone considering setting up a commercial bank would need to have discussions with the Central Bank at a very early stage. When a licence is granted, the decision is published in the Official Gazette and an entry made in the Register of Banks maintained by the Central Bank.

All institutions engaged in commercial banking in the UAE, apart from branches of foreign banks, must be joint stock limited liability companies established by law or decree (article 79). They must have a paid-up capital of no less than Dh40 million (article 80). This capital requirement came into force on 30 June 1982 and led to a restructuring of capital by many of the smaller UAE banks during the months leading up to that date. In the case of local branches of foreign banks, the Central Bank must be satisfied that funds of at least Dh40 million are retained for the UAE operations. At least 10% of the annual net profits must be allocated to a special reserve until the balance of the special reserve equals 50% of the capital for local companies or 100% for branches of foreign banks.[1] The Articles and Memorandum of Association of a commercial bank must comply with these requirements and any changes to the articles or memorandum must be approved by the Central Bank before they become effective.

For the purposes of supervision the Central Bank regards all UAE branches of a commercial bank as part of a single entity and only one licence is required to enable a multi-branch commercial bank to trade. However, Central Bank consent is required for the opening, closing or relocation of any branch.

A commercial bank may not cease operations or merge with another bank without the prior authorisation of the Central Bank,[2] who will only give such authority if they are satisfied that the arrangements will not prevent the bank from meeting its obligations to customers and other creditors.

A commercial bank may have its licence withdrawn by the Central Bank and its name deleted from the Register of Banks for any of the following reasons,[3] in which case the bank must also be liquidated:

(a) On the request of the bank concerned.

(b) If it has not commenced operations within one year of registration.

(c) If it has ceased trading for more than one year.

(d) If it is declared bankrupt.

(e) If it merges with another bank.

(f) If its liquidity or solvency are endangered.

---

[1] Union Law 10 of 1980 art. 81   [3] Union Law 10 of 1980 art. 88
[2] Union Law 10 of 1980 art. 87

(g) If it has seriously contravened Union Law 10 of 1980 or the various regulations and instructions issued by the Central Ban k under that law.

Commercial banks may not engage in non-banking operations.[4] In particular a commercial bank shall not:

(a) Carry on commercial or industrial activities or acquire or trade in goods.

(b) Acquire immovable property except for housing its business or staff.

(c) Hold or deal in its own shares.

(d) Purchase shares or bonds issued by commercial companies (excluding bonds guaranteed by the government or public sector institutions) to the extent of more than 25% of its own funds.

A bank may break these rules if it obtains goods, property or shares in settlement of a debt, in which circumstances time limits are laid down before which the assets must be sold.

Restrictions on banking operations[5] include the prohibition of loans to directors and staff without Central Bank consent, a restriction whereby advances for the construction of buildings may not exceed 20% of total deposits (except for banks which specialise in granting estate loans and are authorised to do so by the Central Bank) and a prohibition on taking its own shares as security for customer credit facilities. Banks can issue their own travellers' cheques only with Central Bank consent. There are restrictions on persons who can act as directors or managers of a commercial bank.

The Central Bank has powers[6] to make any instructions to commercial banks including prudential ratio requirements, the maximum proportion of a bank's funds which can be lent to one customer, and levels of interest and commission payable on deposits or chargeable on loans.

In addition to the minimum share capital of Dh40 million laid down by law, banks must now maintain capital and reserves of at least one fifteenth of total assets. Capital and reserves includes inner reserves but excludes provisions or other balances which are not free reserves. However, subordinated loans may be regarded as part of capital and reserves provided that:

(a) They have a minimum original term of five years.

(b) They do not exceed 25% of the other components of 'capital and reserves'.

(c) A copy of the loan agreement is filed with the Central Bank.

(d) An amortisation factor is applied to loans with less than five years to maturity.

Total assets should be calculated net of all provisions against assets and should exclude contra accounts and property loans which have been refinanced through the Real Estate Committee.

1.7 Laws and regulations: investment banks

Investment banks are not permitted to accept customer deposits having a term of less than two years; deposits may be taken from their main offices, local or foreign banks or financial markets. The rules for the licensing and operating of investment banks are not laid down in law but left to the discretion of the Central Bank. It is likely that many of the rules relating to commercial banks, particularly those for minimum capital and special reserves, would be invoked by the Central Bank as requirements for the obtaining of an investment banking licence.

1.8 Laws and regulations: financial institutions

The definition of a financial institution in Union Law 10 of 1980 (Section 1.2 above) is not precise and appears to embrace various types of investment company as well as banking-related businesses; within a group of companies it is possible that the holding company could be a financial institution if its main function is to advance funds to subsidiaries to enable them to carry on their trades.

Financial institutions may not accept deposits, which implies that they may not borrow funds from the general public. Borrowing is permitted from head offices, local or foreign banks or financial markets. These institutions require a Central Bank licence to operate, which can be revoked for the same reasons as for a commercial bank. Financial institutions are required to follow directives issued by the Central Bank as part of its credit policy or for the sound functioning of the institution concerned.

The Central Bank has issued general rules to be followed by financial institutions wishing to obtain a licence. The major rules may be summarised as follows:

(a) The institution must be a joint stock limited liability company established by law or decree.

(b) The capital must be no less than Dh50 million denominated in shares of Dh100 of which at least 70% must be owned by UAE nationals or institutions owned wholly by UAE nationals.

(c) There are restrictions on the payments of fees, commissions, etc. in connection with new issues of shares.

(d) The objects of the company must be defined in detail and must be confined to credit, lending or financial operations, participation in existing or future projects, investment in movable assets or such other objects as may be agreed with the Central Bank.

(e) At least two thirds of the board of directors, including the Chairman, shall be UAE nationals.

(f) The Articles of Association must require that the company shall comply with all Central Bank rules and regulations.

1.9 Laws and regulations: financial and monetary intermediaries

The Central Bank is empowered to establish licensing and supervision arrangements and rules for the professional obligations of financial and monetary intermediaries but at the present time no such rules have been issued.

1.10 Laws and regulations: representative offices

The Central Bank is also given powers to issue regulations dealing with representative offices of foreign banks.

---

[4] Union Law 10 of 1980 art. 90
[5] Union Law 10 of 1980 arts 91 and 92
[6] Union Law 10 of 1980 arts 95 and 96

1.11 Ability of foreign banks to operate through branches and subsidiaries

It is extremely unlikely that a foreign bank would currently be permitted to establish a wholly-owned local subsidiary with a licence to trade in the banking sector in the UAE. It could seek to establish a local company with majority UAE shareholders in which it has a minority stake (of 40% or less) but, for any wholly-owned operation, the practical alternatives are a branch or a representative office.

There is a widely held view that there are too many banks in the UAE at the moment and the Central Bank required all foreign banks already operating in the UAE to reduce their UAE branches to eight or less by the end of 1983. The foreign banks have followed this directive. For the same reason the Central Bank has ceased issuing any licences for foreign banks to establish new commercial banking operations for the time being, although licences to set up representative offices continue to be granted on occasions. Any foreign bank wishing to establish a presence in the UAE would need to discuss their proposals with the Central Bank, whose attitude will vary according to the prevailing economic and financial climate as well as the proposals put to them.

1.12 Methods of incorporation

Locally incorporated joint stock banks can be chartered by law or decree. Establishing a company by law is rare; this is normally reserved for government institutions. A joint stock company is usually established by decree of the Ruler of the Emirate in which it is registered. The form of the Memorandum and Articles of Association, the amount of capital and the extent of registration fees would all be subject to agreement by the Ruler's office. Before a decree is granted the names of the prospective shareholders must also be made known, and for a banking company it is likely that the Ruler of the relevant Emirate and/or the Central Bank would require all or most of the shares to be owned by UAE nationals or companies which are themselves wholly owned by UAE nationals.

1.13 Areas of the country subject to special laws

There are no general rules issued by the Central Bank dealing with Islamic banking practice. However, the Central Bank has expressed its willingness to co-operate with the development of Islamic banks and believes that they can function within the framework of the existing rules and regulations.

There are no special rules for offshore banks. Because there are no exchange controls or equivalent restrictions, UAE banks are free to conduct business throughout the world. However, the authorities have not encouraged the establishment of banks solely involved in international business, and with the large offshore banking centre of Bahrain situated less than 300 miles away there is little pressure at this time for widespread introduction of this form of banking in the UAE.

2 ACCOUNTING REQUIREMENTS

2.1 Introduction

Articles 101 to 107 of Union Law 10 of 1980 deal with the subjects of annual financial statements and periodical statistical returns to the Central Bank by commercial banks. These articles are supplemented by a number of Central Bank circulars which prescribe the format of certain accounting information. For local banks the Articles of Association, which are subject to approval by the Ruler of the Emirate in which the bank is registered, may contain additional accounting requirements, although these do not follow any standard form. The rules for banking operations other than commercial banks are not specified in law, but the Central Bank generally requires that the same regulations should be followed where they are applicable.

2.2 Annual financial statements

Financial statements on a Gregorian calendar year basis must be prepared and audited for each commercial bank in the UAE. Accounts covering the operations of all branches in the UAE of each bank, whether local or foreign, must be drawn up on a consolidated basis and must include a balance sheet and profit and loss account. A circular lays down the detailed information that must be contained within the annual financial statements that are required to be submitted to the Central Bank. A format which meets these requirements is given in Appendix I. The submission must be made by 30 April in each year and, for a local bank, after the financial statements have been approved by members in general meeting.

It is important to recognise that this format relates solely to the financial statements that must be submitted to the Central Bank. Local banks can, and almost all do, prepare different financial statements for circulation among shareholders, other banks and third parties. The latter statements tend to contain less information, particularly in areas such as inner reserves and provisions against doubtful loans. These published financial statements are not subject to any laid down disclosure requirements.

2.3 Audit requirements

Financial statements for submission to the Central Bank must be audited. The published financial statements for local banks are also audited because this is invariably required by the Articles of Association. Before 31 May in each year a series of forms must be submitted to the Central Bank in which details of the qualifications and experience of the nominated audit firm and its staff are provided. If a bank does not appoint auditors the Central Bank is empowered to do so on its behalf. The auditor may not be a director, member of staff or regular consultant with the bank to which he is assigned. The auditors' report on the financial statements for submission to the Central Bank must include opinions as to whether:

(a) Proper books of account have been maintained by the bank.

(b) The balance sheet and profit and loss account are in agreement with the books and records of the bank.

(c) The financial statements comply with the accepted practice of financial institutions and on that basis give a true and fair view of the financial position of the bank and the result of its operations.

(d) The auditing team has obtained all information and explanations considered necessary for their audit.

2.4 Confidentiality

Financial statements submitted to the Central Bank, as well as all monthly returns and other data, are treated confidentially and are not available for public inspection. The only financial information published by the Central Bank is statistical data on an aggregate basis.

2.5 Advertising of financial statements in newspapers

Each commercial bank trading in the UAE is required to advertise extracts from its audited financial statements in a local newspaper of wide circulation. The detailed requirements are:

(a) Advertising must be for three consecutive business days within four months of the balance sheet date (i.e. before 30 April).

(b) For a local bank, it is preferable to advertise the consolidated results of operations throughout the world including those of subsidiaries.

(c) Foreign banks may advertise either worldwide consolidated figures (with the consent of the Central Bank) or their local financial statements. In practice, foreign banks usually opt for the former.

(d) Advertised financial statements must include a balance sheet, profit and loss account, material footnotes, the name of the auditors and details of any qualification in the audit opinion.

(e) Additional information may be provided but must not be misleading.

(f) The only disclosure requirement is that the advertised figures must show deposits from customers separately from deposits from banks.

3 FORMAT AND CONTENTS OF PUBLISHED FINANCIAL STATEMENTS AND ACCOUNTING POLICIES

3.1 Introduction

There are no regulations dealing with the format, style and contents of published financial statements or the accounting policies that they have followed therein. The comments made in the general chapter on Middle East bank accounting are substantially applicable to banks in the UAE. However, certain matters can usefully be emphasised.

3.2 Inner reserves

Some UAE banks maintain inner reserves which vary in size from modest to very substantial amounts in relation to the disclosed equity. Similarly the disclosed profit or loss for the year can be affected a little or considerably by the annual transfer to or from inner reserves.

3.3 Loan loss provisions

All UAE banks make provision against bad and doubtful loans based upon the estimated shortfalls on ultimate recoveries. Some banks have general as well as specific provisions. Banks do not normally quantify the amount provided during the year or the extent of the accumulated provision.

3.4 Taxation

There is no taxation payable by local banks in the UAE and, accordingly, tax and deferred tax accounting policies are of no relevance to their financial statements. However, at the time of obtaining approval to establish themselves in the UAE, branches of most foreign banks are contracted to pay a percentage of their profits to the Ruler of those Emirates in which they operate.

4 KEY RATIOS

The Central Bank requires that total assets of commercial banks (including foreign branches) shall not exceed fifteen times their capital and reserves. This requirement is the principal ratio to which UAE banks must adhere. The Central Bank also expects that advances to non-bank customers should not exceed non-bank deposits, although it will allow individual banks to extend their advances in agreed circumstances.

Apart from the above, the Central Bank has not yet made use of its powers under the law to set other ratio limits.

5 ACCOUNTING RETURNS OTHER THAN FINANCIAL STATEMENTS

5.1 Introduction

The Central Bank is empowered to request such information and statistical data as it deems necessary (article 105) and the format and frequency of these returns, which are designed by the Central Bank, will vary from time to time.

5.2 Current requirements for returns made at least monthly

The weekly and monthly returns currently required to be submitted are:

(a) Banking return Form 1: detailed statement of assets and liabilities including an analysis of balances with head office, branches and other banks in the UAE (monthly).

(b) Banking return Form 6: statement by country of balances with head office, branches and other banks abroad (monthly).

(c) Detailed breakdown of assets, liabilities and forward contracts denominated in UAE dirhams and showing net position of the bank in the local currency (weekly).

(d) Balance of payments return I: remittances abroad (excluding payments for imports) and sales of foreign currencies and travellers' cheques (monthly).

(e) Balance of payments return II: remittances received from abroad (excluding receipts for exports) and purchases of foreign currencies and travellers' cheques (monthly).

5.3 Current requirements for quarterly returns

Quarterly returns which are in force at the present time are:

(a) Banking return Form 2: statement of bank credit to residents by customers' economic activity.

(b) Banking return Form 3: ownership of deposits.

(c) Banking return Form 14: interest paid on deposits by residents and charged on loans to residents.

(d) Banking return Form 5: maturity pattern of time deposits.

(e) Banking return Form MBC: movement of bank credit granted to and utilised by residents, categorised by industry.

(f) BSD Form 1: analysis by currency of foreign currency amounts due to and from head office and branches and other banks and of foreign exchange positions, spot and forward.

(g) BSD Form II: details of loans to directors and staff and their business interests, totals of past due loans by industry and movements on loan loss provision.

(h) Banking return Form MA1: maturity analysis of liabilities and claims by sector.

(i) Banking return Form MA2: maturity analysis of contingent accounts (guarantees, letters of credit, etc).

5.4 Current requirements for reporting credit risks

The Central Bank has recently established a risk bureau. Each month every bank submits on Form RB-5 details of all credit risks (including unused facilities and contingent liabilities) for each customer whose exposure exceeds Dh500,000. Any bank is then entitled to enquire of the risk bureau the extent of total notified credit extended to any person or company.

6 CONCLUSION

Almost all of the regulations referred to in this chapter have been introduced or amended during the past three years and it is likely that this rapid change will continue in the future.

The Central Bank is making considerable advances in the extent of its supervision over the banking sector and, in time, this will no doubt be reflected in the form of financial statements of UAE banks as well as in the conduct of their business.

APPENDIX

Financial statements for submission to the Central Bank
Format which complies with Central Bank requirements

UAE Bank Limited

Balance sheet at 31 December 19xx

Liabilities	(Dh000)	(Dh000)	Assets	(Dh000)	(Dh000)
Customers' deposits, of which			Cash and deposits with Central Bank		xxx
Current accounts	xxx		Deposits with other banks, of which		
Savings accounts	xxx		Banks abroad	xxx	
Time deposits	xxx		Banks in the UAE	xxx	xxx
Other deposits	xxx	xxx			
			Investments (Securities)		xxx
Borrowing from branches abroad		xxx	Loans, advances and overdrafts, of which		
Borrowing from other banks, of which			Secured	xxx	
Banks abroad	xxx		Unsecured	xxx	xxx
Banks in the UAE	xxx	xxx	Bills discounted		xxx
Borrowing from Central Bank		xxx	Fixed assets (Note 5)		xxx
Capital account (Note 4)			Other assets		xxx
Authorised, of which	xxx				
Issued and fully paid		xxx	Total assets		xxx
Reserves, of which					
For bad and doubtful debts	xxx		**Contra accounts** (Memorandum)		
Statutory reserve	xxx				
General reserve	xxx		Bank's liabilities against letters of credit opened		xxx
Reserve for contingencies	xxx	xxx			
Retained earnings		xxx	Bank's liabilities against letters of guarantee issued		xxx
Other liabilities		xxx	Bank's liabilities against other acceptances and endorsements		xxx
Inter-branch transactions		xxx			
Total liabilities		xxx	Total assets		xxx

The attached Notes 1 to 5 form part of these financial statements.

The attached Notes 1 to 5 form part of these financial statements.

323

UAE Bank Limited

Profit and loss account
for the year ended 31 December 19xx

Income	(Dh000)	(Dh000)
Interest received, of which		
On deposits with banks in the UAE	xxx	
On deposits with banks abroad	xxx	
Other (of which Dhxxx governmental)	xxx	xxx
Income from securities		xxx
Income from other investments, of which		
Rent	xxx	
Other	xxx	xxx
Commissions and brokerage, of which		
Transfers	xxx	
Documentary credit	xxx	
Other	xxx	xxx
Gains on foreign exchange		xxx
Other income		xxx
Capital	xxx	
Receipt of bad debts	xxx	
Other	xxx	xxx
Total income		**xxx**

Expenditure	(Dh000)	(Dh000)
Interest paid on:		
Customers' deposits (of which Dhxxx governmental)	xxx	
Other banks' deposits	xxx	
Branches' deposits	xxx	
Borrowing from Central Bank	xxx	xxx
Commission paid on:		
Transfers	xxx	
Documentary credits	xxx	
Other	xxx	xxx
Other current expenditure		xxx
Wages and salaries		xxx
Overtime and other extra payments		xxx
Staff training		xxx
Other expenditure on staff		xxx
Premises		xxx
Duties and taxes		xxx
Other administrative expenditure		xxx
Consumption of fixed and durable assets		xxx
Appropriations, of which		
For bad and doubtful debts	xxx	
Proposed dividend	xxx	
Transfer to general reserve	xxx	
Transfer to statutory reserve	xxx	
Transfer to reserve for contingencies	xxx	xxx
Investment expenditure		xxx
Total expenditure		**xxx**
Net adjustment to retained profit		xxx

The attached Notes 1 to 5 form part of these financial statements.

The attached Notes 1 to 5 form part of these financial statements.

UAE Bank Limited

Notes to the financial statements
31 December 19xx

1 Background

The bank was incorporated in the Emirate of .... in 19 .... under a charter granted by H.H. Sheikh ...., Ruler of ....and operates from the following branches:
Head Office:
Branches:
Sub-branches:

2 Format of financial statements

These financial statements have been prepared in the format required by circular 449 issued by the UAE Currency Board under articles 40 and 41 of Union Law No. 2 of 1973, and accordingly provision for bad and doubtful debts has been shown as part of Reserves.

3 Accounting policies

The accounting policies adopted by the bank are set out below and are consistent with those adopted in 1982.

(a) Foreign currencies

Assets and liabilities in foreign currencies have been translated to UAE Dirhams at middle-market rates of exchange current at the end of the year. Gains and losses are taken to profit and loss account.

(b) Investments

Listed investments are stated at the lower of cost and market value. Unlisted investments are stated at the lower of cost and estimated value at the balance sheet date.

(c) The following loans, advances and overdrafts are classified by the bank as secured facilities:

(i)   Guaranteed by prominent businessmen in the UAE without tangible security.
(ii) Where securities are deposited with the bank by way of an equitable mortgage without a formal charge in favour of the bank.
(iii) To the Rulers of the Emirates, their families and projects sponsored by them.
(iv) To government departments.
(v)   To the extent of funds retained by customers in fixed deposits, current and savings accounts.

(d) Depreciation

Freehold land is not depreciated. The cost of other fixed assets is written off by equal instalments over their expected useful lives.

4   Share capital   (Dh000)

Authorised	xxx
	xxx
Issued and fully paid	xxx
	xxx

The directors approved the issue of .... ordinary shares for cash at face value by a resolution dated ....

5   Fixed assets

The estimated useful lives of the assets for the calculation of depreciation are as follows:

Freehold buildings	x years
Leasehold property and improvements	Over period of lease
Office furniture and equipment	x years
Motor vehicles	x years

	Freehold land and buildings (Dh000)	Leasehold property and improvements (Dh000)	Others (Dh000)	Total (Dh000)
Cost or valuation:				
At 31 December 19x1	xxx	xxx	xxx	xxx
Additions during year	xxx	xxx	xxx	xxx
Cost of disposals	xxx	xxx	xxx	xxx
At 31 December 19x2	xxx	xxx	xxx	xxx
Depreciation:				
At 31 December 19x1	xxx	xxx	xxx	xxx
Charge for year	xxx	xxx	xxx	xxx
Relating to disposals	xxx	xxx	xxx	xxx
At 31 December 19x2	xxx	xxx	xxx	xxx
Net book amounts:				
At 31 December 19x2	xxx	xxx	xxx	xxx
At 31 December 19x1	xxx	xxx	xxx	xxx

325

CHAPTER 17

SINGAPORE

FANG AI LIAN and NATARAJAN SUBRAMANIAN

1 GENERAL INFORMATION

The financial system in Singapore as it is today is much more sophisticated compared to what it was two decades ago. Its development has been aided by various government measures introduced over the years, particularly during the 1970s. The improvement in the financial system has facilitated the flow of funds into the economy and widened the scope for various financing activities.

The financial system is relatively free of restrictions. The regulations which do exist are largely to ensure that financial institutions are prudent in their operations and that depositors are protected. There is a free flow of funds in and out of Singapore since exchange control was abolished in June 1978.

Since 1970 the number of financial intermediaries has also increased. This had led to a greater variety of financial instruments being available to those with surplus funds, as well as new sources of financing for those in need of funds. The various financial markets have also been further developed thus contributing to the improvement in the financial system.

Apart from the commercial banks, finance companies and insurance companies, other organisations in the financial system include fairly recently introduced institutions such as merchant banks, international money brokers, discount houses and gold dealers. Except for one commercial bank and one insurance company, which the government partly owns, all the institutions are in the private sector.

Within the last 10 years new financial instruments and papers have become available. Negotiable certificates of deposit, both in Singapore dollars and US dollars, are now issued by several banks. Commercial paper and government securities of a wider range of maturities are also available. Gold certificates have been introduced to investors. Following the establishment of the Asian dollar market in Singapore, depositors also have the opportunity to place funds in foreign currencies with institutions which are licensed to operate the Asian Currency Units (ACU). With the entry of more foreign banks, many of which are licensed to undertake offshore banking, the banking system has become more international. There is greater opportunity for interest arbitrage and speculation in foreign exchange.

1.1 Organisations covered by banking regulations

All commercial banks have to comply with the provisions of the Banking Act 1970, Bank Notices and administrative guidelines issued by the Monetary Authority of Singapore (MAS).

Finance companies are regulated by the Finance Companies Act 1967 and also by Notices and administrative guidelines issued by the MAS.

There is no specific legislation governing the activities of merchant banks and discount houses. However, these institutions are also regulated by the MAS and therefore have to comply with a different set of guidelines and regulations issued by the MAS. Where merchant banks have ACUs they are indirectly regulated under the Banking Act. However, for ACUs certain provisions of the Banking Act are exempted by the MAS.

1.2 Summary of major types of bank

Private sector

(a) Commercial banks

Commercial banks are licensed by the Monetary Authority of Singapore. Approval from the MAS is also needed for the opening of a branch office or a sub-branch. The Monetary Authority grants three types of licence, namely, full licences, restricted licences and offshore bank licences. Before 1971 there was only one type of licence for all banks. To develop Singapore as a financial centre, more banks were to be admitted. However, it was recognised that in view of the small size of the Singapore economy, the existing banks could adequately meet the domestic banking needs and the licensing of more banks could lead to undue competition for deposits. The scope for Singapore's growth as a financial centre was perceived to be in offshore banking. Foreign banks, with their international connections and expertise, could also be of benefit to Singapore. Thus a differentiation in bank licences was introduced. The main differences between the three types of banking licence are as follows:

(a) A full bank licence allows a bank to engage in all types of activities permitted under the Banking Act. These activities are broadly the same as those undertaken by any commercial bank elsewhere. All the 13 locally incorporated banks and the 24 foreign banks which were established before 1971 are fully licensed banks.

(b) A restricted bank licence enables a bank to undertake transactions similar to that of fully licensed banks, except that in its deposit collection it has to observe a limit on the amount it may accept per deposit. It may take in deposits of not less than S$250,000 per deposit. It is also not allowed to operate savings accounts nor to open any branches. The 13 banks with restricted licences are all foreign banks.

(c) An offshore bank licence allows a bank to engage in wholesale banking with non-residents. In its dealings with residents, an offshore bank may extend credit and provide such facilities as opening of letters of credit, issuing trust receipts and giving overdrafts up to a total limit of S$30 million. It may not accept fixed term, savings and other interest-bearing deposits from residents. Like the restricted banks, offshore banks are also not permitted to establish branches. There are 71 banks with offshore banking licences. They are branches of banks from more than 10 countries, including the United States, the United Kingdom, other countries in Europe and Latin America, Japan, Malaysia, and Australia.

Other than in the difference in the type of licence, banks are also distinguished by those with and without ACUs. Of the 122 commercial banks, 109 have approval to operate ACUs. Banks may apply to the MAS for approval to transact in the Singapore-based Asian dollar market. They have to set up a separate bookkeeping unit for their ACU where all transactions in the Asian dollar market are recorded. The purpose of setting up separate bookkeeping units is to isolate the movement of funds in and out of the Asian dollar market so that any disruptive effects on the domestic monetary system would be minimised. All restricted offshore banks have ACUs. Of the 37 banks with a full licence, both local and foreign, only 24 have ACUs.

Banks have been free to quote their own interest rates since the abolition of the cartel system of interest rate quotations in 1975. A few banks tend to lead the market in interest rate changes. Some of the bank charges are fixed by the Association of Banks, of which nearly all banks are members.

(b) Finance companies

Finance companies accept deposits and extend credit, like the commercial banks, but they are different in many other respects. Their history is also much more recent.

Most of the finance companies were set up in the 1950s, but a licence to operate a finance company was needed only from 1967 with the passing of the Finance Companies Act. Legislation was introduced as the mushrooming of finance companies led to growing concern over the lack of proper control and protection of depositors' moneys.

Unlike the commercial banks, there is a uniform licence for finance companies. All the 34 finance companies are locally incorporated. Sixteen of the finance companies are affiliated to banks. The banks had set up wholly-owned finance company subsidiaries to provide financing services, mainly consumer durable goods financing and mortgage loans. For some banks their finance companies served as substitutes for additional bank branches and sources for deposit collection. The bank-affiliated finance companies are known to channel some of the deposits they collect to their parent bank. The finance companies have a total of 132 offices. Their total assets as at the end of December 1983 amounted to S$6.5 billion.

Finance companies may accept fixed and savings deposits but not demand deposits. They therefore do not provide customers with cheque account facilities. The main areas of activity of the finance companies are hire purchase financing and mortgage financing. They also engage in lease financing and accounts receivable financing. Another significant difference between finance companies and commercial banks is that finance companies do not finance international trade. They do so only indirectly through trade financing, where they may open letters of credit on behalf of the local importer or through inventory financing. For this type of financing they provide funds against storage of goods in warehouses. Some of the finance companies concentrate on housing mortgages, while others specialise in hire purchase financing, mainly for motor vehicles and machinery.

Compared to banks, the activities which finance companies may engage in are restricted. They are not permitted to operate in the Asian dollar market nor to issue negotiable certificates of deposit. They are also not allowed to deal in gold nor engage in foreign exchange transactions.

(c) Merchant banks

The first approved merchant bank was set up in Singapore only as recently as 1970. Prior to this, merchant banking was conducted by some of the commercial banks. At the end of December 1983 there were 51 merchant banks. Some of the merchant banks are branches of institutions overseas, while others are joint ventures between local and foreign partners. The merchant banks engage in a wide range of activities. They include wholesale banking in the offshore market, underwriting and flotation of stocks and bonds, lending to residents, providing investment and financial advisory services and dealing in gold and foreign exchange. As a group, the predominant activity of merchant banks is offshore wholesale banking. Of the 51 merchant banks, 48 have the approval to operate ACUs, that is, to deal in the offshore market. Over 80% of the assets of merchant banks as a group are from their ACUs. Total assets of merchant banks as at the end of December 1983 were S$23.6 billion.

The merchant banks are generally less homogeneous than the commercial banks or finance companies. There is a certain degree of specialisation, the area depending on the shareholders and the expertise available. Some merchant banks concentrate on corporate financial services, some on offshore banking and others are engaged in varied activities.

(d) Asian Currency Units

'Asian Currency Unit' is a term used to describe the bookkeeping unit of a financial institution which has been given approval by the Monetary Authority of Singapore to operate in the Asian dollar market. Financial institutions with ACUs are allowed to accept time and call deposits and to borrow or lend in currencies other than Singapore dollars. As at the end of December 1983 there were 159 ACUs, of which 109 were those of commercial banks, 48 of merchant banks and two of an investment company.

Before the total liberalisation of exchange control in June 1978, ACUs were free to deal with non-residents, but transactions with residents were subject to various restrictions, including ceilings on the amount they could accept as deposits from residents and the loans they could make. ACUs may now deal freely with residents.

Asian Currency Units may transact business with other ACUs and with banks, both in Singapore and abroad. They are also permitted to invest in foreign currency securities and deal in third currencies. Other activities they may engage in are the opening of letters of credit, discounting of bills and the issuing of guarantees, all of which have to be in currencies other than the Singapore dollar. The operators of ACUs pay tax at a concessionary rate of 10% on income earned on their activities, other than loans to residents which are taxed at the normal rate of 40%.

One of the objectives of requiring financial institutions wishing to operate in the Asian dollar market to set up separate bookkeeping units was to facilitate the implementation of the concessionary tax rate scheme. Another objective of the separation was to isolate the domestic economy from the possible disruptive flow of foreign currency funds in the monitoring of monetary aggregates for the purpose of formulating monetary policy.

The maximum size of the assets/liabilities of ACU operations is determined by the MAS. This varies among the ACUs. However, institutions with increased activity may apply for a larger limit on the size of their book.

Although over 20 foreign currencies are accepted and dealt with by the ACUs, the US dollar predominates. More than 90% of transactions conducted by the ACUs are in US dollars.

(e) Discount houses

There are four discount houses in Singapore, three of which were set up in 1972 and the last in 1974. They are modelled along the lines of the London discount houses. The discount houses act as the intermediary between the banks and other financial institutions on the one hand and the MAS on the other for transactions in the money markets. They accept short-term funds from commercial banks, either on an overnight or call basis, and invest these funds in assets prescribed by the MAS. The instruments which discount houses are allowed to hold are treasury bills, Singapore dollar negotiable certificates of deposit, short-term government bonds and commercial bills. The discount houses underwrite the weekly treasury bill issue, conducted by the MAS. The total assets of the discount houses as at the end of December 1983 amounted to S$2.3 billion.

The discount houses not only invest in the primary issue of treasury bills and Singapore dollar NCDs, but are also active in the secondary market for such instruments. In addition they trade in commercial bills, and to a lesser extent government securities, in the secondary market.

The shareholders of the four discount houses are the Post Office Savings Bank, financial institutions abroad and some of the local banks.

Discount houses do not participate in the foreign exchange or gold markets. Their role is essentially to stimulate competition among banks and thus to help in the development of a more active domestic money market.

Public sector

(a) Central Provident Fund Board

The Central Provident Fund Board (CPF) is a statutory authority, set up under the Central Provident Fund Act, to administer the government's social insurance scheme. Since its establishment in 1955 the CPF has evolved into a major financial institution in terms of the size of its resources and its influence on domestic savings.

All employees in the private sector earning more than S$200 a month have to be members and their contributions are matched by contributions from their employers. Effective July 1984, the combined contribution is 50% (shared equally by employer and employee) of the employee's monthly wage. Maximum monthly wage to which this applies is S$5,000 effective July 1984.

The objective of the fund is to provide workers with a lump sum at retiring age of 55 (or earlier under certain conditions) and to purchase flats built by the public sector authorities.

Contributions are greatly in excess of expenditure and the fund had grown to S$19.0 billion by the end of 1983, making it larger than any commercial bank and about one third of the total assets of all commercial banks combined.

The fund is required to invest its surpluses in long-term government bonds mostly with a life of 10-15 years and these are normally held to maturity. The proceeds of sale of these bonds are in turn largely invested abroad as the government does not, at the present time, require the funds for public sector investment.

The CPF has a powerful effect on the money supply as it drains off funds which would otherwise be left in the banking system and sometimes the MAS has to intervene in the money sector to counteract this liquidity squeeze.

The investment policies of the CPF are being changed to some extent and this will help to ease liquidity pressures.

The CPF pays its members interest on their outstanding balances. This is 6% per annum and is credited to the member's account quarterly. The interest earned (which is tax free) may not be withdrawn but is left to accumulate in the members' accounts.

(b) Post Office Savings Bank

The Post Office Savings Bank (POSB) is the national savings bank. Founded in 1877 as a department of the Post Office it became independent in 1972 with the objective of encouraging thrift and mobilising domestic savings for use in the public sector.

Besides offering savings and checking accounts it provides Giro facilities for the transfer of funds. However, it can only accept deposits from individuals and public institutions, including clubs and societies, but not from companies.

The growth rate has been high and its total funds amounted to S$5.9 billion at the end of 1983 with some 2.5 million account holders.

It has 122 separate offices including some counters at post offices. These are mostly equipped with online facilities and automatic bank tellers so as to compete with other financial institutions.

At least 50% of its assets have to be invested in long-term government securities (which, however, include loans to statutory boards and government owned companies). It offers mortgage loans through a separate subsidiary and it has made equity investments in private companies, including a merchant bank. However, the balance of its funds are mainly invested in the inter-bank market where it places overnight money and makes term loans to banks and finance companies.

Interest paid by the POSB on savings deposits is generally lower than the rates for fixed deposits with banks and finance companies. For deposits above S$100,000, the POSB pays an even lower rate. This two-tier interest rate structure was introduced in September 1978. However, unlike those of banks and finance companies, interest earnings on POSB deposits are tax exempt. Furthermore, deposits with the POSB are guaranteed by the government.

(c) The Monetary Authority of Singapore

Singapore does not have a central bank such as found in most countries. However, through its agency, the Monetary Authority of Singapore (MAS), the government carries out many of the functions normally performed by a central bank. The only major function which the MAS is not responsible for is the issue of currency. This is entrusted to another organisation, the Board of Commissioners of Currency.

Set up under the Monetary Authority of Singapore Act 1970 the MAS started functioning in January 1971 and took over the central banking functions which had previously been performed by several government departments.

The MAS has five main functions. These are:

(1) To serve as banker, fiscal agent and financial adviser to the government:

The MAS provides current and deposit account facilities for the government and it manages the public debt. This latter task includes the issuing and servicing of government bonds and it also floats, on the overseas financial market, government loans. However, the management of the official foreign reserves is now in the hands of the Government of Singapore Investment Corporation. The MAS also provides financial facilities on behalf of the government for international agencies such as the International Monetary Fund, the World Bank and the Asian Development Bank.

(2) To act as banker to banks and other financial institutions:

The MAS acts as banker to banks, finance companies and discount houses, thus serving two purposes. Firstly, enabling daily settlement of balances arising from the centralised clearing of cheques and remittances, including balances with the government and secondly, controlling the money supply by requiring a minimum cash deposit to be held with it. In the case of the discount houses the MAS will also act as a lender of last resort.

(3) To promote monetary and exchange rate stability:

As well as controlling the minimum cash deposit to be maintained with it the MAS operates in the money market by lending, buying, selling, discounting and rediscounting securities, treasury bills, commercial bills and government securities. It has a rediscount window for import and export bills. The rediscounting of export bills is at a concessionary rate in order to promote exports. Its monetary policy is designed to achieve the government's overall economic policy objective and at times it intervenes in the foreign exchange market in order to smooth out movements in the Singapore dollar, which has been floating since June 1973.

(4) To supervise and regulate the banking and financial sector:

The MAS is responsible for the licensing of all banks and finance companies and for the registration of insurance companies. It is the approving authority for discount houses and merchant banks wishing to operate in Singapore. Institutions also have to seek the approval of the MAS to operate Asian Currency Units.

(5) To develop financial markets, introduce new instruments and license institutions, with the objective of nurturing Singapore's growth as a financial centre:

In consultation with the Ministry of Finance and the Ministry of Trade and Industry, the MAS formulates policies and implements measures for the development of Singapore as a financial centre. It was responsible for the establishment and development of the Singapore-based Asian dollar market, for the complete liberalisation of exchange control in 1978 and for the introduction of new instruments such as the Singapore dollar and US dollar negotiable certificates of deposit. As part of its development strategy for the 1980s, it will further develop the various financial markets through greater liberalisation of activities, provision of tax incentives and the more liberal entry of financial institutions. Measures will be introduced to attract, for example, funds management to Singapore, to develop further the capital market and offshore reinsurance activities. In line with the government's call to increase productivity through increased automation, the MAS is working closely with banks to establish the automated cheque clearing system while banks have been encouraged to computerise and to establish automated teller-machines.

1.3 Supervisory authorities

As mentioned in the preceding Section, the MAS supervises and regulates the banking and financial sector.

The MAS administers the Banking Act, the Finance Companies Act and Notices and guidelines it issues. It is thus responsible for ensuring the orderly development of the financial system and for upholding high standards of banking and commercial practices. It regulates the activities of the financial institutions and supervises them. In the discharge of its function as the regulatory authority, it has to process and evaluate applications for banking licences to ensure that only select, sound financial institutions are admitted. It promotes the development of financial skills by ensuring that proper training and education are provided by the financial institutions.

In its capacity as the supervisory authority, the MAS is authorised to inspect banks and finance companies. In the inspection of these institutions, emphasis is placed on capital adequacy, asset structure, soundness of control systems and management. The MAS conducts its supervision by examining statistical returns and other information which the financial institutions are required to submit periodically. Institutions which deviate from statutory provisions or which are assessed to be veering towards unsound business practices are informed of their weaknesses. These are rectified through consultations with the MAS. In the final analysis, the MAS has the mandate to withdraw the licences and the approvals necessary for these institutions to operate. However, such drastic steps are taken only in exceptional cases.

Furthermore, under the Banking and Finance Companies Acts, all banks and finance companies are required to appoint annually an external auditor approved by the MAS to audit its accounts each year. The auditors' reports on the financial statements as well as management letters on internal control and a supplemental letter on compliance with MAS guidelines have to be submitted to the MAS.

The functions of the external auditors are explained in Section 2.7.

1.4 Status of supervisory authorities

Supervisory authorities referred to in Section 1.3 are required under the terms of the Banking Act 1970 and Finance Companies Act 1967.

1.5 Laws and regulations governing banks
1.6 Application of general company law to banks
1.7 Sources of laws and regulations

The Banking Act 1970 and the Finance Companies Act 1967 were passed for the protection of depositors and for the proper control of the activities of commercial banks and finance companies. The MAS was set up in 1970 to supervise the various banking organisations.

As mentioned in Section 1.2, all commercial banks, ACUs and finance companies are licensed by the MAS. Merchant banks and discount houses do not require licences but require the approval of the MAS before commencement of operations.

For specific regulations governing the various types of banking organisations, reference needs to be made to Section 1.1. General company law also applies to banking organisations.

The main provisions of the various regulations are as follows:

(a) Commercial banks

(a) A bank incorporated in Singapore, is required to have a minimum paid-up capital of S$3 million net of any debit balances in its profit and loss account. The minimum paid-up capital for a bank whose head office is outside Singapore is the equivalent of S$6 million, net of any debit balance in its profit and loss account. The foreign bank is also required to hold not less than S$3 million in Singapore in the form of assets approved by the MAS.

(b) A minimum cash balance has to be maintained with the MAS. Since July 1975 this has been kept at 6% of a bank's liabilities base. The minimum cash balance has been as low as 3% and as high as 9%. The variation in the minimum cash balance is one of the instruments used by the MAS to implement its monetary policy.

(c) Banks have to hold a minimum amount of liquid assets. This is 20% of a bank's liabilities base and comprises a first tier liquid assets ratio amounting to 10% and a second tier of another 10%. The assets eligible for inclusion in the first tier are cash, balances with the MAS in excess of the statutory minimum, funds placed with discount houses, treasury bills and other government securities with less than one year to maturity. Assets which qualify for the second tier are government securities of over one year's maturity and bills of exchange. For the latter, the maximum permitted is 5% of the bank's liabilities base.

(d) The total facilities, including guarantees, which a bank may extend to a single customer, were limited to 60% of a bank's capital funds but this is being phased down to 30% in 1984. However, with approval from the Monetary Authority this may be raised to 100%. This limit does not cover the government nor another bank borrower.

(e) The amount which a bank may invest is subject to a limit of 40% of its capital funds, while the value of immovable property which it may own is also limited to not more than 40% of its capital funds.

(f) A bank is not allowed to engage in commercial trading activity including import and export whether on its own account or on a commission basis. It is not prohibited by the Banking Act from establishing a subsidiary company to carry out commercial trading activities but such a step will not be well received by the MAS.

(g) A reserve fund has to be maintained. So long as the size of the reserve fund forms less than 50% of a bank's paid-up capital, it has to transfer at least 50% of its net profits to the fund. If the percentage of reserve fund to paid-up capital is between 50% and 100% it has to transfer at least 25% of its net profits to the fund. If the reserve fund exceeds the paid-up capital, the bank need only transfer 5% of its profits to the reserve fund. Foreign banks may apply for exemption from this provision.

(h) A bank has to submit regular statistical returns to the Monetary Authority. Income and expenditure statements have to be submitted annually. The books of the bank may be inspected by the MAS at any time.

(i) A bank is required to appoint annually an auditor, approved by the MAS, to audit its accounts each year. The auditor's report, together with the balance sheet and profit and loss account of the bank has to be sent to the MAS.

(b) Finance companies

(a) Finance companies are required to maintain a minimum cash balance with the MAS. This cash ratio is 6% of a finance company's liabilities base. In addition they observe a liquid assets ratio of 10%.

(b) A finance company with paid-up capital exceeding S$2 million has to transfer part of its annual net profit to a reserve fund. This proportion varies depending on the size of the reserve fund. For example, if the size of the reserve fund is less than half the paid-up capital, at least 30% would have to be transferred to the fund. If the reserve fund is larger than the paid-up capital, only 5% of net profits need be transferred to the fund.

(c) The investment by a finance company in any company may not exceed 25% of its paid-up capital and reserves. However, this ceiling may be increased to 50% with the approval of the MAS.

(d) Investments of finance companies in immovable property may not exceed 25% of their paid-up capital and reserves.

(e) The books of finance companies may be inspected by the MAS at any time.

(f) Regular statistical returns have to be submitted to the MAS.

(c) Merchant banks

(a) Merchant banks are not permitted to collect Singapore dollar deposits from individuals, nor to issue promissory notes or other commercial paper. They are not permitted to offer checking and savings facilities.

(b) Merchant banks may collect deposits from banks and other financial institutions.

(c) Merchant banks may not open branches.

(d) Periodical statistical returns have to be submitted to the MAS.

(d) Asian Currency Units

Operators of Asian Currency Units have to comply with the Banking Act applicable to commercial banks and the terms and conditions laid down by the MAS. However, they are exempted from some of the provisions of the Banking Act, such as the need to hold minimum cash balances with the MAS and to observe the minimum liquid assets ratio.

(e) Discount houses

(a) The maximum amount which discount houses may borrow is 30 times their paid-up capital. The gearing ratio was 40 times in 1974 and was reduced, following the increase in the paid-up capital and reserves of the four discount houses. The total paid-up capital and reserves was S$73 million as at the end of December 1983. Thus the lending capacity of the discount houses is slightly over S$2 billion.

(b) Discount houses have to observe an assets ratio. They are required to hold 70% of their assets in government securities. They may hold the remaining 30% in higher yielding commercial papers.

(c) The deposits which discount houses may accept have to be at least S$50,000 per deposit. Although they are not prohibited from accepting deposits from individuals and corporations, discount houses refrain from competing with commercial banks in this respect. They may not offer current or savings account facilities.

(d) Discount houses are required to balance their books at the end of each trading day. If they are in deficit they may turn to the MAS for 'last resort' loans to enable them to square their positions. Generally, they would rediscount treasury bills or commercial papers with the MAS before resorting to the lender of last resort facility. Discount houses in surplus would use the excess funds for purchase of short-dated treasury bills, government bonds or commercial bills from the MAS.

(e) Periodical statistical returns have to be submitted to the MAS.

1.8 Ability of foreign banks to operate through branches and subsidiaries

At present, for commercial banking operations, the MAS will only issue foreign banks with an offshore bank licence to operate one branch in Singapore. Subsidiaries are not permitted. As the thrust of the Singapore government's policy is towards offshore banking, ACU licences are normally issued to the branches of foreign banks.

Finance companies have to be incorporated as companies with a proper share capital structure (see Section 1.5). At present, as the government considers that the domestic banking needs are adequately met by existing banks and finance companies, the MAS is unlikely to issue any further finance companies' licences.

Like finance companies, approved merchant banks and discount houses have to be incorporated as companies with proper capital structures. Foreign banks therefore have to incorporate subsidiaries in Singapore in order to carry out such operations. As mentioned before, approval to operate has to be obtained from the MAS.

Applications to operate in Singapore are very carefully evaluated by the MAS so as to ensure that only select, sound financial institutions are admitted. The MAS also requires foreign experienced personnel to head the main banking operations. *Curriculum vitae* of these personnel have to be submitted to the MAS for review and approval.

1.9 Level of supervisory control for branches and subsidiaries of foreign banks

Foreign banks operating in Singapore are accorded the same level of supervisory control as local banks. (See Sections 1.5 to 1.7.)

1.10 Methods of incorporation

The incorporation of companies and registration of branches of foreign banks are governed by the Companies Act, cap. 185. The requirements of the Singapore Companies Act are very similar to the UK Companies Act.

1.11 Areas within the country subject to special laws

None.

2 ACCOUNTING

2.1 Laws and regulations governing accounts
2.2 Application of general company law
2.3 Roles of legislature and supervisory authority
2.4 Extent to which requirements as to returns and accounts are prescribed by laws and regulations

The Companies Act, the Banking Act and the guidelines and Notices issued by the MAS regulate the information to be included in annual financial statements of both Singapore incorporated banks as well as branches of foreign banks.

The Registrar of Companies ensures compliance with the Companies Act, while the MAS ensures that the provisions of the Banking Act and the guidelines of and Notices issued by the MAS are met with.

2.5 Obligations to furnish accounts

2.5.1 Accounting periods and times of furnishing

2.5.2 Form of accounts to be furnished

2.5.3 Mandatory accounting dates

Annual audited financial statements are required to be prepared for all banks. A foreign bank is only required to prepare an audited statement of assets and liabilities and the profit and loss account arising out of its branch or consolidated branches' operations in Singapore. In the case of locally incorporated banks, the audited financial statements together with the directors' report must be presented at an annual general meeting of shareholders not later than 18 months after incorporation of the company and subsequently at intervals of not more than 15 months.

All banks, whether incorporated in or outside Singapore, are required to publish the following information in four local daily newspapers within six months of the annual year end.

(1) A copy of its latest audited annual balance sheet, and a copy of the profit and loss account, together with any notes thereon, and a copy of the report of the auditors.

In the case of a bank incorporated outside Singapore, the above-mentioned statements may be in such a manner as to comply with the law for the time being applicable in the place of its corporation or origin.

(2) The full and correct names of all persons who are directors for the time being of the bank.

(3) The names of all subsidiary companies for the time being of the bank.

Banks incorporated outside Singapore must include the above details in respect of their worldwide operations and not merely the Singapore operations.

No mandatory accounting periods are prescribed.

In addition to the publication in the newspapers, financial statements are also required to be filed with the Registrar of Companies and the Monetary Authority of Singapore. A branch of a foreign incorporated bank must also submit the audited financial statements of the bank within two months of the holding of the bank's annual general meeting.

The audited financial statements also form the basis for submission of the required information to the revenue authorities.

2.6 Requirements as to accounts (a) prior to incorporation (b) prior to commencement of trading and (c) in order to continue trading

Prior to incorporation or commencement of operations, foreign banks have to apply for an appropriate licence from the MAS. Such applications have to be accompanied by consolidated worldwide financial statements of foreign banks.

In order to continue trading, all banks have to furnish financial statements as stated in Section 1.5 to the relevant authorities.

2.7 Audit requirements

Every bank shall appoint annually an auditor approved by the MAS.

The duties of an auditor appointed under the Banking Act shall be:

(a) To carry out, for the year in respect of which he is appointed, an audit of the accounts of the bank.

(b) To make a report in accordance with section 174 of the Companies Act on the annual financial statements referred to in Section 2.5 for both banks incorporated in Singapore and branches of foreign banks.

The auditors' report shall be attached to the annual financial statements and submitted to both the MAS and Registrar of Companies.

Also, for MAS purposes, auditors are required to certify certain additional information to the MAS.

More recently, the MAS has also required auditors for all banks to comment on the adequacy of those loan provisions having a material effect on financial statements, compliance with the Companies Act, Banking Act, Notices and guidelines issued by the MAS and all relevant laws and regulations.

2.8 Acceptability to fiscal authorities of accounts submitted to supervisory authority

Under the Banking Act the MAS may, at its absolute discretion, regard the annual accounts as having been duly audited for the purposes of the Banking Act if such accounts are accompanied by a report of an approved auditor which complies as far as it is practicable with the provisions of the Companies Act.

Therefore, annual accounts submitted to the Registrar of Companies are acceptable to the MAS in form and content.

The MAS has allowed certain exceptions and modifications to the form and content of the directors' report and the financial statements. Such exceptions and modifications are accepted by the Registrar of Companies and are referred to in the auditors' report.

2.9 Submission of accounts to any authority other than by requirement of law

There are no other requirements other than those already mentioned.

2.10 Application of laws and regulations to foreign banks operating through branches and subsidiaries

This has been covered under Section 2.5.

2.11 Availability of accounts for public inspection

The requirement for banks to publish their annual financial statements in the four local daily newspapers (Chinese, English, Malay and Tamil) makes a significant amount of their financial information public knowledge (see Section 2.5).

Additionally, all documents, including annual audited financial statements filed with the Registrar of Companies, are considered public documents under the Companies Act and are therefore available for public inspection at the offices of the Registrar of Companies, notwithstanding the exceptions allowed. Most financial statements of banks are moving towards greater disclosure, in line with current accounting trend.

3 FORMAT, STYLE AND CONTENTS OF ACCOUNTS

3.1 Extent to which format is laid down by statute, supervisory authority, generally accepted accounting practice or otherwise

3.2 Description of format

3.3 Extent to which contents are prescribed by statute, supervisory authority, generally accepted accounting practice or otherwise

3.4 Disclosure of specific items required other than those required by general law

3.5 Exemptions from disclosure allowed in respect of banking items

3.6 Hidden reserves

3.7 Requirements as to consolidated accounts

The main disclosure requirements are those stipulated under the Companies Act. Although financial statements generally comply with International Accounting Standards, banks have been given special dispensation by the local accounting body in Singapore from complying with IAS Standards on preparation of consolidated accounts (IAS3) and disclosure of information in financial statements (IAS5).

The format of the financial statements are prescribed by the MAS. While the form should be adhered to as far as applicable, flexibility is allowed in the layout of accounts and also notes to be annexed for certain items. The format of the accounts is shown in Appendix I. Banks are encouraged to give additional information wherever considered necessary.

The MAS has determined certain exceptions and modifications to the form and content of the directors' report and the financial statements. These are:
(1) Banks would be allowed to make undisclosed transfers to and from reserves before arriving at published profits, particularly movements in and out of contingency accounts and reserves for bad and doubtful debts. However, such movements should be disclosed to and approved by the Authority.
(2) Banks would be allowed to avoid showing the charge for income tax as a deduction from published profits.
(3) Banks would be allowed to show their investments without having to disclose their market value. However, the basis of valuation, whichever method is adopted, should be shown.
(4) Banks would be allowed to show fixed and other assets without having to show accumulated depreciation and write-off separately. The method of valuation adopted should be shown.

The Companies Act requires every holding company to present audited group financial statements. In cases where group financial statements are not prepared or where only accounts of some of the subsidiaries are consolidated, the accounts of the subsidiaries not consolidated must be attached to the accounts. These accounts must be in form and content similar to those presented at the annual general meeting of the subsidiaries. The MAS has, however, directed that where a bank is a holding company the accounts of the bank shall only be consolidated with directly-owned banking subsidiaries. Directly-owned non-banking subsidiaries may be excluded as well as sub-subsidiaries irrespective of whether these carry on banking or non-banking activities.

In addition to the annual audited financial statements banks are also required to submit certain additional information to the MAS in accordance with the format determined by the Authority. This information should be prepared and certified correct by the external auditors. The format of this information is shown in Appendix II.

The additional information is not required to be furnished to any other government authority.

Also, as referred to in Sections 1.5 to 1.7, banks have to submit regular statistical information to the MAS.

4 ACCOUNTING POLICIES

4.1 Responsibility for laying down accounting policies

Accounting policies adopted in the preparation and presentation of financial statements are not governed by the Companies Act nor the Banking Act. These policies, in the main, follow generally accepted accounting practice and the disclosure thereof has been made mandatory following the adoption in 1976 of the International Accounting Standard No. 1 by the Singapore Society of Accountants. The Standard applied to all financial statements for periods commencing on or after 1 January 1977.

4.2 Particular accounting policies

4.2.1 Foreign exchange

Foreign currency assets and liabilities are converted into Singapore dollars at rates approximating those ruling at balance sheet date. Profit and loss account items are converted at rates ruling at transaction dates.

Forward exchange contracts, except those entered into for 'swap' purposes, are valued at the year end closing market rates applicable to their respective maturities.

All exchange differences arising from the above are taken to the profit and loss account.

In the case of 'swap' transactions which are entered into in connection with loans and deposits, the resultant profit or loss is apportioned over the period of the transaction.

4.2.2 Deferred tax

Provision is usually made for the deferred tax effect (using the liability method) of the difference between the operating profit and taxable profit arising from short-term timing differences.

4.2.3 Specific and general provisions for bad and doubtful debts

4.2.4 Treatment of provisions in accounts

Specific provision is made for losses on loans and advances which are assessed by the management to be bad or doubtful, based on the borrower's debt servicing ability and security. Additionally, the management may decide to build up a general loan loss provision. Interest charged on bad and doubtful debts is held in a suspense account rather than being taken to the profit and loss account.

Both specific and general provisions for loan losses and interest suspense are shown as deductions from loans in the balance sheet.

4.2.5 Premiums and discounts on investments (amortise, write off, etc.)

Premiums and discounts are usually evenly spread over the period from the date of purchase to the date of maturity of such investments.

Some banks on the other hand choose to write off premiums in the year the securities are purchased.

4.2.6 Offsets, i.e. to what extent can assets and liabilities be set off against each other (legally or in practice)

In general, balances with the same entity are disclosed separately. However, where there are specific arrangements of set-off then balances with the same entity are reported net.

4.2.7 Goodwill

Goodwill arising from consolidation is either:
(i) Amortised over a period of time through the profit and loss account.
(ii) Written off as and when it arises through the profit and loss account or direct to reserves.

Reserve on consolidation is credited direct to a separate reserve account.

4.2.8 Consolidation

The consolidated accounts include the accounts of the bank and all its subsidiaries made up to the end of the financial year. (See also comments on consolidation requirements under Section 3.)

Assets and liabilities of foreign subsidiaries are translated into Singapore dollars at rates of exchange closely approximating rates ruling at balance sheet date. Profit and loss account items are translated at the average rates of exchange in effect during the year or at rates closely approximating rates ruling at balance sheet date.

Translation differences resulting therefrom are either dealt with through the profit and loss account or through reserves.

4.2.9 Revaluations of assets

In one of MAS's Notices to banks, banks are advised to refrain from writing up their assets, such as landed properties. The MAS will therefore not give favourable consideration to any applications from banks for upward revaluation of their assets. Banks are instead encouraged to build up their inner strength through building up of hidden reserves.

4.2.10 Instalment finance and leasing including basis of recognition of income

(i) Lease rentals are credited to income on an accrual basis.
Leased assets are stated at cost less depreciation. Depreciation is calculated to write off the cost of assets concerned, less their residual value, on a straight line basis over the periods of the related leases.
(ii) Term charges and hire purchase are credited to the profit and loss account, either by apportioning such charges equally over the period in which monthly instalments are due or computed under the 'rule of 78' method.

4.2.11 Dealing assets

(i) Treasury bills are stated at face value less earned interest or, like government securities, are stated at the lower of cost and market value on an aggregate basis.
Cost for such securities is stated after adjustments for premiums and discounts as stated in Section 4.2.5.
(ii) Quoted shares, loan stocks and bonds are stated at the lower of cost and market value on an aggregate basis.
(iii) Unquoted shares are stated at cost less provision for diminution in value which is considered permanent. The share of results of associated companies is not usually included in the profit and loss account, except in so far as dividends have been received or are receivable. Provision for diminution in value is usually based on the earning capacity of the companies and their net tangible asset backing.

As can be deduced from above, there is no differentiation between dealing and investment assets.

4.2.12 Pensions

Contributions to the Central Provident Fund (see Section 1.2) are considered employee costs. These do not require separate disclosure in the profit and loss account.

Where additional pension schemes are set up for employees, the provision set aside each year will require separate disclosure in the profit and loss account while the accumulated provisions set up will be shown separately in the accounts as a deferred liability.

4.2.13 Depreciation

Fixed assets are stated at cost less accumulated depreciation.

Depreciation of fixed assets is usually provided on a straight line basis over the estimated useful life of the asset or, in the case of leasehold property, over the term of the lease, if shorter. Assets out on lease are depreciated over the period of the respective leases.

5 WINDOW DRESSING

The need for regular submission of statistical information to the MAS, as well as the requirement for annual audited accounts to be submitted to both the MAS and the Registrar of Companies, act as deterrents against window dressing.

6 AMOUNTS REQUIRED TO BE MAINTAINED BY LAW OR OTHERWISE

These requirements relate to:
(i)   Minimum capital.
(ii)   Reserve funds.
(iii) Minimum cash balance.
(iv)   Minimum liquid assets.

All the above requirements have been dealt with in Sections 1.5 to 1.7.

Also, as required under the Bank Notice 609 issued to Banks, the MAS requires banks to submit additional information relating to items in its annual balance sheet and profit and loss account in accordance with the form laid down in Appendix II. This information has to be certified correct by external auditors.

7 KEY RATIOS

There are no specific ratios laid down by either the Companies Act, Banking Act or Notices and guidelines issued by the MAS.

Apart from the conventional ratios like earnings per share and dividend cover, banks in Singapore would only publish ratios such as loans to deposit and net assets per share.

Little information is published on what ratios are used by banks for their own internal use but these would be work done on risk asset analysis and liquidity ratios.

The general provision for such bad debts is set at rates varying from ½% to 1½% of outstanding loans.

8 ACCOUNTING RETURNS OTHER THAN ACCOUNTS

8.1 By whom required
8.2 Nature of requirements

Under the Banking Act, every bank shall send to the MAS and the Chief Statistician:

(i)   Not later than 15 days after the last day of each month a statement in the form set out in the first schedule to that Act showing the assets and liabilities of its banking offices and branches in Singapore at the close of business on the last business day of the preceding month.

(ii)   Not later than one month after the last day of each quarter of a calendar year a statement in the form set out in the second schedule to that Act giving an analysis of loans and advances of its banking offices and branches in Singapore as at 31 March, 30 June, 30 September and the 31 December, respectively.

(iii) Not later than six months after the close of its financial year a statement in the form set out in the third schedule to that Act showing the income and expenditure in respect of its banking business in Singapore.

9 TAXATION

9.1 General method of taxation
9.2 Accounts as basis for taxation
9.3 Adjustments permitted or required
9.4 Effect of tax considerations on presentation of accounts

(a) General

Any company or individual whose income accrues in or is derived from Singapore is required to pay tax on such income. For individuals, foreign income received in Singapore is also subject to income tax. The rate of income tax for companies, whether resident or non-resident, is 40%.

The tax year or year of assessment is the same as the calendar year. Income assessed for taxation in any year is the income derived in the preceding year. However, a company which operates in Singapore may choose an accounting year which differs from the calendar year. In such a case, the income assessed will be that of the preceding 12 months of the accounting year.

There is no statutory date for filing tax returns in Singapore. Normally, income tax forms are sent out by the Inland Revenue Department in January. Any company which does not receive a tax return by the end of March in a tax year is obliged to inform the Inland Revenue Department of the omission within two weeks. The income tax forms have to be completed and submitted to the Inland Revenue Department within 21 days of the date the forms were issued. A company may apply for an extension of the deadline but it will have to provide its estimated income. Taxes have to be paid within 30 days of the date of issue of the 'Notice of Assessment'. However, arrangements can be made for payment to be made in instalments. The maximum allowed instalment period is January to October in the year of assessment.

(b) Taxation on income of banks, merchant banks and finance companies

Income of banks, merchant banks and finance companies is taxed on a net basis. The computation of profits is based on normal accounting principles and in accordance with specific provisions of the Income Tax Act. Audited financial statements form the bases of taxation and appropriate adjustments are made thereto. Expenses incurred wholly and exclusively in the production of income are tax deductible. However, in cases where an expenditure is not incurred solely for producing income, a part of the expenditure can be deducted if the company is able to quantify the amount which is incurred in generating the income.

Expenses which are deductible have actually to be incurred. Deductions may not be made for general provision or reserves for anticipated losses or for contingent liabilities. Specific provisions for bad and doubtful debts may be deducted but the amount provided for has to be acceptable to the Comptroller of Income Tax.

Capital allowances are granted for expenditure on plant and machinery used in the business. However, the depreciation provided by the financial institutions is disregarded for tax purposes. Instead, statutory capital allowances computed on a straight line basis are applied. In the year of acquisition, an 'initial allowance' equal to one fifth of the capital expenditure may be claimed by the financial institutions in addition to the annual capital allowances. When an asset is sold or disposed of, the difference between the tax written-down value and the proceeds of the sale may be taken into account when computing profits for that year of assessment.

Assets which are leased under a genuine lease agreement in the course of business remain the property of the lessor, who is then entitled to claim these capital allowances. When assets are sold on hire purchase, the hirer and not the financial institution is entitled to claim the capital allowance.

(c) Investment of banks and finance companies

There is no capital gains tax in Singapore. However, the acquisition and disposal of investments by banks and finance companies is considered to be a part of their normal business. Hence gains or losses associated with investments are taken into account for tax purposes. If the investments are in subsidiary companies, whose business is incidental to the bank or finance company, for example a trustee or nominee company, then any gains or losses would not be considered in the tax computation.

(d) Taxation on Asian Currency Unit operations

To encourage offshore banking activity, the government has granted tax concessions to operators of ACUs. Income earned by the ACUs is taxed at the reduced rate of 10% instead of 40%. Income derived from the following activities is taxed at the concessionary rate:
(1) Granting of loans to non-residents to be used outside Singapore and in currencies other than the Singapore dollar. Interest on such loans should not be borne directly or indirectly by a resident.
(2) Opening, advising or confirming letters of credit related to offshore trade transactions.
(3) Financing or refinancing of offshore trade.

(4) Foreign currency inter-trade or inter-ACU transactions covering loans, deposits, bankers' acceptances on bills relating to offshore trade, negotiable certificates of deposit.
(5) Managing underwriting, broking and investing in bonds, debentures, fixed or floating rate notes and certificates of deposit, in currencies other than the Singapore dollar.
(6) Providing advisory financial services to non-residents.
(7) Transactions in foreign exchange with banks or other ACUs.
(8) Transactions in gold with other ACUs, the Gold Exchange of Singapore or with non-residents.

To determine net offshore income eligible for the tax concession, the financial institutions have to apportion indirect expenses, including depreciation allowances, between income derived from operations of their ACU and their other operations.

(e) Dividends and branch profits

Under Singapore law, a company is regarded as a resident if the control and management of its business is in Singapore. Hence banks incorporated in Singapore are treated as residents while foreign banks are considered as non-residents.

Dividends paid by a resident company are subject to withholding tax at the rate of 40%. However, where the dividend has been paid out of taxed profits, the tax already paid is imputed to the dividend and no additional tax needs be paid. Recipients of dividends paid out of profits of ACUs taxed at 10% are exempt from further taxation in Singapore. Net profit after tax of a branch of a foreign company operating in Singapore may be freely repatriated. There is no additional remittance tax to be paid on such profits.

(f) Withholding tax on interest

Interest earned on deposits with approved commercial and merchant banks in Singapore is exempted from tax if it accrues to non-residents. Such persons should not by themselves or in association with others carry on a business in Singapore nor have a permanent establishment in Singapore. For non-residents, interest derived from all other sources is subject to withholding tax at the 40% rate, or at a lesser rate as provided by any relevant double taxation agreement.

Interest on deposits with finance companies is taxable, whether received by a resident or a non-resident.

Interest paid by the Singapore branch of a foreign bank to its head office or to a branch outside Singapore is exempted from withholding tax.

(g) Other tax concessions

Interest from certain government bonds is tax free if received by an individual or a trading company. For banks and other financial institutions the concession rate for similar bonds is 20%.

Interest from Asian dollar bonds approved by the Minister for Finance, which is received in Singapore, is exempted from Singapore tax if it is received by a non-resident individual or a company that does not operate in Singapore nor has a permanent establishment in Singapore.

(h) Double taxation agreements

Singapore has concluded double taxation agreements with 23 countries. Singapore branches of foreign banks do not qualify for any relief in Singapore for any foreign taxes paid on income of the Singapore branch. In practice, however, deductions are allowed when computing branch profits for any foreign withholding tax paid on interest income received by the Singapore branch.

(i) Presentation of accounts

Presentation of accounts are determined by the Banking Act and Companies Act. Therefore income tax considerations should not affect presentation of accounts.

10 INTERPRETATION OF ACCOUNTS

10.1 Adequacy of information as to contents and disclosure

10.2 Audit and reliability of information

The requirements of the Companies Act can at best only disclose the minimum information desirable for users of financial statements for making evaluations and financial decisions. Introduction of standards, particularly IAS 5, seek to redress this inadequacy. However, the exceptions and modifications to finance statements allowed by the MAS as detailed in Section 3 can only result in less public disclosure by banks.

To ensure reliability of information, annual accounts as previously stated have to be examined by auditors approved by the MAS.

10.3 Comparability between different banks on the basis of published accounts or publicly available returns

Banks in Singapore are generally not prepared to disclose more than the minimum disclosure requirements. The amount of income tax charged in the accounts is usually not disclosed and profit is stated net of income tax. With the exception of one publicly listed bank, the published accounts of banks do not disclose the total interest income and expense. These items are considered useful indicators of the bank's performance.

The format of accounts generally adopted by banks in Singapore is presented in Appendix I.

APPENDIX I

Pro forma profit and loss accounts

	$	$
Net profit for the year after providing for taxation, diminution in value of assets, contingencies and after making transfers from/to reserves		xxx
after crediting:		
Gross income from investments in subsidiaries	xxx	
and after charging:		
Depreciation of fixed assets	xxx	
Directors' remuneration	xxx	
Auditors' remuneration	xxx	
Add: Balance brought forward from previous year		xxx
		xxx
Deduct:		
1 Transfer to reserve fund	xxx	
2 Interim dividend of xxx less income tax of xxx% paid on	xxx	
3 Proposed final dividend of xxx less income tax at xxx%	xxx	
		xxx
Unappropriated profit carried forward		xxx

Pro forma balance sheet

	$	$
SHARE CAPITAL		
Authorised		
xxx shares of $x each	xxx	
Issued and fully paid		
xxx shares of $x each		xxx
GENERAL RESERVE		xxx
REVENUE RESERVE		
Profit unappropriated		xxx
Total of capital and reserves		xxx
CURRENT LIABILITIES AND PROVISIONS		
Current, fixed, savings accounts and other deposits of customers	xxx	
Deposits and balances of bankers and agents	xxx	
Bills and drafts payable	xxx	
Other liabilities including provisions and other reserves	xxx	
Proposed dividend (net)	xxx	
		xxx
AMOUNTS OWING TO SUBSIDIARY COMPANIES		xxx
		xxx
ACCEPTANCES, GUARANTEES AND EXCHANGE CONTRACTS ON BEHALF OF CUSTOMERS PER CONTRA		xxx
		xxx

	$	$
CURRENT ASSETS		
Cash and balances with bankers and agents		xxx
Money at call and short notice		xxx
Bills receivable less provision		xxx
Singapore government securities including Singapore treasury bills (state method of valuation)	xxx	
Other government securities including treasury bills (state method of valuation)	xxx	
		xxx
Other investments (state method of valuation)		
Quoted shares in corporations	xxx	
Unquoted shares in corporations	xxx	
		xxx
Loans and advances		
Less provision for bad and doubtful debts		xxx
Other accounts		xxx
SUBSIDIARY COMPANIES		
Shares (state method of valuation)	xxx	
Amounts owing by subsidiary companies	xxx	
		xxx
FIXED ASSETS		
Land, buildings, office equipment, furniture and fittings less amounts written off (state method of valuation)		xxx
		xxx
CUSTOMERS' LIABILITY FOR ACCEPTANCES, GUARANTEES AND EXCHANGE CONTRACTS PER CONTRA		xxx
		xxx

APPENDIX II

Additional information required by MAS

Name of Bank................

Additional information

PART I
BALANCE SHEET ITEMS

			Amount
(A)	(i)	Total credit facilities* outstanding graded:	
		– Substandard	_____
		– Doubtful	_____
		– Bad	_____
		Less: Amount estimated to be recoverable	_____
		Amount estimated to be irrecoverable	_____
	(ii)	Specific provision for bad and doubtful debts	
		– Loans and advances	_____
		– Bills receivable	_____
	(iii)	General Provision for loans	_____

(B) Short- and long-term investment securities:

	Original cost	Par value	Premium charged to expense	Discounts accrued as income	Diminution in value		Net book value	Market value (ex-interest in case of debt-securities)
					Provision made	Amount written off		
(i) Singapore government securities and Singapore treasury bills								
(ii) Other government securities and treasury bills								
(iii) Investment in subsidiary companies: – Quoted – Unquoted								
(iv) Investment in associated companies – Quoted – Unquoted								
(v) Other investments: Equity investment – Quoted – Unquoted Other papers – Quoted – Unquoted								

* Inclusive of bills discounted

		Amount
(C)	Bank premises and other immovable property:	

(C) Bank premises and other immovable property:

    (i)   Original cost of property   _____

    (ii) Amount written off   _____

    (iii) Provision for depreciation/losses   _____

    (iv) Market value/Estimated market value*
         (indicate date property was last valued by
         professional valuers)   _____

    To provide list of properties, addresses and
    other details

(D) Capital reserves:

    (i)   Share premium reserves   _____

    (ii) Revaluation reserves   _____

    (iii) Other capital reserves   _____

(E) Revenue reserves:**

    (i)   Statutory reserves   _____

    (ii) Other revenue reserves   _____

    (iii) Unappropriated profit or loss   _____

(F) Other provision and reserves for losses or
    contingencies   _____

    Give breakdown of provisions and other
    reserves (indicating purposes) classified under
    the item 'Other liabilities including provisions
    and other reserves' in the balance sheet

(G) To provide breakdown of items listed in
    'Other accounts'   _____

(H) (i)   Total deposits of non-bank customers   _____

    (ii) Deposits and balances of bankers and
         agents   _____

(I) Where applicable, the following items should
    be attached:

(i)   List of outstanding credit facilities utilised by companies
    in which the bank directly or indirectly holds 5% or
    more of the issued share capital.

(ii) List of loans and other credit facilities in which any of
    the bank's directors (including parents, spouse and
    children) has an interest.

(iii) List of assets of the bank that have been mortgaged or
    pledged with other banks, financial institutions, etc., as
    securities for funds provided to the bank or any party by
    way of deposits, loans, advances or any other means.

   * Delete as appropriate

   ** Statutory reserve is that which is set up for compliance with
section 18(1) of the Banking Act. Other revenue reserve is that which is
set up in excess of statutory reserve

PART II
PROFIT AND LOSS ACCOUNT

(i)   A copy of the audited Profit and Loss Account showing
    details of the income and expenditure of the bank, and

(ii) A copy of the Profit and Loss Appropriation Account
    are attached.

....

Chicf Executive Officer

....

Principal Financial Officer

We confirm that the financial data stated herein are in
accordance with the financial books and records of the bank
from which the audited statutory accounts of the bank are
prepared.

....

External Auditors

CHAPTER 18

SOUTH AFRICA

ANDRE BOTHA

1 GENERAL INFORMATION

1.1 Organisations covered by banking regulations

Banking in South Africa is controlled by a variety of banking institutions of which the following types are the most important:
- Commercial banks.
- General banks.
- Merchant banks.
- Discount houses.
- The Reserve Bank (central bank).

The first four categories come under the jurisdiction of the Banks Act.[1]

The banking scene is principally dominated by the commercial and general banks with the merchant banks offering, in the main, specialised financial advice and other financial services.

In addition there is the National Finance Corporation and the Land and Agricultural Bank of South Africa (the Land Bank) which have been incorporated under their own Acts.

These banks are regulated by the Registrar of Banks (see Section 1.4 below) who is instrumental in carrying out the monetary policy formulated by the Reserve Bank (see below). The Reserve Bank will act according to guidelines laid down by the government.

1.2 Summary of major types of bank

(a) Commercial banks

The commercial banks provide mainly a retail service. This service includes the acceptance of savings and time deposits, the providing of cheque account facilities, the provision of short-term finance in the form of overdrafts, the discounting of trade bills and the provision of spot foreign exchange and forward cover for foreign exchange transactions for customers.

(b) Discount houses

The discount houses act as intermediaries between the banking system and the Reserve Bank, specialising in the mobilisation of call and other moneys and facilitating an efficient market in treasury bills and other short-term instruments.

(c) General banks

General banks provide corporate services, some of which are not provided by the commercial banks. They accept deposits but in most cases do not provide cheque account facilities. General banks also underwrite share issues and discount hire-purchase and leasing paper.

(d) Merchant banks

Merchant banks primarily provide professional financial advice rather than being involved in retail banking. They accept deposits and bills for discounting and generally operate in the money market, including buying and selling of government and municipal bonds. They are also involved in foreign exchange transactions.

The definitions of the above-mentioned four types of bank have one common denominator, the acceptance of deposits. A financial institution that offers similar services out of its own funds does not fall within the scope of the Banks Act.

None of the types of bank mentioned above are precluded from offering the type of services rendered by another type of bank, as long as it is registered according to the function which constitutes the major part of its operations.

(e) The National Finance Corporation (NFC)

The NFC is jointly owned by the Reserve Bank, commercial banks and a variety of other financial institutions. The NFC's prime objective is that of residual depositary of surplus funds and to provide greater scope for co-operation and consultation among the country's financial institutions. The interest rates payable on these deposits are less than those of the discount houses and merchant banks. The NFC invests these funds in government treasury bills, Land Bank bills and government loan stock, etc. The NFC as a matter of policy will always accept deposits. If the NFC becomes underinvested the Reserve Bank will assist it by selling from its own portfolio, government treasury bills and other similar instruments.

---

[1] Act No. 44 of 1958

(f) Land and Agricultural Bank of South Africa (Land Bank)

The Land Bank was established to provide finance at low rates of interest for farmers in respect of the purchase of land, improvements to farms, purchase of stock and agricultural requirements generally, and loans to agricultural co-operatives, which in turn also provide credit to farmers.

(g) The South African Reserve Bank

The South African Reserve bank is privately owned and quoted on the Johannesburg stock exchange.

The main object for the formation of the Reserve Bank was the centralising of the issue of bank notes.

The other main functions of the bank can be summarised as follows:
(1) Bankers' bank and lender of last resort.
(2) Buying and selling of government securities (certain restrictions are imposed on this bank in respect of trading in such securities) and in addition the Reserve Bank acts as agent to the government for the issue of treasury bills.
(3) Banker to the government.
(4) Custodian of the foreign reserves.
(5) Formulation of monetary policy in conjunction with the Treasury and Minister of Finance.

No further reference will be made to the NFC, Land Bank and Reserve Bank as these are unique institutions, governed by their own Acts of Parliament and under the control of boards of directors appointed in terms of the respective Acts.

(h) Insurance companies, pension funds and building societies

These institutions, which account for a major proportion of individual savings, are all regulated by their own Acts and not by the Banks Act.

(i) Post Office Savings Bank

The Post Office Savings Bank is also regulated by its own Act and does not fall under the Banks Act.

1.3 Supervisory authorities
1.4 Status of supervisory authorities

The Banks Act establishes the office of the Registrar of Banks and appoints an officer called the Registrar of Banks who is responsible, under the control of the Minister of Finance, for the administration of the Act which is applicable to the following banks:[2]
 − Commercial banks.
 − Discount houses.
 − General banks.
 − Merchant banks.

Technical advisory committee in terms of banking and building society legislation

The Minister of Finance[3] appoints a committee which advises on alteration/improvement of the Banks Act.

Authorities set up by the banking industry

The following associations have no supervisory authority but merely act as spokesmen for the bankers which they represent.

Association of General Banks and Finance Houses

The Association of General Banks is not a cartel or price fixing body, but does impose certain standards of conduct on its members in respect of general leasing and suspensive sale business, and consumer affairs. It represents the industry in discussions with the authorities and other bodies on a wide range of matters. Members are kept informed of matters affecting their interests and of technical and legislative developments on a regular basis.

Clearing Bankers Association

The objects of the Association of Clearing Bankers which includes the main commercial bankers offering cheque clearing facilities are:
(a) To provide a forum for the consideration of matters of policy and material interest concerning member banks.
(b) To act as a communication medium between the banks and other parties.
(c) To deal with, advance and promote any other matters of interest to member banks and to foster co-operation between such banks. It is not a price fixing cartel.

Merchant Bankers Association

Similar objects to those of the Clearing Bankers Association but applicable to merchant banks.

1.5 Laws and regulations governing banks

The prime law governing banking is the Banks Act, No. 23 of 1965. This Act gives power to the Minister of Finance[4] to make regulations consistent with that Act, and officers of the banks are obliged to follow these regulations.

A summary of the main laws and regulations is contained in Appendices I and II.

1.6 Application of general company law to banks

All banking institutions are subject to the provisions of the Companies Act, with certain minor exclusions in respect of banks.

No person shall carry on the business of a banking institution unless that person has been registered as a banking institution of a particular class.[5]

The only provisions of the Companies Act that do not apply to banking institutions and external companies (foreign companies) are those provisions which are inconsistent with that of the Banks Act.[6]

Foreign banks (external companies) doing banking business in South Africa must also register as banks. In addition they will have to comply with the Companies Act provisions embodied in sections 322 to 336; the most important sections are:

---

[2] Section 3 Banks Act
[3] Section 53 Banks Act
[4] Section 50 (1) Banks Act
[5] Section 7 Banks Act
[6] Section 3 (b) Companies Act

322	Registration of memorandum of incorporation of an external company.
323/328	Effect of such a registration of memorandum of incorporation of an external company/and changes to memorandum of incorporation.
324	Power of external company to own immovable property in South Africa.
325	External company to have an auditor.
326	External company to have a representative to receive official notices.
327	Register of directors, managers and secretaries.
329	Keeping of accounting records and lodging of annual financial statements and interim report.
330	Lodging of annual returns to Registrar of Companies (Prescribed Forms).

Certain foreign banks only have a representation in South Africa. As they act as agents only and do not do business in South Africa they need not be registered as banking institutions. (See also Section 1.8.)

1.7 Sources of laws and regulations

Laws are enacted by parliament and regulations are made by a Minister under powers conferred on him by a particular Act, e.g. as mentioned in Section 1.5 the Minister of Finance may make regulations under powers conferred on him by the Banking Act.

1.8 Ability of foreign banks to operate through branches and subsidiaries

Before a foreign bank[7] can open a representative office in South Africa it must obtain the permission of the Registrar of Banks and provide him with the name and address of the representative and office.

This representative office would not be able to carry on banking business. If a foreign bank wishes to open a branch that will carry on banking business in South Africa it would have to register itself as an external company[8] and apply to the Registrar of Banks for a licence. However, under present conditions the latter is unlikely to be granted (see below).

While subsidiaries have been incorporated in the past and have been registered as banking institutions, the Financial Institutions Amendment Act of 1976 requires the foreign bank's shareholding to be reduced to not more than 50% in accordance with a programme agreed with the Minister of Finance.

Furthermore, a bank in South Africa may not register shares held by a foreign bank (or its associate) in excess of 30% of its shares in issue, or the shares held by an individual and his associates in excess of 10%, unless the Minister of Finance gives his agreement.

It should be noted that the authorities regard the banking industry as overcrowded and it is unlikely that a new bank would be allowed to be registered. However, it might be possible to purchase an existing bank.

1.9 Level of supervisory control for branches and subsidiaries of foreign banks

In the event of a foreign bank having a representative office in South Africa, there are certain minimum requirements that must be complied with.[9] However, if banking business is carried on in South Africa supervisory controls would be the same as for any bank in South Africa.

1.10 Methods of incorporation

There is only one method of incorporation of a bank in South Africa today and that is by means of the registration of a public company. Before the registration of a bank will be allowed by the Registrar, a person who intends to carry on the business of a banking institution must apply to the Registrar for permission to establish such a banking institution.[10]

The Registrar shall only grant such permission if the applicant satisfies him that the establishment of such an institution will be in the public interest. Only a registered banking institution may carry on banking business[11] and the Registrar of Banks may[12] require unregistered persons to furnish such information as he requires.

1.11 Areas within the country subject to special laws

There are no areas in the country subject to special laws but it should be noted that there are strict exchange control regulations in force for South African residents.

2 ACCOUNTING

2.1 Laws and regulations governing accounts

The laws governing accounts of banks are the Bank Act which requires[13] a bank to submit its accounts to the Registrar of Banks and the Companies Act which governs the disclosure requirements for the accounts. In addition there are certain specific sections of the Companies Act with which a banking institution has to comply. These sections are as follows:

282	Duties of auditor.
286	Duty to make out annual financial statements and to lay them before an annual general meeting.
299 (1)	Requirement for directors to lay before the annual general meeting a directors' report as part of the annual financial statements as to the state of the company's affairs, business and profit and loss of the company and its subsidiaries, and which deals with every other matter which is material for the appreciation by the members of the state of affairs of the company. The directors' report shall comply with the 4th schedule requirements applicable thereto. (See section 286 (3) of the Companies Act/definitions – re accounts.)
300	Describes the auditors' duties as to the annual financial statements and other matters.

---

[7] Section 27 Banks Act
[8] Section 322 Companies Act
[9] Section 27 D of Banks Act
[10] Section 4 Banks Act

[11] Section 7 Banks Act
[12] Section 8 Banks Act
[13] Section 37 Banks Act

301 (1) Describes the format of the auditors' report and
(2) the duties of the auditor when he is unable to make such a report.

The accounts of banking institutions are thus governed by the Banks Act, Companies Act and its relevant accounting disclosure schedule and South African General Accepted Accounting Practice (GAAP).

Bank controlling companies are governed by similar Acts and regulations as set out above for banking institutions.

2.2 Application of general company law

As all major banking institutions are incorporated as public companies under the Companies Act, these accounts are governed by that Act and its relevant accounting disclosure requirements.

2.3 Roles of legislature and supervisory authority

Parliament is instrumental in the passing of the various Acts such as the Banks Act and the Financial Institutions Amendment Acts. The State President appoints the Registrar of Banking Institutions (Registrar of Banks) who is responsible for the administration of that Act.[14] The Registrar of Banks shall be responsible for the functions assigned to him by the Minister of Finance.

2.4 Extent to which requirements as to returns and accounts are prescribed by laws and regulations

The Banks Act and Regulations[15] lay down the requirements for the submission of various returns and prescribe the form and content of such returns.

There is no specific prescribed form in the Banks Act for the form and content of banking accounts, other than that as set out in the Companies Act. The Companies Act is applicable to all banking institutions incorporated thereunder and it should be noted that there is a statutory obligation in respect of public companies to issue an interim report in respect of the first six months of its financial year.[16]

2.5 Obligations to furnish accounts

2.5.1 Accounting periods and times of furnishing
2.5.2 Form of accounts to be furnished

A balance sheet, income statement (profit and loss account) and other reports referred to in the Companies Act which includes the audit report, directors' report and notes to the financial statements (also known as the annual financial statements) must be furnished to the Registrar of Banks within three months after the end of the financial year to which they relate.[17]

A copy of the accounts and a copy of the group accounts, if any, shall be despatched not less than 21 days before the date of the annual general meeting of the company to members and other persons entitled to receive notice.

A bank shall, on the day on which it sends such copies to its members, forward to the Registrar of Companies under the cover of the prescribed form:
(a) A copy of the accounts and group accounts.

(b) A copy of the accounts of every private company which is a subsidiary of that bank. On application, banks could be exempted from filing the accounts of private companies.[18]

The half-yearly interim report must be issued within three months after the end of the first six months of its financial year[19] and also be sent to the Registrar of Banks and Registrar of Companies.[20]

2.5.3 Mandatory accounting dates

None.

2.6 Requirements as to accounts (a) prior to incorporation (b) prior to commencement of trading and (c) in order to continue trading

No provision is made in section 4 of the Banks Act or in section 63 of the Companies Act for the submission of accounts prior to incorporation. The sections mentioned deal with the incorporation requirements of banking institutions and companies in the Banks and Companies Acts respectively.

A banking institution[21] which has been registered provisionally (see Section 1.10 above) shall not accept a deposit or grant an advance until it has furnished proof to the Registrar of Banks that it has a certain amount of paid-up capital and unimpaired reserve funds (see Section 6.1 below for further details).[22]

Although no formal requirements for accounts prior to commencement of trading are made in the Banks or Companies Act it could, however, be assumed that the above-mentioned information required could be furnished in the form of a financial statement of accounts.

Non-submission of accounts will not stop a bank from trading under the Banks Act or Companies Act[23] but it should be noted that a bank could lose its registration if it neglects to render the returns required by the Banks Act.

2.7 Audit requirements

The Banks Act[24] and Companies Act[25] set out the duties of the auditor relevant to the annual financial statements (accounts) of companies including banks.

It should be noted that in addition to the general company law requirements for the standard audit report as set out in the Companies Act,[26] the Banks Act[27] requires that the following paragraphs be included in the audit report on a bank's accounts:

---

14 Section 3 Banks Act
15 Section 13 Banks Act
16 See part IV of 4th schedule to Companies Act
17 Sections 37 and 38 Banks Act
18 Section 302 Companies Act
19 See part IV of 4th schedule Companies Act
20 Companies Act Form CM34
21 Section 4 (5) Banks Act
22 Section 14 Banks Act
23 Sections 302 (5) and 441 Companies Act
24 Section 37 (1) Banks Act
25 Section 300 Companies Act
26 Prescribed by section 301 Companies Act
27 Section 37 (2)

– Whether the securities and all records of the company are being properly and safely preserved.

– Whether the control of the bank over its branches and agencies is adequate and whether its instructions to the employees in its branches and agencies have been properly carried out.

An auditor need not visit every branch and agency of a banking institution to carry out an audit unless circumstances demand such action.

The governing body of a banking institution shall, within three months of the date of registration or provisional registration of that banking institution, appoint an auditor until the conclusion of the first succeeding annual general meeting.[28] The banking institution shall at the annual general meeting appoint an auditor from the conclusion of that annual general meeting to the next annual general meeting. When, however, the assets of the bank exceeds R2 million a second auditor, who will be independent of the other auditor, must be appointed.[29]

2.8 Acceptability to fiscal authorities of accounts submitted to supervisory authority

The accounts submitted to the members, Registrar of Banks and Registrar of Companies are similar to those submitted to the Receiver of Revenue (fiscal authority). In addition to the published accounts the Receiver of Revenue, however, requires further information in respect of certain items such as:
– Provisions and reserves.
– Bad debts.
– Repairs and maintenance.
– Overseas travelling expenses.

The accounts, detailed income statement and other information as described above, are submitted annually to the Receiver of Revenue under cover of the prescribed Income Tax Form IT 14 and signed by the Public Officer. Correspondence and assessments from the Fiscal Authorities are served on the Public Officer.

2.9 Submission of accounts to any authority other than by requirement of law

The Department of Statistics annually requires details of certain balance sheet items. It is authorised by law to obtain such information from companies but does not formally require copies of the accounts.

The banks listed on the Johannesburg stock exchange are required annually to submit their accounts to the Johannesburg stock exchange. There are various regulations that listed companies must abide by, such as submitting draft copies of all documentation to be sent to shareholders, 21 days before such submission to shareholders, to the Manager – Listings of the Johannesburg stock exchange for his approval.

2.10 Application of laws and regulations to foreign banks operating through branches and subsidiaries

A South African subsidiary of a foreign bank is subject to the same laws and regulations which apply to other banking institutions in South Africa and in this connection it should be noted that a banking institution carrying on business in South Africa must be registered as a public company under the Companies Act.

A foreign bank with a branch operating in South Africa must be registered as an external company under the Companies Act and, as such, it is required[30] to keep accounting records, submit interim reports and lodge annual financial statements similarly to other companies in South Africa. (See Sections 2.1, 2.2, 2.4 and 2.5 above.)

In the case of a representative office it is only necessary to comply with the requirements set out in Section 1.8 above; on informing the Registrar of Banks as to the name and address and any change therein of a foreign representative, no accounts need be furnished because the foreign representative is not doing business in South Africa.

See Section 1.8 for the restrictions on a foreign bank operating in South Africa.

2.11 Availability of accounts for public inspection

All accounts and other documentation relating to banking institutions (the majority of which are public companies) which are submitted to the Registrar of Companies (see Section 2.5) are available for inspection or copy by the general public at the office of the Registrar of Companies,[31] unless exemption is given by the Registrar.[32]

Certain returns submitted by banking institutions to the Registrar of Banks are also available for public inspection. See Appendix II and Section 8 below.

In addition to the accounts being available at the Registrar of Companies Office, for listed companies such information would be available on request from the registered offices of the company and the Johannesburg stock exchange.

3 FORMAT, STYLE AND CONTENTS OF ACCOUNTS

3.1 Extent to which format is laid down by statute, supervisory authority, generally accepted accounting practice or otherwise

With a few minor exceptions all South African registered banking institutions are public companies, incorporated and registered under the Companies Act and therefore their accounts have to comply with the requirements of the Act as applicable to banking companies.[33]

One of the requirements of the Companies Act is that accounts must be prepared in accordance with generally accepted accounting principles.[34]

---

[28] Section 35 (1) (a) Banks Act
[29] Section 35 (1) (b) Banks Act
[30] Section 329 Companies Act
[31] Section 9 Companies Act
[32] Section 9 (4) Companies Act
[33] 4th schedule to Companies ACt including part V thereof
[34] Section 286 (3) Companies Act

6.1 Minimum capital and reserves[41]

Each banking institution must maintain in South Africa a paid-up share capital and unimpaired reserve funds, together amounting to not less than the greater of
(i) R200,000 or
(ii) 6% of its liabilities to the public in South Africa (excluding liabilities under acceptances) plus 4% of its liabilities under acceptances, contingent liabilities under promissory notes, bills and other similar instruments endorsed by it.
There are certain minor exceptions to the above rules.

6.2 Minimum reserve balances with the Reserve Bank[42]

Each banking institution must maintain an interest free reserve balance with the Reserve Bank amounting to not less than 8% of its short-term liabilities to the public in South Africa (excluding liabilities under acceptances). In determining the amount of its short-term liabilities to the public (excluding liabilities under acceptances) banking institutions may make certain approved deductions and omissions and bring into account its demand liabilities on an average daily basis.

6.3 Minimum liquid assets[43]

Details of current minimum liquid asset requirements to be held by banking institutions are given in Appendix V.

6.4 Minimum prescribed investments[44]

Every banking institution is required to maintain in South Africa prescribed investments of an amount not less than 13% of its long-term liabilities to the public in South Africa.

Of these prescribed investments, an amount equal to not less than 6% of its long-term liabilities is to consist of securities issued by the government which are ranked as prescribed investments. These percentages are from time to time varied by the Minister of Finance by Notice in the Government Gazette.

6.5 Banking institutions must maintain a covered domestic position

Every banking institution[45] must maintain assets (other than claims) situated in South Africa and assets consisting of claims payable in the currency of South Africa, of an aggregate value not less than the sum of:
– The amount of its liabilities payable in the currency of South Africa;
and
– The paid-up capital and unimpaired reserve funds which it is required to maintain.
The Minister of Finance may exempt any banking institution from the provisions of this Section, to the extent and for the period and on the conditions determined by him. A commercial bank is exempt from these requirements in certain specified circumstances.

The liabilities of a banking institution which are payable in the currency of South Africa shall be a prior charge (as against all other liabilities) on the assets which it is required to maintain for its covered domestic position.

6.6 Conclusion

The percentages and basis of calculation of the prescribed minimum amounts mentioned above may from time to time be varied by the Minister by Notice in the Government Gazette and consequently the information given here will need to be checked to ensure its current relevance.

See Appendix V for further details of these requirements.

7 KEY RATIOS
7.1 Regulatory

Key ratios required to be maintained by a banking institution are prescribed in terms of the Banks Act and are recorded in Section 6 above. The significant ratios required are as follows:
(1) Minimum capital and reserves.
(2) Share capital requirements for discount houses.
(3) Minimum reserve balance.
(4) Minimum liquid assets.
(5) Minimum prescribed investments.
(6) Maintenance of covered domestic position.
These ratios are computed and monitored on the periodic returns[46] submitted by the banking institutions to the Registrar of Banks in terms of the Regulations to the Banks Act (i.e. BA Forms).

All banking institutions must at all times display a copy of their latest statement of assets and liabilities[47] in a conspicuous place in every building in South Africa in which they carry on business. While these returns are required by regulation to be submitted to the Registrar of Banks, the information contained therein is not readily available to investors, analysts and shareholders but is available for scrutiny and copy at the offices of the Registrar of Banks.[48] Generally speaking, no reference is made in the financial statements of banking institutions to the statutory ratios computed above.

8 ACCOUNTING RETURNS OTHER THAN ACCOUNTS

A number of returns are required to be filed by bank institutions with the Registrar of Banks and these are summarised below:
– A monthly return[49] must be filed containing information on whether the banking institution maintained the

---

[41] Section 14 (1) Banks Act
[42] Section 16 Banks Act
[43] Section 17 Banks Act
[44] Section 18 (1) Banks Act
[45] Section 20 Banks Act
[46] BA Forms, see Appendix II
[47] BA Form 9, see Appendix II
[48] Section 48 Banks Act
[49] Section 13 (1) (a) Banks Act – Return Form BA7

required 'liquid assets', prescribed investments and the reserve balances with the Reserve Bank.

— A quarterly return[50] must be filed of assets and liabilities of the banking institution as at the close of the last business day of that quarter. At least one quarter must be audited.[51] The latest copy of this return must be displayed in every building where the bank carries on its business.

— A return[52] together with the quarterly return described above must be filed, to be able to determine whether the institution maintained the paid-up capital and unimpaired reserve funds and the 'prescribed assets' to maintain a covered domestic position.

— A banking institution must furnish the Registrar of Banks with details of its shareholders, the number of shares held and whether they are domiciled in South Africa or abroad.[53]

The Registrar of Banks issues instructions to banking institutions by means of the RB (Registrar of Banks) circulars. Arising from these circulars certain accounting and other returns must be forwarded to the Registrar of Banks. A summary of the most important returns is set out in Appendix VI.

9 TAXATION

9.1 General method of taxation

One Act[54] contains the rules for collection of income tax from all taxpayers, distinguishing only between individuals and companies, with banks falling under the latter category.

The tax system is based on source with all real and deemed South African receipts and accruals constituting gross income. The timing of items for inclusion in gross income is based on receipt or prior accrual (i.e. whichever occurs first). Exempt income and allowable deductions are subtracted from gross income in order to determine taxable income.

Because only South African source income is taxed, a South African bank usually encounters few instances of double taxation. Specific allowance for foreign tax credit is provided where deemed South African source income in the form of interest or royalties is involved. Most double taxation conventions also provide for additional foreign tax credit relief.

Company and other tax rates are set each year for mining and non-mining income. The company tax rate applicable for the year ending 31 March 1983 was 46.2% in respect of non-mining income.

9.2 Accounts as basis for taxation

As accounts form the basis for taxation, for all practical purposes the banks' financial statements will form the basis for determining taxable income with various adjustments being made to the accounting profit. Additions to accounting profit will include items charged against income relating to revenue expenditure not in production of income or for purposes of trade, capital expenditure and losses, provisions and reserves.

In addition, income received in advance will be added back to arrive at taxable income. Deductions will include allowances for doubtful debtors, unearned profit on instalment sales, investment in hotel and manufacturing equipment or buildings (leased by the banks) and prepaid expenditure. Income from foreign sources and dividends received are also deductible.

Depreciation allowances on movable assets used in the business may vary from those used for accounting purposes.

Should the end result be a loss it is carried forward annually, until offset against future profits. A loss may not be carried back for deduction from prior profits.

9.3 Adjustments permitted or required

Accounting adjustments which vary the net profit from the figure reported to shareholders are discouraged but not specifically prohibited.

9.4 Effect of tax considerations on presentation of accounts

Those banks which take advantage of the exemption provisions of the Companies Act will not normally disclose the charge for taxation, although reference is occasionally made to it in the accounting policies in the notes to the accounts. Apart from this tax considerations have no effect on the presentation of the accounts.

9.5 General

The Income Tax Act provides for the deduction of Non-resident Shareholders Tax on dividends and interest remitted to non-resident (foreign) shareholders. This tax amounts to between 10 and 15% of the income.

10 INTERPRETATION OF ACCOUNTS

10.1 Adequacy of information as to contents and disclosure

The adequacy of the information contained in the accounts of banking institutions has to be considered in the light of the Companies Act, whether the bank avails itself of the disclosure exemptions granted in terms of the Companies Act, and published 'Statements of Generally Accepted Accounting Practice' applicable in South Africa. Several banks follow a policy of full disclosure of profits but, generally speaking, the effectiveness of the interpretation of financial statements of banking institutions is reduced where advantage is taken of the above-mentioned exemptions. From the point of view of both the shareholder and financial analyst, the information disclosed is not adequate for more than a superficial interpretation of the financial statements but additional information can be obtained by reference to

---

[50] Section 13 (1) (b) Banks Act — Return Form BA9
[51] Section 13 (4) Banks Act
[52] Section 13 (1) (c) Banks Act — Return Form BA8
[53] Section 34 (5) Banks Act
[54] Income Tax Act No. 58 of 1962

APPENDIX VI

Summary of returns

1 RB Circular 3/1943, 94/1966 (1)

Special return of trust assets at 31 December to be furnished to Reserve Bank.

2 RB 13/1944

Provides for insurance cover against negligence and dishonesty of employees and prescribed minimum amounts that the Banking Institution should be insured for. An annual audited certificate re adequacy of amount is also required. (See also Section 45 of the Banks Act.)

3 RB 16/1947

Commented on the desirability of receiving auditors' reports suggesting improvements in accounting systems of banking institutions. It is clearly impracticable in the current day except for extreme cases. Auditors are also reminded to note and report undesirable practices carried on by banking institutions.

4 RB 140/1976

Banking institutions need not disclose the liability on acceptances which they have obtained in their own names on behalf of clients from foreign banks as a liability to the public. They must, however, disclose the amount of such bills in their quarterly statement (Form BA9) by way of a note.

5 RB 144/1977

Banking institutions are requested to submit together with their quarterly statement of assets and liabilities, details of all reserves not shown in the balance sheet (e.g. hidden reserves). Details of all losses written off against such reserves are also to be furnished similarly. This information would not be made available to the general public.

6 RB 150/1978

Details, together with the quarterly statement of assets and liabilities, of amounts of loans, guarantees, acceptances, etc. (not forward exchange contracts) owing by a person or group of associated persons, which exceeds 10% of the paid-up capital and unimpaired reserves of the banking institution. The name and total amount owing by the company and/or person which exceeds the laid-down limits must be disclosed.

If there were no such companies and/or persons where the exposure exceeded 10% of the capital and unimpaired reserves a certificate to that effect must be furnished.

7 RB 161/1979

Details to be submitted together with the quarterly statement of assets and liabilities in respect of leasing business, distinguishing between (a) financial leasing and (b) operational leasing, which constitutes the total leasing (in merchandise of date of this return).

8 Repurchase agreements

From 1 October 1983, banking institutions must report the information regarding liabilities under repurchase agreements by way of a note on the BA7 and BA9 forms.